DATE DUE

1. All pupils in the school are entitled to use the library and to borrow books.

2. Reference books, such as encyclopedias and dictionaries, are to be used only in the library.

3. Reserved books may be borrowed for one period, or at the close of school, and should be returned before the first class the following school day.

4. All other books may be retained for two weeks.

5. A fine is charged for each day a book is kept overtime.

6. Injury to books beyond reasonable wear and all losses shall be paid for.

7. No books may be taken from the library without being charged.

THE
Chicago Tribune
COOKBOOK

THE
Chicago Tribune
COOKBOOK

CONTEMPORARY AND CLASSIC FAVORITES

EDITED BY JEANMARIE BROWNSON

CHICAGO REVIEW PRESS

Library of Congress Cataloging-in-Publication Data

The Chicago Tribune cookbook / edited by JeanMarie Brownson.—1st ed.
  p.   cm.
  Includes index.
  ISBN 1-55652-069-7 : $24.95
  1. Cookery.   I. Brownson, JeanMarie.   II. Chicago Tribune
(Chicago, Ill.)
  TX714.C47   1989
  641.5—dc20   89-15899
                                                            CIP

CHICAGO TRIBUNE STAFF

Cookbook Editor: JeanMarie Brownson

Food Editor: Carol Haddix

Writers: Beverly Dillon, Marcia Lythcott, Steven Pratt, William Rice,
  Margaret Sheridan, Barbara Sullivan, Patricia Tennison

Art Director/Designer: Kevin Fewell

Photo Editor: Dorothy B. Anderson

Business Managers: Kevin Dabe, John Lux

Editorial Production Assistant: Darren Szrom

Chicago Tribune Photographers: Tony Berardi, Bob Fila, Bill Hogan, Chris Walker

Jacket Design: Fran Lee and Kevin Fewell

Illustrations: Fran Lee

1 2 3 4 5 6 7 8 9 10

Published by Chicago Review Press, Incorporated
  814 N. Franklin Street, Chicago, Illinois, 60610

ISBN 1-55652-069-7

CONTENTS

INTRODUCTION

Most people are surprised to learn that there is a working kitchen in the middle of *The Chicago Tribune*'s newsroom. Today, only a handful of newspapers around the country have a test kitchen. *The Tribune*'s kitchen, complete with gas and electric ranges, microwave oven, two refrigerators, dishwasher and stocked cupboards, is a vital part of the daily newspaper.

While city desk reporters are busy covering Chicago's colorful political scene, our test kitchen staff may be creating a recipe or sampling a tried-and-true classic. Food writers may be interviewing a famous chef, testing the latest piece of kitchen equipment or conducting a comparative tasting on a new product. Meanwhile, the color photography studio located next to the test kitchen is a flurry of activity, with photographers and food stylists composing luscious food photographs.

The Chicago Tribune has been a premier source of excellent, timely, practical food advice and recipes for more than 75 years. "The big development of the modern newspaper," said *Chicago Tribune* editor James Keeley in 1912, "will be along the lines of personal service. . . . The newspaper must be of service today, not only in politics and morals, but it must also be of social service."

Over the years *Tribune* readers came to rely on Jean Eddington and Mary Meade, pen names for various members of the food staff. In 1957, the newspaper's Food Guide was launched, with Ruth Ellen Church as editor; it immediately became essential weekly reading for cooks and homemakers throughout the Midwest.

In recent years, we have endeavored to combine culinary service with the need for information about new food products, new methods of cooking, diet and health, shopping and the world of food away from home.

But the heart of our food coverage continues to be recipes. In an average year, *The Tribune* test kitchen prepares more than 1,000 recipes for the Thursday Food Guide, Sunday Home section and *Sunday* magazine. Along with a talented photography staff, the kitchen also produces more than 100 color and 250 black-and-white food photographs.

Our recipes come from a rich diversity of sources: *Tribune* staff members, regular contributors, caterers, cookbook authors, chefs from around the world and our readers.

Almost daily, the test kitchen conducts a taste panel of selected recipes. The kitchen staff, food editors and writers then taste and rate finished dishes on a score sheet. Lively discussions arise when staff members disagree on the amount of butter needed in a sauce or the perfect way to cook asparagus. If the tested recipe is a dessert, chances are it will first be devoured and then discussed.

After testing and photography, each recipe is edited or rewritten to ensure that it is readable, easy to follow and, above all, accurate.

Over the years we have tested and sampled recipes from around the world. Many of these have been clipped and filed by readers and staff members alike to cook again and again. Every year there are favorites we all fantasize about—the macadamia nut tart from a local bakery, a reader's Oriental noodle salad, the prizewinning gumbo, a columnist's pumpkin pie.

In the pages that follow is the cream of that crop, more than 600 of the very best recipes that have appeared in *The Chicago Tribune* during the 1980s, along with some from prior decades.

In gathering these recipes we could not help but recall their origins and the fun we've had meeting their creators. We will never forget the time that Oriental cooking teacher Ken Hom prepared a chicken dish on the spur of the moment, or the day chef Paul Prudhomme arrived with enough crab fritters and jambalaya to feed 50 fortunate reporters.

Then there was the day Chinese cooking teacher Nina Simonds came for a thirty-minute interview and ended up cooking with us for three hours, all the while telling stories about her adventures in China, which included teaching chefs to use a food processor.

Speaking of food processors, columnist Jane Salzfass Freiman once worked with the test kitchen staff to find the best food processor on the market. After the extensive testing we had enough shredded cabbage and sliced carrots for gallons of coleslaw.

Food Guide editor Carol Haddix treated us to her mother's Thanksgiving apple cornbread stuffing recipe the same year writer Margaret Sheridan whipped up her grandmother's mashed rutabaga. And we enjoyed abundance again when we conducted an apple pie contest that brought more than 200 recipes from our readers.

In addition to cooking at *The Tribune*, we have often ventured through the city, across the nation and even abroad in search of a new recipe or cooking method such as risotto with corn and red peppers and Thai pork satay.

Former Taste section editor Carol Rasmussen and test kitchen director JeanMarie Brownson could be seen early one July morning cooking corn in the Cook's Garden at Cantigny Gardens and Museum, in Winfield, Illinois, for a story on the differences between freshly picked and supermarket corn-on-the-cob. Leftover cobs were brought back to the test kitchen and assistant editor Marcia Lythcott cooked up her famous bacon-fried corn.

The Tribune publishes recipes that reflect contemporary lifestyles. The profusion of fresh produce available today in many varieties is evident in the more than 100 salad and vegetable recipes.

America has become even more of a melting pot with food of all cuisines making inroads in our daily eating habits. Here you'll find recipes for Italian pastas, French bouillabaisse, Moroccan stew, Oriental stir-fries, Mexican pot roast and Indian vegetables.

Tribune readers place high priority on convenience and saving time in the kitchen. Therefore, the Food Guide frequently features recipes made with the use of the microwave oven and the food processor. Those included in this book are Middle Eastern eggplant spread, hollandaise sauce, turbot with basil and cauliflower with red pepper sauce.

Nostalgic favorites, such as roast beef and Yorkshire pudding and oven-fried chicken, have been updated by reducing the amount of salt, sugar and animal fat without sacrificing flavor or quality.

There is continuity amid change, however. These recipes and the ancillary information contained in this volume are a continuation of *The Tribune's* tradition of reader service. They are intended to help cooks prepare meals that bring sustenance and pleasure. And to these cooks, we dedicate this book.

We may live without poetry, music and art;
We may live without conscience, and live without heart;
We may live without friends; we may live without books;
But civilized man cannot live without cooks.

—E. R. Bulwer-Lytton

THE
Chicago Tribune
COOKBOOK

SUGGESTED MENUS

HEARTY BREAKFAST

Apple juice
Baked apple pancake, *page 86*
Breakfast sausage, *page 284*
Coffee, hot chocolate

THANKSGIVING DINNER

Curried cream of acorn squash soup, *page 123*
Turkey with herbed cornbread stuffing and pan gravy, *page 355*
Marbled mashed potatoes, *page 410*
Green beans with garlic almonds, *page 401*
Onion compote, *page 404*
Pumpkin pecan pie, *page 566*
Cranberry-banana nut bread, *page 519*
Zinfandel, milk

AN ITALIAN PICNIC

Cold tomato-basil soup with pesto sauce, *page 128*
Muffalata, *page 197*
Amaretto cheesecake, *page 550*
Soave, flavored sparkling water

A SOUTHERN COUNTRY SUPPER

Crispy oven-fried chicken, *page 335*
Jalapeño pepper corn pudding, *page 397*
Creamy coleslaw, *page 443*
Herbed biscuits, *page 525*
Key lime pie, *page 563*
Iced tea with mint, *page 58*

A TEX-MEX BRUNCH

Green chili Bloody Marys, *page 60*
Scrambled eggs with chorizo, *page 84*
Sliced honeydew
Skillet cornbread, *page 518*
Frozen mango whip, *page 598*

MEXICAN APPETIZER PARTY

Spicy bean dip, *page 16*
Guacamole, *page 20*
Melted cheese casserole, *page 23*
Salsa, *page 20*
Crisp tortilla chips, *page 14*
Green chili Bloody Marys, margaritas, *pages 60, 65*

TAILGATE PARTY

Greek-style grilled chicken, *page 337*
Pasta shell salad with tomato and zucchini, *page 163*
Tarragon green bean salad in tomato cups, *page 450*
Whole-wheat millet bread, *page 449*
Walnut refrigerator cookies, *page 620*
Hot cider

SWEET TABLE FOR 25

Buttermilk lemon cake, *page 546*
Flourless chocolate cake with orange liqueur, *page 539*
Fresh fruit tarts, *page 568*
Macadamia nut tart, *page 571*
Peppercorn cookies, *page 619*
Rhubarb lemonade punch, *page 60*, coffee

MEATLESS DINNER

Vegetable chili with red beans, *page 426*
Cactus salad with toasted chilies, *page 440*
Cheddar-onion corn muffins, *page 523*
All-American apple pie, *page 558*
Apple spritzers, *page 57*, beer

WINTER WARM-UP DINNER

Mexican-style pot roast with vegetables, *page 277*
Romaine salad with Camembert dressing, *page 438*
Warm flour tortillas
Golden rice pudding, *page 580*
Mexican beer, milk

MEDITERRANEAN DINNER

Couscous with lamb stew and vegetables, *page 308*
Cucumber and mint salad, *page 444*
Baklava, *page 584*
Iced tea with mint, *page 58*, zinfandel

ST. PAT'S CELEBRATION

Creamy corned beef and pasta, *page 162*
Fresh asparagus with butter and parsley, *page 386*
Irish soda bread, *page 521*
Easy pear crisp, *page 572*
Beer, milk

FALL GAME DINNER

Grilled squab with wild mushroom sauce, *page 370*
Sweet and sour red cabbage, *page 391*
Potatoes Anna, *page 406*
Homemade rye buns, *page 497*
Fudgy flourless chocolate cake, *page 540*
Burgundy, sparkling cider

EASTER DINNER

Sugar-baked ham, *page 302*
Buttered new potatoes and peas with watercress, *page 409*
Tropical fruit salad with honey-lime dressing, *page 481*
Easter twists, *page 508*
White chocolate coconut cake, *page 549*
Iced tea, *page 58*, rosé

PASTA PARTY

Hot goat cheese and herbed tomato sauce dip, *page 22*
Linguini with shrimp and sun-dried tomatoes, *page 157*
Green bean, radicchio and endive salad with thyme vinaigrette, *page 436*
Country Parmesan herb bread, *page 500*
Tangerine sherbet, *page 599*
Chardonnay, sparkling water

WINTER HOLIDAY DINNER

Chicken and veal terrine, *page 26*
Crown roast of lamb with lemon and herbs, *page 306*
Steamed butternut squash with ginger, *page 414*
Broccoli with lemon, *page 389*
Beet and mâche salad with walnuts, *page 434*
Buttermilk cranberry muffins, *page 521*
Cold cranberry soufflé, *page 587*
Chocolate hazelnut cake, *page 538*
Bordeaux, milk

ORIENTAL LUNCH PARTY

Salmon Oriental, *page 219*
Rice with lemon rind and fresh herbs, *page 169*
Colorful broccoli stir-fry, *page 389*
Poached cinnamon pears, *page 589*
Tangerine tea, *page 59*

SOUTHERN SHORE SUPPER

Cheese wafers, *page 15*
Sparkling orange mint juleps, *page 61*
Batter-fried soft-shell crabs, *page 242*
Brown rice pilaf, *page 172*
Spicy okra and tomato salad, *page 453*
Strawberry ice cream, *page 595*
Iced tea, *page 58*

Bistro Meal

Duck liver pâté, *page 25*
Clay-pot chicken with 40 cloves of garlic, *page 333*
Potato gratin with cepes, *page 407*
Autumn salad with goat cheese, *page 433*
Hot French apple tart, *page 570*
Beaujolais, coffee

Chicago Sunday Supper

Chicago-style deep-dish pizza, *page 183*
Green salad with oregano dressing, *page 485*
Frango chocolate brownies, *page 626*
Beer, milk

Fourth of July Backyard Party

Grilled herbed pork roast, *page 291*
Grilled beets, *page 387*
Boiled corn with lemon butter, *page 395*
Red jacket picnic salad, *page 460*
Lemon meringue pie, *page 564*
Daiquiris, *page 64*, sodas

Summer Concert Picnic

Cream of cucumber soup, *page 129*
Curried turkey salad, *page 465*
Cherry pecan muffins, *page 522*
Almond nougat crispies, *page 624*
Iced tea with mint, citrus spritzers, *pages 58 and 62*

Family Weekend Lunch

Cheese and bacon hot dogs; chili dogs; Reuben hot dogs, *pages 202, 203, 204*
Kohlrabi slaw, *page 449*
Peanut butter cookies, *page 618*
Frothy lemon coolers, *page 58*

SEAFOOD SAMPLER

Angels on horseback, *page 43*
Steamed Manila clams with spicy sauce, *page 38*
Scallops in lemon grass sauce, *page 243*
Basil fried rice, *page 168*
Tossed salad with shallot vinaigrette, *page 486*
Cassis and blackberry sorbet, *page 597*
Chardonnay, sauvignon blanc, sparkling water

LIGHT, LOW-FAT LUNCH

Mushroom ginger soup, *page 106*
Light and easy lasagna, *page 149*
Sesame broccoli and cauliflower salad, *page 442*
Pear lemon ice, *page 598*
Hot tea, coffee

TWENTY-MINUTE DINNER

Turbot with basil, *page 227*
Romaine lettuce with garlic croutons, *page 437*
Easy cooked rice, *page 168*
Rhubarb orange sauce over vanilla ice cream, *page 601*
Sparkling water, milk

APPETIZERS

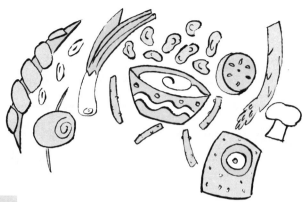

From the most humble salted peanuts to the most elegant of terrines, appetizers are beloved.

The word means "to tease the appetite," but appetizers (or nibbles or hors d'oeuvres or whatever you call them) can be much more than just teasers. For many people, the perfect meal is a smattering of appetizers and then dessert. They can be fun, handed out in the kitchen as they're made, or elegantly served as a first course for a formal dinner.

In putting together this section of appetizers from *The Tribune*, we noted certain trends. The microwave oven is becoming increasingly important, an everyday fact of life, and it certainly extends to appetizers. One recipe calls for cooking a whole eggplant in the microwave oven; that never would have occurred to most of us a few years ago.

Another trend is "grazing," that growing penchant toward eating a little bit of this and a little bit of that. We've included several recipes that can be grouped together for your grazing delight.

Cheese has always been a popular appetizer ingredient, but the advent of goat cheese is fairly recent in this country. Included here are several recipes using that flavorful cheese, with suggestions for substitutes in case it is a little too flavorful for you.

Raw vegetables continue winning popularity contests at informal parties because they can be consumed without guilt. So we've gathered a variety of dips and spreads that can be served with these vegetables to keep them interesting.

Fresh fish always adds an elegant touch to a cocktail party or when served as a first course. The recipes that follow range from simple mussels vinaigrette to sophisticated oysters in cream sauce.

And finally, today's restaurants offer a myriad of interesting taste and texture combinations as starters to a meal. Gone are the days when shrimp cocktail was the the only appetizer listed. So we have collected a handful of our favorite appetizer recipes from Chicago-area chefs and restaurants.

A tease, a nibble, or a whole meal. These are recipes that have pleased us over the years, and we think they'll please you too.

APPETIZERS

CRISP SNACKS

Crispy sugared peanuts

Creole pecans

Indian-style nuts

Crisp tortilla chips

Sesame pita chips

Cheese wafers

DIPS & SPREADS

Spicy bean dip

Creamy vegetable dip

Green peppercorn dip

Eggplant spread

Crab and fish spread

Fresh tomatillo sauce

Salsa

Guacamole

Layered avocado dip

Hot goat cheese and herbed
tomato sauce dip

Melted cheese casserole

PÂTÉS & TERRINES

Chicken liver pâté with pistachios

Duck liver pâté

Chicken and veal terrine

Eggplant terrine with sun-dried
tomato mayonnaise

WARM DISHES

Japanese beef and asparagus rolls

Asparagus tempura

New potatoes with horseradish cream
and caviar

Pork meatballs with apricot
dipping sauce

Pumpkin fritters

Thai pork satay

Sautéed radicchio with shallots
and goat cheese

Oysters with endive and cream

Steamed Manila clams with
spicy sauce

Meat-filled turnovers

Passover "egg rolls"

Pot stickers

Spicy veal puffs with mustard
cream sauce

Angels on horseback

Samosas with mint chutney

COLD DISHES

Caponata in red cabbage leaves

Blackened carpaccio with
chili mayonnaise

Mushrooms with ancho chilies

Pea pods stuffed with crabmeat

Prosciutto wrapped green beans

Mussels vinaigrette

Salmon with basil vinaigrette

Smoked turkey canapes with
honey mustard

Steak tartare

The following flavored-nut recipes are so good they're hard to resist. After coating as described below, keep nuts in covered tins or jars no longer than two weeks to assure maximum freshness and flavor.

CRISPY SUGARED PEANUTS

About 4 cups
Preparation time: 10 minutes
Baking time: 45 minutes

1 cup sugar
½ cup cornstarch
1 teaspoon ground cinnamon
  Pinch salt
2 egg whites, slightly beaten
¼ cup cold water
4 cups dry-roasted unsalted peanuts

1. Heat oven to 250 degrees. Sift sugar, cornstarch, cinnamon and salt into shallow pan. Mix egg whites and water in shallow bowl.

2. Dip peanuts into egg white mixture. Drain off excess liquid and roll in sugar mixture. Spread on greased baking sheet.

3. Bake until crisp, about 45 minutes. Break up with spatula. Cool on wire rack.

CREOLE PECANS

About 3 cups
Preparation time: 5 minutes
Cooking time: 5 minutes

1 teaspoon each: cayenne pepper, dried leaf thyme
½ teaspoon each: onion powder, salt, freshly ground pepper
¼ teaspoon garlic powder
3 tablespoons unsalted butter
3 cups pecan halves or cashews

1. Mix spices in small bowl. Melt butter in medium skillet. Stir in nuts; cook and stir over medium heat until lightly toasted, about 3 minutes. Add spices. Toss to coat well. Cool on baking sheet on wire rack.

INDIAN-STYLE NUTS

About 5 cups
Preparation time: 15 minutes
Cooking time: 5 minutes

1   **cup dry-roasted unsalted cashews or macadamia nuts**
1   **cup dry-roasted unsalted peanuts**
1   **cup Brazil nuts or walnuts, halved**
1   **cup hazelnuts**
1   **cup dark raisins**
1   **tablespoon curry powder**
¾   **teaspoon each: ground cumin, ground coriander**
¼   **teaspoon each: cayenne pepper, salt**
6   **tablespoons unsalted butter**

1. Mix nuts and raisins in large bowl. Mix spices in small bowl. Melt butter in large skillet. Add nuts and spices. Toss well to coat. Cook and stir over medium heat until nuts are lightly toasted, about 3 minutes. Cool on baking sheet on wire rack.

Packaged corn chips or tortilla chips are OK, but for something special, serve these homemade chips.

CRISP TORTILLA CHIPS

6 appetizer servings
Preparation time: 5 minutes
Cooking time: 15 minutes

12 **large corn tortillas**
    Vegetable oil for deep-frying
    Salt to taste

1. Cut tortillas into sixths. Heat a small amount of oil in large nonstick skillet until hot but not smoking. Add a few tortilla pieces at a time; fry, turning, until crisp and golden, about 1 minute. Remove with slotted spoon. Drain on paper towels.

2. Sprinkle with salt while still warm. If made in advance, reheat in a 250-degree oven on a baking sheet.

Pita bread can be transformed into a crisp, crunchy snack simply by brushing the bread with butter and baking it until crisp. Serve the pita chips with vegetable dips or eggplant spread.

SESAME PITA CHIPS

6 appetizer servings
Preparation time: 15 minutes
Baking time: 15 minutes

3 **round pita pocket breads, each about 6 inches diameter**
½ **cup (1 stick) butter, melted**
1 **tablespoon sesame seeds**
   Salt, garlic salt or onion salt to taste

1. Heat oven to 350 degrees. Cut each bread into quarters. Split each quarter in half. Brush split side of bread with butter.

2. Put in single layer onto baking sheet, buttered side up. Sprinkle with sesame seeds. Bake until crisp and golden, about 15 minutes. Season lightly with desired salt.

Use good, sharp Cheddar cheese, such as a New York Herkimer, for these delicious and crispy crackers. They're like nuts—you can't stop eating them.

CHEESE WAFERS

About 5 dozen
Preparation time: 15 minutes
Chilling time: 30 to 60 minutes
Baking time: 10 to 12 minutes

2 **cups all-purpose flour**
1 **teaspoon salt**
¼ **teaspoon each: dill weed, cayenne pepper**
⅛ **teaspoon freshly ground pepper**
⅔ **cup cold unsalted butter or margarine**
¾ **cup grated Cheddar cheese**
4 **to 5 tablespoons ice water**

1. Mix flour, salt, dill weed, cayenne pepper and black pepper in large bowl. Cut in butter until mixture resembles coarse crumbs. Stir in cheese. Gradually add ice water. Mix with a fork until dough gathers into a ball. Roll into a log, about 1½ inches in diameter. Refrigerate, wrapped in wax paper, until firm, 30 to 60 minutes.

2. Heat oven to 400 degrees. Unwrap log and cut it into ¼-inch-thick slices. Put onto baking sheets. Bake until crisp and bottoms are golden, 10 to 12 minutes. Cool on wire rack. Store in covered tin.

Why go out and buy bean dip in those little tin cans when it is so simple to make? It also is less costly. This dip is best served warm with sturdy tortilla chips and either homemade or bottled salsa.

SPICY BEAN DIP

About 2 cups
Preparation time: 10 minutes
Cooking time: 5 minutes

2 tablespoons vegetable oil

1 large yellow onion, minced

1 large clove garlic, minced

1 can (15 ounces) pinto beans

¾ cup shredded Monterey Jack cheese with jalapeños

Hot pepper sauce to taste

Diced avocado for garnish

Crisp tortilla chips for serving

Salsa for serving (see recipe, page 20)

1. Heat oil in medium saucepan. Add onion and garlic; cook and stir over medium heat until tender and lightly browned, about 5 minutes.

2. Puree beans with their liquid in food processor or blender. Stir into onion mixture. Stir in cheese and hot pepper sauce. Refrigerate at this point if making in advance.

3. To serve, heat over low heat just until hot and most of cheese is melted. Garnish with avocado. Serve with tortilla chips; pass salsa.

Creamy vegetable dip is just the thing to serve with a platter of fresh raw vegetables. Use plain yogurt for a lower-calorie version and add lots of hot pepper sauce for spice if desired.

CREAMY VEGETABLE DIP

About 2¾ cups
Preparation time: 10 minutes
Standing time: 20 minutes

1 cup plain yogurt or sour cream
1 cup mayonnaise
¼ cup each, minced: red bell pepper, green pepper
2 tablespoons each, minced: fresh parsley, fresh dill, fresh chives
Dash hot pepper sauce
Pinch salt
Assorted raw vegetables

1. Mix all ingredients, except assorted raw vegetables, in medium bowl. Let stand at least 20 minutes before serving. Serve with assorted raw vegetables.

Here is an easy dip to make, and the combination with raw vegetables makes it a sure hit with those watching their weight. If you'd like a more tangy taste, try substituting plain low-fat yogurt for the sour cream.

GREEN PEPPERCORN DIP

About 1½ cups
Preparation time: 10 minutes
Chilling time: 1 hour

4 ounces softened cream cheese
⅓ cup each: sour cream, mayonnaise
2 tablespoons each, minced: green onion, fresh parsley
2 tablespoons drained bottled green peppercorns
1 tablespoon lemon juice
1 clove garlic
½ teaspoon paprika
Dash hot pepper sauce
Salt to taste
¼ cup minced celery
Assorted raw vegetables and crackers

1. Put cream cheese, sour cream and mayonnaise in blender or food processor; process until smooth. Add remaining ingredients except celery, raw vegetables and crackers. Process until smooth. Stir in celery.

2. Refrigerate until cold, about 1 hour. Serve with vegetables and crackers.

Using the microwave oven to cook the eggplant for this spread cuts down on the time and eliminates having to wash another pan. If eggplant has never been one of your favorites, try this. You might change your mind.

EGGPLANT SPREAD

About 2 cups
Preparation time: 15 minutes
Chilling time: 30 minutes
Microwave cooking time: 7 to 9 minutes

1 **medium eggplant**
¼ **cup each: minced onion, minced fresh parsley**
2 **tablespoons each: olive oil, fresh lemon juice**
1 **teaspoon salt**
1 **clove garlic, minced**
⅛ **teaspoon freshly ground pepper**
1 **large tomato, diced**
¼ **cup finely chopped walnuts**
 Pita chips, crackers or bagel chips for serving

1. Pierce eggplant several times with the tines of a fork, then put it on paper towels or microwave-safe plate in the microwave oven. Microwave on high (100 percent power) until eggplant softens and skin shrivels, 7 to 9 minutes, turning over after 5 minutes. Refrigerate until cool to the touch, about 30 minutes.

2. Peel eggplant; cut off and discard stem end. Cut lengthwise in half. Roughly cut up eggplant and put into food processor or blender. Add onion, parsley, oil, lemon juice, salt, garlic and pepper. Process with on/off turns until smooth. Stir in tomato and nuts.

3. Serve with pita chips, crackers or bagel chips.

■ *This fish spread has two "tricks." One is the use of the microwave oven, which makes it a speedy spread to prepare, and the second is that it tastes a lot more expensive than it is. Mixing cooked orange roughy, flounder, sole or turbot with crabmeat gives the taste illusion of all crabmeat.*

CRAB AND FISH SPREAD

About 3 cups
Preparation time: 10 minutes
Microwave cooking time: 5 to 7 minutes
Chilling time: 30 minutes

1 pound skinless orange roughy, flounder, sole or turbot fillets
1 jar (12 ounces) cocktail sauce
4 to 6 tablespoons prepared horseradish
1 package (6 ounces) frozen crabmeat, thawed, well drained
Celery sticks, Belgian endive leaves, crackers or bagel chips for serving

1. Arrange fish on microwave-safe plate with thickest portion toward outside of plate. Cover with plastic wrap, vented at one corner. Microwave on high (100 percent power) until fish starts to separate and flake, 5 to 7 minutes, rearranging fish after 3 minutes. Drain well. Let stand 1 minute to finish cooking.

2. Flake fish with fork to help cool; drain. Cover well and refrigerate until cool, 30 minutes.

3. Combine cocktail sauce and horseradish in large bowl. Taste and adjust seasoning. Stir in fish and most of the crabmeat, reserving the prettier whole pieces of crab for garnish.

4. Spoon onto serving dish and garnish with reserved crabmeat. Serve with celery sticks, Belgian endive leaves, crackers or bagel chips.

■ *Tomatillos, small green fruit incased in a papery husk, are the base of this salsa. Tomatillos are often labeled green tomatoes but are really related to the Cape gooseberry, not the tomato. For the freshest taste, the salsa should be prepared just before serving.*

FRESH TOMATILLO SAUCE (Salsa verde)

About 2½ cups
Preparation time: 15 minutes

8 tomatillos, husks removed
2 cloves garlic
½ teaspoon salt
1 medium white onion, chopped
1 serrano pepper, seeded, minced
½ cup fresh cilantro (coriander) leaves

1. Add tomatillos to boiling water in large saucepan. Boil 1 minute. Drain; rinse in cold water.

2. Grind garlic with salt in blender or molcajete (Mexican mortar and pestle). Do not puree. Add onion and serrano pepper; mix lightly. Mix in tomatillos, a few at a time; mix in cilantro. Taste and adjust seasonings. Serve immediately.

■ *Is there anyone who hasn't succumbed to the love of Mexican foods, including that all-important salsa? It can be made as hot or as mild as you want it, says Chicago-based writer and Mexican cooking authority Judy Hevrdejs. Serve it with chips as an appetizer or as an accompaniment to eggs, tacos or grilled meats and fish.*

SALSA

About 2 cups
Preparation time: 10 minutes

4 **very ripe plum tomatoes**

1 **very ripe slicing tomato**

¾ **cup finely chopped white onion**

½ **cup chopped fresh cilantro (coriander)**

2 **to 3 jalapeño peppers, seeded, minced**

Pinch salt

1. Coarsely chop tomatoes; put into small bowl. Add remaining ingredients. Toss to mix.

■ *Cooking expert Jolene Worthington says the best way to make her recipe for guacamole is the simple way—by hand. An ordinary fork will do the job. She recommends Haas avocados (they have a black-green skin with a pebbly surface) or other California avocados.*

GUACAMOLE

About 2½ cups
Preparation time: 15 minutes

1 **small ripe tomato, peeled, seeded, diced**

3 **tablespoons minced green onion, white part only**

2 **serrano or jalapeño peppers, seeded, minced**

1 **tablespoon finely chopped fresh cilantro (coriander)**

¼ **teaspoon coarse (kosher) salt**

2 **ripe avocados, preferably Haas**

1. Combine and toss all ingredients, except avocados, in small bowl. Mash mixture gently with large fork to release juices of tomato.

2. Cut one avocado in half; discard pit. Using a large spoon, scrape the flesh from the shell, making sure to scrape the dark green layer next to the skin. Mash the avocado with a large fork to chunky consistency. Add to bowl. Repeat with second avocado. Mix well. Taste, and add salt if needed.

THE CHICAGO TRIBUNE COOKBOOK

This layered avocado dip can be a meal in itself. Tell your guests to dig their chips down to the bottom of the serving dish to make sure they get the full array of ingredients.

LAYERED AVOCADO DIP

20 appetizer servings
Preparation time: 30 minutes

8 large ripe avocados, peeled, pitted, diced
4 cans (4 ounces each) chopped green chilies (mild or hot, to taste), drained
1 cup plain yogurt
3 tablespoons fresh lemon juice
2 tablespoons minced fresh cilantro (coriander)
6 small cloves garlic, minced
10 dashes hot pepper sauce, or to taste
2 cups sour cream
4 medium tomatoes, peeled, seeded, chopped
1 cup chopped green onions
2 cups finely shredded lettuce
1 cup shredded Cheddar or Monterey Jack cheese
   Tortilla chips for serving

1. Put half the avocados, chilies, yogurt, lemon juice, cilantro, garlic and hot pepper sauce in food processor or blender; process until almost smooth. Remove to medium bowl. Repeat with remaining half of these ingredients.

2. Spread avocado mixture onto large platter. Spread sour cream over mixture. Sprinkle with tomatoes, green onions and lettuce. Top with cheese. Serve with tortilla chips.

NOTE: To make ahead, reserve avocado pits. Process avocado mixture; put into bowl and put pits into middle of mixture. Cover tightly with plastic wrap and chill until serving time. Remove pits and assemble just before serving.

■ *This recipe for goat cheese dip comes from Chicago's Cafe Ba-Ba-Reeba! which serves an array of Spanish tapas. Garlic-flavored bread slices or crackers are a natural to serve with this flavorful dip.*

HOT GOAT CHEESE AND HERBED TOMATO SAUCE DIP

6 appetizer servings
Preparation time: 30 minutes
Chilling time: 3 hours
Cooking time: 1 hour

CHEESE SPREAD

- 6 ounces mild French goat cheese, such as Montrachet
- 6 ounces domestic goat cheese, or more of the French goat cheese
- 2 tablespoons fresh rosemary leaves, minced
- 1 tablespoon fresh thyme leaves, minced
  Pinch white pepper

TOMATO SAUCE

- 2 tablespoons olive oil
- ½ onion, diced
- ½ cup diced fresh fennel (or ½ cup diced celery and ½ teaspoon fennel seeds)
- 1 small carrot, diced
- 6 small cloves fresh garlic
- 1 can (15 ounces) Italian-style plum tomatoes, drained, diced
- 1 tablespoon tomato paste
- 2 teaspoons dried basil
- 1 teaspoon sugar
  Salt, pepper to taste

TOPPING AND GARNISH

- 6 tablespoons coarse homemade bread crumbs
  Black olives, preferably Niçoise
  Garlic bread slices for serving

1. For cheese spread, put both goat cheeses, rosemary, thyme and white pepper into large bowl. Mix with wooden spoon until smooth. Scrape onto wax paper or aluminum foil; roll up into a log shape. Refrigerate at least 3 hours or overnight.

2. For tomato sauce, heat oil in large saucepan. Add onion, fennel, carrot and garlic. Cook over medium heat until soft, about 15 minutes. Stir in tomatoes, tomato paste, basil, sugar, salt and pepper. Simmer, uncovered, 35 minutes. Put into food processor or blender. Process until almost smooth.

3. Heat oven to 500 degrees. Put about ½ cup tomato sauce into bottom of six 5½-inch gratin or other shallow ovenproof dishes. Top each with one-sixth of the goat cheese log. Sprinkle each with 1 tablespoon bread crumbs.

4. Bake until warm, but do not melt cheese, 5 to 10 minutes. Garnish with olives. Serve with garlic bread for dipping.

Food writer Judy Hevrdejs' recipe for a traditional Mexican appetizer, queso fundido, is simple but good. To serve, you'll need warmed tortillas, spicy salsa and plenty of napkins.

MELTED CHEESE CASSEROLE
(Queso fundido)

4 appetizer servings
Preparation time: 20 minutes
Cooking time: 7 minutes

Vegetable oil
1 cup coarsely chopped onions
3 cups shredded Monterey Jack cheese
2 plum tomatoes, seeded, coarsely chopped
2 poblano peppers, roasted, peeled, seeded, cut in strips
12 warmed flour or corn tortillas
Salsa (see recipe, page 20)

1. Heat oven to 450 degrees. Brush an ovenproof 9- or 10-inch skillet lightly with oil. Add onions and sauté lightly until transparent. Remove to small plate.

2. Sprinkle half the cheese into the skillet. Arrange onions, tomatoes and pepper strips over cheese. Sprinkle with remaining cheese.

3. Bake until cheese is melted and bubbly, about 5 minutes. To serve, scoop cheese into a warm tortilla. Add salsa to taste. Roll up to eat.

NOTE: If you wish, sliced, pimiento-stuffed green olives, mushrooms or cooked and drained chorizo can be substituted for the tomatoes or peppers.

■ *Pistachio nuts add both an interesting texture and taste to this pâté. Like most pâtés, it has the advantage of improving with age. You can make it a week ahead of time and simply leave it in the refrigerator.*

CHICKEN LIVER PÂTÉ WITH PISTACHIOS

About 3 cups
Preparation time: 35 minutes
Cooking time: 10 minutes
Chilling time: 24 hours

1 **pound chicken livers, trimmed of membranes and fat**
1 **medium onion, sliced**
1 **cup chicken stock or broth**
1 **bay leaf**
½ **teaspoon each: dried leaf thyme, salt**
1 **cup (2 sticks) unsalted butter, softened**
2 **tablespoons cognac or brandy**
1 **teaspoon salt or to taste**
½ **teaspoon freshly ground pepper**
¼ **teaspoon ground ginger**
½ **cup chopped natural colored pistachio nuts**
1 **cup crème fraîche or whipping cream, whipped**
  Toast points, apple slices, raw vegetables for serving

1. Combine chicken livers, onion, stock, bay leaf, thyme and ½ teaspoon salt in medium saucepan. Heat to boil over medium heat; reduce heat to low. Barely simmer, covered, until livers are just tender, 6 to 8 minutes. Remove from heat; let stand 10 minutes. Drain; discard bay leaf.

2. Put livers, butter, cognac, salt, pepper and ginger into food processor or blender. (If using blender, process in two batches.) Process with on/off turns until smooth. Transfer to large bowl; stir in nuts. Refrigerate covered, 15 minutes.

3. Fold crème fraîche into liver mixture. Taste and adjust seasonings. Spoon into 3-cup terrine, packing slightly. Refrigerate covered at least 24 hours, or up to 1 week.

4. Serve with toast points, apple slices and raw vegetables.

Leslee Reis serves this luscious duck liver pâté at her restaurant, Cafe Provençal, in Evanston, Illinois. Home cooks may not be able to purchase duck livers but you can freeze livers from ducks until you have a total of one pound (from about 5 ducks). Or simply substitute fresh chicken livers.

DUCK LIVER PÂTÉ

8 appetizer servings
Preparation time: 45 minutes
Cooking time: 30 minutes
Chilling time: 3 hours

1¼ cups (2½ sticks) unsalted butter
1 small onion, finely chopped
1 clove garlic, finely chopped
1 small tart apple, peeled, coarsely grated
1 pound duck or chicken livers, trimmed of membrane and fat
¼ cup port
1 tablespoon brandy
¼ cup whipping cream
Fresh lemon juice to taste
Salt, freshly ground pepper to taste
Homemade melba toast, toast points or French bread

1. Melt ½ cup butter in medium skillet. Add onion and garlic; cook and stir over low heat until soft and golden, 15 to 20 minutes.

2. Add grated apple; continue cooking 2 minutes longer, stirring. Add livers and cook on medium heat, tossing, until livers are cooked but still pink inside, 3 to 4 minutes. Transfer mixture to food processor or blender.

3. Deglaze pan with port and brandy, raising heat and scraping away any brown bits sticking to bottom of skillet. Add to processor along with cream.

4. Process with on/off turns until smooth (if using blender, process in 2 batches). Push mixture through a fine sieve or tamis; let cool.

5. Return liver to food processor. Add remaining ¾ cup softened butter by tablespoons, running machine until all butter is incorporated. Season to taste with lemon juice, salt and pepper.

6. Spoon pâté into individual ramekins or 3-cup terrine. Cover with plastic wrap and refrigerate until firm, about 3 hours.

7. Serve with homemade melba toast, toast points or good French bread.

The combination of veal and chicken in this light terrine makes a loaf that is perfect for a picnic and also elegant enough to grace a more formal party. The word terrine is derived from the pan used to cook the mixture. A lining of thinly sliced bacon and ham keeps the moisture in and adds subtlety to the flavor.

CHICKEN AND VEAL TERRINE

8 to 10 appetizer servings
Preparation time: 45 minutes
Cooking time: 1¼ hours
Chilling time: Overnight

1 cup firmly packed fresh basil or spinach leaves
1 pound boneless veal shoulder cubes
3 boneless chicken breast halves, skinned
¼ pound veal fat cubes
7 green onions, minced
1 egg, slightly beaten
¼ cup each: pine nuts, brandy
2 cloves garlic, minced
1 teaspoon salt
¼ teaspoon freshly ground pepper
¾ pound each, thinly sliced: bacon, ham
Thinly sliced bread, assorted mustards for serving

1. Put basil (or spinach) into large saucepan with water that clings to leaves. Cook and stir over medium-high heat until leaves wilt, about 30 seconds. Drain in colander.

2. Cut ¼ pound of the veal into ¼-inch cubes; set aside. Cut enough of the chicken breasts in ¼-inch cubes to yield ⅓ cup; set aside.

3. Cut remaining chicken breasts into 1-inch cubes. Put into food processor or meat grinder; process until coarsely ground. Transfer to bowl.

4. Put remaining veal and veal fat into food processor or meat grinder. Process until finely ground. Add to ground chicken. Stir in veal cubes, chicken cubes, onions, egg, pine nuts, brandy, garlic, salt and pepper until well mixed. Fry 1 tablespoon of the mixture in small skillet until cooked through. Taste and adjust seasonings.

5. Line 6-cup enameled cast-iron terrine or 8 by 4-inch loaf pan with bacon so bottom and sides are completely covered. Line pan with ham slices. Firmly pack half the meat mixture into pan. Top with basil leaves. Top with a layer of ham. Firmly pack remaining meat mixture over ham. Top meat mixture with a layer of ham.

6. Fold overhanging bacon over ham. Add more bacon slices so mixture is completely covered. Cover tightly with aluminum foil. Cover terrine with lid. (If using loaf pan, cover with two more thicknesses of foil.)

7. Set terrine into larger pan filled with hot water. Bake until meat mixture registers 150 degrees on thermometer, about 1¼ hours.

8. Remove from oven; remove lid but not foil. Let cool on rack 1 hour. Put into a large dish. Set baking sheet on top of terrine. Top baking sheet with a brick or heavy cans to squeeze out juices. Refrigerate with the weights overnight.

9. Cut into very thin slices. Serve with thinly sliced bread and assorted mustards.

Cookbook author and Tribune *columnist Abby Mandel created this beautiful terrine from ordinary eggplants and extraordinary sun-dried tomatoes.*

EGGPLANT TERRINE WITH SUN-DRIED TOMATO MAYONNAISE

8 appetizer servings
Preparation time: 45 minutes
Draining time: 30 minutes
Cooking time: 1 hour 20 minutes
Chilling time: Overnight

2 **large eggplants, 2½ pounds total**
   Salt
¼ **cup each: unsalted butter, olive oil**
1 **medium onion, minced**
3 **large cloves garlic, minced**
   Freshly ground pepper to taste
2 **large roasted red bell peppers (see note)**
10 **large basil leaves, plus additional for garnish**
   Sun-dried tomato mayonnaise (recipe follows)

1. Trim ends from eggplants, then cut lengthwise into ⅜-inch-thick slices. Toss with 2 teaspoons salt; stand on sides in colander and let drain for 30 minutes. Rinse with cold water and pat dry.

2. Heat oven to 400 degrees. Melt butter with oil in 8-inch skillet. Add onion, garlic, ½ teaspoon salt and pepper. Cook over low heat until completely soft, about 8 minutes.

3. Brush both sides of eggplant with onion mixture. Arrange in single layer on baking sheets and cover tightly with aluminum foil. Bake until soft, 18 to 20 minutes. Reduce oven temperature to 300 degrees.

4. Line 5-cup terrine or loaf pan with plastic wrap. Cover entire bottom of terrine with half the red pepper. Arrange half the eggplant in terrine, fitting into corners and distributing as evenly as possible. Add as follows: a layer of large basil leaves, remaining red pepper, another layer of basil and remaining eggplant.

5. Put terrine into larger baking pan and place on oven rack. Pour boiling water into large pan so it comes halfway up sides of terrine. Bake for 50 minutes. Cover with piece of plastic wrap and press down on eggplant to level and compact it. Cool slightly, then refrigerate overnight or up to 2 days.

6. To serve, invert terrine onto platter and remove plastic wrap. Cut into ¾-inch slices with electric or serrated knife. Serve with a dollop of mayonnaise and garnish with basil leaves.

NOTE: To roast peppers, cut 4 sides from each pepper and place, skin side up, on baking sheet lined with aluminum foil. Broil 6 inches from heat source until skin is completely charred. Place in paper bag and seal tightly. When cool enough to handle, slip off skin.

SUN-DRIED TOMATO MAYONNAISE

About 1⅛ cups

6 **sun-dried tomatoes**
⅛ **teaspoon saffron threads**
1 **large egg yolk**
1 **tablespoon fresh lemon juice**
1 **teaspoon each: red wine vinegar, Dijon mustard**
  Cayenne pepper to taste
½ **cup each: extra-virgin olive oil, safflower oil**
  Salt

1. Put tomatoes into small dish and cover with hot water. Let soak 10 minutes, then squeeze dry and cut into quarters. Put saffron in small dish with 1 teaspoon hot water and let soak 10 minutes.

2. Put egg yolk, lemon juice, vinegar, mustard and cayenne pepper into food processor or blender and mix 1 minute. With motor running, slowly add oil in thin steady stream. When it has thickened, add saffron with water it was soaked in, and tomatoes. Mix until almost smooth. Add salt to taste. Can be made up to 4 days in advance and refrigerated.

This attractive dish, thin beef slices rolled around bright green asparagus, can be served as part of a Japanese meal or with cocktails. The rolls can be assembled in advance but should be cooked just before serving.

JAPANESE BEEF AND ASPARAGUS ROLLS

6 appetizer servings
Preparation time: 45 minutes
Cooking time: 10 minutes

1 **pound piece beef tenderloin, trimmed**
1 **pound fresh asparagus, trimmed**
1 **teaspoon sesame seeds**
  Cornstarch
2 **tablespoons vegetable oil**
½ **cup water**
6 **tablespoons soy sauce**
3 **tablespoons sugar**
2 **tablespoons mirin or white wine**
  Shredded lettuce for garnish
  Sesame seeds for garnish

1. Cut beef crosswise into ¼-inch-thick slices. Pound slices between two sheets of heavy plastic until ⅛-inch thick.

2. Lightly peel asparagus stalks. Cut stalks into 3- to 4-inch lengths. Put 3 to 4 asparagus pieces in center of slice of beef. Sprinkle lightly with sesame seeds. Roll up, tucking in ends, to enclose asparagus.

3. To cook, dredge beef rolls lightly in cornstarch. Heat oil in skillet large enough to hold rolls in single layer. Add rolls; cook over medium-high heat until well browned on all sides, 3 to 4 minutes. Pour off all but about 1 tablespoon pan juices. Mix water, soy sauce, sugar and mirin in small bowl. Pour into skillet. Cover and simmer until beef is tender, about 3 minutes.

4. Remove rolls to cutting board. Boil pan juices until slightly thickened. Cut rolls diagonally in half. Place on serving plate lined with lettuce. Spoon sauce over all. Sprinkle with sesame seeds. Serve immediately.

Numerous raw vegetables can be dipped into tempura batter and fried but fresh asparagus is especially good prepared in this manner.

ASPARAGUS TEMPURA

8 appetizer servings
Preparation time: 10 minutes
Chilling time: 1 hour
Cooking time: 10 minutes

DIPPING SAUCE
 2 **tablespoons each: soy**
    sauce, water
1½ **teaspoons mirin**
 ½ **teaspoon sugar**
ASPARAGUS TEMPURA
 2 **cups ice water**
1⅔ **cups all-purpose flour**
 1 **egg yolk**
 ⅛ **teaspoon baking soda**
 3 **cups vegetable oil for**
    deep-frying
 2 **pounds thin asparagus,**
    trimmed, chilled

1. For dipping sauce, combine all ingredients in small bowl.

2. For tempura, combine ice water, flour, egg yolk and baking soda in medium bowl; whisk until smooth. Cover and refrigerate until thoroughly chilled, about 1 hour.

3. Heat oil in wok or deep saucepan to 375 degrees. Dip asparagus into batter; let excess drain off. Deep-fry in batches until golden brown, 1 to 2 minutes. Remove from oil with slotted spoon. Drain on paper towels. Serve immediately with dipping sauce.

Food consultant Diane Hugh created this recipe for The Tribune. *These tender potatoes stuffed with a rich cream mixture are the best served slightly warm.*

NEW POTATOES WITH HORSERADISH CREAM AND CAVIAR

8 appetizer servings
Preparation time: 20 minutes
Cooking time: 40 minutes

 2 **dozen small new**
    potatoes
    Olive oil
    Coarse (kosher) salt
    Juice of 1 lemon
 2 **cups sour cream**
 3 **tablespoon freshly**
    grated or well-
    drained prepared
    horseradish
 1 **to 2 ounces red or**
    black caviar, drained

1. Heat oven to 400 degrees. Brush potatoes lightly with oil. Place in single layer on a baking sheet. Bake until fork-tender, 30 to 40 minutes. Sprinkle with salt and lemon juice. Cool 15 minutes or just long enough so they can be handled.

2. Meanwhile, combine sour cream and horseradish in small bowl. Let stand at room temperature.

3. To assemble, cut a small piece off one end of the potato so potato sits level. Cut ¼-inch piece off the other end. Scoop out flesh with a small spoon or melon baller leaving a ¼-inch-thick shell. Fill with sour cream mixture. Top with caviar. Serve immediately.

■ *Oriental appetizers have been popular at parties for years and with good reason. They add an exotic touch with a minimum of expense. These pork meatballs are best made right before serving but can be deep-fried a few hours in advance and reheated in the oven if necessary.*

PORK MEATBALLS WITH APRICOT DIPPING SAUCE

6 to 8 appetizer servings
Preparation time: 1 hour
Cooking time: 25 minutes

DIPPING SAUCE

- ½ **cup apricot preserves**
- ⅓ **cup cider vinegar**
- 2 **tablespoons hoisin sauce**
- 1 **tablespoon hot chili paste with garlic or hot pepper sauce to taste**
- 1 **tablespoon peanut oil**

MEATBALLS

- 1 **pound ground pork**
- 2 **eggs, slightly beaten**
- 6 **tablespoons all-purpose flour**
- 4 **water chestnuts, coarsely chopped**
- 2 **green onions, minced**
- 2 **cloves garlic, minced**
- 1 **teaspoon each: baking powder, minced fresh ginger**
- ½ **teaspoon salt**
  Pinch white pepper
- 1 **small loaf (8 ounces) French bread**
- 3 **to 4 cups vegetable oil for deep-frying**

1. For dipping sauce, mix all ingredients in small saucepan. Cook and stir over low heat for 10 minutes. Cool. (Sauce can be made ahead and refrigerated covered.)

2. For meatballs, mix all ingredients except bread and oil in large bowl. Let stand about 10 minutes.

3. Cut bread into ¼-inch-thick slices. Cut slices into ¼-inch cubes; place on a tray.

4. To shape meat, dip hand into water to prevent sticking. Shape pork mixture into 24 balls. Roll each ball in bread cubes, covering completely. Lightly squeeze outside of ball so that bread sticks.

5. Heat oil in wok or deep saucepan to 350 degrees. Deep-fry meatballs, a few at a time, until golden brown, 2 to 4 minutes. Remove with slotted spoon. Drain on paper towels.

6. Arrange on platter and serve with dipping sauce.

The taste of fresh pumpkin is tantalizing, and not just in pie; fritters make a wonderful dish and can be used as an appetizer as well as a side dish. Each egg-batter fritter is light and soufflé-like. Be sure to keep the oil temperature at a constant 375 degrees by using a thermometer and adjusting the heat. This insures that the batter browns quickly enough to seal out excess oil.

PUMPKIN FRITTERS

6 appetizer servings
Preparation time: 30 minutes
Standing time: 1 hour
Cooking time: 15 minutes

3 cups peeled seeded finely diced pumpkin
1¼ cups all-purpose flour
⅛ teaspoon salt
2 large eggs, separated
1 cup buttermilk or sour milk
¼ cup butter, melted, cooled
Vegetable oil for deep-frying

1. Add pumpkin to boiling water in large saucepan. Cook until crisp-tender, 3 to 5 minutes. Drain; rinse under cold water to stop the cooking. Pat dry on paper towels.

2. Mix flour and salt in large bowl. Lightly beat egg yolks in small bowl; stir in buttermilk and butter. Gradually stir into flour mixture until smooth. Do not overmix. Let batter stand for 1 hour.

3. Heat oil in deep saucepan to 375 degrees. Beat egg whites in small bowl until stiff but not dry. Gently fold into batter. Add pumpkin. Stir just to mix.

4. Carefully drop batter from a ¼ cup measure into hot oil. Deep-fry, a few at a time, turning once, until puffed and golden, 2 to 3 minutes. Remove with slotted spoon. Drain on paper towels. Serve immediately.

VARIATIONS: For a spicy appetizer, add 1½ cups finely diced boiled ham and 3 large jalapeño peppers, seeded and minced, to the batter. Serve with salsa.

For a brunch treat, add 3 tablespoons sugar to the batter. After frying, sprinkle with cinnamon-sugar while hot. Serve with coffee.

This classic Thai appetizer for pork on skewers is from Saard Kongsuwan at Roong-Petch Restaurant in Chicago. For home cooks, praise from family and friends should more than justify the extra effort of making the sauce and cucumber salad that are served with the pork. Thai ingredients are available at most Oriental markets or see sources on pages 669–70.

THAI PORK SATAY

8 to 10 appetizer servings
Preparation time: 1 hour
Marinating time: 1 hour
Cooking time: 10 minutes

10 **black peppercorns**
 1 **teaspoon whole coriander seeds**
½ **teaspoon ground cumin**
¾ **teaspoon salt**
½ **white onion, diced**
 6 **tablespoons water**
 7 **cloves garlic, halved**
 2 **stalks fresh lemon grass, thinly sliced**
 2 **slices galangal (laos), minced, about 2 tablespoons**
 2 **pounds pork tenderloin, trimmed**
 2 **teaspoons fish sauce (nam pla)**
½ **teaspoon turmeric**
    Peanut sauce (recipe follows)
    Sweet-sour cucumbers (recipe follows)
    Vegetable oil, milk for brushing

1. Put peppercorns, coriander, cumin and ¼ teaspoon of the salt into mortar. Grind with pestle until almost a powder. (Or use an electric spice or coffee grinder.) Put into blender. Add onion, water, garlic, lemon grass and galangal. Process until mixture forms a smooth thick paste.

2. Cut pork crosswise into ¼-inch-thick slices. Pound slices between two sheets of heavy plastic until ⅛-inch thick. Cut in half.

3. Put pork into large bowl. Add fish sauce, turmeric and remaining ½ teaspoon salt. Add 5 tablespoons of the garlic-onion mixture. Mix well to coat all slices. Refrigerate covered for 1 hour. (Save remaining garlic-onion mixture for other use.)

4. Meanwhile, make peanut sauce and sweet-sour cucumbers. Soak wooden or bamboo skewers in water for at least 15 minutes; drain.

5. Prepare charcoal grill or preheat broiler. Thread pork onto skewers. Grill or broil, 6 inches from heat source, brushing with oil and a little milk to prevent drying, 2 minutes. Turn; cook second side 2 minutes. Serve immediately with peanut sauce for dipping. Pass cucumbers.

PEANUT SAUCE | About 1⅔ cups

1 cup unsweetened
    coconut milk
⅓ cup each: smooth
    peanut butter, water
1 tablespoon packed
    dark brown sugar
½ teaspoon cayenne
    pepper
    Pinch salt

1. Put coconut milk, peanut butter and water into small saucepan. Heat to simmer over low heat, stirring constantly. Cook and stir until oils rise to the surface. Stir in sugar, cayenne pepper and salt. Taste and adjust seasonings. Remove from heat.

SWEET-SOUR CUCUMBERS | About 3 cups

¾ cup sugar
½ cup each: water,
    distilled white
    vinegar
    Pinch salt
1 large cucumber
½ large white onion
2 jalapeño peppers,
    thinly sliced

1. Put sugar, water, vinegar and salt into small saucepan. Heat to boil; simmer until sugar dissolves. Remove from heat; cool.

2. Remove ends from cucumber; peel if desired. Cut cucumber lengthwise into quarters; cut quarters into ⅛-inch-thick slices. Cut onion into thin slices.

3. Put cucumber, onion and cooled vinegar mixture in large bowl. Mix well. Serve garnished with peppers.

■ *Radicchio, shallots, Belgian endive and goat cheese are relatively recent additions to American supermarkets. They are combined here for a sophisticated appetizer.*

SAUTÉED RADICCHIO WITH SHALLOTS AND GOAT CHEESE

4 appetizer servings
Preparation time: 30 minutes
Cooking time: 10 minutes

Shallot vinaigrette (see recipe, page 486)

6 ounces mild goat cheese, such as Montrachet, cut into 8 slices

2 tablespoons butter

1 tablespoon olive oil

5 large shallots, sliced

8 ounces radicchio or red cabbage, shredded

3 small heads Belgian endive, sliced

Freshly ground pepper to taste

Crusty French bread

1. Make shallot vinaigrette. Arrange 2 goat cheese slices on each salad plate.

2. Heat butter and oil in large skillet over medium heat. Add shallots; cook and stir just until limp, about 2 minutes. Stir in shredded radicchio; cook and stir for 2 minutes. Stir in Belgian endive; cook and stir until crisp-tender, 5 to 6 minutes.

3. Pour half of the shallot vinaigrette into vegetable mixture. Stir just until heated through. Immediately spoon vegetable mixture over cheese slices, dividing evenly. Sprinkle with pepper. Serve immediately with slices of crusty French bread. Pass remaining shallot vinaigrette.

The highly acclaimed restaurant, Tallgrass, in Lockport, Illinois, sometimes serves this recipe for an elegant oyster first course. The oysters, poached in their own liquid, are topped with a cream/endive mixture. One word of advice: fresh oysters, in the shell, should be used rather than the pre-shucked oysters that are sometimes available.

OYSTERS WITH ENDIVE AND CREAM

12 appetizer servings
Preparation time: 45 minutes
Cooking time: 30 minutes

3 heads Belgian endive
1 cup water
  Juice of 1 lemon
  Pinch salt
3 dozen oysters in the shell
2 tablespoons chopped shallots
1 cup whipping cream
1½ cups (3 sticks) unsalted butter, softened
  Freshly ground white pepper to taste
1 ripe tomato, peeled, seeded, diced

1. Cut endive into ½-inch-thick slices. Put into saucepan with water, lemon juice and salt. Heat to simmer. Cook, stirring occasionally, until endive is very tender, 15 to 20 minutes.

2. Drain endive. Puree in food processor or blender; set aside.

3. Carefully shuck oysters over bowl to save their liquid. Put oysters into a separate bowl.

4. Reserve deep half of each oyster shell. Discard shallow half. Rinse reserved shells. Arrange on baking sheet and put into 200-degree oven to warm.

5. Heat reserved oyster liquid to simmer in medium-size heavy-bottomed saucepan. Gently poach oysters in this liquid for 1 minute. Remove oysters with slotted spoon; keep warm.

6. Add shallots to oyster liquid; boil gently until reduced to a glaze. Stir in cream and endive puree. Boil gently until about the consistency of sour cream and reduced enough to coat the back of a spoon. Cool 3 to 5 minutes.

7. Vigorously whisk in butter, a tablespoon at a time, over very low heat, until incorporated and frothy. Do not boil. Add pepper to taste.

8. Put oysters into warmed shells. Spoon warm sauce over all. Garnish with tomato. Serve immediately.

■ *This recipe for spicy clams is from Le Mikado, a pan-Asian restaurant in Chicago. Either small, tender Manila clams or Littleneck clams may be used. The amount of chopped, dried chilies can be increased or decreased according to taste preferences.*

STEAMED MANILA CLAMS WITH SPICY SAUCE

2 to 4 appetizer servings
Preparation time: 15 minutes
Standing time: Several hours
Cooking time: 5 minutes

SPICY SAUCE
- 1 cup: fish stock or bottled clam juice
- 1 cup chicken broth
- ½ cup chopped green onions
- 2 tablespoons tamari or soy sauce
- 1 tablespoon minced garlic
- 2 teaspoons each: sugar, grated fresh ginger
- 1 teaspoon each: crushed red pepper flakes, chopped fresh cilantro (coriander)

- Rind of 1 lemon (yellow part only)
- 4 dozen Manila or Littleneck clams, scrubbed clean

1. Put all ingredients, except lemon rind and clams, into glass bowl. Stir and let sit several hours or overnight.

2. Remove rind from lemon with zester (or remove with paring knife and cut into very fine strips).

3. Put clams into large pan. Add sauce mixture. Cover and cook over high heat just until clams open, about 5 minutes. Do not overcook.

4. Serve clams with broth ladled over in wide soup bowls. Sprinkle with lemon rind.

It isn't a quick recipe, but the taste combination of meat with almonds, raisins and spices wrapped in a cheese pastry is worth the effort, for you and your guests.

MEAT-FILLED TURNOVERS

16 appetizer servings
Preparation time: 45 minutes
Chilling time: 4 hours
Baking time: 25 minutes

CHEESE DOUGH
- 1 cup (2 sticks) unsalted butter, softened
- 1 package (8 ounces) cream cheese, softened
- ¼ teaspoon salt
- 2 cups all-purpose flour

FILLING
- ½ pound ground beef round
- 4 green onions, minced
- 2 cloves garlic, minced
- ¼ cup each: slivered almonds, dark raisins
- ½ teaspoon dried leaf oregano
- ¼ teaspoon each: dried marjoram, freshly ground pepper, salt
- ⅛ teaspoon ground cinnamon
- Pinch cayenne pepper or to taste
- 1 egg yolk mixed with 1 tablespoon whipping cream or milk

1. For dough, cream butter and cream cheese in large mixer bowl until smooth. Beat in salt. Using a wooden spoon, stir in flour to form a stiff dough. Gather dough into a ball. Refrigerate covered at least 4 hours or up to 24 hours.

2. For filling, mix beef, onions and garlic in large skillet. Cook and stir over medium heat until beef is no longer pink. Remove from heat. Drain off fat. Add almonds, raisins, oregano, marjoram, pepper, salt, cinnamon and cayenne pepper. Mix well. Taste and adjust seasonings.

3. Heat oven to 350 degrees. Roll out dough on lightly floured surface into a rectangle about ⅛-inch thick. Cut into 3½-inch circles. Put about 1 teaspoon of the meat mixture in center of a circle. Moisten edge of circle with egg yolk mixture. Fold over and press edge firmly to enclose filling. Repeat with remaining dough and filling.

4. Put filled turnovers onto baking sheet. Brush tops with egg yolk mixture. Bake until golden brown, about 25 minutes. Serve hot.

■ *You don't have to wait until Passover to enjoy these "egg rolls" as an appetizer, says cooking teacher Lois Levine. Use lean ground beef, such as round steak, to cut down on the fat.*

PASSOVER "EGG ROLLS"

10 appetizer servings
Preparation time: 20 minutes
Cooking time: 30 minutes

CREPES
- 3 **large eggs**
- 1 **cup water**
- ¼ **cup (½ stick) margarine, melted**
- ¼ **cup potato starch**
- ½ **teaspoon sugar**
- ¼ **teaspoon salt**
- **Margarine for frying**

MEAT FILLING
- 1 **pound ground beef round**
- 1 **can (6 ounces) tomato paste**
- 1 **medium onion, chopped**
- 1 **large egg, slightly beaten**
- ¼ **cup raisins**
- 1 **large clove garlic, chopped**
- ¼ **teaspoon each: garlic powder, salt, freshly ground pepper**

1. For crepes, put all ingredients into food processor or blender; process until well mixed, 10 to 15 seconds. (Or beat with electric mixer until well blended.)

2. To fry, melt 1 teaspoon margarine in well-seasoned 6-inch skillet. Use about 3 tablespoons of batter for each crepe, or enough batter to cover entire pan bottom. Cook over medium heat until edges are brown, about 1 minute. Loosen edges with long spatula. Slip spatula under middle of crepe and with fingers flip crepe over. Cook second side only 30 seconds.

3. Repeat until all batter is used. Stir batter before cooking each crepe because potato starch may settle to bottom.

4. For filling, mix all filling ingredients in small bowl. Put a crepe, browned side up, on work surface. Spoon about 2 tablespoons of filling down middle. Fold crepe up compactly, envelope-style, to completely enclose filling.

5. Place seam-side down in lightly oiled skillet over medium-high heat. Fry until brown and crisp on all sides, 10 to 15 minutes. (Or bake on baking sheet in 350-degree oven, brushing occasionally with melted margarine, until brown, about 30 minutes.)

NOTE: Crepes may be made ahead and frozen. Layer with plastic wrap or wax paper and place in freezer bag. Try other fillings such as vegetables or fill with ice cream and/or fresh fruit and top with melted chocolate.

Pot stickers (pan-fried dumplings) don't have to be ordered in a Chinese restaurant; they can be made in your kitchen. The food processor makes short work of the dough.

POT STICKERS

2 dozen
Preparation time: 1 hour
Standing time: 1 hour
Cooking time: 10 minutes

WRAPPERS
- **2 cups all-purpose flour**
- **¼ teaspoon salt**
- **⅔ cup tepid water**

FILLING
- **4 dried Chinese black mushrooms**
- **½ pound ground pork**
- **1 cup finely shredded cabbage**
- **1 large egg, beaten**
- **¼ cup minced green onions**
- **2 tablespoons dry sherry**
- **2 teaspoons minced fresh ginger**
- **1 teaspoon each: soy sauce, Oriental sesame oil, oyster sauce**
- **1 small clove garlic, minced**
- **¼ teaspoon freshly ground white pepper**

COOKING
- **4 tablespoons vegetable oil**
- **½ cup hot water**
- **Apricot dipping sauce (see recipe, page 32)**
- **Spicy dipping sauce (see recipe, page 38)**

1. For wrappers, put flour and salt into food processor. Process until mixed. With machine running, add water in slow steady stream until dough forms a loose ball. Knead on lightly floured surface about 30 seconds. Wrap in plastic wrap and let rest about 1 hour.

2. For filling, soak mushrooms with enough hot water to cover them in small bowl until soft, about 20 minutes. Drain; discard stems. Finely chop caps. Mix mushrooms and remaining filling ingredients in medium bowl.

3. Divide dough in half. Wrap one half in plastic. Set aside.

4. Divide remaining half into 12 equal pieces. Roll each piece on lightly floured surface in a circle about 3 inches in diameter with center slightly thicker than edges.

5. Put about 2 teaspoons of the filling onto each dough circle. Fold in half, making a half-moon shape. Crimp and pleat the edges of dough together, making a crescent shape. Let sit on floured surface covered loosely with wax paper. Repeat until all dough and filling are used.

6. To cook, heat large heavy skillet over medium heat until hot. Pour about 2 tablespoons oil into skillet. Arrange dumplings, flat side down, in oil. Fry until bottoms are pale gold, about 2 minutes. Pour in ½ cup hot water, cover immediately and cook 5 minutes. Drain off excess liquid. Add 2 more tablespoons oil to skillet. Fry until bottoms are crisp-golden, about 3 minutes. Serve immediately with apricot dipping sauce and/or spicy dipping sauce.

■ *Frozen filo dough, sometimes spelled phyllo, is a packaged product that makes life in the kitchen easier without sacrificing quality. A few precautions make working with commercial filo dough even easier: The dough must be defrosted exactly as directed on the package; take care not to puncture or twist the package, or the dough may rip. Keep the dough covered with a cloth when not using it.*

This delicious first course sits atop a pool of tangy cream sauce that helps blend the flavors and textures of the spicy veal and the crisp filo. For finger food simply make the rolls or triangles half the size specified, omit the sauce and serve the puffs with some mustards for dipping.

SPICY VEAL PUFFS WITH MUSTARD CREAM SAUCE

6 first-course servings
Preparation time: 1 hour
Baking time: 25 minutes

½ **pound each: ground veal, ground pork**

½ **cup coarse homemade bread crumbs**

½ **medium green pepper, minced**

4 **green onions, minced**

1½ **teaspoons minced fresh thyme or ½ teaspoon dried**

¼ **teaspoon each: dry mustard, salt, freshly ground pepper**

12 **sheets filo dough, thawed according to package directions**

½ **cup (1 stick) unsalted butter, melted**

Mustard cream sauce (recipe follows)

Parsley sprigs, for garnish

1. Mix veal, pork, bread crumbs, green pepper, green onions, thyme, mustard, salt and pepper in medium bowl.

2. Heat oven to 375 degrees. Carefully unwrap filo dough. Lay all the dough out flat on a clean towel. Cover dough with another towel that has been dampened and wrung out well.

3. Remove one sheet to a clean towel with short end facing you. Brush lightly with melted butter. Fold lengthwise in half to form a long strip. Brush with butter. Put 2 tablespoons of the meat filling onto bottom end of strip slightly left of strip's center. Holding the left corner in place, fold the right corner over the filling to form a triangle at the bottom of the strip. Fold triangle up the strip keeping the triangle shape; continue folding in this manner until filling is completely enclosed and you have a neat triangle shape. (The folding motions are the same as in folding the flag. If you wish to make rolls, simply fold sides of dough over filling and roll up.)

4. Repeat to use up filling and dough. Put folded (or rolled) pieces onto baking sheet.

5. Brush tops with butter. Bake until crisp and golden, about 25 minutes. To serve, put a pool of the sauce onto each serving plate. Set 2 baked puffs on top of the sauce. Garnish with parsley.

MUSTARD CREAM SAUCE | About 1 cup

½ cup dry white wine
¼ cup minced shallots
2 cups whipping cream
1 tablespoon unsalted butter, softened
1 to 2 tablespoons country-style Dijon mustard
Salt, freshly ground pepper to taste

1. Put wine and shallots into small nonaluminum saucepan. Heat to boil. Boil gently until wine is reduced to about 1 tablespoon.

2. Stir in cream. Boil gently until cream is reduced to about 1 cup and sauce coats the back of a spoon, about 10 minutes. Strain into bowl. Stir in butter until melted. Stir in mustard, salt and pepper to taste.

The name of this appetizer is something of a teaser in itself. Does it mean that oysters prepared in this manner will transport an oyster-lover right to heaven? This sumptuous appetizer, from the late food writer Roy Andries de Groot, should be served straight from the oven, sizzling hot. The "angels" can be eaten right off a toothpick, or on a small round of buttered toast.

ANGELS ON HORSEBACK

6 to 8 servings
Preparation time: 45 minutes
Cooking time: 15 minutes

24 thin slices medium-lean, country-style bacon
24 medium-sized oysters, freshly shucked
2 tablespoons anchovy paste
Juice of 2 lemons
24 small rounds of buttered toast, optional
Parsley or watercress sprigs for garnish

1. Heat oven to 425 degrees. Separate bacon slices, trim off rind. Place an oyster in the center of each bacon slice. Touch oyster on each side with a tiny dab of anchovy paste and a spritz of lemon juice. Use less than ¼ teaspoon anchovy paste for each oyster.

2. Roll up oyster, encasing it in bacon, tucking in the sides like an envelope. Hold it together by carefully sliding onto a wooden skewer.

3. Arrange skewers so each end is supported in baking pan; the angels must not touch the pan. Bake in center of oven until bacon is thoroughly crisp and light golden in color, 5 to 9 minutes.

4. Slide angels off skewers onto toast, or put onto warm platter. Garnish with parsley. Serve immediately.

■ *This Indian appetizer recipe comes from cooking teacher Rajana Bhargava, who says she cooks in a sari. You can use an apron instead.*

SAMOSAS WITH MINT CHUTNEY

24 appetizer servings
Preparation time: 1½ hours
Chilling time: 1 hour
Cooking time: 40 minutes

DOUGH

- 2 **cups sifted all-purpose flour**
- 6 **tablespoons vegetable oil**
- 1 **teaspoon salt**
- ½ **cup water**

FILLING

- ¼ **cup vegetable shortening, vegetable oil or margarine**
- 2 **teaspoons each: cumin seeds, fennel seeds**
- 2 **or 3 jalapeño or serrano peppers, seeded, minced**
- 6 **medium potatoes, boiled, peeled, cut into ¼-inch cubes**
- ½ **cup shelled peas**
- 4 **teaspoons ground coriander**
- 2 **teaspoons each: curry powder, lemon juice**
- 1 **teaspoon salt, or to taste**
  Vegetable oil for deep-frying
  Mint chutney (see recipe, page 648)

1. For dough, mix flour, oil and salt in large bowl. Add water slowly; knead to a hard dough. Knead an additional 10 minutes (keep hands oiled so dough won't stick). Cover dough with plastic wrap and refrigerate at least 1 hour.

2. For filling, heat shortening over medium heat in large skillet for 2 minutes. Add cumin seeds, fennel seeds and jalapeño peppers; cook 1 minute. Add potatoes and peas; cook and stir until mixture looks dry, about 10 minutes. Remove from heat; stir in coriander, curry powder, lemon juice and salt.

3. Knead dough for 1 minute; divide in half. Cut each half into 12 equal pieces. Roll each piece into a ball. Put one ball at a time onto lightly floured work surface. Keep remaining dough covered. Roll into a 7-inch circle. Cut the circle in half (each semicircle will make 1 samosa).

4. Put a small bowl of water next to work surface. Out of each semicircle, form a cone: moisten half of the straight edge with water. Fold the dry half of the straight edge so it overlaps the moistened portion by ¼ inch. Press the overlapped edges securely together to seal. Drop about 1 teaspoon of the filling into the cone. Moisten the open end of the cone and pinch the open end shut, closing the cone in a triangular shape; press tightly to seal.

5. Repeat with remaining dough and filling. (Samosas can be shaped a few hours ahead of time; keep loosely covered in refrigerator. Let them warm at room temperature 30 minutes before frying.)

6. Heat oil in deep saucepan to 350 degrees. Add 8 to 10 samosas and deep-fry, turning occasionally until evenly brown and flaky, about 10 minutes. Remove with slotted spoon. Drain on paper towels. Repeat to fry all samosas. Serve with mint chutney.

Caponata is an Italian medley of vegetables flavored generously with olive oil, garlic and often olives, capers and raisins for a unique flavor combination. Serve it either as a side dish or as directed here.

CAPONATA IN RED CABBAGE LEAVES

8 appetizer servings
Preparation time: 25 minutes
Standing time: 30 minutes
Cooking time: 40 minutes

2	medium eggplants, about 1 pound each, cut into ¾-inch cubes
	Salt
5	tablespoons olive oil
2	ribs celery, chopped
2	green peppers, seeded, chopped
2	medium onions, halved, thinly sliced
1	large clove garlic, minced
4	medium tomatoes, diced
⅓	cup sliced pitted black olives
¼	cup dark raisins
2	tablespoons red wine vinegar
1½	tablespoons drained capers
16	small red cabbage or radicchio leaves
	Freshly ground pepper to taste
¼	cup toasted pine nuts

1. Sprinkle eggplant generously with salt. Let drain on paper towels for 30 minutes. Rinse; pat dry.

2. Heat 1 tablespoon of the oil in large skillet; add celery, green peppers, onions and garlic. Cook and stir over medium-high heat until onions are translucent, about 3 minutes. Remove from skillet with slotted spoon. Add remaining oil to skillet; heat. Stir in eggplant; cook until golden, about 10 minutes.

3. Stir in onion mixture, tomatoes, olives, raisins, vinegar and capers. Cook, stirring occasionally, over low heat, until eggplant is tender, about 20 minutes. Let cool to room temperature.

4. Meanwhile, add cabbage leaves, a few at a time, into a large pot of boiling water. Cook until leaves are crisp-tender and flexible, about 1 minute. Remove from water with slotted spoon and rinse under cold water to stop the cooking. Repeat with remaining leaves.

5. To serve, stir pepper and pine nuts into eggplant mixture. Spoon some of the mixture into center of each cabbage leaf. Wrap leaf around mixture and eat out of hand.

Several trendy mid-eighties ingredients and techniques are combined in a single restaurant recipe from the American Grill in Glenview, Illinois. Cooking spice-coated meat (or more commonly, fish) over high heat is a Cajun technique. Carpaccio was originally a raw beef appetizer served at Harry's Bar in Venice but here it is teamed with chili mayonnaise, an invention of the American Southwest. The result is an explosive but enjoyable amalgamation.

BLACKENED CARPACCIO WITH CHILI MAYONNAISE

6 appetizer servings
Preparation time: 45 minutes
Chilling time: 2 to 3 hours

2 **tablespoons each:
  paprika, freshly
  ground white pepper**
1 **tablespoon each:
  dried basil,
  cayenne pepper,
  chili powder,
  ground cumin,
  garlic powder,
  onion powder,
  dried leaf oregano,
  salt**
1¼ **pound piece beef
  tenderloin, well
  trimmed**
3 **tablespoons clarified
  butter**
  Lettuce leaves
  **Chili mayonnaise
  (recipe follows)**
2 **firm tomatoes,
  chopped**
6 **sprigs fresh cilantro
  (coriander) for
  garnish**

1. Mix spices together in bottom of large flat dish. Dip beef in butter; then roll in spice mixture until beef is heavily coated on all sides.

2. Heat large heavy skillet, preferably cast-iron, over medium-high heat until very hot. Put beef into skillet. Cook until one side is blackened, about 5 minutes. Immediately turn and cook until blackened all around. Remove to plate; refrigerate immediately. (Beef will be blackened outside and very rare inside.) Refrigerate until thoroughly cold, 2 to 3 hours.

3. Arrange lettuce leaves in single layer over 6 chilled dinner plates. Using an electric knife, cut beef into very thin slices. Arrange slices over lettuce.

4. Top each serving with a dollop of chili mayonnaise. Garnish with tomato and cilantro.

NOTE: Keep beef in coldest section of the refrigerator right up until serving time.

CHILI MAYONNAISE | About 1 cup

1 **cup homemade
  mayonnaise (see
  recipe, page 487)**
½ **teaspoon cayenne
  pepper**
¼ **teaspoon chili powder**

1 **jalapeño pepper,
  seeded, minced**

1. Mix mayonnaise, cayenne pepper, chili powder and jalapeño together in small bowl. Cover and refrigerate until needed.

The following recipe is from Leslee Reis, owner of Cafe Provençal in Evanston, Illinois. She has paired dried ancho chilies with mushrooms for a hearty appetizer that can be served year round.

MUSHROOMS WITH ANCHO CHILIES

16 appetizer servings
Preparation time: 30 minutes
Soaking time: 30 minutes
Cooking time: 20 minutes

2 **ounces dried mushrooms, such as cepes or porcini (see note)**

3 **cups hot water**

3 **dried ancho chilies**

½ **cup olive oil**

2 **jalapeño peppers, seeded, minced, optional**

4 **ounces pancetta, sliced, cut into strips (see note)**

2 **teaspoons minced fresh garlic**

2 **pounds fresh button mushrooms, wiped clean, halved or quartered if large**

1 **to 2 tablespoons fresh lemon juice**

Salt, freshly ground pepper to taste

¼ **cup minced fresh parsley**

1. Soak dried mushrooms in hot water until softened, about 30 minutes. Strain and reserve soaking liquid and mushrooms separately.

2. Slit ancho chilies open and remove seeds and stems. Cut into ¼-inch-wide strips.

3. Heat oil in large heavy-bottomed skillet until hot but not smoking. Add dried mushrooms, ancho chilies and jalapeño peppers. Cook and stir over high heat 1 minute. Reduce heat to medium; add pancetta. Cook and stir until the pancetta begins to turn golden, 2 to 3 minutes.

4. Stir in garlic; cook and stir until garlic begins to turn golden, about 2 minutes. Stir in reserved soaking liquid from mushrooms. Heat to a boil; boil gently until liquid reduces to a glaze, 5 to 10 minutes.

5. Stir in fresh mushrooms, lemon juice, salt and pepper. Cook and stir over medium heat until most of the moisture has evaporated, about 5 minutes. Remove from heat. Let cool. Sprinkle with parsley. Serve at room temperature.

NOTE: Dried cepes and porcini are available at gourmet food shops. Other dried mushrooms, such as chanterelles or shiitakes, may be substituted. Pancetta, a type of unsmoked Italian bacon, is available at Italian markets. Salt pork or lightly smoked bacon may be substituted.

The cocktail hour is back in vogue, but instead of serving heavy canapes try refreshing pea pods filled with a spicy crab mixture. They can be made several hours ahead of time.

PEA PODS STUFFED WITH CRABMEAT

12 appetizer servings
Preparation time: 30 minutes
Cooking time: 1 hour

½ **pound fresh snow pea pods**

2 **packages (6 ounces each) frozen crabmeat, drained well**

¼ **cup each: mayonnaise, chili sauce**

2 **tablespoons finely chopped celery**

1 **tablespoon each: minced fresh parsley, drained small capers**

⅛ **teaspoon each: salt, freshly ground pepper**

1. Remove strings from pea pods. Drop into large pot of boiling water; cook until pods turn bright green, about 10 seconds. Drain; rinse under cold water to stop the cooking. Split pods open.

2. Mix remaining ingredients in large bowl. Taste and adjust seasonings. Stuff each pea pod with about 1 teaspoon of the crab mixture. Refrigerate, covered, until serving time.

Tender green beans, marinated in olive oil and lemon juice, are wrapped in a piece of prosciutto or ham for a light appetizer. To save on preparation time, have the prosciutto sliced by the butcher.

PROSCIUTTO WRAPPED GREEN BEANS

12 appetizer servings
Preparation time: 20 minutes
Cooking time: 10 minutes

1 **pound fresh green beans, ends trimmed**

3 **tablespoons olive oil**

2 **tablespoons fresh lemon juice**

¼ **teaspoon each: salt, freshly ground pepper**

18 **thin slices prosciutto or smoked ham**

2 **lemons, cut into wedges**

1. Add beans to large pot of boiling water. Boil, uncovered, until beans are bright green and crisp-tender, about 6 minutes. Drain; rinse under cold water to stop the cooking.

2. Mix oil, lemon juice, salt and pepper in large bowl. Add beans. Refrigerate, stirring occasionally, 10 minutes.

3. Drain beans; reserve marinade. Cut prosciutto slices crosswise in half. Wrap several beans in each piece of prosciutto. Arrange on platter. Drizzle with reserved marinade. Sprinkle with pepper. Garnish with lemon wedges.

Tapas are Spanish noshing food. Small, appetizer-size portions made from all manner of ingredients, tapas have been served for centuries in Spain. The following recipe for mussels vinaigrette comes from Cafe Ba-Ba-Reeba! in Chicago.

MUSSELS VINAIGRETTE

4 appetizer servings
Preparation time: 30 minutes
Cooking time: 5 minutes

2 dozen mussels, scrubbed, debearded

1 small each, seeded, cut into ¼-inch dice: green pepper, red bell pepper, yellow bell pepper

½ cup olive oil

¼ cup red wine vinegar

1 hard-cooked egg, chopped

2 tablespoons chopped fresh parsley

½ teaspoon salt
Pinch freshly ground pepper

1. Put mussels into large pot. Add 1 inch of water; set pot over high heat. Cover and steam just until mussels open, 3 to 5 minutes. Drain.

2. Remove one side of mussel shell leaving mussel on remaining shell. Mix remaining ingredients. Spoon a dollop of the mixture over each mussel. Serve immediately.

A take-off on the Japanese dish, sashimi, or raw fish fillets, this recipe has a decidedly Western touch with a basil vinaigrette.

SALMON WITH BASIL VINAIGRETTE

2 appetizer servings
Preparation time: 20 minutes
Chilling time: 15 minutes

¼ cup each: vegetable oil, red wine vinegar

1 green onion, slivered

2 teaspoons minced fresh basil leaves

¼ teaspoon each: coarse (kosher) salt, coarsely ground black pepper

½ pound skinless salmon fillet
Basil sprigs for garnish

1. Mix oil, vinegar, onion, basil, salt and pepper in small bowl. Taste and adjust seasonings.

2. Cut salmon in half. Put each piece between 2 sheets of heavy plastic wrap. Pound gently until uniformly about ⅛-inch thick. Remove 1 sheet of plastic wrap. Put salmon onto serving plate with remaining sheet of plastic wrap side up. Remove sheet of wrap. Repeat with second piece.

3. Drizzle each lightly with vinaigrette. Refrigerate 5 to 15 minutes to chill slightly. Garnish with basil sprigs.

Simple ingredients such as smoked turkey, mustard and honey, when combined on good-quality bread, can serve as party fare. These finger sandwiches can be made up to 4 hours in advance.

SMOKED TURKEY CANAPES WITH HONEY MUSTARD

12 to 14 appetizer servings
Preparation time: 30 minutes

½ **cup country-style Dijon mustard**

2 **tablespoons honey**

1 **loaf (16 ounces) thin-sliced pumpernickel bread**

2 **heads Boston lettuce, leaves separated**

20 **thin slices smoked turkey breast, about 2 pounds**

1. Mix mustard and honey in small bowl. Spread bread slices on one side with mustard mixture. Top half of the bread slices with a lettuce leaf and then a turkey slice. Top with a second piece of bread to make a sandwich.

2. Cut sandwiches into halves or quarters depending on size of bread. Arrange on platter. Refrigerate, tightly covered, up to 4 hours.

A good steak tartare is dependent on the freshest meat possible and very clean equipment for preparing it. You might choose to serve the meat plain and allow your guests to add their own ingredients and garnishes to taste.

STEAK TARTARE

6 appetizer servings
Preparation time: 45 minutes

1 pound boneless lean beef, preferably tenderloin or top round

ACCOMPANIMENTS

Chopped fresh flat-leaf parsley

Chopped drained capers

Chopped cornichons or dill pickles

Chopped pitted Niçoise olives

Minced red or white onion

Minced garlic

TO SERVE

Salt, freshly ground black pepper to taste

Lettuce leaves

1 or 2 raw egg yolks

Cherry tomatoes

Sliced pumpernickel or dark rye bread

1. Shortly before serving, trim all fat and membranes from beef. Cut meat into small cubes. Finely chop the cubes, using a very sharp chef's knife on a cutting board. (Or, use a food processor with on/off turns.) Refrigerate meat, covered.

2. Arrange accompaniments in small dishes near serving table.

3. To serve, mix a little salt and pepper into meat and shape into a mound. Put onto a lettuce-lined platter. Make a well in center of meat and drop in egg yolk. Garnish with tomatoes.

4. At the table, mix egg yolk and other accompaniments into meat to desired tastes. Serve with bread.

BEVERAGES

During the Prohibition era, Chicago developed a world-wide reputation as a beverage center. Unfortunately, the focus was on the celebrity gangsters who made or stole illicit booze.

Before "the noble experiment," the city's inhabitants enjoyed locally made beers, wines from vineyards in Ohio and Missouri as well as far-off France, and sublime cocktails produced by talented mixologists at numerous bars and nightclubs. Then, as now, important coffee companies were located in the city.

Some famous Roaring Twenties drinks are popular still, though the multi-martini business lunch has largely evaporated here as elsewhere. Chicago tourists have brought back from overseas a taste for many other mixed drinks, brandies, cordials and aperitifs in the years since the end of World War II. Beers from around the world are readily available and the local beer industry is enjoying a resurgence with the opening of several micro-breweries. Our most popular wines now come from the vineyards of California, while imports flood in from such traditional Western European suppliers as France, Italy, Spain and Germany as well as new sources such as Australia.

Meanwhile, statistics show that the most popular beverages of all in Chicago and across the nation are soft drinks.

The trigger for much of this activity involving beverages is a search by consumers for enhanced flavor, variety and novelty. But another important factor is health concerns. Whole new industries have sprung up to provide plain and flavored bottled waters, nonalcoholic or low-alcohol beer and wine, sparkling fruit juices and wine coolers. Bartenders routinely prepare "mocktails" or "virgin" drinks made without alcohol, while people entertaining at home are well advised to offer some alternatives to alcoholic beverages.

All this is reflected in the recipes in this chapter. Readers of *The Tribune* have always been eager for beverage recipes to help them entertain. Those presented here include holiday punches and eggnogs, blender and iced tea drinks for summer, contemporary champagne cocktails and a tasty assortment of nonalcoholic cocktails.

BEVERAGES

NONALCOHOLIC

Apple spritzer

Cranberry nog

Frothy lemon cooler

Iced tea

Indian spiced tea

Tangerine tea

Rhubarb lemonade punch

Green chili Bloody Mary

Not so old-fashioned
   old-fashioned

Sparkling orange mint julep

ALCOHOLIC

Cajun martini

Citrus spritzer

Champagne variations

Papaya daiquiri

Raspberry slush

Margarita

Classic Southern eggnog

Mary Meade's eggnog

Cider punch

Holiday punch

Sake-pineapple punch

Sparkling apricot punch

Rum risk punch

This nonalcoholic spritzer is especially appropriate when Midwestern apples are being harvested and fresh apple cider is in abundance.

APPLE SPRITZER

1 serving
Preparation time: 2 minutes

¾ **cup apple cider, preferably unfiltered**
¼ **cup club soda**
 Ice
 Green apple slice, lemon wedge, optional

1. Mix apple cider and club soda together in 10-ounce old-fashioned glass. Fill with ice. Garnish with green apple slice or lemon wedge.

For those who find traditional eggnog too rich, this nonalcoholic version reduces the milk and adds the fruit flavor and Christmas color of cranberry.

CRANBERRY NOG

12 servings
Preparation time: 15 minutes

6 **large eggs, separated**
1 **cup confectioners' sugar**
2 **cups cranberry juice cocktail, cold**
1 **cup cold milk**
2 **cups cold whipping cream**
 Ground cloves to taste

1. Whisk egg yolks in large nonaluminum bowl until thick and lemon-colored. Whisk in half of the sugar. Whisk in cranberry juice, a little at a time, until blended. Whisk in remaining sugar until dissolved. Whisk in milk. (Recipe can be prepared to this point several hours in advance.)

2. To serve, beat egg whites until stiff but not dry. Beat cream until soft peaks form. Fold cream into egg whites, then into cranberry juice mixture. Sprinkle with cloves. Ladle into small glasses.

NOTE: An alcoholic version may be made by substituting cranberry-flavored liqueur for all or part of the cranberry juice. Or, for a peach version, substitute peach-flavored brandy for the cranberry juice.

This lemon cooler is based on the fresh lemonade sold at stands at state fairs and festivals. Simply composed of lemons, sugar, water and ice, it quenches thirst and refreshes the palate.

FROTHY LEMON COOLER

2 to 4 servings
Preparation time: 10 minutes

5 large lemons
2 cups each: ice water, crushed ice
½ cup sugar

1. Cut lemons crosswise in half. Squeeze lemon juice through sieve into glass measure; there should be about 1 cup. Put half of the lemon juice, water, ice and sugar into blender container. Blend at high speed until frothy.

2. Pour into tall, chilled pitcher. Repeat with remaining ingredients. Serve immediately.

Tastings in The Tribune *test kitchen proved that when it comes to ice tea, the real thing is superior to the instant substitute. Try this recipe on one of those summer scorchers.*

ICED TEA

2 quarts
Preparation time: 5 minutes

2 quarts water
6 heaping tablespoons loose black tea or 15 tea bags
Ice cubes

1. Put 1 quart of water in a nonaluminum pan with tight-fitting lid. Heat to boil. When water boils furiously, add tea. Cover pan immediately and remove from heat. Steep 3 to 5 minutes (no longer or tea will be bitter).

2. Put remaining 1 quart cold water in large, heatproof bowl or 2-quart pitcher. Stir tea; pour through fine sieve into bowl. Serve immediately over ice cubes in tall glasses.

NOTE: If refrigerated, tea may become cloudy. It may also become cloudy if steeped too long. The cloudiness doesn't impair flavor or quality, but if you wish to make it clear again, add a little boiling water.

Here's a delightful variation to serve to company at teatime or after an Indian meal to refresh the palate.

INDIAN SPICED TEA

6 servings
Preparation time: 10 minutes

6 cups water
6 tablespoons Darjeeling tea
4 to 5 green cardamom pods
½-inch piece cinnamon stick, broken up
2 to 3 whole cloves
Half-and-half, sugar, optional

1. Heat water to boil. Add tea and spices to preheated tea pot. Pour in boiling water. Cover. Let steep 4 minutes.

2. Strain into cups. Serve with half-and-half and sugar, if desired.

Spice and citrus make an extra-refreshing, reviving hot tea.

TANGERINE TEA

4 servings
Preparation time: 5 minutes
Cooking time: 5 minutes

2 cups cold water
1½ cups fresh tangerine or orange juice
¼ cup sugar
¼ teaspoon ground cinnamon
⅛ teaspoon ground cloves
2 tea bags

1. Heat water to boil in medium nonaluminum saucepan. Stir in tangerine juice, sugar and spices. Heat to boil; cook and stir until sugar is dissolved. Remove from heat.

2. Add tea bags; cover; let steep 5 minutes. Mix; serve hot or chilled over ice.

Reader Jean E. Reeb of Woodstock, Illinois, contributed this unusual, nonalcoholic fruit punch. For best results, chill the base mixture for several hours. Add the lemon-lime soda just before serving.

RHUBARB LEMONADE PUNCH

12 servings
Preparation time: 10 minutes
Cooking time: 20 minutes
Chilling time: Several hours

4 to 5 cups fresh or frozen diced rhubarb
3 cups water
1 can (6 ounces) frozen lemonade concentrate
¼ to ½ cup sugar to taste
1 bottle (16 ounces) lemon-lime carbonated soda, cold

1. Put rhubarb, water, lemonade concentrate and sugar into large, nonaluminum saucepan. Heat to simmer; cook, covered, over low heat until rhubarb is very soft, about 20 minutes. Press mixture through fine strainer into pitcher. Discard pulp. Refrigerate until chilled, several hours.

2. To serve, pour the rhubarb mixture over ice cubes in small punch bowl. Slowly pour in lemon-lime soda. Serve immediately.

NOTE: Sparkling water or club soda can be substituted for the lemon-lime soda.

In this drink from the popular Chicago outpost of Southwestern cooking, the Blue Mesa Restaurant, spice—not alcohol—provides the lift.

GREEN CHILI BLOODY MARY

4 servings
Preparation time: 15 minutes

1 quart tomato juice
2 tablespoons Worcestershire sauce
1 tablespoon chopped, canned hot or mild green chilies, to taste
1 teaspoon freshly ground pepper
¼ teaspoon salt, or to taste
Hot pepper sauce to taste
Celery salt
Ice cubes
1 zucchini, sliced into sticks

1. Mix tomato juice, Worcestershire sauce, green chilies, pepper, salt and hot pepper sauce in a blender. Process until smooth.

2. Sprinkle a small amount of celery salt in saucer. Wet rims of four 12-ounce brandy snifters or tall glasses with water. Twirl wet rims in celery salt. Fill snifters with ice. Add tomato juice mixture. Garnish each snifter with a zucchini stick.

NOTE: One jigger (3 tablespoons vodka) may be added to each drink if desired.

Here's a first-rate "mocktail" from one of Chicago's most famous watering holes, The Pump Room.

NOT SO OLD-FASHIONED OLD-FASHIONED

1 serving
Preparation time: 4 minutes

1 **each: orange slice,
   maraschino cherry**
2 **dashes Angostura
   bitters**
1 **teaspoon sugar or low-
   calorie sweetener to
   taste**
   Ice cubes
½ **cup sparkling water**

1. Mash together orange and cherry in old-fashioned glass. Add bitters, sugar, ice cubes and sparkling water. Stir well. Serve.

This nonalcoholic mint julep is flavored with fresh orange juice as well as fresh mint for a refreshing summer drink.

SPARKLING ORANGE MINT JULEP

6 to 8 servings
Preparation time: 15 minutes
Standing time: Overnight

¾ **cup each: freshly
   squeezed orange
   juice, sugar**
½ **cup water**
3 **cups lightly packed
   fresh mint leaves**
   Crushed ice
1 **bottle (32 ounces) club
   soda**
   **Sprigs of fresh mint
   for garnish**

1. Heat orange juice, sugar and water in small saucepan over medium heat. Cook and stir until sugar dissolves, 5 minutes; cool. Put mint leaves in large bowl or jar with tight-fitting lid. Pour orange juice mixture over leaves. Cover lightly; refrigerate overnight or up to 24 hours.

2. Strain mint mixture. Fill six 10-ounce glasses with crushed ice. Add ¼ cup mint mixture and ½ cup club soda. Mix with long-handled spoon. Add a sprig of fresh mint to each glass and serve.

When famous Cajun chef Paul Prudhomme first told us about his Cajun martini, we thought it would be too wicked to enjoy. Surprisingly, the picantness of the hot pepper adds flavor to the vodka or gin without making it too hot to drink. Served very cold with crisp crackers or salted nuts, it's a drink that won't last long.

CAJUN MARTINI

15 servings
Preparation time: 5 minutes
Chilling time: 8 to 16 hours

1 jalapeño pepper
1 unopened fifth of gin or vodka
Dry vermouth
Pickled green tomatoes, okra, eggplant or olives on toothpicks, optional

1. Slice jalapeño pepper lengthwise without cutting through stem. Open bottle of gin or vodka. Put pepper in bottle. Fill remaining airspace with vermouth. Recap bottle; refrigerate 8 to 16 hours.

2. Remove pepper. Store bottle in refrigerator until ready to use.

3. To serve, fill pitcher with ice and pour in martini. Strain into serving glasses. Garnish with pickled vegetables on toothpicks.

Here's a refreshing cocktail to serve at summer parties. The alcohol is optional.

CITRUS SPRITZER

4 servings
Preparation time: 10 minutes

1 cup each: orange juice, unsweetened pineapple juice
Juice of 1 lemon and 1 lime
½ cup vodka, optional
1⅓ cups cold club soda or carbonated mineral water
Cracked ice
Maraschino cherries and lemon slices for garnish

1. Mix fruit juices, vodka and club soda in tall pitcher. Serve over ice with cherries and lemon slice.

Champagne is a wonderful aperitif all by itself, and that's how the very best should be served. But moderately priced bubbly can be dressed up to suit any mood or occasion. Here are several fruitful additions to consider.

CHAMPAGNE VARIATIONS

SUMMER BLISS: Float a wedge of poached fresh peach in a glass of pink champagne.

BERRY BUBBLY: Put 1 teaspoon berry-flavored liqueur into bottom of champagne glass. Fill glass with brut or extra-dry champagne. Garnish with any kind of berry such as strawberry, blueberry, raspberry or black raspberry.

ORANGE KISS: Put 1 tablespoon orange-flavored brandy or liqueur into bottom of champagne glass. Add 2 teaspoons brandy. Fill glass with brut or extra-dry champagne. Garnish with orange twist.

LEMON FIZZ: Fill a stemmed dessert glass with lemon ice or lemon sorbet. Pour several tablespoons of extra-dry champagne over top. Garnish with mint sprig.

CLASSIC MIMOSA: Mix equal parts extra-dry champagne and orange juice.

KIR ROYALE: Put a teaspoon of crème de cassis (black-currant liqueur) into bottom of champagne glass. Fill glass with brut or extra-dry champagne.

BUBBLING PASSION: Put 3 tablespoons passion-fruit liqueur into bottom of champagne glass. Fill glass with brut or extra-dry champagne. Garnish with lemon twist.

The daiquiri, named for a town in Cuba, is one of the world's most versatile cocktails. This version features the tropical flavor of papaya. Be sure to use fresh lime juice.

PAPAYA DAIQUIRI

2 servings
Preparation time: 15 minutes

2 cups peeled, seeded
   papaya cubes
   (1 large papaya)
⅓ cup light rum
3 tablespoons
   confectioners' sugar
2 tablespoons fresh lime
   juice
1 cup crushed ice
   Lime slices,
   strawberries, mint
   sprigs for garnish

1. Put papaya, rum, sugar and lime juice into blender. Process until smooth. Add ice; blend until frothy. Pour into glasses. Garnish. Serve immediately.

VARIATIONS: *Peach daiquiri:* Substitute 2 cups diced, peeled peaches and ¼ cup dark rum for the papaya and light rum.

Slushy strawberry daiquiri: Substitute 4 cups partly frozen hulled strawberries, halved for papaya. Omit the ice.

This intensely flavored drink smells as delicious as it tastes.

RASPBERRY SLUSH

1 to 2 servings
Preparation time: 10 minutes

½ pint fresh raspberries
3 tablespoons
   confectioners' sugar
2 tablespoons raspberry-
   flavored liqueur, such
   as Chambord
3 tablespoons light rum
1 teaspoon lime juice
1 cup crushed ice

1. Puree raspberries in blender. Push through a sieve to remove seeds. Put raspberry puree, sugar, liqueur, rum and lime juice into blender. Process until smooth. Add ice; blend until frothy. Pour into glasses.

NOTE: One box (10 ounces) quick-thaw frozen raspberries, thawed, pureed and sieved may be substituted. Omit the sugar.

■ *Hispanics have contributed their unique culinary heritage to Chicago's melting pot, including that potent liquor, tequila. This is* The Tribune *test kitchen's version of a classic tequila cocktail.*

MARGARITA

1 serving
Preparation time: 5 minutes

3 tablespoons tequila
2 tablespoons orange-flavored liqueur (such as Triple Sec)
Juice of ½ large lime or 2 small limes
1 handful chopped ice
1 glass with a salt-coated rim

1. Put tequila, orange-flavored liqueur, lime juice and chopped ice into a blender container and turn on for a few seconds. Pour the drink to within ¼ inch of the salty rim.

■ *In general, eggnog enjoys greater popularity in the South than anywhere else. Perhaps that's because of the healthy shot of bourbon Southern cooks use to spike their punch. Here's the classic recipe.*

CLASSIC SOUTHERN EGGNOG

30 servings
Preparation time: 25 minutes

12 large eggs, separated
1½ cups sugar
1 quart milk
One fifth good-quality Kentucky bourbon
1 quart whipping cream
Freshly grated nutmeg

1. Beat egg yolks until very light and foamy. Gradually add 1 cup of sugar; beat until creamy. Add milk and beat until thoroughly mixed. Pour into large serving bowl and add bourbon.

2. Beat cream in large bowl until soft peaks form when the beater is lifted. Do not overbeat.

3. Beat egg whites in large bowl until foamy; gradually beat in remaining ½ cup sugar. Beat until soft peaks form when the beater is lifted.

4. Add whipped cream to egg yolk mixture; then fold in egg whites. Mix gently. Sprinkle with nutmeg. Serve immediately.

NOTE: Some say that flavor improves with time; so this, as all eggnogs, can be stored in the refrigerator from a few hours to two days before serving. However, reserve the egg whites, to be beaten and blended into the eggnog just before serving.

Beverages

A lady for all seasons in the post–World War II era, The Tribune*'s Mary Meade (like Betty Crocker, a mythical personality) crafted food and drink for her Midwestern readers. This recipe appeared in the 1955 book* Mary Meade's Kitchen Companion.

MARY MEADE'S EGGNOG

20 servings
Preparation time: 15 minutes
Chilling time: 24 hours

6 large egg yolks
1 cup each: sugar, rum, orange-flavored brandy
½ cup cognac or brandy
1½ quarts milk
3 cups whipping cream, whipped
6 egg whites, beaten stiff
Nutmeg to taste

1. Beat egg yolks in large mixer bowl until very thick and light. Gradually beat in sugar. Gradually beat in rum, orange-flavored brandy and cognac. Refrigerate 1 hour, stirring occasionally.

2. Add milk slowly; fold in whipped cream and egg whites. Store covered in refrigerator 1 day before serving. Sprinkle each serving with nutmeg.

A legacy of punches has come down to us from the hard-drinking eighteenth century Americans and immigrants who settled the Heartland. They not only left us recipes but beautiful punch bowls, cups and ladles that are collectors' items today.

Fill a beautiful punch bowl with this cider punch and you will create a gathering place, as well as a conversation piece, at a party.

CIDER PUNCH

6 to 8 servings
Preparation time: 15 minutes
Standing time: 30 minutes

1 quart unsweetened apple cider
1 cup dry sherry
Grated rind of ½ lemon
½ cup superfine sugar
Juice of 1 lemon
Freshly grated nutmeg to taste
½ cup brandy
2 thin strips of rind from an unwaxed cucumber
Lemon slices, whole cloves or cinnamon sticks for garnish

1. Mix cider and sherry and lemon rind in punch bowl. Let stand for 30 minutes.

2. Add sugar, lemon juice and nutmeg. Stir to dissolve sugar. Refrigerate until serving time.

3. Just before serving, stir in brandy. Garnish with cucumber rind and lemon slices. Serve in punch cups.

The wine list was exceptional at the now-closed Tango restaurant in Chicago and the bartenders, as well as the cooks, found novel ways to use the fruit of the vine.

HOLIDAY PUNCH

30 servings
Preparation time: 15 minutes

1   bottle (750 ml.)
    nouveau Beaujolais,
    cold
3   cups cranberry juice
    cocktail, cold
2   cups light rum, cold
¾   cup cranberry-flavored
    liqueur, cold
    Juice of two limes,
    cold
6   cups boysenberry (or
    raspberry) sherbet,
    softened
3   pesticide-free
    gardenias for garnish
2   bottles (750 ml. each)
    sparkling white wine,
    cold

1. Mix nouveau Beaujolais, cranberry juice, rum, cranberry-flavored liqueur and lime juice in punch bowl. Stir in 2 cups of the sherbet until smooth.

2. Divide remaining sherbet into scoops and float these on top of the punch. Garnish punch bowl with gardenias.

3. To serve, fill punch glass half full, being sure to get some of the sherbet in the glass. Pour in enough well-chilled sparkling wine, kept cold on the side, to fill glass.

Shilla, a Korean restaurant in Chicago, serves this deliciously refreshing cocktail. It goes well with almost any Oriental appetizer.

SAKE-PINEAPPLE PUNCH

12 servings
Preparation time: 10 minutes

9   cups unsweetened
    pineapple juice
1½ cups light rum
¾   cup each: sake, peach-
    flavored brandy
    Ice cubes
12 orange slices for
    garnish
12 maraschino cherries
    for garnish

1. Put pineapple juice, rum, sake and brandy into large pitcher. Refrigerate until very cold.

2. Pour into tall glasses filled with ice. Garnish each with an orange slice and cherry. Serve immediately.

A vivid centerpiece for a Yuletide gathering comes from the celebrated restaurant for celebrities, The Pump Room, in the Omni Ambassador East Hotel in Chicago.

SPARKLING APRICOT PUNCH

About 20 half-cup servings
Preparation time: 10 minutes
Freezing time: Overnight

ICE RING
3 cups each: ginger ale, cranberry juice cocktail
Fresh cranberries

PUNCH
2 cups cranberry juice cocktail, cold
1 can (14 ounces) apricot nectar, cold
¾ cup orange-flavored liqueur
2 bottles (750 ml. each) Spanish sparkling wine, cold
Orange slices, lemon slices, sprigs fresh mint for garnish

1. Fill an 8-cup ring mold (or a holly wreath mold or any Christmas holiday mold such as a Christmas tree) with ginger ale and 3 cups cranberry juice cocktail. Sprinkle very liberally with fresh cranberries; freeze overnight.

2. Mix 2 cups cranberry juice cocktail, apricot nectar and orange-flavored liqueur in punch bowl. Unmold ice ring; place in center of punch. Add sparkling wine.

3. Serve in chilled champagne glasses with a garnish of orange and lemon slices and sprigs of fresh mint.

A bartender at Chicago's City Tavern restaurant created this combination of tropical flavors that makes a hit at parties in winter as well as summer.

RUM RISK PUNCH

30 servings
Preparation time: 20 minutes

4 cups amber or gold rum, cold
4 cups each, cold: cranberry juice cocktail, pineapple juice, orange juice
1 cup lemon sour mix, cold
6 tablespoons orange-flavored liqueur
Ice cubes

1. Mix rum, cranberry juice cocktail, pineapple juice, orange juice, sour mix and orange-flavored liqueur in punch bowl. Mix well. Serve over ice.

EGGS & BREAKFAST

Which came first? The breakfast or the egg?

The two go hand in hand, although dishes based on eggs easily overlap into lunch, brunch and supper. Eggs are definitely one of our most versatile and useful foods; they are low in calories and high in nutrients. The only caveat, which we have become increasingly aware of in recent years, is the high cholesterol content of egg yolk. The days are probably gone when a "mess of eggs" was an every-morning staple.

But what a selection of recipes we can choose from when we do eat eggs. Soufflés, crepes, frittatas, omelets. The variety is endless.

In this selection, we have given you some of the best of the egg dishes we have tested and enjoyed over the years. Two recipes—the oven French toast and the pecan-topped toast casserole—can be made the night before, a delicious nod to the person who wants a wonderful, elegant breakfast without standing at the stove for an hour in the morning.

Most of these recipes are fit either for company or for the family. Eggs benedict, for example (a breeze with the hollandaise whipped up in the blender), are a special occasion morning tradition in many homes. They also are a dish worthy of elegant entertaining.

Homemade pancakes and waffles are another treat for most people. The recipes included here have special flavor additions such as ginger and chocolate to elevate them to new heights.

Just remember that eggs like to be handled gently. With that in mind, enjoy.

Eggs

Baked eggs with mushrooms
    and potatoes

Cheddar cheese soufflé

Curried egg salad

Crab egg foo yung

Egg, bacon and cheese bake

Egg crepes with red peppers
    and mushrooms

Make-ahead poached eggs

Basic omelet

Mexican omelet with avocado topping

Omelet with chicken, tomato
    and cheese

Morel and asparagus omelet

Scrambled eggs with chorizo

Potato and pepper frittata

Eggs Benedict

Breakfast

Baked apple pancake

Ginger pancakes with cinnamon
    butter

Pumpkin flapjacks with cider
    walnut syrup

Chocolate waffles with poached
    strawberries

Waffles with ginger pear
    topping

Oven French toast

Pecan-topped toast casserole

Savory Cheddar bread pudding

Cheese blintzes

■ *This recipe for an egg casserole was contributed by Irene Ulanov, of Northbrook, Illinois, for a story in the Food Guide on hearty meatless meals. It may be served for brunch or as a supper entree.*

BAKED EGGS WITH MUSHROOMS AND POTATOES

4 to 6 servings
Preparation time: 30 minutes
Cooking time: 40 minutes

¼ cup (½ stick) butter

3 small red potatoes, thinly sliced

½ pound fresh mushrooms, wiped clean, sliced

1 small yellow onion, sliced

6 large eggs, at room temperature, separated

½ cup half-and-half
   Pinch cayenne pepper
   Salt to taste

1 green pepper, seeded, chopped

½ cup chopped green onions

1 cup shredded sharp Cheddar cheese

3 tablespoons chopped fresh parsley

1. Melt butter in large skillet over medium heat. Add potatoes, mushrooms and yellow onion. Sauté until potatoes are crisp-tender, about 10 minutes. Remove from heat; set aside.

2. Heat oven to 350 degrees. Mix egg yolks, half-and-half, cayenne and salt in small bowl. Beat egg whites until stiff but not dry.

3. Spread potato mixture evenly over bottom of a buttered 13 by 9-inch baking dish. Pour egg yolk mixture over potatoes. Spread green pepper, green onions and ¾ cup of the cheese over egg yolk mixture. Spoon beaten egg whites evenly over all. Sprinkle with remaining cheese.

4. Bake until puffed and top is golden, about 20 minutes. Serve immediately garnished with parsley.

Soufflés have a reputation for being difficult. Each soufflé brings with it moments of anxiety. Will it rise? Or will it fall flat before it gets to the table?

Soufflés are simple to prepare if three basic rules are followed: don't overbeat the egg whites; fold them ever-so-gently into the batter; serve the soufflé as soon as it is done.

This soufflé makes a rich and satisfying main course. For variety try substituting an aged Swiss, Comte or Havarti cheese for the Cheddar.

CHEDDAR CHEESE SOUFFLÉ

6 servings
Preparation time: 20 minutes
Cooking time: 40 minutes

¼ cup each: butter, all-purpose flour
1 teaspoon dry mustard
½ teaspoon salt
   Pinch cayenne pepper
1 cup hot milk
5 large egg yolks
½ pound sharp Cheddar cheese, shredded, about 2 cups
7 large egg whites
½ teaspoon cream of tartar

1. Melt butter in small saucepan; blend in flour. Cook and stir for 1 minute. Stir in mustard, salt and cayenne pepper. Gradually add hot milk; cook and stir until thickened and smooth. Cool mixture.

2. Heat oven to 375 degrees. Beat egg yolks in large mixer bowl until thick and lemon-colored. Gradually beat in sauce; stir in cheese.

3. Beat egg whites in medium bowl until foamy; gradually beat in cream of tartar; beat until stiff but not dry.

4. Gently fold egg whites into cheese mixture. Spoon into ungreased 1½-quart soufflé dish. With a teaspoon, draw a circle around the top of soufflé mixture 1 inch from edge.

5. Bake until puffed and golden, about 35 minutes. Serve immediately.

This recipe was developed in The Tribune *test kitchen as a way to use up all those leftover Easter eggs. But there's no need to wait until Easter to hard-cook some eggs for this salad.*

CURRIED EGG SALAD

6 to 8 servings
Preparation time: 25 minutes

¾ **cup mayonnaise**
2 **tablespoons each:**
   mango chutney,
   minced fresh cilantro
   (coriander)
2 **teaspoons prepared**
   horseradish
   Juice of 1 lime
½ **teaspoon curry powder**
   or to taste
⅛ **teaspoon cayenne**
   pepper
1 **medium green pepper,**
   seeded, diced
1 **medium McIntosh**
   apple, cored, diced
5 **green onions, minced**
12 **hard-cooked large**
   eggs, chilled (see
   note)
1 **ripe avocado, peeled,**
   chopped, optional
   Salt, freshly ground
   black pepper to taste

1. Mix mayonnaise, chutney, cilantro, horseradish, lime juice, curry powder and cayenne pepper in large bowl. Stir in green pepper, apple and onions.

2. Peel and dice eggs. Add eggs and avocado to mayonnaise mixture. Toss well to mix. Add salt, pepper and additional curry powder to taste. Refrigerate covered up to 48 hours.

3. To serve, fill pita pockets with some shredded lettuce and then some of the egg salad. Or, add 1 cup drained flaked tuna, cooked shrimp or diced boneless cooked chicken to mixture; serve in cantaloupe halves if desired.

NOTE: To hard-cook eggs, immerse eggs in cold water in a saucepan, heat the water to full boil and then remove pan from heat. Let eggs stand in the hot water 15 to 20 minutes; then plunge immediately into cold water and let stand for 5 minutes. Hard-cooked eggs will keep refrigerated for up to 10 days; do not store at room temperature.

Here's a dish from columnist Beverly Dillon that will put some Oriental zip in your mealtime. The two accompanying sauces may be made in advance, stored in jars with tightly fitting lids and refrigerated for up to two days. Let them come to room temperature before serving.

CRAB EGG FOO YUNG

3 to 4 servings
Preparation time: 15 minutes
Soaking time: 30 minutes
Cooking time: 5 minutes

6 to 8 dried black
   Chinese mushrooms
3 large eggs
1 can (6½ ounces) lump
   crabmeat, drained,
   flaked
1 cup fresh bean
   sprouts, rinsed,
   drained
1 can (8 ounces) water
   chestnuts, drained,
   coarsely chopped
2 tablespoons each:
   chopped green onion,
   soy sauce
1 tablespoon chopped
   fresh cilantro
   (coriander)
½ teaspoon minced garlic
2 to 3 tablespoons
   vegetable oil
   Ginger sauce
   (recipe follows)
   Hot mustard sauce
   (recipe follows)

1. Soak mushrooms in hot water to cover until soft, about 30 minutes. Squeeze out as much water as possible. Remove and discard stems. Dice mushroom caps.

2. Lightly beat eggs in medium bowl. Add crabmeat, bean sprouts, water chestnuts, onion, soy sauce, cilantro and garlic. Stir gently to mix.

3. Heat 2 tablespoons oil in large skillet over medium heat. Fill a ¼-cup measure with egg mixture. Gently put into skillet, press to flatten slightly with the back of a spatula. Cook until bottom is almost set, 1 to 2 minutes. Turn; cook other side until bottom is golden, yet still a bit moist, about 1 minute. Arrange on platter, cover lightly with aluminum foil to keep warm. Continue cooking until all batter is used.

4. Serve with ginger sauce and hot mustard sauce.

GINGER SAUCE | About ⅓ cup

¼ cup soy sauce
1 tablespoon each: dry
   sherry, light brown
   sugar, grated fresh
   ginger
½ teaspoon white wine
   vinegar

1. Mix all ingredients in small bowl.

HOT MUSTARD SAUCE | About 2 tablespoons

2 tablespoons dry
   mustard
Dash Oriental sesame
   oil
Warm water to
   moisten

1. Mix all ingredients until mixture has a thin, smooth consistency.

Madeleine Reinke includes these baked eggs in her breakfasts at the Inn at Union Pier in Union Pier, Michigan. It's an individualized and tasty rendition of the classic bacon and eggs breakfast.

EGG, BACON AND CHEESE BAKE

4 servings
Preparation time: 15 minutes
Baking time: 10 minutes

  Vegetable oil
4 large eggs
¼ cup half-and-half
2 to 3 slices bacon,
   cooked, drained,
   crumbled
3 tablespoons shredded
   Swiss cheese
4 teaspoons chopped
   fresh parsley
  Paprika
  Parsley sprigs for
   garnish

1. Heat oven to 450 degrees. Coat 4 ovenproof ceramic ramekins, egg cups or muffin tins with oil. Crack 1 egg into each cup. Put 1 tablespoon half-and-half over each.

2. Top each with ¼ of the bacon, cheese, chopped parsley and paprika. Bake until eggs are set, about 10 minutes. Serve garnished with parsley sprigs.

This dish, created by Beverly Dillon, uses roasted red peppers as a hearty sauce for mushroom-filled egg crepes. The crepes may be served for brunch, supper or as a first course for a formal dinner.

The most time-consuming part of this recipe is roasting the red peppers, but they may be prepared in advance and refrigerated up to several days.

EGG CREPES WITH RED PEPPERS AND MUSHROOMS

4 servings
Preparation time: 45 minutes
Cooking time: 30 minutes

ROASTED RED PEPPER SAUCE
- 5 **medium red bell peppers**
- 1 **cup whipping cream**
- 2 **tablespoons fresh lemon juice**
- 1 **tablespoon minced fresh tarragon or ½ teaspoon dried**
- ½ **teaspoon salt**
- ¼ **teaspoon freshly ground pepper**
- **Dash hot pepper sauce**

FILLING
- 2 **tablespoons each: butter, olive oil**
- 1½ **pounds mixed fresh mushrooms, such as button, oyster or shiitake**
- 1 **tablespoon minced shallots or green onion**

EGG CREPES
- 8 **large eggs, lightly beaten**
- 6 **tablespoons water**
- ½ **teaspoon each: salt, freshly ground pepper**
- 2 **to 3 tablespoons butter for cooking**
- **Fresh tarragon sprigs for garnish**

1. To roast red peppers, preheat broiler. Put peppers on broiler pan. Broil 4 to 6 inches from heat source until skins are blistered and slightly charred. Wrap in foil; let stand until cool. Put onto cutting board; remove stems and seeds. Using a paring knife, peel away charred skin. Cut peppers into ¼-inch-wide strips; you should have about 2 cups.

2. For roasted red pepper sauce, put 1 cup of the roasted peppers, cream, lemon juice, tarragon, salt, pepper and hot pepper sauce into food processor. Process until smooth. Put into saucepan and heat until warm.

3. For filling, heat butter and oil over medium high heat in large heavy skillet. Add mushrooms and shallots. Cook, stirring occasionally, over medium heat, until mushrooms give up their water and are lightly browned. Add remaining red pepper strips; cook just to heat through. Remove from heat; set aside.

4. For crepes, put eggs, water, salt and pepper into medium bowl. Whisk to blend. Melt 1 teaspoon butter over low heat in an 8-inch nonstick crepe pan or skillet. Add ¼ cup of the mixture to pan. Cook until set, about 1 minute. Carefully lift edge, turn and cook other side 30 seconds. Stack crepes between sheets of waxed paper. Continue to cook until all the mixture is used. You should have 8 crepes. Loosely cover crepes with foil to keep warm.

5. To assemble, divide roasted red pepper sauce among 4 individual serving plates. Tip plate to lightly spread sauce over bottom. Put some of the mushroom filling into center of crepe and fold crepe into quarters. Gently put two filled crepes on top of sauce on each plate. Top with additional mushroom mixture. Garnish with tarragon. Serve immediately.

Poached eggs are simple to prepare once the technique of slipping the eggs into the simmering water is mastered. Practice on the family before making them for company. This recipe allows the eggs to be prepared several hours in advance of serving. To serve, the eggs are simply reheated in a bowl of hot water.

MAKE-AHEAD POACHED EGGS

6 servings
Preparation time: 5 minutes
Cooking time: 3 to 4 minutes

2 tablespoons distilled white vinegar
12 large eggs

1. Set a large bowl of cold water near cooking surface.

2. Heat 3 quarts water and the vinegar to boil in large high-sided skillet; reduce heat to low simmer. (Bubbles should just barely break on the surface.) Break 1 egg at a time into a small cup. Hold the cup as close to water surface as possible, then let egg slip out into water. Immediately push white over yolk with a large spoon. Proceed with remaining eggs. Poach until whites are set and yolks are still soft, 3 to 4 minutes.

3. Carefully remove eggs from water with slotted spoon and put into cold water. When cool, lift eggs, one at a time, from water; trim edges even with scissors. Return to cold water. Refrigerate if prepared in advance.

4. To serve, put eggs into large bowl of hot (not boiling) water. Let stand until heated, about 1 minute. Remove with slotted spoon; drain on paper towels.

An omelet is such a basic dish—eggs, with the addition of just about anything you want, cooked to a puffy, browned, savory perfection. Yet it triggers a touch of fear in many home cooks. Here's a practical, step-by-step procedure from The Tribune test kitchen.

BASIC OMELET

1 omelet
Preparation time: 5 minutes
Cooking time: 5 minutes

2 or 3 large eggs, at room temperature
1 tablespoon each: butter, water
Optional: chopped fresh herbs, or ⅓ cup of any desired filling
Salt, freshly ground pepper to taste

1. Warm eggs to room temperature. Cold eggs hitting a hot pan will produce a tough omelet. Do not salt the raw eggs; that will toughen them, too. Salt may be added with the filling or at the table.

2. The pan should be hot, but not too hot: turn the burner up high. When the pan is hot, add butter. It should melt and foam, but not brown or burn. If it does, toss it, wipe the pan, let it cool a few seconds and start over. When the butter stops foaming the pan is ready for the eggs.

3. Add water to the eggs. Mix with a fork just enough to mix eggs and the water. Don't overmix. Add optional herbs.

4. Quickly add eggs to the pan and stir gently as if making scrambled eggs. Then cook, without stirring, just until slightly less than desired doneness. (How done is done? Americans tend to prefer their omelets hard, while the French prefer theirs soft and runny.) Top with optional filling, if desired.

5. To roll the omelet out of the pan, tip the pan so the omelet rolls into itself when you lift the top edge with a spatula.

6. Reverse your grip on the pan's handle so that you're holding it from underneath; tilt the pan until nearly vertical and continue rolling the omelet onto the serving plate. Serve immediately.

■   *Salsa, either bottled or homemade, is the key to this zesty omelet that is suitable for either brunch or a vegetarian dinner. Toasted flour tortillas, Mexican rice or refried beans and a tossed salad make traditional accompaniments.*

MEXICAN OMELET WITH AVOCADO TOPPING

2 servings
Preparation time: 10 minutes
Cooking time: 5 minutes

1 avocado, peeled, pitted, diced
2 tablespoons plain yogurt or sour cream
1 tablespoon minced fresh cilantro (coriander)
1 teaspoon lemon juice
4 large eggs, lightly beaten
2 tablespoons each: water, butter
½ cup chunky-style salsa, medium to hot as desired

1. Mix avocado, yogurt, cilantro and lemon juice in small bowl. Whisk eggs and water in separate small bowl.

2. Heat butter in 10-inch nonstick skillet. Add egg mixture. Cook, stirring lightly with fork, until mixture begins to set on bottom. Then cook, without stirring, until set. Spoon salsa down middle of omelet. Loosen edges with spatula. To roll the omelet out of the pan, tip the pan so the omelet rolls into itself when you lift the top edge with a spatula. Reverse your grip on the pan's handle so that you're holding it from underneath; tilt the pan until nearly vertical and continue rolling the omelet onto plate.

3. Top with avocado mixture. Serve immediately.

NOTE: Diced ham, crisp-cooked bacon or cooked, crumbled sausage may be added.

Omelets are a wonderful way to use leftover chicken or turkey. Sunday brunch or supper is a perfect time for this dish. The recipe may be prepared ahead through step four and finished just before serving.

OMELET WITH CHICKEN, TOMATO AND CHEESE

6 servings
Preparation time: 25 minutes
Cooking time: 30 minutes

6 tablespoons butter
3 tablespoons finely chopped onion
2 cups peeled, seeded, chopped tomatoes
2 sprigs fresh thyme, chopped or ½ teaspoon dried leaf thyme
1 bay leaf
Salt, freshly ground pepper to taste
3 tablespoons all-purpose flour
1 cup chicken broth
½ cup whipping cream or half-and-half
1 cup finely cubed, cooked chicken breast, turkey, shrimp or crabmeat
1 egg yolk
¼ cup shredded Swiss, Gruyère or Fontina cheese
10 large eggs
3 tablespoons freshly grated Parmesan cheese

1. Heat 1 tablespoon of the butter in small saucepan; add onion. Cook, stirring until wilted; add tomatoes, thyme, bay leaf, salt and pepper. Simmer, stirring occasionally, about 10 minutes. Set aside.

2. Heat 2 tablespoons of the butter in small saucepan over medium heat; whisk in flour until blended. Cook and stir 1 minute. Add broth; cook, whisking vigorously until smooth and thickened. Add cream; heat to boil. Simmer, stirring often, about 5 minutes. Add salt and pepper to taste. Set aside.

3. Mix chicken, turkey, shrimp or crabmeat with 3 tablespoons of the cream sauce; set aside.

4. Stir egg yolk into remaining cream sauce. Add Swiss cheese, salt and pepper. Cook, stirring, just until the cheese melts. Set aside.

5. Preheat broiler. Set all ingredients and broiler-proof platter near work surface.

6. To cook, beat eggs with pinch of pepper. Add 6 tablespoons of tomato mixture. Heat remaining 3 tablespoons butter in 12-inch omelet pan or nonstick skillet. When hot, add eggs. Cook stirring, until omelet is set on bottom but moist in center. Spoon creamed chicken down center; add remaining tomato mixture. Quickly turn omelet out into platter.

7. Spoon remaining cream sauce over omelet. Sprinkle with Parmesan cheese. Broil until cheese is golden. Serve immediately.

Morels, those highly prized wild mushrooms, have a certain mystique about them, so the combination of morels and asparagus makes this a very elegant omelet.

MOREL AND ASPARAGUS OMELET

2 servings
Preparation time: 15 minutes
Cooking time: 15 minutes

8 **fresh morels (see note)**
6 **fresh asparagus spears**
2 **tablespoons shredded Swiss cheese**
4 **large eggs**
2 **tablespoons water**
  Freshly ground pepper
2 **teaspoons unsalted butter**
  Salt to taste

1. Soak fresh morels in lightly salted warm water for a few minutes.

2. Snap off ends of asparagus. Lightly peel stalks. Heat 2 inches of water to boil in large skillet; add asparagus. Cook until crisp-tender, about 2 minutes. Drain well. Dice the stalks. Set tips aside for garnish.

3. Mix morels, diced stalks and cheese in small bowl.

4. For each omelet, beat 2 eggs, 1 tablespoon water and pepper in medium bowl until combined. Heat 9-inch omelet pan or nonstick skillet over medium-high heat until hot. Add 1 teaspoon butter; swirl pan until butter is melted.

5. Quickly pour in egg mixture; stir gently with a fork until eggs begin to set. Then cook, without stirring, just until almost set. Spread half of morel mixture and pinch of salt over omelet. Loosen edge with spatula. Tip the pan so the omelet rolls into itself when you lift the top edge with a spatula. Reverse your grip on the pan's handle so that you're holding it from underneath; tilt the pan until nearly vertical and continue rolling the omelet onto plate.

6. Repeat for second omelet. Garnish each with 3 of the reserved asparagus tips. Serve immediately.

NOTE: If fresh morels are unavailable, you may substitute dried morels. Soak in very hot water to cover until softened, about 20 minutes. Strain; use soaking water for flavoring soups and sauces.

Writer Judy Hevrdejs contributed this recipe for the classic Mexican combination of spicy chorizo sausage and eggs. Chorizo is a Mexican sausage with a unique flavor, found in Mexican food stores and other specialty stores.

SCRAMBLED EGGS WITH CHORIZO
(Huevos con chorizo)

4 servings
Preparation time: 10 minutes
Cooking time: 5 minutes

¼ **pound chorizo sausage, casing removed**

6 **large eggs**

2 **tablespoons butter**
Salt, freshly ground pepper
Minced fresh cilantro (coriander), optional

1. Crumble chorizo into medium skillet. Cook over low heat until dry and crumbly. Drain off liquids.

2. Beat eggs lightly. Melt butter in medium skillet over medium heat. Add eggs; cook, stirring constantly. When eggs are half-cooked, stir in chorizo. Finish cooking eggs. Season with salt and pepper. Sprinkle with cilantro. Serve immediately.

A frittata is an Italian omelet. This one, chock-full of potatoes, peppers and green onions, may be served for brunch but it is also hearty enough for a light supper or vegetarian entree.

POTATO AND PEPPER FRITTATA

6 servings
Preparation time: 15 minutes
Cooking time: 11 minutes

2 **tablespoons butter**

4 **small red potatoes, about ½ pound, cooked, cut into ½-inch chunks**

1 **each, seeded and diced: medium red bell pepper, green pepper**

⅓ **cup sliced green onions**

8 **large eggs, lightly beaten**

½ **teaspoon salt**

¼ **teaspoon each: freshly ground black pepper, cayenne pepper**

1. Heat oven to 375 degrees. Melt 1 tablespoon of the butter in 10-inch ovenproof, nonstick skillet over low heat. Add potatoes, red bell pepper, green pepper and onions. Sauté vegetables until light brown. Remove with slotted spoon to bowl.

2. Mix eggs, salt, black pepper and cayenne pepper in large bowl. Add sautéed vegetables; stir to mix.

3. Heat remaining butter in same skillet over low heat. Pour in egg mixture. Cook until light brown on bottom, 2 to 3 minutes. Remove from stove top. Bake until eggs are set, 8 to 10 minutes.

4. Loosen edges; slide onto plate. Serve hot or cool to room temperature. Cut into wedges.

In many homes, eggs Benedict is a dish that is synonymous with a leisurely breakfast on a special occasion. Fresh orange juice, coffee and eggs Benedict with hollandaise. Just be sure to watch the cholesterol intake for the rest of the day.

Hollandaise was a rather complicated sauce before the advent of the blender and the food processor. Now it only takes moments to make. If you like it tart, increase the amount of lemon juice.

EGGS BENEDICT

6 servings
Preparation time: 30 minutes
Cooking time: 10 minutes

12 **poached eggs (see recipe, page 79)**

HOLLANDAISE SAUCE

4 **large egg yolks, at room temperature**

1 **tablespoon each: fresh lemon juice, hot water**

¼ **teaspoon each: salt, freshly ground white pepper**

1 **cup (2 sticks) unsalted butter, melted and hot**

TO ASSEMBLE

2 **tablespoons butter**

12 **slices Canadian bacon or ham, cut ¼-inch thick**

6 **English muffins, split, toasted**

Minced fresh parsley for garnish

1. Make poached eggs.

2. For hollandaise sauce, put egg yolks, lemon juice, hot water, salt and pepper into blender; process 3 seconds. With machine running, pour in melted butter in slow, steady stream. Process until sauce is thick and creamy, about 1 minute. (To keep sauce warm, pour into glass measure; cover with plastic wrap; set in pan of hot water. Or, pour into insulated vacuum bottle.)

3. To assemble, heat 2 tablespoons butter in large skillet; add Canadian bacon. Cook until browned on both sides. Keep warm.

4. Put poached eggs in large bowl of hot water to reheat. Drain well.

5. Arrange 2 muffin halves on each plate. Put 1 bacon slice and 1 poached egg on each muffin half. Spoon about 2 tablespoons hollandaise sauce over each. Garnish with parsley.

The batter for this pancake is similar to that of a Yorkshire pudding or a popover. It puffs up very high in the oven, then deflates quickly when removed. The apples look best when thinly sliced rather than chopped. The juice from the apples, butter and sugar combine to form a syrup in the bottom of the pan so no other syrup is needed when serving.

A cast-iron, enameled cast-iron or heavy anodized aluminum skillet is required to produce crispy edges and a golden brown bottom. A nonstick skillet will do, and clean-up will be easier, but the edges of the pancake won't crisp as nicely.

BAKED APPLE PANCAKE

2 to 4 servings
Preparation time: 30 minutes
Cooking time: 20 to 30 minutes

2   **Granny Smith apples**
2   **teaspoons ground cinnamon**
½   **cup each: granulated sugar, packed light brown sugar**
1   **cup milk**
4   **large eggs**
1   **cup all-purpose flour Pinch salt**
4   **tablespoons unsalted butter**

1. Heat oven to 425 degrees. Lightly oil a well-seasoned, ovenproof, 10-inch cast-iron or enameled cast-iron skillet with sloping sides.

2. Peel apples. Cut in quarters; remove core. Cut into thin slices. Mix apples, cinnamon and sugars in medium bowl.

3. Put milk and eggs into blender or food processor. Process until well mixed. Add flour and salt. Process until smooth.

4. Melt butter in prepared skillet over medium heat. Add apple mixture. Cook, stirring, until sugars have melted and apples are well coated with mixture, about 5 minutes.

5. Gently pour batter over apples. Bake until puffed, edges are golden and apples tender, about 20 to 30 minutes. Serve immediately.

These light and tender pancakes, created in The Tribune *test kitchen by Beverly Dillon, are sure to be winners at your house. Perfect for a fall breakfast, they may be served with homemade applesauce.*

GINGER PANCAKES WITH CINNAMON BUTTER

4 servings
Preparation time: 45 minutes
Cooking time: 25 minutes

¾ **cup milk**

¼ **cup melted butter**

1 **large egg, lightly beaten**

¾ **cup each: all-purpose flour, confectioners' sugar**

2 **teaspoons baking powder**

½ **teaspoon ground ginger**

¼ **teaspoon salt**

¾ **cup quick-cooking oats**

½ **cup finely chopped pecans**

¼ **cup finely chopped crystallized ginger**

4 **to 6 tablespoons butter, for cooking**

Cinnamon butter (recipe follows)

Applesauce, either homemade or bottled

1. Mix milk, melted butter and egg in small bowl. Sift together flour, confectioners' sugar, baking powder, ginger and salt in large bowl. Stir in oats, pecans and ginger. Stir milk mixture into flour mixture until blended. Let stand a few minutes.

2. Heat large nonstick griddle or 2 skillets until hot. Melt a little butter on griddle or skillet over medium heat until bubbly but not brown. Spoon about 3 tablespoons batter per pancake onto the griddle. Cook until bubbles appear uniformly across top. Turn; cook second side until golden, about 2 minutes total. Repeat, using more butter as needed, to use up all batter. Keep cooked pancakes warm in 220-degree oven.

3. Serve with cinnamon butter and applesauce.

CINNAMON BUTTER

About ½ cup

½ **cup (1 stick) unsalted butter, softened**

1 **tablespoon brown sugar**

⅛ **teaspoon ground cinnamon**

1. Beat butter, brown sugar and ground cinnamon in electric mixer until well blended and fluffy. Spoon into small serving dish; refrigerate to firm slightly.

Eggs & Breakfast

87

■ *These hearty pancakes, also created by Beverly Dillon, are packed with flavor from canned pumpkin and spices. They may be served with maple syrup or an easy-to-make cider walnut syrup.*

PUMPKIN FLAPJACKS WITH CIDER WALNUT SYRUP

8 servings
Preparation time: 35 minutes
Cooking time: 20 minutes

CIDER WALNUT SYRUP

- 2 **cups packed light brown sugar**
- 1 **cup unsweetened apple cider or apple juice**
- ½ **cup coarsely chopped walnuts**
- ¼ **teaspoon ground cinnamon**

FLAPJACKS

- 1½ **cups each: whole-wheat flour, all-purpose flour**
- 1 **cup old-fashioned rolled oats**
- 2 **tablespoons sugar**
- 1 **tablespoon baking powder**
- 2 **teaspoons baking soda**
- 1 **teaspoon each: salt, ground cinnamon**
- ½ **teaspoon each: ground ginger, ground nutmeg**
- ¾ **cup (1½ sticks) unsalted butter, cut into small pieces**
- 4 **large eggs, separated**
- 1 **quart buttermilk**
- ½ **cup canned solid-pack pumpkin**
- 6 **tablespoons butter for cooking**

1. For cider walnut syrup, mix all ingredients in medium saucepan. Boil, stirring occasionally, 3 minutes. Remove from heat. Keep warm.

2. For flapjacks, put flours, rolled oats, sugar, baking powder, baking soda, salt, cinnamon, ginger and nutmeg in food processor. Process until blended. Add butter; process with on/off turns until mixture resembles coarse crumbs.

3. Beat egg whites in small mixer bowl until soft peaks form. Beat egg yolks, buttermilk and pumpkin in large mixer bowl until smooth. Using a wooden spoon, stir in flour mixture just until blended. Fold in beaten egg whites.

4. Heat large nonstick griddle or 2 skillets until hot. Melt a little butter on griddle. Spoon batter onto griddle in several places, making 3-inch round pancakes. Cook until bubbles appear uniformly across top. Turn; cook second side until golden, about 2 minutes total. Repeat using more butter as needed. Serve immediately with warm syrup.

Chocolate waffles? Michael Foley's Chicago restaurants, Printer's Row and Foley's, are known for their unusual culinary combinations, and this recipe for chocolate waffles is no exception. It works and it's delicious, especially topped with the warm, sweetened strawberries.

CHOCOLATE WAFFLES WITH POACHED STRAWBERRIES

6 servings
Preparation time: 25 minutes
Standing time: 30 minutes
Cooking time: 20 minutes

WARM POACHED STRAWBERRIES

2½ **pints fresh strawberries, hulled**

1¾ **cups sugar**

Juice of 1 small lemon

2 **cups water**

1 **vanilla bean, or ½ teaspoon vanilla extract**

WAFFLES

1¼ **cups all-purpose flour**

½ **cup unsweetened cocoa powder**

¼ **cup sugar**

1 **teaspoon baking powder**

½ **teaspoon each: baking soda, salt**

1¾ **cups milk**

3 **large eggs, separated**

¼ **cup (½ stick) butter, melted**

Whipped cream, mint sprigs for garnish

1. Put strawberries into bowl; spoon 1 cup of the sugar and lemon juice over berries. Let sit about 30 minutes.

2. Put remaining ¾ cup sugar, water and vanilla bean into large saucepan. Cook and stir until sugar dissolves. Add strawberries; heat to simmer; poach over low heat, until almost tender 1 to 3 minutes. Do not overcook. Cool slightly.

3. Lightly brush waffle grids with vegetable oil. Close waffle iron and preheat according to manufacturer's directions.

4. For waffles, sift together flour, cocoa, sugar, baking powder, baking soda and salt. Lightly beat in milk and egg yolks.

5. Beat egg whites until stiff but not dry. Fold into batter along with butter. Bake waffle batter in batches according to manufacturer's directions.

6. Serve waffles while hot, topped with warm poached strawberries. Garnish with whipped cream and mint.

These waffles have just enough spice in them to give them a lively kick. The pear topping may be varied by using red and green Bartletts, Bosc or Comice pears. It's the tiny Seckel pears, however, that lend an unbeatable touch of elegance.

WAFFLES WITH GINGER PEAR TOPPING

4 to 6 servings
Preparation time: 20 minutes
Baking time: 20 minutes

GINGER PEAR TOPPING

½ cup each: granulated sugar, packed dark brown sugar, water

3 ripe pears, peeled, cored, sliced, about 2 cups

1 tablespoon minced fresh ginger

WAFFLES

2 large eggs, separated

1½ cups milk

½ cup vegetable oil

1¾ cups all-purpose flour

2 tablespoons granulated sugar

1 tablespoon baking powder

½ teaspoon each: salt, ground ginger

⅛ teaspoon mace

1. For pear topping, heat sugars and water in medium saucepan over medium heat until sugars dissolve. Stir in pears and ginger. Simmer, stirring often, until pears are tender, about 10 minutes. Cool until warm.

2. For waffles, lightly brush waffle grids with vegetable oil. Close waffle iron and preheat according to manufacturer's directions.

3. Beat egg whites in small bowl until stiff but not dry. Beat egg yolks in large bowl until thick and lemon colored. Continue beating while adding milk and oil. Add dry ingredients and beat just until smooth. Do not overmix. Fold in beaten whites.

4. Bake waffle batter in batches according to manufacturer's directions.

5. Serve immediately with warm pear topping.

French toast is usually a stand-and-serve-from-the-stove dish. The cook stands and everyone else sits and eats. That situation is remedied with the following recipes. You make these French toast casseroles the night before, then just pop them in the oven and they'll bake while you're reading the morning paper.

OVEN FRENCH TOAST

6 servings
Preparation time: 15 minutes
Chilling time: Overnight
Baking time: 45 to 50 minutes

1 **loaf (8 ounces) French bread, cut into 1-inch-thick slices**
3 **cups milk**
8 **large eggs**
4 **teaspoons sugar**
1 **tablespoon vanilla extract**
¾ **teaspoon salt**
2 **tablespoons butter, cut into small pieces**
   Maple syrup or honey

1. Generously butter 13 by 9-inch baking dish. Fill dish with bread slices so dish is completely covered with bread and filled to the top.

2. Mix milk, eggs, sugar, vanilla and salt in large bowl. Pour over bread. Cover with foil. Refrigerate, covered, overnight.

3. Heat oven to 350 degrees. Remove toast from refrigerator and uncover; it is not necessary to bring casserole to room temperature. Dot top with butter.

4. Bake, uncovered, until puffed and golden, 45 to 50 minutes. Let stand 5 minutes before serving. Serve with maple syrup or honey.

PECAN-TOPPED TOAST CASSEROLE

6 to 8 servings
Preparation time: 20 minutes
Chilling time: Overnight
Baking time: 40 minutes

1 loaf (8 ounces) French bread, cut into 1-inch-thick slices

1½ cups each: milk, half-and-half

6 large eggs

1 teaspoon vanilla extract

⅛ teaspoon each: freshly ground nutmeg, ground cinnamon

TOPPING

1 cup packed light brown sugar

½ cup (1 stick) unsalted butter, softened

2 tablespoons dark corn syrup

1 cup coarsely chopped pecans

1. Generously butter 13 by 9-inch baking dish. Fill dish with bread slices so dish is completely covered with bread and filled to the top.

2. Mix milk, half-and-half, eggs, vanilla, nutmeg and cinnamon in a large bowl. Pour over bread. Refrigerate, covered, overnight.

3. Heat oven to 350 degrees. Remove toast from refrigerator and uncover. For topping, mix brown sugar, butter and corn syrup. Stir in pecans. Dollop evenly over bread slices. Bake, uncovered, until puffed and golden, about 40 minutes. Let stand 5 minutes before serving.

Warm, creamy bread pudding is comfort food. This recipe is comfort food with a robust Cheddar flavor perfect for brunch.

SAVORY CHEDDAR BREAD PUDDING

4 servings
Preparation time: 20 minutes
Baking time: 45 minutes

1 **small onion, minced**
4 **tablespoons plus 2 teaspoons butter**
8 **slices whole-wheat bread, toasted**
2 **cups shredded sharp Cheddar cheese**
3½ **cups milk**
4 **large eggs**
¼ **teaspoon salt**
⅛ **teaspoon pepper**

1. Cook onion in 2 tablespoons of the butter in small skillet over medium heat until limp and translucent, about 2 minutes.

2. Spread each bread slice evenly on one side with 1 teaspoon butter. Cut slices into quarters. Arrange half of the bread in single layer over bottom of buttered 11 by 7-inch baking pan, buttered side up. Sprinkle half the onion over bread. Sprinkle with 1 cup of the cheese. Repeat to make a second layer.

3. Heat oven to 325 degrees. Beat milk, eggs, salt and pepper in medium bowl. Pour over bread mixture. Let stand 15 minutes.

4. Bake until puffed and golden, about 40 minutes. Serve immediately.

A blintz is like a stuffed pancake—a rich, stuffed pancake. The filling in this recipe is a combination of ricotta cheese, sugar and butter. The whole thing is topped, of course, with sour cream. And if you really want richness, finish up by pouring a little strawberry or maple syrup over the entire dish.

CHEESE BLINTZES

4 servings
Preparation time: 25 minutes
Standing time: 1 hour
Cooking time: 20 minutes

BATTER

1½ **cups milk**

¾ **cup all-purpose flour**

1 **large egg, lightly beaten**

2 **tablespoons melted butter**

CHEESE FILLING

½ **pound ricotta cheese**

1 **tablespoon sugar**

1 **teaspoon vanilla extract**

½ **teaspoon grated lemon rind**

⅓ **cup butter, about**
Sour cream, sliced strawberries, maple or strawberry syrup for serving, optional

1. For batter, mix milk, flour, egg and melted butter in medium bowl until smooth. Strain through fine sieve. Cover; let stand 1 hour.

2. For filling, beat cheese, sugar, vanilla and lemon rind with electric mixer until smooth.

3. Melt 1 teaspoon of the butter in 8-inch crepe pan or nonstick skillet. Pour 3 tablespoons batter into pan; immediately rotate pan to swirl batter over entire surface of pan. Cook over medium heat until blintz is brown around edges, about 2 minutes. Remove to a sheet of wax paper. Repeat with remaining butter and batter; separate each blintz with wax paper.

4. Put 2 tablespoons cheese filling near bottom edge of blintz. Fold in sides to partly cover filling; roll up to enclose filling. Heat remaining butter in large skillet. Add blintzes in single layer. Cook over medium heat, turning, until golden on all sides, about 5 minutes. Transfer to warm platter. Serve immediately with sour cream, and sliced strawberries and syrup.

SOUPS & STOCKS

I n bygone eras, when women spent much of their time in the kitchen, a pot of stock often simmered slowly on the back burner. It provided, among other things, the basis for any number of good, nourishing soups.

Those times definitely have passed, but soups still are an important part of the modern diet and stocks still can give them an extra fullness and flavor. Soups often come at the beginning of the meal. Sometimes they are so delicious it's a shame to leave them and proceed to the next course.

Thick hearty soups, lumpy with chunks of meat and vegetables, are so filling that with a crust of bread they make a meal in themselves. They are full-bodied peasant soups often made from what is available or left over from other meals. Soup frequently is a dish that turns discards into dinner; it lets little go to waste.

Other soups are lighter—pureed, refined, dressed up in china tureens and served in delicate porcelain. There are cold soups for hot-weather eating or soups made with fruit.

Not the least of the advantages of soup is that it can be very nourishing and very healthful. Soups often are rich in nutrients. Bean and other legume soups are full of protein, as are those with meat. Most soups, with the exception of the heavily creamed ones, are low in fat, especially if the stock used to construct them has been defatted with care.

The long simmering stock is pretty much passé in all but the largest restaurants and hotels, but it still can be made to order at home, and it especially warms a kitchen on a cold winter's day.

Unlike other kitchen preparations, stocks make use of vegetable ends and pieces, bones, shells and other detritus from meal preparation. The essence of these throw-away ingredients is extracted through slow simmering.

Stocks are the foundation of many soups, supplying the underlying flavor, like the cello and bass parts in a culinary orchestration.

STOCK-MAKING TIPS

When making a stock, try to trim away as much fat as practical from the bones and meat pieces.

Bones, especially marrow bones, add gelatin and thus thickening to the stock as well as nutrients and flavor.

Tops and ends of celery and carrots, turnip and potato peelings and other vegetable scraps also can be used in stock. Eventually they will be strained away. Some cooks even save vegetable scraps by storing them in a plastic bag in the freezer until they are needed for a stock.

Stocks, with the exception of fish stock, can be frozen for 4 to 6 months. Some cooks freeze reduced stock in ice cube trays so that it will be available in small amounts as needed.

Fish heads, tails, bones and seafood shells make excellent ingredients for a fish stock, also called a fumet, but remember that fish stocks should be used only for fish and seafood preparations. Also they do not keep more than a day or two in the refrigerator or a month in the freezer.

When cooking stocks, use a heavy pot, ideally twice as high as round, or place an asbestos pad between the pot and the fire so that the stock can be simmered at a very low temperature. A stock never should be allowed to boil, or "laugh," as some say. It should only "smile" gently.

Depending on the kind of stock you are making, carefully skim off the foam that rises to the surface in the early stages of simmering. This is especially important when making a clear stock.

An onion stuck with two or three cloves and/or a bouquet garni (a tied bunch of parsley, bay leaf and thyme) add to the stock flavor.

After the stock has cooked for a while, turn off the heat and allow it to cool enough so that any fat will rise to the surface of the liquid. Skim the fat off with a spoon or ladle or, if this is difficult, a folded paper towel. If you want to remove a maximum amount of fat, cool the stock in the refrigerator until the fat rises to the top and congeals into a solid or semi-solid mass. This is much easier to remove.

SOUPS

Beef mushroom barley soup

Creamy split pea soup

Cuban black bean soup

Escarole and bean soup

Lentil soup

Lithuanian beet soup

Mushroom ginger soup

Pumpkin soup with Illinois Brie

Oriental spinach and tofu soup

Chicken and avocado soup

Turkey soup with angel-hair pasta

Goulash soup

Meatball minestrone

Mexican meatball soup

Quick tortilla soup

Bouillabaisse

New England clam chowder

Jalapeño cheese soup

Vietnamese combination soup

Duck and sausage gumbo

Curried cream of acorn squash soup

Superbowl chicken and andouille
  sausage gumbo

Cream of cauliflower soup

Cream of patty pan squash soup

Cream of red pepper soup

COLD SOUPS

Cold tomato-basil soup with
  pesto sauce

Cream of cucumber soup

Curried cream of eggplant soup

Cold gingered avocado soup

Fruit gazpacho with mint

STOCKS

Basic beef or veal stock

Rich chicken broth

Turkey stock

Fish stock

Lobster, shrimp or crayfish stock

This recipe is a good example of a soup that is a whole meal in itself. Eat it with a little crusty bread on a cold winter's night or just after a morning of cross-country skiing.

BEEF MUSHROOM BARLEY SOUP

6 to 8 servings
Preparation time: 25 minutes
Cooking time: 2¼ hours

2 tablespoons vegetable oil

2 pounds boneless beef stew, cut into ½-inch cubes

1 can (16 ounces) whole tomatoes, crushed

3 packages (¼ ounce each) dried mushrooms, crumbled

3 quarts water

4 medium carrots, grated

2 medium onions, minced

1 cup medium pearl barley

2 cloves garlic, minced

1 teaspoon each: salt, paprika

½ teaspoon each: dried leaf thyme, freshly ground pepper

¼ teaspoon each: dried basil, celery salt, dried summer savory

⅛ teaspoon ground cloves

1 can (10½ ounces) beef broth

1. Heat oil in large dutch oven over medium heat. Add beef in single layer; cook until well browned on all sides. Repeat to brown all beef. Return all beef to dutch oven; add tomatoes, dried mushrooms and 3 quarts water. Heat to boil; reduce heat to low. Simmer, covered, 30 minutes.

2. Stir in carrots, onions, barley, garlic, salt, paprika, thyme, pepper, basil, celery salt, summer savory and cloves. Simmer, covered, stirring occasionally, until beef is tender, about 1½ hours.

3. If desired, cool soup slightly, then cover and refrigerate overnight. Remove fat from surface. Before serving, add beef broth and heat slowly to simmer. Taste and adjust seasonings.

■ *Creamy split pea soup, created by JeanMarie Brownson,* The Tribune *test kitchen director, is a five-star production that features a lowly ham bone. The added fennel gives it a special touch. Do not add any salt, as the ham will do that adequately.*

CREAMY SPLIT PEA SOUP

6 to 8 servings
Preparation time: 30 minutes
Cooking time: 2¼ hours

2 tablespoons butter
2 small leeks, split lengthwise, rinsed, chopped
2 medium carrots, peeled, chopped
1 medium onion, chopped
½ cup minced fresh fennel bulb or celery ribs
2 large cloves garlic, minced
2 quarts rich chicken broth (see recipe, page 134), or substitute canned broth
1 pound green split peas
1 ham bone with some meat or 2 ham hocks, about 1½ pounds
   Bouquet garni (see note)
1 package (10 ounces) frozen peas (optional)

TO SERVE
4 cups large cubes day-old French bread
   Vegetable oil
   Whipping cream, optional

1. Heat butter in 6-quart dutch oven over medium heat until hot. Add leeks, carrots, onion, fennel and garlic. Cook and stir until vegetables are limp, about 10 minutes. Stir in broth, split peas, ham bone and bouquet garni. Simmer uncovered over low heat, stirring occasionally, until peas are very tender, about 2 hours.

2. Remove and discard bouquet garni. Remove ham bone or hocks to cutting board. Add frozen peas to soup; stir until thawed. Puree soup in batches in blender or food processor. Return to dutch oven.

3. Chop any meat from bones and add meat to soup. Reheat soup. Add more broth if needed to thin soup to desired consistency.

4. For croutons, fry bread cubes in a small amount of oil in large skillet over medium heat until crisp and golden on all sides. Drain on paper towels.

5. To serve, ladle soup into bowl. Drizzle a little whipping cream into center of soup. Sprinkle with croutons.

NOTE: For bouquet garni, tie 3 bay leaves; ½ teaspoon each: dried leaf thyme, dried marjoram; 4 parsley sprigs and 10 black peppercorns in a double thickness of cheesecloth.

One of the pleasures of traveling to Florida, especially Miami, is sampling the black bean soups in various Cuban restaurants. But the late food writer Roy Andries de Groot explained that the black beans and rice date back to the time when black Moors occupied white Christian Spain. For centuries the dark colored soup with its mound of white rice was known as Moros y Christianos (Moors and Christians), he said. He also cautioned that to preserve the delicate balance of flavors, follow the recipe precisely.

CUBAN BLACK BEAN SOUP

6 to 8 servings
Preparation time: 40 minutes
Soaking time: Overnight
Cooking time: 2 to 5 hours

2 **pounds dried black beans or black turtle beans**
2 **teaspoons baking soda**
2 **cups dry white wine**
8 **medium yellow onions, coarsely chopped**
3 **medium green peppers, seeded, coarsely chopped**
¼ **pound piece salt pork, cut into ½-inch cubes**
2 **cups olive oil**
½ **pound piece dark smoked bacon, with rind**
1 **medium ham bone, with lean meat on it**
6 **cloves garlic, thinly sliced**
4 **whole bay leaves**
2 **tablespoons white wine tarragon vinegar**
1 **tablespoon coarse (kosher) salt**
 Freshly ground pepper to taste

TO SERVE

3 **cups cooked white rice**
1 **cup finely diced red onion**

1. Heat 4 quarts of cold water to a rolling boil. Meanwhile, pick over and rinse black beans. When the water is bubbling hard, add beans while maintaining the boil. Then boil hard for 4 more minutes. Remove from heat; cover, let soak about 1 hour.

2. When the timer rings, test the water with your fingertip; it should be hot but not stinging. Using a wooden spoon, stir in baking soda. Let stand, covered, at room temperature overnight.

3. Drain beans. Rinse thoroughly in a colander under cold water. Put beans, wine and enough cold water to cover beans by ½ inch in 6- or 8-quart dutch oven. Heat to simmer over low heat.

4. Mix yellow onions, green peppers and salt pork in large bowl. Heat oil in large skillet over medium heat until hot but not smoking. Add onion mixture. Cook and stir until light brown, about 10 minutes. Stir onion mixture into beans.

5. Add bacon, ham bone, garlic, bay leaves, vinegar, salt and pepper. Simmer, covered, until beans are tender; after about 2 hours they will be edible, but they will be better after 3 hours; they will be superb after 5 hours. They will be even better if allowed to cool and reheated the next day.

6. Before serving, remove bacon and ham bone. Cut meat from these into large dice; return meat to beans. Discard bone. Taste and adjust seasonings.

7. To serve, ladle soup into warm deep soup bowls. Put scoop of rice into center. Sprinkle with red onions.

Tribune food and wine columnist William Rice featured this simple soup in a Sunday magazine column on real Italian food. The recipe is adapted from Romeo Salta's out-of-print cookbook, The Pleasures of Italian Cooking. *Rice says the soup has "perfect pitch" in terms of flavor and represents a standard of simple refinement.*

ESCAROLE AND BEAN SOUP

6 servings
Preparation time: 15 minutes
Soaking time: 1 hour
Cooking time: 2½ hours

2 **cups dried white beans**
2 **slices salt pork or bacon, chopped**
1 **cup chopped onions**
2 **tablespoons all-purpose flour**
2 **teaspoons salt**
½ **teaspoon freshly ground pepper**
1 **bunch escarole, shredded**

1. Rinse beans. Put into large saucepan; add cold water to cover. Heat to boil; remove from heat; let soak 1 hour.

2. Drain beans. Return beans to pan; add fresh water to cover (about 2 quarts). Heat to boil over medium heat. Reduce heat to low; simmer, covered, until beans are almost tender, about 1½ hours.

3. Cook salt pork in large skillet over medium heat until browned. Add onions; cook and stir until soft. Stir in flour; cook and stir 1 minute. Stir flour mixture into beans; add salt and pepper. Cook over low heat, stirring occasionally, for 30 minutes. (Recipe can be done ahead to this point.)

4. Add shredded escarole; cook until beans are very tender, about 30 minutes more. Taste and adjust seasonings.

Few soups are more peasant-like than one made with lentils. But in the hands of a chef like Dennis Terczak, co-owner of Chez Jenny and Sole Mio restaurants in Chicago, this simple, nourishing dish becomes a minor work of art. The secret, once again, is in the stock.

LENTIL SOUP

12 to 14 servings
Preparation time: 25 minutes
Cooking time: About 4 hours

3 smoked ham hocks
1 quart water
2 tablespoons butter
1 pound fresh mushrooms, sliced
2 each, finely diced: carrots, ribs celery, onions
8 cloves garlic, finely chopped
5 bay leaves
2 tablespoons rubbed sage
1 tablespoon dried leaf thyme
5 quarts basic beef or veal stock or rich chicken broth (see recipes, pages 133–34), or substitute canned broth
3 tomatoes, peeled, seeded, finely chopped
3 cups dried lentils
1 cup frozen green peas, thawed
Salt, freshly ground pepper to taste
Garlic bread, toast or croutons for serving

1. Put ham hocks and water into medium saucepan. Simmer, covered, over low heat until tender, about 1½ hours. Strain; reserve broth. Remove meat from bones and chop fine; discard bones.

2. Melt butter in 8-quart stock pot or dutch oven. Add mushrooms, carrots, celery, onions, garlic, bay leaves, sage and thyme. Cook and stir over medium heat until vegetables are tender and golden, about 10 minutes.

3. Stir in reserved hock broth and meat, beef stock, tomatoes and lentils. Heat to boil; reduce heat to low. Simmer, partially covered, stirring occasionally, until lentils are very tender, about 2½ hours.

4. Stir in peas, salt and pepper. Serve with garlic bread, toast or croutons.

This Lithuanian soup is a cousin to the more robust borscht favored in other parts of the Soviet Union. The dried mushrooms are a traditional Lithuanian touch.

LITHUANIAN BEET SOUP

6 servings
Preparation time: 40 minutes
Cooking time: 1 hour

4 to 6 medium beets
1 ounce dried mushrooms such as cepes, porcini or shiitakes
¼ cup hot water
1 tablespoon unsalted butter
1 medium onion, thinly sliced
1 teaspoon sugar
3 cups basic beef or veal stock or rich chicken broth (see recipes, pages 133–34), or substitute canned broth
1 to 2 tablespoons fresh lemon juice
Salt, freshly ground pepper to taste
Fresh parsley for garnish

1. Scrub beets clean. Cut tips and root ends off beets. Put beets in large saucepan with water to cover. Cover and heat to boil; reduce heat to low. Cook until fork-tender, 20 to 30 minutes. Remove from heat. Strain beets, reserving beets and 2 cups of the cooking liquid separately.

2. While beets are cooking, soak mushrooms in ¼ cup hot water until soft.

3. When beets are cool enough to handle, peel and cut into ½-inch cubes. Melt butter in a 4-quart saucepan; add onion and cook over medium heat until tender, about 2 minutes.

4. Add beets and sugar to pan. Cook until sugar is melted and vegetables are glazed, 3 to 5 minutes. Add stock, beet cooking liquid, mushrooms and their soaking liquid to vegetables. Simmer over low heat until flavors are blended, about 20 minutes. Add lemon juice, salt and pepper. Garnish with parsley.

■ *In a microwave soup, as in most conventionally cooked soups, flavors will heighten if it is made ahead then reheated. If making the soup ahead, reduce the fresh ginger to ½ teaspoon. After reheating, taste the soup and add more ginger as desired. To add more, put ginger and ¼ cup soup broth in a cup and microwave on high for 30 seconds. Return mixture to soup.*

MUSHROOM GINGER SOUP

2 to 3 servings
Preparation time: 20 minutes
Microwave cooking time: 12 to 16 minutes

½ **pound fresh mushrooms, wiped clean, sliced very thin**

½ **cup minced onion**

1 **large carrot, grated**

1 **teaspoon minced fresh ginger**

2 **cups basic beef stock (see recipe, page 133), or substitute canned broth**

¼ **teaspoon ground nutmeg**

⅛ **teaspoon freshly ground pepper**

Salt to taste

2 **tablespoons minced fresh cilantro (coriander)**

2 **green onions, white and first 2 inches of green, chopped**

1. Put mushrooms, onion, carrot and ginger in 3-quart microwave-safe casserole. Cover with plastic wrap vented at one corner. Microwave on high (100 percent power), stirring twice, until mushrooms are tender and have released juices, 8 to 10 minutes.

2. Stir in beef stock. Cover with plastic wrap. Microwave on high until simmering, 4 to 6 minutes. Stir in nutmeg, pepper and salt. Sprinkle with cilantro and green onions. Serve.

NOTE: Soup also can be served cold. Refrigerate, covered, at least 3 hours before serving.

This rich pumpkin soup, featuring Illinois Brie cheese, is from Michael Carmel, a chef/instructor at the Cooking and Hospitality Institute of Chicago.

PUMPKIN SOUP WITH ILLINOIS BRIE

12 servings
Preparation time: 40 minutes
Cooking time: 1 hour

1 cup (2 sticks) unsalted butter
4 to 5 cups chopped raw pumpkin
1 cup minced onions
½ cup each, minced: carrot, celery, leek
1½ cups all-purpose flour
4 quarts rich chicken broth (see recipe, page 134), or substitute canned broth
1 teaspoon salt
½ teaspoon each: ground cinnamon, mace, ground nutmeg, freshly ground pepper
¼ to ½ cup hazelnut or praline-flavored liqueur
2 cups whipping cream or half-and-half, optional
5 to 6 ounces firm domestic Brie cheese, diced
1 cup (2 sticks) unsalted butter, optional

1. Melt butter in 6- or 8-quart dutch oven or stock pot. Add pumpkin, onions, carrot, celery and leek. Cook, covered, over medium heat, stirring occasionally, 15 minutes. Stir in flour; mix well. Gradually stir in broth, salt, cinnamon, mace, nutmeg and pepper. Simmer, stirring often, over low heat, 45 minutes.

2. Stir in ¼ cup of the liqueur, cream if using and diced cheese. Simmer until cheese melts, about 5 minutes. Remove from heat. Taste and adjust seasonings, adding more liqueur if needed. If desired, stir in butter for a richer flavor. Soup can be strained or pureed if a creamy texture is desired.

3. Serve hot. If desired, serve soup in hollowed-out individual pumpkins.

This soup with an Oriental flavor has a minimum of ingredients and needs only a limited amount of cooking. So it is essential to have the freshest spinach and the highest quality chicken broth for the best results.

ORIENTAL SPINACH AND TOFU SOUP

6 servings
Preparation time: 20 minutes
Cooking time: 20 minutes

1 **pound fresh spinach**
3 **tablespoons vegetable oil**
¼ **teaspoon sugar**
3 **cups rich chicken broth (see recipe, page 134), or substitute canned broth**
2 **tablespoons cornstarch, dissolved in ¼ cup water**
1 **package (16 ounces) tofu, drained, cubed**
1 **teaspoon soy sauce**
½ **teaspoon Oriental sesame oil to taste**

1. Rinse spinach thoroughly; remove tough stems. Tear into bite-size pieces. Heat oil in large heavy saucepan over medium heat. Add spinach; stir-fry until wilted and bright green, about 1 minute. Stir in sugar. Remove spinach with slotted spoon. Wipe out saucepan.

2. Put broth into saucepan. Heat to boil over medium heat. Whisk in cornstarch mixture. Cook and stir until smooth and thickened. Stir in spinach, tofu cubes, soy sauce and sesame oil. Heat just until warm. Serve immediately.

Simple, Mexican-style chicken soup is thick with chunks of avocado and cheese. Serve it with toasted warm tortillas and a tossed salad for a casual lunch or supper.

CHICKEN AND AVOCADO SOUP

4 servings
Preparation time: 30 minutes
Cooking time: 25 minutes

5 **cups rich chicken broth (see recipe, page 134)**
1 **whole chicken breast, split**
6 **fresh cilantro (coriander) sprigs**
¼ **teaspoon crushed red pepper flakes or to taste**
2 **ripe avocados, peeled, seeded, sliced**
1 **package (6 ounces) white Mexican cheese or brick cheese, cubed**
   Thin slices of fresh lime for garnish

1. Heat broth to simmer in large saucepan. Add chicken breast; simmer over low heat until chicken is opaque, 15 to 20 minutes. Remove chicken from broth. Remove and discard skin and bones. Tear meat into thin shreds.

2. Put chicken shreds, cilantro sprigs and pepper flakes into broth. Heat to simmer over low heat. Add avocados and cheese cubes. Serve immediately, garnished with lime slices.

■ *The problem of using Thanksgiving leftovers is an annual one, but this method for getting the most from the turkey carcass is an elegant end for the old bird. It is best looking when the broth is clear so be careful to skim the stock as it cooks.*

TURKEY SOUP WITH ANGEL-HAIR PASTA

6 servings
Preparation time: 45 minutes
Cooking time: 2 hours

1 **cooked turkey carcass**
1 **cup dry sherry or dry white wine**
3 **quarts turkey stock or rich chicken broth (see recipe, page 134), or substitute canned broth**
1 **large leek, halved lengthwise, rinsed, sliced**
½ **cup chopped onion**
   Bouquet garni (see note)
4 **cups diced, boneless, skinless, cooked turkey**
2 **medium carrots, sliced**
1 **tablespoon minced fresh ginger**
1 **teaspoon soy sauce**
   Salt, optional
¼ **pound dried angel-hair pasta**
2 **cups shredded fresh spinach**

1. Heat oven to 350 degrees. Cut turkey carcass into pieces. Put into roasting pan. Bake until browned, about 30 minutes. Remove bones to large dutch oven. Pour sherry into roasting pan. Heat to boil over medium heat, scraping up browned bits from bottom of pan. Add sherry to bones.

2. Add stock, leek, onion and bouquet garni to bones. Heat to boil; reduce heat. Simmer, partially covered, skimming surface scum occasionally, 1 hour.

3. Remove and discard bouquet garni. Remove bones; remove any meat on bones and add back to soup. Add diced turkey, carrots, ginger and soy sauce. Cook until carrots are crisp-tender, about 10 minutes. Taste and adjust seasonings, adding salt if necessary.

4. Add pasta noodles and spinach to soup. Cook just until pasta is al dente and spinach wilts, about 3 minutes. Serve immediately.

NOTE: For bouquet garni, tie 2 bay leaves, 1 sprig parsley, 12 black peppercorns and ¼ teaspoon dried leaf thyme in a double thickness of cheese-cloth.

VARIATION: For chicken soup with angel-hair pasta, you may substitute 3 pounds chicken bones, such as necks, backs and wings for the turkey carcass and 4 cups diced, skinless, boneless chicken for the turkey meat.

Thick, hearty and old-fashioned, this goulash soup is cooked in a microwave oven—cutting the cooking time in half. To ensure tender meat, the microwave should be set at medium power. Use canned broth if you must, but if you happen to have homemade stock, you will see how much better your soup can be.

Goulash Soup

6 servings
Preparation time: 30 minutes
Microwave cooking time: 1 hour

2 **tablespoons butter**

2 **large onions, chopped, about 1¼ cups**

1 **clove garlic, minced**

1 **pound boneless beef chuck, cut into ½-inch cubes**

¼ **cup all-purpose flour**

3 **cups basic beef stock (see recipe, page 133), or substitute canned broth**

1 **tablespoon each: tomato paste, sweet Hungarian paprika**

¾ **teaspoon caraway seeds**

½ **teaspoon ground ginger**

¼ **teaspoon cayenne pepper or to taste**

3 **medium red potatoes, cubed**

2 **carrots, peeled, diced**

1 **green pepper, seeded, diced**

1 **tomato, peeled, seeded, chopped**

Salt, freshly ground pepper to taste

Sour cream

1. Microwave butter in a 3-quart microwave-safe bowl on high (100 percent power) until melted, about 30 seconds. Stir in onions and garlic. Microwave on high until onions are soft, about 2 minutes. Toss beef cubes with flour. Add to onion mixture; microwave on high, stirring, until beef loses its pink color, about 5 minutes.

2. Stir in beef stock, tomato paste, paprika, caraway, ginger and cayenne pepper. Microwave, covered, on medium (50 percent power), stirring often, until beef is almost tender, 20 to 30 minutes.

3. Stir in potatoes and carrots. Microwave on medium until potatoes are fork-tender, 10 to 15 minutes. Stir in green pepper and tomato. Microwave on medium until green pepper is crisp-tender, 5 to 10 minutes. Let stand 10 minutes. Add salt and pepper. Serve with a dollop of sour cream.

Another good soup for during or after a game of football or soccer is this Italian minestrone from columnist Beverly Dillon. To transport it to a tailgate party, heat the soup to a boil, then pack it into an insulated, wide-mouthed container.

MEATBALL MINESTRONE

12 servings
Preparation time: 1 hour
Cooking time: 3 hours

SOUP

⅓ cup olive oil
1 cup coarsely chopped onions
2 large cloves garlic, minced
4 large carrots, peeled, thinly sliced
1 fennel bulb, tops removed, coarsely chopped
1 large green pepper, seeded, diced
2 each, thinly sliced: zucchini, yellow squash
1½ cups green beans, cut into 1-inch lengths
2 ribs celery, cut into ½-inch pieces
1 medium cabbage, shredded, about 4 cups
10 cups basic beef stock (see recipe, page 133), or substitute canned broth
1 can (28 ounces) Italian-style plum tomatoes
1 can (15 ounces) tomato puree
1 can (6 ounces) tomato paste
1 tablespoon each: dried basil, Italian seasoning, dried leaf oregano

ingredients continued on next page

1. For soup, heat oil in 9-quart dutch oven over medium heat. Add onions and garlic; cook and stir for 5 minutes. Add carrots, fennel, green pepper, zucchini, yellow squash, green beans and celery. Cook and stir for 5 minutes. Add cabbage; cook 5 minutes longer.

2. Add stock, tomatoes, tomato puree, tomato paste and seasonings. Heat to boil. Reduce heat to low; simmer, covered, 2½ hours. (Soup can be made ahead up to this point and refrigerated up to 24 hours.)

3. Meanwhile, heat oven to 400 degrees. Grease a 13 by 9-inch baking pan. Mix all meatball ingredients together in medium bowl. Shape into 1-inch balls. Place meatballs in single layer in prepared pan. Bake, turning meatballs occasionally, until brown on all sides, 15 to 20 minutes.

4. Remove meatballs from baking pan and drain on paper towels. (Meatballs may be made ahead and frozen up to 1 month.)

5. To serve, heat soup to simmer. Add meatballs, red kidney beans, white beans, corn, macaroni and wine. Cook, over medium heat, stirring occasionally, until macaroni is tender and meatballs are heated through, about 15 minutes.

6. Serve in large soup bowls. Pass grated Parmesan cheese.

1 teaspoon freshly
   ground pepper
½ teaspoon salt or
   to taste

MEATBALLS

1 pound each: ground
   beef round, mild
   Italian sausage,
   casing removed
1 cup fresh bread
   crumbs
1 medium onion,
   finely chopped
⅓ cup milk
¼ cup minced flat-leaf
   Italian parsley
2 eggs, slightly beaten
2 tablespoons dried
   Italian seasoning
1 teaspoon each: salt,
   freshly ground
   pepper, fennel seeds,
   crushed
1 large clove garlic,
   minced

TO SERVE

1 can (15 ounces) each,
   drained: red kidney
   beans, white beans,
   corn kernels
1 cup each: uncooked
   elbow macaroni,
   dry red wine
   Freshly grated
   Parmesan cheese for
   serving

Small pork and beef meatballs enliven this typical Mexican soup. Either beef or chicken broth can be used as the soup base.

MEXICAN MEATBALL SOUP
(Sopa de albondigas)

6 servings
Preparation time: 30 minutes
Cooking time: 30 minutes

MEATBALLS

- 2 **slices white bread**
- ¼ **cup milk**
- ½ **pound each: ground pork, ground beef round**
- 2 **tablespoons chopped fresh parsley**
- 1 **tablespoon minced white onion**
- 1 **egg, slightly beaten**
- 1 **clove garlic, minced**
- ¼ **teaspoon each: salt, freshly ground pepper**

SOUP

- 1 **tablespoon oil**
- 1 **small white onion, minced**
- 1 **clove garlic, minced**
- 5 **cups basic beef stock or rich chicken broth (see recipes, pages 133–34), or substitute canned broth**
- 2 **tablespoons tomato paste**
- 1 **medium carrot, peeled, diced**
- 1 **medium or 2 small zucchini, diced**
- 2 **whole tomatoes, seeded, cubed**
- 2 **tablespoons minced fresh cilantro (coriander) leaves**

1. For meatballs, soak bread in milk in small bowl until moistened. Squeeze bread dry; put bread into medium bowl. Stir in pork, beef, parsley, onion, egg, garlic, salt and pepper. Shape into bite-size meatballs.

2. Cook meatballs in nonstick skillet over medium heat until light brown on all sides, about 10 minutes. Drain on paper towels.

3. For soup, heat oil in large saucepan over medium heat. Add onion and garlic; cook and stir until softened. Stir in stock and tomato paste. Simmer 10 minutes.

4. Add meatballs and carrot. Simmer until meat is thoroughly cooked, about 20 minutes. Add zucchini and tomatoes. Simmer until vegetables are tender, 5 to 10 minutes. Stir in cilantro. Taste and adjust seasonings with salt and pepper. Serve immediately.

This is a fast version of the classic Mexican soup. It can be served as a starter for a Mexican meal or the main course for a hearty lunch. The dried chilies are available in most Mexican markets; they will keep on the shelf indefinitely.

QUICK TORTILLA SOUP

4 servings
Preparation time: 10 minutes
Cooking time: 20 minutes

1 **can (46 ounces) chicken broth**

2 **tablespoons each: tomato paste, minced white onion**
  Salt, freshly ground pepper to taste

8 **stale corn tortillas**
  Vegetable oil

2 **dried chilies pasilla**

2 **tablespoons chopped fresh cilantro (coriander) leaves**
  Grated añejo or Parmesan cheese

1. Heat broth, tomato paste and onion to simmer in large saucepan. Simmer 10 minutes. Add salt and pepper.

2. Meanwhile, cut tortillas into small wedges. Pour oil to a depth of ⅛ inch in large nonstick skillet. Heat oil over medium heat until hot but not smoking. Add a few tortilla wedges. Fry, turning until crisp and golden, 1 to 2 minutes. Drain on paper towels. Repeat with remaining tortilla wedges. Add dried chilies to oil, fry until puffed and crisp, about 30 seconds. Drain on paper towels; crumble when cool.

3. To serve, ladle broth mixture into hot serving bowls. Drop tortilla pieces, crumbled chilies, cilantro and cheese into soup. Stir once; serve immediately.

When the magical word bouillabaisse *is pronounced on the French Riviera, says William Rice in his* Sunday *magazine column, the waiter soon brings a copious quantity of rich, robust fish stew. While no one can quite agree on the exact true bouillabaisse recipe, the following version from Chicago's Le Perroquet restaurant contains an ample supply of rouille, a red-hot condiment with a mayonnaise-consistency.*

BOUILLABAISSE

6 servings
Preparation time: 1 hour
Cooking time: 40 minutes

2 quarts fish stock (see recipe, page 135)
2 ribs celery, diced
1 each, diced: large carrot, large onion
1 leek, white part only, diced
1 large head garlic, unpeeled, but cut in half
¼ cup olive oil
2 cups dry white wine
1 cup brandy
6 sprigs parsley
3 bay leaves
1 tablespoon each, minced: fresh tarragon, fresh thyme (or 1 teaspoon each dried)
1 generous pinch saffron threads
1 can (28 ounces) Italian-style plum tomatoes, drained, coarsely chopped
1 tablespoon tomato paste
  Salt, freshly ground white pepper to taste
24 mussels, scrubbed clean, debearded
1 pound halibut steak or monkfish fillet, cut into cubes

1. Make fish stock.

2. Cook celery, carrot, onion, leek and garlic in olive oil in large dutch oven over low heat until tender. Add wine and brandy; boil over medium heat until liquid is reduced by half.

3. Tie parsley, bay leaves, tarragon, thyme and saffron in cheesecloth. Add to the pot along with fish stock, tomatoes and tomato paste. Stir well. Simmer over low heat 25 minutes. Add salt and pepper. Strain through fine sieve; discard vegetables and cheesecloth bag. (Recipe may be done ahead to this point. Refrigerate covered up to 2 days.)

4. Pour broth into large dutch oven. Heat to boil over medium heat, then add mussels and cover the pan. Simmer, covered, 3 minutes, then add fish cubes. Simmer, covered, 2 minutes, then add shrimp and scallops. Cook, uncovered, until shrimp and scallops are just firm, about 3 minutes. Remove from heat.

5. Divide fish and shellfish among 6 bowls. Spoon hot broth over each portion. Garnish with julienned carrot, zucchini and langoustine. Serve with bread and rouille. There will be broth left for second helpings.

24 medium shrimp,
     peeled, deveined

24 sea scallops

    Julienned carrot,
     julienned zucchini for
     garnish

    Whole cooked
     langoustines or
     shrimps for garnish

12 thin slices French
     bread, optional

 1 cup rouille (recipe
     follows), optional

ROUILLE | About 1 cup

¼ cup each, chopped:
     pimiento, well-cooked
     potato

4 cloves garlic

½ teaspoon cayenne
     pepper

⅓ cup olive oil

3 tablespoons warm fish
     broth

    Salt to taste

1. Put pimiento and potato into food processor or blender. Add garlic and cayenne pepper. Process until well mixed. With machine running, add oil in slow, steady stream until smooth and thickened. Then add broth, salt and additional cayenne pepper.

Clam chowder is a tradition that goes backs to the first settlers in the New World, and there's been very little change in its basic structure. This recipe, adapted from The Barclay Hotel in Chicago, is a quick and simple method for this hearty dish. Using fresh clams makes a world of difference in the taste.

NEW ENGLAND CLAM CHOWDER

8 servings
Preparation time: 20 minutes
Cooking time: 25 minutes

3 **ounces salt pork, minced**
¾ **cup (1½ sticks) unsalted butter**
1 **cup finely chopped onions**
3 **cups peeled, cubed red potatoes**
6 **bottles (8 ounces each) clam juice**
1½ **cups whipping cream or half-and-half**
3 **cups fresh, minced clams, preferably quahogs**
   Freshly ground pepper to taste
   Minced fresh parsley for garnish

1. Cook salt pork in medium dutch oven over medium heat until transparent, 2 to 3 minutes. Add butter; cook over low heat 1 minute. Do not allow butter to take on color. Add onions; cook and stir until transparent, about 4 minutes.

2. Add potatoes and clam juice. Heat to boil over medium heat; simmer until potatoes are tender, about 10 minutes. (Soup can be prepared ahead to this point.)

3. Stir in cream. Heat to simmer over medium-low heat. Add clams; simmer until clams are tender, about 3 minutes. Do not boil. Add pepper to taste. Sprinkle with parsley.

NOTE: If thicker consistency is desired, add a mixture of 2 tablespoons cornstarch and ¼ cup water to soup before adding clams; cook and stir until thickened.

A recipe submitted to The Tribune *Food Guide by reader Martha F. Davis of Chicago shows that there is always a new combination of ingredients to be tasted.*

JALAPEÑO CHEESE SOUP

6 to 8 servings
Preparation time: 25 minutes
Cooking time: 25 minutes

2 **cups canned chicken broth or vegetable bouillon**

2 **medium red potatoes, peeled, diced**

1 **cup diced tomato**

½ **cup finely chopped onion**

1 **teaspoon minced garlic**

6 **tablespoons each: butter, all-purpose flour**

1 **quart hot milk**

2 **teaspoons caraway seeds**

¼ **teaspoon salt, or to taste**

⅛ **teaspoon freshly ground pepper**

3 **cups coarsely shredded Monterey Jack cheese with jalapeño peppers**

1. Mix broth, potatoes, tomato, onion and garlic in large saucepan. Heat to boil over high heat. Cover; reduce heat to medium; simmer for 10 minutes.

2. Melt butter in medium saucepan; stir in flour. Cook and stir over medium heat for 3 minutes. Gradually stir in milk. Cook and stir until smooth and thickened, about 7 minutes. Remove broth mixture from heat. Stir milk mixture into broth.

3. Stir in caraway seeds, salt and pepper. Stir in cheese. Cook and stir until cheese melts and soup is well heated.

Vietnamese combination soup has as many variations as French bouillabaisse or Italian spaghetti. This version, from Lam Ton, owner of the Mekong restaurants in Chicago, combines seafood, pork and chicken.

VIETNAMESE COMBINATION SOUP
(Lau thap cam)

6 to 8 servings
Preparation time: 1 hour
Soaking time: 8 hours or overnight
Cooking time: 3½ to 4½ hours

4 ounces large dried squid
2 pounds chicken bones (wings, necks, backs, etc.)
1 pound pork bones
4 carrots, peeled, sliced
3 ribs celery, sliced
3 quarts water
Few pinches each: sugar, salt
5 dried Chinese black mushrooms
½ pound napa (also called celery cabbage)
1 whole chicken breast, boned, skinned, split
½ pound raw, peeled shrimp, deveined, tails left on
¼ pound piece lean boneless pork, cut into ⅛-inch-thick matchsticks
½ pound fresh mushrooms, sliced, browned in butter
1 can (8 ounces) bamboo shoots, drained
Fish balls (recipe follows)

1. Put dried squid in bowl, cover with boiling water. Let stand until softened, 8 hours or overnight. Drain, cut squid into ⅛-inch matchsticks.

2. Meanwhile, put chicken bones, pork bones, carrots and celery into large dutch oven. Add 3 quarts water or enough to cover bones by 1 inch. Heat to boil over high heat; add sugar and salt. Reduce heat to low. Simmer, partly covered, skimming surface scum occasionally, 3 to 4 hours.

3. Strain through fine sieve; there should be about 6 cups. If you have more, simmer until reduced to that amount.

4. Meanwhile, put black mushrooms in a separate bowl and cover with boiling water. Let stand until soft, about 30 minutes. Drain and cut each mushroom into 3 pieces.

5. Heat a pot of water to a boil, drop napa pieces into boiling water; cook for 30 seconds. Remove from water, drain and reserve.

6. Cut chicken breast into 1-inch cubes. Put chicken, squid, black mushrooms, shrimp, pork, fresh mushrooms, bamboo shoots and fish balls into a large saucepan.

7. Heat the 6 cups broth to boil. Pour boiling broth over ingredients in saucepan. Turn heat to simmer; cook until pork is completely cooked, about 5 minutes.

8. Arrange napa around sides of a Mongolian hot pot or substitute a large serving casserole with raised sides.

**Several sprinklings
each: Oriental sesame
oil, freshly ground
white pepper**
**Few sprigs fresh
cilantro (coriander)**
**Oriental chili sauce,
optional**

9. Using a soup ladle, scoop up all solid ingredients from saucepan with small amount of broth and arrange it all over top of napa. There should be a little broth and a lot of meat and vegetables.

10. Sprinkle a few drops of sesame oil over top of dish. Then sprinkle with white pepper. Garnish with cilantro. Serve immediately. Pass hot chili sauce.

FISH BALLS

**1 pound each, chopped:
skinless white fish
fillets, lean boneless
pork**
2 teaspoons cornstarch
**1 teaspoon each: baking
powder, freshly
ground pepper, salt,
sugar**

1. Put fish and pork through medium blade of food chopper or process with on/off turns in food processor until coarsely chopped. Stir in remaining ingredients. Mix very well. Shape into 1-inch balls.

Gumbos don't get much richer than this one but the taste is worth the indulgence. Duck and andouille sausage add flavor and texture to this main-course soup-stew created by test kitchen director JeanMarie Brownson.

DUCK AND SAUSAGE GUMBO

8 servings
Preparation time: 1 hour
Cooking time: 1¼ hours

⅔ cup vegetable oil

2 ducks, about 4 pounds each, quartered

⅔ cup all-purpose flour

1 pound andouille sausage or smoked Polish sausage, cut into ¼-inch-thick slices

2 cups each: chopped yellow onions, chopped celery

1 cup chopped green onions

⅔ cup chopped green pepper

¼ cup chopped fresh parsley

5 large cloves garlic, minced

2 quarts rich chicken broth (see recipe, page 134), or substitute canned

3 bay leaves, crumbled

2½ teaspoons salt, or to taste

1 teaspoon each: dried leaf thyme, freshly ground black pepper, or to taste

¼ teaspoon cayenne pepper, or to taste

2½ to 3 tablespoons filé powder

Cooked rice

Hot pepper sauce to taste

1. Heat oil in 7- or 9-quart heavy dutch oven over medium heat. Add duck quarters in single layer. Cook until brown on all sides. Remove and reserve duck.

2. Add flour to hot oil and stir until smooth. Cook and stir constantly, over medium-high heat, until roux is color of cinnamon. Remove from heat.

3. Stir in sliced sausage, yellow onions, celery, green onions, green pepper, parsley and garlic. Cook and stir over medium heat until vegetables are crisp-tender, about 10 minutes.

4. Stir in ½ cup of the chicken broth scraping up browned bits from bottom of pan. Stir in browned duck parts, bay leaves, salt, thyme, black pepper and cayenne pepper. Stir in remaining broth. Heat to boil over medium heat. Skim off surface scum. Reduce heat to low; simmer, uncovered, until duck is tender, 30 to 40 minutes. Taste and adjust seasonings.

5. Remove duck pieces from gumbo. (Recipe can be made ahead to this point; refrigerate duck pieces separately. Before reheating remove solidified fat from surface.)

6. Skim all fat from surface of gumbo. Remove skin and bones from duck and discard. Cut meat into thin shreds.

7. To serve, reheat gumbo; add duck meat. Heat to boil. Remove from heat; let simmer die down. Add filé powder and stir. Let stand 5 minutes.

8. Serve in soup bowls over rice. Pass hot pepper sauce.

Simple acorn squash is seasoned with the exotic overtones of curry, apple and smoked ham in the following soup. It is perfect for making after Thanksgiving when there's plenty of turkey carcass to use for a rich stock.

CURRIED CREAM OF ACORN SQUASH SOUP

6 servings
Preparation time: 40 minutes
Cooking time: 2 hours

6 small acorn squash
4 tablespoons butter
2 leeks, white part only, coarsely chopped, about 1 cup
1 medium carrot, diced
5 cups rich chicken broth or turkey stock (see recipe, page 134), or substitute canned broth
2 small ham hocks
1 medium apple, peeled, cored, diced
1 bay leaf
¾ teaspoon curry powder, or to taste
½ teaspoon dried chervil
¼ teaspoon freshly ground pepper
2 cups half-and-half
2 teaspoons fresh lemon juice
Salt to taste
1½ cups bread cubes
¾ cup shredded Gruyère or Swiss cheese

1. Remove a small slice from top of each squash. Remove seeds from squash with a spoon. With melon baller scoop out flesh leaving a ½-inch-thick shell. Put flesh into measuring cup. There should be about 5 cups. If necessary, cut a small slice off bottom of each squash so they stand upright. Reserve shells in a baking pan.

2. Heat 2 tablespoons of the butter in large non-aluminum dutch oven. Add leeks and carrot; cook and stir until soft, about 5 minutes. Stir in squash flesh, chicken broth, ham hocks, apple, bay leaf, curry powder, chervil and pepper. Heat to boil; reduce heat to low. Simmer, uncovered, stirring often, until squash is very tender, about 1 hour.

3. Remove ham hocks to small bowl and reserve. Remove and discard bay leaf. Using slotted spoon, transfer solids in pan to a blender or food processor. (Leave broth in pan.) Add half-and-half to solids; process until pureed. Set aside.

4. Heat broth in pan to a gentle simmer. Simmer, uncovered, until mixture reduces to 2 cups. Stir squash puree mixture into reduced broth. (Recipe can be done ahead to this point; refrigerate covered, up to several days.)

5. Remove and dice meat from ham hocks; stir into soup. Reheat soup; add lemon juice and salt.

6. Heat remaining 2 tablespoons butter in large nonstick skillet. Add bread cubes. Sauté until golden. Remove from heat.

7. To serve, preheat broiler. Ladle soup into reserved squash shells. Sprinkle bread cubes over top. Sprinkle with cheese. Broil until cheese browns. Serve immediately.

Cajun Chef Paul Prudhomme sat in judgment for The Tribune *Food Guide's 1986 Great Gumbo Contest and picked Annamarie Bannos' gumbo as the best from more than 100 recipes. The amount of crushed red pepper and cayenne pepper may be reduced for those with heat-sensitive palates.*

SUPERBOWL CHICKEN AND ANDOUILLE SAUSAGE GUMBO

16 to 18 servings
Preparation time: 1½ hours
Cooking time: 6½ hours

ROUX

2 **cups each: all-purpose flour, vegetable oil**

GUMBO

½ **bunch celery, diced**

6 **green peppers, seeded, diced**

3 **red bell peppers, seeded, diced**

4 **green onions, diced**

1 **red onion, diced**

½ **white onion, diced**

2 **each, seeded, minced: jalapeño peppers, serrano peppers**

1 **clove garlic, minced**

5 **bay leaves**

1½ **tablespoons each: dried basil, dried leaf oregano, dried leaf thyme, freshly ground white pepper**

1 **tablespoon crushed red pepper flakes**

1½ **teaspoons cayenne pepper**

1 **jar (2.2 ounces) Cajun spice for poultry, such as Chef Paul Prudhomme's Louisiana Cajun Magic**

1. For roux, mix flour and oil in roasting pan. Bake at 250 degrees, stirring often, until mixture is color of dark red clay, about 5 hours or more. Remove from oven. (See note on alternate method.)

2. For gumbo, put all vegetables, peppers and garlic into 12-quart heavy-bottomed dutch oven or stockpot. Cook and stir over medium-high heat until vegetables are limp, 10 to 15 minutes. Stir in bay leaves, basil, oregano, thyme, white pepper, crushed red peppers, cayenne pepper and half of the Cajun spice mixture. Mix thoroughly over medium heat.

3. Stir in half of the roux. Gradually stir in chicken broth until well blended. Cook and stir over medium heat until thickened. Stir in remaining roux if thicker consistency is desired.

4. Cook cubed sausage in nonstick skillet over medium heat until slightly browned, 5 to 10 minutes. Drain off excess grease and add sausage to simmering gumbo mixture.

5. Mix chicken with remaining Cajun spice mixture. Cook in large nonstick skillet over medium heat until chicken is browned, 5 to 10 minutes. Add to gumbo. Simmer gumbo over medium heat, stirring often, for 1 hour.

6. Just prior to serving, heat gumbo to boil. Turn off heat. Add filé powder. Stir well. Add water if needed to thin to desired consistency. Serve hot with a spoonful of cooked rice.

**6 quarts rich chicken
    broth (see recipe,
    page 134)**
**2 pounds andouille
    sausage or smoked
    Polish sausage, cubed**
**2½ pounds cubed,
    boneless, skinless
    chicken breasts**
**½ cup filé powder
    Cooked white rice**

NOTE: To make roux on top of stove, put flour and oil into large skillet. Cook and stir over medium-high heat until mixture is dark reddish-brown in color, 20 to 30 minutes. To freeze gumbo, prepare recipe through step 5. Freeze solid up to 1 month. Reheat and finish gumbo as directed in step 6 before serving.

Many people dislike cauliflower, but this soup, based on a classic recipe, will change their minds. Try it on cauliflower haters you know.

CREAM OF CAULIFLOWER SOUP

4 servings
Preparation time: 15 minutes
Cooking time: 20 minutes
Chilling time: Several hours

**1 head cauliflower,
    broken into flowerets**
**4 cups rich chicken broth
    (see recipe, page
    134), or substitute
    canned broth**
**4 slices bread, crusts
    removed, chopped**
1½ cups half-and-half
**2 tablespoons dry white
    wine**
¼ teaspoon salt
**⅛ teaspoon freshly
    ground white pepper**
**2 tomatoes, peeled,
    seeded, diced,
    drained**
**2 tablespoons finely
    chopped fresh dill**

1. Cook cauliflower in broth in large saucepan over medium heat until very soft, about 20 minutes. Puree in batches in food processor or blender. Return puree to saucepan.

2. Meanwhile, soak bread in half-and-half in small bowl. Puree in food processor or blender; stir into soup. Cook soup, stirring often, over low heat until heated through. Stir in wine, salt and pepper. Taste and adjust seasonings.

3. To serve, ladle soup into serving bowls. Top with a spoonful of tomatoes; sprinkle with dill.

NOTE: This soup is also delicious served cold.

Patty pan squash, also known as asparagus squash, became very popular a few years ago in their miniature variety. The large patty pan can also be used in this soup but more cooking time will be required. Several variations follow the initial recipe which can be served either hot or cold.

CREAM OF PATTY PAN SQUASH SOUP

6 to 8 servings
Preparation time: 25 minutes
Cooking time: 35 minutes

2 **pounds miniature patty pan squash, trimmed**
4 **tablespoons unsalted butter**
1 **clove garlic, minced**
5 **cups rich chicken broth (see recipe, page 134), or substitute canned broth**
½ **teaspoon each: salt, freshly ground pepper**
¾ **cup whipping cream**
1 **egg yolk**
2 **to 3 tablespoons minced fresh chives**

1. Slice 4 of the miniature squash into thin rounds to be used for garnish. Dice remaining squash. Melt 2 tablespoons of the butter in large saucepan. Add garlic and diced squash. Sauté until tender but not brown, about 10 minutes.

2. Stir in chicken broth, salt and pepper. Simmer until squash is very tender, about 20 minutes. Puree in batches in food processor or blender. Return puree to saucepan.

3. Mix cream and egg yolk in small bowl. Stir into pureed squash mixture. Cook and stir over low heat until mixture thickens slightly. Do not boil. Remove from heat.

4. For garnish, melt remaining 2 tablespoons butter in large skillet. Add reserved squash slices. Sauté until golden. Serve soup with a sautéed squash slice floating on top and sprinkled with chives.

NOTE: This soup is also delicious served cold.

VARIATIONS: *Indian flavor:* Add ¼ to ½ teaspoon curry powder to hot or cold soup. Top each serving with a spoonful of plain yogurt.

Tex-Mex: Add 2 tablespoons minced fresh cilantro (coriander) and ¼ teaspoon hot pepper sauce to hot or cold soup. Garnish with crisply fried tortilla strips.

Cold mint: Add 1 to 2 tablespoons minced fresh mint to cold soup. Garnish with mint sprig.

This simple soup defies ethnic definition. It combines Italian, Mexican and Central European styles of cooking. The result is superb.

CREAM OF RED PEPPER SOUP

6 servings
Preparation time: 20 minutes
Cooking time: 50 minutes

4 **red bell peppers**
2 **medium onions, minced**
2 **cloves garlic, minced**
1 **tablespoon vegetable oil**
4 **cups rich chicken broth (see recipe, page 134), or substitute canned broth**
¼ **teaspoon cayenne pepper**
   Sour cream, minced, seeded jalapeño pepper, fresh cilantro (coriander) leaves for garnish

1. To roast red peppers, preheat broiler. Put peppers onto broiler pan. Broil 4 to 6 inches from heat source until skins are blistered and slightly charred. Wrap in foil; let stand until cool. Put onto cutting board; remove stems and seeds. Using a paring knife, peel away charred skin.

2. Cook onions and garlic in oil in dutch oven over medium heat until tender, about 10 minutes. Add chicken broth, chopped red peppers and cayenne pepper. Cook, stirring often, over low heat until peppers are very tender, about 20 minutes.

3. Cool slightly; puree in batches in blender or food processor. Return puree to saucepan. Cook over low heat until heated through. Serve garnished with a dollop of sour cream, minced jalapeño pepper and cilantro leaves.

One of the pleasures of summer lunching in Chicago's Magnificent Mile along Michigan Avenue is Avanzare's outdoor cafe. One indelible memory from a noontime stop there is of the tomato-basil soup with its dollop of pesto sauce floating in the center. The soup should sit on ice for at least a half hour before serving to ensure that the flavors blend. That, after all, is the secret.

COLD TOMATO-BASIL SOUP WITH PESTO SAUCE

6 to 8 servings
Preparation time: 40 minutes
Chilling time: 2 hours

12 **very ripe garden tomatoes, cored**

½ **cup packed fresh basil leaves, julienned or finely chopped**

Tomato juice, if needed

Red wine vinegar to taste

Extra-virgin olive oil to taste

Salt, freshly ground white pepper to taste

3 **cloves garlic, peeled, lightly bruised**

Pesto sauce (recipe follows)

1. Make a small x-shaped cut in back of each tomato. Heat large pot of water to boil. Drop tomatoes into boiling water. Boil 1 minute; drain well. Let sit at room temperature until cool enough to handle. Peel and discard skin.

2. Set a fine strainer over a large bowl. Cut tomatoes in half horizontally. Squeeze out juice and seeds into strainer. Using a spoon, push on seeds and juice to catch juice in bowl. Discard seeds.

3. Finely chop tomatoes in food processor or by hand. Do not puree. Add tomatoes to juice. Add basil. If necessary, add a little tomato juice to thin soup slightly.

4. Season with vinegar, oil, salt and pepper to taste. Add garlic. Refrigerate, or set bowl over a large bowl of ice, about ½ to 2 hours before serving. Remove garlic.

5. Top each serving with a small spoonful of pesto sauce.

PESTO SAUCE | About 2 cups

1 cup tightly packed
  fresh basil leaves
½ cup pine nuts, toasted,
  cooled
2 large cloves garlic
½ cup each: freshly
  grated Parmigiano-
  Reggiano cheese
  (imported Parmesan)
  and Pecorino Romano
  cheese
½ cup olive oil
  Salt to taste

1. Put basil, pine nuts and garlic in a grinder or mortar and pestle. Grind until fine, but do not puree.

2. Stir in remaining ingredients. If making in advance, cover the surface with a little oil and then plastic wrap to avoid color change. Pesto sauce can be kept refrigerated up to 1 week.

NOTE: If freezing the sauce, pack tightly into a freezer container. Cover the surface with plastic wrap. Cover tightly with lid. Freeze solid. Sauce will keep for several weeks.

Cool, crisp cucumbers refresh the palate on warm summer days. This creamy soup, made from cucumbers and tangy yogurt and sour cream, is delicately flavored with curry for a summer cool-down.

CREAM OF CUCUMBER SOUP

4 servings
Preparation time: 25 minutes
Cooking time: 35 minutes
Chilling time: Several hours

3 large cucumbers
1 tablespoon butter
¼ cup diced onion
1 can (13¾ ounces)
  chicken broth
½ teaspoon salt, or to
  taste
¼ to ½ teaspoon curry
  powder to taste
¼ teaspoon freshly
  ground pepper
½ cup each: plain yogurt,
  sour cream

1. Peel cucumbers; cut lengthwise in half. Remove seeds. Chop coarsely.

2. Melt butter in dutch oven over medium heat. Add onion; cook and stir until limp. Stir in cucumbers, broth, salt, curry powder and pepper. Increase heat to high; heat to boil. Reduce heat to low; simmer until cucumbers are very tender, about 30 minutes. Remove from heat. Cool slightly.

3. Puree in batches in food processor or blender. Stir in yogurt and sour cream. Process until well blended. Refrigerate until very cold.

This unique cold soup uses eggplant, which is not a common soup ingredient, and just a hint of curry. Make it a day ahead of a luncheon party and let it chill overnight.

CURRIED CREAM OF EGGPLANT SOUP

6 servings
Preparation time: 30 minutes
Cooking time: 1 hour
Chilling time: 4 hours or overnight

1 **medium eggplant**
2 **tablespoons butter**
1 **cup finely chopped onions**
2 **cloves garlic, minced**
1 **can (16 ounces) whole tomatoes, drained**
2 **cups rich chicken broth (see recipe, page 134), or substitute canned**
¼ **teaspoon each: curry powder, freshly ground pepper**
1 **cup whipping cream or half-and-half**
Salt to taste
Minced parsley for garnish

1. Heat oven to 450 degrees. Put eggplant onto baking sheet. Bake, turning occasionally, until eggplant is very soft and collapsed, about 30 minutes. Cool; halve and scrape pulp into bowl.

2. Heat butter in dutch oven over medium heat; add onions and garlic. Cook and stir until onion is tender, 3 to 5 minutes. Stir in eggplant pulp, tomatoes, chicken broth, curry powder and pepper. Heat to boil; reduce heat to low. Simmer, uncovered, stirring often, 30 minutes.

3. Puree mixture in food processor or blender. Put into large bowl. Stir in cream and salt. Refrigerate, covered, 4 hours or overnight. Serve very cold, garnished with parsley.

Creamy, ripe avocados add a rich dimension to cold soups. Serve a bowlful of this ginger-flavored avocado soup with pita chips or Melba toast.

COLD GINGERED AVOCADO SOUP

8 servings
Preparation: 20 minutes

3 **large ripe avocados, peeled, cubed**

1 **cup plain yogurt or sour cream**

½ **cup mayonnaise**

1 **small bunch green onions, sliced**

¼ **cup each: fresh lemon juice, fresh parsley leaves**

2 **tablespoons grated, peeled fresh ginger**

3 **cups canned chicken broth, cold**

Salt, freshly ground white pepper to taste

Minced parsley for garnish

1. Put avocados into food processor or blender. Add yogurt, mayonnaise, onions, lemon juice, parsley and ginger. Process until pureed.

2. With machine running, slowly pour in chicken broth until completely mixed. Add salt and pepper. Serve soup immediately or refrigerate up to 1 hour. Sprinkle with parsley.

Melons, the base of the following soup, are at the sweetest end of the gourd family, which also includes cucumbers and squash. They are among the earliest cultivated vegetables. There is no need to follow the suggested ingredients slavishly because the possibilities for pleasing combinations are limited only by one's imagination.

FRUIT GAZPACHO WITH MINT

6 to 8 servings
Preparation time: 45 minutes
Chilling time: Several hours

6 pounds fresh melon, such as crenshaw, honeydew, cantaloupe, canary or a combination

2 cups diced, seeded watermelon

1 Bartlett pear, cored, diced

1 cup seedless green or red grapes, halved

½ cup each: fresh raspberries, halved, seeded Bing cherries

Juice of each:
1 orange,
1 large lime

3 tablespoons light rum, optional

2 tablespoons minced fresh mint

1 tablespoon sugar or honey

Pinch ground cloves

Plain yogurt for serving

Minced fresh mint for garnish

1. Cut melons in half. Remove seeds. Cut melon away from rind. Put half of the melon into blender or food processor. Process until pureed. Transfer to large nonaluminum bowl.

2. Dice remaining melon. Stir into puree. Stir in watermelon, pear, grapes, raspberries, cherries, orange juice, lime juice, rum, 2 tablespoons mint, sugar (or honey) and cloves. Refrigerate, covered, until very cold.

3. Taste and adjust seasonings, adding more sugar or honey as desired. Serve in bowls topped with a dollop of yogurt and a sprinkle of mint.

Following are recipes for five basic stocks. Use them as outlines, filling in with what you have on hand.

In a pinch, you can use beef, chicken, ham or vegetable concentrate to enhance your soups and sauces, but remember there is no substitute for a stock you make yourself. Cubes and concentrates have a lot of salt. They not only lack real flavor, they lack the love a good stock thrives on.

BASIC BEEF OR VEAL STOCK

About 2½ quarts
Preparation time: 20 minutes
Cooking time: 3 to 4 hours

4 **to 6 pounds beef or veal bones (especially marrow and knuckle bones) and beef or veal scraps**

5 **quarts water**

3 **to 6 ribs celery or celery cuttings and leaves**

2 **medium carrots, chopped**

1 **onion, stuck with 2 or 3 whole cloves**

1 **medium leek, chopped**

1 **tomato, chopped or tomato scraps**

8 **black peppercorns**

1 **bay leaf**
  Parsley sprigs
  Other vegetable cuttings

1. Put all ingredients into large stockpot. Heat to boil; reduce heat to simmer. Simmer, partly covered, skimming off surface scum, until liquid is reduced by half, 3 to 4 hours.

2. Strain through fine sieve. Cool; then refrigerate, covered, until cold. Remove solidified fat from surface. Store in refrigerator up to 1 week or freeze solid up to several months.

NOTE: For brown beef or veal stock, heat oven to 400 degrees. Put bones in a single layer in roasting pan. Roast bones, turning often, until dark brown but not burned. Proceed with recipe as directed.

Rich Chicken Broth

About 6 cups
Preparation time: 20 minutes
Cooking time: 2 hours

4 to 5 pounds chicken backs, wings, necks and bones or carcass (avoid liver and heart)
3 quarts water
2 ribs celery, halved
1 medium carrot, halved
1 white onion, quartered
1 medium leek, split in half
4 parsley sprigs
8 black peppercorns

1. Put all ingredients into large saucepan or small stockpot. Heat to boil; reduce heat to simmer. Simmer, partly covered, skimming off surface scum, until liquid is reduced by half, about 2 hours.

2. Strain through fine sieve. Cool, then refrigerate, covered, until cold. Remove solidified fat from surface. Store in refrigerator up to 1 week or freeze solid up to 3 months.

Turkey Stock

About 3 cups
Preparation time: 15 minutes
Cooking time: 2½ hours

1 each: medium onion, rib celery, carrot
Turkey neck and giblets
1 quart water
¼ cup parsley sprigs

1. Heat oven to 350 degrees. Chop vegetables. Place vegetables, turkey neck and giblets in small roasting pan. Bake, turning often, until browned on all sides, about 1 hour. Transfer to medium saucepan.

2. Place roasting pan with juices directly over stove burner turned on to high heat. When drippings sizzle, add 1 cup water and heat to boil, scraping all brown bits from pan. Pour this liquid into saucepan with giblet mixture. Add remaining 3 cups water and parsley.

3. Heat to boil over high heat and simmer 1½ hours. Strain and measure. If stock does not yield over 3 cups, add water to compensate. Cool, then cover and refrigerate. Store in refrigerator up to 3 days or freeze solid up to 2 months.

Fish stock should be used only for fish or seafood dishes unless a recipe specifically calls for it. Chicken or beef stock sometimes can be added to fortify the stock. Fish heads and tails often are available at supermarket fish counters but some now are charging for them. Bones from halibut, cod, pike and sea bass make an exceptionally tasty stock.

FISH STOCK
(Fumet)

About 6 cups
Preparation time: 20 minutes
Cooking time: 30 to 40 minutes

2 ribs celery, chopped
1 each, chopped:
   medium onion,
   medium carrot
2 tablespoons butter or
   vegetable oil
3 pounds fish heads,
   bones, tails (avoid
   strong fish such as
   buffalo fish,
   mackerel, mullet and
   salmon)
2 quarts water
¼ cup dry white wine
2 tablespoons lemon
   juice or white vinegar
6 black peppercorns
2 whole cloves
1 teaspoon dried leaf
   thyme
1 bay leaf

1. Sauté celery, onion and carrot in butter or oil in bottom of stockpot until translucent, about 3 minutes. Add remaining ingredients. Heat to boil; reduce heat to simmer. Simmer, uncovered, skimming off surface scum, for 30 minutes. (Longer cooking will impart a bitter flavor.)

2. Strain through fine sieve. Cool, then refrigerate covered until cold. Store in the refrigerator up to 2 days or freeze solid up to 1 month.

This rich crayfish stock can be used as a base for fish soups, chowders, fish stews and sauces to be served with fish. If crayfish shells are not available you may substitute crab, lobster or shrimp shells.

LOBSTER, SHRIMP OR CRAYFISH STOCK

About 1 quart
Preparation time: 10 minutes
Cooking time: 30 minutes

2 to 3 pounds lobster heads and shells, shrimp shells or crayfish heads and tail shells
1 rib celery
1 small onion stuck with 1 clove
2 bay leaves
4 black peppercorns
2 sprigs parsley

1. Put fish shells into a 4-quart saucepan. Add remaining ingredients and cold water to cover all by 2 inches. Heat to boil; reduce heat to simmer. Simmer uncovered for 30 minutes.

2. Strain well, pressing hard on shells to extract all the liquid. Simmer strained liquid in large saucepan until reduced to about 1 quart. Cool, then refrigerate, covered, until cold. Store in the refrigerator up to 2 days or freeze solid up to 1 month.

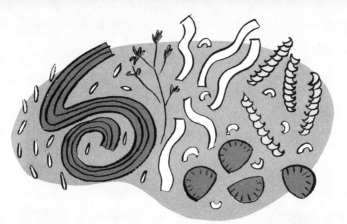

PASTA, RICE & OTHER GRAINS

Probably no other type of food has influenced American tastes in the last few years as much as pasta. Not just a passing trend riding on the popularity of Italian cuisine, pasta has permeated the fabric of American cooking and has found a flavorful place in many food styles other than Italian.

Evidence suggests that spaghetti was invented by the Chinese, centuries before it adorned tables in Rome, and that intrepid explorer Marco Polo brought it back to Italy, where it became a national dish.

And it should be, because spaghetti and other pastas are nourishing and healthful, although only lately have they been regarded as such. For a while, pasta, breads and other grain products were thought to be fattening, but medical research shows that well-made pasta is rich in complex carbohydrates and carries its own in protein content. Although it is not shy in calories, pasta certainly has fewer than the olive oil with which it often is coated.

Basic pasta is little more than flour and water. Yet a few well-trained Oriental chefs are able to take a volleyball-size heap of this paste-like mix and literally turn it into thousands of amazing, spaghetti-thin strands by tossing, stretching and turning the dough in the air with their bare hands. The feat takes about 10 years to learn and it is quite a trick to watch.

Less dexterous individuals content themselves by rolling the dough out thin, then cutting and shaping it into various forms such as linguini, tortellini, ravioli and tagliatelle. The addition of fat and eggs to the basic dough helps provide more flavor and body, though it is not necessary.

Many variations of pasta are available in the well-stocked supermarket at a wide range of prices. Most of it is commercially produced and dried, from both domestic and foreign sources. But the more expensive, freshly made pasta also has become popular, often sold in specialty food shops and a few supermarkets in such flavors as spinach, tomato, mushroom and even chocolate.

Making your own fresh pasta is not that difficult, especially if someone has given you a pasta machine to take the tedium out of the exercise. For the discriminating pasta eater, there is no substitute for fresh. Still, the simplicity of storing and cooking dried pasta makes it an essential staple in the modern kitchen.

Italians believe pasta is best when cooked al dente, literally "to the tooth," so that the strands or pieces are soft and pliable but still firm enough to cause a slight resistance when chewed. A little experience with overcooked and undercooked pasta should help you find the right stage to remove it from the heat. Fresh pasta takes much less time to cook, so you should pay close attention to the pot.

College students used to test spaghetti for doneness by slinging a strand against the wall to see if it would stick. When it stuck it meant the spaghetti was done. For the sake of cleanliness, the bite test should suffice.

RICE

Although rice is an entirely different grain than wheat, it is like pasta in that it will extend the flavor of meats and vegetables and especially sauces. And like pasta, rice lends itself to a wide variety of dishes.

It is a mainstay of Chinese, Japanese, Korean, Thai, Vietnamese and Indian cooking. The Italian risotto and the Spanish paella, both based on rice, are two of the world's finest culinary preparations.

The most common rice is polished white, enriched with some vitamins, but with most of the rice bran removed. Brown rice has some of the bran left and thus offers more vitamins and fiber. Both white and brown rice are good sources of complex carbohydrates and some protein. Rice combined with beans makes an almost perfect protein food, supplying nearly all of the body's daily nutritive requirements.

Basmati rice from India often is called the premier of rice. With its nutty flavor and separate long grains, it is basic to several fine Indian preparations.

OTHER GRAINS

Other grains are gaining a long-deserved popularity. Although cornmeal is an American tradition, it also has been accepted heartily in the form of Italian polenta, and is found in more and more American restaurants. Bulgur, a cracked whole wheat, is eaten in salads; couscous, a steamed and dried semolina, teams with stews; and the South American quinoa, a nutty flavored grain, is slowly finding its way into North American cupboards for cereal or casseroles. These grains provide a great variety of flavors and textures that are a welcome stand-in for pasta or rice.

PASTA

Homemade noodles

Spaghetti sauce with Italian sausage
    and meatballs

Fiesta spaghetti sauce and meatballs

Bolognese sauce

Four cheese sauce

Special pesto sauce

Spinach pesto sauce

Meaty baked lasagna

Light and easy lasagna

Fettucini Alfredo

Fettucini with wild mushrooms

Spaghetti with spicy topping

Skinny spaghetti

Spaghetti with chunky tomato sauce
    and fried calamari

Pasta with broccoli, cheese
    and bacon

Pasta primavera

Linguini with shrimp and
    sun-dried tomatoes

Linguini with bay scallops,
    goat cheese and red peppers

Penne St. Martin

Peasant rigatoni

Ravioli rustica

Creamy corned beef and pasta

Orzo with feta cheese and
    green onions

PASTA SALADS

Pasta shell salad with tomato
    and zucchini

Mozzarella, tomato and linguini salad

Pasta salad with smoked mussels

Sesame noodle salad

Chicken and cheese pasta salad

RICE & OTHER GRAINS

Easy cooked rice

Basil fried rice

Rice with lemon rind and fresh herbs

Afghanistan baked rice pilaf

Red beans and brown rice

Brown rice pilaf

Wild rice and mushroom casserole

Wild rice cakes

Risotto with corn and red peppers

Vegetable couscous with
    cilantro chutney

Basic cooked quinoa

Quinoa chicken salad

Making noodles from scratch is not only satisfying but results in more flavorful pasta. Whether your personal pasta is prepared for guests or family, they are sure to appreciate your efforts. This basic recipe uses eggs in the dough, which makes the noodles even richer.

HOMEMADE NOODLES

6 servings
Preparation time: 45 minutes
Resting time: 30 minutes
Cooking time: 3 minutes

4   **cups sifted all-purpose flour**
1   **teaspoon salt**
4   **large eggs**
2½ **tablespoons olive oil**

1. Mix flour and salt in large mixer bowl. Make well in center. Break eggs into center; add oil. Using a dough hook on an electric mixer at low speed, or a large wooden spoon, gradually draw flour from edges of bowl into egg mixture to form a stiff dough. Knead on lightly floured surface until very smooth and elastic, about 10 minutes. Cover with plastic wrap; let rest 30 minutes.

2. Divide dough into quarters; cover 3 of the quarters. Put 1 quarter through rollers of pasta machine according to manufacturer's directions. Or, roll with a rolling pin into a very thin sheet. (Sprinkle dough with flour to prevent sticking.)

3. Cut dough in thinnest cutter portion of pasta machine or use a sharp knife and cut into very thin strands as for linguini noodles. Let noodles dry on a flour dusted baking sheet while rolling and cutting remaining dough.

4. Cook noodles in large pot of boiling salted water until al dente (tender but still firm), 1 to 3 minutes. Drain; serve immediately.

NOTE: Cut noodles can be dried overnight; turn occasionally, then store in airtight jar up to several days. Cook as directed.

This sauce recipe is from Food Guide reader Dolores Kaiser. If you make the sauce a day ahead of serving, the flavors will mellow. The sauce can be frozen; freeze the cooked meatballs and sausage separately—it will make reheating easier.

SPAGHETTI SAUCE WITH ITALIAN SAUSAGE AND MEATBALLS

6 servings
Preparation time: 30 minutes
Cooking time: 3½ hours

1 can (28 ounces) tomato puree
3 cans (6 ounces each) tomato paste
3 cloves garlic, crushed
1 each, minced: carrot, celery rib
1 tablespoon each: dried leaf oregano, salt
2 teaspoons each: dried basil, sugar
½ teaspoon ground allspice
⅛ teaspoon freshly ground pepper
3½ cups water

ITALIAN MEATBALLS AND SAUSAGE

1½ pounds ground beef round
½ cup fine dry bread crumbs
1 egg
1½ teaspoons each: dried basil, dried leaf oregano
½ teaspoon each: garlic powder, freshly ground pepper, salt
2 tablespoons olive oil
1 pound mild Italian sausage

TO SERVE
1 pound spaghetti noodles, cooked, drained
Freshly grated Parmesan cheese

1. Mix tomato puree, tomato paste, garlic, carrot, celery, oregano, salt, basil, sugar, allspice, pepper and 3½ cups water in dutch oven. Heat to boil; reduce heat. Simmer, partly covered, over very low heat, stirring occasionally, 3 hours.

2. Meanwhile, for Italian meatballs and sausage, mix beef, bread crumbs, egg, basil, oregano, garlic powder, pepper and salt in a large bowl. Shape into 1½-inch round balls. Cut sausage into 2½-inch lengths.

3. Heat oil in large skillet; add meatballs and sausage. Cook over medium heat, turning occasionally, until golden brown and cooked through, 20 to 30 minutes. Drain off fat.

4. Stir meatballs and sausage into sauce. Simmer 30 more minutes.

5. Serve over spaghetti noodles. Pass Parmesan cheese.

During the 1985 Fiesta Italiana celebration in Chicago, Geri DeStefano won the spaghetti sauce contest with this recipe. She serves the sauce over cooked spaghetti or ravioli.

FIESTA SPAGHETTI SAUCE AND MEATBALLS

12 servings
Preparation time: 1½ hours
Cooking time: 3 to 6 hours

MEATBALLS

- 2 **pounds ground beef chuck**
- 4 **large eggs**
- ½ **cup each: chopped white onion, green onions, fresh parsley**
- ½ **cup shredded Fontinella cheese**
- ¾ **cup fine, dry, seasoned bread crumbs**
- ½ **teaspoon each: seasoned salt, garlic powder, salt-free herb and spice mixture**
- ¼ **teaspoon freshly ground pepper**

SAUCE

- ½ **cup pure virgin olive oil**
- 1 **cup each: chopped white onions, green onions, green peppers**
- 5 **cloves garlic, crushed**
- 1½ **pounds Italian sausage, removed from casings, crumbled**
- 1 **pound each: beef tenderloin strips, pork shoulder arm or blade steaks**
- 2 **cans (15 ounces each) Italian-style tomato sauce**

ingredients continued on next page

1. For meatballs, mix all ingredients in large bowl. Shape into 2-inch meatballs.

2. For sauce, heat olive oil in 9-quart heavy-bottomed dutch oven over medium-high heat. Add white onions, green onions, green peppers and crushed garlic. Cook and stir until crisp-tender, about 2 minutes.

3. Add meatballs in single layer over medium heat. Cook, turning, until brown on all sides, about 10 minutes. Remove meatballs to large bowl; set aside.

4. Add sausage, beef strips and pork in single layer. Cook over medium heat until brown on all sides, 15 to 20 minutes. Set aside with meatballs.

5. Stir remaining sauce ingredients into onion mixture. Simmer 20 minutes.

6. Transfer to large crock pot; add browned meats and any juice that has accumulated. Cook, covered, on low setting, 4 to 5 hours. Or leave in dutch oven and simmer, covered, over very low heat, for 2 hours, stirring very frequently to prevent scorching. Taste sauce as it cooks and adjust seasonings accordingly.

NOTE: Sauce can be frozen up to 2 months.

1 can (29 ounces)
   tomato puree
1 can (28 ounces)
   Italian-style plum
   tomatoes
1 can (15 ounces) Italian
   tomato sauce
1 can (12 ounces)
   tomato paste
½ cup each: chopped
   fresh parsley,
   shredded Fontinella
   cheese

1 teaspoon each: dried
   leaf oregano, dried
   basil, Italian
   seasoning, salt-free
   herb and spice
   mixture
½ teaspoon each: garlic
   powder, freshly
   ground pepper
1 bay leaf

In Highwood, a suburb north of Chicago where Elsa Amidei and her husband Marco run their Pastificio Pasta store, good Italian cooking means simplicity—a cuisine without tricks. Elsa's sauces, including the following Bolognese and four cheese sauce reflect that simplicity but brim with flavor.

BOLOGNESE SAUCE

4 servings
Preparation time: 20 minutes
Cooking time: 2 hours

¼ cup each: olive oil,
   butter
1 each, finely chopped:
   medium onion, carrot,
   celery rib
¾ pound each: ground
   beef round, ground
   veal
1 can (16 ounces)
   Italian-style plum
   tomatoes, crushed
1½ cups chicken or beef
   broth
1 teaspoon dried basil
   Pinch dried leaf
   oregano
   Salt, freshly ground
   pepper to taste
1 medium clove garlic
1 pound noodles,
   cooked, drained

1. Heat olive oil and butter in large saucepan. Add chopped vegetables and sauté gently until onion is golden and soft, 10 to 15 minutes.

2. Add ground meats. Cook over low heat until brown, 15 to 20 minutes. Separate meat into little bits with wooden spoon, taking care that the meat does not stick to the pan.

3. Add crushed tomatoes. Heat to boil; add broth, basil, oregano, salt and pepper. Simmer, uncovered, over low heat, stirring often, until desired consistency, about 1½ hours.

4. Remove pan from heat and immediately crush in clove of garlic. Stir. Let rest for 10 minutes before serving over noodles.

This luscious sauce is often served with green and white pasta. The cooked pasta should be added to the sauce as soon as the sauce is finished. Serve immediately after mixing.

FOUR CHEESE SAUCE

4 to 6 servings
Preparation time: 15 minutes
Cooking time: 20 minutes

2 **cups whipping cream**
¼ **cup unsalted butter**
⅓ **pound Gorgonzola cheese**
⅓ **pound each, cubed: Bel Paese, Italian Fontina cheese**
   Freshly grated Parmesan cheese, such as Parmigiano-Reggiano, to taste
   Salt, freshly ground pepper to taste
1 **pound noodles, such as half spinach noodles and half egg noodles, cooked, drained**
   Minced parsley for garnish

1. Heat cream in a medium-size nonaluminum saucepan over low heat, watching that it does not come to a boil. Add butter, Gorgonzola, Bel Paese and Fontina cheeses. Cook and stir over low heat until melted and mixture is of rich consistency, about 20 minutes. Stir in Parmesan cheese until melted. Add salt and pepper.

2. Stir cooked noodles into hot sauce. Serve immediately, garnished with parsley.

Pesto, a blend of basil, garlic, olive oil, pine nuts and Parmesan cheese, is a classic Italian sauce that should be part of any good cook's repertoire. This version, from Chicago herb expert Jim Haring, will not disappoint you.

SPECIAL PESTO SAUCE

4 to 6 servings
Preparation time: 10 minutes

4　cups chopped fresh
　　basil leaves, about 6
　　ounces
¾　cup pine nuts, about 4
　　ounces
1½　cups shredded or 1
　　cup finely grated
　　cheese (⅔ Parmesan
　　and ⅓ Romano)
3　cloves garlic, quartered
1　cup olive oil
¼　cup (½ stick) unsalted
　　butter

Juice of ¼ lemon
Fresh pepper to taste

1. Put all ingredients into food processor fitted with metal blade. Process until finely chopped but not pureed. Serve over hot pasta.

NOTE: Other suggested uses for pesto sauce: stir into hot soup; substitute for mayonnaise in chicken salad or on sandwiches. Serve on grilled meats and hamburgers, or stuff into broiled mushroom caps.

When the fresh basil season starts to diminish, try this variation of pesto sauce. Here, the addition of spinach gives the sauce a unique flavor as well as texture and color.

SPINACH PESTO SAUCE

4 servings
Preparation time: 25 minutes
Cooking time: 10 minutes

½　of a 10-ounce package
　　frozen chopped
　　spinach, thawed
½　cup each: olive oil,
　　freshly grated
　　Parmesan cheese
5　tablespoons minced
　　fresh basil leaves
2　tablespoons each:
　　toasted pine nuts,
　　softened butter
1　clove garlic, minced
　　Pinch each: ground
　　anise, freshly ground
　　black pepper
　　Salt to taste

1　package (12 ounces)
　　linguini or other
　　pasta noodles

1. Put spinach in a sieve: press hard to extract all excess liquid. Put into food processor or blender. Add oil, Parmesan cheese, basil, pine nuts, butter, garlic, anise, pepper and salt. Process until smooth. Taste and adjust seasonings.

2. Cook noodles in large pot of boiling water until al dente. Drain well. Toss with sauce. Serve immediately.

This hearty lasagna is adapted from one by New York restaurateur Romeo Salta in his out-of-print book The Pleasures of Italian Cooking.

MEATY BAKED LASAGNA

4 to 6 servings
Preparation time: 45 minutes
Cooking time: 1½ hours

TOMATO SAUCE

- 2 **slices bacon, diced**
- 2 **tablespoons olive oil**
- ½ **cup each: chopped onions, grated carrots**
- 1 **rib celery, chopped**
- 4 **fresh basil leaves, chopped, or** ½ **teaspoon dried**
- 2 **cans (28 ounces each) Italian-style plum tomatoes, sieved**
- 1½ **teaspoons salt**
- ½ **teaspoon freshly ground pepper**

LASAGNA

- 4 **tablespoons butter**
- 2 **tablespoons flour**
- 1½ **teaspoons salt**
- ¾ **cup milk**
- ½ **pound each, chopped: chicken livers, Italian sausage removed from casing**
- 2 **tablespoons olive oil**
- 1 **pound lasagna noodles, cooked, drained**
- ½ **pound prosciutto, or cooked ham, chopped**
- 1½ **cups freshly grated Parmesan cheese**

1. For tomato sauce, cook bacon in olive oil in large saucepan over medium heat, 2 minutes. Stir in onions, carrots, celery and fresh basil. (If using dried basil, add in step 2.) Cook and stir until vegetables are soft, about 10 minutes.

2. Stir in tomatoes, salt, pepper and dried basil if using. Heat to boil; reduce heat to low; simmer, partly covered, 1 hour. Taste and adjust seasonings. Use 3 cups of the tomato sauce for the lasagna; remaining sauce can be frozen.

3. For lasagna, melt 2 tablespoons of the butter in small saucepan. Blend in flour and half of the salt. Add milk; cook and stir over medium-low heat until smooth and thick. Cook over very low heat 5 minutes.

4. Melt 1 tablespoon of the butter in skillet over medium-high heat. Add livers; cook 2 minutes. Add sausage meat and remaining salt; cook 10 minutes, stirring occasionally. Drain.

5. Put a layer of lasagna noodles over bottom of oiled 13 by 9-inch baking dish. Arrange as many successive layers as possible of the tomato sauce, sausage mixture, white sauce, prosciutto, grated cheese and noodles. End with noodles and grated cheese. (Recipe may be prepared ahead to this point.)

6. Heat oven to 400 degrees. Dot top of lasagna with remaining 2 tablespoons butter and bake until top is browned, about 15 minutes. Cut into squares and serve from dish.

Jeanne Jones, in her popular "Cook It Light" column in the Food Guide, adapts readers' recipes to be lower in fat, cholesterol and sodium. This lasagna is not only healthful, it has a winning flavor.

LIGHT AND EASY LASAGNA

12 servings
Preparation time: 45 minutes
Cooking time: 3 hours

3 **medium onions, chopped**

3 **garlic cloves, finely chopped**

2 **cans (28 ounces each) Italian-style plum tomatoes, undrained**

2 **cans (12 ounces each) Italian tomato paste**

1 **cup chopped fresh parsley**

2 **teaspoons dried leaf oregano, crushed**

½ **teaspoon each, crushed: dried leaf thyme, dried marjoram**

½ **teaspoon freshly ground pepper**

½ **pound lasagna noodles**

1 **pound part-skim ricotta cheese**

½ **pound part-skim mozzarella cheese**

2 **ounces imported Parmesan cheese, grated**

1. Put onions and garlic in large saucepan. Cook, covered, over low heat until tender, adding a little water if necessary to prevent scorching. Add tomatoes, tomato paste, parsley, oregano, thyme, marjoram and pepper. Simmer, covered, stirring occasionally, about 2 hours.

2. Cook lasagna noodles in boiling water until al dente, about 12 minutes. Drain in colander; rinse with cold water. Drain well.

3. Heat oven to 350 degrees. Cover bottom of lightly oiled 13 by 9-inch baking dish with ¼ of the sauce. Add layer of lasagna noodles. Top with ⅓ of the ricotta cheese, then ⅓ of the mozzarella. Sprinkle with ¼ of the Parmesan cheese. Cover with ¼ of the sauce. Repeat procedure 2 more times. Sprinkle remaining Parmesan cheese on top.

4. Bake until sauce is bubbly and cheese is melted, about 45 minutes. Let stand 10 minutes before serving.

One of the classic Italian pasta dishes, fettucini Alfredo is featured in almost every traditional Italian restaurant. It is not complicated to make. The important thing is to be sure the pasta is cooked al dente.

FETTUCINI ALFREDO

2 to 4 servings
Preparation time: 10 minutes
Cooking time: 10 minutes

½ **pound fettucini**
1 **clove garlic, minced**
½ **cup (1 stick) unsalted butter**
½ **cup whipping cream**
½ **cup freshly grated Parmesan cheese**
  Salt, freshly ground white pepper to taste
  Chopped fresh parsley for garnish

1. Cook fettucini in large saucepan of boiling water until al dente. Drain well.

2. Meanwhile, melt butter in large saucepan. Add garlic; cook and stir 1 minute. Stir in cream; heat to boil. Add drained fettucini and toss well. Sprinkle with cheese, salt and pepper; toss again. Garnish with parsley. Serve immediately.

You may use any fresh wild mushrooms in the following recipe, if you're lucky enough to find them. You may use fresh or dried pasta, but the fresh will absorb the sauce better. Serve this dish with a Barbaresco or another rich red Italian wine.

FETTUCINI WITH WILD MUSHROOMS

4 to 6 servings
Preparation time: 20 minutes
Cooking time: 10 minutes

½ **pound wild mushrooms, such as oyster, shiitake or a mixture**
3 **tablespoons butter**
2 **slices bacon, cut into small pieces**
1 **medium carrot, peeled, diced**
1 **medium onion, cut into thin slices**
1 **rib celery, diced**
1 **can (14 ounces) Italian-style plum tomatoes, drained, chopped**
1 **clove garlic, peeled, minced**
Freshly ground pepper to taste
1 **cup beef stock or broth**
1 **pound fettucini, preferably fresh**
Salt to taste
Freshly grated Parmesan cheese

1. Wipe mushrooms clean with damp paper towels. Chop coarsely. Heat 2 tablespoons of the butter and bacon in high-sided skillet. Cook, stirring occasionally, until bacon is cooked but not crisp.

2. Add carrot, onion and celery. Cook, covered over low heat until vegetables are soft, 5 to 7 minutes. Raise heat and add mushrooms. Cook and stir until mushrooms begin to give off liquid, about 2 minutes. Add tomatoes, garlic and several grinds of pepper. Stir briefly, then add stock.

3. Heat to boil; reduce heat to simmer; cover and cook for 15 minutes. (Recipe may be done ahead to this point. Refrigerate sauce and reheat before completing the recipe.)

4. Cook fettucini in large pot of salted water, until al dente, about 3 minutes for fresh and 10 to 12 minutes for dried. (Fresh pasta will do a much better job of absorbing the sauce.)

5. Put remaining tablespoon of butter in large bowl. Drain pasta, then toss it with the butter. Add about half of the sauce along with a liberal amount of Parmesan. Toss to mix; add salt and pepper. Distribute among warm bowls. Spoon remaining sauce over pasta. Pass additional Parmesan at the table.

NOTE: One to two cups chopped or shredded cooked poultry can be added to the sauce.

Here is a recipe for spaghetti with an unusual sauce that will make your taste buds stand up and cheer.

SPAGHETTI WITH SPICY TOPPING

4 servings
Preparation time: 30 minutes
Cooking time: 20 minutes

3 tablespoons vegetable oil
1 tablespoon mustard seeds
2 cups finely sliced whole green onions
1 tablespoon very finely minced garlic
½ pound mushrooms, thinly sliced
2 pounds ripe tomatoes, peeled, finely chopped
1 teaspoon finely grated fresh ginger
¼ cup minced fresh cilantro (coriander) or parsley
1 to 2 jalapeño peppers, seeded, minced, or to taste
1 each, diced: red bell pepper, green pepper
2 zucchini, thinly sliced
½ teaspoon salt
   Freshly ground pepper to taste
½ pound spaghetti or linguini noodles, cooked, drained

1. Heat oil in large skillet over medium heat. When hot, add mustard seeds, green onions and garlic. Stir-fry until onions are soft, 3 minutes. Add mushrooms; cook and stir 1 minute.

2. Add tomatoes, ginger, cilantro and jalapeño peppers. Stir-fry over medium heat until some of the liquid has evaporated, about 7 minutes. Stir in peppers and zucchini; cook until vegetables are crisp-tender, 3 to 5 minutes. Add salt and pepper. Taste and adjust seasonings.

3. Put pasta in a colander and run hot tap water over it to reheat. Drain, transfer to serving platter with raised sides and toss with spicy topping. Serve immediately.

This recipe comes from the fifties theme restaurant Ed Debevic's in Chicago. Some people might refer to this as vermicelli, but Ed likes to call it "skinny spaghetti."

SKINNY SPAGHETTI

6 servings
Preparation time: 20 minutes
Cooking time: About 3 hours

8 **hot Italian sausages (3 ounces each)**

7 **tablespoons olive oil**

⅔ **cup chopped onion**

1 **tablespoon minced garlic**

2 **cans (28 ounces each) whole tomatoes, seeded, chopped**

1 **can (15 ounces) tomato puree**

2½ **cups water**

1 **teaspoon salt**

¼ **teaspoon each: freshly ground pepper, dried leaf oregano**

2 **green peppers, seeded, cut into 1½-inch chunks**

1 **red bell pepper, seeded, cut into 1½-inch chunks**

1 **tablespoon salt, optional**

1 **pound vermicelli**
 Freshly grated Parmesan cheese

1. Brown sausages in 1 tablespoon of the olive oil in large saucepan. Add onion and garlic; cook until tender. Add tomatoes, tomato puree, water, 1 teaspoon salt, pepper and oregano. Stir to blend, cover and simmer over low heat, 2 to 3 hours. Stir occasionally. Taste and adjust seasonings.

2. Heat 2 tablespoons of the olive oil in large skillet. Add green and red bell pepper chunks; cook over high heat until softened and slightly charred.

3. Remove sausages from sauce and slice each one into 4 pieces. Return sliced sausage to sauce and stir in cooked peppers. (Recipe may be done ahead to this point.)

4. Heat a large pot of water to a boil. Add 1 tablespoon salt if desired. Return to boil; add vermicelli and cook until al dente. Drain well.

5. Toss vermicelli with remaining 4 tablespoons olive oil. Transfer to plates or bowls and top with sauce, making sure everyone receives an equal amount of sausage. Serve at once. Pass Parmesan cheese at the table.

Some people believe the feasting that accompanies St. Joseph's Day stems from the drought that struck Sicily in the Middle Ages. Prayers to St. Joseph were answered by rain and a restoration of the crops, so people brought food to the town plazas to share with others, especially the poor.

Beverly Dillon devised a delicious entree of spaghetti with calamari for St. Joseph's Day, March 19, 1988.

SPAGHETTI WITH CHUNKY TOMATO SAUCE AND FRIED CALAMARI

6 servings
Preparation time: 45 minutes
Cooking time: 30 minutes

VEGETABLE MIXTURE
- 2 **tablespoons olive oil**
- 2 **teaspoons minced garlic**
- 1 **cup coarsely chopped onions**
- 1 **pound fresh zucchini, cut in half lengthwise then into ½-inch slices**
- ½ **pound fresh mushrooms, trimmed, cut in half if large**
- 1 **each, halved, seeded and sliced: green pepper, red bell pepper**

TOMATO SAUCE
- 1 **can (28 ounces) Italian-style plum tomatoes**
- 1 **can (12 ounces) tomato paste**
- ½ **cup each: water, olive oil**
- ½ **teaspoon each: crushed red pepper flakes, sugar**
- 1 **teaspoon each: dried leaf oregano, salt**
- ½ **cup minced fresh parsley**

1. For vegetable mixture, heat 2 tablespoons olive oil in large skillet over medium-high heat. Add garlic, onions, zucchini, mushrooms and peppers. Cook over medium heat, stirring occasionally, until crisp-tender. Remove vegetables from pan with slotted spoon to side dish; reserve.

2. For tomato sauce, mix tomatoes, tomato paste, water, olive oil, red pepper flakes, sugar, oregano and salt in large saucepan. Heat to boil over high heat. Reduce heat; add parsley; stir to break up tomatoes. Cook until slightly thickened, about 5 minutes. Keep warm.

3. For calamari, defrost if frozen, rinse well under cold running water. Pat dry on paper towels. Cut into ½-inch rings. Heat oil in heavy skillet over medium-high heat.

4. Put flour into one small bowl, put bread crumbs into another and put eggs into a third. Toss calamari, a few pieces at a time, in flour. Then dip the pieces into egg and gently toss them in bread crumbs, coating them well.

5. Fry, a few pieces at a time, in hot oil until golden, about 3 minutes. Drain on paper towels and reserve.

6. To assemble, add reserved vegetables and peas to tomato sauce. Gently stir to mix; cook just to reheat.

CALAMARI

1 **pound frozen or fresh, cleaned calamari (squid)**

3 **cups vegetable oil for frying**

1 **cup all-purpose flour**

3 **cups homemade seasoned bread crumbs**

2 **eggs, lightly beaten**

TO ASSEMBLE

1 **box (10 ounces) frozen green peas, defrosted**

1 **pound spaghetti noodles, cooked, drained**

½ **cup to 1 cup freshly grated Parmesan cheese, optional**

7. Arrange cooked spaghetti on large serving platter. Spoon vegetable-tomato sauce over spaghetti. Arrange fried calamari over top. Sprinkle with freshly grated Parmesan cheese, if desired.

Seven simple ingredients are combined in this hearty, comforting dish that can be a main course or side dish. Almost any small pasta, such as pastina, orzo, small shells or even elbow macaroni can be used.

PASTA WITH BROCCOLI, CHEESE AND BACON

4 servings
Preparation time: 15 minutes
Cooking time: 15 minutes

½ **pound sliced smoked bacon**

1 **package (6 ounces) pastina, orzo or other small pasta noodles**

1 **large bunch fresh broccoli**

¼ **cup unsalted butter**

¾ **cup freshly grated Parmesan cheese**

Salt, freshly ground pepper to taste

1. Cook bacon in large skillet until lightly browned. Drain off fat; crumble bacon. Reserve bacon.

2. Cook pasta according to package directions; drain well.

3. Trim tough ends from broccoli stalks. Separate flowerets from stalks. Lightly peel stalks. Slice stalks into ½-inch pieces. Drop broccoli into boiling water. Cook, uncovered, until crisp-tender, 3 to 5 minutes. Drain well.

4. Melt butter in large skillet. Add pasta, broccoli, cheese and bacon. Toss to mix and heat through. Add salt and pepper to taste. Serve immediately.

■ *Attention! Use this recipe only as a guide. Substitute any pleasing combination of vegetables fresh from the garden or farmer's market as they come into season. Make sure to vary the vegetables to create textural interest as well as a colorful presentation. Fresh herbs also greatly enhance the flavor of the dish.*

PASTA PRIMAVERA

4 servings
Preparation time: 30 minutes
Cooking time: 15 minutes

½ **pound vermicelli noodles, regular or whole-wheat**

6 **tablespoons extra-virgin olive oil**

2 **large carrots, lightly peeled, sliced on diagonal**

10 **asparagus stalks, about ½ pound, stalks lightly peeled, diced**

1 **teaspoon minced fresh garlic**

2 **red bell peppers, roasted, peeled, diced**

1 **cup thinly sliced mushrooms**

½ **cup shelled fresh or frozen peas**

½ **cup diced prosciutto or ham**

3 **tablespoons each, minced: fresh basil, fresh parsley**

1 **teaspoon minced fresh oregano or ¼ teaspoon dried**

6 **tablespoons freshly grated Parmesan cheese**

Salt, freshly ground black pepper to taste

Fresh basil sprigs for garnish

1. Cook noodles in boiling water until al dente. Drain. Toss with 2 tablespoons of the oil.

2. Meanwhile, put carrot slices into boiling water; boil 3 minutes. Drain. Place asparagus pieces in boiling water; boil 2 minutes. Drain.

3. Heat a large skillet. Add remaining 4 tablespoons of the oil and heat over medium heat. Add garlic and carrots; cook and stir until tender, about 3 minutes. Add asparagus; cook and stir until crisp-tender, about 2 minutes.

4. Stir in red peppers, mushrooms, peas, prosciutto, basil, parsley and oregano. Cook and stir 2 minutes. Add noodles, cheese, salt and pepper. Toss to mix and heat through. Serve immediately, garnished with basil sprigs.

Cooking teacher Ann Bloomstrand, of Glen Ellyn, Illinois, says this recipe can be done in 30 minutes, but you need to be organized. If you wish, substitute fresh peas for the frozen. Blanch them for one minute in the pasta cooking water by slipping them in, in a strainer. It won't affect the flavor of the pasta.

LINGUINI WITH SHRIMP AND SUN-DRIED TOMATOES

4 servings
Preparation time: 15 minutes
Cooking time: 15 minutes

¼ **cup olive oil**

1½ **pounds large raw shrimp, shelled, deveined**

3 **green onions, chopped**

1 **or 2 garlic cloves, minced**

½ **cup each: thinly sliced sun-dried tomatoes, dry white wine**

1 **cup whipping cream**

1 **package (6 ounces) frozen snow pea pods, thawed, patted dry**

1 **tablespoon dried basil**

½ **pound linguini noodles Salt, freshly ground pepper to taste**

1. Start a pot of water boiling for the pasta. Heat olive oil in large skillet over medium-high heat. Add shrimp; sauté until just pink, 3 to 4 minutes. Remove with slotted spoon to large serving bowl.

2. Add green onions, garlic and tomatoes to oil. Sauté until onions are tender, about 3 minutes. Add wine; cook for 3 more minutes. Add cream, peas and basil. Cook over medium heat, until slightly thickened, about 3 more minutes. Add shrimp to cream mixture. Add salt and pepper to taste. Heat through.

3. Meanwhile, cook pasta in boiling water until al dente, about 5 minutes. Drain. Put in serving bowl. Add shrimp mixture. Toss well.

NOTE: Two boneless chicken breasts or 1 pound fresh scallops can be substituted for shrimp. Broccoli can replace snow pea pods.

This recipe comes from Ann Topham and Judy Borree, of Fantome Farm in Ridgeway, Wisconsin, where they run a goat farm and make goat cheese.

LINGUINI WITH BAY SCALLOPS, GOAT CHEESE AND RED PEPPERS

2 servings
Preparation time: 15 minutes
Cooking time: 10 minutes

½ **pound fresh linguini**

3 **tablespoons butter**

½ **cup each: chopped leeks, thinly sliced red bell pepper**

8 **ounces bay scallops**

4 **ounces fresh goat cheese**

1 **to 2 tablespoons whipping cream**

Salt, freshly ground black pepper, cayenne pepper to taste

Chopped fresh parsley for garnish

1. Cook pasta in boiling water until al dente. Drain.

2. Meanwhile, melt 2 tablespoons of the butter in large skillet over medium-high heat. Add leeks and red pepper; sauté until tender, 3 to 4 minutes. Stir in scallops and remaining 1 tablespoon butter. Sauté over medium heat until scallops are opaque, about 1 minute. Stir in cheese and cream until blended and heated through. Season with salt, black pepper and cayenne.

3. Toss scallop mixture with hot drained pasta. Sprinkle with parsley. Serve immediately.

THE CHICAGO TRIBUNE COOKBOOK

Tony Terlato, president of Paterno Imports, a wine importing firm in Chicago, first tasted this dish on the island of St. Martin in the Caribbean. It has become one of his favorite dishes. Use macaroni type pasta such as penne or mostaccioli.

PENNE ST. MARTIN

6 servings
Preparation time: 20 minutes
Cooking time: 30 minutes

⅓ **cup olive oil**
1 **tablespoon butter**
3 **cloves garlic, cut in half**
2 **pounds ripe plum tomatoes, chopped, or 1 can (32 ounces) Italian-style plum tomatoes, drained**
6 **ounces small button mushrooms, quartered**
1 **sprig fresh rosemary, leaves removed and minced**
5 **or 6 fresh basil leaves, finely chopped**
1 **cup shelled peas**
  Pinch cayenne pepper
  Salt, freshly ground black pepper to taste
1 **pound dried penne, rigatoni or mostaccioli**
⅓ **cup whipping cream**
¾ **cup freshly grated Parmesan cheese**

1. Heat olive oil and butter with garlic in large saucepan. Cook until garlic is golden, then remove the pieces and discard.

2. Add tomatoes to oil; simmer until tomatoes are soft, about 4 minutes. If using fresh tomatoes, turn into a strainer to drain, then return to pan. Add mushrooms; cook and stir 5 minutes. Add rosemary, basil, peas, cayenne, salt and black pepper. Cook until peas are tender, about 5 minutes. (Recipe may be made ahead to this point.)

3. Heat water to boil in large pot. Add salt, then penne. Cook until al dente, about 8 minutes. Drain; transfer to serving bowl.

4. While pasta is cooking, stir cream into sauce; cook until heated through.

5. Pour hot sauce over penne, add half the Parmesan and toss to mix. Pass the remaining Parmesan at the table.

Why this is called peasant pasta is anybody's guess. It is a very satisfying dish from chef Robert Chavis at Convito Italiano restaurants and gourmet shops in Chicago and Wilmette, Illinois.

PEASANT RIGATONI

4 servings
Preparation time: 20 minutes
Cooking time: 20 minutes

1 **pound rigatoni**
1 **cup olive oil**
3 **cloves garlic**
1 **teaspoon crushed red pepper flakes**
½ **of a 2-ounce can anchovy fillets packed in olive oil**
1 **pound broccoli flowerets, steamed or boiled for 3 minutes**
Salt, freshly ground pepper to taste
Pecorino-Romano or Parmigiano-Reggiano cheese, for grating

1. Cook rigatoni according to package directions until al dente. (Timing will vary according to whether the pasta is packaged or fresh.) Drain.

2. Put olive oil, garlic and pepper flakes in large skillet over low heat. Cook until garlic is golden; remove from skillet and discard. Add anchovy fillets to oil; cook and stir until dissolved. Stir in broccoli flowerets; cook and stir until crisp-tender, 2 to 3 minutes.

3. Add rigatoni; toss to mix. Add salt and pepper. Serve immediately, topped with grated cheese.

Barry Bursak, owner of the avant-garde Chicago store, City, used this recipe when he was amateur guest chef for a day at friend Erwin Drechsler's Metropolis Cafe, also in Chicago.

RAVIOLI RUSTICA

6 servings
Preparation time: 1 hour
Cooking time: 15 minutes

DOUGH

¼ **cup semolina flour**
¾ **cup all-purpose flour**
1 **large egg**
1 **teaspoon olive oil**

FILLING

¾ **pound ricotta cheese**
¼ **pound freshly grated Parmesan cheese**
  Salt, freshly ground pepper to taste

SAUCE

1 **large onion, cut into paper thin slices, left to breathe for 2 hours**
1 **dried hot red chili**
2 **cups olive oil**
½ **cup finely ground green olives**
1 **teaspoon each: dried rosemary, dried leaf oregano, dried basil, rubbed sage, dried celery leaves**
  Olive oil
  Freshly grated Parmesan or Romano cheese for serving

1. For dough, put flours, egg and 1 teaspoon oil into food processor. With machine running, gradually add water, a few drops at a time, until dough forms into a ball. Remove and let rest covered for 30 minutes.

2. For filling, mix ricotta cheese, Parmesan cheese, salt and pepper together in bowl.

3. Using rolling pin on floured surface, or pasta machine according to manufacturer's directions, roll out dough into long, paper-thin sheets.

4. Spoon filling onto dough every few inches. Cover with second sheet of dough and cut into squares with ravioli cutter. Repeat to use up all dough and filling. Cover ravioli with clean towel and set aside until ready to cook.

5. For sauce, sauté onion and red chili in 2 cups olive oil until onion begins to brown. Add ground olives, rosemary, oregano, basil, sage and celery leaves. Remove red chili.

6. Heat water to boil in large pot. Add salt and a few spoonfuls of olive oil. Add ravioli to boiling water. Cook until dough is tender, 3 to 5 minutes. Remove and drain.

7. Place ravioli on heated plate. Spoon sauce over all. Pass cheese.

This dish was created in the test kitchen to use up St. Patrick's Day leftovers. It was voted one of The Tribune *Food Guide's 10 best recipes of 1985.*

CREAMY CORNED BEEF AND PASTA

4 servings
Preparation time: 40 minutes
Cooking time: 20 minutes

8 ounces small shell-
shaped pasta noodles
1 tablespoon olive oil
2 tablespoons butter
1¼ cups chopped leeks,
white part only
2 cups each: whipping
cream, cubed cooked
corned beef
¼ teaspoon freshly
ground pepper
⅛ teaspoon ground
nutmeg
1 tablespoon each:
freshly grated
Parmesan cheese,
chopped fresh parsley

1. Cook noodles according to package directions. Drain. Toss with oil. Put onto serving platter. Cover to keep warm.

2. Melt butter in large saucepan. Add leeks; cook until wilted, 3 to 4 minutes. Stir in cream. Boil gently over high heat until thickened and reduced to 1½ cups. Add corned beef, pepper and nutmeg. Cook and stir 1 minute. Pour over pasta. Sprinkle top with Parmesan cheese and parsley.

Pasta has made the rounds of several countries and often gets incorporated into all kinds of dishes. In this 1984 recipe from Tribune *reader Sadie Porto of Harwood Heights, Illinois, Greek feta cheese is combined with orzo, a rice-shaped pasta.*

ORZO WITH FETA CHEESE AND GREEN ONIONS

4 servings
Preparation time: 10 minutes
Cooking time: 12 minutes

1½ cups orzo or other
small pasta
1½ teaspoons salt
2 teaspoons butter or
margarine
1 large green onion,
sliced
½ cup crumbled feta
cheese

1 teaspoon each:
chopped fresh
parsley, freshly
ground pepper

1. Heat 3 quarts water to boil in large saucepan. Add orzo and salt. Cook, stirring occasionally, until al dente, about 10 minutes. Drain well.

2. Melt butter in medium skillet; add green onion. Cook and stir for 3 minutes. Stir in hot, cooked orzo, feta cheese, parsley and pepper. Toss well, serve immediately.

Pasta salad has been popular for years, a trend that refuses to die. Perhaps that is because it serves its purpose so well. Nearly a decade ago Margie Korshak, a Chicago public relations executive known for her fashionable sense, provided The Tribune with this simple recipe. Preparation time is only 28 minutes, which makes it an appropriate summer dish for working people.

Remember that if you are using fresh, homemade pasta it will absorb more liquid than dried pasta. Most pasta salads are best served at room temperature, not cold.

PASTA SHELL SALAD WITH TOMATO AND ZUCCHINI

4 servings
Preparation time: 20 minutes
Cooking time: 8 minutes
Chilling time: 2 hours

½ **pound small pasta shells**
2 **tomatoes, peeled, seeded, chopped**
1 **zucchini, julienned**
¼ **cup olive oil**
   Juice of 1 lemon
2 **tablespoons red wine vinegar**
⅛ **to ¼ teaspoon crushed red pepper flakes**
   Salt, freshly ground pepper to taste

1. Cook pasta shells in boiling water until al dente, about 8 minutes. Drain; rinse under cold water until cold. Mix with remaining ingredients. Cover, refrigerate 1 to 2 hours. Taste and adjust seasonings.

Here's a dish that can be made in 25 minutes. It's just the thing for a spur-of-the-moment lunch.

MOZZARELLA, TOMATO AND LINGUINI SALAD

6 servings
Preparation time: 15 minutes
Cooking time: 10 minutes

1 **pound linguini noodles**
   Salt
1 **tablespoon olive oil**
2 **pounds mozzarella**
   cheese, cubed
2 **bunches watercress,**
   stems removed
2 **cloves garlic**
12 **small tomatoes,**
   quartered, seeded
   Freshly ground pepper
   to taste

1. Cook linguini in 4 quarts boiling salted water with 1 tablespoon oil until al dente, 7 to 10 minutes.

2. Drain, rinse under cold water. Put into large serving bowl; stir in mozzarella cubes.

3. Put watercress in food processor or blender; process until chopped. Add garlic and tomatoes; process until coarsely chopped.

4. Season sauce with salt and pepper. Toss all but ¼ cup of the sauce with pasta. Pour remaining sauce on top of pasta for garnish. Serve at room temperature.

NOTE: You may substitute 1 cup fresh basil leaves for the watercress.

A great summertime dish uses yellow summer squash and smoked mussels with pasta. The combination is enticing.

PASTA SALAD WITH SMOKED MUSSELS

4 servings
Preparation time: 40 minutes
Cooking time: 10 minutes

½ **pound wagon wheel or other pasta**

1 **tablespoon olive oil**

1 **yellow squash, halved, sliced**

½ **cup extra-virgin olive oil**

5 **tablespoons white wine vinegar**

½ **teaspoon freshly ground pepper**

¼ **teaspoon salt**

3 **tablespoons minced fresh basil or 1 tablespoon dried**

3 **tablespoons minced parsley**

4 **green onions, minced**

1 **green pepper, cored, diced**

1 **red bell pepper, roasted, peeled, diced**

1 **pound smoked shelled mussels**

Bibb or Boston lettuce leaves

1. Cook noodles in large pot of boiling water until al dente. Drain; toss with 1 tablespoon olive oil. Cool.

2. Drop yellow squash into boiling water. Cook 1 minute. Drain; rinse under cold water to stop the cooking. Drain well.

3. Put ½ cup oil, vinegar, pepper, salt, basil, parsley and onions in large bowl. Add green pepper, red pepper, yellow squash and noodles.

4. Toss to mix well. Add mussels; toss to mix. Serve on lettuce leaves.

■ *Did the Chinese really invent pasta? The Chinese pasta salad from Chicago's House of Hunan restaurant proves they certainly have a knack for delicious noodles.*

SESAME NOODLE SALAD

4 to 6 servings
Preparation time: 25 minutes
Cooking time: 5 minutes

½ **pound dried Chinese noodles or linguini noodles**

3 **tablespoons vegetable oil**

5 **tablespoons water**

¼ **cup each: peanut butter, sesame seed paste (see note)**

3 **tablespoons white wine vinegar**

1 **tablespoon Oriental sesame oil**

4½ **teaspoons soy sauce**

¾ **teaspoon hot pepper sauce**

1 **teaspoon sugar**

¼ **teaspoon minced garlic**

1 **cup each: cooked, shredded chicken, thin strips of ham, shredded whole cucumber, fresh rinsed bean sprouts**

1. Cook noodles in large pot of boiling water until al dente, 3 to 5 minutes. Drain. Rinse under cold water; drain thoroughly. Put into large bowl; add vegetable oil; toss to coat. Refrigerate.

2. Mix water, peanut butter and sesame paste in large bowl until smooth. Stir in vinegar, sesame oil, soy sauce and hot pepper sauce. Mash sugar and garlic together in wooden bowl or on wooden board. Stir into sesame mixture until sugar is dissolved.

3. Add cold noodles. Toss gently to coat noodles with sauce.

4. Put noodles onto platter. Arrange chicken, ham, cucumber and bean sprouts over noodles. Toss together just before serving.

NOTE: Sesame seed paste is available in Oriental food markets. If unavailable, substitute 3 tablespoons peanut butter and 1 tablespoon Oriental sesame oil.

The microwave oven helps out in making pasta salad with chicken easy to prepare. The bacon, chicken and cheese create a perfect harmony of flavor.

CHICKEN AND CHEESE PASTA SALAD

2 servings
Preparation time: 15 minutes
Cooking time: 10 minutes

2 slices bacon, chopped
1 cup small shell-shaped noodles
3 tablespoons red wine vinegar
1 teaspoon Dijon mustard
½ teaspoon sugar
4½ tablespoons oil
1½ cups chopped, cooked, white meat chicken
½ cup each: diced Swiss or Cheddar cheese, chopped black olives
½ green pepper, chopped
Salt, freshly ground pepper to taste
Lettuce leaves for serving

1. Put bacon into microwave-safe 2-quart casserole. Microwave on high (100 percent power), until crisp, about 2 minutes. (Or, cook bacon in small skillet until crisp.) Drain bacon on paper towels.

2. Cook noodles in large pot of boiling water until al dente. Drain; rinse under cold water; drain well.

3. Mix vinegar, mustard and sugar in large bowl. Gradually whisk in oil until smooth. Add noodles, bacon and remaining ingredients except lettuce. Toss to mix. Refrigerate, covered, at least 1 hour. Serve over lettuce leaves.

If you need a step-by-step recipe for rice, this one should fit the bill precisely.

Easy Cooked Rice

4 to 6 servings
Preparation time: 5 minutes
Cooking time: 15 to 20 minutes

1½ cups long-grain white rice
3 cups water
1 tablespoon butter or margarine
¼ teaspoon salt

1. Put all ingredients into 2-quart saucepan. Heat to boil over high heat. Reduce heat to low. Simmer, covered, until rice is tender, 15 to 20 minutes. Fluff with fork.

This spicy rice recipe is from Arun's, a popular Thai restaurant in Chicago.

Basil Fried Rice
(Khao phad kraprao)

4 to 6 servings
Preparation time: 20 minutes
Cooking time: 10 minutes

3 tablespoons corn oil
1 teaspoon minced garlic
1 to 2 serrano peppers, seeded, minced, to taste
3 tablespoons ground or minced chicken (about ½ chicken breast)
3 peeled deveined shrimp, coarsely chopped
1½ tablespoons fish sauce (nam pla)
1 teaspoon sugar
3 cups cooked rice
10 to 15 fresh holy basil leaves (kraoprao) (see note)
10 to 12 sprigs fresh cilantro (coriander)
1 lime, cut in 6 wedges

1. Heat 2 tablespoons of the oil in wok or large skillet over medium heat. Add garlic; stir-fry until golden, 2 to 3 minutes.

2. Add serrano peppers; stir-fry 15 seconds. Add chicken; stir-fry while breaking up chicken so it doesn't stick together. Add shrimp; stir-fry 1 minute. Add fish sauce and sugar. Stir well.

3. Add rice; stir-fry until all ingredients are well mixed. Add remaining 1 tablespoon oil and basil; stir-fry until basil softens, about 30 seconds. Transfer to platter. Garnish with cilantro and lime wedges. Squeeze lime onto rice before eating.

NOTE: If holy basil is unavailable, sweet basil leaves (horapa) may be substituted. Look for them in Thai markets.

A simple rice dish, such as this one flavored with lemon rind and fresh dill, is excellent with most meat, poultry and fish.

RICE WITH LEMON RIND AND FRESH HERBS

6 servings
Preparation time: 15 minutes
Cooking time: 15 minutes

1½ **cups long-grain rice**
1½ **tablespoons olive oil**
   Salt, freshly ground
   pepper to taste
 2 **lemons**
 ½ **cup each, minced:**
   fresh parsley, fresh
   dill

1. Heat 6 quarts of lightly salted water to boil in large pot. Slowly add rice, a little at a time, so water continues to boil. Boil, uncovered, until rice is still firm to the bite but no longer raw and hard in center, about 15 minutes. Drain well. Put into large bowl; stir in oil, salt and pepper.

2. Meanwhile, rinse lemons in hot water to remove any wax covering. Use citrus zester to remove rind from lemon into thin slivers. Or, remove rind with a vegetable peeler and then cut into fine slivers with a knife. Mix lemon rind and herbs into warm rice. Serve.

NOTE: Rice may be prepared ahead through step 1, cooled, covered and refrigerated up to 24 hours before serving. Reheat, covered, in a 375-degree oven, about 15 minutes. Then continue with recipe.

The Helmand Restaurant in Chicago contributed this recipe for an Afghanistan-style rice pilaf. It makes a nutty tasting accompaniment to lamb or beef shish kebabs.

AFGHANISTAN BAKED RICE PILAF (Pallou)

6 to 8 servings
Preparation time: 15 minutes
Standing time: 1 hour
Cooking time: 40 minutes

3 cups long-grain rice (preferably basmati rice)
1 tablespoon sugar
8½ cups water
¼ cup vegetable oil
¼ teaspoon each: ground cinnamon, ground cloves, freshly ground black pepper, ground cardamom
1½ teaspoons salt

1. Put rice into sieve; rinse with lukewarm water. Put rice into large bowl; add warm water to cover rice. Let stand 1 hour.

2. Put sugar into small, heavy saucepan. Cook and stir over high heat until sugar liquifies and starts to turn golden. (Be careful not to touch the sugar; it is extremely hot.) Remove pan from heat and let cool 15 minutes.

3. Heat oven to 350 degrees. Add ½ cup of the water to melted sugar; heat to boil over medium heat. Add oil, cinnamon, cloves, pepper and cardamom. Cook and stir until dissolved, 1 to 2 minutes. Remove from heat.

4. Heat remaining 8 cups water to boil in large saucepan over medium-high heat. Add salt. Drain rice and add to the boiling water. Let water return to boil; cook 2 to 3 minutes. During this time test for firmness by biting a grain or breaking it with fingernails; when rice is tender yet firm, drain well.

5. Shape rice into a mound in oiled ovenproof baking dish. Pour sugar mixture over rice and mix gently with rubber spatula until moistened thoroughly. Bake, covered, until golden and grains are distinct yet tender, 30 to 35 minutes.

One of the most nutritionally satisfying meals you can concoct is rice and beans, because it includes a balance of fat, carbohydrates and protein. In this recipe Chicago cooking teacher Nancy Abrams creates a hearty Creole dish, the classic red beans and rice. She emphasizes using the freshest ingredients and prefers using brown rice although traditional long grain white rice is fine.

RED BEANS AND BROWN RICE

6 to 8 servings
Preparation time: 25 minutes
Standing time: Overnight
Cooking time: 2½ hours

1   **pound dried red beans or kidney beans**
6   **cups water**
1   **ham bone, ham hock or carcass from a smoked turkey**
2   **medium onions**
1   **each: carrot, bay leaf**
1   **cup brown rice**
¼   **cup vegetable oil**
2½ **teaspoons salt or to taste**
2   **tablespoons butter or oil**
3   **medium onions, finely chopped**
3   **ribs celery, finely diced**
¼   **cup chopped fresh parsley**
1   **to 2 teaspoons hot pepper sauce to taste**
¼   **teaspoon cayenne pepper**
    Chopped parsley, chopped green onions for garnish

1. Put beans in large bowl; add enough water to cover tops of beans by several inches. Let stand, covered, overnight.

2. Drain beans. Put beans into large dutch oven. Add 6 cups fresh water. Add ham bone, whole onions, carrot and bay leaf. Heat to boil; reduce heat. Simmer, covered, until beans are tender, about 2½ hours.

3. About 45 minutes before beans are finished cooking, cook rice according to package directions, adding ¼ cup oil and 2 teaspoons of the salt.

4. Meanwhile, heat 2 tablespoons butter in large skillet. Add onions and celery; cook and stir over medium heat until vegetables are crisp-tender.

5. When beans are finished cooking, remove bones and trim any bits of meat from them and add to the beans. Discard bones. Discard whole onions and carrot, or, if you like, puree and return to beans. Remove 1 cup cooked red beans and puree; return to pot.

6. Add onion mixture, ¼ cup parsley, hot pepper sauce, remaining ½ teaspoon salt and cayenne pepper. Taste and adjust seasonings. Simmer until hot throughout.

7. Put a scoop of rice on one side of shallow soup bowl. Spoon beans over half of rice. Sprinkle with parsley and green onions.

■ *In Petoskey, Michigan, summer tourists sooner or later happen onto Justin Rashid's American Spoon Foods, a shop and mail-order firm that preserves regional foods. This pilaf, made with dried tart cherries and wild rice, is one way he uses his products.*

BROWN RICE PILAF

8 servings
Preparation time: 10 minutes
Cooking time: 10 minutes

2 **tablespoons butter**
¼ **cup vegetable oil**
1 **medium onion, minced**
2 **large ribs celery,
   coarsely chopped**
4 **cups cooked brown or
   wild rice, or a
   mixture of the two**
¾ **cup (3 ounces) dried
   tart red cherries**
½ **cup (2 ounces) pecans,
   coarsely chopped**
3 **or 4 green onions,
   finely chopped**
   Salt, pepper to taste

1. Melt butter with oil in large skillet over medium heat. Add onion and celery; cook and stir until soft, about 5 minutes.

2. Add rice; cook, stirring occasionally, until heated through, 5 to 7 minutes. Remove from heat. Stir in cherries, pecans, green onions, salt and pepper.

Cooking teacher Jean True gave us this recipe for an article about holiday entertaining. Once this casserole is in the oven you can attend to other things.

WILD RICE AND MUSHROOM CASSEROLE

6 to 8 servings
Preparation time: 10 minutes
Soaking time: 1 hour
Cooking time: 1½ hours

1 **cup wild rice**
1 **pound fresh mushrooms, sliced**
1 **medium onion, chopped**
6 **tablespoons butter**
1¾ **cups long-grain white rice**
3 **cups chicken broth, homemade preferred**
1½ **cups whipping cream**
½ **cup sliced almonds**
2 **teaspoons salt**
¼ **teaspoon freshly ground pepper**
3 **tablespoons freshly grated Parmesan cheese**

1. Rinse wild rice; put into large bowl. Add boiling water to cover. Let soak 1 hour. Drain well.

2. Heat oven to 350 degrees. Cook mushrooms and onion in 1 tablespoon of the butter in large skillet over medium heat until golden, about 5 minutes. Stir in wild rice, white rice, chicken broth, whipping cream, almonds, salt and pepper. Transfer to buttered 2-quart casserole.

3. Bake, covered, until rice is tender, about 1½ hours. Increase oven temperature to 425 degrees. Sprinkle with cheese; dot top with remaining 5 tablespoons butter. Bake until cheese melts, about 5 minutes.

Chef Peter McGinley serves these chewy, earthy wild rice cakes with his special pheasant dish (see recipe, page 372). They are also good served as a side dish to roast beef or pork or as a savory main course for brunch.

WILD RICE CAKES

4 servings
Preparation time: 5 minutes
Cooking time: 35 minutes
Chilling time: 1 hour

2 **tablespoons butter**
½ **small onion, minced**
½ **cup water**
1 **cup wild rice**
3 **cups rich chicken broth (see recipe, page 134), or substitute canned**
¼ **cup diced fresh wild or button mushrooms**
Salt, freshly ground pepper to taste
2 **large eggs**
Vegetable oil or clarified butter

1. Melt 1 tablespoon of the butter in large saucepan. Add onion; cook until caramelized on edges. Add ½ cup water; cook 3 minutes.

2. Add rice; cook and stir 5 minutes. Add chicken broth; heat to simmer over low heat. Simmer, covered, until rice is tender, about 30 minutes. Drain well; put into large bowl. Refrigerate until cold, about 1 hour.

3. Melt remaining 1 tablespoon butter in another saucepan. Add mushrooms; cook over high heat 5 minutes. Add salt and pepper. Refrigerate until cold.

4. Mix cold rice, mushrooms and eggs in large bowl. Heat large well-seasoned or nonstick skillet. Add a thin layer of oil or clarified butter; heat over medium heat. Spoon rice mixture into pan, forming a small cake about 3 inches in diameter. Flatten rice cakes. Cook until golden on both sides, turning gently with a spatula as cakes are fragile. Serve warm.

This recipe if adapted from one served at Valentino's restaurant in Los Angeles. Risotto, a soft rice mixture, is a classic dish of northern Italy.

RISOTTO WITH CORN AND RED PEPPERS
(Risotto peperoni e pannocchie)

4 servings
Preparation time: 40 minutes
Cooking time: 45 minutes

3 red bell peppers
1 onion, chopped, about ¾ cup
¼ cup butter
1 pound Arborio rice, available at Italian stores
¼ cup dry white wine
1 quart beef stock (see recipe, page 133), or substitute canned broth
1 box (10 ounces) frozen corn kernels, thawed
⅔ cup freshly grated Parmesan cheese
1 tablespoon anise-flavored liqueur, optional

1. Cut tops off red peppers; reserve for garnish. Preheat broiler. Put peppers onto broiler pan. Broil 4 to 6 inches from heat source until skins are blistered and slightly charred. Wrap in foil; let stand until cool. Put onto cutting board; remove stems and seeds. Using a paring knife, peel away charred skin. Finely chop peppers.

2. Sauté onion in butter in heavy 4-quart saucepan over medium heat until golden, 2 to 3 minutes. Add rice and mix well until rice is glossy.

3. Add wine; reduce heat to low; simmer until wine is absorbed. Add about ½ cup of the broth; cook and stir until it has been absorbed. Continue adding broth by the ½-cupful, cooking and stirring between each addition until it has been absorbed. The process takes about 30 minutes, at which time rice will be almost tender and consistency will be creamy. Remove rice from heat. Stir in roasted peppers, corn and ½ of the cheese. Mix well over low heat for 4 to 5 minutes. Stir in liqueur.

4. Put risotto into individual serving bowls. Put a reserved red pepper top over each. Sprinkle with remaining cheese.

As a young man growing up in Luxembourg, Chicago restaurateur Andre Schaak learned to appreciate couscous and other Algerian and Moroccan dishes brought back by travelers. This vegetable couscous featured at the former Kitchen Store Cafe in Chicago blends eight vegetables with the exotic flavors of turmeric, cumin, ginger, cilantro and saffron.

VEGETABLE COUSCOUS WITH CILANTRO CHUTNEY

10 servings
Preparation time: 1 hour
Cooking time: 1 hour

1 pound banana peppers
2 large red bell peppers
1 pound fresh okra
2 pounds small carrots
2½ pounds zucchini
1½ pounds yellow squash
3 pounds tomatoes
2 pounds onions
½ cup fresh cilantro leaves (coriander)
4 cloves garlic
½ cup (1 stick) unsalted butter
2 tablespoons turmeric
1 teaspoon each: ground cumin, ground ginger, cayenne pepper
2 pinches powdered saffron
2 quarts rich chicken broth (see recipe, page 134), or substitute canned
3 pounds uncooked couscous
Grilled lamb, optional
Cilantro chutney (see recipe, page 647)

1. Remove seeds from banana peppers and red peppers; cut into eighths. Cut okra and carrots crosswise in half. Cut zucchini and yellow squash into ¼-inch-thick diagonal slices. Cut tomatoes and onions into eighths. Chop cilantro and garlic.

2. Melt butter in large dutch oven or stockpot over medium heat. Add onions; cook and stir until softened, about 5 minutes. Add tomatoes; cook over low heat, stirring often, for 30 minutes.

3. Add cilantro, turmeric, garlic, cumin, ginger, cayenne and saffron. Stir well. Add chicken broth; heat to boil. Add okra, banana peppers and carrots. Heat to boil; reduce heat. Simmer 10 minutes.

4. Add red peppers, zucchini and yellow squash; simmer 20 minutes.

5. Meanwhile, soak couscous in 1 quart water on large jelly-roll pan. Rake with your fingers to soak and separate grains evenly. Let stand 15 minutes. Drain well.

6. Remove 3 cups of the cooking liquid to a 10-quart stockpot. Put a large colander into the pot. Line with wet cheesecloth. Turn heat to medium. Add couscous to the colander. Steam, covered, until hot, about 20 minutes. Do not stir.

7. Put couscous onto large platter. Make a well in the center. Add vegetables with slotted spoon. Serve with grilled lamb. Pass cooking liquid to spoon over all. Pass cilantro chutney.

Quinoa, an ancient grain grown in the Andes mountains of South America, is a relatively new addition to food choices in our supermarkets. This grain, which is reminiscent in flavor to bulgur or toasted wheat, contains more high-quality protein than any other grain and is considered one of the best sources of protein in the vegetable kingdom.

Serve cooked quinoa as an alternative to rice or pasta. It can be cooked in water or flavored broth of your choice. For variety, try adding chopped fresh herbs, grated cheese or pepper.

BASIC COOKED QUINOA

About 3 cups
Preparation time: 5 minutes
Cooking time: 15 minutes

1 **cup quinoa**
2 **cups water or broth**
   Dash salt

1. Rinse quinoa thoroughly, either using a strainer or by running water over quinoa in a saucepan. Drain off excess water.

2. Place quinoa, 2 cups water and salt in 1½-quart saucepan. Heat to boil. Reduce heat to simmer; simmer, covered, until all water is absorbed, about 15 minutes. Grains will turn from white to transparent and should still be slightly chewy. Fluff with fork before serving.

This quinoa salad makes an excellent light main course. It is also delicious served cold or at room temperature for a picnic or casual supper.

Quinoa Chicken Salad

4 servings
Preparation time: 20 minutes
Cooking time: 5 minutes

2 **cups uncooked quinoa (see recipe, page 177)**
3 **tablespoons olive oil**
1 **red bell pepper, seeded, diced**
¼ **cup chopped green onions**
1 **clove garlic, minced**
1 **can (4 ounces) peeled, chopped green chilies, drained**
2 **cups diced, cooked, skinless, boneless chicken**
1 **can (15½ ounces) red kidney beans, drained**
3 **tablespoons fresh lemon juice**
2 **tablespoons minced fresh parsley**
½ **teaspoon each: salt, freshly ground pepper**
¼ **teaspoon each: ground cumin, ground coriander**

1. Cook quinoa according to recipe.

2. Heat 1 tablespoon of the oil in large skillet over high heat. Add red pepper, green onions and garlic. Sauté until vegetables are crisp-tender, 2 to 3 minutes.

3. Stir in cooked quinoa, chilies, chicken and kidney beans. Cook and stir until heated through. Stir in remaining 2 tablespoons oil, lemon juice, parsley, salt, pepper, cumin and coriander. Serve hot or at room temperature.

PIZZA &
SANDWICHES

Chicagoans would love to claim their city as the home of "real" pizza, but historical evidence suggests a larger story, one that predates pepperoni and even, gasp, sun-dried tomatoes.

When you talk pizza, you have to start way back, about 30 centuries ago, when the Etruscans from Asia Minor brought a humble bread to northern Italy. The ancient Italians took the crude Etruscan bread and, once cooked, topped it with oil and herbs and used it instead of a plate to sop up broth. (Flavored bread still exists today in Italy as *focaccia*.)

The Greeks who colonized southern Italy then added their own touch by baking the topping with the bread and eating it as a main meal. Modern pizza lovers may find the ancient Greek toppings—oil, garlic, onions, vegetables, olives and cheese—surprisingly familiar.

In the mid-sixteenth century, the tomato arrived in Italy via Spain, and the Neapolitans quickly slapped it on their daily bread. But it wasn't until 1889, when Raffaele Esposito honored pizza-loving Queen Margherita with the colors of Italy (tomatoes for red, herbs for green, and mozzarella cheese for white) that pizza reached its final stage.

Well, perhaps not final. Consider some of the recipes included in this chapter: prosciutto–goat cheese pizza, leek and mushroom pizza, whole-wheat pizza, thin-crust pizza and, of course, Chicago deep-dish and stuffed pizza.

Clearly, pizza is still evolving—and so is another foodstuff with a proud history, the sandwich. The meat-stuffed bread slices that the Earl of Sandwich enjoyed in the eighteenth century have evolved into delicious variations. The sandwich recipes that we have particularly enjoyed and selected for this cookbook include the avocadowich, a reuben hot dog and a smoked duck breast sandwich with leeks.

The last chapter on both pizza and sandwiches, it seems, has yet to be written.

PIZZA

Chicago-style deep-dish pizza

Chicago-style stuffed pizza

Chicago-style stuffed spinach
pizza

Chicago-style thin-crust pizza

Pizza with wild leeks and
mushrooms

Prosciutto–goat cheese pizza

Stuffed broccoli pizza

Whole-wheat pizza

SANDWICHES

Avocadowiches

Meatless burritos

Chorizo bread sandwich loaf

Chicken sandwiches with lemon
basil mayonnaise

Grilled ham and cheese sandwiches

Layered corned beef
sandwich loaf

Muffalata

Pan bagnat in pita

Mexican open-face bean and
cheese sandwiches

Shrimp poor boys

Smoked duck breast sandwiches
with leeks

Steak and cheese sandwiches

Summer pizza sandwiches

Cheese and bacon dogs

Chili dogs

Reuben hot dogs

Chicago is the city where deep-dish pizza was born, and this is the recipe that The Tribune test kitchen developed to try to duplicate one of the best versions, from Gino's East Pizzeria. If you like a lot of crunch on your crust, sprinkle additional cornmeal in the pan before adding the dough.

CHICAGO-STYLE DEEP-DISH PIZZA

6 servings
Preparation time: 1 hour
Cooking time: 1 hour

CRUST
1 cup water
¼ cup vegetable shortening
1½ tablespoons sugar
2¼ teaspoons salt
1½ packages active dry yeast
½ cup warm water (105 to 115 degrees)
¾ cup yellow cornmeal
3 to 3½ cups all-purpose flour
Vegetable oil

FILLING
1 can (28 ounces) Italian-style plum tomatoes
2 tablespoons vegetable oil
1 small onion, chopped
1 small green pepper, chopped
1 clove garlic, minced
¾ teaspoon dried leaf oregano
½ teaspoon each: fennel seeds, salt
¼ teaspoon freshly ground pepper
¼ pound fresh mushrooms, sliced
1 pound mild Italian sausage

1 package (10 ounces) mozzarella cheese, thinly sliced
½ cup freshly grated Parmesan cheese

1. Heat oven to 425 degrees. For crust, heat 1 cup water, shortening, sugar and salt until shortening melts; cool to 105 to 115 degrees warm. Dissolve yeast in ½ cup warm water; let stand until bubbly. Mix yeast and shortening mixtures in large bowl. Add cornmeal. Add 2 cups flour; beat well. Stir in enough additional flour to make a soft dough. Turn onto lightly floured surface; knead, working in more flour as needed until smooth and elastic.

2. Brush a round, 12-inch pizza pan (at least 2 inches deep) with oil. Press dough evenly over bottom and up sides of pan. Bake at 425 degrees 5 minutes.

3. For filling, drain tomatoes in colander, chop tomatoes and return to colander; set aside to drain. Cook onion, green pepper, garlic and spices in 2 tablespoons oil in medium saucepan over medium-high heat until onion and green pepper are tender. Stir in well-drained tomatoes and mushrooms; cook lightly; remove from heat.

4. Remove sausage from casing; crumble into pizza crust. Arrange mozzarella slices over sausage. Top with tomato mixture; sprinkle with Parmesan cheese. Bake until crust is golden brown, about 45 minutes. Let stand 5 minutes before serving.

■ *Another Chicago wonder, stuffed pizza, comes with the cheesy filling hidden inside a double layer of crust and the tomato sauce on top. This version was developed by* The Tribune *test kitchen using Giordano's stuffed pizza as a guide.*

CHICAGO-STYLE STUFFED PIZZA

6 servings
Preparation time: 45 minutes
Cooking time: 45 minutes

CRUST

1 package active dry yeast

1¼ cups warm water (105 to 115 degrees)

1 tablespoon melted vegetable shortening

2 tablespoons sugar

1 teaspoon salt

4¼ to 4½ cups all-purpose flour
Vegetable oil

FILLING

1½ pounds mild Italian sausage

1 medium each, chopped: onion, green pepper

1 tablespoon vegetable oil

½ teaspoon salt

1 package (10 ounces) mozzarella cheese, thinly sliced

¼ pound fresh mushrooms, sliced

TOPPING

1 can (28 ounces) Italian-style plum tomatoes, drained, chopped

½ teaspoon Italian seasoning

¼ teaspoon fennel seed

⅓ cup freshly grated Parmesan cheese

1. Dissolve yeast in water in large bowl; let stand until bubbly. Add shortening, sugar and salt. Stir in 2 cups flour. Stir in enough flour to form a soft dough. Turn dough onto lightly floured surface; knead, working in more flour as needed until smooth and elastic.

2. Divide dough into thirds. Cover and set one-third aside. Roll two-thirds of the dough into 14-inch circle. Brush a 12-inch pizza pan (at least 2 inches deep) lightly with oil. Press dough evenly over bottom and up sides of pan.

3. Heat oven to 425 degrees. Remove sausage from casing; crumble into crust. Cook onion and green pepper in 1 tablespoon oil in small skillet over medium-high heat until tender. Stir in salt; sprinkle vegetables over sausage. Top with mozzarella cheese and mushrooms.

4. For topping, cook tomatoes and spices in medium saucepan, over medium heat 10 minutes, breaking up tomatoes with a fork. Roll out remaining one-third of dough into 12-inch circle. Set over filling in pan. Crimp edges of top and bottom crust together to seal well. Pierce top crust with fork.

5. Spread tomato sauce over top. Sprinkle with Parmesan cheese. Bake until crust is golden, 45 minutes. Let pizza stand 10 minutes before serving.

For a satisfying meal-in-one, try this spinach and mushroom-stuffed pizza.

CHICAGO-STYLE STUFFED SPINACH PIZZA

6 servings
Preparation time: 1 hour
Rising time: 1 hour
Cooking time: 1 hour

CRUST

- 1 tablespoon sugar
- 2 envelopes active dry yeast
- 2 cups warm water (105 to 115 degrees)
- ⅓ cup vegetable oil
- 4 to 6 cups all-purpose flour

SAUCE

- 2 tablespoons olive oil
- 1 clove garlic, minced
- 1 can (28 ounces) crushed tomatoes with added puree
- 2 teaspoons dried leaf oregano
- 1½ teaspoons dried basil
- ¼ teaspoon each: salt, freshly ground pepper

FILLING

- 3 packages (10 ounces each) frozen, chopped spinach, thawed, well-drained
- 2½ cups shredded mozzarella cheese
- ½ pound fresh mushrooms, sliced, optional
- ½ cup each, freshly grated: Parmesan cheese, Romano cheese
- 2 cloves garlic, minced
- 2 tablespoons olive oil
- 1 teaspoon dried basil
- ¼ teaspoon each: salt, freshly ground pepper

1. For crust, dissolve sugar and yeast in water in large bowl; let stand until bubbly. Stir in ⅓ cup oil. Stir in 4 cups of the flour until smooth; stir in remaining flour as needed until stiff dough forms. Knead on lightly floured surface until smooth and elastic. Put into greased bowl. Turn to coat top. Let rise, covered, in warm place until doubled in bulk, about 1 hour.

2. For sauce, heat 2 tablespoons oil in large saucepan over medium-high heat; add garlic, cook 2 minutes. Stir in tomatoes, oregano, 1½ teaspoons basil, ¼ teaspoon salt and pepper. Simmer until very thick, 30 minutes.

3. For filling, mix remaining ingredients in large bowl.

4. Heat oven to 450 degrees. Punch down dough. Let rest 10 minutes. Roll two-thirds of the dough into 16-inch circle. Fit into lightly oiled 12-inch pizza pan (at least 2 inches deep); let sides overhang.

5. Put spinach mixture into center of dough and smooth evenly over surface. Roll remaining dough on lightly floured surface to 12-inch circle. Put over filling. Crimp edges; cut excess dough at edges so dough is level with top crust. Pour sauce over dough to cover. Bake until dough is golden, 20 to 40 minutes. Let stand 10 minutes before serving.

Pizza & Sandwiches

For those who like it thin, The Tribune *test kitchen developed this recipe, using the pizza from Chicago's The Home-Run Inn as a trusty model.*

CHICAGO-STYLE THIN-CRUST PIZZA

6 servings
Preparation time: 25 minutes
Cooking time: 30 minutes

CRUST
1 **package active dry yeast**
¾ **cup warm water (105 to 115 degrees)**
1½ **teaspoons vegetable shortening, melted**
1 **tablespoon sugar**
½ **teaspoon salt**
2 **to 2½ cups all-purpose flour**
Vegetable oil

TOPPING
½ **pound mild Italian sausage**
1 **medium each, chopped: onion, green pepper**
1 **can (8 ounces) pizza sauce**
1 **package (10 ounces) mozzarella cheese, thinly sliced**
⅓ **cup freshly grated Parmesan cheese**
¼ **pound fresh mushrooms, sliced**

1. For crust, dissolve yeast in water in large bowl; add shortening, sugar and salt. Stir in 1 cup flour. Gradually stir in remaining flour to form a soft dough. Turn onto lightly floured board; knead until smooth and elastic.

2. Heat oven to 425 degrees. Roll dough to 16-inch circle. Fit into lightly oiled 14-inch pizza pan (at least ¾-inch deep); crimp edges to form a slight rim.

3. Remove sausage from casing: crumble into skillet. Cook over low heat until cooked through about 10 minutes. Remove sausage with slotted spoon; set sausage aside.

4. Cook onion and pepper, in drippings left in skillet, over medium-high heat until tender. Spread pizza sauce over dough. Top with sausage, onion mixture and mozzarella cheese. Sprinkle with Parmesan cheese, then mushrooms. Bake until crust is golden, about 15 minutes.

Wild mushrooms such as shiitake, porcini or morels add a distinctive taste to fresh pizza. If you can't find wild leeks, available in the spring, tender green onions will do.

PIZZA WITH WILD LEEKS AND MUSHROOMS

2 to 4 servings
Preparation time: 1 hour
Rising time: 1½ to 2½ hours
Baking time: 15 to 20 minutes

CRUST

- ¾ **cup warm water (105 to 115 degrees)**
- 1 **envelope dry active yeast**
- **Pinch sugar**
- 2 **tablespoons olive oil**
- 2 **cups flour, about**
- ½ **cup wheat germ**
- ¼ **teaspoon salt**
- **Cornmeal**

TOPPING

- **Olive oil**
- 3 **wild leeks, white part only, or 6 green onions, thinly sliced**
- 1 **cup fresh wild mushrooms, halved if large**
- 4 **ripe plum tomatoes, thinly sliced**
- ½ **teaspoon minced fresh thyme or ¼ teaspoon dried**
- ¼ **cup freshly grated Parmesan cheese**
- **Freshly ground pepper**

1. For crust, dissolve water, yeast and sugar in large bowl; let stand until bubbly. Stir in oil, 1 cup of the flour, wheat germ and salt. Stir well. Stir in remaining flour as needed until a soft, sticky dough forms. Put into greased bowl; turn to coat top with oil. Let rise, covered, in warm place until doubled in bulk, about 1½ hours.

2. Punch down dough. If time allows, let rise a second time.

3. Heat oven to 450 degrees. Divide dough in half. Roll each half into a very thin circle. Put onto baking sheets sprinkled with cornmeal.

4. For topping, brush each dough circle heavily with olive oil. Cook leeks in 2 tablespoons olive oil in medium skillet over medium heat until almost tender, about 10 minutes. Add mushrooms and cook 5 minutes. Arrange a layer of sliced tomatoes over dough, leaving a 1-inch border on all sides. Sprinkle with cooked leeks and mushrooms. Sprinkle each with half of the thyme, cheese and pepper.

5. Bake until dough is nicely crisp, 15 to 20 minutes. Cool a few minutes before serving.

Sometimes the trick to a good pizza is to let your imagination roll, as in this prosciutto and goat cheese version from the Metro.

PROSCIUTTO–GOAT CHEESE PIZZA

3 servings
Preparation time: 30 minutes
Rising time: 1 hour
Cooking time: 10 to 14 minutes

¼ cup warm water (105 to 115 degrees)

1½ teaspoons sugar

1 package active dry yeast

2 teaspoons olive oil

1½ teaspoons salt

3 to 4 cups all-purpose flour

1 cup warm water

3 ounces sliced mozzarella cheese

3 medium tomatoes, seeded, diced

1 teaspoon coarse (kosher) salt, about

1 medium, each julienned: red onion, red bell pepper

3 ounces prosciutto julienned, tossed with 1 tablespoon olive oil

6 ounces goat cheese, crumbled

6 fresh basil leaves for garnish

1. Dissolve ¼ cup water, sugar and yeast in large bowl; let stand until bubbly. Add oil and salt; stir well. Add 1 cup flour; stir until smooth. Add 1 cup water. Then add remaining flour, 1 cup at a time, until dough forms. Turn out onto floured surface; knead until smooth and elastic, about 10 minutes. Put into greased bowl; turn once to oil top. Let rise, covered in warm place until double in bulk, about 1 hour.

2. Heat oven to 475 degrees. Pat dough into 3 circles, each measuring about 8 inches in diameter. Put onto lightly greased cookie sheets.

3. Top each with ⅓ of the mozzarella. In order listed, sprinkle each with ⅓ of the tomatoes, salt, onion, red pepper, prosciutto and goat cheese. Bake until cheese has melted and crust edges are brown, 10 to 12 minutes. Garnish with basil leaves.

This broccoli-stuffed pizza is a close version to the popular one served at Edwardo's restaurants in Chicago.

STUFFED BROCCOLI PIZZA

8 servings
Preparation time: 1 hour
Rising time: 1 hour
Baking time: 40 to 50 minutes

WHOLE-WHEAT CRUST

- 2 tablespoons sugar
- 2 packages active dry yeast
- 2 cups warm water (105 to 115 degrees)
- 3 cups each: whole-wheat flour, all-purpose flour
- 7 tablespoons vegetable oil

TOMATO SAUCE

- 1 can (28 ounces each) Italian-style plum tomatoes, drained, chopped
- 1 can (14 ounces) whole tomatoes, drained, chopped
- 2 tablespoons each: olive oil, minced fresh basil (or 1 teaspoon dried)
- 1 teaspoon each: dried oregano, salt
- 1 clove garlic, minced

BROCCOLI FILLING

- 3 to 4 stalks broccoli, cooked, chopped, about 4 cups
- 2 pounds mozzarella cheese, shredded
- ¼ cup olive oil
- 4 teaspoons minced garlic
- 1 teaspoon salt
- ½ teaspoon freshly ground pepper

1. For crust, dissolve sugar and yeast in water in large bowl; let stand until bubbly. Gradually stir in flours and oil until stiff dough forms. Knead on lightly floured surface until smooth and elastic. Put into greased bowl; turn once to grease top. Let rise, covered, in warm place until doubled in bulk, about 1 hour.

2. Lightly grease 12-inch pizza pan (at least 2 inches deep). Divide dough in half. Roll out 1 half into ¼-inch-thick circle; fit into prepared pan. Press up sides of pan and allow edges to overlap the sides.

3. For sauce, mix all ingredients in medium bowl. For broccoli filling, mix all ingredients in large bowl. Heat oven to 500 degrees.

4. Spread broccoli filling over crust. Roll out remaining dough on floured surface into ¼-inch-thick circle. Lay over filling. Crimp top and bottom crust edges together. Trim off excess dough. Spread tomato sauce over dough.

5. Bake until crust is golden, 40 to 50 minutes. Cool on wire rack 10 minutes before serving.

When we asked readers to recommend their favorite pizza restaurants in town, Victoria Becker nominated her own North Side home where she whips up this whole-wheat pizza, generously topped with sauce and chunks of cheese.

WHOLE-WHEAT PIZZA

6 to 8 servings
Preparation time: 1 hour
Rising time: 1 hour
Cooking time: 1 hour

CRUST

- **3 packages active dry yeast**
- **2½ cups warm water (105 to 115 degrees)**
- **½ cup (1 stick) butter, melted, cooled**
- **1 teaspoon salt**
- **6 to 8 cups whole-wheat flour**

SAUCE AND FILLING

- **¼ cup olive oil**
- **2 cans (28 ounces each) Italian-style plum tomatoes**
- **1½ medium onions, finely chopped**
- **1 green pepper, finely chopped**
- **7 tablespoons Italian seasoning for pizza, such as Dell' Alpe**
- **4 cloves garlic, chopped**
- **3 cans (6 ounces each) tomato paste**
- **¾ pound hot Italian sausage, removed from casings**
- **1 tablespoon soy sauce**
- **1 teaspoon garlic salt**
- **¼ teaspoon freshly ground pepper**

ingredients continued on next page

1. For crust, dissolve yeast in water in large bowl; let stand until bubbly. Stir in butter and salt. Gradually stir in enough of the flour until soft dough forms. Knead until smooth and elastic. Put dough into greased bowl; turn to grease top. Let rise, covered, in warm place until doubled in bulk, about 1 hour.

2. Meanwhile for sauce, put olive oil into large skillet. Stir in tomatoes, chopped onion, chopped green pepper, 5 tablespoons of the Italian seasoning and garlic. Simmer over low heat about 15 minutes, breaking up tomatoes as you stir. Stir in tomato paste. Simmer 15 minutes. Taste and adjust seasonings.

3. Mix sausage with soy sauce, garlic salt and pepper in medium bowl.

4. Heat oven to 400 degrees. Punch down dough. Divide in half; refrigerate one half for other use. Roll other half of dough to ¼-inch thick. Fit into lightly oiled 12-inch pizza pan (at least 2 inches deep). Roll up edges to make a shallow bowl. Bake until set, 5 to 8 minutes.

5. Spoon 3 cups of sauce over dough (see note). Top with sausage mixture and mushrooms. Arrange green pepper slices and onion rings over all. Top with cubed cheese. Sprinkle with 2 tablespoons of the remaining Italian spice mixture.

6. Bake until dough is golden and crisp, cheese is melted and sauce is bubbly, 20 to 25 minutes.

1 can (8 ounces)
    mushrooms, drained,
    sliced
1 green pepper, seeded,
    sliced into rounds
1 large onion, sliced,
    rings separated
5 ounces each, cubed:
    mozzarella cheese,
    provolone cheese

NOTE: Remaining sauce will keep refrigerated for 1 week, or frozen solid up to 2 months. Remaining dough can be shaped into a loaf and baked at 350 degrees about 25 minutes, or until golden and bottom sounds hollow when tapped. Or refrigerate dough for up to 2 days and use for pizza.

The Honora family of Chicago came up with this unusually fine sandwich, which is pita bread stuffed with mashed avocados plus onion, black olives, eggs, tomato, cheese and celery.

AVOCADOWICHES

4 to 6 servings
Preparation time: 30 minutes
Heating time: 10 minutes

1 large, ripe avocado
1 tablespoon lemon juice
4 green onions, finely
    sliced
1 can (2¼ ounces)
    sliced, ripe olives,
    drained
2 hard-cooked eggs,
    chopped
1 small tomato, peeled,
    seeded, chopped
½ cup shredded Cheddar
    cheese
2 ribs celery, diced
    Garlic salt to taste
    Hot pepper sauce to
    taste
4 or 5 pita pocket
    breads, halved
3 cups shredded iceberg
    lettuce

1. Peel and pit avocado. Mash avocado and lemon juice with a fork in large bowl until well blended. Stir in onion, olives, eggs, tomato, cheese and celery. Season to taste with garlic salt and hot pepper sauce. Cover and refrigerate as long as 2 hours.

2. To serve, wrap bread in foil and heat at 350 degrees for 10 minutes, or until hot. Or, place in plastic bag and microwave on medium (50 percent power) about 50 seconds.

3. Stuff a portion of lettuce, then the avocado mixture into each warm bread half. Serve.

Tortillas are the main breadstuff of Mexico. In this recipe, featured as a Food Guide Recipe of the Week several years ago, the stuffing for the burritos is meatless and the sauce hot and spicy.

MEATLESS BURRITOS

4 to 6 servings
Preparation time: 20 minutes
Cooking time: 15 minutes

3 **green onions, finely chopped**

1 **clove garlic, minced**

3 **tablespoons vegetable oil**

2 **cans (15 ounces each) pinto beans, drained**

1 **package (10 ounces) frozen corn, thawed**

2 **tablespoons minced fresh cilantro (coriander) leaves**

1 **tablespoon minced fresh parsley**

Hot pepper sauce, salt, freshly ground pepper to taste

10 **large flour tortillas**
Vegetable oil
Quick red sauce (recipe follows)
Shredded Monterey Jack cheese
Sour cream, tomato wedges, fresh cilantro sprigs for garnishes

1. Cook onions and garlic in 3 tablespoons oil in large skillet over high heat until soft but not brown, 3 minutes. Stir in beans, mashing with spoon. Stir in corn, cilantro, parsley, hot pepper sauce, salt and pepper.

2. Heat oven to 300 degrees. Brush each tortilla lightly with oil on both sides. Wrap in aluminum foil; bake until hot, 5 to 10 minutes.

3. Preheat broiler. Spoon hot bean mixture down center of each tortilla; fold over ends. Place seam side down on heatproof platter.

4. Spoon quick red sauce over center of burrito, sprinkle with cheese. Broil until cheese is melted, 2 to 3 minutes. Garnish with sour cream, tomato wedges and cilantro.

QUICK RED SAUCE

About 1½ cups

1 **can (8 ounces) whole tomatoes**

1 **small onion, halved**

1 **clove garlic, halved**

1 **can (4 ounces) peeled green chilies**

1. Put tomatoes, onion, garlic, green chilies, parsley, oregano and cilantro leaves in food processor or blender. Process until coarsely chopped. Transfer to small saucepan; stir in wine vinegar, oil, hot pepper sauce, salt and pepper to taste. Heat until warm.

ingredients continued on next page

THE CHICAGO TRIBUNE COOKBOOK

1 tablespoon chopped
fresh parsley

1 teaspoon each: dried
oregano, chopped
fresh cilantro
(coriander)

2 tablespoons red wine
vinegar

1 tablespoon vegetable
oil

Hot pepper sauce, salt,
pepper to taste

For this original recipe from the Chicago Baking Company, the sausage filling is baked inside the bread.

CHORIZO BREAD SANDWICH LOAF

4 servings
Preparation time: 25 minutes
Rising time: 1 hour
Cooking time: 1 hour

1 pound chorizo sausage

1 medium onion, minced

1 cup tomato sauce

2 tablespoons chopped
fresh cilantro
(coriander) leaves

½ teaspoon salt

¼ teaspoon freshly
ground pepper

1 package (2 pounds)
frozen bread dough,
thawed

1. Remove casing from chorizo (sausage falls apart when casing is removed). Put sausage and onion into skillet; cook over low heat, until lightly browned. Pour off all excess fat. Add tomato sauce, cilantro, salt and pepper; cook over low heat 25 minutes.

2. Roll dough on lightly floured surface into 12 by 10-inch rectangle. Spread sausage mixture over dough leaving a 1-inch margin around all sides.

3. Roll up dough jelly-roll fashion. Put onto baking sheet with seam side down; tuck ends under. Let rise, covered in warm place until doubled in bulk, about 1 hour.

4. Heat oven to 400 degrees. Bake until golden and crusty, about 35 minutes. Remove bread from oven; cool on wire rack 3 hours.

Beverly Dillon developed this portable sandwich as the perfect choice for a picnic at the Ravinia Park summer concerts in Highland Park, Illinois.

CHICKEN SANDWICHES WITH LEMON BASIL MAYONNAISE

4 sandwiches
Preparation time: 15 minutes
Cooking time: 4 minutes
Chilling time: About 2 hours

LEMON BASIL MAYONNAISE
- 1 egg yolk
- 2 tablespoons fresh lemon juice
- ¼ cup loosely packed fresh basil leaves
- 1 large clove garlic
- ¼ teaspoon each: salt, freshly ground pepper
- 1 cup olive oil

SANDWICHES
- 2 cans (13¾ ounces each) chicken broth
- ¼ cup each: fresh lemon juice, white wine
- 2 bay leaves
- 1 teaspoon each: dried basil, dried tarragon, salt
- ½ teaspoon freshly ground pepper
- ¼ teaspoon crushed red pepper flakes
- 2 whole chicken breasts, split into 4 halves
- 4 croissant rolls, split
- 1 small head leaf lettuce
- 1 large ripe tomato, thinly sliced

1. For lemon basil mayonnaise, put egg yolk, lemon juice, basil, garlic, salt and pepper in food processor or blender. Process until smooth. With machine running, add oil in steady stream until ingredients thicken, scraping down sides of container once or twice. (Mayonnaise will keep in jar with tight-fitting lid up to 2 to 3 days.)

2. For sandwiches, put broth, lemon juice, white wine, bay leaves, basil, tarragon, salt, pepper and red pepper flakes into large nonaluminum saucepan. Heat to boil over high heat. Add chicken breasts; be sure the liquid covers chicken. Reduce heat to low; cover, and simmer 4 minutes. Remove pan from heat. Keep chicken covered. Let chicken breast cool in broth.

3. When chicken breasts are cool, remove from broth, reserving broth. Strain broth into large bowl; you will have about 4 cups. Cover with plastic wrap, refrigerate and reserve for soup or other use.

4. Discard skin from chicken breast. Separate meat from bones. Thinly slice chicken breast and reserve.

5. Spread cut side of each croissant roll with lemon basil mayonnaise. Arrange sliced chicken, lettuce and sliced tomatoes, dividing evenly among croissants to make 4 sandwiches.

Croque *means "crunch" in French, and crunchy the croque monsieur is. The sandwich can be found in two versions: croque monsieur and croque madame. The masculine version is the original classic. The croque madame is a lighter adaptation that leaves out the prosciutto completely or at least reduces the amount used. This recipe can be doubled or tripled as the circumstances dictate.*

GRILLED HAM AND CHEESE SANDWICHES
(Croque monsieur)

2 servings
Preparation time: 10 minutes
Cooking time: 5 minutes

4 **thick slices good-quality French-style bread**
 Softened butter
8 **slices Swiss or Gruyère cheese, about 4 ounces**
6 **very thin slices prosciutto ham, about 2 ounces**
 Dijon mustard
1 **egg**
3 **tablespoons milk**
2 **tablespoons butter**
1 **tablespoon vegetable oil**
 Tomato wedges
 Cornichon pickles

1. Spread bread slices generously on one side with softened butter. Top buttered side of 1 slice with 2 slices of the cheese. Top with 3 slices of prosciutto. Spread prosciutto very lightly with mustard. Top with 2 more slices of cheese. Put a second slice of bread, buttered-side down, on top to make a sandwich. Repeat for second sandwich.

2. Whisk egg and milk together in shallow dish. Heat a large skillet until hot over medium heat. Dip sandwiches in egg mixture; turn to coat with egg mixture on all sides. Let excess drain off. Add butter and oil; heat until butter is melted. Add sandwiches; reduce heat to low. Cook, turning once and flattening slightly with a spatula until golden brown on both sides and cheese is warm and slightly melted. Remove to plate. Pass extra mustard. Serve with tomatoes and pickles.

Beverly Dillon developed this perfect St. Patrick's Day sandwich, which includes corned beef and sautéed cabbage on thick wedges of Irish soda bread.

LAYERED CORNED BEEF SANDWICH LOAF

4 servings
Preparation time: 30 minutes
Cooking time: 40 minutes

4 tablespoons softened butter

1 cup coarsely chopped green cabbage

1 large onion, coarsely chopped

¼ teaspoon each: dill weed, salt, pepper

1 round loaf of bread (about 1 to 1½ pounds), such as Irish soda bread or sourdough bread

About 6 fresh spinach leaves

8 to 10 slices Swiss cheese

¾ pound thinly sliced corned beef

¼ cup (½ stick) butter, melted

Stone ground or country mustard, optional

1. Heat 1 tablespoon of the butter in skillet over medium heat. Add cabbage and onion. Sauté, just until crisp-tender, about 10 minutes. Stir in dill, salt and pepper. Cool slightly.

2. Heat oven to 350 degrees. Cut small slice horizontally from top of bread; reserve this slice. Hollow out bread to make ½-inch-thick shell. Spread inside of bread shell and reserved top slice with remaining 3 tablespoons of softened butter.

3. Arrange spinach leaves, overlapping to completely cover inside of bread shell.

4. Arrange half of the cheese over spinach, trimming cheese to fit. Spoon cabbage-onion mixture over cheese. Lay corned beef slices over cabbage mixture. End with remaining cheese slices. Top with reserved bread slice.

5. Brush outside of bread with melted butter. Wrap assembled stuffed bread in heavy-duty aluminum foil, leaving top slightly open to allow heat to escape while bread heats in oven.

6. Put foil-wrapped bread on cookie sheet and bake in oven just to heat through, about 30 minutes. Remove, unwrap, cut into wedges. Serve with mustard.

The secret to this muffalata (a layered sandwich on round Italian bread) from Wheeling's Pomodoro's restaurant is to make the olive oil dressing the night before and let the flavors marinate.

MUFFALATA

2 sandwiches
Preparation time: 20 minutes
Chilling time: Overnight

6 tablespoons virgin olive oil

4 tablespoons red wine vinegar

2 tablespoons each, finely chopped: celery, pitted green olives

1 tablespoon each, finely chopped: red onion, green or red bell pepper

1 tablespoon fresh lemon juice

2 cloves garlic, finely minced

¼ teaspoon each: dried leaf thyme, freshly ground pepper, crushed fennel seed

⅛ teaspoon cayenne pepper

2 muffalatas or round Italian rolls

6 slices each: mortadella, capocollo sausage, aged Swiss cheese, mild provolone cheese

2 large leaves leaf lettuce

10 or 12 thin red onion rings

8 slices tomato

1. At least one day before using, put oil, vinegar, celery, olives, chopped onion, bell pepper, lemon juice, garlic, thyme, black pepper, crushed fennel and cayenne pepper in small bowl. Mix well. Refrigerate overnight. (Mixture will keep at least 2 weeks in refrigerator.)

2. Slice muffalatas in half lengthwise with serrated knife. For each sandwich, lay a single layer of mortadella on bottom of roll. Top with layer of capocollo, a layer of Swiss, a layer of provolone, lettuce leaf, 5 or 6 red onion rings and 4 tomato slices.

3. Spoon 5 tablespoons of olive mixture over the tomato slices. Use top of roll to cover sandwich. Serve immediately.

This easy-to-assemble sandwich packs plenty of taste, including a briny punch from anchovies and olives.

PAN BAGNAT IN PITA

2 sandwiches
Preparation time: 20 minutes

2 **pita breads with pockets**
1 **can (6½ ounces) tuna, drained, flaked**
3 **to 4 tablespoons best French virgin olive oil**
6 **leaves green leaf lettuce, shredded**
1 **small firm tomato, chopped**
2 **hard-cooked eggs, chopped**

½ **red or green bell pepper, chopped**
6 **flat anchovy fillets, drained, minced**
6 **to 8 small black olives in brine, pitted, sliced**

1. Split pita bread open. Mix remaining ingredients in large bowl. Toss well to mix. Taste and adjust seasonings. Serve in pita pockets.

These hearty Mexican-style bean sandwiches get extra depth from cheese and bacon, making them suitable for a light dinner. Bolillo rolls can be found in Mexican bakeries.

MEXICAN OPEN-FACE BEAN AND CHEESE SANDWICHES
(Molletes)

6 servings
Preparation time: 30 minutes
Cooking time: 10 minutes

6 **bolillos, or substitute small French-type rolls, or use 5-inch sections of French bread**
1 **can (16 ounces) refried beans**
12 **slices bacon, cooked, drained, crumbled**
2 **cups shredded Monterey Jack cheese**
Salsa (see recipe, page 20)

1. Heat oven to 450 degrees. Split bolillos lengthwise. Tear out only a small amount of the soft interior of the bolillos. Place rolls cut-side down on a cookie sheet. Place in oven to toast lightly, about 3 minutes.

2. Spread cut-side of toasted rolls with refried beans. Sprinkle with some of the bacon, then sprinkle with cheese. Arrange on baking sheet. Heat in oven until cheese is bubbly and golden, about 10 minutes. Watch carefully so cheese does not burn. Sprinkle with remaining bacon. Serve molletes hot with salsa.

Spicy shrimp sandwiches with a chili sauce are the perfect main course for a casual company luncheon or supper.

SHRIMP POOR BOYS

6 servings
Preparation time: 45 minutes
Cooking time: 5 minutes

SAUCE

¾ **cup chili sauce or catsup**

1 **tablespoon orange marmalade**

1 **tablespoon brown mustard or country-style Dijon mustard**

½ **teaspoon Worcestershire sauce**

2 **to 3 drops hot pepper sauce**

SANDWICHES

6 **rectangular sandwich rolls**

1 **bag (16 ounces) frozen, small shrimp**

1 **head leaf lettuce**

1 **cup milk**

2 **large eggs**

1¾ **cups all-purpose flour**

¼ **cup yellow cornmeal**

1 **tablespoon baking powder**

1 **teaspoon each: cayenne pepper, salt, pepper, paprika, garlic powder, onion powder, dried leaf oregano**

½ **teaspoon dried leaf thyme**

¼ **teaspoon dry mustard**

1 **cup vegetable oil, preferably peanut oil**

3 **tablespoons butter**

1. For sauce, mix all ingredients in small bowl. For sandwiches, split rolls ¾ of the way through; remove some of the bread from each side to make more room for filling.

2. Thaw shrimp following package directions. Pat dry on paper towel. Remove core from lettuce; wash and separate leaves. Pat dry on paper towel.

3. Whisk milk and eggs in small bowl until well mixed. Mix flour, cornmeal, baking powder, cayenne, salt, pepper, paprika, garlic powder, onion powder, oregano, thyme and dry mustard in large bowl until well mixed. Add shrimp; toss gently to coat. Transfer shrimp to sifter; shake off excess flour over pan.

4. Add shrimp to milk mixture. Gently turn to make sure shrimp are all moistened. Drain off liquid. Return shrimp to flour mixture. Toss gently with fingertips to coat again in seasoned flour.

5. Heat oil and butter in large skillet to 300 degrees. Add a few shrimp at a time, shaking off any excess flour. Cook, turning until golden, about 1 minute. Remove with slotted spoon. Drain on paper towels. Repeat until all shrimp are cooked.

6. Line each roll with lettuce; spoon in shrimp, dividing evenly among the rolls. Spoon on sauce. Serve immediately.

To make an unusual sandwich, start with unusual ingredients such as thinly sliced smoked duck breast and julienned leeks, a specialty at Mitchell Cobey Cuisine, a gourmet food shop in Chicago.

SMOKED DUCK BREAST SANDWICHES WITH LEEKS

2 sandwiches
Preparation time: 15 minutes
Cooking time: 45 minutes

1 **boneless smoked duck breast, about ¾ pound, with fat and skin on**
2 **leeks**
  Green peppercorn mustard (or any strong seed mustard)
4 **slices whole-wheat Italian bread**
2 **small clusters each: green, red and purple grapes for garnish**

1. Remove fat and skin from fully cooked duck breast; cut fat and skin into chunks. Set meat aside. Put fat and skin into baking pan. Bake at 350 degrees until fat is liquid and skin is crisp, 30 to 45 minutes.

2. Remove pan from oven and remove cracklings (fried pieces of skin) from fat to paper towels to drain. Discard fat (or save for frying potatoes later). Meanwhile, cut breast meat into very thin slices for sandwiches.

3. Cut root ends off leeks; cut away any tough parts of the green tops. Split leeks in half lengthwise and wash thoroughly under cold running water to get out soil. Cut leeks into julienne strips (the size of matches) with a sharp knife. Toss drained cracklings with leeks in a bowl.

4. Apply mustard liberally to 2 slices of whole-wheat bread. Layer duck slices over mustard, dividing evenly. Sprinkle leek/crackling mixture over duck slices.

5. Top sandwiches with slices of whole-wheat bread. Garnish with grapes.

A Philadelphia-style cheese steak sandwich is difficult to find in other cities. To help you along, however, Beverly Dillon created this recipe.

STEAK AND CHEESE SANDWICHES

6 servings
Preparation time: 15 minutes
Marinating time: Overnight
Cooking time: 5 minutes

½ cup each: cider vinegar, Italian salad dressing
4 tablespoons vegetable oil
1 tablespoon soy sauce
1 clove garlic, minced
1 bay leaf
¼ teaspoon freshly ground pepper
1½ pounds flank steak
2 medium onions, sliced, separated into rings
2 medium green peppers, seeded, cut into ½-inch strips
6 French-style rolls
6 slices provolone cheese

1. Mix vinegar, salad dressing, 2 tablespoons of the oil, soy sauce, garlic, bay leaf and pepper in large bowl. Add steak; turn so meat is covered with marinade. Cover with plastic wrap and refrigerate overnight.

2. Heat remaining 2 tablespoons oil over medium-high heat in large skillet. Add onions and peppers; cook until just crisp-tender. Remove with slotted spoon to small bowl; set aside.

3. Heat oven to 200 degrees. Cut rolls halfway through lengthwise; wrap in foil and place in oven until warmed through.

4. Remove steak from marinade and drain. Cut steak against grain into ⅛-inch-thick strips. Add to skillet and cook, stirring, over medium-heat until rare, 1 to 2 minutes. Remove from skillet; divide evenly on bottom halves of rolls. Divide onion-pepper mixture evenly over meat; cover each with a slice of cheese.

5. Put into oven to melt cheese. Cover top with remaining half of roll and serve. The cut roll can be brushed with some of the pan juices if desired.

Two favorites in one: the taste of spicy pizza sauce and the convenience of a bagel. Select a good quality olive oil to drizzle on top.

SUMMER PIZZA SANDWICHES

3 servings
Preparation time: 10 minutes
Broiling time: 4 minutes

3 bagels
1 can (8 ounces) pizza sauce
1 tablespoon each: minced fresh basil, fresh oregano (or 1 teaspoon each dried)
½ teaspoon minced fresh garlic or ⅛ teaspoon garlic powder
1 large ripe tomato, cut into 6 slices
6 thin slices mozzarella cheese
Olive oil

1. Preheat broiler. Cut bagels crosswise in half. Toast or broil until golden.

2. Meanwhile, mix pizza sauce, basil, oregano and garlic in small bowl. Spread sauce evenly over toasted bagel halves. Top with a tomato slice and cheese slice. Drizzle lightly with olive oil. Broil until cheese is golden.

NOTE: Thinly sliced prosciutto or ham can be added to this open-face sandwich, if desired.

Beer—a natural with hot dogs—is added right into the topping for this unusual cheese and bacon dog.

CHEESE AND BACON DOGS

8 servings
Preparation time: 10 minutes
Cooking time: 20 minutes

1 tablespoon butter
½ cup beer
½ pound shredded Cheddar cheese
1 egg, beaten
1 teaspoon Worcestershire sauce
¼ teaspoon curry powder
Pinch paprika
Dash red pepper sauce
Salt, pepper to taste
8 cooked hot dogs
8 toasted hot dog buns

8 slices bacon, cooked, crumbled

1. Melt butter in medium saucepan; add beer. When beer is warm, stir in cheese. Stir over low heat until cheese melts. Stir in egg and seasonings. Do not boil.

2. Spoon hot sauce over 8 hot dogs on buns. Top with bacon.

When a plain hot dog won't do, top it with yet another meal: spicy ground beef and beans.

CHILI DOGS

8 servings
Preparation time: 15 minutes
Cooking time: 1 hour

½ **pound ground beef**
1 **large onion, finely chopped**
1 **large clove garlic, minced**
1½ **teaspoons chili powder**
1 **teaspoon ground cumin**
½ **teaspoon salt**
¼ **teaspoon freshly ground pepper**
1 **large green pepper, seeded, chopped**
1 **can (10 ounces) peeled tomatoes, drained, chopped**
1 **tablespoon tomato paste**
1 **cup canned kidney beans**
8 **cooked hot dogs**
8 **hot dog buns**

1. Cook meat, onion and garlic in large saucepan over medium heat until brown. Stir in seasonings. Cook, stirring, 5 minutes. Stir in green pepper, tomatoes and tomato paste. Simmer, stirring occasionally, 1 hour.

2. Stir in kidney beans. Cook until beans are thoroughly heated. Spoon over hot dogs on buns.

NOTE: Sour cream, chopped onion or shredded Cheddar cheese can be served with chili dogs.

■ *Sauerkraut is the key element here, providing the juicy tang that defines a reuben sandwich or hot dog.*

REUBEN HOT DOGS

8 servings
Preparation time: 10 minutes

1 **cup mayonnaise**
¼ **cup chopped onion**
3 **tablespoons chili sauce**
1 **teaspoon each:**
   hickory-flavored
   barbecue sauce,
   Worcestershire sauce
   Dash hot pepper sauce
   Salt, freshly ground
   pepper to taste
8 **cooked hot dogs**
8 **hot dog buns**
1 **can (16 ounces)**
   sauerkraut, drained,
   rinsed
½ **pound sliced Swiss**
   cheese

1. Preheat broiler. Mix together first six ingredients in a small bowl; season to taste with salt and pepper.

2. Spread sauce over hot dogs on buns; top with sauerkraut and sliced cheese. Broil until cheese melts.

THE CHICAGO TRIBUNE COOKBOOK

FISH & SEAFOOD

I f this cookbook had been written 20 years ago, the fish chapter would have been dramatically different. Like fresh vegetables, fresh fish have captured the imagination of both restaurant chefs and home cooks. Americans are eating more fish than ever, and for the same reason: good health.

As Americans try to shift away from a diet heavy with red meat, the void has been filled by chicken and fish—and not just the favorite fillet of sole of yesterday's generation. Blessed by a location in the middle of a massive transportation system that spreads to either coast, the Midwest is an ideal post for receiving fresh shipments from the Atlantic, Pacific and Gulf coastal states—shipments loaded with pristine belon oysters from Maine or still-wriggling sardines from Monterey. Fresh—not frozen—shrimp find their way up from Louisiana, and the nearby Great Lakes provide a wealth of freshwater fish.

In this chapter you will find skate as well as scallops, and fresh tuna instead of canned. Fish often are given a decidedly Oriental touch, which typifies current trends in the food field. Shrimp and salmon, of course, remain strong favorites and deserve the extra space we have given them here. We also have balanced cooking techniques with ideas for the grill and microwave oven, as well as the conventional stove.

Who can resist stir-fried shrimp? Or a classic baked fish with olive oil and tomatoes? Or let your imagination go. These recipes will lead the way.

How to Pick the Freshest Fish

No fish tastes good unless it is fresh and well cared for. To test for freshness in whole fish, look for bulging eyes, reddish gills, scales that stick firmly to the fish, and flesh that is firm to the touch. There should be no odor, especially around the gills or the belly. For fillets, look for flesh that has a shiny gleam and is void of discoloration, especially browning or yellowing around the edges. Again, as a final test of freshness, smell the fillets after they have been rinsed; they should smell sweet and somewhat like a cucumber—not "fishy."

How to Store Fresh Fish

Fish should be refrigerated or frozen as soon as possible to avoid bacteria which grows quickly at room temperature. Remove fish from its store package, rinse under cold water to remove surface bacteria and odors, and pat dry.

To store fish, place the fillets or whole fish on a wire rack over a deep dish or pan. If the fish needs to be held longer than a few hours, fill the pan with ice cubes, but don't let the ice touch the fish. Cover the fish and pan with tightly wrapped plastic wrap or foil. Store in the refrigerator as close to 32 degrees as possible. Cook the fish within a day.

How to Store Shellfish

Oysters, clams and mussels should be stored in loosely covered containers in a damp atmosphere at about 35 degrees. Store live lobsters in the refrigerator in moist packing (seaweed or damp newspaper strips). Do not store in air-tight containers or in water. Fresh scallops, freshly shucked oysters and clam meat should be stored in containers, surrounded by ice, if possible.

How to Freeze a Fish

To hold fish for longer than a day, freezing is best. Rinse the fillets, steaks or whole fish under cold running water and pat dry. Wrap tightly in plastic wrap, squeezing out the air, then wrap in aluminum foil. Most fish will freeze well for up to two weeks, but avoid refreezing fish because the delicate flesh breaks down, and the fish may become soft. When buying frozen fish, look for solidly frozen packages that show no evidence of refreezing.

Thaw fish slowly in the refrigerator. Keep the fish in its original wrapping and count on about 8 hours per pound. Lobster will take a little more time, shrimp, slightly less. Frozen fillets can be cooked without thawing, if you wish.

How Much to Buy

For each serving, buy 1 pound of whole fish, ¾ pound dressed (head and tail removed), ½ pound fish steaks or ⅓ pound fillets.

How to Tell When a Fish Is Perfectly Cooked

To test for doneness in fish, insert a thermometer at the thickest portion. The thermometer should register 135 degrees. At 140 degrees, the tissues break down and juices escape. Another way to test for doneness is to press the fish with your finger. When a soft-fleshed fish is done, the pressed spot will return to its original shape. A more reliable method and one that works well both in conventional and microwave cooking is to check for translucency: a fish is done when the flesh is opaque.

FISH COOKING METHODS

There are almost as many methods of cooking fish as there are varieties. Baking is an ideal way to treat large, whole fish, especially if you make good use of the natural juices. Steaming and microwave cooking fish are excellent ways to cut back on extra fats. Poached fish pick up extra flavors from the liquid they are cooked in. Americans love to grill, and fish—particularly firm steaks such as halibut or salmon—are beautiful when cooked over the open fire. Indoors, you can duplicate the texture of a grill by broiling.

Fish & Seafood

Saltwater Fish

Oven-baked cod with tomatoes

Grilled halibut with mustard
  cream sauce

Pan-fried porgy

Red snapper firepot

Red snapper in orange sauce

Sweet and sour snapper

Thai whole fried red snapper

Broiled salmon with sesame-sauced
  green beans

Grilled salmon with anchovy butter

Salmon Oriental

Salmon mousse with beurre blanc

Sea bass Provençal

Grilled shark with tomato-feta relish

Deep-fried skate and onions

Swordfish with spicy basil butter

Puffy broiled tilefish

Orange roughy with tarragon

Tuna fillets Creole

Turbot with basil

Shellfish

Spicy boiled crayfish

Mussels with marinara sauce

Lobster salad with avocado
  mayonnaise

Sautéed soft-shell crabs

Soft-shell crabs with walnut-
  tarragon vermicelli

Batter-fried soft-shell crabs

Scallops in lemon grass sauce

Scallops in red butter sauce

Garlic prawns

Shrimp de Jonghe

Stir-fried shrimp on rice

Quick Oriental shellfish ragout

Lemon-dill dry cure for
  smoked fish

Freshwater Fish

Marinated grilled bass with
  green tomato relish

Grilled fillet of catfish with
  Dijon mustard

Cornmeal-fried catfish with
  barbecue sauce and sweet
  potato hush puppies

Uptown fish with saffron rice

Coho Berteau

Whitefish with golden tomato
  butter sauce

Spicy fried smelt

Batter-fried Cajun smelt

Food Guide reader Angie Gulino gave us a recipe for oven-baked fish fillets for serving as part of a St. Joseph's Day table. In addition to cod, she uses this simple recipe with several other fish, including perch and turbot.

OVEN-BAKED COD WITH TOMATOES

2 to 4 servings
Preparation time: 15 minutes
Baking time: 20 minutes

½ **cup olive oil**
1 **pound cod fillets, or perch or turbot**
1 **cup undrained canned plum tomatoes, coarsely chopped**
½ **medium onion, sliced**
2 **tablespoons minced fresh parsley**
 Salt, freshly ground pepper to taste

1. Heat oven to 350 degrees. Rinse fish under cold water; pat dry on paper towels. Put fish in 13 by 9-inch baking dish oiled with some of the olive oil. Put tomatoes and onion over fish. Sprinkle with parsley, salt and pepper. Drizzle remaining oil over fillets.

2. Bake, uncovered, until fish almost flakes easily, about 20 minutes.

NOTE: Any remaining juice from the baked fish can be used as sauce over pasta or cooked rice.

This recipe was created by Chicago chef Dennis Terczak. He prepared the dish at a 1984 U.S. Culinary Olympics fund-raiser dinner in Geneva, Illinois.

GRILLED HALIBUT WITH MUSTARD CREAM SAUCE

4 servings
Preparation time: 10 minutes
Grilling time: 15 minutes

4 **halibut fillets (6 to 8 ounces each)**
½ **cup dry white wine**
1¼ **cups whipping cream**
1 **to 2 tablespoons Dijon mustard**
 Salt, freshly ground pepper to taste
¼ **cup vegetable oil**
20 **asparagus, trimmed, steamed**

1. Prepare grill. Rinse fish under cold water; pat dry on paper towels.

2. Boil wine in small saucepan over medium heat until reduced by half. Add cream; heat to boil. Simmer 2 minutes; remove from heat. Whisk in mustard, salt and pepper to taste.

3. When coals are covered with gray ash, brush one side of fish with oil. Sprinkle with salt. Grill, 6 inches from heat source, until fish almost flakes easily, about 3 minutes per side.

4. Put just enough sauce onto each serving plate to cover bottom. Put fish and asparagus on top of sauce. Serve immediately.

■   The Tribune *test kitchen devised this recipe for porgy, a relatively new fish in 1980 but much more common today.*

PAN-FRIED PORGY

4 servings
Preparation time: 10 minutes
Cooking time: 5 minutes

1½ **pounds porgy fillets,
    about 8 fillets**
 1 **cup milk**
 ½ **cup each: cornmeal,
    all-purpose flour**
 1 **teaspoon each: lemon
    pepper, seasoned salt**
 ½ **cup vegetable oil**
 ¼ **cup (½ stick) unsalted
    butter**
    **Fresh parsley, lemon
    wedges**

1. Rinse fish under cold water; pat dry on paper towels. Pour milk in large shallow dish. Mix cornmeal, flour, lemon pepper and salt in second dish.

2. Heat oil and butter in heavy 12-inch skillet over medium-high heat. Dip fish in milk, then into cornmeal mixture, pressing coating onto fish. Shake off excess. Cook, a few fillets at a time, turning once, until lightly browned, about 2½ minutes on each side.

3. Transfer to warm platter. Keep warm in 250-degree oven while cooking remaining fillets. Garnish with parsley and lemon.

Younghee Na of Chicago wowed the judges with this dramatic red snapper firepot, then stood aghast as she was awarded first place in the 1985 Seafood Recipe Contest cosponsored by The Tribune *and the Chicago Fish House.*

RED SNAPPER FIREPOT

4 to 6 servings
Preparation time: 40 minutes
Marinating time: 30 minutes
Cooking time: 40 minutes

½ **pound flank steak**

MARINADE

3 **tablespoons soy sauce**

2 **teaspoons each:**
   Oriental sesame oil,
   toasted sesame seeds

1 **green onion, minced**

2 **cloves garlic, minced**
   Pinch sugar

FIREPOT

8 **large shrimp**

½ **pound fresh bean curd**
   (tofu)

1 **pound red snapper**
   fillets

12 **large, fresh clams,**
   cleaned

1 **small carrot, peeled,**
   thinly sliced, cooked
   until crisp-tender

6 **green onions, cut**
   diagonally into 2-inch
   pieces

SAUCE

¼ **cup soy sauce**

2 **tablespoons each:**
   water, rice vinegar

1 **tablespoon each:**
   dry sherry, Oriental
   sesame oil, toasted
   sesame seeds

2 **green onions, minced**

2 **cloves garlic, minced**

1 **teaspoon salt**

½ **teaspoon each: sugar,**
   crushed red pepper
   flakes or to taste

1. Cut steak lengthwise in half. Cut each half crosswise into strips as thin as possible, ⅜-inch thick at most. Mix marinade ingredients in small bowl. Add meat; toss to coat well. Let marinate at least 30 minutes.

2. For firepot, peel and devein shrimp, keeping tails intact. Cut bean curd into 2 by 2 by ⅔-inch pieces. Cut snapper into 2-inch pieces. Scrub clams clean. Prepare carrot and 6 green onions as directed.

3. For sauce, mix all ingredients in small bowl; stir until salt and sugar are dissolved. Divide evenly into small, individual bowls.

4. Heat large deep skillet over medium heat. (Grease lightly with vegetable oil if necessary.) Add marinated beef; stir-fry until pinkness is gone. Add 3 cups water; heat to boil. Reduce heat to medium-low. Simmer, covered, 30 minutes.

5. Add red snapper, clams, shrimp, carrot and bean curd, arranging snugly in groups. The liquid should barely cover the ingredients at this point, but if not, add more water. Heat to boil. Adjust heat to medium-high; cook, uncovered, until fish flakes easily and clams have opened slightly, 5 to 7 minutes.

6. Add green onions, making room for them between ingredients; continue to cook 30 seconds.

7. Serve in wide soup bowls. Pass sauce.

Fish & Seafood

213

■ *To test microwave-oven covering techniques for fish,* Tribune *writer Patricia Tennison cooked this red snapper two ways: covered with plastic wrap and with paper towels. Tasters found the fish tasted the same, but the plastic-wrapped version was more moist. With no added fat, and a little cornstarch instead of butter and flour to thicken the juices, this red snapper dish has only 128 calories and 2 grams of fat per serving.*

RED SNAPPER IN ORANGE SAUCE

4 servings
Preparation time: 10 minutes
Marinating time: 15 minutes
Microwave cooking time: 3½ to 4½ minutes

1 **pound red snapper fillets**
1 **medium orange**
2 **garlic cloves, minced**
2 **tablespoons each: light soy sauce, dry white wine**
¼ **teaspoon cornstarch, dissolved in 1 tablespoon cold water**

1. Rinse fish under cold water; pat dry on paper towels. Use zester or grater to remove orange rind, being careful to scrape lightly and avoid bitter white pith. Mince rind; wrap loosely in plastic wrap.

2. Mix 2 tablespoons of orange juice squeezed from the orange, garlic, soy sauce and wine in small bowl. Put fish, skin side down, on microwave-safe plate; pour orange juice mixture over all. Let stand at room temperature, turning fish once, 15 minutes.

3. Arrange fish, skin side down, so that thickest portion is toward rim of plate. If end of fillet is thin, tuck under meatier portion of fillet. Cover tightly with plastic wrap, turning back a small corner to make a vent.

4. Microwave on high (100 percent power) until fish is firm and flakes when touched with a fork, 3 to 4 minutes. Drain juices from fish into microwave-safe 1-cup glass measure. Cover fish and let stand on counter. Stir cornstarch mixture into juices. Microwave on high until sauce boils and thickens, about 30 seconds. Stir well. Pour over fish; sprinkle reserved orange rind on top.

■ *At Arun's, a Thai restaurant in Chicago, strips of red snapper are fried until crisp, then mixed with quick-fried vegetables, and even a little pork for a delicious dish. A light sweet and sour sauce ties it all together.*

The sweet and sour sauce can be used with either the accompanying red snapper recipe, or other stir-fried favorites.

SWEET AND SOUR SNAPPER

2 servings
Preparation time: 10 minutes
Cooking time: 10 minutes

1 pound red snapper fillets
2¼ cups vegetable oil
1 teaspoon minced garlic
½ cup thinly sliced pork, optional
2 shiitake mushrooms, thinly sliced
1 medium onion, sliced
½ cup each, sliced: green and red bell peppers
1 cup sweet and sour sauce (recipe follows)

1. Rinse fish under cold water; pat dry on paper towels. Cut snapper into pieces 2 by 3 inches.

2. Heat 2 cups oil in deep saucepan or wok to 375 degrees. Deep-fry fish, 2 pieces at a time until crispy, 2 to 3 minutes. Set aside; keep warm.

3. Heat remaining ¼ cup oil in large skillet. Add garlic; cook until golden, 2 to 3 minutes. Add pork and mushrooms; cook and stir until pork is no longer pink, 2 to 3 minutes.

4. Add onion, peppers and sauce; cook and stir 5 minutes. Add snapper pieces; gently mix snapper in sauce. Serve immediately.

SWEET AND SOUR SAUCE

About 1½ cups

½ cup plus 1 tablespoon water
⅓ cup sugar
¼ cup vinegar
1 teaspoon salt
2 tablespoons each: tomato paste, cornstarch

1. Mix ½ cup water, sugar, vinegar and salt in small saucepan over medium heat; heat to boil. Whisk in tomato paste.

2. Dissolve cornstarch in 1 tablespoon water. Reduce heat under sauce, quickly stir in cornstarch. Cook and stir until smooth and thickened, 1 to 2 minutes.

A recipe for delicious, fried, whole red snapper came from Chanpen Ratana, owner of the Thai Room restaurant in Chicago. She prefers to fry the whole fish in a deep-fryer or deep kettle in a basket to keep the fish from falling apart. After frying, the oil can be strained and stored in an air-tight container to use for cooking other fish.

THAI WHOLE FRIED RED SNAPPER

2 servings
Preparation time: 30 minutes
Cooking time: 20 minutes

1 whole, cleaned red snapper, 1 to 1½ pounds
  Corn oil for deep-frying
2 tablespoons corn oil
2 teaspoons minced garlic
⅛ pound coarsely chopped pork, about ⅓ cup
¼ cup dried Chinese black mushrooms, soaked in hot water, sliced
2 tablespoons slivered fresh ginger
¾ cup light chicken or pork broth or stock
2 tablespoons each: Thai fish sauce (nam pla), sugar
1 tablespoon each: soy sauce, brown bean sauce
1½ teaspoons cornstarch dissolved in 2 tablespoons cold water
4 green onions, thinly sliced
1 small onion, coarsely chopped
1 small carrot, slivered
1 tablespoon slivered jalapeño pepper

1. Rinse fish under cold water; pat dry on paper towels. With sharp knife, score both sides of fish about ½-inch deep in crisscross pattern. Pat fish dry.

2. Heat enough corn oil in large dutch oven or deep-fryer to completely cover fish to 375 degrees. Deep-fry whole fish, turning occasionally, until skin is very crisp and golden brown, 10 to 15 minutes. Drain fish on paper towels; put on warm platter.

3. Meanwhile, heat 2 tablespoons oil in wok or large skillet; stir-fry garlic until golden. Stir in pork, mushrooms and ginger. Stir-fry until pork loses its color.

4. Stir in broth, fish sauce, sugar, soy sauce and bean sauce. Stir in cornstarch mixture, cook and stir until mixture thickens. Stir in green onions, chopped onion, carrot and jalapeño pepper. Cook until vegetables are crisp-tender, 2 minutes. Pour over fish; serve.

This Japanese-style recipe uses warm sake and soy sauce to marinate broiled salmon. The salmon is served with fresh green beans that have been tossed with a toasted sesame seed sauce. Both dishes are served warm, rather than hot, for a fuller flavor.

BROILED SALMON WITH SESAME-SAUCED GREEN BEANS

4 servings
Preparation time: 30 minutes
Cooking time: 15 minutes

4 salmon fillets, each about 1-inch thick

½ cup plus 2 tablespoons soy sauce

⅓ cup sake

1 teaspoon finely grated lemon rind

1 pound fresh green beans, trimmed

¼ cup sesame seeds

2 tablespoons mirin

1 tablespoon sugar

1. Preheat broiler. Rinse fish under cold water; pat dry on paper towels. Place in single layer on broiler pan. Broil, 6 inches from heat source, until fish flakes easily when tested with fork, about 10 minutes.

2. Meanwhile, heat ½ cup of the soy sauce and sake to boil in small saucepan. Remove from heat; add lemon rind. Pour hot sauce mixture over fish. Let stand while preparing green beans.

3. Boil beans in salted water just until crisp-tender, about 5 minutes. Drain; rinse under cold water to stop the cooking. Cut beans into thin strips.

4. Put sesame seeds in small skillet; cook and stir over low heat until very lightly toasted; do not allow to turn golden. Immediately remove sesame seeds to dish to cool. When cool, grind sesame seeds with mortar and pestle or spice grinder to a paste. Add 2 tablespoons soy sauce, mirin and sugar; stir well.

5. Put beans into bowl; spoon sesame sauce attractively over beans. Toss just before serving. Serve with salmon.

■ *Designed to celebrate the fresh ingredients of spring, this salmon entree was part of a menu developed in the test kitchen by Beverly Dillon that also included a salad of marinated asparagus and tender green beans, crisp French bread and sliced strawberries with pound cake.*

GRILLED SALMON WITH ANCHOVY BUTTER

6 servings
Preparation time: 20 minutes
Grilling time: 10 minutes

½ cup (1 stick) unsalted butter, softened

Juice of 1 lime, about 1½ tablespoons

3 anchovy fillets, patted dry

2 medium shallots, halved

½ teaspoon dried basil

¼ teaspoon freshly ground pepper

6 salmon steaks, each about ¾-inch thick

2 lemons, cut into wedges

1. Prepare grill.

2. Put butter, lime juice, anchovies, shallots, basil and pepper in food processor or blender. Process until it becomes a smooth paste.

3. When coals are covered with gray ash, rinse fish under cold water; pat dry on paper towels. Grill fish, 4 to 5 inches from hot coals, basting often with anchovy butter, until fish is opaque and almost flakes, 4 to 5 minutes per side. Put onto platter; brush with any remaining butter. Garnish with lemon wedges.

Chef John Terczak was cooking at Bigg's in Chicago when he gave this wonderful salmon recipe to The Tribune test kitchen. It was an immediate hit with all who attended the taste panel.

SALMON ORIENTAL

4 servings
Preparation time: 40 minutes
Cooking time: 20 minutes

¼ **cup whipping cream**

½ **cup (1 stick) plus 6 tablespoons cold unsalted butter, cut into small pieces**

3 **tablespoons light (low-sodium) soy sauce**

Juice from ½ lemon

4 **salmon fillets (5 to 7 ounces each), each about 1-inch thick, skinned, boned**

Freshly ground pepper

Olive oil

1 **small head napa cabbage, chopped, about 4 cups**

1 **small red bell pepper, seeded, diced**

2½ **tablespoons finely chopped fresh ginger**

2 **green onions, thinly sliced on an angle**

12 **plump raspberries**

1 **teaspoon black sesame seeds**

2 **tablespoons sliced pickled ginger**

1 **cup finely chopped fresh parsley**

1. Prepare grill. Or preheat broiler.

2. Gently boil cream in medium saucepan until reduced to 1½ tablespoons. Working off and on very low heat, whisk in butter, several pieces at a time, until sauce is frothy. (Butter must melt without becoming liquid; do not boil.) Off the heat, stir in soy sauce and lemon juice. Taste and adjust seasonings. Strain through fine sieve into small bowl. Keep in warm place until ready to serve. Do not reheat.

3. When coals are covered with gray ash, rinse fish under cold water; pat dry on paper towels. Season with pepper; coat lightly with olive oil. Grill or broil fish, 6 inches from heat source, turning once, until fish is opaque and almost flakes, about 10 minutes. Keep warm.

4. Heat ¼ cup olive oil in large sauté pan or wok over high heat. Add cabbage, red pepper, fresh ginger and green onions. Toss until vegetables are heated through and crisp-tender, about 5 minutes.

5. Distribute vegetables equally over 4 dinner plates. Put salmon fillet in middle; put 3 raspberries on the edges. Spoon some of the soy butter over each fillet. Sprinkle with sesame seeds; garnish with pickled ginger. Cover entire plate, including outside rim, with parsley. Serve immediately.

■ *If you use the microwave oven to make a fish mousse, you can eliminate the water bath necessary for the conventional oven cooking technique. Patricia Tennison developed this delicate salmon and scallop mousse for which you don't even have to butter the custard cups.*

The accompanying simple, elegant butter sauce will whip into shape easily if the butter is at room temperature. To heat, microwave the finished sauce on high power for only 10 to 15 seconds, then store in an insulated bottle to keep warm.

SALMON MOUSSE WITH BEURRE BLANC

6 servings
Preparation time: 30 minutes
Microwave cooking time: 11 to 14 minutes

1 **pound salmon fillets, skinned**
½ **pound sea scallops**
⅓ **cup minced fresh dill**
2 **tablespoons lemon juice**
1 **cup cold whipping cream**
½ **teaspoon each: grated lemon rind, salt**
⅛ **teaspoon freshly ground white pepper**

BEURRE BLANC
2 **tablespoons each: dry white wine, lemon juice**
1 **tablespoon minced shallots**
¾ **cup (1½ sticks) unsalted butter, cut into pieces, softened**
Pinch salt

Fresh dill sprigs for garnish
Red salmon roe for garnish

1. Rinse salmons and scallops under cold water; pat dry on paper towels. Cut into ½-inch pieces. Mix scallops and one-quarter of the salmon in small bowl with dill and lemon juice. Refrigerate.

2. Put remaining three-quarters of the salmon into food processor. Process with on/off turns until coarsely chopped. Add cream, lemon rind, salt and pepper. Process only until mixed.

3. Spread half of salmon-cream mixture equally over bottom of six 6-ounce custard cups. Arrange reserved scallops and salmon on top. Spoon remaining salmon-cream mixture into cups to fill each to the top. Cover with plastic wrap. Press down firmly on plastic wrap to pack mixture firmly into cups.

4. Microwave on medium (50 percent power) 2 minutes. Then microwave on low (30 percent power) until edges are firm and knife inserted in middle comes out almost dry, 6 to 8 minutes (or 135 degrees in center on an instant-read thermometer). Let stand 5 minutes.

5. Meanwhile, for beurre blanc, put wine, lemon juice and shallots in 1-quart microwave-safe bowl. Microwave on high (100 percent power) until liquid is reduced to about 1 tablespoon, 3 to 4 minutes. Vigorously whisk in butter until sauce is foamy. Taste and adjust seasonings.

6. Pour some of the beurre blanc onto each serving plate. Turn salmon mousse out onto small plate; transfer to center of plate with sauce. Garnish with dill sprig; scatter salmon roe over beurre blanc.

NOTE: The mousse will have a fuller flavor if served slightly warm or at room temperature. To store for up to 2 days, cover with plastic wrap and refrigerate. Let stand at room temperature 10 minutes; unmold and serve.

Olive oil—a monounsaturated fat that is believed to help reduce cholesterol—is added to this sea bass recipe for flavor. You can eliminate the olive oil, if you like, and drop 13.5 grams of fat from the entire recipe.

SEA BASS PROVENÇAL

4 servings
Preparation time: 10 minutes
Microwave cooking time: 6 to 6½ minutes

4 sea bass or sole fillets, about 1 pound total

1 can (16 ounces) plum tomatoes, drained, chopped

1 green pepper, seeded, julienned

1 small onion, sliced ⅛-inch thick

1 tablespoon olive oil

2 garlic cloves, minced

¼ teaspoon each: dried leaf oregano, sugar

⅛ teaspoon each: salt, freshly ground black pepper

¼ teaspoon cornstarch dissolved in 1 tablespoon cold water

¼ cup sliced black olives

1. Rinse fish under cold water; pat dry on paper towels. Mix tomatoes, green pepper, onion, olive oil, garlic, oregano, sugar, salt and pepper in 2-quart microwave-safe casserole. Cover tightly with plastic wrap, turning back a small corner to make a vent. Microwave on high (100 percent power) 2 minutes.

2. Push vegetables to side. Arrange fish in casserole skin side down with thickest portion to outside. If one end of fillet is thin, tuck under meatier portion of fillet. Spoon vegetables over fish. Cover tightly with plastic wrap, turning back a small corner to make a vent.

3. Microwave on high until fish is opaque and almost flakes, 3½ to 4 minutes. Drain juices into 1-cup microwave-safe glass measure. Cover fish; let stand on counter.

4. Stir cornstarch mixture into juices. Microwave on high until sauce boils and thickens, about 30 seconds. Stir well. Pour sauce over fish and vegetables. Sprinkle olives over all.

Garden-fresh tomatoes contrast beautifully with the bite of vinegar and slightly sharp taste of feta cheese in this recipe inspired by a similar dish served at Shaw's Crab House in Chicago. Quality olive oil truly does have a different flavor, one that comes through even in small quantities.

GRILLED SHARK WITH TOMATO-FETA RELISH

4 servings
Preparation time: 25 minutes
Grilling time: 5 to 8 minutes

2 **large tomatoes, peeled, seeded, chopped**
¼ **cup diced feta cheese**
3 **tablespoons minced flat-leaf parsley**
2 **tablespoons extra-virgin olive oil**
2 **tablespoons minced fresh basil or 1 teaspoon dried**
1 **tablespoon red wine vinegar**
⅛ **teaspoon minced garlic**
   Salt, freshly ground pepper to taste
1½ **pounds fresh shark or tuna steaks, about 1-inch thick**
   Olive oil
   Tomato wedges, fresh parsley for garnish

1. Prepare grill or preheat broiler.

2. For relish, mix tomatoes, cheese, parsley, 2 tablespoons oil, basil, vinegar, garlic, salt and pepper in medium bowl.

3. When coals are covered with gray ash, rinse fish under cold water; pat dry on paper towels. Brush lightly with olive oil. Grill or broil fish, about 6 inches from heat source, turning once, until medium-rare, 5 to 6 minutes (7 to 8 minutes for medium).

4. Put fish on warm serving plates. Put a spoonful of the relish alongside fish. Garnish with tomato wedges and parsley. Serve immediately.

NOTE: This recipe also makes a great fresh fish salad. Prepare the relish as directed. Then grill fish to medium, about 7 to 8 minutes. Cool fish to room temperature. Coarsely shred into large bowl. Add relish; toss to mix. Serve over torn lettuce leaves with a drizzle of olive oil and a sprinkle of freshly ground black pepper. Garnish with additional hunks of feta cheese.

Underutilized fish such as skate are bargains in disguise, as seen in this recipe from The Tribune *test kitchen. Skate, like scallops, doesn't have bones, but check the edges of the fillets for any tough pieces of skin that may remain.*

DEEP-FRIED SKATE AND ONIONS

3 to 4 servings
Preparation time: 25 minutes
Marinating time: 2 hours
Cooking time: 15 minutes

1 **pound skate fillets**
½ **cup olive oil**
¼ **cup fresh lemon juice**
4 **slices onion, separated into rings**
1 **tablespoon finely chopped fresh parsley**
2 **cloves garlic, finely chopped**
¾ **teaspoon salt**
¼ **teaspoon each: dried leaf oregano, freshly ground pepper, dried leaf thyme**
   Oil for deep-frying
1½ **cups all-purpose flour**
2 **teaspoons baking powder**
3 **carrots, cut into julienne strips, steamed until crisp-tender**
   Lemon wedges
   Dijon mustard, optional

1. Rinse fish under cold water; pat dry on paper towels. Cut into 2-inch pieces. Mix olive oil, lemon juice, onion rings, parsley, garlic, ½ teaspoon salt, oregano, pepper and thyme in shallow, nonmetal dish. Add fish; toss to coat. Refrigerate, covered, 2 hours.

2. Heat 2 inches of oil in deep saucepan or deep-fryer to 375 degrees. Mix flour, baking powder and remaining ¼ teaspoon salt in bowl.

3. Remove fish and onions from marinade; drain. Dredge fish in flour mixture, shaking off excess. Deep-fry fish, a few pieces at a time, until fish is opaque and coating is browned, 2 to 2½ minutes. Drain; keep warm while preparing remaining fish. Dredge onion rings in remaining flour and deep-fry until golden.

4. Arrange fish and onions on warm platter. Garnish with steamed carrots and lemon wedges. Serve with mustard.

■ *Swordfish on the grill succeeds due to the meaty texture of the fish. For added flavor, this recipe adds jalapeño pepper, garlic and basil to the butter topping.*

SWORDFISH WITH SPICY BASIL BUTTER

4 servings
Preparation time: 15 minutes
Grilling time: 10 minutes

¼ cup (½ stick) unsalted butter, softened
1 tablespoon each, minced: onion, fresh basil or 1 teaspoon dried
½ teaspoon each, minced: garlic, fresh ginger, jalapeño or serrano pepper
4 swordfish fillets, about 8 ounces each

1. Prepare charcoal grill or preheat broiler.

2. Put butter into small bowl. Beat until fluffy. Add onion, basil, garlic, ginger and jalapeño pepper. Mix well. Refrigerate until needed.

3. When coals are covered with gray ash, rinse fish under cold water; pat dry on paper towels. Grill or broil fish, 6 inches from heat source, until fish is opaque and almost flakes, 7 to 10 minutes.

4. Put fish onto serving plates. Put a dollop of the flavored butter on top of each hot fish fillet. Serve immediately.

NOTE: If desired, you can also gently heat this mixture and use it as a hot butter sauce.

■ *Tilefish, native to the Atlantic Ocean, eat a diet of shrimp, lobster and clams, giving them a delicate and sweet flavor. In this recipe beaten egg white is mixed with tartar sauce for a puffy topping.*

PUFFY BROILED TILEFISH

2 to 4 servings
Preparation time: 10 minutes
Broiling time: 12 minutes

1 pound tilefish fillets
Salt, freshly ground pepper to taste
2 tablespoons melted butter
¼ cup tartar sauce
1 egg white, beaten stiff

1. Preheat broiler. Rinse fish under cold water; pat dry on paper towels. Put fillets on well-oiled broiler pan. Season with salt and pepper and brush with melted butter.

2. Broil, 4 inches from heat source, until fish is opaque and almost flakes easily with fork, 8 to 10 minutes.

3. Meanwhile, gently fold tartar sauce into beaten egg white. Spread over fish and broil until topping is golden, about 2 more minutes. Serve immediately.

■ *Patricia Tennison suggests covering fish fillets with plastic wrap while microwaving them to keep them moist, as in her orange roughy with tarragon.*

ORANGE ROUGHY WITH TARRAGON

2 to 4 servings
Preparation time: 15 minutes
Microwave cooking time: 4 to 6 minutes

1 **pound orange roughy fillets (or sole, flounder, turbot or other mild white fish)**
2 **tablespoons olive oil**
   Juice from ½ lemon
8 **large sprigs of fresh tarragon or 1½ teaspoons dried**
¼ **teaspoon each: salt, freshly ground pepper**

1. Rinse fish under cold water; pat dry on paper towels. Mix olive oil, lemon juice, tarragon, salt and pepper on microwave-safe plate. Add fish to oil mixture and turn. Arrange fish on plate with thickest portion to the outside, tucking under thinnest part of fillet for more even cooking. Let stand 10 minutes to marinate.

2. Cover fish tightly with plastic wrap. Microwave on high (100 percent power) until fish is just opaque and firm to the touch, 2 to 4 minutes. Lift fish—and tarragon sprigs, if using—carefully to another plate. Cover lightly to keep warm.

3. Put plate with juices back in the microwave. Do not cover. Microwave on high to slightly reduce juices, about 2 minutes. Stir well. Pour over fish and serve.

NOTE: If fish flakes and breaks up as you move it, you've cooked it too long; make a note to cook it 1 minute less next time, then check the fish every 20 seconds.

Broiled fresh tuna, sprinkled with herbs and spices, is presented on a creamy mustard and horseradish sauce, then topped with chopped avocado. The idea and the skills needed to cook it up in The Tribune *test kitchen earned Dorothy DeVries-Wolf of Palatine, Illinois, third place in the 1986 Seafood Contest sponsored by* The Tribune *and the Chicago Fish House.*

TUNA FILLETS CREOLE

2 servings
Preparation time: 40 minutes
Cooking time: 20 minutes

1¼ cups fish stock or chicken broth

½ cup whipping cream

2 tablespoons country-style Dijon mustard

1 generous teaspoon prepared horseradish

1 teaspoon catsup

2 fresh tuna fillets (or swordfish or halibut), about 6 ounces each

Vegetable oil

Salt, freshly ground pepper to taste

Lemon juice

Fresh or dried minced thyme

Chopped fresh parsley

Garlic powder, optional

1 avocado, peeled, chopped, sprinkled with lime juice

1. Put fish stock in small nonaluminum saucepan. Boil gently until reduced by half. Add cream. Boil gently until thick enough to coat back of spoon, about 5 minutes. Stir in mustard, horseradish and catsup. Keep warm.

2. Preheat broiler. Rinse fish under cold water; pat dry on paper towels. Lightly oil fish. Sprinkle lightly with salt, pepper, lemon juice, thyme, parsley and garlic powder. Broil, on lightly oiled broiler pan, 6 inches from heat source, until instant-read thermometer registers about 130 degrees. Turning isn't necessary.

3. Mix a few tablespoons of the sauce with the avocado. Divide remainder of sauce between 2 serving plates. Put fish on top of sauce. Top with avocado-sauce mixture.

Carlos' restaurant in Highland Park has won rave reviews from restaurant critics for its outstanding food, thanks to talented chef Roland Liccioni. The Tribune challenged Liccioni to create a recipe especially for the microwave oven. Here is the result: a simple yet refined fish entree.

TURBOT WITH BASIL

2 servings
Preparation time: 15 minutes
Marinating time: Overnight
Microwave cooking time: 1½ minutes

2 boneless skinless turbot fillets, 3 ounces each, or other lean white fish

1 large tomato, peeled, diced

1 teaspoon olive oil

3 fresh basil leaves, julienned

½ teaspoon coarse (kosher) salt

2 teaspoons fresh lemon juice

1 teaspoon butter

1. Rinse fish under cold water; pat dry on paper towels. Mix tomato, olive oil, basil and salt in small bowl or cup. Put each fish fillet on microwave-safe plate. Pour tomato mixture over each fillet. Cover with plastic wrap and refrigerate overnight.

2. To serve, sprinkle each fillet with 1 teaspoon lemon juice and dot with ½ teaspoon butter. Cover with plastic wrap. Microwave each plate separately on high (100 percent power) until fish is opaque, about 1½ minutes. Let stand, covered, 1 minute. Then carefully drain off excess juice into a small dish to serve with rice or noodles. Serve fish immediately.

■ *Jim Guth, owner of Chicago Caterers, personally attends each of his catered parties to keep in touch with the host. Guests often can expect the unexpected from Guth, such as this grilled bass with green tomato relish.*

MARINATED GRILLED BASS WITH GREEN TOMATO RELISH

8 servings
Preparation time: 30 minutes
Marinating time: 1 to 1½ hours
Grilling time: 20 minutes

MARINADE

- 1 **cup olive oil**
- ½ **cup fresh lime juice**
- ¼ **cup chopped fresh herbs (such as basil, parsley, tarragon)**
- 3 **tablespoons Dijon mustard**
- 1 **tablespoon each: chopped lime rind, paprika, coarsely ground black pepper**
- 2 **teaspoons drained capers**
- 3 **cloves garlic, minced**
- 1 **teaspoon each: salt, cayenne pepper**

FOR FISH

- 8 **bass fillets, about 4 pounds total**
- 2 **red onions, halved**
- 2 **bunches green onions**
- 1 **lemon, cut into wedges**
  Minced flat-leaf parsley for garnish
  Green tomato relish (recipe follows)

1. For marinade, mix all ingredients in large non-aluminum dish. Rinse fish under cold water; pat dry on paper towels. Add fish and onions to marinade. Refrigerate, covered, turning occasionally, 1 to 1½ hours.

2. Prepare grill or preheat broiler. Heat oven to 350 degrees. Remove fish and onions from marinade. Lightly score fish skin with the tip of a sharp knife.

3. Grill or broil onions, 6 inches from heat source, until crisp-tender, 5 to 10 minutes. Add fish, skin side up; cook 3 minutes. Turn fish skin side down, continue cooking, another 2 minutes. Transfer fish to baking pan. Bake until fish almost flakes easily with fork, about 5 minutes. Continue grilling onions until tender.

4. Serve fish surrounded with grilled onions, lemon wedges and parsley. Pass green tomato relish.

Green Tomato Relish | 8 servings

1½ cups sugar
1 cup white vinegar
6 medium green
   tomatoes, chopped
2 medium red tomatoes,
   chopped
1 medium red bell
   pepper, seeded,
   chopped
½ cup each: olive oil,
   minced fresh cilantro
   (coriander) leaves
2 tablespoons Dijon
   mustard
6 cloves garlic, minced
1 jalapeño pepper,
   seeded, minced, or
   1 teaspoon crushed
   red pepper flakes
1 bunch green onions,
   sliced

1. Put all ingredients, except green onions, in large nonaluminum saucepan. Simmer over low heat, stirring often, until most of the liquid has evaporated and vegetables are very tender, about 2 hours. Cool. Stir in green onions. Refrigerate until chilled.

Catfish is catching on because of its mild, white flesh. Instead of frying it in the southern tradition, try grilling it and serving it with a Dijon mustard sauce.

Grilled Fillet of Catfish with Dijon Mustard

4 servings
Preparation time: 10 minutes
Standing time: 30 minutes
Grilling time: 10 minutes

   Mesquite or hickory
   chips, optional
4 catfish fillets
3 tablespoons Dijon
   mustard
   Salt, freshly ground
   pepper to taste
   Vegetable oil

1. Prepare grill. Soak wood chips in water at least 20 minutes. Rinse fish under cold water; pat dry on paper towels.

2. Coat each side of each catfish fillet with ¾ tablespoon mustard. Let stand 30 minutes. Salt and pepper to taste.

3. When coals are covered with gray ash, sprinkle wood chips over coals. Brush grill rack lightly with oil. Put fish in oiled grill basket. Grill, 6 inches from coals, until fish almost flakes, 3 to 5 minutes per side. Serve immediately.

Beverly Dillon created this recipe for down-home–style fried catfish complete with hush puppies. She suggests using farm-raised catfish for a milder taste; it is becoming more available in supermarkets and fish stores.

For a flavorful twist on hush puppies, two cups of mashed sweet potatoes are added to the cornmeal batter along with onions and seasonings. Use a light hand when stirring; overmixing will give the hush puppies a tough texture.

CORNMEAL-FRIED CATFISH WITH BARBECUE SAUCE AND SWEET POTATO HUSH PUPPIES

6 servings
Preparation time: 10 minutes
Cooking time: 15 minutes

1 **cup buttermilk**

2 **large eggs**

2 **cups each: stone-ground yellow cornmeal, all-purpose flour**

1 **tablespoon each: salt, paprika, onion powder**

2 **teaspoons each: cayenne pepper, freshly ground black pepper, salt, dry mustard**

Vegetable oil for deep-frying

3 **pounds catfish fillets (see note)**

Homemade barbecue sauce (recipe follows)

Sweet potato hush puppies (recipe follows)

1. Beat buttermilk and eggs in shallow dish. Mix cornmeal, flour, salt, paprika, onion powder, cayenne pepper, black pepper, salt and dry mustard in another shallow dish.

2. Pour oil to depth of about 2½ inches in deep-fryer or deep saucepan. Heat oil to 350 degrees.

3. Rinse fish under cold water; pat dry on paper towels. Dip each fillet into buttermilk mixture. Hold over bowl to allow excess to drip off into bowl. Then dredge fillets in cornmeal mixture, pressing mixture firmly into the fish; gently shake off any excess.

4. Deep-fry fish, a few at a time, in hot oil, until golden brown and crisp, about 5 minutes. Remove with slotted spoon. Drain on paper towels; keep warm while frying the remaining fish. Serve immediately with barbecue sauce and hush puppies.

NOTE: Other fresh fish fillets, or even frozen fillets, such as whiting, may be substituted.

Homemade Barbecue Sauce | About 1 cup

½ cup each: catsup, chili
  sauce
1 tablespoon each:
  orange juice,
  prepared yellow or
  Dijon mustard, brown
  sugar
2 teaspoons each: lemon
  juice, Worcestershire
  sauce
1½ teaspoons chili powder
¼ teaspoon each:
  cayenne pepper,
  freshly ground black
  pepper

1. Mix all ingredients in small bowl. Spoon into jar with tight-fitting lid. Refrigerate up to 2 weeks.

Sweet Potato Hush Puppies | 6 servings

1 cup buttermilk
3 large eggs, lightly
  beaten
1 large or 2 medium
  sweet potatoes,
  cooked, mashed,
  about 2 cups
2 green onions, chopped
1½ cups each: stone-
  ground yellow
  cornmeal, all-purpose
  flour
1 tablespoon sugar
2 teaspoons baking
  powder
½ teaspoon salt
  Vegetable oil for deep-
  frying (see note)

1. Beat buttermilk and eggs in large bowl. Beat in sweet potatoes and onions.

2. Mix cornmeal, flour, sugar, baking powder and salt in large bowl. Make a well in center of dry ingredients. Pour egg mixture into well. Using a fork, stir just enough to moisten dry ingredients. Do not overmix.

3. Pour oil to depth of about 2½ inches in deep-fryer or deep saucepan. Heat oil to 350 degrees.

4. To cook hush puppies, carefully drop batter by the tablespoonful into hot oil. Do not crowd. Fry gently, turning with slotted spoon until dark golden brown on each side and cooked through, 2 to 3 minutes. Remove to paper towels to drain. Cover lightly with foil to keep warm. Repeat to fry all the batter.

NOTE: You may use the same oil in which you have fried the catfish.

"Exciting," and "the best aroma—you could smell this across the room," the judges said of the following recipe which William H. Schmit III of Chicago submitted and cooked up in the test kitchen to win first place in the 1984 Tribune Food Guide Seafood Recipe Contest.

UPTOWN FISH WITH SAFFRON RICE

4 servings
Preparation time: 30 minutes
Marinating time: 30 minutes
Cooking time: 10 minutes

½ **pound catfish fillets or swordfish, whitefish or shrimp**

½ **pound fresh shrimp**

3 **green onions, white and green parts reserved separately**

2 **stalks lemon grass**

1 **small piece fresh ginger, 1-inch long by ½-inch square**

¼ **teaspoon saffron powder or a pinch of saffron threads**

1¼ **tablespoons fish or shrimp sauce or 1½ teaspoons light soy sauce**

1 **tablespoon Oriental chili paste**

Saffron rice (recipe follows)

2 **tablespoons oil**

1 **medium yellow onion, minced**

½ **cup thick unsweetened coconut milk**

Small bunch fresh cilantro (coriander), chopped

Chopped green onion tops for garnish

1. Rinse fish under cold water; pat dry on paper towels. Remove bones and skin of catfish. Cut into small pieces. Shell and devein shrimp.

2. Slice white part of green onions into extremely thin ringlets. Slice the lemon grass even thinner (use only the very whitest part). Peel ginger and cut into thin julienne. Put green onions, lemon grass and ginger into a large glass bowl. Add saffron, fish sauce and chili paste. Mix well. Add catfish and shrimp; cover with plastic wrap. Refrigerate 20 to 30 minutes.

3. Meanwhile, make the rice recipe that follows.

4. Heat oil in a heavy saucepan until it pops. Reduce heat to low, add minced onion and sauté slowly until transparent. Add fish mixture, increase heat to medium; sauté until shrimp start to curl and look cooked, about 2 minutes.

5. Add coconut milk; stir carefully, bringing to slight bubble. Reduce heat; simmer another 2 minutes. Do not overcook.

6. Serve spooned over saffron rice. Sprinkle liberally with cilantro and green onions.

SAFFRON RICE | 4 servings

2 cups chicken broth
    (or water and 1 large
    chicken bouillon
    cube)
Pinch saffron threads
1½ teaspoons oil or butter
1 medium onion, cut into
    long strips
1 cup long-grain rice

1. Heat broth to boil; put into glass measure; add saffron. Heat oil in medium saucepan over medium heat. Add onion; sauté until transparent. Turn heat to high, and while stirring vigorously, add rice. Stir until rice is covered with oil and smells as if it will start burning soon. Quickly add broth mixture. Heat to boil; cover tightly and reduce heat to very low and simmer for 15 minutes.

2. Remove from heat and set lid ajar; let rest for a few minutes. Serve warm.

NOTE: Lemon grass, chili paste, fish sauce and unsweetened coconut milk are available at most Oriental or Thai grocery stores.

Terry Roy of Chicago walked away with the first-place prize (a trip to France to study French cooking) in the 1986 Seafood Recipe Contest cosponsored by The Tribune and the Chicago Fish House. Her winning recipe? An elegantly simple treatment for coho salmon.

COHO BERTEAU

2 to 4 servings
Preparation time: 20 minutes
Cooking time: 10 minutes

⅓ cup butter
1 avocado, peeled, finely
    chopped
    Juice of ½ lemon
1 red bell pepper,
    roasted, peeled,
    julienned
3 tablespoons vegetable
    oil
1 pound baby coho
    fillets (see note)
4 to 6 pea pods,
    julienned
    Seasoned salt, freshly
    ground pepper to
    taste

1. Mix butter, avocado, lemon juice and red pepper in small saucepan. Rinse fish under cold water; pat dry on paper towels.

2. Heat oil in large skillet. Add fish and pea pods in single layer. Sauté over medium-high heat until fish almost flakes, about 2 minutes per side. Remove to serving platter. Season with salt and pepper.

3. Heat avocado mixture until barely warm. Spoon over fish and serve immediately.

NOTE: Whole baby coho may be used instead of fillets; cooking time will be slightly longer.

From the heart of the Midwest comes this Great Lakes whitefish with golden tomato butter sauce featured at Harlan "Pete" Peterson's Tapawingo restaurant in Ellsworth, Michigan. Use tweezers to help remove pin bones from the whitefish fillets.

WHITEFISH WITH GOLDEN TOMATO BUTTER SAUCE

6 servings
Preparation time: 25 minutes
Cooking time: 15 minutes

1½ cups chopped golden tomatoes (see note)

¼ cup each: white wine vinegar, fresh lemon juice

2 tablespoons minced shallots

¾ to 1 cup (1½ to 2 sticks) cold, unsalted butter, cut in ½-inch pieces

Salt, freshly ground white pepper, sugar and lemon juice to taste

6 fresh whitefish fillets, 8 to 10 ounces each, trimmed, with pin bones removed

½ cup all-purpose flour

3 tablespoons clarified butter

Golden cherry or pear tomatoes, halved for garnish (see note)

Snipped chives for garnish

Minced red bell pepper for garnish

New potatoes, steamed until crisp-tender

Assorted miniature vegetables, steamed until crisp-tender

1. For sauce, heat chopped tomatoes to boil in small nonaluminum saucepan. Simmer gently until reduced to ½ cup. Push pulp through fine sieve. Reserve.

2. Heat vinegar, lemon juice and shallots to boil in second nonaluminum saucepan. Cook until reduced to 1½ tablespoons. Stir in tomato pulp.

3. Remove saucepan from heat; immediately beat in chilled butter, piece by piece, until sauce is smooth and creamy. Season with salt, pepper and, if desired, a pinch of sugar and lemon juice. Do not allow sauce to boil. Keep warm.

4. Rinse fish under cold water; pat dry on paper towels. Spread flour over bottom of large plate. Stir in salt and pepper to taste. Coat fish fillets lightly.

5. Heat clarified butter in large skillet over medium heat until medium-hot. Add fish in single layer, skin side up. Cook 3 minutes. Turn fish over; cook skin side down until flesh is just opaque. Repeat with remaining fish, adding a little more butter if necessary. (To speed the process, cook fish in 2 skillets at same time.)

6. Spoon tomato butter sauce onto 6 warm dinner plates. Put a fillet on each plate. Garnish with cherry tomatoes, chives and red pepper. Serve with new potatoes and miniature vegetables.

NOTE: Out of season, use canned Italian plum tomatoes and red cherry tomatoes in place of golden tomatoes.

John Husar's favorite way of eating smelt calls for hot and spicy tomato juice cocktail. "Some people use beer, or even lemon-lime soda," says Husar, The Tribune's outdoors writer. "If you don't like the tomato juice flavor, you can soak the fish in cocktail mix for Bloody Marys. The result is super."

SPICY FRIED SMELT

3 to 4 servings
Preparation time: 15 minutes
Marinating time: 1 to 2 hours
Cooking time: 10 minutes

1½ **pounds fresh smelt, cleaned**

1 **cup hot and spicy tomato juice cocktail**

1¼ **cups buttermilk baking mix**

¼ **teaspoon each: salt, freshly ground pepper**

⅛ **teaspoon garlic powder**

Vegetable oil for frying

¼ **cup freshly grated Parmesan cheese**

1. Rinse smelt under cold water; pat dry on paper towels. Pour juice over smelt in large nonaluminum bowl. Refrigerate, covered, 1 to 2 hours.

2. Mix buttermilk baking mix, salt, pepper and garlic powder in shallow dish.

3. Pour oil to depth of 1 inch in large skillet. Heat to 350 degrees.

4. Remove smelt from juice; dredge in flour mixture. Fry in hot oil, turning, until crisp and golden, 3 to 4 minutes. Remove with slotted spoon. Drain on paper towels. Repeat to fry all smelt. Serve immediately, sprinkled with Parmesan cheese.

Whether just pulled from Lake Michigan or from the grocery fish section, the taste of smelt benefits from this Cajun batter-fried recipe.

BATTER-FRIED CAJUN SMELT

4 to 5 servings
Preparation time: 20 minutes
Standing time: 30 minutes
Cooking time: 5 minutes

Dipping sauces (recipes follow)

2 pounds fresh, cleaned smelt

1¼ cups milk

2 large eggs

½ cup each: yellow cornmeal, all-purpose flour

1 teaspoon each: sugar, salt

¼ teaspoon each: cayenne pepper, onion powder, garlic powder, freshly ground black pepper, dried leaf thyme, dried basil

Vegetable oil for deep-frying

1. Make dipping sauces.

2. Rinse smelt under cold water; pat dry on paper towels. Refrigerate, covered.

3. Beat milk and eggs in large shallow dish. Stir in remaining ingredients, except oil, until smooth. Let batter sit about 30 minutes.

4. Pour oil to depth of 2 inches in deep-fryer or deep saucepan. Heat oil to 350 degrees. Maintain oil at 350 degrees by adjusting heat during frying process.

5. Dip a few smelt into batter; let excess batter drain off. Deep-fry smelt, a few at a time, turning with slotted spoon, until golden, 2 to 3 minutes. Remove with slotted spoon; drain on paper towels. Repeat to fry all smelt. Serve immediately with dipping sauces.

HOT MUSTARD DIPPING SAUCE

About ⅓ cup

¼ cup dry mustard powder

2 teaspoons Oriental sesame oil

1 to 2 tablespoons warm water

1. Put mustard and oil into small bowl. Add enough warm water to make a thin, smooth sauce. Let stand 15 minutes before serving.

QUICK REMOULADE DIPPING SAUCE | About 1⅔ cups

½ cup each: mayonnaise, chili sauce

1 small green pepper, diced

1 rib celery, minced

2 green onions, minced

2 tablespoons fresh lemon juice

1 tablespoon each: country-style Dijon mustard, minced fresh parsley

½ teaspoon paprika

⅛ teaspoon cayenne pepper

1. Mix all ingredients in small bowl. Let stand 15 minutes before serving. Taste and adjust seasonings.

The Cajun cooking craze made them popular, but little excuse is needed to enjoy crayfish, the "little lobsters" from Louisiana. This recipe uses ice cubes to cool down the liquid when cooking live crayfish. The ice prevents overcooking, and the crayfish cooling in their liquid will soak up more flavor before they're served.

SPICY BOILED CRAYFISH

6 to 8 appetizer servings
Preparation time: 15 minutes
Cooking time: 20 minutes

5 pounds live crayfish

3 stalks celery, chopped

1 medium onion, chopped

1 lemon, quartered

2 tablespoons cayenne pepper

1 tablespoon each: salt, whole allspice

2 teaspoons whole black peppercorns

10 whole cloves

¼ teaspoon nutmeg

Several trays of ice cubes

Lemon wedges

Hot pepper sauce

1. Rinse crayfish very well to remove dirt. Put crayfish into large pot of cool water; let stand 20 minutes.

2. Heat 6 quarts water to boil in 9- or 12-quart stockpot. Add remaining ingredients through nutmeg. Heat to boil; reduce heat. Simmer, partly covered, over medium heat 15 minutes.

3. Return cooking liquid to boil; drain crayfish well. Add crayfish to cooking liquid. Heat to boil again. As soon as water boils, remove from heat. Immediately add several trays of ice cubes to stop the cooking. Stir well. Let stand 20 minutes. Drain well.

4. Serve chilled with lemon wedges squeezed over and a dash of hot pepper sauce.

Inspired by the herby, aromatic version of this dish at Bruna's restaurant in Chicago, this Tribune test kitchen recipe treats fresh mussels to a simmered marinara sauce.

MUSSELS WITH MARINARA SAUCE

4 servings
Preparation time: 45 minutes
Cooking time: 25 minutes

4 pounds fresh mussels in the shell

½ cup each: water, white wine

¼ cup olive oil

2 medium onions, chopped

1 tablespoon minced garlic

1 can (28 ounces) Italian-style plum tomatoes with basil

1 green pepper, seeded, diced

2 whole green hot finger peppers

¼ teaspoon each: dried basil, dried leaf oregano

⅛ teaspoon each: sugar, salt, freshly ground pepper

½ pound fresh mushrooms, sliced

3 tablespoons minced flat-leaf parsley

1. Scrub mussels clean under running water, using a stiff-bristle brush. Cut off stringy beard from shells with knife or scissors. Put into large kettle; add water and wine. Set aside.

2. Heat oil in large skillet until hot. Add onion and garlic; cook and stir until golden brown. Stir in tomatoes, green pepper, whole finger peppers, basil, oregano, sugar, salt and pepper. Simmer, stirring often and breaking up tomatoes, 15 minutes.

3. Set pan of mussels over high heat. Heat to boil; cover pan tightly; cook just until mussels open slightly, 3 to 4 minutes. Do not overcook. Strain over bowl to catch cooking liquid. Stir ½ cup of the cooking liquid and mushrooms into tomato sauce. Adjust seasonings in sauce to taste. Sprinkle with parsley.

4. At this point, you may simply stir mussels into sauce. Serve with lots of napkins and eat with fingers, breaking open mussels and using shell to scoop up sauce. Or, for a more formal presentation, remove mussels from shells before adding to sauce. Serve over cooked pasta if desired.

For Valentine's Day, Fresh Starts Bakery and Catering in Flossmoor, Illinois, suggested this lobster salad for two. A generous serving of gently simmered lobster tail with a dollop of avocado mayonnaise and a raspberry vinaigrette make an indulgent main course.

LOBSTER SALAD WITH AVOCADO MAYONNAISE

2 servings
Preparation time: 30 minutes
Cooking time: 6 minutes

1 large or 2 small
   lobster tails

LOBSTER POACHING LIQUID

1¼ cups dry white wine

¼ cup each: raspberry-
   flavored liqueur,
   water

   White part of 1 leek,
   julienned

   Juice of 1 lemon

RASPBERRY VINAIGRETTE

⅔ cup walnut oil

⅓ cup raspberry vinegar
   (see recipe, page
   648) or store-bought

¼ cup raspberry puree
   (see note)

1 tablespoon sugar

¼ teaspoon white pepper

SALAD

4 cups torn, assorted
   salad greens

1 ripe avocado, peeled,
   sliced

1 large grapefruit,
   peeled, sectioned

¼ cup shredded radicchio
   or red cabbage

AVOCADO MAYONNAISE

½ ripe avocado

¼ cup mayonnaise
   Salt, pepper to taste

1. Thaw lobster tails if frozen. Put lobster poaching ingredients into medium saucepan. Heat to simmer. Add lobster tails; return to simmer. Simmer until lobster is pink and meat is opaque, 4 to 6 minutes, depending on size. Drain; cool lobster. Remove meat from shells and slice into rounds.

2. For raspberry vinaigrette, put all ingredients into jar with tight-fitting lid. Shake well.

3. For salad, arrange salad greens on serving plates. Arrange lobster slices, avocado slices and grapefruit sections over greens. Put a small pile of shredded radicchio in center of salad.

4. For avocado mayonnaise, mash avocado and mayonnaise in small bowl. Stir in salt and pepper.

5. Serve salad with a dollop of avocado mayonnaise in middle. Drizzle with raspberry vinaigrette. Pass remaining vinaigrette. Serve immediately.

NOTE: For raspberry puree, push ½ cup fresh or frozen raspberries through fine sieve to extract seeds.

Available only for a few months in late spring and early summer, soft-shell crabs—Maryland blue crabs that have shed their shells in their growing season—are one of America's true delicacies. Crabs really need no embellishment, but the simple sauces below from The Tribune test kitchen add interest to a do-it-yourself crabfest. Allow two large or three small crabs per person.

SAUTÉED SOFT-SHELL CRABS

2 servings
Preparation time: 15 minutes
Cooking time: 7 minutes

Dipping sauces
(recipes follow),
optional
6 soft-shell crabs,
cleaned, rinsed
Flour seasoned with
pepper
3 tablespoons unsalted
butter
Lemon wedges,
parsley for garnish

1. Make dipping sauces.

2. Pat crabs dry. Dredge lightly in flour; shake off excess. Heat butter in large, well-seasoned skillet over medium heat. Add crabs in single layer. Cook, turning once, until crispy and browned, 4 to 7 minutes depending on size. Remove from skillet with slotted spatula.

3. Serve immediately with desired dipping sauce. Garnish with lemon wedges and parsley.

TERIYAKI SAUCE | About ½ cup

½ cup teriyaki sauce
1 tablespoon each,
julienned: fresh
ginger, green onions
¼ teaspoon wasabi
powder (Japanese
green horseradish)
Pinch sugar

1. Mix all ingredients in small bowl.

BLACK BUTTER
(BEURRE NOIR) | About ⅔ cup

⅔ cup unsalted butter
1 teaspoon minced
parsley
2 tablespoons fresh
lemon juice
Salt, freshly ground
pepper to taste

1. Heat butter in small skillet until well browned but not burned. Add parsley and cook 1 minute. Add lemon juice, salt and pepper. Serve hot.

Beverly Dillon devised this recipe for sauteed soft-shell crabs served on a bed of vermicelli and toasted walnuts. It's rich and oh-so-satisfying.

SOFT-SHELL CRABS WITH WALNUT-TARRAGON VERMICELLI

2 servings
Preparation time: 20 minutes
Cooking time: 10 minutes

¼ **pound vermicelli noodles**

7 **tablespoons butter**

⅓ **cup coarsely chopped walnuts**

¼ **cup finely chopped fresh parsley**

1 **teaspoon dried tarragon**

¼ **cup all-purpose flour**

¼ **teaspoon each: salt, freshly ground pepper**

4 **soft-shelled crabs, cleaned, rinsed**

1 **tablespoon fresh lemon juice**

Lemon wedges, parsley for garnish

1. Cook vermicelli according to package directions until al dente. Drain; keep warm.

2. Melt 1½ tablespoons of the butter in large skillet over medium heat. Add walnuts; cook until lightly browned, about 1 minute. Add parsley and tarragon. Toss to mix and cook about 1 minute. Remove skillet from heat; transfer mixture with slotted spoon to small bowl.

3. Put flour, salt and pepper in large, shallow dish. Dredge crabs lightly in flour mixture; shake off excess.

4. Heat 4 tablespoons of the remaining butter in same skillet until hot. Add crabs in single layer. Cook over medium-high heat, turning occasionally, until crispy and browned, about 5 minutes. Transfer to 2 serving plates. Sprinkle with lemon juice and keep warm.

5. Add remaining butter to skillet; heat until melted. Add vermicelli and walnut mixture. Toss until well mixed. Divide evenly onto plates. Garnish with lemon wedges and parsley. Serve immediately.

This recipe for batter-fried crabs from Bob Chinn's Crab House, Wheeling, Illinois, is an excellent introduction to eating soft-shell crabs. The crunchy batter convinces the diner to eat the whole thing. And the simple ingredients don't distract from the fine crab flavor. Chin suggests that they be served with tartar sauce or a fresh lemon wedge and cold beer or white wine.

BATTER-FRIED SOFT-SHELL CRABS

4 to 6 servings
Preparation time: 10 minutes
Cooking time: 5 minutes

Safflower or corn oil for frying
4 **large eggs**
2 **cups milk**
1 **teaspoon salt**
12 **to 16 medium-size soft-shell crabs, cleaned, rinsed**
1 **cup all-purpose flour**

1. Pour oil to depth of 1 inch in heavy skillet, electric fry pan or deep-fryer. Heat to 360 degrees.

2. Lightly beat eggs in large bowl. Stir in milk and salt. Add crabs; soak 2 to 3 minutes. Remove crabs to large dish or platter.

3. Toss flour over crabs and pat lightly but firmly on both sides. Fry in single layer, turning, until golden brown, 2 to 4 minutes, depending on size. Remove with slotted spatula. Drain on paper towels. Serve immediately or hold for short time on a paper-lined pan in a 200-degree oven.

Chef Roland Liccioni's cooking style combines nouvelle cuisine with Oriental influences, as seen in this lemon grass-spiked butter sauce for scallops from Carlos' restaurant in Highland Park.

SCALLOPS IN LEMON GRASS SAUCE

4 servings
Preparation time: 30 minutes
Cooking time: 25 minutes

2   **cups dry chablis**
1   **shallot, minced**
1   **branch lemon grass, finely chopped**
1   **cup whipping cream**
3   **tablespoons butter, cut into pieces**
    Freshly ground white pepper to taste
1   **tablespoon olive oil**
1   **pound sea scallops or peeled deveined shrimp, rinsed, patted dry**
5   **fresh shiitake mushrooms, julienned**
¼   **teaspoon minced fresh ginger**

1. Mix chablis, shallot and lemon grass in medium nonaluminum saucepan. Cook over medium heat until reduced to fine glaze, about 10 minutes. Add cream; boil gently until thickened, about 2 minutes. Vigorously whisk in butter. Add pepper. Taste and adjust seasonings. Strain through fine sieve. Keep warm.

2. Preheat broiler. Heat oil in large skillet over medium heat until hot. Add scallops; cook until tender, 1 to 2 minutes. Do not overcook. Add mushrooms and ginger; heat thoroughly. Stir mixture into sauce.

3. Portion mixture into 4 small, heat-proof casseroles or au gratin dishes. Broil until top is lightly browned, about 1 minute. Serve immediately.

Basically a tangy tomato beurre blanc to enhance fresh scallops, this recipe won Susan M. Swett, of Glencoe, Illinois, second place in the 1984 Tribune Food Guide Seafood Recipe Contest. The judges particularly liked the taste and aroma from the garlic and tarragon vinegar and the perfectly textured sauce that just clings to the scallops.

SCALLOPS IN RED BUTTER SAUCE

4 to 6 servings
Preparation time: 30 minutes
Cooking time: About 2 hours

1 **can (28 ounces) whole tomatoes, undrained**
1 **cup dry white wine**
¼ **cup white wine tarragon vinegar**
8 **shallots, peeled**
4 **cloves garlic, peeled**
6 **sprigs fresh tarragon**
1¾ **teaspoons coarse (kosher) salt**
1 **teaspoon sugar**
½ **teaspoon freshly ground pepper**
1 **cup (2 sticks) unsalted butter, at room temperature**
1½ **pounds bay or sea scallops, rinsed, patted dry**
Chopped parsley for garnish
French bread for serving

1. Mix tomatoes, wine, vinegar, shallots, garlic, tarragon, salt, sugar and pepper in 2 to 2½-quart heavy-bottomed nonaluminum saucepan. Heat to boil over medium heat; reduce heat to low. Boil gently, uncovered, stirring often, until thick and most of the liquid has evaporated.

2. Push mixture through fine sieve into 2-cup glass measure. Push through as much of the solids as possible to yield about 1¾ cups. If more than 1¾ cups, return to saucepan and simmer until reduced to that amount. Remove from heat. (Sauce may be made ahead up to this point. Refrigerate covered for a few days or freeze solid up to 6 months.)

3. Put ¼ cup of the sauce and ¼ cup of the butter in large skillet; set aside.

4. Put remaining sauce in small saucepan; heat to boil over medium-high heat. Reduce heat to very low; cook, stirring often, until the consistency of tomato paste, about 1 hour. (Watch carefully because sauce burns easily.)

5. Vigorously beat in remaining 12 tablespoons butter, 1 tablespoon at a time, removing pan from heat whenever the butter appears to be melting rather than thickening or foaming. When all the butter has been incorporated and sauce is thick and foamy, remove from heat.

6. Heat skillet with butter and sauce over high heat to boil. Add scallops; cook and stir until opaque and tender, 2 to 5 minutes, depending on size. Do not overcook.

THE CHICAGO TRIBUNE COOKBOOK

7. Divide scallops evenly among serving plates, using a slotted spoon to drain off the liquid. Put a heaping tablespoon of sauce over scallops. Sprinkle with parsley. Serve immediately with French bread to sop up the extra sauce.

■ *Only a few ingredients are listed in this recipe from Arun's restaurant in Chicago, but don't let that fool you. The fish sauce and garlic add up to plenty of flavor for prawns.*

GARLIC PRAWNS
(Goong kratiam prik-Thai)

4 servings
Preparation time: 10 minutes
Cooking time: 10 minutes

¼ **cup vegetable oil**
1 **tablespoon minced garlic**
1 **pound prawns or large shrimp, peeled, tails left intact, deveined**
2 **tablespoons fish sauce (nam pla)**
½ **teaspoon minced fresh cilantro (coriander)**
¼ **teaspoon each, freshly ground: black pepper, white pepper**

1. Heat oil in large skillet over medium heat. Add garlic; cook and stir until garlic is translucent, 2 to 3 minutes.

2. Stir in shrimp, fish sauce, cilantro and peppers. Cook and stir over medium heat until shrimp is opaque, about 3 minutes. Serve immediately.

■ *Shrimp de Jonghe, a Chicago classic, has endured Prohibition police raids (which closed Henri de Jonghe's Monroe Street hotel and restaurant where the dish was created) and modern low-fat eating trends. This simple-to-make recipe is a close approximation of the delicious original.*

SHRIMP DE JONGHE

4 servings
Preparation time: 30 minutes
Cooking time: 15 minutes

1½ **quarts water**
 ½ **small onion, sliced**
 1 **rib celery, halved**
 3 **black peppercorns**
 1 **bay leaf**
 ¼ **teaspoon salt**
1½ **pounds large raw shrimp in the shell**
 ½ **cup (1 stick) unsalted butter, melted**
 2 **tablespoons dry sherry or white wine**
1½ **cups coarse French bread crumbs**
 2 **tablespoons minced fresh parsley**
 1 **tablespoon minced shallots**
 2 **cloves garlic, minced**
 ½ **teaspoon imported sweet paprika**
 ⅛ **teaspoon cayenne pepper**

1. Put water, onion, celery, peppercorns, bay leaf and salt into large saucepan. Heat to boil. Add shrimp; cover and return to boil. Drain immediately.

2. Peel shrimp and put into large bowl. Add half of the melted butter and sherry. Toss to mix.

3. Heat oven to 400 degrees. Mix remaining melted butter and bread crumbs in small bowl. Stir in parsley, shallots, garlic, paprika and cayenne pepper.

4. Spoon half of the shrimp mixture into buttered 1½-quart baking dish. Top with half of the bread crumbs. Top with remaining shrimp mixture. Top with remaining bread crumbs. Bake until crumbs are lightly browned, about 10 minutes. Serve immediately.

The Tribune *test kitchen developed this stir-fry recipe for cooks who are in a hurry. The cooking time is very quick, and the vegetables and shrimp can be prepared ahead.*

STIR-FRIED SHRIMP ON RICE

4 servings
Preparation time: 15 minutes
Cooking time: 15 minutes

1 cup raw rice
1 tablespoon vegetable oil
4 green onions, sliced
1 tablespoon minced fresh ginger
1 clove garlic, sliced
1 box (6 ounces) frozen snow pea pods, thawed
1 small zucchini, sliced
1 small yellow squash, sliced
1 small red bell pepper, seeded, diced
1 pound shelled, medium shrimp
1 to 2 tablespoons soy sauce to taste
1 to 2 teaspoons Oriental sesame oil to taste
Fresh cilantro (coriander) sprigs for garnish

1. Cook rice according to package directions.

2. Meanwhile, heat oil in large skillet over medium heat. Add green onions, ginger and garlic. Stir-fry 1 minute.

3. Add pea pods, zucchini, squash and red pepper. Stir-fry over medium-high heat until vegetables are crisp-tender, 2 to 4 minutes. Add shrimp; stir-fry just until shrimp turn pink, 2 minutes.

4. Stir in soy sauce and sesame oil. Serve immediately over cooked rice. Garnish with cilantro.

A combination of scallops and shrimp are used in this recipe from chef Kevin Shikami of Jimmy's Place in Chicago. The cooking time is very short once all the ingredients have been prepared. To avoid overcooking the delicate shellfish, have all the ingredients next to the stove before starting.

QUICK ORIENTAL SHELLFISH RAGOUT

2 servings
Preparation time: 25 minutes
Cooking time: 5 minutes

¼ cup clarified butter or olive oil

8 jumbo sea scallops

12 medium shrimp, peeled, deveined

1 large tomato, peeled, seeded, diced

3 green onions, chopped into ¼-inch pieces

1 teaspoon grated fresh ginger

½ cup dry white wine

2 teaspoons fermented black beans, rinsed

Few sprigs fresh cilantro (coriander), minced

6 tablespoons butter, softened

Salt, cayenne pepper to taste

1. Heat large skillet over medium-high heat until hot. Add clarified butter. Add scallops; sear on all sides, then add shrimp and sear on both sides. Add tomato, green onions and ginger; stir to heat, then add white wine. Cook over medium-high heat to reduce it slightly, about 2 minutes.

2. Stir in black beans and cilantro. While shaking the pan and stirring over medium heat, add softened butter until incorporated and sauce is foamy. Do not boil. Season with salt and cayenne pepper. Serve immediately.

Anyone with a covered grill can smoke fish or shellfish for wonderful appetizers or entrees. For this recipe for the Sunday *magazine*, Paul A. Camp and JeanMarie Brownson had excellent results smoking salmon steaks, small whole rainbow trout and mussels and oysters in their shells. Once the fish is on the grill and the lid is in place, don't peek. You want all of the rich smoky flavor in the fish, not in your face.

LEMON-DILL DRY CURE FOR SMOKED FISH

Enough for 4 pounds fish
Preparation time: 10 minutes

3 tablespoons each: coarse (kosher) salt, packed dark brown sugar
1 tablespoon grated lemon rind
2 teaspoons minced fresh dill or ½ teaspoon dried
2 teaspoons freshly ground black pepper
2 large cloves garlic, minced
¼ teaspoon ground coriander seed

1. Mix all ingredients in small bowl.

To grill-smoke whole fish, fish steaks and fillets: Rub the dry cure into fish. If smoking whole fish, rub dry cure in cavity of fish as well. Refrigerate fish, covered, about 30 minutes per inch of thickness.

To prepare grill, place a drip pan of heavy-duty aluminum foil in center of grill. Put a small pile of coals on either side of the drip pan (9 coals per side is enough to smoke 4 pounds of fish). Heat coals until a white ash forms. Temperature when covered should be 150 to 200 degrees.

Cover a handful of hickory chips in water, and soak about 30 minutes. Lightly oil the grill grate.

Rinse fish well. Pat dry. Let stand on a wire rack a few minutes to dry completely. When grill is ready, drain chips and sprinkle over coals.

Position fish on grate over drip pan. Cover grill. Smoke at a temperature between 150 to 200 degrees just until fish is opaque and almost flakes. (For example, small, whole rainbow trout require about 35 minutes.)

To grill-smoke shellfish: After grill has reached temperature, add hickory chips. Position fresh mussels, clams or oysters in the shell over drip pan. Cover grill. Smoke at a temperature between 150 and 200 degrees, just until shellfish open slightly, about 10 to 15 minutes. (All of the oysters may not visibly open; we suggest opening and tasting for doneness.) Do not overcook.

MEAT

With its famous stockyards and bold appetites, Chicago became the nation's number one meat-and-potatoes city in the halcyon days before and after the turn of the century. Now, with the turn of yet another century only a decade away, the stockyards are long gone and American attitudes toward meat have changed considerably.

Although hearty appetites and great steak houses still are very much a part of the city's culinary scene, concerns about health and nutrition have led to a decrease in the amount of meat we eat. These same concerns have prompted beef and pork producers to change breeding and feeding practices to lower the percentage of fat on animals coming to market.

The public is intrigued, and often bewildered, as research scientists seek to unravel the mysteries of cholesterol found in meat and published reports claim positive as well as negative effects on the body. There is concern as well about drugs used to stimulate growth and feeding practices. A small but significant proportion of the population has been demanding "free-range," hormone-free, low-fat beef and veal and is willing to pay a premium for it.

Through all the controversy, and despite the swing to buying poultry, there is ample evidence that Americans continue to prize red meat. Steaks, chops and roasts still have a place at family meals at home and diners frequently choose prize cuts of beef, veal, pork and lamb when enjoying a special meal in a restaurant.

The recipes that follow affirm a trend away from the steak-and-potatoes era, away from serving large roasts and massive steaks plainly cooked. Indeed, it provides striking evidence of the vast degree to which international methods of cooking and flavoring meat have permeated the Midwest.

The largest number are inspired by the cooking of Mexico and the American Southwest. Next come recipes combining meat with Oriental ingredients. Some of them use Oriental cooking techniques as well, while others are examples of the recent culinary cross-pollinization called "East-West" cuisine.

Not that tradition is ignored. This chapter also contains treasured family recipes for roast beef and Yorkshire pudding, corned beef hash, meat loaf mild and spicy and a brisket of beef from Jewish cookery, along with recipes for baking ham, stirring up a tasty chili and roasting elegant crown roasts of pork and lamb.

It is worth noting, however, the differences in these meat recipes from those that might have been published a quarter of a century ago, or perhaps even at the end of the last decade.

Many of today's cooks are coming into the kitchen without the background and exposure their mothers (or grandmothers) enjoyed. They need more basic cooking information in the recipes. Also, the reconfiguration of our meats, especially pork, has made it necessary to revise cooking times and even develop alternate methods for cooking this "new," leaner product.

There are many more recipes for grill cooking. No longer is grilling a summer ritual reserved for male cooks. Due to the flavor it imparts and the speed with which low-fat cuts can be cooked, this method of cooking has become a favorite way for cooks of both sexes to prepare meat. Also, kitchen equipment innovations allow some cooks to grill indoors.

Today we have an increased reliance on kitchen technology. The microwave oven has emerged as an important kitchen tool. It makes defrosting frozen meat, even individual portions, a cinch, and is capable of reheating prepared meat without overcooking it. The repertory of creative microwave meat dishes is growing.

Much more emphasis on cooking for company on weekends has spurred a strong demand for recipes for entertaining. This, in turn, has greatly increased requests for recipes from restaurant chefs.

As readers have sought quick-to-make recipes to suit their busy lifestyles, they have asked less frequently for recipes for cheaper but tougher cuts that require long cooking. There is considerably less interest as well for recipes for offal such as sweetbreads, kidneys and brains.

Due to changing public taste in favor of meat that is less well done and moist, and the development of leaner meats, cooking times have been reduced for many of today's cuts.

And finally, due to our recently acquired love of spice, and to health concerns, many of the meat entrees here are likely to be served with vegetable-based salsas and relishes instead of the complex, butter-enriched sauces of French haute cuisine.

MEAT

BEEF

Beef and peppers on vermicelli

Beef brisket

Roast brisket with barbecue sauce

Beef Niçoise with olives and
red peppers

Japanese beef with soy
dipping sauce

Beef barbecued Korean-style

Beef stew with red wine

Beef stew with spinach and
cilantro chutney

Bowl of red

Roast beef with gravy and
Yorkshire pudding

Spicy mustard beef tenderloin with
oven roasted potatoes

Basic corned beef

Corned beef hash

Hamburgers American-style

Hamburgers with green peppercorns

Spinach burgers

Just great meat loaf

Cajun meat loaf

Picadillo enchiladas

Beef and bean tostadas

Mexican-style pot roast with
vegetables

Steak fajitas with smoky salsa

Stuffed flank steak

Rolled sirloin with
prosciutto and sage

Steak au poivre

Barbecued oxtails

PORK

Breakfast sausage

Maple glazed bacon

Heartland chili

Butterflied pork chops with
polenta and mushroom sauce

Grilled teriyaki pork chops

Braised pork in tortillas

Chicago-style barbecued ribs

Down-home barbecued pork

Grilled herbed pork roast

Garlic and spinach pork roast

Plum-glazed pork roast

Crown roast of pork with fruit
and rice stuffing

Pork tenderloin with apricot relish

Pork cutlets with ginger-lime sauce

Stir-fried pork in a basket

Sausage and pepper skillet dish

Filipino sausage and bok choy

Hungarian-style family sausage

Fresh ham with sage and rosemary

Sugar-baked ham

Ham and sausage jambalaya

LAMB

Lamb patties with yogurt sauce

Grilled butterflied leg of lamb with
herb marinade

Crown roast of lamb with
lemon and herbs

Roast rack of lamb

Couscous with lamb stew and
vegetables

Moroccan meat pie

Lamb shanks with barley and garlic

VEAL

Veal apples
Veal cutlets with red peppers
Spinach-stuffed veal breast
Sliced veal with anchovy sauce
Braised veal shanks
Veal tarragon stew with
   tiny dumplings
Sautéed calf's liver

RABBIT

Spiced rabbit with salsa-flavored
   sauce

Here is a quickly prepared main course from The Tribune *test kitchen—about 40 minutes from start to finish. Pale noodles, tender beef and flavorings are complemented by the visual appeal of tricolored pepper chunks.*

BEEF AND PEPPERS ON VERMICELLI

4 servings
Preparation time: 30 minutes
Cooking time: 10 minutes

1 **pound boneless beef sirloin**

1 **cup canned beef broth**

3 **tablespoons soy sauce**

2 **tablespoons each: red wine, cornstarch**

2 **teaspoons Oriental sesame oil**

¼ **teaspoon crushed red pepper flakes**

1 **each, large: green pepper, red bell pepper, yellow bell pepper**

½ **pound vermicelli**

2 **tablespoons peanut oil**

1 **small yellow onion, thinly sliced**

2 **green onions, sliced**

4 **teaspoons minced fresh ginger**

2 **large cloves garlic, minced**

Salt, freshly ground pepper to taste

1. Cut meat into very thin slices. (To facilitate slicing, meat may be put into freezer until partly frozen, about 15 minutes.)

2. Mix broth, soy sauce, wine, cornstarch, sesame oil and red pepper flakes in small bowl. Remove seeds from green, red and yellow peppers. Cut into 1-inch chunks.

3. Cook noodles according to package directions until al dente. Drain; toss with 1 tablespoon of the peanut oil; keep warm.

4. While noodles cook, heat remaining 1 tablespoon peanut oil in wok or large skillet. Add yellow onion, green onions, ginger and garlic. Stir-fry 1 minute.

5. Add meat; stir-fry 1 minute. Add peppers; stir-fry until vegetables are crisp-tender, about 2 minutes. Stir broth mixture well, then stir into meat mixture. Cook and stir until thickened, about 2 minutes. Add salt and pepper.

6. Put noodles onto platter. Spoon meat mixture on top of noodles. Serve immediately.

Long cooking is needed to make the brisket cut tender. Be sure to remove surface fat from the gravy. Serve with rice or a grain such as bulgur. This recipe comes from a Chicago resident, Sophie Berger, who has been cooking Passover Seder meals for a crowd for many years.

BEEF BRISKET

8 servings
Preparation time: 20 minutes
Baking time: 3 to 3½ hours

5 pounds first cut beef brisket (do not include end portion, which is too fatty)

Gravy darkener, such as Kitchen Bouquet

Salt, freshly ground pepper to taste

Garlic powder to taste

3 medium cloves garlic

3 large onions, diced

½ cup catsup

1. Heat oven to 350 degrees. Trim off fat from brisket. Brush brisket lightly on both sides with gravy darkener. Then season both sides lightly with salt, pepper and garlic powder.

2. Place brisket in heavy metal roasting pan or dutch oven with cover. Put garlic cloves through press and spread garlic on top of beef. Sprinkle onions and 2 tablespoons water over beef.

3. Bake, tightly covered, for 2 hours. Uncover, add 2 tablespoons of the catsup plus 2 to 3 additional tablespoons water and several drops of gravy darkener. Rotate cover slightly so that it still covers most of brisket, but one end is open. This will allow roast to brown but not dry out.

4. Continue baking until beef is tender, 1 to 1½ hours more. While brisket cooks, small amounts of water can be added to pot if needed. At the end of the cooking time, there should be enough gravy to submerge lower half of beef. But at no time should brisket be completely submerged.

5. Allow to cool slightly. Then cut brisket in very thin slices at an angle against the grain. Slices will be long, thin and lean.

6. For gravy, scrape the browned spots and sediment which have adhered to the sides of the roasting pan. Mix these scrapings into the gravy. If necessary, add additional water to extend gravy. Add remaining catsup to thicken, along with a few additional drops of gravy darkener so that finished gravy has a red/brown cast. Taste to adjust seasoning.

NOTE: If cooking ahead of time, pour gravy into small clean roasting pan. Carefully arrange brisket slices in gravy, taking care that slices are moistened with gravy completely. Cover roaster and refrigerate brisket. Reheat over very low heat before serving.

In 1984, reader Joyce Klein won The Tribune's Jewish Mother Cooking Contest and had her brisket selected as one of the year's 10 Best Recipes. Her comment: "I could never serve eight to ten people on this recipe; we loved it so much, four people ate the whole thing."

ROAST BRISKET WITH BARBECUE SAUCE

8 servings
Preparation time: 30 minutes
Cooking time: 3½ to 4 hours

1 **beef brisket, about 4 pounds**
2 **cloves fresh garlic, minced, or garlic salt to taste**
3 **large onions, quartered**
1 **green pepper, cut into squares**
4 **potatoes, peeled, halved**
4 **large carrots, cut into 1½-inch pieces**
1½ **cups water**
¾ **cup each: barbecue sauce, chili sauce**
   Salt, freshly ground pepper to taste

1. Heat oven to 425 degrees. Rinse brisket in cold water. Rub with garlic. Put into roasting pan, fat side up, leaving enough room around meat for carrots and potatoes. Bake until top is brown, about 30 minutes.

2. Add onions and green pepper to pan, continue to bake until onion edges start to turn brown. If too brown, add ½ cup water. Turn meat over and bake until second side is brown, about 20 minutes.

3. Add potatoes, carrots, 1½ cups water, barbecue sauce and chili sauce. Bake, uncovered, basting frequently, for 2 hours. Reduce oven temperature to 350 degrees; cover with foil or a roast cover. Bake until meat is fork-tender, 30 to 60 minutes.

4. Put meat on serving plate; surround with potatoes and vegetables. Season pan juices with salt and pepper; pass with meat.

Clay pot cookers produce exceptionally flavorful stews. Soaking the pot before cooking is essential. This recipe, from writer Lee Thompson, uses thyme, olives and orange flavoring, all common to the region around Nice in southern France. Fresh red bell pepper pieces will provide a better texture contrast than bottled.

BEEF NIÇOISE WITH OLIVES AND RED PEPPERS

6 servings
Preparation time: 25 minutes
Cooking time: 2 to 2½ hours

½ **pound pork rind**
1 **pound small white onions**
3 **pounds boneless beef (round, rump or chuck, all fat removed), cut in 2-inch chunks**
1 **teaspoon dried leaf thyme or 1 tablespoon fresh**
  Salt, freshly ground pepper to taste
1 **cup medium-size, black, pitted olives, drained**
1 **two-inch piece of dried orange peel, or substitute fresh**
½ **cup brandy**
6 **red bell peppers, peeled, seeded, quartered or substitute bottled, drained**
  Minced fresh parsley for garnish

1. Soak clay pot and cover in lukewarm water for 15 minutes or more.

2. Put pork rind in saucepan with cold water to cover. Heat to simmer for 15 minutes. Rinse under cold water; cut rind in ½-inch squares.

3. To peel onions easily, put into saucepan of boiling water for 1 minute. Drain; rinse under cold water. Peel.

4. Drain clay pot. Spread half of the pork rind on the bottom of the pot. Sprinkle beef with thyme, salt and pepper; place in pot. Spread remaining pork rind, onions and olives over beef. Add orange peel. Pour brandy over.

5. Put covered into cold oven. Set oven temperature to 400 degrees and cook until very tender, 2 to 2½ hours. Twenty minutes before you expect meat to be ready, distribute red peppers over stew. Garnish with parsley.

NOTE: While the clay pot yields the best results, this recipe can be prepared in a dutch oven. To do so, omit step 1. Follow directions in steps 2 and 3. Heat 3 tablespoons vegetable oil over medium heat in 4-quart dutch oven. Brown meat in single layer. Drain off oil. Stir in 1 cup beef broth or water. Proceed with step 4 except layering ingredients in the dutch oven. Bake, covered, in a preheated 325-degree oven, until beef is fork-tender, 1 hour 45 minutes to 2 hours. Add red peppers as directed.

This recipe, from the Japanese restaurant, Suntory, in Chicago, has been adapted for home cooks. It offers contrasts in texture and temperature. The shredded daikon is cool; the wasabi is spicy hot. The sauce is sweet; the salt-and-vinegar marinated meat is savory. This may be served as a summertime main course or a year-round cocktail party hors d'oeuvre.

JAPANESE BEEF WITH SOY DIPPING SAUCE

2 main-course servings or
8 appetizer servings
Preparation time: 25 minutes
Marinating time: 30 minutes
Cooking time: 5 minutes

2 **tablespoons each: soy sauce, rice vinegar, sake**

2 **beef filet steaks, each 2 inches thick and about 8 ounces**

1 **small daikon, peeled**

3 **tablespoons wasabi powder**

DIPPING SAUCE

3 **tablespoons soy sauce**

2 **tablespoons sake**

¼ **teaspoon sugar**

3 **green onions, finely chopped**

1. Mix soy sauce, rice vinegar and sake in small nonaluminum dish. Add steaks. Marinate in the refrigerator 30 minutes.

2. Meanwhile, cut daikon into very fine shreds with a food processor or grater. Mix wasabi powder with just enough warm water to make a thick paste. Arrange daikon and wasabi on serving plates.

3. For dipping sauce, mix soy sauce, sake and sugar in small bowl.

4. Preheat broiler. Remove steaks from marinade and place on broiler pan. Broil, 4 inches from heat source, turning once, for 5 minutes. Do not overcook. Center of steaks should be very rare.

5. To serve, cut steaks into very thin slices. Arrange slices on prepared plates. Sprinkle slices with green onion. Serve immediately with dipping sauce.

NOTE: Daikon (Japanese radish) and wasabi powder (Japanese horseradish) are available at most Oriental markets. For appetizers, arrange sliced beef on platter with daikon and wasabi paste. Pass sauce for dipping.

■ *Sugar and spice make a very nice Oriental treat in this recipe for Korean-style barbecued beef from Shilla restaurant in Chicago. To complete the menu, start with a noodle soup, grill some eggplant or zucchini to go with the beef and offer fresh fruit and cookies for dessert.*

BEEF BARBECUED KOREAN-STYLE
(Bul goki)

6 servings
Preparation time: 20 minutes
Marinating time: 30 minutes
Cooking time: 5 minutes

6 **rib-eye steaks, about 6 ounces each**

6 **small cloves garlic, minced**

6 **tablespoons each: water, Oriental sesame oil, soy sauce**

6 **teaspoons sugar**
Freshly ground pepper
Lettuce leaves, cooked rice, hot bean paste for serving

1. For easiest slicing, freeze meat until partly solid, about 1 hour. Using a very sharp knife, slice meat into thin strips large enough so they do not fall through the grill grate or broiler pan.

2. Mix remaining ingredients except lettuce leaves, rice and hot bean paste in nonaluminum dish. Add beef strips. Marinate, turning occasionally, about 30 minutes.

3. Meanwhile, prepare a hibachi or charcoal grill or preheat broiler. When coals are covered with a white ash, drain marinade off beef. Grill or broil beef, about 4 inches from heat source, turning once, until meat just begins to crisp yet remains juicy and pink inside. Time will depend on thickness of meat, usually 2 to 4 minutes.

4. Immediately remove meat from grill to a large platter. Serve with lettuce leaves and rice. Drizzle with hot bean paste or additional soy if desired.

VARIATION: For kalbi, Korean barbecued short ribs, substitute 2¼ pounds boneless beef short ribs (save bones for other use). Cut meat into 1-inch cubes. Marinate as directed in step 2, but increase marinating time to 1 to 2 hours. Cook as directed in step 4. Grilling time will be slightly longer, but take care to keep meat slightly pink in the center to prevent toughening.

NOTE: Hot bean paste can be purchased at Oriental food markets.

A contemporary version of France's boeuf bourguignonne *was developed for* The Tribune *by Beverly Dillon. Any dry red wine will be satisfactory, but avoid "cooking wine," an inferior product that contains salt. The vegetables are added in sequence so they will not be overcooked when the stew is ready.*

BEEF STEW WITH RED WINE

6 servings
Preparation time: 40 minutes
Cooking time: 1½ to 2 hours

3 tablespoons butter

2 cups frozen pearl onions

1 cup chopped white part of leek or yellow onion, about 1 large leek

2 pounds boneless round steak or beef chuck, cut into 1-inch cubes

¼ cup all-purpose flour

½ teaspoon each: freshly ground pepper, dried marjoram, salt, dried leaf thyme

3 cups beef stock (see recipe, page 133), or substitute canned broth

2 cups dry red wine

1 pound carrots, trimmed, peeled, cut into 1-inch pieces

1 pound potatoes, peeled, cut into 1-inch cubes

1 each: green pepper, red bell pepper

½ pound fresh mushrooms, sliced

1 cup frozen peas

¼ cup minced parsley, optional

1. Heat 2 tablespoons of the butter in large dutch oven over medium-high heat. Add pearl onions; sauté until lightly browned and tender, stirring often, about 10 minutes. Remove with slotted spoon to side dish. Reserve.

2. Add remaining butter to same pan. Add leek. Cook over medium heat just until wilted, about 10 minutes. Add meat in single layer. Cook and stir until meat is brown on all sides.

3. Add flour, pepper, marjoram, salt and thyme. Cook, stirring until well mixed and flour has also browned, 1 to 2 minutes. Add beef stock and wine; heat to boil. Reduce heat to medium-low; cover pan. Simmer until meat is tender, about 1 hour.

4. Add carrots and potatoes; simmer, covered, 20 more minutes. Cut peppers in half, seed and cut into 1-inch pieces. Add peppers, mushrooms and peas to meat. Simmer, covered, until all vegetables are tender, about 10 more minutes. Uncover; increase heat to high and boil gently to thicken juices slightly. Stir in pearl onions. Sprinkle with parsley.

■ *Fresh cilantro, also known as coriander, plays a major role in this recipe from The Helmand, an Afghanistan restaurant in Chicago. Though pungent, its flavor dissipates over time. If possible, make the chutney on the day you plan to serve it. You'll want something sweet and creamy, like rice pudding or ice cream for dessert.*

BEEF STEW WITH SPINACH AND CILANTRO CHUTNEY

4 servings
Preparation time: 45 minutes
Cooking time: 1¾ hours

3 tablespoons vegetable oil
1 medium yellow onion, chopped
1 pound boneless beef top round, cut into 1-inch cubes
3 cloves garlic, chopped
1 teaspoon ground coriander seed
　Salt, freshly ground pepper to taste
3 cups water
2 bunches fresh spinach, washed, dried, chopped
1 bunch green onions, chopped
¼ teaspoon ground cinnamon
　Cooked rice
　Cilantro chutney (see recipe, page 647)

1. Heat oil in a skillet over medium heat. Add yellow onion; cook and stir until brown. Add cubed meat. Season with 2 cloves of the garlic, ground coriander, salt and black pepper. Cook until meat is browned on all sides, about 5 minutes.

2. Add 2 cups of the water. Simmer, partly covered, stirring occasionally, until meat is tender, about 1 hour.

3. Add spinach, green onions, remaining garlic, cinnamon and black pepper. Stir in remaining 1 cup water. Cook, uncovered, until water is absorbed, 15 to 20 minutes. Stir occasionally. Taste and adjust seasonings. Serve with cooked rice and cilantro chutney.

In Texas, old-timers call chili "a bowl of red." Cornbread is a good accompaniment. Beverly Dillon created it as the centerpiece of a menu to serve on Valentine's Day.

BOWL OF RED

8 servings
Preparation time: 20 minutes
Cooking time: 30 to 60 minutes

2 tablespoons vegetable oil

2 cups coarsely chopped onions, about 4 medium

1 teaspoon chopped garlic, about 2 cloves

2½ pounds coarsely ground beef chuck

1 pound coarsely ground pork

3 tablespoons chili powder

1½ tablespoons ground cumin

2 teaspoons each: dried basil, dried leaf oregano, freshly ground pepper

1½ teaspoons salt

1 teaspoon dry mustard

1 can (6 ounces) tomato paste

2 cans (28 ounces each) whole tomatoes, undrained, chopped

2 cans (15 ounces each) kidney beans, drained

1½ cups dry red wine

Freshly chopped parsley

Toppings: chopped onion, grated Cheddar cheese, sour cream, sliced olives

1. Heat oil in large dutch oven over medium heat. Add onions and garlic; cook until wilted but not brown. Add meats and cook until lightly brown, breaking up with wooden spoon. Drain off excess fat.

2. Stir in chili powder, cumin, basil, oregano, pepper, salt and dry mustard. Cook and stir over low heat for 2 minutes. Add tomato paste. Stir to mix and cook for 2 minutes.

3. Stir in tomatoes, kidney beans and wine. Cook, uncovered, stirring occasionally, at least 15 minutes or up to 1 hour. Stir in parsley. Taste and adjust seasonings.

4. Put desired toppings in small bowls. Pass toppings with chili.

Traditional roast beef Sunday dinner in the English style at Melanie Atkinson's home, in Wheaton, Illinois, "is a command performance," wrote Patricia Tennison in 1985. The menu, a tradition through three generations, also includes Yorkshire pudding, English peas, cucumber and onion salad and homemade pie or chocolate cake.

ROAST BEEF WITH GRAVY AND YORKSHIRE PUDDING

6 servings
Preparation time: 15 minutes
Cooking time: About 1 hour

1 beef rib roast,
   3 to 4 pounds
Garlic powder
Bay leaves

GRAVY

¼ cup all-purpose flour
2 cups beef stock or
   broth (see recipe,
   page 133), or
   substitute canned
   broth
Gravy darkener, such
   as Kitchen Bouquet,
   optional
Salt, freshly ground
   pepper to taste
Yorkshire pudding
   (recipe follows)

1. Remove roast from refrigerator 1 to 2 hours before cooking to reach room temperature.

2. Heat oven to 500 degrees. Set roast fat side up on rack in roasting pan. Season with garlic powder. Top with bay leaves. Insert meat thermometer into middle without touching bones.

3. Place in oven. Immediately reduce oven temperature to 350 degrees. For medium-rare, cook 18 to 20 minutes per pound, or until meat thermometer registers 140 degrees. (Meat temperature will rise about 10 degrees after removing from oven.) Remove roast from oven; transfer to serving platter. Let stand 20 minutes before carving.

4. Meanwhile, pour fat and juices from roasting pan into heat resistant, see-through container such as a 2-cup glass measuring cup. Let stand for a minute so the fat rises to top and dark pan drippings sink to bottom. Return about 4 tablespoons of fat to roasting pan. Discard rest of fat from measuring cup, taking care not to pour off drippings. Add drippings back to pan.

5. Set roasting pan over medium hot burners on stove. Heat fat and drippings, scraping and mixing in brown bits from bottom of pan. Mix flour and beef stock in small bowl until smooth. Stir into pan. Cook, whisking constantly until thickened, smooth and desired consistency, about 5 minutes. Add gravy darkener if desired. Taste and adjust seasonings with salt and pepper. Strain into serving bowl. Serve with Yorkshire pudding.

YORKSHIRE PUDDING

6 servings
Preparation time: 10 minutes
Baking time: 25 minutes

⅓ **cup flour**

½ **teaspoon salt**

½ **cup whole milk, at room temperature**

1 **egg, at room temperature**

1 **tablespoon vegetable shortening**

1. Mix flour and salt in medium bowl. Mix milk and egg in separate bowl. Gradually stir milk mixture into flour until smooth. Let stand, loosely covered, at least 1 hour.

2. Heat oven to 450 degrees. Put shortening in 9-inch metal pie pan. Place in oven for 2 minutes to melt.

3. Add batter to pie pan. Bake until puffy and golden, 15 to 20 minutes. Keep oven door closed while baking. Remove from pan, cut into pie-like wedges, and serve immediately.

An imaginatively seasoned roast can be the centerpiece of a special-occasion meal. Start with smoked salmon or caviar and blinis and serve a tossed salad on the side with the beef. Chateauneuf-du-Pape or another Rhone red wine will not be overwhelmed by the peppercorns and mustard.

SPICY MUSTARD BEEF TENDERLOIN WITH OVEN ROASTED POTATOES

6 servings
Preparation time: 45 minutes
Cooking time: 45 to 50 minutes

1 teaspoon each: black peppercorns, whole allspice, sage leaves, dried leaf thyme, salt

2 tablespoons Dijon mustard

2 teaspoons green peppercorns, drained, mashed

1 trimmed beef tenderloin, about 3 pounds

1 or 2 thin pieces of beef fat, about ½ pound, to cover tenderloin

4 bay leaves

18 small new red potatoes, peeled, halved

3 tablespoons softened butter

2 to 3 tablespoons oil

½ cup dry red wine

1. For spice mixture, put spices into spice grinder, coffee mill or blender. Process until finely ground. Store in covered jar up to 1 week.

2. Mix mustard and mashed green peppercorns in small bowl.

3. Using a very sharp knife, make a lengthwise cut down the center of tenderloin, cutting through two-thirds of the tenderloin. Lay tenderloin open like a book. Flatten slightly with meat pounder.

4. Spread mustard mixture inside of meat. Sprinkle 1 teaspoon of the spice mixture over mustard. Roll meat back to its original shape. Lay beef fat over meat; top with bay leaves. Tie meat securely in several places with kitchen string to form a compact shape. Refrigerate, covered, up to 1 day. Let stand at room temperature 1 hour before roasting.

5. Add potatoes to boiling water; cook 5 minutes; drain well. Pat dry.

6. Heat oven to 425 degrees. Rub outside of roast with softened butter. Press remaining spice mixture into butter. Put into roasting pan. Rub potatoes with oil and place around roast in pan.

7. Roast at 425 degrees. For rare, cook 6 to 8 minutes per pound, or until meat thermometer registers 130 degrees. (Meat temperature will rise about 10 degrees after removing from oven.) Baste potatoes occasionally with pan juices. Let meat and potatoes stand on serving platter for 10 minutes.

8. Meanwhile, pour wine into pan juices set over medium heat. Cook and stir, scraping up browned bits from bottom of pan, until mixture boils. Pour into serving dish.

9. Remove string and fat from tenderloin. Slice meat thinly. Pass pan juices.

This easy preparation comes from columnist Peter Kump. Be sure the carving knife is well sharpened, or the cutting will be more trouble than the cooking.

BASIC CORNED BEEF

6 to 8 servings
Preparation time: 10 minutes
Cooking time: 3 hours

1   **corned beef, 4 to 6 pounds (brisket is best)**
2   **teaspoons black peppercorns**
2   **cloves garlic, unpeeled**
1   **onion, peeled, quartered**
1   **bay leaf**

1. Put all ingredients in nonaluminum dutch oven. Add cold water to cover by 2 to 3 inches. Heat to boil; reduce heat to low. Simmer covered, until a long-tined fork pierces the meat easily, about 3 hours.

2. Allow the corned beef to sit on cutting board for at least 10 minutes before carving. Slice as thin as possible. Serve with vegetables for dinner or with rye bread and mustard or horseradish for sandwiches.

NOTE: When making corned beef and cabbage (or other vegetables, such as carrots, onions, turnips or potatoes) it is better to boil or steam the vegetables in a separate pot. Cooking them in the water with the meat will result in greasy vegetables.

■ *This was a Mary Meade Recipe of the Week in March 1980. The meat cake will break up when you turn it. Just pat it back into shape.*

CORNED BEEF HASH

4 servings
Preparation time: 20 minutes
Cooking time: 30 to 35 minutes

3 to 3½ cups finely chopped, cooked corned beef

1 pound potatoes, peeled, cooked, diced

½ cup chopped onion

¼ teaspoon ground nutmeg

⅛ teaspoon freshly ground pepper

2 tablespoons butter or margarine

¼ cup whipping cream or half-and-half

1. Mix corned beef, potatoes, onion, nutmeg and pepper in large bowl.

2. Melt butter in large skillet over medium-high heat. Pat corned beef mixture evenly over bottom of pan. Press down firmly. Pour cream evenly over mixture. Cook until golden brown on bottom, 15 to 20 minutes.

3. Turn browned portions over with pancake turner. Cook until golden brown on bottom, about 15 more minutes. Serve immediately.

■ *Add corn relish and call the following recipe from Chicago's Hamburger Hamlet the "Heartland Burger."*

HAMBURGERS AMERICAN-STYLE

4 servings
Preparation time: 25 minutes
Cooking time: 10 minutes

2 pounds ground beef round

4 slices American or mild Cheddar cheese

4 thick slices cooked ham, pan-fried

8 slices bacon, cooked until crisp

4 hamburger buns, split Thousand Island salad dressing

4 thick tomato slices

1. Prepare charcoal grill or preheat broiler. Shape ground round into 4 burgers.

2. Grill or broil hamburgers, 6 inches from heat source, turning once, until halfway cooked, about 4 minutes. Top with a slice of cheese, then ham and then 2 pieces of bacon, crisscrossed. Continue grilling until medium-rare, 2 to 6 minutes.

3. Serve on bun bottom. Spread bun top with Thousand Island dressing; top with tomato slice. Serve open face.

Green peppercorns and freshly cracked black peppercorns combine to make a distinctively spicy burger from test kitchen director JeanMarie Brownson.

HAMBURGERS WITH GREEN PEPPERCORNS

4 servings
Preparation time: 15 minutes
Cooking time: 10 minutes

2 **pounds ground beef round**

2 **small cloves garlic, minced**

¼ **cup drained green peppercorns**

1 **egg, beaten**

1 **tablespoon each: brandy, Dijon mustard**

⅓ **cup fine, dry, bread crumbs**

½ **teaspoon freshly cracked black peppercorns**

¼ **teaspoon ground nutmeg**

4 **hamburger buns, split**

4 **thick slices ripe tomato**

1. Prepare charcoal grill or preheat broiler. Mix all ingredients, except buns and tomato, in large bowl. Shape into 4 patties.

2. Grill or broil hamburgers, 6 inches from heat source, turning once, until medium-rare or desired doneness, 6 to 10 minutes. Serve immediately on buns with a slice of tomato.

The popular restaurant chain Hamburger Hamlet created a burger both Popeye and Whimpy can enjoy.

SPINACH BURGERS

4 servings
Preparation time: 30 minutes
Cooking time: 12 minutes

2 **pounds ground beef round**

10 **ounces fresh spinach, washed**

4 **slices Monterey Jack cheese, sliced**

4 **hamburger buns, split, grilled or toasted**

1. Prepare charcoal grill or preheat broiler. Shape ground round into 4 burgers.

2. Drop spinach into boiling water; cook just until bright green. Drain and press out all excess water.

3. Grill or broil hamburgers, 6 inches from heat source, turning once, until halfway done, about 4 minutes. Top with some of the drained spinach and slice of cheese. Press down. Grill until medium-rare, 2 to 6 more minutes.

4. Place on grilled bun; place bun top next to open-face hamburger.

This tasty meat loaf adapted from a recipe by the noted cooking teacher Maurice Moore-Betty fits any occasion. The green peppers and chili sauce add zest. Cut the recipe in half for a family meal, although leftovers will make great sandwiches.

JUST GREAT MEAT LOAF

10 servings
Preparation time: 10 minutes
Baking time: 1 hour, 20 minutes

2   **pounds ground beef (top round or sirloin)**
1   **pound each: ground veal, ground pork**
1   **cup each: cottage cheese, fresh bread crumbs**
1½ **cups finely chopped onions**
3   **eggs, beaten**
1   **cup finely chopped green pepper, about 1 medium**
1   **cup chili sauce**
    Salt, freshly ground pepper to taste
½   **cup each: dry red wine, tomato sauce**

1. Heat oven to 400 degrees. Combine beef, veal and pork in large bowl; mix thoroughly. Add cottage cheese, bread crumbs, onions, eggs, green pepper and ½ cup of the chili sauce. Season with salt and pepper to taste.

2. Divide mixture in half. Put into two 9 by 5-inch loaf pans. Pour ¼ cup of the wine over each meat loaf. Mix the tomato sauce and remaining ½ cup chili sauce in small bowl, spread over each meat loaf.

3. Bake at 400 degrees for 30 minutes, basting frequently with pan juices. Reduce oven temperature to 350 degrees and bake until juices run clear, 50 to 60 more minutes. Let stand 10 minutes before slicing.

When *The Tribune* *kitchen tested recipes from* Chef Paul Prudhomme's *Louisiana Kitchen cookbook in 1984, tasters fell in love with his meat loaf recipe.*

The king of Cajun cooks, Prudhomme is a master at combining flavors, so follow the seasoning quantities exactly. Mashed potatoes belong on the plate with this meat loaf. You won't need a sauce.

CAJUN MEAT LOAF

6 servings
Preparation time: 1 hour
Cooking time: About 1 hour

SEASONING MIX

- **2 whole bay leaves**
- **1 tablespoon salt**
- **1 teaspoon each:
  cayenne pepper,
  freshly ground black
  pepper**
- **½ teaspoon each: white
  pepper, ground
  cumin, ground
  nutmeg**

MEAT MIXTURE

- **¼ cup (½ stick) unsalted
  butter**
- **¾ cup finely chopped
  yellow onions**
- **½ cup each, finely
  chopped: celery,
  green pepper**
- **¼ cup finely chopped
  green onions**
- **2 teaspoons minced
  garlic**
- **1 tablespoon each: hot
  pepper sauce,
  Worcestershire sauce**
- **½ cup each: evaporated
  milk, catsup**
- **1½ pounds ground beef
  round**
- **½ pound ground pork**
- **2 eggs, lightly beaten**
- **1 cup very dry bread
  crumbs**

1. Combine the seasoning mix ingredients in small bowl and set aside.

2. Melt butter in a 1-quart saucepan over medium heat. Add onions, celery, green pepper, green onions, garlic, hot pepper sauce, Worcestershire sauce and seasoning mix. Sauté until mixture starts sticking excessively, about 6 minutes, stirring occasionally and scraping the pan bottom well.

3. Stir in milk and catsup. Continue cooking about 2 minutes, stirring occasionally. Remove from heat and allow mixture to cool to room temperature. Remove bay leaves.

4. Heat oven to 350 degrees. Put ground beef and pork in ungreased 13 by 9-inch baking pan. Add eggs, cooked vegetable mixture and bread crumbs. Mix by hand until thoroughly combined.

5. In the center of the pan, shape the mixture into loaf about 1½ inches high, 6 inches wide and 12 inches long. Bake, uncovered, at 350 degrees 25 minutes, then raise oven temperature to 400 degrees and continue cooking until done, about 35 minutes longer. Serve immediately.

A tangy party preparation of ground beef from old Mexico was part of a Food Guide celebration menu along with chicken and cilantro enchiladas (provided here as a bonus recipe), plus rice, refried beans, a tossed green salad and fresh pineapple chunks and strawberries for dessert.

PICADILLO ENCHILADAS

8 servings
Preparation time: 45 minutes
Cooking time: 40 minutes

PICADILLO FILLING
- 2 tablespoons oil
- 1 medium onion, minced
- 2 small cloves garlic, minced
- 1 pound ground beef round or pork
- 1½ cups crushed tomatoes with added puree
- 2 tablespoons each: dark brown sugar, cider vinegar
- 1 tablespoon hot or mild chili powder
- ¾ teaspoon ground cumin
- ½ teaspoon each: ground cinnamon, ground coriander seed
- ½ cup each: dark raisins, sliced green olives, frozen peas
- ¼ cup slivered almonds

ASSEMBLY
- Vegetable oil for frying
- 12 corn tortillas

SAUCE
- 2 cups canned crushed tomatoes with added puree
- ¼ cup minced fresh cilantro (coriander)
- 1 small onion, minced
- 1 small clove garlic, minced
- 1 tablespoon chili powder
- 1 cup shredded Cheddar cheese
- Sour cream, optional

1. For picadillo filling, heat 2 tablespoons oil in large dutch oven. Add onion and garlic; sauté until transparent, about 2 minutes. Stir in beef. Cook and stir until beef is no longer pink, about 5 minutes.

2. Drain off all but 2 tablespoons of the fat. Stir in tomatoes, sugar, vinegar, chili powder, cumin, cinnamon and coriander. Simmer, covered, for 15 minutes. Stir in raisins, olives, peas and almonds. Simmer, uncovered, about 10 minutes.

3. To assemble, heat ¼ inch oil in nonstick skillet. Add 1 tortilla at a time; fry just until softened. Remove to paper towel. Put ¼ cup of the meat mixture on tortilla. Roll up and place seam side down in 13 by 9-inch baking dish. Repeat to fry and fill tortillas and arrange in dish.

4. Heat oven to 325 degrees. For sauce, put tomatoes, cilantro, onion, garlic and chili powder into food processor. Process until a coarse puree.

5. Pour sauce over all. Sprinkle with cheese. Bake until sauce is bubbly and cheese is melted, about 15 minutes. Serve with a dollop of sour cream.

THE CHICAGO TRIBUNE COOKBOOK

PAPAYA DAIQUIRI

CIDER PUNCH

CAJUN MARTINI, GUACAMOLE, NEW POTATOES WITH HORSERADISH CREAM AND CAVIAR

EGGPLANT TERRINE WITH SUN-DRIED TOMATO MAYONNAISE

CHOCOLATE WAFFLES WITH POACHED STRAWBERRIES

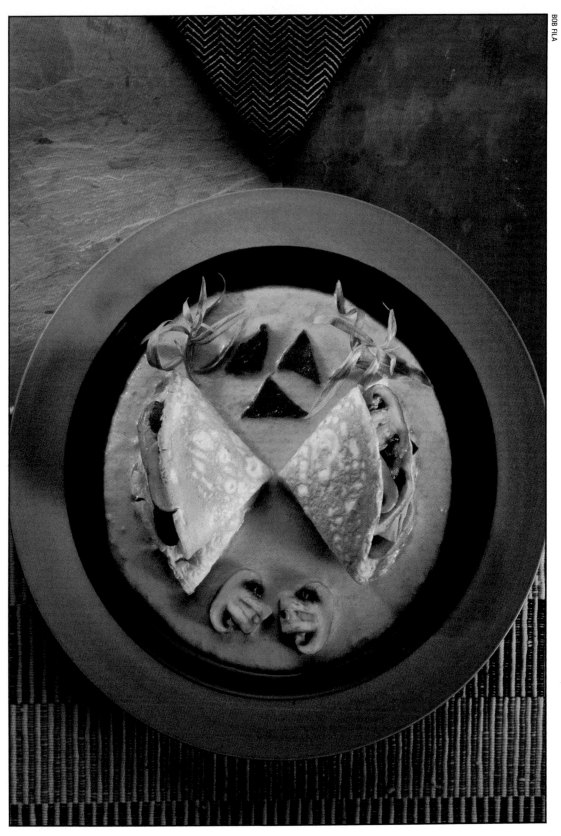

EGG CREPES WITH ROASTED RED PEPPERS AND MUSHROOMS

LITHUANIAN BEET SOUP

BOUILLABAISSE

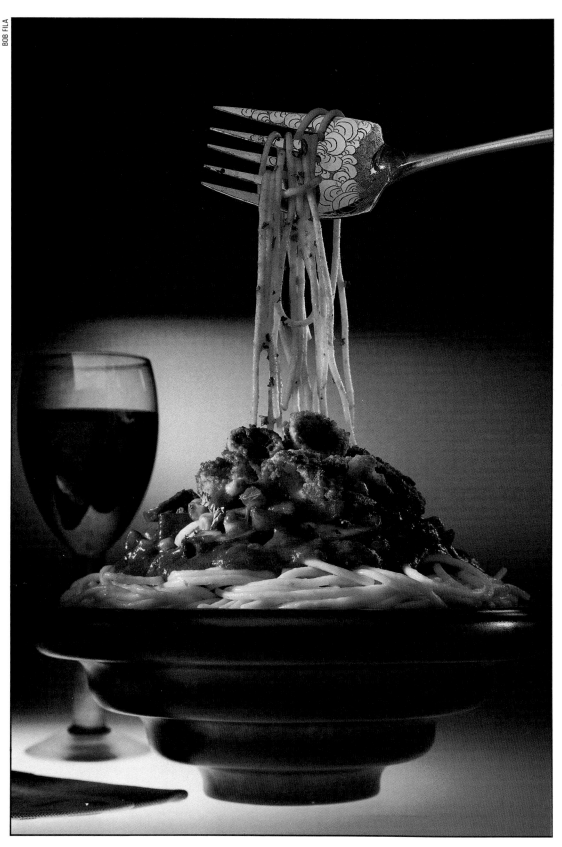

SPAGHETTI WITH CHUNKY TOMATO SAUCE AND FRIED CALAMARI

CHICAGO-STYLE DEEP-DISH PIZZA

WHITEFISH WITH GOLDEN TOMATO BUTTER SAUCE

TURBOT WITH BASIL

**SPICED RABBIT WITH SALSA-FLAVORED SAUCE, DUCK BREAST SALAD
WITH HAZELNUT DRESSING**

PICADILLO ENCHILADAS

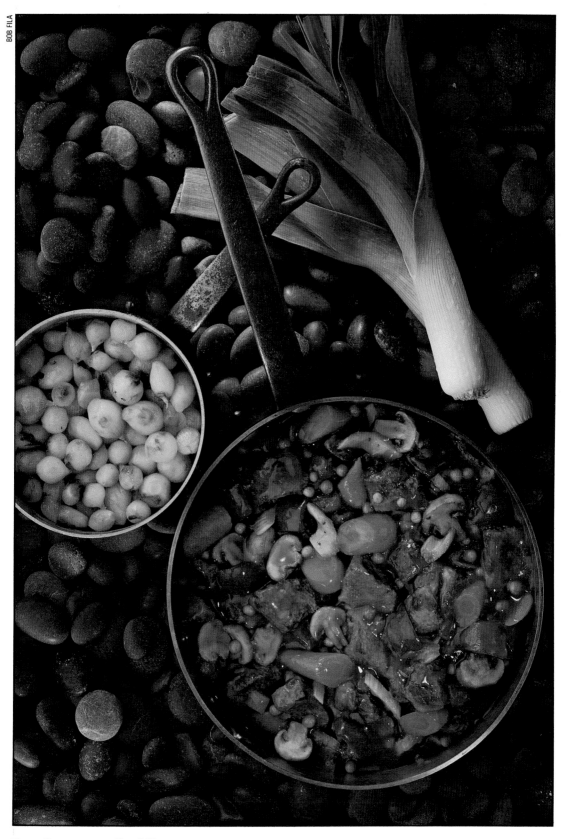

BEEF STEW WITH RED WINE

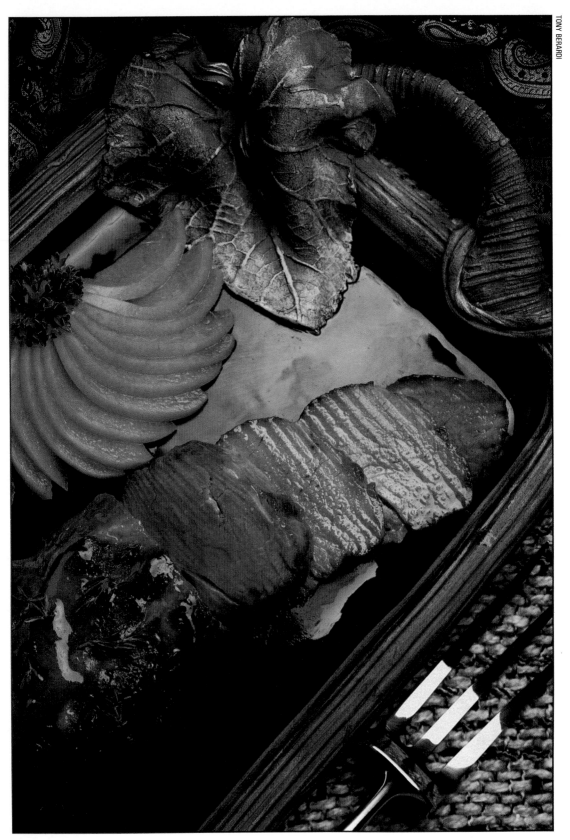

PORK TENDERLOIN WITH APRICOT RELISH

VARIATION: For chicken and cilantro enchilada filling, simmer 3 whole chicken breasts, split, in 5 cups chicken broth or water until chicken is cooked, about 20 minutes. Remove from cooking liquid; reserve cooking liquid for other use. Remove chicken from bones. Discard skin and bones. Pull chicken into shreds. Add 1 minced jalapeño pepper, 1 can (4 ounces) diced green chilies and ¼ cup minced, fresh cilantro. Use to fill tortillas as in step 3 above. Finish dish as directed in steps 4 and 5.

NOTE: Both the picadillo filling and the chicken and cilantro filling can be served in taco shells topped with shredded lettuce and cheese.

Busy Chicago radio disc jockey Terri Hemmert relies on a "tostada with a whole meal on top of it" when she's entertaining with a time deadline. Tasty but messy to eat, this dish is best served informally. She rounds out the menu with beer and ice cream, then takes off for a concert. Her cleanup tip: "Let things soak. Clean up later."

BEEF AND BEAN TOSTADAS

4 servings
Preparation time: 20 minutes
Cooking time: 10 minutes

1 **cup shredded lettuce**
2 **medium-size tomatoes, chopped, seeded**
¼ **cup chopped onion**
1 **cup shredded sharp Cheddar cheese**
1 **pound ground beef chuck**
¼ **teaspoon each: salt, freshly ground pepper**
1 **can (16 ounces) kidney beans, undrained**
  Vegetable oil for frying
8 **fresh corn tortillas**
1 **bottle (16 ounces) salsa, mild, hot or a combination of the two**
  Hot pepper sauce, optional

1. Prepare lettuce, tomatoes, onion and cheese. Put into serving dishes on table.

2. Put beef into large skillet. Cook, stirring occasionally and breaking into small pieces, until no longer pink. Drain off fat. Place cooked meat on paper towels to absorb excess fat. Add salt and pepper.

3. Meanwhile, pour beans into small saucepan. Mash with fork or pastry blender. Set pan over low heat. Stir occasionally, taking care not to burn.

4. Pour oil to depth of ¼ inch in 9-inch skillet. Heat skillet over high heat until a drop of water dropped into the oil splatters. (If oil isn't hot enough, tortillas will be limp, not crisp.) Fry each tortilla separately until firm and a little brown on each side. Use fork to turn occasionally. Also press occasionally in middle so tortilla has a slight curve. Drain tortillas on paper towels.

5. To assemble, spread bean paste on tortillas. Then add ground meat, lettuce, tomatoes, onion, cheese, salsa and hot pepper sauce. Serve immediately.

NOTE: Leftover lettuce, tomatoes and onion, plus some salt and pepper mixed with the meat mixture will make a great salad for the next day.

Beverly Dillon's Mexican pot roast became one of The Tribune*'s 10 favorite recipes of 1985. The chilies are not difficult to work with once they have been softened. They provide more flavor than heat. Marinating the meat with this paste coating adds incredible flavor.*

MEXICAN-STYLE POT ROAST WITH VEGETABLES

6 to 8 servings
Preparation time: 30 minutes
Marinating time: 8 hours or overnight
Cooking time: 2½ hours

4 each: dried pasilla chilies, dried ancho chilies

4 cloves garlic

¼ cup vegetable oil

3 tablespoons fresh lime juice

1 teaspoon ground cumin

½ teaspoon salt

4 pounds beef chuck top blade pot roast

¼ cup vegetable shortening or oil

1 can (28 ounces) Italian-style plum tomatoes, undrained

1 can (13¾ ounces) beef broth

1 pound carrots, peeled, halved

6 to 8 small onions

8 medium red potatoes, halved

2 chayote squash (mirliton) or zucchini, quartered

1. Soak chilies in hot water to cover until softened, about 20 minutes. Drain. Remove and discard veins and seeds.

2. With machine running, drop garlic into food processor or blender. Process until minced. Add drained chilies, oil, lime juice, cumin and salt. Process until a smooth paste.

3. Spread paste over all sides of pot roast. Refrigerate, covered, in a shallow nonaluminum dish 8 hours or overnight.

4. Heat oven to 350 degrees. Melt shortening in large dutch oven. Add roast with paste and cook until brown on both sides. Stir in undrained tomatoes and broth. Heat to simmer; break up tomatoes. Bake, covered, adding more broth or water as needed, for 2 hours.

5. After 2 hours, add carrots, onions, potatoes and squash. Bake, covered, until meat and vegetables are fork-tender, about 30 more minutes.

6. Remove meat and vegetables with slotted spoon to serving platter. Remove fat from pan juices. Pour pan juices over meat and vegetables. Serve meat thinly sliced.

Steak as it's done south of the border makes great party fare. Test kitchen director JeanMarie Brownson created this recipe for a New Year's Eve party. Guests were invited to make their own fajitas, piling on ingredients according to personal whim. The sauce is smoky hot, not smoky pungent. For guests, consider offering a mild sauce as well.

STEAK FAJITAS WITH SMOKY SALSA

8 servings
Preparation time: 1 hour
Marinating time: 4 hours or overnight
Cooking time: 10 minutes

⅓ **cup each: oil, fresh lemon juice**

2 **teaspoons soy sauce**

4 **teaspoons adobo sauce from canned chipotle peppers (see note)**

2 **pounds flank steak or skirt steak**

Smoky salsa (recipe follows)

2 **medium each: green peppers, red bell peppers, white onions**

2 **tablespoons oil**

3 **avocados, peeled, thinly sliced, or guacamole (see recipe, page 20)**

1 **bunch green onions, chopped**

2 **large tomatoes, chopped**

½ **cup minced, fresh cilantro (coriander)**

Sour cream

Shredded lettuce

2 **dozen flour tortillas**

1. Mix ⅓ cup oil, lemon juice, soy sauce and sauce from peppers in large shallow dish. Add steak; turn to coat. Refrigerate covered, turning steak occasionally, at least 4 hours or overnight.

2. Make salsa.

3. Remove seeds from green and red bell peppers; cut into thin strips. Cut white onions into thin slices; separate slices into rings. Heat 2 tablespoons oil in large skillet; add peppers and onions. Sauté until crisp-tender, 3 to 5 minutes. Remove from heat.

4. Shortly before serving, preheat broiler or prepare charcoal grill.

5. Meanwhile, put salsa, sautéed vegetables, avocados, green onions, tomatoes, cilantro, sour cream and lettuce into separate serving dishes.

6. Heat a well-seasoned griddle or cast-iron skillet until hot. Toast tortillas until lightly browned on each side. Wrap in foil to keep warm.

7. Remove steak from marinade and reserve marinade. Broil or grill steak, 6 inches from heat source, turning once, until rare, about 8 minutes.

8. Slice steak on the diagonal into very thin strips. Drizzle with reserved marinade.

9. To serve, put some steak strips onto a flour tortilla; top with desired toppings and salsa. Wrap up and eat out of hand.

NOTE: Chipotle peppers are jalapeño peppers that have been smoked and dried; they are available canned in adobo sauce in Mexican markets.

Smoky Salsa | About 1½ cups

1 **pint cherry tomatoes, hulled, halved**

4 **green onions, quartered**

2 **tablespoons fresh lemon juice**

1 **canned chipotle pepper in adobo sauce, minced, about 1 tablespoon**

10 **sprigs fresh cilantro (coriander)**

½ **teaspoon salt**

1. Put all ingredients into blender or food processor. Process until finely chopped but not pureed. Transfer to serving bowl. Refrigerate up to 2 hours to allow flavors to blend. Taste and adjust seasonings. Serve at room temperature.

Cathy Zordan of Evanston, Illinois, a microwave cooking specialist, developed this recipe. She advises new microwave cooks to get a good microwave cookbook and read it. "Do exactly what it says until you are comfortable," she told The Tribune. *For family meals, she accents this beef dish with fresh vegetables.*

STUFFED FLANK STEAK

6 servings
Preparation time: 15 minutes
Microwave cooking time: 11 minutes

1 beef flank steak, about 1½ pounds
½ cup bottled Italian dressing
2 tablespoons soy sauce

STUFFING

1 medium zucchini, shredded
½ cup each: chopped onion, shredded carrots, diced green pepper
1 cup unseasoned dry stuffing mix
½ teaspoon each: Italian seasoning, salt
¼ cup butter or margarine, melted
¼ cup red wine

1. Marinate steak in Italian dressing and soy sauce in shallow nonaluminum dish in the refrigerator 4 hours or overnight.

2. Remove steak from marinade; reserve marinade. Pat meat dry with paper towel. With sharp knife, butterfly steak by starting at long end, split steak nearly, but not completely, in half horizontally, leaving it hinged on one long side. Open up steak like a book. Using coarser side of meat pounder, pound steak on both sides to about ¼-inch thickness.

3. Mix zucchini, onion, carrots, green pepper, stuffing mix, Italian seasoning, salt and butter in medium bowl. Spread mixture evenly over meat, leaving a 1-inch border on all sides. Roll up meat, starting from long side, jelly-roll fashion. Tie with string in several places along roll to form a compact shape.

4. Put into microwave-safe baking dish. Stir wine into reserved marinade. Brush steak with marinade mixture. Cover with plastic wrap, venting one corner. Microwave on high (100 percent power) for 5 minutes. Baste with marinade mixture. Rotate dish; microwave on medium-high (70 percent power) until tender, 7½ minutes. Let stand, covered, 5 minutes. Serve thinly sliced.

This Italian recipe, from Carlucci's restaurant in Chicago, gives off wonderfully fragrant aromas as it cooks on an open-air grill. It cooks so quickly, you may want to use the grill for a first course as well. Consider grilling shrimp or vegetables. Don't use a pronged fork to turn the meat. The best implement for handling foods on the grill is a pair of metal tongs.

ROLLED SIRLOIN WITH PROSCIUTTO AND SAGE

4 servings
Preparation time: 20 minutes
Standing time: 1 hour
Cooking time: 10 minutes

¼ cup extra-virgin olive oil
2 cloves garlic
4 red bell peppers
4 boneless strip steaks, each ½-inch thick, trimmed of fat
½ teaspoon freshly ground pepper
2 tablespoons fresh sage leaves, coarsely chopped
¼ pound thinly sliced prosciutto
1 small loaf Italian bread

1. Put olive oil in a small bowl. Crush the garlic and add to the oil. Set aside at least 1 hour prior to cooking the steaks.

2. To roast red peppers, preheat broiler. Put pepper onto broiler pan. Broil 4 to 6 inches from heat source until skins are blistered and slightly charred. Wrap in foil; let stand until cool. Put onto cutting board; remove stems and seeds. Using a paring knife, peel away charred skin. Slice into strips.

3. Prepare charcoal grill or preheat broiler.

4. Remove any excess fat from steaks. Flatten steaks between sheets of wax paper or plastic wrap to ⅛-inch thickness. Season with pepper. Place equal amounts of sage on each steak, cover with a thin slice of prosciutto, then roll from the tail up. Secure the flap with a wooden pick.

5. To make garlic croutons, cut the Italian bread into ½-inch slices. Brush generously on both sides with some of the reserved garlic oil. Grill or broil until golden; reserve.

6. Brush steaks with the remaining garlic oil. Grill or broil, 4 inches from heat source, turning once, until medium-rare, 4 to 6 minutes.

7. Remove wooden picks from steaks. Serve the steaks with the croutons and reserved roasted peppers.

Cognac has a place in the kitchen as well as the liquor cabinet. Less elegant brandies are more economical for quantity cooking; but cognac provides a haunting aroma and distinctive flavor nuance to this simple, elegant steak recipe from columnist William Rice. He suggests serving the steak with homemade french fries.

STEAK AU POIVRE

2 servings
Preparation time: 10 minutes
Cooking time: 8 to 10 minutes

1½ **tablespoons black peppercorns**
2 **beef filet steaks, about 5 ounces each, at room temperature**
1 **tablespoon butter**
2 **tablespoons vegetable oil**
Salt to taste
2 **tablespoons cognac**
⅓ **cup crème fraîche or whipping cream**
Watercress sprigs for garnish

1. At least 30 minutes before cooking, crush peppercorns coarsely and spread on plate. Pat both filets into peppercorns, turning to coat both sides.

2. Melt butter with oil in heavy skillet. When very hot, add filets. Cook, turning once, until crisp and dark brown on outside but still rare in center, 8 to 10 minutes. Baste filets and salt lightly after turning.

3. Remove pan from heat, remove filets; pour off grease. Return steaks to pan. Put pan over medium heat; add cognac. Carefully ignite cognac with a long match. Gently shake pan over heat until flame dies. Transfer steaks to plates or platter. Keep warm.

4. Add crème fraîche to pan. As it comes to a boil, scrape bottom with wooden spoon to dislodge brown bits of meat and meat juice. Cook until reduced and slightly thickened, about 2 minutes. Taste and add salt as desired.

5. Pour sauce over filets. Serve garnished with watercress.

Linda Lynn of St. Charles, Illinois contributed this favorite recipe in 1984. Oxtails become wonderfully tender when cooked in this manner, and the sauce will be rich.

BARBECUED OXTAILS

4 to 6 servings
Preparation time: 20 minutes
Cooking time: 2½ hours

2 **whole oxtails, cut into 2-inch pieces, about 3 pounds**
1 **medium onion, finely chopped**
2 **cloves garlic, minced**
1 **can (8 ounces) tomato sauce**
1 **can (6 ounces) tomato paste**
1 **cup catsup**
¾ **cup packed brown sugar**
½ **cup each: water, cider vinegar**
1 **tablespoon each: prepared mustard, Dijon mustard**
1½ **teaspoons ground thyme**

1. Heat oven to 425 degrees. Rinse oxtails; pat dry. Trim off excess fat. Place in dutch oven. Roast for 30 minutes.

2. Reduce oven temperature to 325 degrees. Using a slotted spoon, transfer oxtails to paper towel. Pour off excess fat from pan. Set pan over medium heat. Add onion and garlic; cook and stir until onion is limp, about 3 minutes. Stir in remaining ingredients; heat to simmer. Add oxtails.

3. Bake, covered, until oxtails are very tender, about 2 hours. Add small amounts of water during cooking if needed to keep oxtails moist.

A make-it-yourself breakfast sausage that will stand out on a brunch menu. The fresh basil gives the sausage a wonderful scent and flavor, but many other fresh herbs will work just fine. Experiment to find your favorite, or prepare several different versions for everyone to sample.

BREAKFAST SAUSAGE

4 to 6 servings
Preparation time: 10 minutes
Cooking time: 15 minutes

1   pound ground pork
½   pound ground veal
1½ teaspoons minced
      fresh basil
½   teaspoon each: freshly
      ground black pepper,
      ground sage
¼   teaspoon salt

1. Mix all ingredients in large bowl. Shape into patties about 2½ inches in diameter.

2. Fry in nonstick skillet until golden on all sides, 10 to 15 minutes. Drain on paper towel.

There is some question whether the result of this recipe is bacon or candy, but it is sure to be a conversation piece at breakfast or brunch. This bacon is better with scrambled eggs than fried, and best with waffles.

MAPLE GLAZED BACON

4 servings
Preparation time: 10 minutes
Baking time: 25 minutes

½   pound thick sliced
      bacon
2   tablespoons pure
      maple syrup
1   tablespoon orange
      marmalade
2   teaspoons dry mustard

1. Heat oven to 400 degrees. Line bottom of jelly-roll pan with aluminum foil. Lay wire rack on top of foil. Lay bacon in single layer on rack.

2. Mix syrup, marmalade and mustard in small bowl until well blended. Brush over one side of bacon.

3. Bake 15 minutes. Turn bacon over; brush other side with syrup mixture. Bake until bacon is crisp, 5 to 10 minutes more. Remove from oven; let bacon drip on rack, about 5 minutes. Do not drain on paper towel because bacon will stick. Serve warm.

Rich in flavor, this chili from columnist Beverly Dillon uses cubed pork shoulder instead of the usual ground beef. And in addition to the familiar kidney beans, black beans and corn add interest, texture and color.

HEARTLAND CHILI

6 to 8 servings
Preparation time: 30 minutes
Cooking time: 1½ hours to 2 hours

2 tablespoons vegetable oil

3½ pounds boneless pork shoulder, cut into ½-inch cubes

2 medium onions, chopped

1 tablespoon chopped garlic

3 tablespoons chili powder

1 tablespoon each: dried basil, ground cumin seed, dried leaf oregano

1 teaspoon each: salt, freshly ground pepper

½ teaspoon cayenne pepper or to taste

1 can (13¾ ounces) chicken broth

1 can (14 ounces) whole tomatoes, chopped

1 can (6 ounces) tomato paste

1 each: small green pepper, small red bell pepper

1 can (16 ounces each), drained: red kidney beans, black beans

1 box (10 ounces) frozen corn kernels

GARNISH

1 bunch green onions, diced

Shredded sharp Cheddar cheese

Sour cream

Chopped fresh cilantro (coriander)

1. Heat oil in large dutch oven over medium heat until hot. Add some of the meat in single layer; cook and stir until lightly browned on all sides, about 5 minutes. Remove with slotted spoon; continue to cook until all meat is browned.

2. Return all meat to dutch oven. Add onions, garlic, chili powder, basil, cumin, oregano, salt, pepper and cayenne pepper. Cook and stir 5 minutes. Add chicken broth, tomatoes and tomato paste. Stir to mix. Heat to boil; reduce heat to low. Simmer, covered, stirring occasionally, until meat is fork-tender, about 1½ hours.

3. Remove core and seeds from green and red pepper. Dice peppers. Stir peppers, kidney beans, black beans and corn into chili. Cook until heated through, about 10 minutes.

4. Put garnishes in small serving bowls. Serve chili in wide soup bowls topped with garnishes as desired.

The rustic cooking of Northern Italy inspired this festive feast dish created by Beverly Dillon. It is hearty fare, best enjoyed on a chilly fall or winter day. Polenta is nothing but cornmeal mush, but when the Italians cook it, it tastes nothing like cornmeal. Considering the labor involved, however, do plan to make it ahead.

BUTTERFLIED PORK CHOPS WITH POLENTA AND MUSHROOM SAUCE

6 servings
Preparation time: 40 minutes
Marinating time: 1 hour
Cooking time: 1¼ hours

MARINADE

⅓ cup red wine

¼ cup each: olive oil, loosely packed fresh basil leaves or 2 teaspoons dried

1 tablespoon minced fresh oregano or ¼ teaspoon dried

1 small clove garlic

6 butterflied pork chops, each about 1-inch thick

POLENTA

1½ cups yellow cornmeal

2 cans (13¾ ounces each) chicken broth

½ teaspoon salt

½ cup (1 stick) unsalted butter, softened

1½ cups freshly grated Parmesan cheese

MUSHROOM SAUCE

1 pound mushrooms, sliced

1 tablespoon olive oil

1 can (14 ounces) whole tomatoes

¼ cup loosely packed fresh basil, chopped, or 2 teaspoons dried

1 tablespoon each, minced: shallots, parsley, fresh oregano (or ¼ teaspoon dried)

½ teaspoon minced garlic

1 tablespoon drained capers

¼ teaspoon each: salt, pepper

1. For marinade, put wine, oil, basil, oregano and garlic in blender or food processor. Process until smooth.

2. Put pork chops in shallow glass dish. Pour marinade over chops. Turn once to coat with marinade. Cover with plastic wrap. Refrigerate about 1 hour.

3. Meanwhile, for polenta, butter 13 by 9-inch baking pan. Mix cornmeal and half of the chicken broth in small bowl until smooth. Heat remaining chicken broth and salt in large heavy saucepan over high heat to boil. Stir cornmeal mixture into boiling chicken broth. Return to boil, stirring constantly. Reduce heat to medium low. Simmer, stirring constantly, until mixture is smooth, dry in appearance and pulls away from sides of pan, 40 to 45 minutes. Remove from heat. Stir in butter.

4. Pour into prepared pan. Smooth top. Sprinkle evenly with 1 cup of the cheese. Heat oven to 350 degrees.

5. Bake until cheese is golden, 15 to 20 minutes. Remove from oven. Cool slightly. Cut into 12 squares. (Polenta may be made ahead and reheated just before serving.)

6. Meanwhile, for mushroom sauce, cook mushrooms in oil in large skillet over medium-high heat until golden, about 10 minutes. Add tomatoes, basil, shallots, parsley, oregano and garlic. Heat to boil; reduce heat. Cook and stir, until mixture thickens slightly, about 5 minutes. Add capers, salt and pepper. Keep warm.

7. Prepare charcoal grill or preheat broiler. Remove chops from marinade. Grill or broil, 4 inches from heat source, turning once, until juices run clear, 15 to 20 minutes.

8. To serve, arrange one pork chop on each dinner plate. Add 2 polenta squares. Sprinkle polenta with some of the remaining cheese. Top each with some of the mushroom sauce, dividing evenly. Serve immediately.

NOTE: Mushroom sauce may be made up to one day in advance. Spoon into small bowl. Cover with plastic wrap; refrigerate. To reheat, return to small saucepan and cook over low heat until heated through.

Perfect for a summertime menu, these chops can be served with other Oriental-flavored accompaniments such as fried rice and stir-fried vegetables. Iced tea and fruit for dessert keeps the dinner cool and comfortable.

GRILLED TERIYAKI PORK CHOPS

4 servings
Preparation time: 15 minutes
Marinating time: 4 hours
Cooking time: 20 minutes

¼ **cup each: teriyaki sauce, dry white wine**
2 **tablespoons honey**
1 **small onion, chopped**
1 **clove garlic, minced**
4 **pork chops, about 1-inch thick**

1. Mix teriyaki sauce, wine, honey, onion and garlic in large baking dish. Add pork chops; turn to coat. Refrigerate covered, about 4 hours.

2. Prepare a charcoal grill or preheat broiler. Remove pork chops from marinade. Grill or broil, 6 inches from heat source, basting occasionally with marinade and turning once, until juices run clear, 15 to 20 minutes.

Mexican tortillas get an authentic spicy kick from respected cooking teacher Elaine Gonzalez, of Northbrook, Illinois. She was rated one of the Chicago area's best cooking teachers in a 1987 survey by The Tribune.

BRAISED PORK IN TORTILLAS

4 servings
Preparation time: 20 minutes
Standing time: 30 minutes
Cooking time: 1 hour

1 pound lean boneless pork
1 teaspoon garlic salt
2 tablespoons oil
2 to 3 cloves garlic
2 to 3 fresh chilies japones or any small green chili
1 can (16 ounces) whole tomatoes, undrained, chopped
8 large flour tortillas

1. Cut pork into very small cubes. Sprinkle with garlic salt; let stand 30 minutes.

2. Put pork in medium saucepan with water to cover. Cook, uncovered, until tender, 35 to 45 minutes; drain well.

3. Add oil to pan; fry pork until browned, about 10 minutes. Drain off excess fat. With mortar and pestle, or in a blender, blend garlic cloves with fresh chilies to a paste. Add garlic mixture and tomatoes to pork. Simmer for 15 minutes. Season with salt.

4. Heat tortillas on hot griddle. Spoon about 2 tablespoons hot pork down center of tortilla. Roll up and eat out of hand.

Professional rib master Leon Finney has a wide reputation for his great ribs. While the recipe for the sauce slathered on slabs of ribs at the Leon Finney's Bar-B-Q restaurants in Chicago is a trade secret, The Tribune test kitchen created a similar recipe in 1982.

CHICAGO-STYLE BARBECUED RIBS

4 servings
Preparation time: 30 minutes
Chilling time: Several hours
Cooking time: 1 hour

4 slabs pork baby back ribs, 4 to 6 pounds total
Seasoned salt
1 cup catsup
½ cup plus 1 tablespoon cider vinegar
⅓ cup packed dark brown sugar
2 tablespoons plus 2 teaspoons Worcestershire sauce
2 tablespoons cornstarch
2 teaspoons steak sauce
½ teaspoon each:
seasoned salt,
hickory smoked salt
Hot pepper sauce to taste
Hickory wood chips

1. Generously sprinkle ribs on both sides with seasoned salt. Refrigerate several hours or overnight, if desired. Remove from refrigerator 30 minutes before cooking to allow ribs to come to room temperature.

2. Mix remaining ingredients, except wood chips, in medium-size nonaluminum saucepan. Heat to boil; simmer, uncovered, 30 minutes. Taste and adjust seasonings. (Sauce will keep 2 to 3 weeks in the refrigerator.)

3. Prepare charcoal grill. Soak hickory chips in water to cover for 20 minutes or more.

4. When coals are covered with gray ash, put ribs on grill rack at least 8 inches from charcoal. Cover and grill, until ribs are golden on both sides. Add a handful of drained hickory chips periodically to the charcoal to maintain a steady amount of hickory smoke.

5. Continue grilling until ribs are tender, 30 to 40 minutes. Then baste one side heavily with sauce; grill until sauce is bubbly. Turn and baste second side with sauce; grill until sauce is bubbly. Serve immediately.

NOTE: For the best results, cook with only a moderate amount of charcoal so the grill is not too hot; the longer the ribs take to cook the better the smoke flavor will permeate the meat. Do not allow the ribs to char.

Meat

■ *Chicagoan Lamar Brantley's "down-home" pork received a one-word review: "Yum!"*
Depending on where "down home" is, cooks will slice the pork very thinly and serve it
with sauce on the side; chop it on a wooden cutting board with a knife, or perhaps two
working in tandem; or use a fork to pull the tender meat into shreds. In any event, it
usually winds up on a plate with some cornbread and greens or between 2 slices of
supermarket white bread.

DOWN-HOME BARBECUED PORK

8 servings
Preparation time: 15 minutes
Grilling time: 2 hours

1 pork shoulder blade
   roast, about 4 pounds
3 cups good-old-boy
   barbecue sauce,
   heated (recipe
   follows)

1. Prepare charcoal grill. When coals are covered with a gray ash, arrange coals for the indirect method at sides of grill. Place a drip pan in center. Put roast on grill rack over drip pan. Cover and grill, until meat thermometer registers 160 degrees, about 2 hours. Grill temperature should be maintained at about 325 degrees; add more coals as needed to grill.

2. Let cool 15 minutes before slicing, chopping or shredding. Mix meat with hot barbecue sauce.

GOOD-OLD-BOY BARBECUE SAUCE

About 4 cups

2 small lemons
2 cups natural apple
   cider vinegar
1 bottle (14 ounces)
   catsup
½ cup each:
   Worcestershire sauce,
   prepared mustard
½ cup (1 stick) margarine
2 tablespoons liquid
   smoke
1½ teaspoons each:
   freshly ground
   pepper, cayenne
   pepper, salt, sugar
¾ teaspoon each: ground
   cumin, dried leaf
   oregano

1. Cut ends off lemons; cut lemons into ¼-inch slices. Remove seeds. Put all ingredients, including lemons, in nonaluminum saucepan and cook slowly until all the pulp is cooked from lemon rinds, about 1 hour.

2. Remove rinds; put in blender with a little bit of the sauce, and puree. Put puree back into sauce; heat until hot, a few more minutes.

NOTE: For a mixed grill, you may cook country-style pork ribs or backribs at 350 degrees for 30 minutes while coals are heating. Then grill ribs and chicken (primarily breasts and thighs) over medium-hot coals, 30 minutes, turning and basting with sauce frequently. Cut precooked Polish or Ukrainian sausage into serving pieces. Add to outside edges of grill; continue cooking until chicken and ribs are tender and glazed with sauce, about 15 minutes.

Seasoned in the Italian manner, the aroma of this roast cooking on the grill will stimulate appetites. Finish roast potatoes on the grill as well and serve a giant salad for a first course. A light, slightly chilled red wine from Italy would match the roast well.

GRILLED HERBED PORK ROAST

8 servings
Preparation time: 25 minutes
Cooking time: About 2½ hours

1 **boneless pork top loin roast, rolled, tied, 4 to 6 pounds**

¼ **cup each: extra-virgin olive oil, juniper berries, crushed**

4 **teaspoons each, dried: basil, rosemary**

2 **teaspoons each, dried: tarragon, leaf thyme**

½ **teaspoon freshly ground pepper**

1. Rub roast generously with oil. Mix seasonings. Press mixture over entire surface of roast. Let roast stand at room temperature for 1 hour.

2. Meanwhile, prepare grill. When coals are covered with gray ash, arrange coals for the indirect method at sides of grill. Place a drip pan in center. Put roast on grill rack over drip pan.

3. Cover and grill, until meat thermometer registers 160 degrees, 2 to 2½ hours. Turn roast occasionally during grilling. Grill temperature should be maintained at about 325 degrees; add more coals as needed to grill.

4. Let roast stand 10 minutes before carving. (Meat temperature will rise about 10 degrees.)

■ The Tribune's *test kitchen staff cautions microwave cooks that using only high power overcooks and toughens meats. Therefore it is best to cook meat on the lower power settings and to use a thermometer to check for doneness. The fragrant cheese and spinach filling in this pork roast eliminates the need for a sauce.*

GARLIC AND SPINACH PORK ROAST

6 servings
Preparation time: 30 minutes
Microwave cooking time: 35 minutes

1 **boneless pork top loin roast, rolled, tied, about 3 pounds**
 Freshly ground pepper to taste
1 **package (10 ounces) frozen, chopped spinach, thawed, well drained**
1 **package (3 ounces) cream cheese or Neufchâtel cheese, softened**
3 **green onions, chopped**
2 **cloves garlic, finely minced**
1 **teaspoon dried basil**
½ **teaspoon dried tarragon**
 Several dashes hot pepper sauce
 Salt to taste

1. Lay pork roast out flat on work surface. Sprinkle inside with pepper.

2. Mix spinach, cheese, onions, garlic, basil, tarragon, hot pepper sauce, salt and pepper in small bowl. Spread over inside of pork roast, leaving a 1-inch border.

3. Roll up roast to enclose filling neatly and make a uniform package. Tie securely in several places with kitchen string.

4. Insert microwave thermometer into roast, if used. Put roast, fattest side down, on microwave-safe roasting rack set over microwave-safe drip dish.

5. Microwave on high (100 percent power) 5 minutes. Then microwave on medium (50 percent power) 13 minutes. Turn roast over, fat side up. Microwave on medium until thermometer registers 160 degrees, 13 to 17 minutes. (Total cooking time will be 12 to 16 minutes per pound.) Let stand on counter loosely covered with foil for 10 minutes. (Meat temperature will rise about 10 degrees after removing from oven.)

6. Serve thinly sliced. This roast is also good served cold with assorted mustards.

Oriental cooks are unbeatable when it comes to combining fruit and pork. Serve this roast with white rice and a fruit-friendly green vegetable such as brussels sprouts.

PLUM-GLAZED PORK ROAST

6 to 8 servings
Preparation time: 20 minutes
Cooking time: 2 hours

1 **can (17 ounces) whole red plums**

½ **cup orange marmalade**

¼ **cup rice wine or dry sherry**

¼ **cup soy sauce**

1 **tablespoon chopped crystallized ginger**

1 **clove garlic, minced**

1 **pork top loin rolled roast or shoulder blade, 3 to 4 pounds**

Slivered green onions, for garnish

Orange slices, for garnish

1. Remove pits from plums. Put undrained plums, marmalade, wine, soy sauce, ginger and garlic in small saucepan. Cook, uncovered, over low heat until thickened, about 10 minutes.

2. Heat oven to 350 degrees. Put roast onto rack set in roasting pan. Roast for 1½ hours. Then finish roasting, brushing heavily with glaze every 10 minutes, until meat thermometer registers 160 degrees, about 30 more minutes. (Meat temperature will rise about 10 degrees after removing from oven.)

3. Remove roast to serving platter. Let stand 15 minutes before carving. Garnish with green onions and orange slices. Pass remaining plum glaze.

It's best to have the butcher shape your "crown." Be sure he has made sure the roast will cut into chops easily once it has been presented. Turning the crown ensures even cooking, but can be confusing. The rib bones should point upward when the stuffing, which contains a treasure-trove of intriguing flavors, is added. For presentation, the butcher or a cookware store can provide frilled, colored paper caps to cover each bone-end.

CROWN ROAST OF PORK WITH FRUIT AND RICE STUFFING

8 servings
Preparation time: 30 minutes
Cooking time: About 2 hours

1 **pork crown roast, about 6 pounds**
   Salt, freshly ground pepper, dried leaf thyme, dried rosemary to taste

STUFFING

3 **cups cooked rice**
1 **cup each: chopped apples, chopped celery, currants**
1 **onion, chopped**
¾ **cup chopped dried apricots**
¼ **cup each: chopped dates, melted butter**
1 **teaspoon Worcestershire sauce**
½ **teaspoon ground cinnamon**
¼ **teaspoon each: ground allspice, ground cloves, dried rosemary, dried leaf thyme**

1. Heat oven to 325 degrees. Season meat with salt, pepper, thyme and rosemary. Put in shallow roasting pan, bone side down. Bake 1 hour.

2. Turn roast upright; bake 30 minutes. For stuffing, mix remaining ingredients. Fill center with 2 cups stuffing; cover with foil. Bake 20 minutes.

3. Put remaining stuffing in foil or casserole dish. Put in oven. Bake roast and extra stuffing until meat thermometer registers 160 degrees and extra stuffing is hot. Cooking time is about 30 minutes per pound. Let stand 10 minutes. (Meat temperature will rise about 10 degrees after removing from oven.)

4. To carve, remove stuffing to serving dish. Using a small carving knife, slice down between each rib bone and remove chops one at a time.

A light, very attractive main course featuring the new, leaner pork. Recipe developer Beverly Dillon suggests reinforcing the elegance of the tenderloin by serving it with a mixture of wild rice and mushrooms.

PORK TENDERLOIN WITH APRICOT RELISH

4 servings
Preparation time: 30 minutes
Marinating time: 3 to 6 hours
Cooking time: 45 to 60 minutes

1 whole pork tenderloin, about 1½ pounds

MARINADE

¼ cup apricot preserves

3 tablespoons light soy sauce

¼ teaspoon each: minced garlic, ground ginger, dry mustard, Oriental sesame oil

APRICOT RELISH

1 can (8¾ ounces) apricot halves, drained, pitted

1 orange

1 tablespoon each: minced fresh ginger, minced fresh cilantro (coriander)

1 teaspoon each: cider vinegar, soy sauce

½ teaspoon brown sugar

⅛ teaspoon each: dry mustard, turmeric

TOPPING

3 tablespoons apricot preserves

1 tablespoon Dijon mustard

3 strips bacon

1. Using kitchen string, tie small end of tenderloin under to make a compact shape that will cook evenly. For marinade, mix apricot preserves, soy sauce, garlic, ginger, dry mustard and sesame oil in shallow glass dish. Add tenderloin. Turn to coat well with marinade. Cover with plastic wrap. Refrigerate at least 3 hours or up to 6 hours.

2. Meanwhile, for apricot relish, coarsely chop apricots. Put in bowl. Grate orange rind to measure ½ teaspoon. Remove and discard remaining orange rind. Coarsely chop orange flesh. Add rind and orange flesh to apricots. Add ginger, cilantro, vinegar, soy sauce, brown sugar, dry mustard and turmeric. Stir to mix. Cover with plastic wrap. Refrigerate at least 1 hour or up to 4 hours.

3. For topping, mix apricot preserves and Dijon mustard in small bowl.

4. Heat oven to 375 degrees. Remove tenderloin from marinade. Allow excess marinade to drip off. Put tenderloin into roasting pan. Spread top with apricot-mustard mixture. Lay bacon strips lengthwise over tenderloin.

5. Bake until meat thermometer inserted in center registers 160 degrees, 45 to 60 minutes. Let stand 10 minutes. (Meat temperature will rise 10 degrees.) Serve thinly sliced with apricot relish.

■ *For a vegetable accompaniment to this simple dish, stir-fry some zucchini and red bell pepper strips. The bittersweet candied lime rind is easy to make. Consider using more lime rind and saving what's leftover to garnish ice cream, sherbet or a cake.*

PORK CUTLETS WITH GINGER-LIME SAUCE

4 servings
Preparation time: 40 minutes
Cooking time: 30 minutes

1 large lime
½ cup water
¼ cup brown sugar
1 pound boneless pork cutlets
   Salt, freshly ground pepper to taste
¼ cup (½ stick) butter
1 can (13¾ ounces) chicken broth
1½ tablespoons finely chopped fresh ginger
2 large cloves garlic, minced

1. Remove lime rind with vegetable peeler. Cut rind into fine julienne strips. Squeeze juice from lime; reserve. Mix lime julienne, water and sugar in small saucepan. Heat to boil. Reduce heat; simmer, uncovered, until most of the water has evaporated and rind has candied, 15 to 20 minutes. Remove from heat; set aside.

2. Pound pork to ⅛-inch thickness. Season with salt and pepper. Melt butter in large skillet over high heat. Add pork in single layer; quickly sauté 1 to 2 minutes on each side. Remove to a serving platter and keep warm while making the sauce.

3. Add broth, ginger, reserved lime juice and garlic to skillet. Heat to boil; cook, stirring occasionally, until reduced by half.

4. Pour sauce over pork. Garnish with candied lime rind. Serve immediately.

A quick-cooking party dish, this entree is prettily presented in a basket of mai fun, *or rice sticks. These are thin, dried noodles made of rice flour and water. After deep-frying, rice sticks may be stored in a closed paper bag for 24 hours. As the pork and vegetables are cooked quickly and easily, this means the only tricky step can be completed well before guests arrive.*

STIR-FRIED PORK IN A BASKET

4 servings
Preparation time: 30 minutes
Cooking time: 15 minutes

3 **ounces rice stick noodles**
Oil for frying
1 **pound boneless pork tenderloin**
2 **tablespoons peanut oil**
3 **green onions, minced**
1 **tablespoon minced fresh ginger**
1 **large clove garlic, minced**
1 **medium yellow squash, halved lengthwise, sliced**
1½ **cups fresh snow peas or 1 box (6 ounces) frozen snow peas, thawed**
¼ **cup hoisin sauce**
1 **teaspoon each: Oriental sesame oil, soy sauce or to taste**
Several dashes hot Oriental chili oil
2 **plums, cut into thin slices**
Fresh cilantro (coriander) sprigs or parsley

1. Break and separate rice sticks into 4-inch lengths. Heat 2 inches of oil in wok or deep skillet until hot but not smoking. Add one-quarter of rice sticks and stir quickly. (Stand back from stove as oil may splatter.) As soon as they puff and turn just slightly golden on all sides, about 30 seconds, remove with slotted spoon to paper towels. Drain well. Repeat with remaining rice sticks.

2. Cut pork into ⅛-inch-thick diagonal slices; pat dry with paper towels. Heat empty wok or large skillet over medium-high heat until hot. Add peanut oil; heat until hot. Add green onions, ginger and garlic. Stir-fry 1 minute. Add sliced squash and snow peas to wok. Stir-fry until vegetables are crisp-tender, about 2 minutes. Remove with slotted spoon to a plate.

3. Add pork slices to wok; stir-fry until pork is golden, about 3 minutes. Stir in hoisin sauce, sesame oil, soy sauce and chili oil. Stir-fry until pork is tender and pan juices are slightly thickened, about 3 minutes. Stir in vegetables and plums. Stir-fry until heated through. Remove from heat.

4. Pile the fried rice sticks in basket shape on large platter. Fill with pork mixture. Garnish with cilantro sprigs. Serve immediately.

For a meal in the Italian style, begin with a seafood or vegetable pasta dish and follow these sausages and peppers with slices of Parmesan cheese and fresh fruit.

SAUSAGE AND PEPPER SKILLET DISH

4 servings
Preparation time: 15 minutes
Cooking time: 15 minutes

1 **pound mild Italian sausage**
1 **tablespoon olive oil**
2 **small onions, thinly sliced**
1 **green pepper, seeded, sliced**
1 **red bell pepper, seeded, sliced**
1 **teaspoon dried basil**
½ **teaspoon dried leaf oregano**
1 **cup pitted black olives, halved**
¼ **teaspoon freshly ground pepper**
Salt to taste

1. Cut the sausage into 1-inch pieces. Heat oil in large heavy skillet. Add sausage and onions; sauté over medium heat until sausage is nicely browned and almost cooked, about 10 minutes.

2. Stir in green pepper, red bell pepper, basil and oregano. Cook, stirring occasionally, until sausage is cooked through and vegetables are crisp-tender, 3 to 5 minutes. Stir in olives, pepper and salt. Heat just until hot. Serve.

A sweet and tangy Filipino sausage called longaniza is paired with bok choy for this simple dinner main course. If longaniza is not available, you may substitute Cajun andouille or smoked Polish sausage; cut down cooking time if using fully cooked sausage.

FILIPINO SAUSAGE AND BOK CHOY

6 servings
Preparation time: 25 minutes
Cooking time: 40 minutes

1 **pound longaniza**
   (see note)
1 **cup water**
1 **large head bok choy**
3 **tablespoons peanut oil**
2 **large onions, sliced**
2 **cloves garlic**
¼ **cup beef broth**
¼ **cup cider or malt**
   vinegar
1 **tablespoon soy sauce**
2 **teaspoons cornstarch**
¼ **teaspoon hot red**
   pepper flakes

1. Put sausage into large skillet. Add 1 cup water. Heat to simmer; cook, covered, for 10 minutes. Uncover skillet; cook over medium-low heat until water has evaporated and sausage is crisp on the outside and cooked through, 20 to 25 minutes. Drain on paper towel.

2. Cut bok choy stalks on a diagonal into ½-inch-wide pieces.

3. Heat wok or large skillet until hot; add oil and heat until hot. Add onions and garlic; cook, stirring occasionally, over medium heat until onions are limp and golden, about 10 minutes.

4. Meanwhile, mix broth, vinegar, soy sauce, cornstarch and pepper flakes in small bowl. Slice cooked sausage on diagonal into ½-inch pieces.

5. When onions are done, add bok choy. Stir-fry over medium-high heat until bok choy is crisp-tender, about 5 minutes. Stir in sausage. Stir broth mixture to dissolve cornstarch, then stir the mixture into the pan. Cook and stir until sauce thickens. Serve immediately.

NOTE: Longaniza (Filipino pork sausage) is available at Filipino groceries.

Homemade sausage tastes awfully good when aged in the refrigerator and then cooked on an outdoor grill. This recipe, brought to this country more than 60 years ago from Austria-Hungary by Martin Kaiser, test kitchen director JeanMarie Brownson's grandfather, is served each year at a Labor Day family reunion. If you do not wish to stuff it in the casings, it can be shaped into patties and grilled, broiled or pan-fried.

HUNGARIAN-STYLE FAMILY SAUSAGE

10 to 12 servings
Preparation time: 45 minutes
Chilling time: Overnight
Cooking time: 10 minutes

4 **pounds coarsely ground boneless pork shoulder**

2 **teaspoons salt or to taste**

1½ **heaping tablespoons imported Hungarian sweet paprika**

1 **tablespoon freshly ground pepper**

2 **teaspoons ground allspice**

1½ **cloves fresh garlic, pressed through garlic press**

1 **tablespoon water**
Natural hog casings for 4 pounds meat

1. Mix all ingredients except casings in large bowl. Taste for seasonings by frying a small bit of the mixture in a small frying pan until cooked. Taste and adjust seasoning in raw mixture accordingly.

2. Stuff meat into casings using a sausage stuffer according to manufacturer's instructions. Or slip one casing over the end of a wide funnel; push meat through funnel into casing with the handle of a wooden spoon. Tie off sausages at about 10-inch lengths with kitchen string.

3. Refrigerate, covered, at least overnight or up to 3 days. This allows the flavors to blend.

4. Prepare charcoal grill. When coals are covered with gray ash, grill sausages 6 inches from hot coals, turning occasionally until juices run clear, 15 to 20 minutes. Serve hot.

Leg of pork is called fresh ham when it has not been cured or smoked. The texture of the meat is different than that of a cured ham. The taste is delicious. Serving mashed sweet potatoes and asparagus with the fresh ham would lend color to the plate.

FRESH HAM WITH SAGE AND ROSEMARY

8 servings
Preparation time: 20 minutes
Marinating time: Up to 48 hours
Cooking time: About 3 hours

1 fresh ham, shank or butt portion, about 6 pounds
Olive oil
4 cloves garlic, cut into thin slivers
1½ teaspoons each: dried rosemary leaves, ground dried sage
Freshly ground pepper to taste

1. Remove rind but not the fat from ham; rub ham all over generously with oil. Insert garlic slivers and rosemary leaves into ham, using an ice pick to make small incisions. Rub sage into surface. Sprinkle generously with pepper. Refrigerate, covered, up to 48 hours.

2. Remove ham from refrigerator; let stand, covered, at room temperature 1 hour. Heat oven to 400 degrees.

3. Put ham into large roasting pan. Roast 10 minutes. Reduce oven temperature to 325 degrees. Cook until meat thermometer registers 160 degrees, about 30 minutes per pound. Baste ham frequently with pan juices. Let stand 10 minutes. (Meat temperature will rise about 10 degrees.)

This pretty-to-look-at, sweet-to-taste ham was featured in a Food Guide story by Chicago writer Pat Dailey on how to re-create commercially made, honey-baked hams at home. She discovered that the secret to their crisp exterior did not include honey. Instead granulated sugar is caramelized on the surface with a direct flame. For best results use a propane torch—an unusual piece of kitchen equipment, but handy for this task. (P.S. Julia Child uses a torch to brown the meringue on baked Alaska.)

SUGAR-BAKED HAM

20 to 24 servings
Preparation time: 25 minutes
Cooking time: About 2½ hours

1 **smoked, fully cooked ham, 12 to 16 pounds**
½ **cup sugar**
⅛ **teaspoon ground cloves**

1. Heat oven to 275 degrees. Put ham on large, foil-lined baking sheet. Cut off any brown rind and all but a thin layer of fat. Mix sugar and cloves in small bowl.

2. Carefully using propane torch with low flame, very lightly singe top layer of fat on ham until just softened.

3. Rub sugar mixture over ham, building up a thin layer. Using propane torch with low flame, brown sugar lightly by moving flame across surface of ham.

4. Bake until meat thermometer registers 130 degrees, 10 to 12 minutes per pound, about 2½ hours. Let stand 10 minutes before carving into very thin slices (an electric knife works best).

NOTE: If propane torch is unavailable, the sugar may be browned by placing the ham as close to the broiler element as possible, but not touching it. Then bake as directed.

Spicy, easy Cajun jambalaya is adopted from a recipe by chef Charlie Orr, owner of the Maple Tree Inn in Chicago. He suggests serving the jambalaya with cheddar-onion corn muffins (see recipe, page 523) and pecan pie for dessert.

HAM AND SAUSAGE JAMBALAYA

10 to 12 servings
Preparation time: 45 minutes
Cooking time: 1¾ hours

¼ **cup lard or vegetable shortening**

¼ **cup all-purpose flour**

10 **cups coarsely chopped onions, about 7 large**

1½ **cups diced green pepper, about 1 large**

1 **cup chopped celery, about 3 ribs**

¼ **cup chopped fresh parsley**

1 **tablespoon minced garlic**

3 **pounds diced smoked ham**

1 **pound hot sausage, such as andouille or kielbasa, sliced**

4½ **cups rich chicken broth (see recipe, page 134), or substitute canned broth or water**

2 **teaspoons freshly ground black pepper**

½ **teaspoon salt**

¼ **teaspoon cayenne pepper**

3 **cups raw rice**

Minced fresh parsley for garnish

Hot pepper sauce to taste

1. Melt lard in 8-quart cast-iron or enameled cast-iron dutch oven. Add flour; cook and stir over medium heat until flour is the color of cinnamon, about 10 minutes. Add onions; cook and stir over low heat until tender, about 15 minutes. Add green pepper, celery, parsley and garlic; cook for 2 minutes. Stir in ham and sausage. Cook, covered, for 15 minutes.

2. Add broth, black pepper, salt and cayenne pepper. Simmer for 30 minutes. (This can be prepared in advance and refrigerated up to 2 days or frozen solid up to 1 month.)

3. Heat mixture to simmer. Stir in rice; heat to boil, occasionally stirring gently. Reduce heat; simmer covered, until rice is tender, 30 to 45 minutes. Sprinkle with parsley. Pass hot pepper sauce.

Variety is welcome in meat cookery, even with lamb. So think of this Mary Meade Recipe of the Week, which appeared in the spring of 1980, as a Middle Eastern hamburger. Lamb, the favorite meat in that region, is formed into patties, thoroughly cooked and served in or on pita bread instead of a bun. The cool and tasty sauce is a refreshing alternative to catsup.

LAMB PATTIES WITH YOGURT SAUCE

4 servings
Preparation time: 15 minutes
Cooking time: 8 minutes

SAUCE

- 1 carton (8 ounces) plain yogurt
- ½ cucumber, peeled, diced
- 1 tablespoon grated onion
- 1 teaspoon minced fresh mint leaves
- ¼ teaspoon each: prepared horseradish, salt

PATTIES

- 1 pound ground lamb (or, ½ pound each: ground beef round, ground lamb)
- ⅓ cup each: dried coarse bread crumbs, milk
- 1 egg
- 1 tablespoon chopped fresh parsley
- 1 clove garlic, finely minced
- 1 teaspoon salt
- ¼ teaspoon freshly ground pepper
- 4 pita pocket breads, split open on one end
  Lettuce leaves, tomato wedges

1. For sauce, mix all ingredients in small bowl. Refrigerate until ready to use.

2. Mix lamb, bread crumbs, milk, egg, parsley, garlic, salt and pepper in large bowl. Shape into four patties.

3. Pan-fry in large nonstick skillet over medium heat until browned on both sides and medium-rare in center, about 8 minutes. Serve immediately in pita bread topped with lettuce, tomato wedges and yogurt sauce.

Chicago herb expert Jim Haring offers this easy-to-carve flavorful lamb. Most butchers will bone and butterfly the leg of lamb for you with some advance notice. Because the meat is uneven in thickness, you will be able to offer a choice of rare, medium and well-done lamb. In summertime, wrap potatoes, onions and summer squash in foil and cook them on the grill as well.

GRILLED BUTTERFLIED LEG OF LAMB WITH HERB MARINADE

6 to 8 servings
Preparation time: 20 minutes
Marinating time: Overnight
Grilling time: About 1 hour

1 **cup each: dry red wine, olive oil**
3 **cloves garlic, lightly crushed**
1 **teaspoon coarsely ground pepper**
1½ **ounces fresh rosemary, about six 6-inch branches**
½ **ounce fresh thyme, about twelve 3-inch springs**
1 **large branch fresh sage**
 Salt to taste
1 **leg of lamb, about 6 pounds, boned, butterflied**

1. Mix wine, oil, garlic and pepper in large shallow nonaluminum dish. Coarsely chop herbs. Add to wine mixture along with salt. Mix well. Add lamb; turn to coat thoroughly with the marinade. Cover and refrigerate overnight, turning lamb at least once.

2. Prepare grill. When coals are covered with gray ash, arrange coals for the indirect method at sides of grill. Place a drip pan in center.

3. Remove lamb from marinade. Reserve marinade. Put lamb on grill rack over drip pan. Cover and grill, turning once, until meat thermometer registers 130 degrees for rare, 13 to 15 minutes per pound. Brush frequently with marinade. Grill temperature should be maintained at about 350 degrees.

4. Let meat stand on serving platter for 10 minutes. Temperature will rise about 10 degrees. Serve very thinly sliced.

NOTE: Lamb can be cooked in the oven at 350 degrees. Remove lamb from marinade and set on a rack set in a roasting pan. Cook until meat thermometer registers 130 degrees for rare, 13 to 15 minutes per pound. Brush frequently with marinade.

Former Chicago-area cooking teacher Barbara Tuleja, who now lives in California, suggests having the butcher remove the backbone and trim the rib bones for this elegant lamb roast.

CROWN ROAST OF LAMB WITH LEMON AND HERBS

8 servings
Preparation time: 25 minutes
Baking time: About 1 hour

1   **crown roast of lamb (16 ribs), 5½ to 6 pounds**
1   **large lemon**
1½ **teaspoons each, minced: fresh thyme, fresh marjoram, fresh rosemary (or ½ teaspoon each dried)**
3   **tablespoons olive oil**
    Salt, freshly ground pepper to taste

SHERRIED PAN JUICES
½   **cup each: dry sherry, strong chicken stock**
2   **tablespoons butter, softened**
1½ **tablespoons flour**
2   **bunches watercress, for garnish**

1. Have butcher prepare crown roast of lamb.

2. Wash lemon in hot water to remove any wax coating. Dry well. Using a zester or vegetable peeler, remove thin strips of rind from entire lemon surface.

3. Mix lemon rind, thyme, marjoram, rosemary, olive oil, salt and ⅛ teaspoon pepper in small bowl. Turn roast bone side down. Rub mixture into meat. Marinate at room temperature 30 minutes.

4. Heat oven to 375 degrees. Put roast, bone side up, in shallow roasting pan. Crumple enough foil to fill bottom of roast cavity, so that it will retain circular shape while roasting.

5. Roast, uncovered, until meat thermometer registers 140 degrees for medium-rare, 15 to 17 minutes per pound. To determine temperature, insert thermometer into thickest part of meat without touching bone.

6. When done, remove roast to warm serving platter. Let stand, loosely covered by foil, for 10 minutes before carving.

7. Meanwhile, for sherried pan juices, spoon off all fat from roasting pan. Put pan over high heat for 15 seconds to caramelize any meat juices. Off heat, deglaze pan with sherry, scraping up all browned bits clinging to bottom and sides. Heat to boil. Stir in chicken stock. Pour pan liquids into small saucepan.

8. Mix butter and flour. Heat pan liquids back to a simmer. Whisk in the butter mixture. Add all the meat juices accumulated on the serving platter to pan. Continue simmering for 2 more minutes to blend flavors. Add salt and pepper to taste.

THE CHICAGO TRIBUNE COOKBOOK

9. To serve, remove strings and foil from roast. If necessary, rearrange racks into round shape and salt lightly. For an attractive presentation, fill center of roast with watercress. Serve sherried pan juices to accompany roast at table.

NOTE: Remember that meat continues to cook after it is removed from oven, therefore remove the roast when it is 10 degrees below the desired temperature.

This is the perfect entree for a romantic dinner for two if both partners like garlic. (Parsley effectively counters the lingering taste of garlic. Use some sprigs for garnish and feel free to nibble the leaves.) Crisp green beans and roast or mashed potatoes are traditional accompaniments. If the coating becomes dark brown during cooking, cover it with a piece of foil.

ROAST RACK OF LAMB

2 servings
Preparation time: 10 minutes
Cooking time: 30 minutes

½ **cup fresh bread crumbs**
1 **tablespoon each, minced: fresh parsley, green onion**
2 **teaspoons each: dried basil, dried chervil**
1 **clove garlic, minced**
3 **tablespoons olive oil**
1 **rack of lamb, about 2 pounds**

1. Mix bread crumbs, parsley, onion, basil, chervil and garlic in small bowl. Add enough oil to make a damp mixture that clings together.

2. Heat oven to 400 degrees. Spread crumb mixture over top of lamb. Put onto rack set in roasting pan.

3. Roast until meat thermometer registers 130 degrees for rare, 13 to 15 minutes per pound. Let stand 10 minutes before carving.

Couscous is a grain and also the name of North Africa's favorite stew. The grain, a form of semolina, is much easier to find in markets than it once was. The precooked, or instant, version is perfectly acceptable and allows the cook to omit the difficult, time-consuming ritual of preparing the raw grain. A two-piece cooking pan, the couscousière, allows the grain to cook above the steaming stew. If you wish, the effect can be replicated by placing a colander over a large saucepan, covering the colander and tying a kitchen towel around the gap where the pan and colander meet.

COUSCOUS WITH LAMB STEW AND VEGETABLES

6 to 8 servings
Preparation time: 45 minutes
Cooking time: 1½ hours

Olive oil (about ¼ cup)
4 medium onions, sliced
4 cloves garlic, minced
1½ pounds boneless lamb, cut into 1-inch cubes
Flour
3 tablespoons minced parsley
½ teaspoon salt
¼ teaspoon each: freshly ground black pepper, ground cumin, ground coriander seed
⅛ teaspoon each: saffron threads, cayenne pepper
Pinch ground cinnamon
4 cups rich chicken broth (see recipe, page 134), or substitute canned broth
6 small red potatoes, halved
3 medium carrots, peeled, cut into 1-inch pieces
3 medium zucchini, cut into 1-inch pieces
2 medium yellow squash, cut into 1-inch pieces
1 can (15 ounces) garbanzo beans, drained
2 tomatoes, cut into wedges
1½ cups couscous
⅓ cup golden raisins
Salt, freshly ground pepper to taste
Minced fresh cilantro (coriander) for garnish

1. Heat oil in bottom of large dutch oven. Add onions and garlic; cook over medium heat until onions are golden. Remove onions with slotted spoon.

2. Toss lamb cubes lightly with flour; shake off excess. Add more oil to pan if needed. Add lamb in single layer. Cook, stirring, over medium-high heat, until nicely browned on all sides. Sprinkle with parsley, salt, black pepper, cumin, ground coriander, saffron, cayenne and cinnamon. Cook and stir for 1 minute.

3. Stir in chicken broth. Heat to boil, stirring and scraping up browned bits from bottom of pan. Add onion mixture. Simmer, covered, until meat is almost tender, about 20 minutes.

4. Add potatoes and carrots. Simmer, covered, until potatoes and carrots are crisp-tender, about 20 minutes. Add zucchini, yellow squash and garbanzo beans. Simmer, uncovered, until zucchini is crisp-tender and meat and potatoes are fork-tender, 15 to 20 minutes. Stir in tomatoes. Taste and adjust seasonings, adding salt, pepper and cayenne as desired.

5. Following package directions, use a ladle to remove the required amount of the lamb cooking liquid to a saucepan and prepare couscous. When done, stir in raisins, salt and pepper. Fluff with fork.

6. Place couscous in a mound on serving platter. Pass lamb stew to be ladled over couscous. Serve garnished with cilantro.

■ *Easy to transport in its baking pan, this savory pie can be an exotic treat at a picnic. Beverly Dillon created it for a candlelight supper at Ravinia Park, the open-air amphitheater that is the Chicago Symphony Orchestra's summer home. Serve this with the couscous salad on page 464.*

MOROCCAN MEAT PIE

10 servings
Preparation time: 1 hour
Chilling time: 2 hours
Cooking time: 2¼ hours

MEAT FILLING

- **3 tablespoons each: butter, olive oil**
- **3 pounds boneless lamb shoulder or leg of lamb, cut into ½-inch cubes**
- **2 cups diced onions, about 3 medium**
- **2 cloves garlic, minced**
- **1 cinnamon stick**
- **1 teaspoon ground ginger**
- **½ teaspoon loosely packed saffron threads or ⅛ teaspoon saffron powder**
- **2 cans (16 ounces each) whole tomatoes, chopped**
- **2 tablespoons tomato paste**
- **1 teaspoon each: salt, freshly ground pepper**
- **¼ cup honey**
- **1 teaspoon ground cinnamon**

DOUGH

- **¼ cup homemade bread crumbs**
- **1 box (1 pound) filo dough, thawed**
- **¾ pound (3 sticks) unsalted butter, melted**

1. For filling, put butter, oil, lamb, onions, garlic, cinnamon stick, ginger, saffron, tomatoes, tomato paste, salt and pepper in 6-quart dutch oven with tight-fitting lid. Stir to mix. Chop tomatoes with metal spoon. Add enough water to cover mixture, about 2 cups. Heat to boil. Reduce heat; simmer, covered, until meat is very tender, 1 to 1½ hours. Stir mixture several times during cooking.

2. Remove from heat. Transfer meat with a slotted spoon to a side dish. Pick out cinnamon stick and discard it.

3. Return pan with juices to medium-high heat. Cook, stirring often, until broth is thick and reduced to 2 cups. Stir in honey and ground cinnamon. Remove from heat. Stir meat back into reduced liquid. Refrigerate to cool. (Recipe may be made ahead to this point and frozen. To freeze, spoon into zipper-lock freezer bag. Squeeze out any excess air. Seal shut. Meat mixture may be frozen up to one month.)

4. To assemble, if meat has been frozen, defrost it and reheat just so juices are easier to extract. Put meat filling in strainer over bowl to drain all the juices. Press meat with the back of a wooden spoon to squeeze out as much of the juice as possible. You should have about 2 cups of juice. Reserve meat juices for couscous salad or other use. Spoon meat into a bowl; stir in bread crumbs.

5. Heat oven to 375 degrees. Butter 13 by 9-inch baking pan and place a sheet of filo dough on bottom of the pan. Keep remaining filo covered with towel. Brush lightly with melted butter, then lay in more sheets, buttering each sheet as you go until you have 10 layers. The dough should just fit the pan. If it doesn't, tuck in any excess. It doesn't have to be neat.

6. Spread the meat mixture evenly in the dough-lined pan, then stack another 10 sheets of dough on top, buttering them as you go.

7. Bake for 15 minutes. Reduce oven temperature to 350 degrees. Bake until filo dough is crisp and golden, about 30 more minutes.

8. Let cool 15 minutes before cutting into squares. Serve warm or at room temperature.

NOTE: Filo (or phyllo) pastry dough is available in many supermarket frozen food sections or at Greek groceries.

A prize-winner at the 1982 Gilroy Garlic Festival in California, these lamb shanks are braised. The cooking method takes time but transforms tough cuts into succulently tender meat. The meat is first browned, then partially covered with liquid and cooked at a simmer rather than a boil.

LAMB SHANKS WITH BARLEY AND GARLIC

4 servings
Preparation time: 25 minutes
Cooking time: 2 hours

½ cup (1 stick) plus 2 tablespoons butter

¼ cup olive oil

4 lamb shanks

½ cup each: dry red wine, water

½ teaspoon dried rosemary

30 medium-size cloves garlic, peeled

½ to ¾ pound fresh mushrooms, sliced

1½ cups medium pearl barley

2½ to 3½ cups beef stock (see recipe, page 133), or substitute canned broth

2 tablespoons mint jelly Salt, freshly ground pepper to taste

1. Heat oven to 350 degrees. Heat ¼ cup of the butter and olive oil in large dutch oven. Add shanks in single layer. Cook until brown on all sides. Remove lamb; stir wine and water into pan. Heat, scraping up browned bits from bottom. Replace the lamb and sprinkle with rosemary.

2. Add garlic. Put a sheet of foil over top of pan, then cover with the lid to seal thoroughly. Bake at 350 degrees for 1½ hours.

3. Meanwhile, melt ¼ cup of the butter in large skillet. Add mushrooms; sauté until golden; set aside.

4. Sauté barley in remaining 2 tablespoons butter until golden. Stir in mushrooms. Put into well-buttered, 2-quart casserole. Add 2½ cups of the beef stock. Cover and bake for 30 minutes. Add remaining stock as needed, and cook, uncovered, until liquid is absorbed and barley is done, about 30 more minutes.

5. To serve, arrange lamb shanks around edges of serving platter. Add the garlic cloves to barley and heap in center of platter. Stir mint jelly, salt and pepper into pan juices from shanks. Simmer until flavors have blended, 3 to 5 minutes. Spoon juices over the lamb shanks.

The late Silvio Pinto, chef-owner of Chicago's Sogni Dorati restaurant, loved to create recipes that contained an element of surprise. Here an unlikely filling turns a baked apple into an elegant dinner party treat. This dish needs no accompaniment. Serve it after seafood pasta or before a main course of poultry or meat that does not require a sauce.

VEAL APPLES

8 servings
Preparation time: 30 minutes
Baking time: 40 minutes

FILLING

¼ **pound ground veal**

⅛ **pound ground pork**

1 **teaspoon each, chopped: raisins, walnuts, pine nuts**

¼ **cup chopped onion**

1 **garlic clove, minced**

3 **large eggs**

½ **cup freshly grated Parmesan cheese**

3 **tablespoons chopped fresh parsley**

⅛ **teaspoon ground nutmeg**

Pinch salt, freshly ground pepper

APPLES

8 **Golden Delicious apples**

½ **lemon**

½ **cup homemade, coarse bread crumbs**

8 **teaspoons butter**

¼ **cup water**

MARSALA-SAGE SAUCE

1½ **cups veal stock or chicken broth (see recipes, pages 133–34), or substitute canned broth**

½ **cup dry marsala wine**

Pinch ground dried sage

¼ **cup (½ stick) butter**

Salt to taste

1. Heat oven to 400 degrees. Combine filling ingredients. Mixture should be light and moist.

2. Peel apples. Using a melon baller or spoon, core apples from stem end leaving bottom intact so filling does not leak out. Rub apples with lemon to prevent browning.

3. Stuff apples with veal mixture. Put in roasting dish large enough for apples to sit comfortably. Sprinkle each with 1 tablespoon bread crumbs. Dot each with 1 teaspoon of butter. Add water to bottom of pan. Bake until tender, about 40 minutes.

4. Meanwhile, for sauce, heat veal stock, marsala and sage to boil. Boil gently until reduced to ¾ cup. Vigorously whisk in ¼ cup butter. Add salt to taste. Do not boil. Pour over apples.

Flavorful vegetables add color in this Italian-inspired entree. The trick is not to overcook the peppers so their crisp texture will contrast with the soft veal.

VEAL CUTLETS WITH RED PEPPERS

4 servings
Preparation time: 30 minutes
Cooking time: 10 minutes

½ cup all-purpose flour

4 teaspoons freshly grated Parmesan cheese

½ teaspoon each: salt, pepper, chervil

1 teaspoon dried leaf oregano

4 veal cutlets, each ½-inch thick

2 large red bell peppers

¼ pound fresh mushrooms

10 shallots

2 tablespoons each: butter, olive oil

1 clove garlic, minced

½ cup (1 stick) butter, melted

1 cup dry white wine

¼ teaspoon each: salt, pepper

1. Mix flour, cheese, salt, pepper, chervil and ½ teaspoon of the oregano in shallow dish. Using a flat-sided meat mallet, pound each veal cutlet between wax paper or 2 plastic bags until very thin.

2. Cut peppers in half; remove ends and seeds. Cut into ¼-inch-thick strips. Slice mushrooms ¼-inch thick. Peel shallots. Cut in half lengthwise; if large, cut into fourths.

3. Heat 2 tablespoons butter and oil in large heavy skillet. Add garlic, shallots and mushrooms; cook and stir over medium heat until mushrooms brown slightly. Add peppers; cook and stir until peppers are crisp-tender, about 5 minutes. Remove vegetables to bowl and set aside.

4. Dredge veal in seasoned flour. Dip in melted butter then dredge again in flour. Add more butter and oil to skillet if needed for browning. Add veal in single layer. Cook just until lightly browned on both sides, about 3 minutes total.

5. Remove meat to warm platter; keep warm. Add wine to pan juices. Heat to boil, scraping up all brown pieces and boiling gently until slightly thickened. Add mushroom mixture, remaining ½ teaspoon oregano, salt and pepper. Pour over meat. Serve.

The following recipe works beautifully as an impressive hot entree or chilled as gourmet picnic fare. The key is the versatile stuffing, which tastes great either way. Veal breast often comes with a precut pocket for stuffing; if not ask the butcher to prepare it for you.

SPINACH-STUFFED VEAL BREAST

6 servings
Preparation time: 40 minutes
Cooking time: 2¼ hours

¼ cup (½ stick) butter
1 large green pepper, seeded, diced
2 ribs celery, diced
¼ cup minced fresh parsley
2 large cloves garlic, minced
1 pound ground pork
½ pound ground veal
1 box (10 ounces) frozen chopped spinach, thawed, well drained
3 tablespoons brandy
½ teaspoon each: dried tarragon, dried leaf thyme
¼ teaspoon salt
⅛ teaspoon cayenne pepper
1 veal breast with pocket for stuffing, about 5 to 6 pounds
3 tablespoons oil
1 cup dry sherry

1. For stuffing, melt 2 tablespoons of the butter in large skillet. Stir in green pepper, celery, parsley and garlic. Sauté until crisp-tender, about 3 minutes. Remove from heat. Stir in pork, veal, spinach, brandy, tarragon, thyme, salt and cayenne.

2. Fry a tablespoon of the mixture in a skillet until cooked through and taste for seasonings. Adjust the seasonings in the main mixture accordingly.

3. Heat oven to 325 degrees. Pack stuffing into the pocket of the veal breast. Skewer pocket opening closed.

4. Heat remaining 2 tablespoons butter and oil in large roasting pan over medium heat. Add veal breast. Brown nicely on all sides.

5. Pour sherry into pan. Cover pan tightly with lid or heavy-duty foil. Bake until meat thermometer inserted in meat and stuffing registers 160 degrees, about 2 hours.

6. Serve hot, thinly sliced, with defatted pan juices. Or refrigerate and serve cold, very thinly sliced with assorted mustards.

Here is Chicago chef Jennifer Newbury's version of the Italian classic, vitello tonnato. It's fun to see how many diners will guess that the base of the creamy, delicious sauce is tuna fish. An Italian white wine such as Gavi will match well with this fish and meat combination.

SLICED VEAL WITH ANCHOVY SAUCE
(Vitello tonnato)

6 servings
Preparation time: 20 minutes
Cooking time: 10 minutes

1 can (7 ounces) albacore tuna in water
½ cup each: mayonnaise, extra-virgin olive oil, whipping cream
¼ cup water
5 flat anchovy fillets, rinsed, drained
1½ tablespoons drained capers
6 thin veal cutlets
Salt, freshly ground pepper to taste
1 tablespoon each: olive oil, butter
Arugula or green lettuce, for garnish

1. Drain tuna. Put tuna, mayonnaise, ½ cup oil, cream, water, anchovies and capers into blender. Puree until almost smooth.

2. Season veal cutlets with salt and pepper. Heat 1 tablespoon oil and butter in skillet pan until hot. Add veal in single layer; cook over medium-high heat until brown on both sides, about 2 minutes. Remove to serving plate. Repeat to cook all veal.

3. Cover veal thickly with tuna sauce. Garnish with arugula. Serve warm or at room temperature.

A perfect winter meal, osso buco needs only a crusty Italian bread and a salad to be complete.

BRAISED VEAL SHANKS
(Osso buco)

4 servings
Preparation time: 30 minutes
Cooking time: 2 hours

4 **pounds veal shanks,
   cut in 3-inch lengths**

½ **cup all-purpose flour**

2 **teaspoons salt**

¼ **teaspoon freshly
   ground pepper**

⅓ **cup olive oil**

2 **large carrots, peeled,
   diced**

2 **medium onions,
   minced**

2 **cloves garlic, minced**

1 **rib celery, diced**

1 **can (16 ounces) whole
   tomatoes, chopped**

½ **cup dry red wine**

1 **can (13¾ ounces) beef
   broth**

1 **teaspoon dried basil**

¼ **teaspoon each: dried
   rosemary, dried leaf
   thyme**

1 **bay leaf**

2 **tablespoons minced
   fresh parsley**

2 **teaspoons finely
   grated lemon rind**

1 **clove garlic, peeled,
   minced**

1. Pat veal shanks dry. Mix flour, salt and pepper in large bowl. Dredge veal in flour mixture. Heat oil in large dutch oven. Add veal in single layer. Cook, turning, until brown on all sides. Remove to bowl.

2. Add carrots, onions, garlic and celery to pan. Cook and stir until onions are golden, 5 to 8 minutes. Add tomatoes and wine. Boil gently until liquids are reduced by half. Stir in broth, basil, rosemary, thyme and bay leaf.

3. Return veal to pan. Heat to simmer; cover and simmer until veal is tender but not falling off the bones, 1½ to 2 hours. Remove bay leaf.

4. Mix parsley, lemon rind and garlic. Sprinkle over all. Simmer, covered for 5 more minutes. Serve in wide soup bowls, spooning pan juices over veal.

Louis Szathmary's Bakery restaurant in Chicago served thousands of customers during its long run. This veal tarragon stew with dumplings is just one example of the hearty, satisfying fare enjoyed there. Barbara Kuck, the Bakery's chef-director, says the recipe originally comes from Transylvania and has an "intriguing taste" from the tarragon, bay leaf and vinegar. What she calls intriguing we call incredible.

VEAL TARRAGON STEW WITH TINY DUMPLINGS

8 servings
Preparation time: 30 minutes
Cooking time: 1 hour, 10 minutes

2 **cups minced onions**

¼ **cup (½ stick) butter**

1 **clove garlic**

2 **teaspoons salt**

2 **pounds boneless lean veal, cut into 1-inch cubes**

1 **cup dry white wine**

⅓ **cup distilled white vinegar**

3 **tablespoons chopped flat-leaf parsley**

2 **teaspoons each: dried tarragon, sugar**

1 **bay leaf**

½ **pound mushrooms, sliced**

1½ **cups milk**

¼ **cup all-purpose flour**
   Salt, freshly ground white pepper to taste

1 **cup sour cream**
   Tiny dumplings (recipe follows)

1. Cook onions in butter in dutch oven until transparent. Mash the garlic and 2 teaspoons salt together with the flat surface of a knife until it turns to a pulp. Add to the onions, then add veal, white wine, vinegar, 2 tablespoons of the parsley, tarragon, sugar and bay leaf. Cook, covered, over medium heat until veal is tender, 30 to 40 minutes.

2. Add mushrooms; cook for 3 minutes. Mix milk and flour until smooth. Stir mixture into the veal and heat through until thickened. Taste and adjust seasonings with salt and white pepper.

3. Just before serving, stir in sour cream and remaining 1 tablespoon parsley. Heat until warm; do not boil or sauce will curdle. Serve with tiny dumplings.

Tiny Dumplings | 8 servings

4 slices day-old white bread, preferably hard-crusted French type, or 2 day-old hard rolls

1 cup hot veal stock or chicken broth

3 slices bacon, cooked, crumbled

2 tablespoons finely minced onion, sautéed in 1 tablespoon butter

2 egg whites, lightly beaten

2 tablespoons sour cream

½ teaspoon salt

¼ teaspoon freshly ground white pepper

½ cup all-purpose flour

1 tablespoon finely minced fresh parsley

1. Heat oven to 300 degrees. Cut bread into ¼-inch cubes. Toast in oven until crisp and golden.

2. Put bread cubes in large bowl. Pour hot stock over them. Let stand until cool and well soaked. Add bacon, sautéed onion, egg whites, sour cream, salt and pepper. Stir in flour and parsley. Let stand 30 minutes.

3. With wet hands, form mixture into balls about ¾ inch in diameter. Ease dumplings into lightly salted simmering water. Simmer until tender and dumplings rise to the surface, about 10 minutes. Keep warm in cooking liquid until just before serving. Serve with stew.

The key to the best liver dish in Chicago is fresh liver and a very hot pan, said the late Eli Schulman, who owned Eli's: The Place for Steak, 215 E. Chicago Avenue.

SAUTÉED CALF'S LIVER

4 servings
Preparation time: 20 minutes
Cooking time: 10 minutes

1 **pound calf's liver**
4 **tablespoons vegetable oil, about**
1 **medium onion, coarsely chopped**
1 **green pepper, cored, cut into ½-inch strips**
¼ **pound fresh mushrooms, quartered**
 Flour
 Paprika, salt to taste

1. Using a sharp knife, remove any outer membrane on liver. Then cut out any large veins. Cut into ¼-inch-thick slices.

2. Heat 1 tablespoon of the vegetable oil in large sauté pan over high heat until a drop of water sizzles in the pan. Add onion, green pepper and mushrooms. Cook over high heat until crisp-tender, about 5 minutes. Remove vegetables from pan with slotted spoon and keep warm.

3. Dredge liver slices in flour. Shake off excess. Add remaining oil to pan. Heat oil over high heat until very hot. Add liver in single layer. Sauté, turning once, until the pink color just disappears from the inside meat and outside is very crisp, about 2 minutes.

4. Add vegetables back to pan. Cook just to reheat vegetables. Drain away excess oil. Sprinkle with paprika and salt. Serve immediately.

■ *Chef Aydin Dincer, a culinary innovator, developed this recipe while he was chef of Star Top Cafe, an unconventional and popular restaurant on Chicago's Lincoln Avenue. It represents the trend toward reintroducing game, once a Midwestern staple, on restaurant menus. The chef called this "a very hearty, cold-weather dish" and served it with cracked wheat or brown rice.*

SPICED RABBIT WITH SALSA-FLAVORED SAUCE

4 servings
Preparation time: 40 minutes
Marinating time: Overnight
Cooking time: 50 minutes

Salsa (recipe follows)
2 whole cleaned rabbits
MARINADE
¼ cup chopped fresh parsley
2 tablespoons lemon juice
1 clove garlic, crushed
¾ teaspoon salt
½ teaspoon cayenne pepper
¼ teaspoon ground cumin
Flour for dredging
Vegetable or olive oil
SAUCE
2 cups rich chicken broth (see recipe, page 134), or substitute canned broth
¾ cup dry white wine
1 cup whipping cream

1. Make salsa.

2. Cut rabbits into serving pieces: hind legs, fore legs and loins. Mix marinade ingredients and rub into each piece. Cover and refrigerate overnight. Remove from marinade.

3. Heat oven to 375 degrees. To cook, dredge rabbit pieces in flour; shake off excess. Heat ¼ inch of oil in large skillet until hot but not smoking. Add rabbit pieces in single layer. Cook until golden brown on all sides. Drain on paper towel.

4. Put rabbit in single layer in roasting pan. Bake until juices run clear, about 20 minutes.

5. Meanwhile, for sauce, boil chicken broth and wine in medium saucepan until reduced to about ¼ of the original amount. Add cream; boil gently until reduced enough to lightly coat a spoon. Add salsa to taste, about 4 tablespoons. Serve rabbit immediately with sauce.

SALSA | About 2 cups

1 can (14½ ounces) stewed tomatoes, undrained
1 medium onion, chopped
¾ cup chopped green pepper
2 jalapeño peppers, seeded, minced (or to taste)

¼ teaspoon each: salt, dried oregano
Freshly ground pepper to taste
Vinegar to taste

1. Combine all ingredients in medium bowl. Taste and adjust seasonings. Let stand at least 1 hour before serving. Store in refrigerator.

POULTRY

The Republican Party's 1932 hope for "a chicken in every pot" has become reality. With the advent of modern chicken farming methods, chicken has become one of the best protein bargains around, instead of the luxury, Sunday-only item of Depression days. Chicken is one of the few foodstuffs that has not jumped in price to match the nation's ever-rising inflation.

But it isn't only price that attracts us to this bird, which may soon surpass beef as our favorite protein food. Chicken is one of the stars in the dieter's arsenal of healthful foods. Especially when stripped of its skin, chicken is lower in fat and cholesterol than red meats, thus it is lower in calories, too. Simply roasted or broiled or stir-fried with vegetables, chicken and other birds provide high-quality protein and a minimum of fat.

While other kinds of poultry probably never will catch up to chicken's popularity, several varieties are gaining. Many of the recipes in this chapter reflect that growing choice. Duck, long considered a difficult bird to cook, has become more popular with home cooks who have tried it in restaurants. The advent of duck sold in parts, instead of whole, has helped take the intimidation out of its preparation and many cooks have found that it is as easy as chicken after all.

Turkey, too, is gaining in popularity. What once was a twice-a-year holiday entree has turned into a year-round choice. We've included many unusual recipes here as well as the traditional holiday turkey dishes. Game birds, often raised on farms rather than caught in the wild, also are more available. Cooks can choose from a variety of poultry flavors, from the richness of squab and pheasant to the more delicate taste of guinea hen and quail.

SAFETY

Concern about the safety of chicken in recent years has led many shoppers to avoid supermarket fryers. The problems arose when it was found that a high percentage of flocks are contaminated with salmonella, a bacteria that can cause food poisoning. But with the proper handling of all poultry (and other protein foods such as meats and eggs), salmonella can be rendered ineffective.

First, always keep poultry well chilled. Don't leave it out at room temperature in which salmonella can grow. Thaw frozen poultry in the refrigerator, not on the counter. If speedy thawing is necessary, place the still-wrapped bird in cold water until it is thawed.

Wash poultry inside and out, under cold, running water before cooking. Pat dry. Cut it up on a cutting board that has been scrubbed clean with soap and hot water. After handling poultry, always wash your hands, the knife and the cutting board with soap and hot water before using them for other foods. This will help avoid any cross contamination.

The final step in the fight against salmonella poisoning is to cook all poultry to an internal temperature of 180 degrees on a meat thermometer, a process which kills the microorganism. The thermometer should be inserted in the thickest portion of the thigh meat. Make sure it does not touch the bone. Leftovers should be wrapped well and stored immediately in the refrigerator. If poultry has been stuffed, the dressing should be removed from the bird immediately after cooking and leftovers should be stored separately in the refrigerator. Never cook a bird partially, store it, then cook it completely later.

COOKING TIPS

HOW TO ROAST POULTRY

Roasting is the most common method of cooking poultry and the easiest. Temperatures of 325 to 375 are recommended. Rub the bird well with butter or oil, if you like, for flavor and browning. Place the bird on a greased rack in a roasting pan. During roasting, you may baste the bird with the pan drippings, if you like, but it is not necessary.

Roast to an internal temperature of 180 degrees on a meat thermometer, inserted in the thickest portion of the thigh, but away from the bone. If the bird is stuffed, the center of the stuffing should be 165 degrees.

Allow about 20 minutes per pound roasting time for birds weighing less than 6 pounds. Allow about 15 minutes a pound for birds up to 16 pounds and about 12 minutes a pound for birds more than 16 pounds. If the bird is stuffed, add about 5 minutes more per pound. (See the roasting chart.) Let roasted birds stand for 5 minutes before carving to allow the juices to be absorbed.

HOW TO BROIL POULTRY

Broiling has the advantage of a fast cooking time and it allows the fat to drip off, making a slightly more healthful entree. It is suited to smaller birds that should be split in half or cut up into serving size pieces. The poultry should be placed about 6 inches away from the source of heat to prevent the skin from burning. Broiling needs careful monitoring to avoid burning. Chicken will cook in about 15 to 20 minutes per side.

How to Pan-Fry Poultry

Pan-frying is another popular method for chicken and other types of small poultry. The pieces of chicken may be coated lightly with seasoned flour if you like. The trick in frying is to make sure the oil is hot enough. Otherwise, the coating on the chicken may absorb too much of the fat. To test, sprinkle a drop of water in the oil. If it sizzles strongly, the oil is hot enough. Pan-frying will take about 20 to 40 minutes, depending on the size of the chicken. Turn the pieces often to ensure uniform browning.

How to Poach a Chicken

Poaching chicken is useful when the meat will be used in salads or cut up for casseroles. It can be poached in water to cover or any flavorful broth with herbs or wine. Heat the liquid just to boiling, reduce heat to a simmer and cook the chicken about 30 minutes or until just done.

POULTRY

CHICKEN

Baked chicken with potato "skin"

Chicken breasts marengo

Chicken curry with bamboo shoots

Chicken enchiladas

Clay-pot chicken with 40 cloves
  of garlic

Chicken vesuvio

Crispy oven-fried chicken

Southern-style fried chicken

Greek-style grilled chicken

Chicken in the microwave

Basil chicken goujons

Roast chicken with mushrooms
  and herbs

Roast chicken with lemon and
  rosemary

Smothered chicken and rice

Stir-fried chicken with noodles
  and romaine salad

Stir-fried chicken with walnuts

Crisp oven-roasted capon

Thai chicken in lettuce leaves

ROCK CORNISH HENS

Grilled Rock Cornish hens with
  Italian sausage stuffing

Grilled Rock Cornish hens with
  raspberry sauce

Roast poussin with apple and
  sausage stuffing

Rock Cornish hens with wild
  rice stuffing

TURKEY

Easy Moroccan turkey pie

Mom's foolproof turkey

Turkey with herbed cornbread
  stuffing and pan gravy

Barbecued turkey legs

Smoked turkey breast

Stuffed turkey breast

Herbed turkey gravy

POULTRY STUFFINGS

Apple-cornbread stuffing

Chestnut and sausage stuffing

Herbed cornbread stuffing

Sausage-sage stuffing

Two-bread stuffing

DUCK

Confit of duck

Duck breast salad with
  hazelnut dressing

Ginger glazed duck

Hoisin marinated duck breast

Roast duck with raspberry pink
  peppercorn sauce

OTHER BIRDS

Roast goose with apple stuffing

Grilled squab with wild
  mushroom sauce

Pheasant breast with confit

Guinea hen with orange and
  pomegranate

Grilled quail and polenta

Columnist Jane Salzfass Freiman toasted the New Year's diet resolutions with the following low-calorie entree of chicken breasts and potatoes. It's only 232 calories per portion, and with the help of the food processor, it is quick and easy.

BAKED CHICKEN WITH POTATO "SKIN"

4 servings
Preparation time: 20 minutes
Cooking time: 25 minutes

2 **whole chicken breasts, skinned, split (bones left in)**
¼ **cup firmly packed fresh parsley leaves**
1 **large clove garlic**
¼ **cup Dijon mustard**
1 **medium baking potato (8 ounces), peeled**
1½ **teaspoons olive oil**
   Freshly ground pepper

1. Rinse chicken under cold water; pat dry. Insert metal blade in food processor. Process parsley until minced and, with motor on, add garlic clove to machine. Add mustard and process 10 seconds. Transfer mixture to small bowl; set aside.

2. Change to medium shredding disk. Insert potato sideways in food chute and shred with a firm push; transfer shreds to bowl of cold water and let stand 5 minutes. Rinse and drain thoroughly, then pat potato shreds dry with paper towels. Dry bowl; add potato shreds and toss thoroughly with oil.

3. Heat oven to 375 degrees. Brush each piece of chicken with one-quarter of the mustard mixture. Put chicken, bone side down onto a jelly-roll pan or other flat pan that will fit under broiler. Top each chicken piece with one-quarter of the potato shreds, spreading shreds into a thin, even layer to replace chicken skin. Sprinkle lightly with pepper.

4. Bake until juices run clear when pierced, about 20 minutes. Transfer pan to broiler; broil until "skin" is crisped, about 5 minutes. Serve immediately.

Myrna Greenspan, a Chicago wine wholesaler, shared the following recipe with The Tribune as an example of how to cook with wine. "Many wines impart special flavors and aromas to food," she said, "but not all. When a recipe simply states 'white wine,' be sure to use a dry white wine, nothing too fruity or sweet."

CHICKEN BREASTS MARENGO

6 to 8 servings
Preparation time: 20 minutes
Cooking time: 45 minutes

4 whole chicken breasts, boned, split

½ cup all-purpose flour

1 teaspoon each: salt, dried tarragon

½ teaspoon freshly ground pepper

¼ to ½ cup olive oil

1 medium onion, finely chopped

2 cloves garlic, finely chopped

2 cups stewed tomatoes, crushed

¾ cup dry white wine

½ pound fresh mushrooms, quartered

1 bay leaf

2 tablespoons unsalted butter

16 small white boiling onions, peeled

1 teaspoon sugar

2 tablespoons chopped fresh parsley

1. Rinse chicken under cold water; pat dry. Combine flour, salt, tarragon and pepper in shallow dish. Dredge chicken breasts in flour mixture; shake off excess.

2. Heat ¼ cup olive oil in large high-sided skillet. Sauté breasts, a few at a time, over medium-high heat until well browned on both sides, about 5 minutes. Set aside, covered with foil. Repeat with remaining breasts, adding more oil to skillet, if necessary.

3. When all breasts are browned, add onion and garlic to skillet. Cook and stir until golden. Add tomatoes, white wine, mushrooms and bay leaf. Heat to boil. Transfer contents of skillet to large pot or dutch oven. Add chicken. Cover and simmer over medium-low heat until chicken is tender, about 20 minutes.

4. Meanwhile, melt butter in medium skillet. Add onions and sauté over medium heat until cooked, about 8 minutes. Sprinkle sugar over onions and continue cooking until sugar begins to caramelize.

5. Arrange chicken on warm platter with raised sides. Arrange onions around edges. Garnish with parsley.

Arun's, a Thai restaurant in Chicago, contributed this classic recipe for a Food Guide story on the basics of Thai cuisine. Homemade red curry paste adds the kick to this soup-stew main course.

CHICKEN CURRY WITH BAMBOO SHOOTS
(Kang kai nor mai)

6 servings
Preparation time: 15 minutes
Cooking time: 12 minutes

1 pound boneless, skinless chicken breasts

2 tablespoons each: corn oil, red curry paste (recipe follows)

2 tablespoons fish sauce (nam pla)

2 cups canned unsweetened coconut milk

1 can (8 ounces) thinly sliced bamboo shoots, drained

1½ teaspoons thinly shredded, seeded jalapeño pepper

½ cup fresh sweet basil leaves

Cooked white rice

1. Rinse chicken under cold water; pat dry. Slice chicken breasts into strips. Heat oil in large skillet over medium heat until hot. Add curry paste; cook and stir constantly until the paste smells cooked, about 4 minutes.

2. Stir in chicken and fish sauce; cook and stir over medium heat until chicken turns opaque, about 4 minutes. Add coconut milk and bamboo shoots; heat to boil.

3. Add jalapeño pepper and basil leaves. Simmer 2 minutes. Serve immediately in wide bowls with cooked rice.

RED CURRY PASTE | About 1 cup

7 to 10 small dried red chilies

¼ cup warm water

2 tablespoons chopped lemon grass

1 tablespoon each, chopped: shallots, garlic, fresh ginger

1 tablespoon dried shrimp paste (kapi)

1 teaspoon salt

½ teaspoon dried citrus rind

1. Remove stems and seeds from chilies; keep the seeds in if you desire a hot curry paste. Put chilies and remaining ingredients into a blender. Process, scraping down sides of container occasionally, until a smooth paste. Refrigerate, covered, up to several weeks.

With the use of the microwave oven, chicken enchiladas can be prepared more easily than in the conventional manner. The fresh green sauce, made with cilantro, brings a lively flavor to the dish.

CHICKEN ENCHILADAS

2 servings
Preparation time: 25 minutes
Microwave cooking time: 15 minutes

1 **small onion, minced**
2 **tablespoons each: vegetable oil, all-purpose flour**
2 **cups shredded lettuce**
¼ **cup each: minced fresh parsley, water**
1 **tablespoon minced fresh cilantro (coriander)**
Salt, hot pepper sauce to taste
1 **medium onion, chopped**
1 **clove garlic, minced**
1½ **cups cooked, shredded, dark and white meat chicken (see recipe for chicken in the microwave, page 337)**
2 **canned green chilies, chopped, or to taste**
4 **large corn tortillas**
Vegetable oil
Sour cream
Tomato wedges, chopped green onions, for garnish

1. Put minced onion and 1 tablespoon of the oil into 1-quart microwave-safe bowl. Microwave on high (100 percent power) until onion is soft, about 1 minute. Stir in flour; microwave on high for 1 minute. Stir in lettuce, parsley and water; microwave on high for 6 minutes. Puree in blender or food processor; add an additional 1 to 2 tablespoons of water if necessary for a medium-thick sauce. Add cilantro, salt and hot pepper sauce.

2. Put chopped onion, garlic and remaining 1 tablespoon oil into 2-quart microwave-safe bowl. Microwave on high until soft, about 2 minutes. Stir in chicken, chilies and half of the green sauce; add salt to taste.

3. Brush each tortilla lightly with oil. Put tortillas into 8-inch round microwave-safe baking dish. Microwave, covered, on high until warm and soft, about 1 minute.

4. Spoon one-quarter of the chicken mixture down center of each tortilla. Roll up, arrange on microwave-safe platter or serving dish. Top with remaining green sauce. Put a dollop of sour cream in center of each tortilla. Microwave on high until hot, 2 to 4 minutes. Serve garnished with tomatoes and green onions.

THE CHICAGO TRIBUNE COOKBOOK

Columnist Lee Thompson wrote an ode to the clay pot in one memorable article in the Food Guide. The clay pot makes cooking at high temperatures possible without burning the food within, she wrote, and it gives foods an extra depth of flavor. The classic French dish, chicken with 40 cloves of garlic, is a perfect selection for clay-pot cookery.

CLAY-POT CHICKEN WITH 40 CLOVES OF GARLIC

4 servings
Preparation time: 20 minutes
Cooking time: About 1¼ hours

1 **roasting chicken, 3½ to 4 pounds**
  Juice of ½ lemon
3 **tablespoons butter, softened**
1 **teaspoon each: rubbed sage, ground thyme, ground rosemary**
  Salt, freshly ground pepper to taste
3 **to 4 heads garlic, cloves separated but not peeled (use only large and medium-size cloves)**

1. Soak clay pot and cover in lukewarm water 15 minutes or more. Drain.

2. Rinse chicken under cold water; pat dry. Put chicken into pot. Pour lemon juice into body cavity. Rub chicken with butter, herbs, salt and pepper. Distribute garlic cloves around and over chicken.

3. Put covered pot into cold oven. Set oven temperature to 425 degrees. Bake 50 minutes from time oven reaches this temperature. Remove cover. Baste chicken with juices. Increase oven temperature to 450 degrees. Bake uncovered until breast skin is golden and thigh juices run clear when tested with fork, 10 to 15 more minutes.

NOTE: While the clay pot yields the best results, this recipe can be prepared in a dutch oven. To do so, omit step 1. Follow directions in step 2 except place chicken in a 4-quart dutch oven and pour 2½ cups chicken broth or water over chicken. Bake, covered, in a preheated 350-degree oven, until thigh juices run clear, about 1 hour. Raise oven temperature to 400 degrees; bake until skin crisps, about 15 minutes. After cooking, remove chicken and garlic cloves to platter; keep warm. Simmer pan juices over medium heat until reduced by one-third; season to taste with salt and pepper.

■ *Chicken vesuvio is a true Chicago original, served in almost all the Italian restaurants in town. It's fried and then baked with plenty of garlic, olive oil and potatoes. The following version cuts down the amount of olive oil traditionally used for a less greasy dish.*

CHICKEN VESUVIO

4 servings
Preparation time: 25 minutes
Cooking time: 40 minutes

1 broiler/fryer chicken, about 3 pounds, cut up

⅓ cup all-purpose flour

1½ teaspoons dried basil

¾ teaspoon dried leaf oregano

½ teaspoon salt

¼ teaspoon each: dried leaf thyme, freshly ground pepper

Pinch each: dried rosemary, rubbed sage

½ cup olive oil

3 baking potatoes, cut into lengthwise wedges

3 tablespoons minced fresh parsley

3 cloves garlic, minced

¾ cup dry white wine

1. Rinse chicken under cold water; pat dry. Mix flour, basil, oregano, salt, thyme, pepper, rosemary and sage in shallow dish. Dredge chicken in flour mixture. Shake off excess.

2. Heat oil in 12-inch cast-iron or other ovenproof skillet over medium-high heat until hot. Add chicken pieces in single layer. Fry, turning occasionally (use tongs so chicken will not be pierced), until light brown on all sides, about 15 minutes. Remove with tongs to paper towels.

3. When all chicken is browned, add potato wedges to skillet. Fry, turning occasionally, until light brown on all sides. Remove to paper towels.

4. Heat oven to 375 degrees. Pour off all but 2 tablespoons of the fat from skillet. Put chicken and potatoes back into skillet. Sprinkle with parsley and garlic. Pour wine over all.

5. Bake, uncovered, until potatoes are fork-tender and thigh juices run clear, 20 to 25 minutes. Let stand 5 minutes before serving. Serve with a little of the pan juices.

The best way to make fried chicken has caused heated debate among aficionados. Should one coat it in flour or bread crumbs? Deep-fry it or pan-fry it? Use butter or olive oil? The Tribune set about trying to find the way to make perfect fried chicken by asking local experts and trying our own versions. We came up with the following recipes. The first, an easy, oven-fried version that uses an intriguing coating of whole-wheat bread crumbs and oats, was developed in The Tribune test kitchen.

CRISPY OVEN-FRIED CHICKEN

4 servings
Preparation time: 15 minutes
Standing time: 30 minutes
Baking time: 40 minutes

1 broiler/fryer chicken, about 3 pounds, cut up

3 large eggs

2 tablespoons milk or half-and-half

4 slices day-old whole-wheat bread, cubed

½ cup old-fashioned rolled oats

½ teaspoon each: dried leaf thyme, rubbed sage, salt, freshly ground pepper

½ cup (1 stick) unsalted butter, melted

1. Rinse chicken under cold water; pat dry. Whisk together eggs and milk in large bowl. Add chicken; turn to coat. Let stand 30 minutes.

2. Put bread cubes into food processor or blender. Process with on/off turns until medium-fine crumbs. Add oats, thyme, sage, salt and pepper. Process just to mix. Transfer to shallow dish.

3. Heat oven to 375 degrees. Let excess egg mixture drip off chicken pieces. Dip each piece in melted butter. Put into crumb mixture; turn to coat well with crumbs. Put into buttered 13 by 9-inch baking pan. Drizzle any remaining butter over chicken. Bake until crispy and golden, about 40 minutes. Serve hot or cold.

Jerry's Kitchen, on the Near North Side of Chicago, is known for its good fried chicken, which is coated with an egg and milk mixture, dipped in seasoned flour, and then deep-fried.

SOUTHERN-STYLE FRIED CHICKEN

4 servings
Preparation time: 25 minutes
Soaking time: 1 hour
Cooking time: 20 minutes

1 **broiler/fryer chicken, about 3 pounds, quartered**

MILK MIXTURE

2 **cups milk**

1 **cup water**

1 **egg, beaten**

2 **tablespoons all-purpose flour**

1 **tablespoon sugar**
  Pinch seasoned salt

FLOUR MIXTURE

1 **cup all-purpose flour**

½ **teaspoon each: salt, paprika, onion powder**

¼ **teaspoon freshly ground pepper**
  Vegetable oil for deep-frying

1. Rinse chicken under cold water. Soak chicken pieces in cold, salted water for 1 hour. Drain.

2. For milk mixture, combine milk, water, egg, 2 tablespoons flour, sugar and seasoned salt in large bowl. For flour mixture, combine flour, salt, paprika, onion powder and pepper in shallow dish.

3. Put oil into large deep saucepan or deep-fryer. Heat oil to 350 degrees.

4. Put chicken quarters, one at a time, into milk mixture. Drain off excess. Then dredge in flour mixture to coat thoroughly.

5. Immediately put coated chicken, a few pieces at a time, into 350-degree oil. Deep-fry, turning occasionally, until golden brown and juices run clear, about 20 minutes. Remove chicken to wire rack for a few seconds to drain; serve immediately.

Chicagoan Steve Cotsirilos grills chicken with a Greek flavor. Plenty of lemon and oregano are the secrets to his flavorful entree.

GREEK-STYLE GRILLED CHICKEN

4 to 6 servings
Preparation time: 10 minutes
Marinating time: 12 to 24 hours
Cooking time: 45 minutes

2 **whole broiler/fryer chickens, each about 2 pounds**
2 **tablespoons dried leaf oregano**
4 **teaspoons freshly ground pepper**
1 **teaspoon each: garlic powder, salt**
  Juice of 4 lemons
6 **tablespoons vegetable oil**
2 **tablespoons olive oil**

1. Rinse chickens under cold water; pat dry. Cut in half. Mix oregano, pepper, garlic powder and salt.

2. Rub oregano mixture into chicken. Mix lemon juice and oils in large shallow nonaluminum dish. Add chicken; turn to coat. Refrigerate, covered, turning chicken occasionally, 12 to 24 hours.

3. Prepare grill. When coals are covered with gray ash, remove chicken from marinade and arrange on grill rack. Cover and grill, turning and basting with marinade every 5 to 10 minutes, until juices run clear, about 45 minutes.

Preparing chicken for salads, casseroles and the chicken enchiladas is easy in the microwave oven using the following simple recipe.

CHICKEN IN THE MICROWAVE

6 servings
Preparation time: 10 minutes
Microwave cooking time: 25 minutes

1 **roasting chicken, about 4 pounds**
2 **tablespoons melted butter**
¼ **teaspoon each: salt, freshly ground pepper, paprika**

1. Rinse chicken under cold water; pat dry. Rub chicken with butter. Sprinkle with salt, pepper and paprika. Put into large microwave-safe baking dish or casserole.

2. Microwave, covered, on high (100 percent power), rotating dish 3 times, until tender and thigh juices run clear, about 25 minutes. Let stand, covered, 10 minutes. Remove skin from chicken; remove meat from bones. Use chicken meat in salads, soups and other dishes.

White searing is a cooking technique similar to sautéing. To white sear chicken, cook strips of the meat over medium heat in oil or butter just to seal the outside. Then remove the strips while a sauce is prepared in the skillet. For a final cooking the chicken is returned to the sauce for about 3 minutes. An example of the technique follows from Michigan cooking teacher and chef Yvonne Uhlianuk.

BASIL CHICKEN GOUJONS

2 to 3 servings
Preparation time: 20 minutes
Marinating time: 30 minutes
Cooking time: 15 minutes

2 whole chicken breasts, boned, skinned, split

20 medium-size fresh basil leaves, torn (or substitute 1 teaspoon dried basil)

½ cup plus 2 tablespoons basil vinegar

1 tablespoon olive oil

1 teaspoon minced shallots

½ teaspoon minced garlic

Freshly ground white pepper to taste

¼ cup (½ stick) unsalted butter

1 cup rich chicken broth (see recipe, page 134)

½ cup dry white wine

1 tablespoon tomato paste

Salt to taste

1. Rinse chicken under cold water; pat dry. Pull fillets (the thin strip of meat on underside of breast) free from breast halves. (To remove tendons see note below.) Cut each breast into 4 pieces on a long diagonal. The trimmed fillets and strips of breast are called goujons.

2. For marinade, mix 8 of the basil leaves (or ½ teaspoon of the dried), 2 tablespoons of the basil vinegar, oil, shallots, garlic and pepper in medium bowl. Add chicken goujons; turn to coat well on all surfaces. Let stand uncovered, stirring twice, 30 minutes.

3. Remove goujons from marinade. Shake off excess liquid. Reserve marinade.

4. Melt half of the butter in 10-inch skillet over medium heat. Add goujons; white sear a scant 2 minutes per side. Remove goujons from skillet. Set aside at room temperature.

5. Heat oven to 200 degrees. Pour reserved marinade and remaining ½ cup basil vinegar into skillet. Boil over high heat until reduced by half. Add chicken broth, wine and tomato paste. Cook and stir over high heat scraping up browned bits from bottom of pan. Boil for 2 minutes; then reduce heat to medium-low.

6. Return goujons to sauce; simmer until chicken is tender, about 3 minutes. Remove goujons with slotted spoon, arrange attractively on warm platter. Put into oven while you finish the sauce.

7. Increase heat to high and boil sauce until it thickens slightly. Reduce heat to medium; gradually whisk in remaining 2 tablespoons butter. Add remaining 12 basil leaves (or ½ teaspoon dried). Taste and adjust seasonings adding salt if needed. Pour sauce over chicken. Serve immediately.

NOTE: For best results remove white tendons from chicken breast fillet before cooking. To do so place fillet flat on cutting board with wider end toward you and tendon underneath. Hold end of tendon with tips of your fingers. Insert tip of paring knife between tendon and underneath side of fillet. Angle knife blade slightly downward and move knife firmly and quickly away from your hand toward tail end of fillet, striping tendon free. Discard tendon.

Chef Michael Foley created a method of seasoning chicken by inserting mushrooms and thyme or other herbs under the skin, resulting in meat that is as flavorful as the skin. Try this method with tarragon or dill.

ROAST CHICKEN WITH MUSHROOMS AND HERBS

6 to 8 servings
Preparation time: 30 minutes
Cooking time: 1 hour

3 whole chickens, about 1½ pounds each
Salt, freshly ground pepper to taste
6 bay leaves
2 pounds fresh mushrooms, finely chopped
1½ cups (3 sticks) unsalted butter, slightly softened
1½ teaspoons dried leaf thyme
½ cup chicken broth or water
Cooked egg noodles

1. Rinse chickens under cold water; pat dry inside and outside. Season cavities lightly with salt and pepper; place 2 bay leaves in each cavity.

2. Heat oven to 325 degrees. Mix mushrooms, butter, thyme, ¾ teaspoon salt and ¼ teaspoon pepper in large bowl.

3. Gently separate the skin from breast and thigh meat on each chicken by slipping your fingers between skin and meat. Carefully push mushroom mixture into the resulting pockets. Be certain the mixture is evenly dispersed. Tie legs together.

4. Place chickens on rack in roasting pan, breast side down. Roast for 20 minutes. Turn chickens breast side up; baste with pan juices. Continue cooking until thigh juices run clear when pierced, 30 to 35 minutes. Let chickens rest on platter, loosely tented with foil, while preparing juices.

5. Discard fat from roasting pan; stir in broth. Heat to boil over high heat, while scraping up browned bits from bottom of pan. Boil until mixture is reduced by half. Taste and adjust seasonings if necessary with salt and pepper.

6. Spoon juices over chickens; serve with egg noodles.

A simple roasted chicken gets a big flavor boost from lemon and rosemary in this recipe developed by JeanMarie Brownson in the test kitchen. If you happen to find fresh rosemary in the market, try substituting it for the dried version.

ROAST CHICKEN WITH LEMON AND ROSEMARY

6 servings
Preparation time: 35 minutes
Cooking time: 1½ hours

1 **roasting chicken, about 5½ pounds**
  Salt, freshly ground pepper to taste
1 **lemon**
3 **large cloves garlic, halved**
3 **sprigs parsley**
2½ **teaspoons dried rosemary leaves**
1 **tablespoon vegetable oil**
3 **tablespoons olive oil**
½ **cup chicken broth**
⅓ **cup dry white wine**
3 **tablespoons unsalted butter**
  Chopped parsley for garnish

1. Rinse chicken under cold water; pat dry. Sprinkle cavity with salt and pepper. Remove rind from lemon with zester or vegetable peeler. Cut rind into julienne. Squeeze juice from lemon; reserve juice. Put lemon pulps, garlic, half of the lemon julienne, parsley and 1 teaspoon of the rosemary into cavity of chicken.

2. Heat oven to 375 degrees. Gently separate the skin from breast and thigh meat of chicken by slipping your fingers between skin and meat. Put some of the remaining lemon julienne and rosemary between skin and meat. Repeat with back skin and remaining lemon julienne and rosemary.

3. Brush vegetable oil over bottom of heavy roasting pan. Put chicken in pan; brush generously on all sides with olive oil. Sprinkle with pepper.

4. Roast chicken, basting occasionally with pan juices and chicken broth, until temperature of thigh registers 170 degrees and juices run clear, 1¼ to 1½ hours. Let rest on platter, loosely tented with foil. (Temperature will rise about 10 degrees.)

5. Remove fat from pan juices. Put roasting pan over medium heat; stir in remaining chicken broth and wine. Simmer, scraping up browned bits from bottom of pan until liquid reduces to about ½ cup. Stir in 3 tablespoons lemon juice.

6. Vigorously whisk in butter. Taste and adjust seasonings. Stir in parsley. Serve immediately.

A story celebrating Black History Month in Chicago included the following smothered chicken and rice from caterer Tondalaya Thomas.

SMOTHERED CHICKEN AND RICE

4 servings
Preparation time: 30 minutes
Cooking time: 1 hour

1 **broiler/fryer chicken, about 2½ pounds, cut up**
1 **teaspoon each: salt, freshly ground pepper**
¾ **cup all-purpose flour**
½ **cup vegetable oil or clarified butter**
2 **medium yellow onions, halved, thinly sliced (or 1½ cups chopped green onions)**
3 **cups water**
3 **chicken bouillon cubes**
1 **teaspoon minced garlic**
Easy cooked rice (see recipe, page 168)

1. Rinse chicken under cold water; pat dry. Spread chicken pieces flat on table or cutting board. Sprinkle evenly with half the salt and pepper. Turn all pieces, and repeat with remaining salt and pepper.

2. Thoroughly dredge chicken in flour on all sides. Reserve remaining flour.

3. Heat oil in 10-inch skillet over medium-high heat. Add chicken in single layer. Fry, turning occasionally (use tongs so chicken will not be pierced), until light brown on all sides, about 15 minutes. Remove with tongs to plate.

4. Stir remaining flour into pan juices. Cook and stir, scraping up browned bits from bottom of pan, until flour is light brown. Add sliced yellow onions; cook until dark brown. Remove from heat; cool about 5 minutes.

5. Heat water and bouillon cubes to boil in medium saucepan. Pour bouillon mixture into skillet; cook and stir over medium heat until thickened. Stir in garlic; reduce heat to low. (If using green onions, add at this point.)

6. Add chicken; cook, covered, over very low heat until chicken is tender and thigh juices run clear, 30 to 35 minutes. Serve with rice.

The Tribune *challenged California cooking teacher Ken Hom to whip up a fast meal using chicken when he visited the test kitchen in 1986. He came up with two dishes using chicken legs, a stir-fry entree and a salad using the chicken skin, fried until crispy and placed over romaine lettuce.*

STIR-FRIED CHICKEN WITH NOODLES AND ROMAINE SALAD

2 servings
Preparation time: 25 minutes
Cooking time: 15 minutes

2 **whole chicken legs, thighs and drumsticks**

½ **teaspoon Oriental sesame oil**

Salt, freshly ground pepper to taste

3 **tablespoons peanut oil**

1 **tablespoon each, minced: garlic, fresh ginger**

1 **medium green pepper, seeded, cut into strips**

1 **cup cherry tomatoes, halved**

3 **cups cooked elbow noodles, tossed with 2 tablespoons oil**

SALAD

1 **tablespoon white wine vinegar**

1 **teaspoon country-style Dijon mustard**

¼ **cup olive oil**

3 **cups torn romaine lettuce leaves**

Parsley sprigs for garnish

1. Rinse chicken under cold water; pat dry. Remove skin from chicken legs. Cut skin into strips. Remove meat from bones and cut into strips. Put meat into small bowl; add sesame oil, salt and pepper.

2. Heat wok over medium-high heat until very hot. Add 1 tablespoon of the peanut oil; heat until hot but not smoking. Add chicken skin. Stir-fry until skin is crisp and golden, about 5 minutes. Remove with slotted spoon. Drain on paper towels. Set aside.

3. Pour off fat from wok. Reheat wok over medium-high heat. Add remaining 2 tablespoons peanut oil; heat oil. Add garlic, ginger and chicken. Stir-fry until chicken is no longer pink, about 5 minutes.

4. Add green pepper; stir-fry until green pepper is crisp-tender, about 3 minutes. Add cherry tomatoes; cook just until heated through. Put noodles onto platter. Top with chicken mixture. Keep warm.

5. For salad, mix vinegar and mustard in bottom of serving bowl. Whisk in olive oil until smooth. Add lettuce leaves. Toss to mix. Top with crisp chicken skin. Serve immediately alongside chicken and noodles.

The Tribune's *Cook's Dialogue* column attempts to help readers with cooking questions and recipe requests. When a reader asked for the following recipe from Szechwan House restaurant in Chicago, we were only too glad to get the recipe and test it. The original version calls for a 3½-hour walnut preparation, which we adapted to make it easier for home cooks. Whichever version you use, the results are delicious.

STIR-FRIED CHICKEN WITH WALNUTS

3 to 4 servings
Preparation time: 40 minutes
Standing time: 3½ hours
Cooking time: 20 minutes

1¼ cups sugar
3 tablespoons water
1 cup each: honey,
    walnut halves
2 cups peanut oil
2 whole chicken breasts,
    boned, split
1 egg white
1 tablespoon cold water
2 teaspoons cornstarch
½ teaspoon salt

SAUCE
¼ cup finely shredded
    ginger
2 tablespoons each: soy
    sauce, oyster sauce,
    shao shing wine
    (Chinese rice wine)
2 teaspoons each:
    freshly ground
    pepper, sugar
2 cloves garlic, minced
2 tablespoons water
1 tablespoon cornstarch
4 green onions, shredded

1. Prepare walnuts about 3½ hours before serving: Place sugar and water in large, heavy-bottomed saucepan or frying pan and allow it to liquify over low heat. When liquified, add honey and walnuts and remove from heat. Allow walnuts to soak in mixture for 3 hours. (See note on alternate, quick method.)

2. Put peanut oil into wok or medium-size, heavy-bottomed saucepan. Heat oil to 325 degrees. Using a slotted spoon, drain walnuts from sugar mixture. Carefully drop walnuts, a few at a time, into hot oil. Deep-fry, watching carefully, until crisp, 30 to 60 seconds. Remove walnuts with slotted spoon. Drain on waxed paper.

3. Strain oil through fine sieve. Reserve 1 cup oil for cooking chicken.

4. Rinse chicken under cold water; pat dry. Cut into ½-inch dice. Mix egg white, 1 tablespoon water, 2 teaspoons cornstarch and salt in small bowl. Add chicken; toss to mix. Refrigerate, stirring often, 30 minutes.

5. For sauce, mix ginger, soy sauce, oyster sauce, rice wine, pepper, sugar and garlic in small bowl. Mix 2 tablespoons water and cornstarch in separate bowl.

6. Put reserved 1 cup of oil into wok or large skillet; heat to 350 degrees. Add chicken; cook over medium heat, stirring constantly, until pieces separate, 3 to 4 minutes. Remove chicken with slotted spoon; drain on paper towels. Pour off all but 3 tablespoons of the oil from wok.

7. Add sauce mixture to wok; cook and stir over medium heat, until hot. Add chicken; toss well to coat with sauce. Add cornstarch mixture; cook and stir until thickened and chicken is well coated. Add green onions; cook and stir 1 minute. Stir in walnuts, tossing well to coat with sauce. Serve immediately.

NOTE: If desired, eliminate step 1 and use the following method: Individually dip 1 cup of shelled walnut halves in honey; then dip honeyed nuts in granulated sugar. Continue with recipe from step 2 on.

Chicagoans Judy and Joseph Fell love to entertain; one of their standard entrees is the following moist, oven-roasted capon which fills the house with a wonderful aroma. The Fells accompany the capon with oven-roasted potatoes (seasoned with their herb and salt mixture), a green vegetable and lots of homemade bread.

CRISP OVEN-ROASTED CAPON

6 to 8 servings
Preparation time: 25 minutes
Standing time: 30 minutes
Cooking time: About 1½ hours

1 capon, 5½ to 6
    pounds
    Herb and spice salt
    (recipe follows)
2 or 3 branches fresh
    tarragon or 1½
    teaspoons dried
    tarragon
½ cup (1 stick) unsalted
    butter, cold
¼ cup dry white wine

1. Rinse capon under cold water; pat dry. Let stand at room temperature 30 minutes. Scatter generous amount of herb and spice salt in breast cavity; put tarragon into cavity. Truss openings with kitchen string. Tuck wings underneath and tie legs together. Rub some of the herb and spice salt into the skin.

2. Heat oven to 425 degrees. Put capon on roasting rack, breast up; set in roasting pan. Roast until skin begins to brown, 10 to 15 minutes, then rub butter stick over the breast until 2 tablespoons have melted.

3. Continue roasting, rubbing occasionally with butter, until skin is nicely browned, 35 to 40 minutes. Then reduce oven temperature to 375 degrees. Roast until meat thermometer inserted in thigh registers 170 degrees, 40 to 45 more minutes. Remove from oven and cover loosely with foil. Let rest 10 to 15 minutes. (Meat temperature will rise about 10 degrees.) Carve on cutting board or platter with a rim to save the juices.

4. Skim off fat from pan juices. Pour juices into small saucepan. Pour wine into roasting pan. Heat to boil while scraping up browned bits from bottom of pan. Pour wine into the saucepan along with any accumulated juices from platter. Heat until warm; spoon some over each portion of carved chicken.

Herb and Spice Salt | About ¾ cup

⅔ cup salt

1 heaping tablespoon dried leaf thyme

1 heaping teaspoon freshly ground white pepper

¼ to ½ teaspoon ground cloves

1. Put all ingredients into jar with a tight-fitting lid. Shake to mix. Use on roast poultry, pork and vegetables.

The popularity of Thai food in America keeps growing. The spicy and exotic flavors of ingredients such as ginger, hot chilies and lime juice make the cuisine a refreshing change of pace. The following recipe can be served as an entree or as an appetizer with the chicken rolled up in the lettuce.

Thai Chicken in Lettuce Leaves | 4 to 6 servings
Preparation time: 15 minutes
Marinating time: 30 minutes
Cooking time: 10 to 15 minutes

2 whole large chicken breasts, boned, split

2 egg whites

3 tablespoons plus 1 teaspoon lime juice

1 tablespoon cornstarch

2 to 3 teaspoons hot chili paste with garlic

½ teaspoon salt

3 tablespoons peanut oil

1 cup diced celery

⅔ cup chopped green onions

½ cup diced water chestnuts

¼ cup diced red bell pepper

2 teaspoons minced fresh ginger

2 tablespoons plus 1 teaspoon soy sauce or tamari

16 Boston or other tender lettuce leaves

1. Rinse chicken under cold water; pat dry. Slice chicken breasts into thin strips 1½-inches long and ¼-inch thick. Whisk together egg whites, lime juice, cornstarch, chili paste and salt in large bowl. Add chicken; stir well. Refrigerate for 30 minutes.

2. Heat 1 tablespoon of the peanut oil in a wok or large skillet over medium-high heat. Add celery, green onions, water chestnuts, red pepper and ginger; stir-fry until crisp-tender, 2 to 3 minutes. Remove vegetables from wok.

3. Heat remaining 2 tablespoons peanut oil in wok over medium-high heat. Add chicken with marinade; stir-fry until cooked, about 5 minutes. Add vegetables and soy sauce. Remove from heat.

4. Arrange lettuce on platter with stems toward center. Spoon chicken mixture onto each leaf. Serve immediately.

Rock Cornish hens get an Italian touch in this recipe from Beverly Dillon that's perfect for outdoor grilling. Serve it with a simple pasta salad.

GRILLED ROCK CORNISH HENS WITH ITALIAN SAUSAGE STUFFING

8 servings
Preparation time: 30 minutes
Cooking time: 1 hour, 20 minutes

5   tablespoons olive oil
¾   pound each, removed from casing: mild Italian sausage, hot Italian sausage
½   cup each, diced: onion, celery
1   teaspoon minced garlic
2   slices toasted white bread, cut into ¼-inch cubes
½   cup freshly grated Parmesan cheese
1   egg, lightly beaten
2   tablespoons minced fresh parsley
1   teaspoon dried leaf oregano
½   teaspoon each: dried rubbed sage, dried leaf rosemary, salt, freshly ground pepper
8   Rock Cornish hens, about 1 pound each
     Parsley sprigs for garnish

1. Heat 1 tablespoon of the oil in large skillet over medium heat. Add sausages, onion, celery and garlic. Cook, chopping sausage up as it cooks, until browned, about 20 minutes. Transfer sausage with slotted spoon to large bowl. Add bread cubes, cheese, egg, minced parsley, oregano, sage, rosemary, salt and pepper. Mix well. Cool.

2. Rinse hens under cold water; pat dry. Sprinkle breast cavities with salt. Stuff each breast cavity with equal portions of the sausage mixture. Truss openings with kitchen string. Tuck wings underneath and tie legs together. Rub skin with some of the remaining oil.

3. Prepare grill. When coals are covered with gray ash, arrange hens on grill rack 6 to 8 inches from coals. Cover and grill, basting often with oil, until thigh juices run clear when pierced, 40 to 50 minutes. Let stand on platter 10 minutes. Garnish with parsley.

NOTE: To cook in oven, heat oven to 400 degrees. Put hens in shallow roasting pan, breast side up. Rub well with oil. Cover with foil. Roast, covered, 30 minutes; then uncover and roast, basting often with pan drippings, until golden and thigh juices run clear when pierced, about 20 more minutes.

The rich flavor of Rock Cornish hens is perfect when teamed with fruit such as a raspberry sauce. If you elect to grill the hens, they will have a smoky flavor that adds to the enjoyment.

GRILLED ROCK CORNISH HENS WITH RASPBERRY SAUCE

4 servings
Preparation time: 20 minutes
Cooking time: 45 minutes

4 **Rock Cornish hens, about 1 pound each**
Salt, freshly ground pepper to taste
8 **lemon wedges**
¼ **cup (½ stick) butter, melted**

RASPBERRY SAUCE

1 **package (10 ounces) frozen quick-thaw raspberries, thawed**
1 **tablespoon cornstarch**
2 **tablespoons each: fresh lemon juice, water**
¼ **teaspoon each: ground cardamom, ground ginger**
Lemon wedges, parsley sprigs for garnish

1. Rinse hens under cold water; pat dry. Sprinkle breast cavities with salt and pepper. Stuff each cavity with 2 lemon wedges. Truss openings with kitchen string. Tuck wings underneath and tie legs together. Rub 1 teaspoon of the butter over each hen.

2. Prepare grill. When coals are covered with gray ash, arrange hens on grill rack 6 to 8 inches from coals. Cover and grill, basting occasionally with remaining butter, until thigh juices run clear, 40 to 50 minutes. Let stand on platter 10 minutes.

3. Meanwhile for sauce, push raspberries through fine sieve into small saucepan. Dissolve cornstarch in lemon juice and water. Stir cornstarch mixture, cardamom and ginger into raspberries. Cook and stir over low heat until mixture thickens and clears, 3 to 4 minutes. Taste and adjust seasonings.

4. Remove strings from hens; discard lemon wedges in cavity. Stir any accumulated juices from platter into sauce. Garnish hens with lemon wedges and parsley. Serve with raspberry sauce.

NOTE: To cook in oven, heat oven to 400 degrees. Put hens in shallow roasting pan, breast side up. Rub with butter. Cover with foil. Roast, covered, 30 minutes; then uncover and roast, basting often with pan drippings, until golden and thigh juices run clear when pierced, about 20 more minutes.

■ Poussin *is the French term for baby chicken. These small birds are slightly larger than a Rock Cornish hen, which can be used in place of poussin in the following recipe from chef David Radwine at Chicago's Midland Hotel.*

ROAST POUSSIN WITH APPLE AND SAUSAGE STUFFING

4 servings
Preparation time: 30 minutes
Cooking time: 1¼ hours

4 poussin (baby chicken), about 1¼ pound each (or Rock Cornish hens)

¾ cup chopped onions

½ cup chopped celery

1 apple, cored, chopped

3 tablespoons melted butter

3½ cups toasted, diced bread croutons

¾ pound pork sausage links, cooked, diced

½ cup each: chicken broth, dried apricots, chopped

¼ cup chopped fresh parsley

Salt, freshly ground pepper to taste

1 cup orange juice

1 can (13¾ ounces) beef broth

2 tablespoons flour dissolved in ¼ cup water

GARNISH

Cooked cranberries (recipe follows)

Steamed acorn squash balls (recipe follows)

1. Rinse poussin under cold water; pat dry. Chop giblets and reserve.

2. Cook onions, celery and apple in butter in large skillet over medium heat until crisp-tender, about 5 minutes. Transfer to large bowl. Add croutons, cooked sausage, chicken broth, apricots, parsley and giblets. Toss to mix. Add salt and pepper.

3. Heat oven to 350 degrees. Stuff the breast cavities of poussin with equal amounts of bread mixture. Truss openings with string. Tuck wings underneath and tie legs together. Put into roasting pan. Brush with orange juice; sprinkle with salt and pepper.

4. Roast until meat thermometer inserted in thigh registers 170 degrees, 60 to 70 minutes. Let stand on platter for 10 minutes. (Temperature will rise about 10 degrees.)

5. Meanwhile, for sauce, put roasting pan over medium heat. Stir in beef broth. Heat to boil while scraping up browned bits from bottom of pan. Whisk in dissolved flour. Cook and stir until thickened and smooth. Taste and adjust seasonings. Strain through fine sieve.

6. Serve poussin with sauce. Garnish with cranberries and acorn squash balls.

Cooked Cranberries

Dissolve ¼ cup sugar in ½ cup water in small nonaluminum saucepan over medium heat. Stir in 1 cup cranberries. Cook over low heat just until cranberries are tender, 3 to 4 minutes. Remove from heat, cool. Remove cranberries from syrup with slotted spoon before serving.

Steamed Acorn Squash Balls

Cut acorn squash in half. Scoop out and discard seeds. Using a melon baller, scoop squash into balls. Steam squash balls on a steamer rack over boiling water, covered, until tender, about 10 minutes. Serve warm.

How to survive the holidays without living in the kitchen? We turned to Chicago caterer and teacher Monique Hooker to share a secret for keeping the holidays simple: The following Rock Cornish hens have a wild rice stuffing that can be prepared in advance, then the final cooking time is only 45 minutes.

ROCK CORNISH HENS WITH WILD RICE STUFFING

8 servings
Preparation time: 1 hour
Cooking time: 45 minutes

1 **package (6 ounces) wild rice**

½ **cup raisins**

2 **tablespoons brandy**

2 **oranges**

8 **Rock Cornish hens, about 1 pound each**

½ **cup chopped green onions**

1 **tablespoon butter**

2 **Granny Smith apples, cored, diced**

½ **teaspoon dried leaf thyme**

Salt, freshly ground pepper to taste

8 **slices bacon, cut in half**

2½ **cups dry white wine**

1 **cup chicken broth**

½ **cup mango chutney**

1. Prepare wild rice according to package directions. Refrigerate covered up to several days.

2. Soak raisins in brandy in a small bowl. Grate orange rinds until you have 2½ tablespoons. Rinse hens under cold water; pat dry. Rub the hens inside and out with half of the orange rind; refrigerate.

3. Cook onions in butter in large skillet over medium heat until soft, about 2 minutes. Stir in wild rice, raisin mixture, remaining orange rind, apples, thyme, salt and pepper. Mix well. Refrigerate covered up to several hours.

4. Heat oven to 400 degrees. Stuff the breast cavities of the hens with equal amounts of rice mixture. Truss openings with kitchen string. Tuck wings underneath and tie legs together. Arrange in a roasting pan leaving about 1 inch space between each. Sprinkle with salt and pepper and crisscross each breast with bacon strips.

5. Roast 15 minutes. Then reduce oven temperature to 375 degrees; cook until thigh juices run clear when pierced, 25 to 30 more minutes.

6. Remove to platter and keep warm. Remove any fat from pan juices. Put roasting pan over high heat. Add wine and chicken broth. Heat to boil while scraping up browned bits from bottom of pan. Boil until reduced by half. Stir in chutney. Taste and adjust seasoning.

7. Remove bacon from hens if desired. Spoon some of the sauce over hens. Pass remaining sauce.

Ah, turkey leftovers. Some think they're better than the original roast bird. Here's a novel finale for leftovers, from The Tribune *test kitchen. Reason enough to invite the relatives back again after the holiday.*

EASY MOROCCAN TURKEY PIE

6 servings
Preparation time: 25 minutes
Cooking time: 1 hour

1 **large onion, minced**
3 **cloves garlic, minced**
3 **tablespoons each: butter, olive oil**
1 **cup minced fresh parsley**
2 **tablespoons minced fresh cilantro (coriander)**
2 **cinnamon sticks**
¾ **teaspoon ground ginger**
¼ **teaspoon each: freshly ground pepper, turmeric**
½ **pound whole blanched almonds**
¼ **cup each: vegetable oil, confectioners' sugar**
1 **teaspoon ground cinnamon**
8 **large eggs**
1½ **pounds cooked cubed turkey, about 4 cups**
2 **tablespoons fresh lemon juice**
1 **package (17¼ ounces) frozen puff pastry sheets, thawed**
  Melted butter
  Ground cinnamon
  Confectioners' sugar

1. Cook onion and garlic in butter and olive oil in medium dutch oven over medium heat until tender, about 2 minutes. Stir in parsley, cilantro, cinnamon sticks, ginger, pepper and turmeric. Cook, stirring occasionally, 15 minutes. Remove cinnamon sticks.

2. Meanwhile, cook almonds in vegetable oil in medium skillet over medium heat until golden. Drain almonds on paper towels. When cool, chop coarsely. Mix with ¼ cup confectioners' sugar and 1 teaspoon cinnamon.

3. Beat eggs until mixed; pour into onion mixture. Cook and stir over low heat until mixture is thick and fairly dry. Stir in turkey and lemon juice. Taste and adjust seasonings.

4. Heat oven to 350 degrees. Line a deep 10-inch pie plate with half of the puff pastry; trim and flute edge. Using a slotted spoon, put turkey mixture into pastry-lined pie plate. Sprinkle with almond mixture. Top with remaining half of puff pastry; crimp edges together. Brush with melted butter.

5. Bake until pastry is golden and puffed, about 35 minutes. Cool on wire rack 10 minutes. Sprinkle cinnamon and confectioners' sugar in a decorative pattern over top. Serve warm.

A Tribune *editor, Paul A. Camp, shared the secrets of his mother's perfect-every-time Thanksgiving turkey. The trick, he wrote, is in using a butter-and-broth–soaked towel to cover the bird during roasting.*

MOM'S FOOLPROOF TURKEY

10 to 12 servings
Preparation time: 45 minutes
Cooking time: About 2½ hours

1 **fresh turkey, about 14 pounds**
2 **tablespoons salt**
2½ **cups (5 sticks) unsalted butter, softened**
1 **teaspoon freshly ground pepper**
  Stuffing of choice, if desired, (see recipes, pages 359–63)
2 **cups turkey or chicken stock (see recipes, page 134)**
  Herbed turkey gravy, optional (see recipe, page 358)

1. Remove turkey from refrigerator; rinse it under cold water and pat dry. Let turkey sit 1 hour before cooking so that it will warm to room temperature.

2. Heat oven to 450 degrees. Thoroughly mix salt into 1 cup of the butter. Rub mixture over the interior cavity and exterior of the bird. Sprinkle with pepper inside and out.

3. If using, put stuffing into breast cavity. Truss openings with kitchen string. Tuck wings underneath and tie legs together.

4. Put turkey on oiled rack set in roasting pan with sides at least 3 inches high. Roast, uncovered, 30 minutes.

5. Meanwhile, melt remaining butter. Stir in turkey stock. Soak a clean, white cotton dish towel in this mixture. (Make sure the towel is big enough to cover the turkey when folded in half.)

6. Cover the top and the sides of the turkey with the wet, folded towel making sure none of the towel hangs over the sides of the roasting pan. Reduce oven temperature to 350 degrees; continue cooking until thermometer inserted in thigh registers 170 degrees. Baste every half hour by pouring the remaining butter-stock mixture over the towel (eventually pan drippings can be used for basting). Cooking time is about 2 more hours.

7. Let stand on carving board, covered loosely with foil, at least 15 minutes. (Temperature will rise about 10 degrees.) Remove stuffing from cavity. Serve with turkey gravy.

For Thanksgiving 1988, caterer Marion Mandeltort of Lincolnshire, Illinois, shared her recipes for a heartland dinner, including the following roast turkey.

Both the cornbread for the stuffing and the turkey stock for the gravy can be made a day ahead of time.

TURKEY WITH HERBED CORNBREAD STUFFING AND PAN GRAVY

12 to 14 servings
Preparation time: 1 hour
Cooking time: 3 hours

Herbed cornbread stuffing (see recipe, page 361)
1 fresh turkey, about 16 pounds
Salt to taste
¾ cup (1½ sticks) butter or margarine
1 tablespoon each: dried rosemary, rubbed sage, dried leaf thyme, paprika
1 tablespoon each, minced: fresh parsley, garlic
1 teaspoon freshly ground pepper

PAN GRAVY
2 tablespoons each: flour, butter
2¼ cups turkey stock (see recipe, page 134)
Fresh thyme sprigs for garnish

1. Make herbed cornbread stuffing. Cool.

2. Heat oven to 475 degrees. Rinse turkey under cold water; pat dry. Rub inside of turkey with salt. Spoon cooled stuffing into cavity and neck end of bird loosely to fill. Do not pack in tightly as stuffing will expand. Truss openings with kitchen string. Tuck wings underneath and tie legs together.

3. Melt butter in small saucepan. Add rosemary, sage, thyme, paprika, parsley, garlic and pepper. Simmer over low heat for 5 minutes. Cool.

4. Put turkey on oiled rack set in roasting pan. Rub outside of turkey with butter mixture. Roast, uncovered, 45 minutes. Reduce oven temperature to 400 degrees and loosely tent turkey with aluminum foil. Continue to roast, basting every half hour with pan juices, until thermometer inserted in thigh registers 170 degrees, about 2¼ hours.

5. Let stand on carving board, covered loosely with foil, at least 15 minutes. (Temperature will rise about 10 degrees.) Remove stuffing from cavity.

6. Meanwhile, for gravy, mix flour and butter, mashing together until blended to a paste. Skim off fat from pan juices in roasting pan. Pour turkey stock into roasting pan, set over medium heat and heat to boil while scraping up browned bits from bottom of the pan.

7. Gradually whisk in flour paste. Cook and whisk constantly until thickened. Reduce heat and simmer 5 minutes. Taste and adjust seasonings. Strain if desired. Serve with turkey and stuffing. Garnish with fresh thyme.

Turkey parts are becoming more common at the supermarket. If you like turkey legs, you'll love this barbecued version.

BARBECUED TURKEY LEGS

6 servings
Preparation time: 10 minutes
Marinating time: Several hours or overnight
Cooking time: 1 hour

6 **turkey legs with thighs**
½ **cup bottled barbecue sauce**
¼ **cup each: soy sauce, dry white wine**
1 **tablespoon grated fresh ginger**
1 **teaspoon Worcestershire sauce**
1 **clove garlic, minced**
 Pinch sugar
 Hot pepper sauce to taste

1. Rinse turkey under cold water; pat dry. Cut drumsticks from thighs at joint. Mix remaining ingredients in large nonaluminum bowl. Add turkey. Refrigerate, covered, turning often, several hours or overnight.

2. Prepare grill. When coals are covered with gray ash, remove turkey pieces from marinade. Reserve marinade. Arrange turkey pieces on grill rack 6 inches from coals. Cover and grill, turning frequently, for 20 minutes. Then start basting with marinade. Continue grilling, covered, and basting until juices run clear, 40 to 60 more minutes.

A simple summertime method for turkey breast is to smoke it on a covered grill. Paul A. Camp and JeanMarie Brownson developed the following recipe for The Tribune's Sunday *magazine column.*

SMOKED TURKEY BREAST

8 servings
Preparation time: 15 minutes
Cooking time: 1 to 1½ hours

1 **boneless turkey breast, about 4 pounds**
 Hickory chips

1. Tie turkey breast into even, compact shape with kitchen string. Soak a handful or two of hickory chips in water to cover. Prepare grill. When coals are covered with gray ash, divide coals evenly to sides of the grill and position a drip pan in center.

2. Center the turkey breast over drip pan. Cover and grill until meat thermometer registers 165 degrees, about 1 to 1½ hours. Add more coals as needed. Add soaked and drained hickory chips to coals during the last 30 minutes of cooking. Let turkey stand on platter 10 minutes before carving. Temperature will rise about 10 degrees.

An elegant way to serve turkey is to stuff a turkey breast with sausage and vegetables. It is an ideal entree for smaller dinner parties and won't put a dent in the budget, either.

STUFFED TURKEY BREAST

10 servings
Preparation time: 30 minutes
Cooking time: 2 hours

½ **pound bulk pork sausage, crumbled**

3 **cups coarse dry bread crumbs**

2 **zucchini, shredded, patted dry**

1 **apple, cored, finely chopped**

1 **large red onion, chopped**

2 **eggs, beaten**

¼ **cup brandy**

3 **tablespoons each: chicken broth, minced fresh parsley**

1 **tablespoon finely grated lemon rind**

½ **teaspoon each: rubbed sage, salt**

¼ **teaspoon freshly ground pepper**

1 **whole boneless turkey breast, about 5 pounds**

Melted butter

1. Cook sausage in medium skillet over medium heat until brown; drain off fat. Put sausage into large bowl; stir in bread crumbs, zucchini, apple, onion, eggs, brandy, chicken broth, parsley, lemon rind, sage, salt and pepper. Taste and adjust seasonings.

2. Heat oven to 350 degrees. Put turkey breast, skin side down, onto work surface. Pound turkey breast slightly with meat mallet. Sprinkle with salt and pepper. Spread stuffing over breast, leaving 1½-inch border on all sides. Roll up jelly-roll fashion. Tie securely in several places with string to completely enclose stuffing.

3. Put onto oiled rack set in roasting pan. Brush with butter. Roast until thermometer registers 165 degrees, 1 hour and 40 minutes to 1 hour and 50 minutes. Let stand 10 minutes before slicing. Temperature will rise about 10 degrees. Serve hot. Or, cool completely and refrigerate overnight.

Gravy is the bane of many a cook, especially when the holiday season arrives. Who has time to worry about gravy when so many other dishes require our attention? Former Taste Editor Carol Rasmussen tackled the problem and came up with the following recipe for a simple but flavorful gravy.

HERBED TURKEY GRAVY

About 1 quart
Preparation time: 15 minutes
Cooking time: 30 minutes

½ **cup (1 stick) unsalted butter, softened**

½ **cup all-purpose flour**

1 **quart turkey stock (see recipe, page 134), or substitute strained, defatted pan juices and water**

½ **teaspoon salt, or to taste**

¼ **teaspoon each: freshly ground pepper, crumbled leaf thyme, rubbed sage, or to taste**

1. Mix softened butter and flour in small bowl until smooth. Heat stock to simmer in large saucepan over medium-low heat. While whisking vigorously, add butter mixture 1 tablespoon at a time. Continue whisking until thick and smooth. Add salt, pepper, thyme and sage. Taste and adjust seasonings.

NOTE: If the gravy develops tiny lumps, simply push it through a strainer. Reheat gently. If the gravy thickens a little too much while other things are being prepared, or as it cools at the table, add a little more stock, pan juices, water or dry white wine, then heat gently and serve.

Cornbread adds a sweetness to any stuffing. It can be mixed with white bread or stand on its own. Food Guide Editor Carol Haddix uses it mixed with apples and pecans for any type of poultry. The recipe can be doubled.

APPLE-CORNBREAD STUFFING

About 5 cups
Preparation time: 30 minutes
Cooking time: About 1 hour

1 box (8 ounces) cornbread mix
2 eggs
⅓ cup milk
1 cup pecan halves
3 tablespoons butter
2 medium tart apples, such as Granny Smith
2 ribs celery, diced
1 small onion, finely chopped
¼ cup each: chicken broth, melted butter
½ teaspoon salt, or more to taste
¼ teaspoon each: poultry seasoning, freshly ground pepper

1. Prepare cornbread according to package directions, using 1 egg and ⅓ cup milk. Bake according to directions. Set cornbread aside to dry out. (This may be done a day ahead.)

2. Heat oven to 400 degrees. Put pecans into shallow baking pan. Dot with 3 tablespoons butter. Bake, stirring often, until light brown and fragrant, about 10 minutes. Turn nuts out onto paper towels. Cool completely; chop coarsely.

3. Core and chop apples. Mix apples, celery, onion and pecans in large bowl. Crumble in all of the dry cornbread. Toss lightly. Beat remaining egg with broth, butter, salt, poultry seasoning and pepper. Gradually pour over stuffing mixture while tossing, just to moisten.

NOTE: Use to stuff poultry. Or, spoon into buttered baking dish and bake, covered, at 350 degrees, until heated through, about 30 minutes, then uncover; bake until top is crisp, about 30 more minutes.

■ *Food writer Lee Thompson offers this advice: "My rule of thumb is a minimum of half cup of stuffing per pound of bird. Since I like extra stuffing as well as leftovers, I make at least one cup of stuffing per pound of bird and bake the excess in a separate baking dish." Here's her stuffing recipe using fresh chestnuts.*

CHESTNUT AND SAUSAGE STUFFING

About 6 cups
Preparation time: 25 minutes
Cooking time: 15 minutes

6 tablespoons butter

½ pound bulk pork sausage, crumbled

1 cup each, chopped: onion, celery ribs

3 cups cooked, peeled chestnuts, quartered, about 1½ to 1¾ pounds (see note)

2 cups coarse bread crumbs, from day-old white bread

½ cup fresh parsley leaves, minced

6 tablespoons Madeira or medium-dry sherry

1 egg, lightly beaten

1 tablespoon fresh lemon juice

1 teaspoon each: dried marjoram, dried leaf thyme

   Pinch cayenne pepper

   Salt, freshly ground black pepper to taste

2 to 4 tablespoons whipping cream

1. Melt 1 tablespoon of the butter in large skillet. Add sausage; cook and stir over medium heat until no longer pink, about 5 minutes. Transfer sausage to large mixing bowl using a slotted spoon.

2. Wipe out skillet. Add 1 tablespoon butter to skillet; heat until melted. Add onion and celery; cook and stir until wilted. Add onion mixture and chestnuts to sausage.

3. Melt remaining 4 tablespoons butter in skillet. Add bread crumbs; cook and stir over low heat, stirring frequently, until pale gold and crisp. Stir crumbs, parsley, Madeira, egg, lemon juice, marjoram, thyme, cayenne pepper, salt and black pepper into chestnut mixture. Add cream as needed for moisture.

NOTE: To shell chestnuts, cut a gash around the center of the chestnut shell with a small sharp knife. Bake on a baking sheet in preheated 375-degree oven about 30 minutes. The time varies with size of nut. Remove nuts from oven and keep warm while you are shelling—once cold shell begins to stick.

Caterer Marion Mandeltort uses this hearty cornbread stuffing for her Midwestern-style roast turkey on page 355.

HERBED CORNBREAD STUFFING

About 6 cups
Preparation time: 15 minutes
Cooking time: 10 minutes

Skillet cornbread (see recipe, page 518)

1½ cups cubed toasted white bread

¾ cup minced fresh parsley

1 cup (2 sticks) unsalted butter or margarine

2 medium onions, coarsely chopped

1 each small, chopped: green pepper, red bell pepper

4 ribs celery, coarsely chopped

2 teaspoons each: salt, freshly ground pepper

1 tablespoon each: rubbed sage, dried rosemary, dried leaf thyme (or substitute 1½ tablespoons each of the fresh herbs)

1 cup turkey stock (see recipe, page 134)

2 large eggs, lightly beaten

1 box (10 ounces) frozen corn kernels, thawed

1 cup coarsely chopped walnuts

1. Make cornbread. Crumble in a large bowl and toss with bread cubes and parsley.

2. Melt butter in large skillet. Add onions, green pepper, red bell pepper, celery, salt, pepper, sage, rosemary and thyme. Cook and stir over medium heat until celery and onions are slightly wilted but not browned, about 10 minutes. Remove from heat.

3. Mix turkey stock and eggs in small bowl; pour over cornbread mixture. Add corn and walnuts; toss together lightly. Taste and adjust seasoning.

Tribune writer Barbara Sullivan contributed this recipe for her favorite stuffing. It is sinfully rich and wonderful.

Sausage-Sage Stuffing

About 18 cups
Preparation time: 45 minutes
Drying time: Overnight
Cooking time: 45 minutes

4 loaves (16 ounces each) sliced white bread

2 pounds each: sliced bacon, bulk pork sausage with sage

2 medium onions, diced

4 ribs celery, diced

½ cup (1 stick) unsalted butter

3½ to 4 cups rich chicken broth or turkey stock (see recipes, page 134), or substitute canned

2½ tablespoons poultry seasoning

¼ cup rubbed sage

1 teaspoon freshly ground pepper

½ teaspoon salt

1. Tear bread into chunks. Let stand, uncovered, at room temperature overnight to allow the bread to get slightly stale. (Or, put bread chunks in 200-degree oven, stirring often, until dry, 45 minutes to 1 hour.)

2. Dice bacon. Put bacon, sausage, onions and celery into large deep skillet. Cook, covered with a mesh splatter guard, stirring often, over medium heat until bacon and sausage are thoroughly browned, 30 to 45 minutes. (Drain off fat occasionally during cooking.) Cool mixture slightly; drain off all fat. Transfer mixture to very large bowl with slotted spoon. Do not wash skillet.

3. Melt butter in same skillet over medium heat; stir in 1 cup of the broth. Heat to simmer while scraping up browned bits from bottom of pan; cool slightly.

4. Add bread, poultry seasoning, sage, pepper and salt to bacon mixture. Pour some of the broth mixture over bread mixture; toss to mix. Gradually stir in remaining broth to desired consistency. (This stuffing normally is not crumbly; you won't see any individual white bread chunks.)

5. Taste and adjust seasonings. Stuffing can be made ahead and refrigerated in a covered bowl overnight.

Here's another stuffing recipe from food writer Lee Thompson, who mixes white bread and whole-wheat bread together for color and taste.

TWO-BREAD STUFFING

About 8 cups
Preparation time: 25 minutes
Cooking time: 20 minutes

1 cup (2 sticks) plus 5 tablespoons unsalted butter
2½ cups chopped celery
1½ cups chopped onions
4 cups cubed, firm-textured, day-old white bread
2 cups cubed, firm-textured, day-old whole-wheat bread
2 teaspoons ground sage
½ teaspoon each: dried leaf thyme, dried marjoram
1 teaspoon grated lemon rind
Salt, freshly ground pepper to taste

1. Melt 4 tablespoons butter in large skillet. Add celery and onions; cook over medium heat until wilted, about 5 minutes. Transfer to large bowl.

2. Melt 12 tablespoons butter in same skillet. Add white bread cubes; cook and stir over low heat until golden on all sides, about 10 minutes. Add to celery mixture.

3. Melt remaining 5 tablespoons butter in skillet. Add whole-wheat bread cubes; cook and stir over low heat until golden on all sides, about 5 minutes. Add to celery mixture. Add sage, thyme, marjoram, lemon rind, salt and pepper. Toss until well mixed.

For centuries, French home cooks have preserved duck and goose in fat. Expensive French restaurants would have you believe that the resulting meat, called confit, is very fancy indeed. Actually, it is a simple process, even for home cooks, and it results in poultry with an intensified flavor that can go into bean casseroles, warm salads or can be served hot just as it is.

CONFIT OF DUCK

2 to 4 servings
Preparation time: 25 minutes
Marinating time: Overnight
Cooking time: 2½ hours
Aging time: 1 week

2 **tablespoons coarse (kosher) salt**
1 **teaspoon each: freshly ground pepper, dried leaf thyme**
3 **bay leaves, crumbled**
4 **large duck legs with thighs attached, or whole duck, quartered**
6 **cups (about) rendered duck fat, chicken fat or melted lard (see note)**

1. Mix salt, pepper, thyme and bay leaves in small bowl. Generously rub mixture on each duck leg. Put legs into nonaluminum bowl. Refrigerate, covered, 12 hours or overnight.

2. Heat oven to 300 degrees. Wipe spice mixture off each leg. Heat a few tablespoons of the fat in large dutch oven. Add legs in single layer. Cook over medium heat, turning, until nicely browned on all sides. Remove from heat.

3. Add enough fat to cover duck by 1 inch. Cover pot and bake until duck is fork-tender, 1½ to 2 hours.

4. Ladle some of the warm fat into a ceramic terrine. Refrigerate until fat is solidified. Arrange duck legs on top of fat. Pour in remaining warm fat to cover legs by at least 1 inch. Cover terrine.

5. Store confit in cool place, or refrigerator, at least 1 week before serving. (Keeps up to 4 weeks.)

6. To serve, let terrine sit at room temperature until fat softens. Carefully remove duck from fat. Heat a few tablespoons of the fat in large skillet. Add duck; cook until heated through and skin is very crisp, about 5 minutes. Drain on paper towel. Serve hot.

NOTE: Rendered duck or chicken fat can be made from the skin and pieces of fat found on ducks and chicken. To render, dice skin and fat. Put into heavy-bottomed saucepan. Cook, stirring often, over low heat, until melted. Strain through fine sieve. After making confit, the fat can be strained, kept frozen for several weeks and reused for additional batches of confit.

The chefs at Les Plumes restaurant in Chicago prepare an appetizer salad that's really large enough for an entree. However you serve it, the duck is superb with its dressing of sherry wine vinegar and hazelnut oil.

DUCK BREAST SALAD WITH HAZELNUT DRESSING

4 servings
Preparation time: 45 minutes
Cooking time: 10 minutes

SALAD CUPS
4 large or 8 medium radicchio leaves

1 cup each, torn: Boston lettuce, radicchio, curly endive

1 cup julienned mushrooms

1 cup sliced Belgian endive

¼ pound very thin green beans, cooked, drained, chilled

4 tablespoons hazelnut oil

2 tablespoons sherry wine vinegar

Salt, freshly ground pepper to taste

1 cup toasted blanched hazelnuts

DUCK
2 whole duck breasts, boned, split

1 cup rich chicken broth (see recipe, page 134), or duck stock

1. For salad cups, rinse and refrigerate the large radicchio leaves. Mix torn lettuce, radicchio, curly endive, mushrooms, Belgian endive and green beans in large bowl. Add 3 tablespoons of the hazelnut oil, 1 tablespoon of the vinegar, salt and pepper. Add hazelnuts. Toss to mix.

2. Heat oven to 550 degrees. Rinse duck under cold water; pat dry. Heat a large ovenproof nonstick or well-seasoned skillet over medium heat until hot. Add duck, skin side down. Cook until golden brown, about 5 minutes. Drain off some of the fat from skillet. Roast in oven until medium-rare, about 5 more minutes. Remove duck to plate; keep warm.

3. Pour off all fat from skillet. Add remaining 1 tablespoon vinegar. Cook and stir while scraping up browned bits from bottom of pan. Add chicken broth; cook and stir until stock is reduced by half. Remove from heat, stir in remaining 1 tablespoon hazelnut oil.

4. Strain sauce through fine sieve. Cut duck breast lengthwise into thin slices. Pour some of the sauce onto serving plate. Arrange duck slices on plate. Put 1 large radicchio leaf or 2 smaller leaves onto edge of plate forming a cup. Fill cup with lettuce–green bean mixture. Serve immediately.

Pairing duck with a sweet sauce is an age-old tradition. The sweetness of the sauce often cuts the richness of the meat. Here is an Oriental twist on roast duck that makes use of ginger jam for a sweet, yet spicy flavor.

GINGER GLAZED DUCK

6 servings
Preparation time: 20 minutes
Cooking time: 65 minutes

3 **small fresh ducks, about 3 pounds each**
¾ **cup ginger jam (see note)**
1½ **tablespoons light soy sauce**
¾ **teaspoon Oriental sesame oil**
   Chopped fresh cilantro (coriander), for garnish

1. Heat oven to 350 degrees. Rinse ducks under cold water; pat dry. Cut ducks lengthwise in half through breastbone; spread flat. Cut back of duck in half and remove back bone from each half. Put skin side up onto oiled rack set over drip pan. Roast until golden, about 50 minutes. Pour off pan drippings as they accumulate.

2. Meanwhile, for glaze, mix jam, soy sauce and sesame oil in small bowl. After ducks have cooked 50 minutes, brush with glaze. Then cook, brushing with glaze every 5 minutes, until thigh juices run clear and skin is dark brown and glazed, about 15 more minutes. Put onto serving plates. Sprinkle with chopped cilantro.

NOTE: Ginger jam is available at large supermarkets and specialty food stores. Pineapple jam mixed with 2 tablespoons minced fresh ginger could be substituted.

Another Oriental duck preparation follows, but this one uses hoisin sauce, the Chinese version of barbecue sauce. It's from Chicago caterer Joan Saltzman, who likes to serve it in sandwich form on croissants.

HOISIN MARINATED DUCK BREAST

4 servings
Preparation time: 20 minutes
Marinating time: 8 hours or overnight
Cooking time: 10 to 12 minutes

½ **cup hoisin sauce**
3 **tablespoons honey**
1 **tablespoon each:**
   white vinegar,
   Worcestershire sauce
1 **small clove garlic,**
   finely chopped
2 **whole duck breasts,**
   boned, skinned, split

1. Mix hoisin sauce, honey, vinegar, Worcestershire sauce and garlic in large bowl. Rinse duck under cold water; pat dry. Add duck breasts to hoisin mixture; turn to coat on all sides. Refrigerate, covered, turning occasionally, 8 hours or overnight.

2. Preheat broiler. Remove duck from marinade; put onto oiled broiler rack set over drip pan. Broil, 6 inches from heat source, basting occasionally with marinade, until tender and slightly pink inside, 5 to 6 minutes per side. Serve immediately.

VARIATION: Mix ¼ cup honey and Dijon mustard to taste in small bowl. Spread honey mixture over 4 croissants that have been split. Cut duck breast into thin slices. Pile onto croissant. Serve immediately.

■ *Chef Carolyn Buster of The Cottage restaurant in Calumet City, Illinois, created this roast duck when pink peppercorns first came into the Chicago market. She makes her own raspberry vinegar to use in the dish, but any high-quality bottled raspberry vinegar can be used. This is definitely a company dish.*

ROAST DUCK WITH RASPBERRY PINK PEPPERCORN SAUCE

4 servings
Preparation time: 45 minutes
Cooking time: 3 hours
Cooling time: 1 to 1½ hours

2 **whole ducks, about 4½ pounds each**

2 **ribs celery, chopped**

1 **small Spanish onion, chopped**

1 **carrot, chopped**

2 **cloves garlic, crushed**

6 **to 8 sprigs fresh parsley**

3 **to 4 bay leaves**

10 **to 12 black peppercorns**

Chef's salt (see note)

Vegetable oil

Raspberry pink peppercorn sauce (recipe follows)

1. Heat oven to 350 degrees. Rinse ducks under cold water; pat dry. Put celery, onion, carrot, garlic, parsley, bay leaves and peppercorns into large roasting pan. Put ducks onto vegetables breast side down. Sprinkle lightly with chef's salt.

2. Pour in enough water to come ½-inch up sides of pan. Cover tightly with lid or aluminum foil. Bake for 2½ hours.

3. Carefully remove ducks from liquid. Place on baking sheet; cool completely, breast side up, 1 to 1½ hours. (Recipe may be prepared to this point up to 2 days in advance and refrigerate.)

4. Split ducks in half lengthwise down breast. Remove back bone. Place duck halves, cut side down, on baking tray.

5. About 30 minutes before serving, brush ducks lightly with oil. Heat oven to 450 degrees. Roast ducks until heated through and skin is crisp and golden, 20 to 30 minutes.

6. Meanwhile, make raspberry pink peppercorn sauce. Serve warm with duck.

NOTE: For chef's salt, mix ¼ cup salt, 2½ teaspoons sweet paprika, ¼ teaspoon each: freshly ground white pepper, black pepper and ⅛ teaspoon garlic powder in jar.

Raspberry Pink Peppercorn Sauce | About 2 cups

2 tablespoons sugar

2¼ cups raspberry puree
  (made from fresh or
  frozen raspberries
  pushed through sieve)

3 tablespoons each:
  melted bacon fat,
  pink peppercorns,
  raspberry vinegar

1 bay leaf

¼ teaspoon salt

⅛ teaspoon garlic
  powder

  Pinch freshly ground
  white pepper

1½ tablespoons cornstarch

2 tablespoons crispy-
  fried bacon pieces,
  optional

1. Cook and stir sugar, in medium saucepan over low heat until light brown. Set aside ¼ cup of the raspberry puree. Stir remaining puree, bacon fat, pink peppercorns, vinegar, bay leaf, salt, garlic powder and white pepper into sugar. Cook and stir over low heat until thickened and flavors have blended, 20 to 30 minutes.

2. Dissolve cornstarch in ¼ cup raspberry puree. Stir into sauce. Cook and stir over low heat until sauce thickens, about 3 minutes. Remove from heat; stir in bacon pieces.

Goose is not a common sight on American tables. Too bad. The meat is dark and rich, flavored by its own fat. A fruit stuffing is a perfect, tangy counterpoint in the following recipe.

Roast Goose with Apple Stuffing

6 servings
Preparation time: 30 minutes
Cooking time: 3¼ hours

1 young goose,
  about 10 pounds

½ lemon

  Salt, freshly ground
  pepper to taste

3 slices bacon

1 large onion, diced

2 ribs celery, diced

2 large apples, chopped

1 cup dried prunes,
  soaked, pitted,
  chopped

1½ cups toasted bread
  cubes

1. Rinse goose under cold water; pat dry. Rub inside and out with lemon; sprinkle with salt and pepper.

2. Heat oven to 325 degrees. Cook bacon in large skillet over medium heat until crisp; crumble. Stir onion and celery into bacon fat. Cook until onion is soft. Stir in apples, prunes and bread cubes. Season to taste with salt and pepper.

3. Stuff into breast cavity of goose; truss opening with kitchen string. Tuck wings underneath and tie legs together. Roast until juices run clear and thermometer registers 180 degrees, about 3 hours. Let stand 10 minutes. Remove stuffing to warm serving bowl.

■ *Chef Leslee Reis created a dinner to remember when Julia Child dined at her Cafe Provençal restaurant in Evanston, Illinois. Among the many courses were lobster timbales and this recipe for squab. It's teamed with fresh wild mushrooms and a red wine and rosemary sauce.*

GRILLED SQUAB WITH WILD MUSHROOM SAUCE

6 servings
Preparation time: 45 minutes
Cooking time: 4 hours

6 **farm-raised squabs, about 12 ounces each**
1 **to 2 carrots, cut into 1-inch pieces**
1 **small onion, chunked**
1 **rib celery, cut into 1-inch pieces**
  Vegetable oil
2 **to 3 cups veal stock or rich chicken broth (see recipes, pages 133–34)**
¼ **teaspoon each: dried thyme, dried rosemary (or 1 teaspoon each fresh)**
1 **bay leaf**
12 **ounces fresh mixed wild mushrooms (such as chanterelle, cepe, shiitake, oyster)**
2½ **tablespoons minced shallots**
4 **tablespoons butter, at room temperature**
½ **cup dry red wine, preferably Burgundy**
  Fresh rosemary sprigs
  Salt, freshly ground pepper to taste
  Fresh thyme springs (or dried leaves)

1. Heat oven to 400 degrees. Bone squabs, leaving leg and wig bones intact. (See note.) Refrigerate squabs. Put bones, carrots, onion and celery into roasting pan with 1 to 2 tablespoons oil. Roast until nicely browned, about 30 minutes.

2. Transfer mixture to large heavy saucepan. Add veal stock to cover bones. Stir in ¼ teaspoon thyme, rosemary and bay leaf. Heat to boil; skim off surface scum. Simmer gently 3 hours. (The stock should be skimmed well during simmering to achieve a clear sauce.) Strain well through fine sieve.

3. Meanwhile, separate mushroom caps from stems. Sauté caps with half of the shallots and 1 tablespoon of the butter in small skillet until mushrooms exude their juices and caps are just tender, about 5 minutes. Set aside.

4. Put stems, remaining shallots and 1 tablespoon of the butter into saucepan. Simmer over medium heat 4 minutes. Increase heat; add wine. Boil until liquid reduces by about two-thirds.

5. Stir in strained stock and strained juices from mushroom caps. Simmer until sauce-like consistency is achieved, 45 minutes to 1 hour. Near the end of the simmering, add a couple of sprigs of fresh rosemary. Add salt and pepper to taste. Just before serving, whisk remaining 2 tablespoons butter into sauce. Keep warm, but do not boil or sauce will curdle.

6. Heat oven to 400 degrees. Brush squabs with oil; sprinkle with salt and pepper. Tuck a branch of thyme (or sprinkle lightly with dried thyme) in each cavity. Prepare charcoal grill. When coals are covered with gray ash, arrange squabs on grill rack 6 inches from coals. Grill, turning until golden, about 5 minutes. (Or, broil 6 inches from heat source, turning, until golden, about 5 minutes.) Finish cooking at 400 degrees or until tender and juices run clear, about 10 minutes.

7. Put onto warmed serving plates. Pour sauce around squab. Garnish with sautéed mushroom caps.

NOTE: Cornish hens can be substituted for the squab. Some butchers will bone the birds for you, but be sure to keep the bones for making the sauce. Boned birds are a more elegant presentation and easier to eat. However, if you do not wish to bone the birds, the cooking time at 400 degrees will increase slightly.

Farm-raised pheasant is milder in flavor than wild birds and is often as tender as chicken. Chef Peter McGinley of Les Celebrities restaurant in Chicago's Nikko Hotel demonstrated just how tender it could be in the following recipe that appeared in an article on "Tame Game." The Tribune test kitchen has adapted the recipe for the home cook.

PHEASANT BREAST WITH CONFIT

2 servings
Preparation time: 1 hour
Marinating time: Overnight
Cooking time: 1 hour

1 **pheasant, about 3 pounds**
   Garlic salt
   Crushed black peppercorns
   Dried rosemary
2 **bay leaves**
   Peanut oil

RED ZINFANDEL SAUCE

2 **cups red zinfandel wine**
1 **cup minced mushrooms**
1½ **tablespoons minced shallots**
1 **bay leaf**
1 **cup demi-glace (see note)**
   Salt, white pepper to taste

TO SERVE

   Cranberry conserve (see recipe, page 646)
   Wild rice cakes (see recipe, page 174)

1. Rinse pheasant under cold water; pat dry. Using a sharp knife, remove legs from pheasant without separating thigh and drumstick. Remove breast halves from carcass. Remove skin from breast; refrigerate breast until ready to use. (Wings and carcass can be saved for use in soups and stocks.)

2. Rub legs with garlic salt, crushed peppercorns, rosemary and 1 bay leaf. Cover and let marinate in refrigerator overnight.

3. Heat oven to 300 degrees. Heat 2 inches of peanut oil in large saucepan over medium heat to 300 degrees. Place legs in oil. Cover with foil. Bake until meat is very soft, about 1½ hours. Remove from oven; cool in oil on wire rack.

4. Meanwhile, for sauce, put wine, mushrooms, shallots and 1 bay leaf into medium-size nonaluminum saucepan. Boil gently until reduced by two-thirds. Add demi-glace. Boil until reduced again by one-fourth or until sauce is thick enough to coat a spoon. Season with salt and white pepper to taste.

5. Increase oven temperature to 350 degrees. Melt butter in medium skillet over medium-high heat. Add breast halves. Cook, turning once, until golden, about 4 minutes. Then bake until medium-rare, 3 to 5 more minutes.

6. Remove legs from oil. Heat 2 tablespoons of the oil in large skillet over medium-high heat until hot. Add legs; cook until skin is crisp, about 3 minutes.

7. Thinly slice breast meat and fan out on serving plate. Put legs on plate. Drizzle sauce around meat. Garnish with cranberry relish and wild rice cakes.

NOTE: If you don't have a demi-glace for the sauce, dissolve 2 teaspoons arrowroot or 1 tablespoon cornstarch in 1 cup homemade beef stock and heat until thickened. Use in place of demi-glace.

■ *Guinea hen, though not a new kind of fowl, is new to many Americans. A relative of the pheasant, it is mostly farm-raised today and weighs 2 to 3 pounds. This recipe is one fit for company.*

GUINEA HEN WITH ORANGE AND POMEGRANATE

4 servings
Preparation time: 45 minutes
Cooking time: 5 hours

2 guinea hens, 2 to 2½ pounds each
2 carrots, sliced
1 onion, sliced
1 tomato, halved
3 quarts water
1 cup dry red wine
1 clove garlic, crushed
Bouquet garni (see note)
4 tablespoons orange liqueur
2 tablespoons butter
1 cup pomegranate juice (if fresh, from 3 medium pomegranates, blended and strained) or cranberry juice
½ cup whipping cream
¼ teaspoon grated orange rind
Salt, freshly ground pepper to taste
Julienned orange rind, for garnish

1. Heat oven to 450 degrees. Rinse guinea hens under cold water; pat dry. Cut along breast bones and remove the two breast halves from the bone, leaving skin attached. Remove legs without separating thigh and drumstick. Cover breasts and legs and refrigerate.

2. Chop carcasses and necks. Put into shallow roasting pan with carrots, onion and tomato. Roast in upper third of oven, turning once or twice, until well browned, 20 to 30 minutes.

3. Put bone mixture into stockpot; add 3 quarts cold water. Pour wine into roasting pan. Heat to boil and scrape up browned bits from bottom of pan; add to stockpot with garlic and bouquet garni. Simmer, skimming off surface scum, 4 hours. Strain through cheesecloth. There will be about 1 quart. (Recipe can be made ahead to this point.)

4. Put stock into saucepan. Add 3 tablespoons of the orange liqueur. Boil gently until reduced to 1 cup.

5. Heat oven to 250 degrees. Melt 1 tablespoon of the butter in large heavy skillet over medium-high heat. Add legs, skin side down; sauté until golden, 3 to 4 minutes. Turn and cook 3 to 4 minutes longer. Transfer to platter. Put in oven.

6. Add remaining butter to skillet. Add breasts, skin side down. Sauté until golden, 2 minutes. Turn and cook, until slightly pink inside, about 2 more minutes. Add to platter; cover and keep warm.

7. To the skillet, add the 1 cup reduced stock and pomegranate juice; boil until reduced to 1 cup. Add cream; boil until reduced to 1 cup. Remove from heat; stir in ¼ teaspoon orange rind, remaining 1 tablespoon orange liqueur, salt and pepper.

8. Cut breast halves into thin slices and fan onto dinner plates. Add a leg to each plate and ¼ cup sauce per person. Garnish with julienned orange rind.

NOTE: For bouquet garni, tie 2 sprigs parsley, 2 bay leaves, ½ teaspoon thyme and 5 black peppercorns together in double thickness cheesecloth.

Elegant grilled quail is served on a bed of shaped polenta in this recipe from chef Tony Mantuano of Spiaggia restaurant in Chicago.

Chicken broth or stock, instead of water, helps polenta keep its shape.

GRILLED QUAIL AND POLENTA

4 servings
Preparation time: 10 minutes
Marinating time: 1 to 3 days
Cooking time: 10 to 12 minutes

4 quail
4 garlic cloves, crushed
1 cup loosely packed flat-leaf Italian parsley, chopped
¼ cup olive oil
1 tablespoon juniper berries, crushed
  Grilled polenta (recipe follows)
  Grilled Italian sausage

1. Rinse quail under cold water; pat dry. Put garlic, parsley, oil and juniper berries into shallow glass dish. Add quail; turn to coat well with marinade. Refrigerate, covered, turning quail occasionally for at least 24 hours or up to 3 days.

2. Bring quail to room temperature. Remove quail from marinade, scraping off excess.

3. Prepare charcoal grill. When coals are covered with gray ash, grill quail, 6 inches from coals, turning often, until breast meat is still slightly pink, 8 to 12 minutes. Serve with grilled polenta and Italian sausage.

GRILLED POLENTA

4 servings
Preparation time: 10 minutes
Cooking time: 20 minutes
Chilling time: 3 to 4 hours

2½ cups chicken stock or broth
1 cup fine yellow cornmeal, such as stone-ground
  Salt, freshly ground white pepper to taste
  Vegetable oil

1. Heat chicken broth in large saucepan to simmer. Slowly whisk in cornmeal, salt and pepper. Reduce heat. Simmer, stirring constantly, until mixture is very thick and smooth, about 20 minutes.

2. While mixture is still warm, pour it into ¾-inch layer on buttered baking sheet. Smooth with rubber spatula. Cool in refrigerator until firm, 3 to 4 hours.

3. Prepare charcoal grill. Use cookie cutter to cut polenta into desired shapes. Brush grill rack with oil. Dip one side of polenta in oil and put that side down onto grill. Grill, turning once, until heated through and slightly crisp on both sides, about 3 minutes.

VEGETABLES

A stroll through the produce department of a typical urban supermarket tells a lot about what's going on in America's kitchens today. Amid the pyramids of faithful white potatoes, carrots and corn-on-the-cob are newcomers such as crisp bok choy, pale Belgian endive, purple radicchio and white eggplant.

Seasonal onions are flown in from Maui, Georgia or Washington. Fresh snow peas are available year-round. Mushrooms have exotic shapes and answer to names such as oyster, chanterelle, morel or shiitake. Even potatoes aren't just potatoes when they come in shades of purple or creamy yellow.

Supermarkets bloom with a startling variety of vegetables because this is what Americans want to eat. Armed with statistics telling them they will live a longer and happier life by eating well, consumers are trying to cut back on saturated fats and increase consumption of complex carbohydrates, including fruits and vegetables.

As an example of a healthful food, a half cup of cooked broccoli provides 89 milligrams of calcium, more than 1,000 International Units of vitamin A, 49 milligrams of vitamin C, while only .22 grams of fat and a mere 23 calories. One potato with the skin on provides healthy doses of phosphorus and potassium. And spinach is indeed a powerful ally when you consider that a half cup yields more than 7,000 units of vitamin A.

Thumbing through the chapter, you will find some simple recipes such as fresh asparagus drizzled with butter, and some unusual twists such as grilled fresh beets, squash stuffed with prunes and morel-topped quesadillas.

The cooking techniques are almost as varied as the vegetables. Using recipes from chefs, readers and our own staff members, we show you how to boil, steam, fry, bake, grill, simmer, blanch, braise, sauté, stuff and otherwise delight yourself and your guests with fresh vegetables.

HOW TO BUY FRESH VEGETABLES

When selecting fresh vegetables, look for ones that you would pick to photograph: unblemished, bright colored and firm. Carrots, leeks and other vegetables with leaves should have good colored leaves with no signs of wilting. Check for molds or other signs of poor handling.

HOW TO STORE FRESH VEGETABLES

Most vegetables are stored unwashed and loosely wrapped in the refrigerator. This avoids mold that comes with moisture. Exceptions include white potatoes, sweet potatoes, winter squash, pumpkins, rutabagas, garlic and onions which are best stored in a dark, well-ventilated area. Tomatoes should be held at room temperature until fully ripened, then, if necessary, refrigerated for up to three days.

For best flavor and nutrition, eat fresh vegetables as soon as possible, usually within three days of purchase. New strains of corn-on-the-cob help this vegetable last at least five days in the refrigerator and still taste sweet, but even the new corn will get starchy and dull if held too long.

VEGETABLES

Cooked artichokes with
  basic hollandaise sauce

Moroccan-style artichokes

Artichokes with creamy
  vegetables

Fresh asparagus with butter
  and parsley

Crispy asparagus with tomato
  ginger chutney

Asparagus and prosciutto

Grilled beets

Belgian endive braised with
  chives

Broccoli with lemon

Colorful broccoli stir-fry

Smoky brussels sprouts

Sweet and sour red cabbage

Baked sauerkraut with kirsch

Carrot tzimmes

Steamed cauliflower with
  red pepper sauce

Boiled corn with lemon butter

Bacon-fried corn

Succotash

Jalapeño pepper corn pudding

Baked eggplant with yogurt sauce

Eggplant Parmesan

Baked whole garlic

Green beans with dill

Green beans with garlic almonds

Sautéed mushrooms and
  pearl onions

Deep-fried mushrooms

Morel quesadillas

Onion compote

Crispy light onion rings

Green peas with mint

Potatoes Anna

Potato gratin with cepes

Cheese and bacon-topped
  baked potatoes

Buttered new potatoes and
  peas with watercress

Sautéed potatoes with herbs

Marbled mashed potatoes

Herbed sweet potatoes

Mashed rutabaga with pepper

Spinach with sesame seeds

Spinach with yogurt

Acorn squash with fruit stuffing

Steamed butternut squash with
  ginger

Dixie chayote squash

Stuffed golden squash

Yellow squash casserole

Spaghetti squash with white
  clam sauce

Feta and spinach stuffed tomatoes

Zucchini or green beans in
  fresh tarragon marinade

VEGETABLE COMBINATIONS

Oven-baked ratatouille

Grilled vegetables with
  rosemary vinaigrette

Baked winter vegetables

Celery root and fennel au gratin

Vegetable stir-fry with
  tofu and nuts

Vegetable chili with red beans

■ *At first glance, a fresh artichoke appears to be a cooking challenge. But you can cook artichokes like an expert in any of the three following ways: boiled, steamed or microwaved.*

COOKED ARTICHOKES WITH BASIC HOLLANDAISE SAUCE

4 servings
Preparation time: 20 minutes
Cooking time: 25 to 40 minutes

**4 medium artichokes
Vegetable oil
Lemon juice
Salt
Basic hollandaise
   sauce (recipe
   follows), or melted
   butter**

1. Trim artichoke stems off at base so artichokes sit level. Pull off small lower leaves. Trim off tips of outer leaves. Cut off top quarter of each artichoke.

2. COOKING METHODS

To boil: Place prepared artichokes in saucepan just large enough to hold them upright. Add enough water to fill the pan 3 inches in depth. Add 1 tablespoon each olive oil and lemon juice and a sprinkle of salt to the water. Cover pan; heat to boil. Boil gently until fork-tender and a leaf near center pulls out easily, 25 to 40 minutes. Stand artichokes upside down to drain.

To steam: Place prepared artichokes on rack over about 1½ inches boiling water. Drizzle a little oil, lemon juice and salt over top of each artichoke. Cover and steam until fork-tender and a leaf near center pulls out easily, 25 to 40 minutes.

To microwave: Invert one prepared artichoke in deep, 1-quart microwave-proof cup or bowl; add 3 tablespoons water, 1 teaspoon oil, 1 teaspoon lemon juice and salt to taste. Cover with heavy-duty plastic wrap, then pierce the wrap with a fork to allow steam to escape. Microwave on high (100 percent power) until a leaf near center pulls out easily, 6 to 8 minutes. Let stand 5 minutes.

3. Serve artichokes with hollandaise sauce or melted butter for dipping the base of each leaf.

Basic Hollandaise Sauce | About 1 cup

4 large egg yolks
½ cup (1 stick) unsalted
 butter, softened, cut
 into thirds
2 to 3 teaspoons fresh
 lemon juice
 Salt, freshly ground
 white pepper to taste

1. Put egg yolks and one-third of the butter in top of double boiler. Cook over simmering water until butter melts, stirring rapidly. (Water in bottom of double boiler should simmer, but not touch the top pan.)

2. Add the second third of the butter and continue stirring vigorously. At this stage, the sauce should be somewhat runny. As butter melts and mixture thickens, add remaining butter, stirring constantly. After all the butter is added and melted, the consistency should be thick and fluffy. Remove from double boiler. Using a wooden spoon, stir rapidly for about 2 minutes.

3. Season with lemon juice, salt and pepper. Return to double boiler and stir constantly until heated through, about 2 minutes. Do not let sauce boil at any time. If sauce curdles, immediately stir in 1 to 2 tablespoons boiling water and mix well. If necessary, keep warm in an insulated bottle.

■ *Artichokes are delicious served with lemon butter or a homemade mayonnaise, but when given a Moroccan touch, they reach new flavor heights.*

MOROCCAN-STYLE ARTICHOKES

6 servings
Preparation time: 25 minutes
Cooking time: 30 minutes

6 small artichokes
1 tablespoon each: olive oil, lemon juice

DIPPING SAUCE

⅔ cup olive oil
¼ cup red wine vinegar
¼ cup minced fresh parsley
1 tablespoon each: lemon juice, sweet paprika
2 teaspoons each: ground cumin, minced fresh cilantro (coriander)
1 clove garlic, minced
Salt, freshly ground pepper to taste

1. Trim artichoke stems off at base so artichokes sit level. Pull off small, lower leaves. Trim off tips of outer leaves. Cut off top quarter of each artichoke.

2. Place prepared artichokes in a pan just large enough to hold them upright. Add enough water to fill the pan 3 inches in depth. Add 1 tablespoon each olive oil and lemon juice. Cover pan; heat to boil. Boil gently until fork-tender and a leaf near center pulls out easily, about 30 minutes. Drain well.

3. Arrange in serving dishes. Combine all sauce ingredients in small bowl. Pour over artichokes. Serve warm or at room temperature.

Elegant artichoke bottoms are filled with broccoli, cauliflower and carrots in a cream sauce in this indulgent side dish. Serve it alongside roast beef or broiled salmon.

ARTICHOKES WITH CREAMY VEGETABLES

6 servings
Preparation time: 25 minutes
Cooking time: 40 minutes

2 cans (14 ounces each) artichoke bottoms, drained

2 tablespoons butter

½ cup finely chopped walnuts

1 bunch broccoli, about ¾ pound

1 small head cauliflower, about 1 pound

1 large carrot, peeled, sliced

1 cup whipping cream

2 teaspoons grated lemon rind

¼ teaspoon each: salt, freshly ground pepper

⅛ teaspoon ground nutmeg

1. Butter 13 by 9-inch baking dish. Arrange artichoke bottoms in dish, trimming bottoms if necessary so they sit flat.

2. Heat 1 tablespoon of the butter in small skillet; add nuts. Cook over low heat just until lightly browned, 1 to 2 minutes. (You can wrap nuts in foil and store them up to 2 days.)

3. Remove stems and core from broccoli and cauliflower. Cut into small flowerets. Heat 2 quarts water to boil in large saucepan. Add broccoli and cauliflower; cook until crisp-tender, about 3 minutes. Remove with slotted spoon; rinse under cold water to stop the cooking. Add carrot; cook until crisp-tender, about 5 minutes. Remove with slotted spoon; rinse under cold water to stop the cooking. Refrigerate, covered, up to 1 day.

4. Heat oven to 350 degrees. Put cream into heavy-bottomed large saucepan. Boil gently until reduced to ½ cup. Stir in remaining 1 tablespoon butter, lemon rind, salt, pepper and nutmeg. Add vegetables, except artichokes. Toss to mix.

5. Pile vegetable mixture on artichoke bottoms. Sprinkle tops with nut mixture. Bake until heated through, about 20 minutes. Serve.

Simplicity at its best: butter-drizzled fresh asparagus, topped with a sieved egg and parsley.

FRESH ASPARAGUS WITH BUTTER AND PARSLEY

8 servings
Preparation time: 5 minutes
Cooking time: 10 minutes

3 **pounds fresh asparagus**
3 **tablespoons melted butter (or margarine)**
Salt, freshly ground pepper to taste
1 **hard-cooked egg, sieved**
1 **tablespoon chopped fresh parsley**

1. Trim off tough ends of asparagus. If desired, lightly peel asparagus stalks with a vegetable peeler.

2. Put asparagus in large pot, skillet or baking pan so they lay flat. Cover with boiling water. Bring water back to a boil; cook until crisp-tender, 2 to 4 minutes. Drain.

3. Drizzle with melted butter. Season with salt and pepper. Garnish with sieved egg and parsley.

Stuart Parsons, chef at Eurasia restaurant in Chicago, steams delicate asparagus separately until crisp, then tops them with a thick, aromatic chutney in an example of his modern East-meets-West cuisine.

CRISPY ASPARAGUS WITH TOMATO GINGER CHUTNEY

4 servings
Preparation time: 25 minutes
Cooking time: 10 minutes

2 **tablespoons each: sugar, water**
1 **small onion, finely chopped**
1 **teaspoon chopped jalapeño pepper**
½ **teaspoon finely chopped garlic**
2 **tablespoons wine vinegar**
1 **cup peeled, seeded, chopped tomatoes**
1 **tablespoon minced garlic**
1 **teaspoon chopped, fresh cilantro (coriander)**
⅛ **teaspoon each: ground cardamom, turmeric, ground cinnamon**
1 **pound fresh asparagus, peeled, tough ends removed**

1. For chutney, heat sugar and water in saucepan. Cook and stir until it becomes amber. Add onion, jalapeño and garlic; cook and stir 1 minute. Add vinegar; cook over low heat 2 minutes. Add tomato; cook 5 minutes. Stir in remaining ingredients except asparagus. Simmer for a few minutes and remove from heat.

2. Steam asparagus over boiling water until crisp-tender, 2 to 4 minutes. Heat chutney, pour over asparagus and serve.

A little prosciutto or smoked ham plus Parmesan cheese add a pleasantly salty touch to fresh asparagus. Prepare this dish last before dinner, and serve immediately.

ASPARAGUS AND PROSCIUTTO

4 servings
Preparation time: 10 minutes
Cooking time: 10 minutes

1 **pound fresh asparagus, peeled, tough ends removed**
¼ **cup each: chopped prosciutto or smoked ham, freshly grated Parmesan cheese**
2 **tablespoons each: melted butter, toasted pine nuts or slivered almonds**
1 **tablespoon fresh lemon juice**
1 **teaspoon dried chervil or minced fresh parsley**
Freshly ground pepper to taste

1. Cook asparagus in 3 quarts boiling, salted water until crisp-tender, 2 to 4 minutes. Drain; rinse under cold water. Drain.

2. Put asparagus on broiler-proof serving plate. Mix remaining ingredients; sprinkle over asparagus. Broil 4 inches from heat source, until cheese melts, about 2 minutes. Serve immediately.

Now here is an unusual way to present fresh beets: wrapped in foil with onion, basil and butter, then grilled over hot coals.

GRILLED BEETS

3 servings
Preparation time: 5 minutes
Grilling time: 30 minutes

3 **large beets, peeled if desired**
1 **yellow onion, cut into thirds**
6 **basil sprigs**
3 **tablespoons butter (or margarine)**

1. Prepare grill. Cut beets crosswise in half. Put 2 halves onto large square of heavy duty aluminum foil. Sandwich beet halves with onion slice, 2 basil sprigs and 1 tablespoon butter. Wrap well. Repeat.

2. When coals are covered with gray ash, grill beets 6 inches from hot coals, until very tender (test with fork), 20 to 30 minutes.

Choose crisp, firm, snowy white Belgian endive when selecting it at the produce market. This bitter vegetable can be eaten raw in salad but is equally delicious cooked— particularly braised.

When braising Belgian endive, the trick is to add just the right combinations of other fresh vegetables to balance the bitterness of the endive and give the dish full, rounded flavor. Try this version with grilled pork or veal chops.

BELGIAN ENDIVE BRAISED WITH CHIVES

2 to 3 servings
Preparation time: 15 minutes
Cooking time: 15 minutes

2 tablespoons unsalted butter
1 tablespoon oil
3 large heads Belgian endive
1 small yellow bell pepper, diced
½ cup chicken broth
1 small ripe tomato, cut into wedges
3 slices red onion, rings separated
1 tablespoon minced chives
Salt, freshly ground pepper to taste
¼ cup whipping cream
Minced chives for garnish

1. Heat butter and oil in large heavy-bottomed skillet. Add endive. Cook, turning, until lightly browned, about 5 minutes.

2. Add yellow pepper, chicken broth, tomato, onion and 1 tablespoon minced chives. Heat to simmer. Simmer, covered, over low heat until endive is fork-tender, 10 to 12 minutes.

3. Season with salt and pepper. Remove endive with slotted spoon to serving dish.

4. Heat pan juices to a boil. Boil gently until reduced to about 3 tablespoons. Stir in whipping cream. Boil until thickened, about 1 minute. Taste and adjust seasonings. Pour over endive. Garnish with minced chives.

Fresh broccoli needs nothing more than butter, lemon juice and a touch of salt and pepper for a dish you can eat again and again. If you are watching your cholesterol intake, try substituting a couple of tablespoons extra-virgin olive oil for the butter.

BROCCOLI WITH LEMON

6 to 8 servings
Preparation time: 15 minutes
Cooking time: 8 minutes

3 pounds fresh broccoli
¼ cup (½ stick) butter (or margarine), melted
Fresh lemon juice to taste
Salt, freshly ground pepper to taste

1. Lightly peel broccoli stalks. Separate stalks into even-size pieces.

2. Cook in 6 quarts boiling water until crisp-tender, 6 to 8 minutes. Drain well. Arrange on warm serving platter.

3. Drizzle broccoli with butter, lemon juice, salt and pepper. Serve immediately.

Broccoli, stir-fried with onion, garlic, ginger, peppers, pea pods and water chestnuts, makes a light vegetarian entree or a colorful side dish.

COLORFUL BROCCOLI STIR-FRY

4 servings
Preparation time: 30 minutes
Cooking time: 10 minutes

1 bunch broccoli, about 1½ pounds
3 tablespoons peanut oil
½ small red onion, diced
2 tablespoons grated fresh ginger
2 cloves garlic, minced
1 yellow or green bell pepper, cored, diced
1 red bell pepper, cored, diced
1 package (6 ounces) frozen snow pea pods
1 can (6 ounces) whole water chestnuts, sliced
¼ cup each: teriyaki sauce, dry sherry

2 tablespoons soy sauce
1 tablespoon sesame seeds

1. Using a large knife, cut the broccoli flowerets from stalks. Lightly peel stalks. Cut stalks into ¼-inch-thick slices. Separate flowerets into equal-size pieces.

2. Heat large skillet until hot. Add oil; heat until hot. Add onion, ginger and garlic. Stir-fry until golden, about 2 minutes. Stir in broccoli pieces and peppers. Stir-fry until crisp-tender, about 3 minutes. Stir in remaining ingredients. Cook and stir until broccoli is tender, about 3 minutes. Serve immediately.

NOTE: Serve over cooked brown rice or toss with cooked shell-shaped pasta noodles if desired. Or, stir in 1 pound cooked, shelled shrimp.

Humble brussels sprouts are anything but mundane when paired with hickory-smoked bacon, shallots and almonds. For best results, select fresh, firm brussels sprouts and remove the core with the tip of a paring knife before cooking.

SMOKY BRUSSELS SPROUTS

4 servings
Preparation time: 20 minutes
Cooking time: 15 minutes

2 **cups brussels sprouts, trimmed**

Coarse (kosher) salt

1 **tablespoon butter**

3 **tablespoons sliced almonds**

4 **slices hickory-smoked bacon, diced**

2 **shallots, minced**

Freshly ground pepper, ground nutmeg to taste

1. Carefully cut out core from sprouts with small paring knife. Cook sprouts in large saucepan of boiling, salted water until crisp-tender, 5 to 8 minutes. Drain; rinse under cold water to stop the cooking.

2. Melt butter in small, nonstick skillet. Add almonds; cook, stirring constantly, until lightly toasted. Remove from heat.

3. Heat large skillet until hot. Add bacon; cook and stir until almost crisp, about 3 minutes. Stir in shallots; cook 1 minute. Add brussels sprouts, salt, pepper and nutmeg. Cook and stir until sprouts are heated through. Pour almonds over all. Serve immediately.

Dark brown sugar provides the sweet, and white vinegar the sour, for this homemade treatment of red cabbage.

SWEET AND SOUR RED CABBAGE

6 servings
Preparation time: 20 minutes
Cooking time: 35 minutes

- **4 slices bacon, chopped**
- **1 onion, finely chopped**
- **1 small clove garlic, finely chopped**
- **¼ cup distilled white vinegar**
- **3 tablespoons dark brown sugar**
- **2 teaspoons Dijon mustard**
- **1 teaspoon caraway seeds**
- **½ teaspoon salt**
- **⅛ teaspoon freshly ground pepper**
- **1 medium red cabbage, about 2 pounds, shredded**
- **½ cup canned beef broth**

1. Fry bacon in large, nonaluminum dutch oven over low heat until crisp, about 5 minutes. Add onion and garlic; cook over low heat until onion is soft, about 8 minutes.

2. Stir in vinegar, sugar, mustard, caraway seeds, salt and pepper. Add cabbage, tossing to coat evenly; cover and cook over medium-low heat, stirring occasionally, for 15 minutes.

3. Add beef broth; cook, uncovered, stirring frequently, until cabbage is tender, about 5 minutes. Taste and adjust seasonings, if necessary. Serve hot.

Sauerkraut mellows when baked for an hour in a clay pot, then gets a last minute jolt of kirsch (a colorless, cherry-flavored eau de vie) in the following recipe. Food writer Lee Thompson has fashioned the recipe after one by English writer Elizabeth David.

BAKED SAUERKRAUT WITH KIRSCH

6 servings
Preparation time: 15 minutes
Cooking time: 1 hour 20 minutes

2 **pounds fresh sauerkraut**

1 **cup rich chicken broth (see recipe, page 134), or substitute canned broth**

½ **cup each: dry white wine, chopped onion**

2 **tablespoons melted butter**

10 **crushed juniper berries, or substitute 1 tablespoon gin**

2 **to 3 teaspoons chopped fresh dill or thyme (or ½ to 1 teaspoon dried)**

1 **baking potato, peeled, grated**

2 **to 3 tablespoons kirsch to taste**

1. Soak clay pot and cover in lukewarm water 15 minutes or more. Drain.

2. Rinse sauerkraut under cold water. Put into clay pot; add ½ cup of the chicken broth, wine, onion, butter, juniper berries and dill.

3. Cover pot and place in cold oven. Set oven temperature to 400 degrees. Cook 1 hour.

4. Heat remaining ½ cup chicken broth with potato and stir into sauerkraut. Cook 20 minutes more. Stir in kirsch.

NOTE: While the clay pot yields the best results, this recipe can be prepared in a dutch oven. To do so, omit step 1. Follow directions in step 2 except place mixture in 4-quart dutch oven. Bake, covered, in a preheated 350-degree oven for 45 minutes. Follow directions in step 4.

Perfect for a Passover celebration, this version of tzimmes from Carol and Darwin Apel of Chicago features a moist mixture of carrots and sweet potatoes.

CARROT TZIMMES

8 servings
Preparation time: 30 minutes
Cooking time: 30 minutes

2 **pounds carrots, peeled, cut in ½-inch-thick slices**

3 **raw sweet potatoes, peeled (or substitute canned in natural juice)**

1 **teaspoon granulated sugar**

¼ **teaspoon salt**
   Freshly ground pepper to taste

1 **pound fresh peas, shelled (or 1 package 10 ounces frozen)**

1 **cup cooked beef brisket (see recipe, page 258), optional**

1 **tablespoon each: chicken fat, flour**

1 **teaspoon brown sugar**

1. Cook carrots and sweet potatoes in water to cover until partly, but not completely, soft. (If using canned sweet potatoes, do not add them to carrots; merely drain and reserve for adding later.)

2. Add granulated sugar, salt, pepper and peas to pot. (If using frozen peas, reserve for adding later.) Cook 3 minutes, then strain, reserving liquid and vegetables separately.

3. Heat oven to 325 degrees. Lightly grease 2-quart casserole. Put vegetables in casserole. If using canned sweet potatoes and frozen peas, add now, stirring gently to combine. Cut brisket into long, shred-like strips and add to vegetables, tossing lightly to combine.

4. Melt fat in small saucepan over medium heat; stir in flour. Cook and stir until blended. Add brown sugar and cook until dissolved. Stir in ½ cup of reserved vegetable liquid; mix well. Simmer 1 minute.

5. Pour over vegetable mixture. Bake, covered, 30 minutes. (If you like a drier tzimmes, do not use a cover.) Serve from casserole.

With a microwave oven and a food processor, you can produce this dramatically colored—and healthful—dish in 30 minutes.

STEAMED CAULIFLOWER WITH RED PEPPER SAUCE

4 to 6 servings
Preparation time: 15 minutes
Microwave cooking time: 11 to 14 minutes

1 **head cauliflower,**
    about 2 pounds
3 **tablespoons water**

RED PEPPER SAUCE

1 **tablespoon olive oil**
1 **small white onion,**
    chopped
1 **rib celery, diced**
½ **teaspoon minced garlic**
2 **red bell peppers,**
    roasted, peeled,
    seeded
2 **tomatoes, peeled,**
    seeded, chopped
¼ **teaspoon dried leaf**
    thyme
    Salt, freshly ground
    pepper to taste
    Minced fresh parsley

1. Using sharp paring knife, remove center core from cauliflower. Separate head into 2-inch flowerets.

2. Put flowerets into 2-quart microwave-safe baking dish. Add water. Cover with plastic wrap vented at one corner. Microwave on high (100 percent power), stirring occasionally, until almost fork-tender, 4 to 6 minutes. Let stand, covered, 5 minutes.

3. Meanwhile, for sauce, put oil into 1½-quart microwave-safe casserole. Microwave, uncovered, on high until hot, 45 seconds to 1 minute. Stir in onion, celery and garlic. Microwave, uncovered, on high, stirring once, until crisp-tender, about 2 minutes.

4. Stir in peppers, tomatoes and thyme. Microwave, covered, on high, until very tender, 4 to 5 minutes. Puree in blender or food processor. Taste and adjust seasonings.

5. To serve, ladle sauce onto serving plate. Top with cauliflower flowerets. Garnish with parsley.

NOTE: To substitute broccoli for cauliflower, trim off and discard about 2 inches of the bottom of 2 pounds broccoli stalks. Lightly peel stalks. Arrange stalks in a spoke pattern, with flowerets in center, on a large microwave-safe platter. Sprinkle with 2 tablespoons water. Cover with plastic wrap vented at one corner. Microwave on high (100 percent power) until crisp-tender, 6 to 8 minutes.

Just a touch of lemon juice, basil and paprika mixed into the butter makes fresh corn-on-the-cob even better.

BOILED CORN WITH LEMON BUTTER

4 servings
Preparation time: 10 minutes
Cooking time: 5 minutes

6 tablespoons butter (or margarine), softened
2 tablespoons fresh lemon juice
1 tablespoon minced fresh basil or 1 teaspoon dried
¼ teaspoon each: imported sweet paprika, freshly ground pepper
4 ears fresh corn, husked, rinsed

1. Mix butter, lemon juice, basil, paprika and pepper in small bowl.

2. Add corn to 4 quarts boiling water. Cook until bright gold and crisp-tender, 2 to 4 minutes. Drain. Serve immediately with lemon butter.

When Marcia Lythcott, a Tribune *editor, cooked up this family favorite in* The Tribune *test kitchen, the smoky, rich corn disappeared faster than a double layer chocolate cake.*

BACON-FRIED CORN

4 servings
Preparation time: 20 minutes
Cooking time: 20 minutes

9 strips bacon, diced
1 large onion, chopped
4 cups fresh corn kernels
1 red bell pepper, seeded, chopped
2 tablespoons minced fresh parsley
1 tablespoon milk
Salt, freshly ground pepper to taste

1. Cook bacon in large heavy-bottomed skillet over medium heat until bacon is crisp. Remove bacon with slotted spoon; reserve.

2. Add onion to bacon fat; cook and stir until crisp-tender, about 4 minutes. Add corn and red pepper. Cook and stir until corn is crisp-tender, about 5 minutes. Stir in parsley, milk, salt and pepper. Garnish with bacon pieces.

Tondalaya Thomas, a Chicago caterer, offers this buttery version of succotash, a melting pot of corn, tomatoes, green peppers, onion and lima beans.

SUCCOTASH

4 to 6 servings
Preparation time: 25 minutes
Cooking time: 20 to 25 minutes

4 ears fresh corn,
   husked, rinsed, or
   3 cups frozen corn
   kernels
2 medium tomatoes
½ cup (1 stick) butter
   (or margarine)
2 medium to large
   onions, diced
2 medium green
   peppers, seeded,
   diced
1 clove garlic, minced or
   crushed
1 package (10 ounces)
   frozen baby lima
   beans
   Salt, freshly ground
   white pepper to taste
¼ cup water

1. If using fresh corn-on-the-cob, cut kernels off cob with sharp knife.

2. Cook tomatoes in boiling water for 30 seconds. Slip off skin; dice.

3. Melt butter in large skillet over medium heat until sizzling, but do not allow to brown. Add fresh corn, onions, green peppers and garlic; cook and stir over medium heat until crisp-tender, about 3 minutes. Add lima beans, salt and pepper; cook and stir 3 minutes. (If using frozen corn, add with lima beans.)

4. Add tomatoes and water. Cook, covered, over low heat until vegetables are tender, 15 to 20 minutes.

This rich, soft pudding, featuring a combination of corn and jalapeño peppers, makes a nice side dish to roast or grilled pork. Accompanied by a salad, it could be a main course for brunch.

JALAPEÑO PEPPER CORN PUDDING

6 to 8 servings
Preparation time: 20 minutes
Baking time: 40 to 45 minutes

6 **large eggs, beaten**

¼ **cup each, finely chopped: green pepper, green onions**

1 **to 2 jalapeño peppers, seeded, minced**

2 **cans (16 ounces each) cream-style corn**

1 **pound shredded Cheddar cheese**

2 **tablespoons flour**

¼ **teaspoon salt**

1. Heat oven to 350 degrees. Put eggs, green pepper, green onions and jalapeño pepper in large bowl. Mix to blend. Add corn, cheese, flour and salt. Mix to blend.

2. Pour into greased 13 by 9-inch baking dish. Place dish in larger pan of boiling water. Bake until center is almost firm, 40 to 45 minutes. Cool on wire rack 10 minutes.

The Helmand, an Afghanistan restaurant in Chicago, serves this rich eggplant dish both as an appetizer and an entree. It is also delicious reheated.

BAKED EGGPLANT WITH YOGURT SAUCE

4 servings
Preparation time: 25 minutes
Cooking time: 30 minutes

1 medium to large
  eggplant, cut cross-
  wise into 4 pieces
  Salt
¼ cup vegetable oil
4 each: tomato slices,
  green pepper rings
2 cloves garlic, minced
½ teaspoon freshly
  ground pepper

YOGURT SAUCE
1 cup plain yogurt
½ teaspoon dried mint
¼ teaspoon garlic
  powder

1. Score eggplant slices with knife. Salt each side; let stand on paper towels 15 minutes. Pat dry.

2. Heat oven to 350 degrees. Heat oil in large skillet. Add eggplant in single layer; cook, turning once, until brown, about 4 minutes. Remove with slotted spatula to ovenproof baking dish. Top each with tomato slice.

3. Cook green pepper rings in same skillet about 1 minute. Place over tomato slice. Sprinkle each with minced garlic and pepper.

4. Pour remaining oil from skillet over all. Bake, covered, until eggplant is tender, about 20 minutes.

5. Meanwhile, for yogurt sauce, mix all ingredients in small bowl. Add salt to taste.

6. To serve, spread about 3 tablespoons yogurt sauce on each serving plate. Arrange eggplant portions over sauce. Top with dollop of remaining yogurt sauce. Drizzle pan juices over all.

Food Guide reader Rosalyn Markette contributed this recipe for eggplant Parmesan. She recommends salting the raw eggplant slices and letting them drain to help remove some of their inherent bitterness. Then the slices are sautéed to a golden brown before getting a coating of tomato sauce and cheese.

EGGPLANT PARMESAN

6 servings
Preparation time: 15 minutes
Standing time: 30 minutes
Baking time: 25 minutes

2 **medium eggplants**
   Salt
½ **cup each: sifted flour,**
   fine bread crumbs
1 **teaspoon dried**
   oregano, crumbled
2 **large eggs, well**
   beaten
6 **tablespoons olive oil**
¼ **cup (½ stick) butter**
   (or margarine),
   melted
1 **teaspoon freshly**
   ground pepper
2 **jars (15½ ounces**
   each) spaghetti sauce
½ **cup freshly grated**
   Parmesan or Romano
   cheese
16 **thin slices mozzarella**
   or Swiss cheese

1. Rinse eggplants; pat dry. Do not peel. Cut into ½-inch-thick slices. Sprinkle lightly with salt. Let stand on paper towels 30 minutes. Pat dry.

2. Dredge slices in flour. Mix bread crumbs with oregano in shallow dish. Dip eggplant into beaten eggs, then into bread crumbs.

3. Put olive oil and butter into large skillet. Heat over medium heat. Add eggplant slices in single layer. Sprinkle lightly with pepper. Sauté until golden, about 5 minutes per side. Remove with slotted spatula; drain on paper towels.

4. Heat oven to 325 degrees. Lightly oil 13 by 9-inch baking pan. Cover bottom of pan with a thin layer of spaghetti sauce. Arrange a layer of eggplant slices on top; sprinkle lightly with Parmesan. Put a slice of mozzarella on each. Spoon another thin layer of spaghetti sauce over all. Repeat layers. Bake until thoroughly heated, 20 to 30 minutes.

Baking gives garlic a full, yet mild, flavor and reduces its impact on the breath. Vary the recipe to better suit the food it accompanies by using the same broth flavor as the meat you are serving.

BAKED WHOLE GARLIC

10 servings
Preparation time: 10 minutes
Baking time: 45 minutes

10 whole heads fresh
    garlic
1 cup beef, chicken,
    pork or lamb broth
⅓ cup olive oil
    Salt, freshly ground
    pepper to taste

1. Heat oven to 350 degrees. Peel away as much of the outer skin of the garlic heads as possible but leave individual cloves still covered. Put garlic in single layer in shallow, nonaluminum baking dish.

2. Pour broth over all. Drizzle with oil. Sprinkle with salt and pepper. Bake, partly covered, basting frequently, until heads are soft to the touch, 35 to 45 minutes, depending on the size. If desired, remove cover during the last 10 minutes to allow skins to turn golden.

3. To serve, press the pulp out of the skins onto toasted bread or roasted meats such as beef, chicken, pork or lamb.

While the smell of fresh dill was prominent in The Tribune*'s Cook's Garden, the test kitchen created this buttery treatment of green beans.*

GREEN BEANS WITH DILL

6 servings
Preparation time: 25 minutes
Cooking time: 15 minutes

1½ pounds fresh green
    beans, ends trimmed
1 medium onion, minced
¼ cup (½ stick) butter
    (or margarine)
1 tablespoon minced
    fresh dill
¼ teaspoon salt
⅛ teaspoon freshly
    ground pepper
2 hard-cooked eggs

1. Heat 3 quarts water to boil in large saucepan. Add beans; cook, uncovered, until crisp-tender, 6 to 8 minutes. Drain; rinse under cold water to stop the cooking.

2. Cook onion in butter in large skillet until tender, about 5 minutes. Stir in green beans, dill, salt and pepper. Cook and stir just until heated through.

3. Transfer to serving dish. Garnish with coarsely chopped egg white and sieved egg yolk.

Butter and almonds pick up a mild garlic flavor, then are stirred into tender-crisp green beans in the following recipe.

GREEN BEANS WITH GARLIC ALMONDS

4 to 6 servings
Preparation time: 15 minutes
Cooking time: 10 minutes

1½ pounds fresh green
    beans, ends trimmed
1 clove garlic, minced
¼ cup (½ stick) butter
    (or margarine)
⅓ cup slivered almonds
2 tablespoons lemon
    juice
    Salt to taste

1. Heat 3 quarts water to boil in large saucepan. Add beans, cook, uncovered, until crisp-tender, 6 to 8 minutes. Drain; rinse under cold water to stop the cooking.

2. Cook garlic in butter in large saucepan until soft, stir in almonds. Cook until almonds are light brown. Stir in beans, lemon juice and salt. Cook and stir just until hot. Serve.

Almost any type of fresh mushroom can be used in the following recipe; cooking time will vary slightly depending on mushroom size and natural tenderness. Serve this as a side dish to grilled meats and poultry.

SAUTÉED MUSHROOMS AND PEARL ONIONS

8 servings
Preparation time: 25 minutes
Cooking time: 15 minutes

⅓ cup olive oil
¼ cup (½ stick) butter
1 pound pearl onions,
    peeled
3 large shallots, minced
2 large cloves garlic,
    minced
1 pound oyster,
    chanterelle, button or
    other fresh
    mushrooms, sliced
1 small bunch green
    onions, minced

1. Heat oil and butter in large nonstick skillet over medium heat. Add pearl onions, shallots and garlic. Cook and stir until pearl onions are crisp-tender, about 10 minutes.

2. Add mushrooms and green onions. Cook and stir over medium heat until mushrooms are tender, 3 to 5 minutes. Remove from heat. Serve immediately.

The ingredients are simple, and the results, delicious. To keep the oil hot and the mushrooms crisp, fry only a few mushrooms at a time.

DEEP-FRIED MUSHROOMS

2 servings
Preparation time: 5 minutes
Soaking time: 30 minutes
Cooking time: 2 minutes

2 cups cleaned fresh morels or 1 ounce dried morels, or any other fresh mushroom
Salt
½ cup all-purpose flour
¼ teaspoon baking powder
⅛ teaspoon freshly ground pepper
Vegetable oil for deep-frying

1. If using morels, soak fresh morels in several changes of salted water. Drain; discard water from fresh morels. (If dried morels are reconstituted, reserve soaking water from the morels for use in soups, stock, sauces.) Pat morels dry. If using other mushrooms, simply wipe clean with a damp cloth.

2. Put flour, baking powder and pepper into plastic bag. Add a few mushrooms. Shake well to coat.

3. Heat oil to 365 degrees in deep saucepan or deep-fryer. Deep-fry mushrooms, a few at a time, until golden. Remove with slotted spoon. Drain on paper towels. Serve immediately.

Woodsy-flavored morels get the honored spot on the very top of these cheese-filled quesadillas. The quesadillas can be served for a quick meatless brunch entree or as sophisticated appetizers for a Southwestern-style party.

MOREL QUESADILLAS

2 servings
Preparation time: 5 minutes
Cooking time: 5 minutes

12 **tablespoons small fresh or dried morels**
Salt
¼ **cup (½ stick) butter**
4 **flour tortillas**
4 **slices Monterey Jack cheese**

1. Soak fresh morels in several changes of salted water. Drain; discard water from fresh morels. (If dried morels are used, reconstitute in warm water to cover; reserve soaking water for use in soups, stock, sauces.) Pat morels dry.

2. Heat butter in medium skillet over medium heat. Add morels; cook and stir until golden, about 5 minutes.

3. Heat tortillas, 1 at a time on a comal (tortilla griddle) or in well-seasoned skillet, turning with a spatula. Put a slice of cheese on each tortilla; fold in half; cook until cheese begins to melt.

4. Top each cheese-filled tortilla with 3 sautéed morels. Serve immediately.

For this thick, luscious compote, former Chicago chef Michael Beck bakes tiny onions up to four hours in a low oven to develop flavor, then simmers them with cognac and crème fraîche.

ONION COMPOTE

4 servings
Preparation time: 30 minutes
Cooking time: 2½ to 4½ hours

2 **pounds unpeeled pearl onions or boiling onions (of equal size)**

4 **slices lean bacon, about ¼-inch thick, julienned**

¼ **cup good cognac or brandy**

1½ **cups crème fraîche or whipping cream**

Pinch freshly ground white pepper

Salt to taste

1. Heat oven to 325 degrees. Put onions in single layer on baking sheet. Bake until soft to touch and skin is lightly browned, 2 to 4 hours. (The baking time depends on age of onions; test by squeezing.) Let cool to room temperature.

2. Slice off top on root end. Gently squeeze onion out of skin, being careful to discard any dry outer skin. There should be 1½ to 2 cups.

3. Cook bacon in large heavy-bottomed skillet over medium-low heat, until cooked but not brown. Discard excess fat. Cool slightly.

4. Stir in cognac; cook over low heat. Add onion meat, crème fraîche and pepper. Do not salt. Cook and stir until cream is reduced and thickened, about 25 minutes. Taste and adjust seasonings. Add salt, if desired.

NOTE: This can be prepared one day ahead of time, covered and refrigerated. Reheat gently. Consistency should be like a thick split pea soup.

Deep-frying onion rings in two stages makes them easy to prepare ahead for entertaining. Though not cooked in a loaf shape, these rings resemble the loaf-style fried onion rings found in many restaurants.

CRISPY LIGHT ONION RINGS

4 to 6 servings
Preparation time: 25 minutes
Cooking time: 10 minutes

6 **medium yellow onions**
Vegetable oil for deep-frying
All-purpose flour
Salt, cayenne pepper to taste

1. If using food processor, select onions that will fit into feed tube; thinly slice using 2-mm slicing disk. If using regular or electric knife, cut onions into thinnest slices possible. Separate slices into rings.

2. Pour oil to depth of 3 inches in deep-fryer, wok or deep saucepan. Heat oil to 375 degrees.

3. Toss onion rings lightly in flour; shake off excess. Deep-fry, a few at a time, in oil until very light gold color, about 1 minute. Do not overbrown. Remove with slotted spoon to paper towels. Repeat. Let cool completely. Then cover with foil to keep for up to several hours.

4. When ready to serve, strain oil back into clean pan. Heat to 365 degrees. Deep-fry onions as directed above, this time letting them get a golden color. Drain on paper towels. Sprinkle with salt and cayenne. Serve immediately.

Green peas with mint is a classic flavor combination. The peas should be eaten as close to picking time as possible.

GREEN PEAS WITH MINT

2 servings
Preparation time: 20 minutes
Cooking time: 5 minutes

1½ **to 2 cups fresh shelled peas**
2 **tablespoons butter**
Salt, freshly ground pepper to taste
1 **tablespoon finely chopped fresh mint**
¼ **to ½ teaspoon sugar**

1. If peas are extremely fresh, they do not have to be parboiled in water. If they are older, it is best to parboil by cooking in boiling water until crisp-tender, 2 to 4 minutes. Drain.

2. Heat butter in large skillet; add peas, salt, pepper, mint and sugar. Cook and stir until peas are cooked and heated through, 1 to 2 minutes.

Vegetables

Arguably the most celebrated potato dish of all, potatoes Anna starts with rounds of potatoes baked like a cake, so that the outside is browned and crisp and the center very tender. New York cooking teacher and writer Peter Kump takes you through this famous dish, step-by-step.

POTATOES ANNA

8 servings
Preparation time: 25 minutes
Baking time: 40 to 45 minutes

3 **pounds older, waxy or boiling potatoes**
1 **cup (2 sticks) unsalted butter, clarified (see appendix)**
  Salt, freshly ground pepper, ground nutmeg to taste

1. Peel potatoes and cut into ⅛-inch-thick rounds. Pat dry; if necessary, hold them wrapped in a damp cloth; do not immerse in water. Heat oven to 450 degrees.

2. Pour about ¼ inch of butter in large ovenproof skillet; heat. When skillet is hot, start rapidly arranging the first layer of potatoes, overlapping them in concentric circles. Sprinkle with salt, pepper and nutmeg, then make a second layer of potatoes. Baste with 1 tablespoon of the butter. Continue making layers and basting with butter. Shake the pan from time to time to prevent sticking. Fill the pan to a dome about ½ inch above the top.

3. Press down hard on layers of potatoes with bottom of saucepan. Cover with buttered lid; put onto a baking sheet (to catch any drippings). Bake in upper third of oven 20 minutes.

4. Remove potatoes from oven, uncover, press down again with saucepan. Return to oven uncovered. Press down on potatoes again before baking time is up. Potatoes are done when they're brown and crusty on the outside, 20 to 25 minutes.

5. Drain off excess butter, run spatula around edge of pan, shake pan and unmold onto serving dish.

NOTE: To hold, cover loosely with aluminum foil and keep in a low oven (less than 170 degrees) up to 30 minutes.

VARIATIONS: To make baker's style potatoes, make potatoes Anna with 5 to 6 potatoes and 3 onions. Start with a layer of potatoes, then sliced onions, continuing to a top layer of potatoes. For potatoes sarladaise, make potatoes Anna, adding 1 to 2 truffles, black or white, very thinly sliced as a layer in the middle.

Cepes, one of the most highly prized mushrooms, make a perfect marriage with potatoes. Peter Kump notes in this recipe that if you use dried cepes, soak them for 20 to 30 minutes in hot water, strain, and add the soaking water to the dish.

POTATO GRATIN WITH CEPES

6 servings
Preparation time: 35 minutes
Baking time: 40 minutes

2 **ounces dried cepes**
2 **pounds waxy new potatoes**
½ **small onion, minced**
¼ **cup minced fresh parsley**
½ **cup shredded Gruyère or Swiss cheese**
2 **cloves garlic, minced**
1 **cup crème fraîche or whipping cream**
  Salt, freshly ground pepper, ground nutmeg to taste
  Unsalted butter, melted

1. Soak mushrooms in hot water to cover in small bowl until softened, about 20 minutes. Strain soaking liquid into saucepan; simmer until reduced to ¼ cup. Rinse mushrooms several times to remove grit; chop coarsely.

2. Butter baking dish generously. Peel and slice potatoes into ⅛-inch-thick rounds. Heat oven to 400 degrees.

3. Mix together onion, parsley, ¼ cup of the Gruyère and garlic in small bowl. Mix crème fraîche and reduced mushroom liquid in glass measure.

4. Put a layer of potatoes in prepared baking dish. Season with salt, pepper and nutmeg. Sprinkle some of the onion mixture over it, then add a layer of mushrooms. Continue, finishing with a potato layer.

5. Pour crème fraîche mixture over all. Top with remaining cheese. Drizzle with melted butter. Bake until brown and crusty on top, about 40 minutes.

Vegetables

Stuffed potatoes were a big trend in 1985 when The Tribune *test kitchen created this recipe. They are still good anytime.*

CHEESE AND BACON-TOPPED BAKED POTATOES

4 servings
Preparation time: 15 minutes
Baking time: 1 hour

4 **medium Idaho potatoes**

TOPPING

4 **slices bacon, cooked, crumbled**

1 **package (3 ounces) cream cheese**

1 **cup each, shredded: sharp Cheddar cheese, Muenster cheese**

2 **tablespoons butter**

1 **tablespoon Dijon mustard**

2 **green onions, minced**

½ **teaspoon each: minced fresh parsley, hot pepper sauce**

1. Heat oven to 400 degrees. Thoroughly wash and dry potatoes. Pierce each potato with knife to allow steam to escape. Bake on rack until soft, about 45 minutes. Let sit while preparing topping.

2. Reduce oven to 375 degrees. Put remaining ingredients in small baking dish. Bake just until cheese is melted, about 15 minutes. Mix well.

3. Cut long slit in potatoes; fluff up insides. Spoon cheese topping over potatoes. Serve immediately.

Harbingers of spring, tiny new potatoes, fresh peas and watercress are teamed in this vegetable side dish.

BUTTERED NEW POTATOES AND PEAS WITH WATERCRESS

4 servings
Preparation time: 15 minutes
Cooking time: 20 minutes

1 pound small new potatoes
1 cup each: chicken broth, water
2 tablespoons olive oil
Dash each: salt, freshly ground pepper
1 cup fresh shelled peas or frozen
3 tablespoons unsalted butter
4 green onions, minced
2 cloves garlic, minced
¼ cup minced watercress leaves
2 tablespoons minced fresh parsley

1. Put potatoes, chicken broth, water, oil, salt and pepper into medium saucepan. Heat to boil; reduce heat to medium. Simmer, uncovered, until potatoes are fork-tender, about 15 minutes. Remove potatoes with slotted spoon to bowl. Cut potatoes crosswise in half.

2. Drop peas into simmering potato cooking liquid. Simmer, uncovered, until peas are bright green and crisp-tender, about 2 minutes. Remove from heat.

3. Melt butter in large skillet. Add onions and garlic; cook and stir until wilted, about 2 minutes. Stir in potatoes, peas and cooking liquid. Cook and stir until heated through, about 2 minutes. Stir in watercress and parsley. Transfer to serving dish. Serve immediately.

This recipe is an excellent way to showcase waxy new potatoes and garden-fresh herbs.

SAUTÉED POTATOES WITH HERBS

6 servings
Preparation time: 20 minutes
Cooking time: 25 minutes

16 small new potatoes
5 tablespoons olive oil
2 tablespoons each, minced: fresh parsley, fresh savory (or 1½ teaspoons dried)
2 teaspoons minced fresh sage or ½ teaspoon dried
½ teaspoon salt

¼ teaspoon freshly ground pepper

1. Scrub potatoes; pat dry. Cut potatoes in half if large. Heat olive oil in large skillet. Add potatoes. Cook, shaking pan occasionally until potatoes are crisp-tender, about 20 minutes.

2. Add herbs, salt and pepper. Cook and toss, until potatoes are golden and tender, 2 to 5 minutes. Serve hot, warm or at room temperature.

JeanMarie Brownson, Tribune test kitchen director, elevates potatoes from ordinary fare to the center of attention when orange-colored sweet potatoes and white-colored potatoes are cooked separately and then swirled together in a baking dish. This dish freezes well, making it perfect for hectic holiday entertaining.

MARBLED MASHED POTATOES

8 to 10 servings
Preparation time: 25 minutes
Cooking time: 1 hour, 10 minutes

1½ pounds medium baking potatoes, halved
3 large sweet potatoes, quartered
¼ cup (½ stick) butter
4 large shallots, minced
1 cup sour cream
1 cup whipping cream, whipped
½ teaspoon salt
¼ teaspoon white pepper
⅛ teaspoon freshly ground nutmeg

TOPPING
½ cup fresh homemade bread crumbs
6 tablespoons melted butter
¼ cup minced fresh parsley

1. Cook potatoes separately in boiling water in large saucepans until fork-tender, about 30 minutes. Drain; cool slightly; peel. Push potatoes separately through a ricer into separate bowls. (Or mash with potato masher.)

2. Heat oven to 350 degrees. Melt ¼ cup butter in small skillet; add shallots. Cook and stir until shallots are tender. Stir half of the shallot mixture into each potato mixture. Whisk sour cream into whipped cream. Gently fold half of the cream mixture into each potato mixture.

3. Season each of the potato mixtures with half of the spices. Taste and adjust seasonings. Put some of the sweet potato mixture into 2-quart baking or soufflé dish; top with half of the white potato mixture. Repeat layering. Swirl potatoes with a metal spatula to give a marbled effect.

4. For topping, mix all ingredients. Sprinkle topping over potatoes. Bake until topping is golden and potatoes are hot throughout, 30 to 35 minutes.

NOTE: To freeze, complete recipe through step 3. Freeze well wrapped up to 2 months. Thaw in the refrigerator. Make topping as directed; sprinkle over potatoes. Bake as directed, adding time if necessary to be sure potatoes are hot throughout.

Sweet potatoes are baked, scooped out and beaten with basil and dill, then piped back into the potato shells for attractive, individual portions.

HERBED SWEET POTATOES

6 servings
Preparation time: 15 minutes
Baking time: 1 hour, 10 minutes

6 sweet potatoes
5 tablespoons half-and-half
3 tablespoons softened butter
1 teaspoon each: dried basil, dry mustard
½ teaspoon dried dill weed
⅛ teaspoon each: salt, freshly ground pepper
3 slices bacon, cooked, drained, finely crumbled
Melted butter

1. Heat oven to 400 degrees. Bake sweet potatoes until tender, about 1 hour.

2. Cut off a long section from the top of each, about ½-inch thick. Scoop out flesh from top and bottom to form ¼-inch thick shell.

3. Beat potato flesh with half-and-half, butter and seasonings until light and fluffy. Stir in bacon. Pipe mixture into potato shells, using pastry bag fitted with ½-inch star tip or spoon back into shells. Drizzle with melted butter.

4. Bake until tops are brown and potatoes are heated through, about 10 minutes.

Rutabaga is an old-fashioned vegetable that too many shoppers overlook at the supermarket. This basic recipe brings out the good, natural flavor of this root vegetable. It's from former Tribune *writer Margaret Sheridan's grandmother Karrer in Port Huron, Michigan.*

MASHED RUTABAGA WITH PEPPER

6 to 8 servings
Preparation time: 10 minutes
Cooking time: 15 minutes

2 medium rutabaga, about 1 pound each, peeled, cubed
1 teaspoon sugar
½ cup (1 stick) butter, softened
Freshly ground pepper to taste
Salt, optional, to taste

1. Put rutabaga in large pot. Sprinkle with sugar; add water to cover. Cover and heat to boil over high heat. Reduce heat to medium and cook until fork-tender, about 15 minutes.

2. Drain, add butter and mash with potato masher until coarse texture is achieved. Mash in pepper. Season with salt, if desired. Serve hot.

Fresh spinach takes a decidedly Oriental twist in this easy and very appealing side dish.

SPINACH WITH SESAME SEEDS

6 servings
Preparation time: 20 minutes
Cooking time: 5 minutes

3 **pounds fresh spinach**
6 **green onions, sliced**
6 **tablespoons Oriental sesame oil**
¼ **cup soy sauce, or to taste**
  Pinch salt
2 **tablespoons sesame seeds**

1. Rinse spinach leaves well under running water. Trim off thick stems. Put spinach leaves, with water that clings to leaves, into large pot. Heat over high heat, stirring constantly, until spinach wilts and turns bright green. Immediately remove spinach to colander; rinse with cold water to stop the cooking.

2. Squeeze water from spinach leaves. Chop coarsely. Put into bowl. Stir in onions, sesame oil and 2 tablespoons soy sauce. Taste and add remaining soy and salt as desired to taste.

3. Put sesame seeds into small nonstick skillet. Cook, stirring constantly, over medium-low heat, until lightly toasted. Immediately remove from heat to plate. Let cool.

4. Serve spinach at room temperature sprinkled with sesame seeds.

Indian cooks bring out the flavor of herbs and seeds by sautéing them in oil until the herbs emit a wonderful flavor, as demonstrated in this classic sag paneer from the now-defunct Chicago restaurant Gandhara.

SPINACH WITH YOGURT
(Sag paneer)

6 servings
Preparation time: 25 minutes
Cooking time: 1½ hours

4 large cloves garlic

1 piece fresh ginger, ½- to ¾-inch long and wide

4 to 5 tablespoons oil

4 to 5 yellow onions, about ¾ pound, sliced

3 pounds fresh spinach, well rinsed

½ teaspoon cumin seeds

1½ teaspoons turmeric

1 teaspoon salt

2 to 3 teaspoons fenugreek leaves (methi), crushed

2 cups homemade plain yogurt, or 2 containers (8 ounces each)

½ cup (1 stick) butter

1 tablespoon paprika

1 to 1½ teaspoons ground cumin, to taste

⅛ to ¼ teaspoon cayenne pepper, to taste

1. Put garlic and ginger into blender; process until very finely chopped.

2. Heat 4 tablespoons of the oil in heavy-bottomed dutch oven over medium-high heat until very hot. Sauté onions, stirring often, until light brown at edges, about 20 minutes. Drizzle in more oil, if needed.

3. Meanwhile, cook spinach in boiling water just until tender, about 3 minutes. Drain; puree in food processor or blender. Set aside.

4. Add cumin seeds to onions; cook 30 seconds, stirring constantly, until golden and aromatic. Immediately add garlic mixture and turmeric. Cook and stir 5 minutes.

5. Stir in spinach and salt. Cook, stirring often, 10 minutes. Add fenugreek leaves. Cook, with pan mostly covered, 15 minutes.

6. Stir in yogurt, butter, paprika, ground cumin and cayenne. Cook, partly covered, stirring often, over low heat, until thickened and flavors are well blended, 15 to 20 minutes.

Rather than serve plain acorn squash halves, try this tasty version filled with fresh apples, sweet pineapple and crunchy water chestnuts.

ACORN SQUASH WITH FRUIT STUFFING

6 servings
Preparation time: 15 minutes
Cooking time: 1 hour

3 **small acorn squash**
1 **can (20 ounces) crushed pineapple, drained**
2 **medium apples, cored, diced, about 1½ cups**
4 **ribs celery, chopped**
1 **can (8 ounces) water chestnuts, drained, chopped**
½ **cup each: melted butter (1 stick), packed light brown sugar**
1 **tablespoon soy sauce**
1 **teaspoon dry mustard**
½ **teaspoon ground cinnamon**

1. Heat oven to 350 degrees. Cut each squash in half crosswise, so edges are scalloped. Remove seeds. Bake upside down in baking pan with little water added, until tender, about 45 minutes.

2. Mix remaining ingredients in large bowl. Drain water from baking pan. Turn squash right side up and fill with fruit mixture. Bake until heated through, about 15 minutes.

The microwave oven is ideal for shortening the cooking time needed for butternut squash. Two pounds of squash cook in only 8 minutes. In this recipe, they also absorb extra flavor from fresh ginger.

STEAMED BUTTERNUT SQUASH WITH GINGER

6 servings
Preparation time: 15 minutes
Microwave cooking time: 8 minutes

2 **pounds butternut squash, peeled, seeded**
2 **tablespoons each: minced fresh ginger, water, butter**
Salt, freshly ground pepper to taste
Ground nutmeg to taste

1. Cut squash into 1½-inch cubes. Put squash, ginger and water into 2-quart microwave-safe baking dish. Cover with plastic wrap vented at one corner.

2. Microwave on high (100 percent power) until crisp-tender, 6 to 8 minutes. Drain; add butter, nutmeg, salt and pepper. Stir until butter melts. Serve hot.

Also called mirliton or christophene, chayote squash is a mild-tasting squash that marries well with this peppery, butter-rich baked dish.

DIXIE CHAYOTE SQUASH

8 to 10 servings
Preparation time: 45 minutes
Cooking time: 1¼ hours

SEASONING MIXTURE

- **2 whole bay leaves**
- **2 teaspoons freshly ground white pepper**
- **½ teaspoon cayenne pepper or to taste**
- **1 teaspoon each, dried: leaf thyme, basil**
- **½ teaspoon freshly ground black pepper**

SQUASH

- **5 medium chayote squash (also called mirliton, substitute zucchini or yellow squash)**
- **1 cup (2 sticks) unsalted butter**
- **3 medium onions, chopped**
- **2 medium green peppers, seeded, chopped**
- **4 ribs celery, chopped**
- **⅓ cup chicken broth**
- **3 cloves garlic, minced**
- **1½ cup coarse homemade bread crumbs**

1. Heat oven to 350 degrees. For seasoning mixture, combine all ingredients. Peel; seed and chop chayote squash.

2. Melt half of the butter in large skillet over medium heat. Add half of the onions, half of the green pepper and half of the celery; cook and stir over medium-high heat until tender, about 15 minutes.

3. Stir in remaining onions, green pepper, celery, seasoning mixture, broth and garlic. Cook and stir 2 minutes. Add remaining butter; cook and stir until melted while scraping bottom. Add chopped chayotes; sauté 2 minutes.

4. Transfer to 13 by 9-inch baking dish. Bake, covered, 25 minutes. Sprinkle with bread crumbs; bake, uncovered, until brown, about 25 minutes.

Carolyn Buster, chef/owner of The Cottage Restaurant in Calumet City, Illinois, elevates squash to a stuffed dish suitable for party fare.

STUFFED GOLDEN SQUASH

8 servings
Preparation time: 20 minutes
Standing time: 1 hour
Cooking time: 45 minutes

24 **pitted prunes**
24 **walnut halves**
½ **cup packed light brown sugar**
¼ **cup (½ stick) butter, melted**
1½ **teaspoons ground cinnamon**
½ **teaspoon ground nutmeg**
Rind of 1 orange, optional

SQUASH
4 **small (3 inches diameter) acorn squash, preferably golden**
8 **tablespoons each: light brown sugar, butter**
Salt, freshly ground white pepper to taste
2 **tablespoons bourbon**

1. Stuff each prune with walnut half. Put into 8-inch baking dish. Mix ½ cup sugar, melted butter, cinnamon and nutmeg in small bowl; pour over prunes. Stir in orange rind, if desired. Add water to cover, about 3 cups. Let stand 1 hour.

2. Heat oven to 425 degrees. For squash, cut each squash in half. Remove seeds and center pulp. Put 1 tablespoon brown sugar and butter into each half. Put into large baking pan. Sprinkle with salt and pepper.

3. Cover prunes; bake prunes and squash until liquid on prunes is bubbling and syrupy and squash is glazed with butter and sugar and is fork-tender, about 45 minutes. Occasionally baste edge of squash with butter mixture in center.

4. Remove prunes and squash from oven. Pour bourbon over prunes; carefully ignite. Spoon 3 prunes into center of each squash. Serve.

The addition of a white sauce, cheese and a crunchy cracker-crumb top turns ordinary yellow squash into a rich, creamy and comforting meatless entree or side dish.

YELLOW SQUASH CASSEROLE

6 to 8 servings
Preparation time: 30 minutes
Baking time: 20 minutes

3 **medium yellow squash or zucchini**
9 **tablespoons butter**
2 **small onions, finely chopped**
3 **tablespoons all-purpose flour**
½ **cup each: milk, half-and-half**
1½ **cups shredded sharp Cheddar cheese, about 6 ounces**
   Salt, freshly ground pepper to taste
1 **cup coarse cracker crumbs, such as saltines**
   Minced fresh parsley for garnish

1. Cut squash lengthwise in half; then cut into ½-inch-thick slices. There should be about 3 cups.

2. Melt 3 tablespoons of the butter in large skillet over medium heat. Add squash and onions; cook until squash is crisp-tender, 5 to 10 minutes. Strain off pan juices into glass measure.

3. Heat oven to 350 degrees. Melt 3 tablespoons of the butter in medium saucepan over low heat. Stir in flour; cook and stir 1 minute. Slowly stir in milk, half-and-half and pan juices from squash. Cook until smooth and thickened, about 5 minutes. Remove from heat; stir in cheese, salt and pepper until cheese melts.

4. Mix cheese sauce and squash in 8-inch square baking dish. Sprinkle with cracker crumbs. Dot top with remaining 3 tablespoons butter. Bake until bubbly and golden, about 20 minutes.

If it looks like spaghetti, why not treat it like spaghetti? Strands of fresh spaghetti squash are topped with a light, wine-enhanced clam sauce in this quick microwave recipe. Or, instead of the clam sauce, try topping the cooked squash with butter, black pepper and Parmesan cheese, or a fresh tomato sauce.

SPAGHETTI SQUASH WITH WHITE CLAM SAUCE

4 servings
Preparation time: 20 minutes
Microwave cooking time: 23 minutes

1 **spaghetti squash, about 3 pounds**
2 **tablespoons olive oil**
1 **small onion or 5 shallots, minced**
2 **to 3 cloves garlic, minced**
2 **cans (10 ounces each) shelled clams and their juice**
⅓ **cup dry white wine**
   Freshly ground pepper to taste
¼ **cup minced fresh parsley**
   Salt to taste
   Freshly grated Parmesan cheese

1. Pierce squash in several places with sharp knife or fork. Put squash on paper towel in microwave. Microwave on high (100 percent power) turning occasionally until squash is soft to the touch, 13 to 15 minutes. Let stand 5 minutes.

2. Cut in half; remove and discard seeds. With a fork, comb the squash to pick up the flesh in strands; put into warm serving bowl.

3. For sauce, put oil, onion and garlic into medium-size microwave-safe baking dish. Microwave on high until onions are soft, about 2 minutes.

4. Strain clam juice into onions; reserve clams. Stir wine and pepper into onion mixture. Microwave, covered, on high until simmering, 2 to 4 minutes. Stir in clams, parsley and salt; microwave on high until hot, 2 minutes.

5. Pour over squash. Serve sprinkled with cheese.

Big, summer-ripe tomatoes star when filled with feta cheese and spinach.

FETA AND SPINACH STUFFED TOMATOES

4 servings
Preparation time: 15 minutes
Baking time: 12 to 14 minutes

4 large ripe tomatoes
Salt
1 package (10 ounces) frozen chopped spinach, cooked, well drained
4 ounces feta cheese, crumbled
½ cup each, minced: onion, fresh parsley
¼ teaspoon each, dried: leaf oregano, leaf thyme
Freshly ground pepper to taste

1. Remove tops of tomatoes, using a zigzag cut. Scoop out tomato pulp leaving a ½-inch-thick shell. Chop pulp and put into medium bowl. Salt insides of tomatoes; drain upside down on paper towels.

2. Add spinach, cheese, onion, parsley, oregano, thyme, salt and pepper to tomato pulp. Mix well.

3. Heat oven to 325 degrees. Spoon spinach mixture into tomatoes. Put tomatoes in buttered baking dish. Bake, covered, until hot and cheese melts, 12 to 14 minutes.

When summer zucchini and green beans are at their peak, try mixing them with this light tarragon marinade. Small, light-colored zucchini usually will be sweeter than large, deep-green ones.

ZUCCHINI OR GREEN BEANS IN FRESH TARRAGON MARINADE

4 servings
Preparation time: 15 minutes
Marinating time: 30 minutes to 2 hours

1 **pound small zucchini or fresh trimmed green beans**
  Salt

MARINADE

3 **tablespoons olive oil**
2 **tablespoons each: vegetable oil, white wine vinegar**
4 **green onions, finely chopped**
2 **to 3 teaspoons minced fresh tarragon, to taste, or 1 teaspoon dried**
1 **teaspoon Dijon mustard**
¼ **teaspoon each: sugar, salt, freshly ground pepper**

1. Cut zucchini into thin slices. Sprinkle lightly with salt; let drain on paper towel 20 minutes. Do not cook. (If using green beans, drop beans into boiling water; cook until crisp-tender, 5 to 8 minutes. Drain; rinse under cold water to stop the cooking.)

2. For marinade, mix remaining ingredients in bottom of large bowl. Add zucchini or drained beans. Refrigerate, covered, at least 30 minutes, or up to several hours. Stir occasionally.

3. Serve at room temperature as a vegetable or salad course, or toss with chilled, cooked pasta for a quick pasta salad.

Cooking teacher Jean True, of Glen Ellyn, Illinois, devised this simple oven-baked version of the classic vegetable dish, ratatouille. Try using leftovers as an omelet filling, hamburger topping or cold salad in a lettuce cup.

OVEN-BAKED RATATOUILLE

6 servings
Preparation time: 15 minutes
Draining time: 1 hour
Cooking time: 2½ hours

1 eggplant, cut into ½-inch cubes
Salt
½ cup olive oil
2 large onions, sliced
2 large cloves garlic, minced
½ cup minced fresh parsley
2 teaspoons salt, or to taste
1 teaspoon each, dried: basil, leaf thyme
½ teaspoon freshly ground pepper
6 zucchini, thickly sliced
2 green or red bell peppers, seeded, cut into chunks
4 large ripe tomatoes, coarsely chopped, or 1 can (40 ounces) tomatoes

1. Sprinkle eggplant cubes with salt. Let drain on paper towels 1 hour. Pat dry.

2. Heat oven to 300 degrees. Heat 2 tablespoons of the oil in large ovenproof casserole or dutch oven. Add onions and garlic; cook and stir 2 minutes. Mix parsley, salt, basil, thyme and pepper.

3. Layer eggplant, zucchini and peppers separately over onions, sprinkling each layer with some of herb mixture before adding next vegetable. Drizzle remaining oil over top.

4. Bake, covered, 1½ hours. Add tomatoes. With a spatula, lightly turn vegetables to mix. Continue to bake until vegetables are tender, about 1 more hour. If ratatouille is too soupy, bake it uncovered to allow the excess moisture to evaporate.

■ *Almost all vegetables grill well. And with a little planning, tonight's dinner can become tomorrow's lunch. After grilling your steak or chicken for dinner, throw the vegetables on the grill to cook over fading coals. Basting vegetables with the vinaigrette as they cook also enhances flavor.*

GRILLED VEGETABLES WITH ROSEMARY VINAIGRETTE

4 servings
Preparation time: 15 minutes
Grilling time: 20 minutes

⅓ to ½ **cup extra-virgin olive oil**
¼ **cup red wine vinegar**
1 **tablespoon country-style Dijon mustard**
¼ **teaspoon each: salt, freshly ground pepper**
¼ to ½ **teaspoon minced fresh rosemary leaves or dried to taste**
  Assorted vegetables for grilling

1. Put ⅓ cup oil, vinegar, mustard, salt, pepper and ¼ teaspoon rosemary into jar with tight-fitting lid. Shake well to mix. Taste and add more oil and rosemary as desired.

To grill bell peppers: Place whole peppers 4 to 6 inches from hot coals. Grill, turning often, until skin is slightly charred and flesh is crisp-tender, 15 to 20 minutes. Remove from grill and put into paper bag, close bag and let sit for 10 minutes. Remove from bag, discard charred skin, core and seeds. Cut into slices and toss lightly with vinaigrette.

To grill eggplant, zucchini and yellow squash slices: Place slices 6 inches from hot coals. Grill, turning and brushing with vinaigrette until crisp-tender, 3 to 5 minutes.

To grill onions: Place green onions or medium unpeeled white onions 6 inches from hot coals. Grill, turning often, until slightly charred and crisp-tender, 5 to 10 minutes. Remove peel before slicing and tossing with vinaigrette.

To grill green beans: Place beans on a sheet of heavy-duty aluminum foil. Brush with vinaigrette. Grill 6 inches from hot coals until crisp-tender, about 5 to 10 minutes depending on the thickness.

2. Serve grilled vegetables hot with any remaining vinaigrette.

This dish will look like mashed potatoes, but what a wonderful taste surprise: fennel, celery root and apples, flavored with mace and smoothed with cream.

BAKED WINTER VEGETABLES

6 to 8 servings
Preparation time: 45 minutes
Cooking time: 1 hour, 45 minutes

½ **cup whipping cream**

2 **large eggs**

1 **medium bulb fennel**

6 **large Idaho potatoes, about 3½ pounds, peeled, diced**

1 **medium celery root (celeriac), about 1½ pounds, peeled, diced**

1 **medium tart apple, pared, cored, diced**

1½ **teaspoons salt**

½ **teaspoon freshly ground pepper**

¼ **teaspoon mace**

3 **tablespoons softened butter**

¼ **cup coarse homemade bread crumbs**

1 **tablespoon chilled butter**

1. Mix cream and eggs in small bowl until well blended. Remove leafy tops from fennel bulb and reserve for garnish. Chop fennel stalks and bulb.

2. Put chopped fennel, potatoes, celery root and apple in large dutch oven. Add water to cover; heat to boil over high heat. Reduce heat; simmer until vegetables are fork-tender, 45 minutes to 1 hour.

3. Drain vegetables well. Return vegetables to dutch oven. Mash vegetables over medium heat until smooth. Make a well in center of mashed vegetables. Pour the egg mixture into well, then mash again, incorporating the egg mixture into the vegetables until light and fluffy. Add salt, pepper and mace.

4. Use 3 tablespoons butter to coat the inside of 2-quart baking dish. Add mashed vegetables. Sprinkle with bread crumbs. Dot top with 1 tablespoon chilled butter. Dish may be refrigerated, covered, at this point overnight.

5. Heat oven to 375 degrees. Bake, uncovered, until hot throughout and golden brown, 35 to 45 minutes. Serve garnished with leafy fennel tops.

A subtle fennel taste, as well as hearty cheese and bacon, enliven celery root in this easy baked dish.

CELERY ROOT AND FENNEL AU GRATIN

6 servings
Preparation time: 30 minutes
Cooking time: 40 minutes

1 large bulb fresh fennel, about 1 pound, tops removed, bulb sliced

1 small celery root (celeriac), about 1 pound, peeled, sliced

⅓ cup softened butter
Salt, freshly ground pepper to taste

½ cup each: shredded Gruyère or Swiss cheese, freshly grated Parmesan cheese

1 small bunch green onions, chopped

3 slices bacon, cooked, crumbled

1 cup whipping cream

½ cup beef broth

2 tablespoons all-purpose flour

1. Heat oven to 350 degrees. Cook fennel and celery root in boiling water until crisp-tender, 3 to 4 minutes. Drain; rinse under cold water; pat dry.

2. Layer half of the fennel and celery root in 12 by 8-inch baking dish. Dot with half of the butter; sprinkle with salt and pepper. Combine Gruyère and Parmesan cheese. Sprinkle three-quarters of cheese mixture over fennel mixture. Top with three-quarters of onion and bacon. Add remaining fennel, celery root and butter. Sprinkle with remaining cheese, onion and bacon.

3. Mix cream, broth and flour. Pour over mixture. Bake until vegetables are tender and top is golden, 30 to 35 minutes.

VARIATION: For potato and turnip au gratin, substitute 1 pound boiling potatoes, peeled, sliced and 1 pound small white turnips, peeled, sliced for the fennel and the celery root. Parboil potatoes and turnips in boiling water until tender, 5 to 10 minutes. Drain well. Assemble as directed above. Baking time will be about 5 minutes longer.

This brightly colored dish is as healthful as it is beautiful. Be sure that you heat the peanut oil until very hot so that the vegetables fry up to a crisp texture.

VEGETABLE STIR-FRY WITH TOFU AND NUTS

4 servings
Preparation time: 25 minutes
Cooking time: 20 minutes

SAUCE
- ½ **cup dry-roasted, unsalted cashews or peanuts**
- ½ **cup hot water**
- ¼ **cup cider vinegar**
- 2 **tablespoons soy sauce**
- 1 **tablespoon molasses**
- ¼ **teaspoon crushed red pepper flakes**

STIR-FRY MIXTURE
- 1 **package (16 ounces) fresh tofu, drained**
- 1 **small bunch fresh broccoli**
- 2 **ribs celery**
- 1 **red bell pepper, seeded**
- 3 **tablespoons peanut oil, about**
- 1 **red onion, thinly sliced**
- 1 **tablespoon minced fresh ginger**
- 1 **clove garlic, minced**
- ¼ **cup dry-roasted, unsalted cashews or peanuts**
- **Soy sauce to taste**
- ½ **to 1 teaspoon Oriental sesame oil**
- **Cooked rice**
- **Minced fresh cilantro (coriander), for garnish**

1. For sauce, mix all ingredients in blender or food processor; process until smooth. Set aside near cooking area.

2. Pat tofu dry; cut into 1-inch cubes. Lightly peel broccoli stalks. Cut stalks into ¼-inch-thick diagonal slices. Cut flowerets into 1-inch lengths. Cut celery into ¼-inch-thick diagonal slices. Dice red bell pepper.

3. Heat peanut oil in wok or large skillet until very hot but not smoking. Add onion, ginger and garlic. Stir-fry until onions are crisp-tender, 2 to 3 minutes. Add broccoli stalks, celery and red bell pepper; stir-fry until vegetables are crisp-tender, 6 to 8 minutes.

4. Stir in the broccoli flowerets and the sauce; cook and stir until heated through and flowerets are crisp-tender, about 3 minutes.

5. Add tofu cubes and cashews; cook until heated through, 2 to 3 minutes. Add soy sauce to taste and sesame oil. Serve over rice, garnished with minced cilantro.

This chili—a second-helpings-for-everyone favorite in our test kitchen—is so hearty in texture and flavor that you won't miss the meat.

VEGETABLE CHILI WITH RED BEANS

6 to 8 servings
Preparation time: 30 minutes
Soaking time: Overnight
Cooking time: 2 hours

1 **cup dried red kidney beans (see note)**
2 **tablespoons olive oil**
2 **medium onions, chopped**
2 **cloves garlic, minced, about 1 teaspoon**
½ **pound mushrooms, wiped clean, sliced**
1 **can (28 ounces) crushed tomatoes with added puree**
1 **can (15 ounces) tomato sauce**
3 **tablespoons tomato paste**
2 **tablespoons chili powder**
2 **small zucchini, ends removed, sliced**
2 **red bell peppers, seeded, chopped**
1 **or 2 jalapeño peppers, to taste, seeded, chopped**
½ **teaspoon each: salt, freshly ground pepper**
1 **package (10 ounces) each: frozen corn, frozen lima beans**
  Crushed red pepper flakes, optional

1. Put red beans into large bowl. Add cold water to cover. Let soak overnight.

2. The next morning, drain the beans. Put beans into a large pot and add fresh water to cover. Heat to boil; cover and simmer until almost tender, about 1 hour. Drain.

3. Heat olive oil in large dutch oven. Add onions and garlic; cook and stir 1 minute. Add mushrooms and cook until slightly browned. Stir in drained beans, crushed tomatoes, tomato sauce, tomato paste and chili powder; heat to boil.

4. Reduce heat to simmer and add zucchini, red peppers, jalapeño peppers, salt and pepper. Simmer, covered, until vegetables are crisp-tender, about 30 minutes.

5. Stir in corn and lima beans; cook until heated through, 5 to 10 minutes. Taste and adjust seasonings. Serve with crushed red pepper flakes if desired.

NOTE: One can (16 ounces) red kidney beans, drained, can be substituted for the dried beans. Omit steps 1 and 2.

SALADS &
SALAD
DRESSINGS

Salad making, like a good teacher, coaxes creativity out of cooks. With a variety of raw materials available in an array of colors, shapes, textures, tastes and flavors, creating a salad is an easy outlet for the most timid cook.

Salads do not require the patience and precision of a pâtissier or the speed and dexterity of an experienced chef. They are virtually failure-proof and forgiving.

Unlike making a cake or grilling fish, most mistakes can be caught before they happen. A dressing, a bit too tart, can be adjusted. Greens beyond their prime can be combined into the classic, wilted lettuce salad. The ease with which ingredients can be substituted gives cooks plenty of freedom.

Thanks to the ease of international transportation, growing seasons are nearly passé. Cooks in the Midwest can have raspberries in winter and asparagus in December. And thanks to agriculture sleuths, the produce with foreign passports, such as mâche, Belgium endive, radicchio, clementines, are at last being grown in this country.

Today, salad roams the menu. It bows as an appetizer or first course, with the entree, as a palate refresher or even dessert.

But a glance over three decades of recipes from *Chicago Tribune* Food Guide files shows that salad has not always been a victor in culinary liberation.

Back in the fifties, those days of "square meals" and meat-vegetable-starch mentality, salad had a niche. Like the best man in the bridal party, it was the uncontested accompaniment to the main course. And it was usually dressed with creamy neon-bright orange dressing.

Toward the end of the decade, salad went technicolor. It jiggled like a burlesque queen, thanks to fruit-flavored gelatin. It debuted in new shapes, layers and forms. Sweetened mayonnaise bound layers. Cream cheese became mortar in jellied vegetable rings or between layers of drained fruit cocktail.

Then came a French influence. During the sixties and seventies, salad's role broadened. It jockeyed for several positions—as appetizer, first course or after the entree. As standard issue at lunch or brunch, it married quiche as the entree of choice, accompanied by, of course, a glass of white wine.

In the eighties, salads truly emerged as entrees, those hot/cold unions of chilled greens with strips of warm, grilled meat, chicken or fish. Salad became the meal.

So anything goes. It's a salad maker's choice. Those favorites—the Caesar, Waldorf, potato salad, Cobb, curried turkey salad—are served as tradition dictates. Or they appear in updated versions. The most simple assortment of crisp, leafy greens tossed with olive oil and an herb-flavored vinegar stands on its own.

As salads have come of age, so have dressings. An extensive repertoire isn't necessary. Mastering a basic vinaigrette or mayonnaise is all the cook needs to do. Variations evolve with additions of herbs or spices and imagination. Honey and a splash of lemon juice transforms mayonnaise into a dressing for fruit salad. That same base, cut with plain yogurt and flavored with fresh dill, suits grilled salmon as a dip or a sauce.

NOTES

If all greens are not used immediately, store unwashed, in a tightly covered container or plastic bag in the refrigerator. Wash as needed.

In washing greens, cut away any discolored or wilted parts. Wash gently but thoroughly. Pat dry with clean, soft paper towel.

Know the taste of greens and use their flavors as contrasting ingredients. Mix a slightly bitter green such as chicory or curly endive with a leaf lettuce. Offset the bitter taste of escarole or arugula with a milder taste such as romaine.

How much salad should you make? According to food authority, the late James Beard, figure two cups of loosely packed greens per person, or a bit less if the salad contains other ingredients.

In making a large amount of tossed salad, it is best to add dressing at the last minute and only on the greens to be used. Unused greens will maintain freshness and texture longer if stored undressed. Store leftovers in plastic freezer bags in the refrigerator.

If the greens are not as flavorful as they appear, pep them up with a few splashes of fresh lemon juice. Be sure to serve with an assertive dressing.

SALADS & SALAD DRESSINGS

LEAFY SALADS

Autumn salad with goat cheese

Beet and mâche salad with walnuts

Caesar salad

Green bean, radicchio and endive
  salad with thyme vinaigrette

Romaine lettuce with garlic croutons

Romaine salad with Camembert
  dressing

VEGETABLE SALADS

Avocado salad with balsamic
  vinaigrette

Cactus salad with toasted chilies

Chayote with vinaigrette

Sesame broccoli and cauliflower salad

Creamy coleslaw

Cucumber salad with paprika

Cucumber and mint salad

Dilled asparagus vinaigrette

Eggplant and pepper salad

Grilled vegetables with spicy
  bean salad

Herbed hearts of palm salad

Kohlrabi slaw

Korean zucchini salad

Tarragon green bean salad in
  tomato cups

Mushroom and sun-dried tomato
  salad

Red cabbage and noodle slaw

Spicy okra and tomato salad

Original Cobb salad

Tomato, mozzarella and basil salad

POTATO SALADS

Garlic potato salad

French potato salad

Potato salad with baked garlic
  and goat cheese

Potato salad with Polish sausage

Potato salad with red peppers
  and dill

Red jacket picnic salad

Warm German potato salad

SUBSTANTIAL SALADS

Pork salad on red cabbage with
  shallots

Crab salad Louis

Couscous salad

Curried turkey salad

Main-dish bulgur salad

Middle Eastern tabbouleh

Oriental noodle salad

Poached salmon salad with
  mustard dressing

Quick chef's salad

Shrimp and mussel salad with
  cumin vinaigrette

Shrimp and vegetable rice salad

Salad Niçoise

Oriental chicken salad

Cajun chicken salad with honey
  jalapeño dressing

FRUIT SALADS

Blueberry gelatin

Carrot apple salad

Fresh fruit salad with creamy
 yogurt dressing

Layered garden salad with fruit

Simple Waldorf salad

Waldorf salad with curried
 mayonnaise

Tropical fruit salad with
 honey-lime dressing

Curried cabbage and fruit salad

SALAD DRESSINGS

Creamy black peppercorn dressing

Creamy cilantro dressing

Chive vinaigrette

Creole mustard vinaigrette

Oregano dressing

Shallot vinaigrette

Warm bacon and shallot dressing
 with basil shreds

Basic mayonnaise

Herb mayonnaise

■ *Ford Motor Company's loss was the food world's gain when Harlan "Pete" Peterson gave up automotive design in the mid-seventies to pursue his passion, cooking. Today, he owns Tapawingo, a gem of a restaurant in Ellsworth, Michigan. He is that state's unpaid cheerleader for regional ingredients, and he has shared many culinary ideas with* The Tribune *Food Guide. One follows.*

AUTUMN SALAD WITH GOAT CHEESE

6 to 8 servings
Preparation time: 25 minutes

6 **ounces goat cheese, blue-veined preferred**

3 **tablespoons cider vinegar**

1 **tablespoon Dijon mustard**

1 **egg yolk**

⅔ **cup each: olive oil, vegetable oil**

Salt, pepper to taste

1 **head each, rinsed, trimmed: romaine, escarole and frissee or curly endive**

1 **small bulb fresh fennel, cut into julienne strips**

½ **small red cabbage, cut into julienne strips**

2 **tablespoons chopped fresh chives**

1. Put half of the goat cheese, vinegar, mustard and egg yolk in blender or food processor. Process until smooth. With machine running, add oils in slow steady stream. Add salt and pepper. Crumble remaining cheese and reserve to sprinkle over salads.

2. Prepare the greens, fennel and cabbage. (Recipe may be prepared ahead to this point.)

3. Mix greens, fennel and cabbage in large bowl. Add a generous amount of dressing and toss to mix.

4. Arrange portions on plates. Sprinkle with crumbled goat cheese and chives before serving.

NOTE: Remaining dressing may be refrigerated up to several days.

Fresh beets are cooked most easily by baking, skins on, says New York cooking teacher Peter Kump. Cook the beets just as you would a potato, until tender. If the grocer is out of Belgian endive, or price strikes it from the budget, substitute with romaine.

BEET AND MÂCHE SALAD WITH WALNUTS

4 servings
Preparation time: 20 minutes
Cooking time: 10 minutes

½ cup walnut halves

VINAIGRETTE

1½ tablespoons red wine vinegar

1 teaspoon Dijon mustard

¼ teaspoon freshly ground pepper

5 tablespoons safflower oil (1 to 2 tablespoons may be walnut oil)

2 large heads Belgian endive, about ½ pound

4 to 6 bunches mâche (lamb's lettuce), about ¼ pound

2 cooked beets, peeled, finely diced

1. Heat oven to 350 degrees. Put walnuts on baking sheet. Bake until toasted, being careful not to burn them, about 10 minutes. They should have a nice aroma when ready.

2. Mix vinegar, mustard and pepper in small bowl. Whisk in oil in slow, steady stream until smooth.

3. Wipe endive and pull off larger outside leaves for garnish. Cut the smaller ones on the diagonal into ¾-inch-wide slices.

4. Rinse mâche well to remove any sand, cut off roots and separate the leaves. Toss with endive slices.

5. Just before serving, place whole endive leaves on serving plate with tips pointing out. Toss lettuces with beets and put in the middle of plate. Garnish with toasted walnuts and serve with vinaigrette.

More interesting than arguing over the origin of Caesar salad—that controversial dish of romaine, garlic, egg, croutons, lemon, olive oil and Parmesan cheese—is tossing one for friends. Leave the anchovies out if you must, or add them according to taste as did Caesar Cardini, a Mexican restaurant owner and alleged creator of the salad back in the 1920s.

CAESAR SALAD

4 servings
Preparation time: 20 minutes
Chilling time: 30 minutes
Cooking time: 5 minutes

1 **large head romaine lettuce**
Olive oil
3 **cloves garlic, peeled, halved**
3 **cups French bread cubes**
Salt to taste
4 **anchovy fillets, minced**
1 **large egg (see note)**
Juice of 1 small lemon
¼ **cup olive oil**
⅓ **cup freshly grated imported Parmesan cheese**
Freshly ground pepper to taste
6 **anchovy fillets for garnish**

1. Rinse lettuce leaves under cold running water. Break leaves into bite-size pieces, removing and discarding thick ribs. Wrap leaves, with water that clings to leaves, in paper towel. Put into plastic bag. Refrigerate to crisp, about 30 minutes or longer.

2. For croutons, pour thin layer of olive oil over bottom of 10-inch skillet. Heat oil until hot but not smoking. Add 2 of the halved garlic cloves; cook 1 minute. Add bread cubes in single layer. Toss well. Cook, tossing cubes occasionally, until lightly toasted on all sides. Remove garlic if it begins to burn. Transfer croutons to paper towels. Sprinkle lightly with salt.

3. Use remaining garlic to rub over insides of large salad bowl. Put minced anchovies, egg and lemon juice into bottom of the salad bowl. Beat vigorously with a fork until well blended. Gradually stir in ¼ cup olive oil.

4. Add lettuce leaves, Parmesan cheese and pepper. Toss to mix. Sprinkle with croutons. Arrange anchovy fillets over top. Serve immediately.

NOTE: If desired, egg may be simmered in the shell in boiling water for 1 minute before using.

Salads & Salad Dressings

■ *Paul A. Camp, a* Tribune *editor, kicked off summer with a discourse on salad. "If there is a trick to great salad making," he wrote in the* Sunday *magazine in June 1984, "it is creating tension among the ingredients." In this recipe the slight bitterness of Belgian endive is contrasted against the mildness of French green beans. The salad dressing plays mediator.*

GREEN BEAN, RADICCHIO AND ENDIVE SALAD WITH THYME VINAIGRETTE

4 servings
Preparation time: 25 minutes
Cooking time: 3 minutes

2 **heads each: radicchio (Italian red chicory), Belgian endive, Bibb lettuce**

1 **cup French green beans or small green beans, halved lengthwise**

⅓ **cup extra-virgin olive oil**

3 **tablespoons red wine shallot vinegar, or substitute 3 tablespoons red wine vinegar and 1 teaspoon minced fresh shallots**

3 **tablespoons minced fresh thyme or 2 teaspoons dried**

Salt, freshly ground pepper to taste

1. Rinse radicchio, endive and lettuce under cold water. Separate leaves and remove tough veins. Tear into bite-size pieces. Wrap in paper towels; put into plastic bag. Refrigerate until crisp, 10 to 20 minutes.

2. Meanwhile, drop green beans into boiling water. Boil, uncovered, until crisp-tender, 2 to 3 minutes. Drain; rinse under cold water to stop cooking.

3. Mix oil, vinegar, thyme, salt and pepper in jar with tight-fitting lid. Shake well. Taste and adjust seasonings.

4. To serve, arrange greens on large serving platter. Sprinkle with green beans. Drizzle with dressing. Toss to coat. Serve immediately.

Garlic is sensitive to heat. It burns easily and imparts a bitter taste. When preparing these croutons, keep an eye on the cloves and cook over medium heat. Patience pays off.

ROMAINE LETTUCE WITH GARLIC CROUTONS

4 servings
Preparation time: 10 minutes
Cooking time: 4 minutes

3 **very thin slices white bread**

¼ **cup plus 3 tablespoons olive oil**

2 **small cloves garlic, peeled**

2 **teaspoons each: Dijon mustard, red wine vinegar**

Salt, freshly ground pepper to taste

1 **head romaine lettuce, rinsed, torn into bite-size pieces**

1. Trim away bread crusts. Cut slices into ½-inch cubes. Heat 3 tablespoons of the oil in large skillet; add garlic and bread cubes. Cook and stir until bread is golden on all sides, 3 to 4 minutes. Discard garlic.

2. Put mustard, vinegar, salt and pepper into bottom of large serving bowl. Whisk in remaining ¼ cup oil in very slow, steady stream until smooth.

3. Add lettuce; toss to coat with dressing. Sprinkle with croutons. Serve immediately.

Apples, cheese and nuts work well as dessert. This salad takes that union a step further. If the dressing is too rich or thick for your taste, cut it with buttermilk or plain yogurt. It keeps well in the refrigerator for about a week.

ROMAINE SALAD WITH CAMEMBERT DRESSING

6 servings
Preparation time: 15 minutes

1 **head romaine lettuce, rinsed, torn into bite-size pieces**

1 **red apple, cored, thinly sliced**

½ **cup each: sliced mushrooms, chopped walnuts**

3 **ounces soft-ripened Camembert cheese, at room temperature, rind removed**

1 **teaspoon Dijon mustard**

2 **tablespoons sherry wine vinegar**

⅓ **cup vegetable oil Salt, freshly ground pepper to taste**

1. Mix lettuce, apple, mushrooms and walnuts in large serving bowl.

2. Beat cheese and mustard to smooth paste; gradually beat in vinegar; gradually beat in oil, salt and pepper. Mix before serving. Pass with salad.

NOTE: If dressing is prepared in advance, bring to room temperature before serving.

Having the proper ingredients is key to the success of this salad. Avocados, perfectly ripe, are crucial. So is balsamic vinegar. Not only does its flavor tie the ingredients of this salad together, it prevents the salad from tasting overly sweet. Tart but with no hint of sharpness, balsamic vinegar works with the subtle avocado taste to make a simple salad spectacular.

AVOCADO SALAD WITH BALSAMIC VINAIGRETTE

4 servings
Preparation time: 25 minutes

3 small fresh beets
1 cup fresh, shelled peas
VINAIGRETTE
⅓ cup balsamic vinegar
3 tablespoons minced fresh chervil or flat-leaf parsley
2 tablespoons each: peanut oil, olive oil
2 tablespoons minced shallot or green onion
Pinch each: minced fresh garlic, cayenne pepper
Salt, freshly ground black pepper to taste
SALAD
1 medium cucumber, peeled
1 bunch red leaf lettuce, rinsed
2 ripe avocados
Juice of ½ lemon
1 bunch watercress, rinsed, trimmed

1. Cook beets in boiling water until crisp-tender, about 15 minutes. Drain; rinse under cold water. Peel. Cut into thin slices. Drop peas into boiling water just until bright green and crisp-tender, 2 to 3 minutes. Drain; rinse under cold water.

2. For vinaigrette, mix all ingredients in jar with tight-fitting lid. Toss the sliced beets with some of the vinaigrette. Toss peas with some of the vinaigrette.

3. Cut cucumber lengthwise in half. Scoop out seeds. Cut into ¼-inch slices. Toss cucumber slices with some of the vinaigrette.

4. Cut lettuce leaves into thin shreds. Cut avocados in half. Remove seed. Peel. Cut into thin slices. Sprinkle with lemon juice.

5. Arrange lettuce on serving plates. Arrange avocado slices near lettuce. Arrange cucumber, peas and beets around avocado. Garnish with watercress. Sprinkle with some of the remaining vinaigrette and serve.

Flavor explodes in this recipe with fresh cilantro, garlic, onion and cheese. The cactus leaves play a supporting role to those assertive tastes. If cactus is unavailable you may substitute fresh green beans but shorten the cooking time slightly. If you like aromatic firecrackers, include the chilies pasilla. They require toasting to bring out their flavor. But the time spent is worth the effort.

CACTUS SALAD WITH TOASTED CHILIES

6 to 8 servings
Preparation time: 20 minutes
Cooking time: 30 minutes

1½ **pounds fresh cactus leaves (nopales) (see note)**
2 **tablespoons butter**
1 **tablespoon olive oil**
2 **large white onions, halved, sliced**
2 **cloves garlic, minced**
¾ **cup canned chicken broth**
   Salt, freshly ground pepper to taste
⅔ **cup loosely packed fresh cilantro (coriander), chopped**
½ **cup freshly grated asiago or Parmesan cheese**
2 **chilies pasilla, toasted, optional (see note)**

1. Using a small paring knife or vegetable peeler, carefully remove the "eyes" (where the thorns were) on the cactus leaves. Cut leaves into ½-inch-wide strips.

2. Heat butter and oil in large skillet until hot. Add onions and garlic; sauté for 2 minutes. Add cactus leaves. Sauté over high heat for 5 minutes. Stir in chicken broth. Heat to boil; reduce heat. Simmer, covered, until leaves are crisp-tender, about 15 minutes.

3. Uncover and simmer until broth is almost evaporated, about 5 minutes. Remove from heat. Stir in salt, pepper and half of the cilantro. Transfer to a serving platter. Sprinkle with remaining cilantro and the cheese. Crumble and sprinkle the toasted chilies over all. Serve warm or at room temperature.

NOTE: Fresh cactus leaves are available at large supermarkets and Mexican groceries. Chilies pasilla are long, dark, dried chilies. To toast, wipe clean with dry cloth, put whole chilies into a hot, dry, heavy skillet. Cook, turning often, until chilies darken and become aromatic, about 3 to 5 minutes. Remove from heat and cool. Chilies will be brittle when cooled.

Chayote squash has the size and shape of an avocado but the creamy pale green skin of a summer squash. A vegetable with Caribbean roots, it can be used in recipes calling for summer squash or zucchini. Like most squash, it is a candidate for marinating because it picks up assertive flavors.

CHAYOTE WITH VINAIGRETTE

8 servings
Preparation time: 15 minutes
Cooking time: 14 minutes
Chilling time: Overnight

4 chayote squash (mirliton)

1 cup fresh or frozen corn kernels

½ cup each: chopped red bell pepper, chopped green pepper, sliced green onions

¼ cup minced fresh cilantro (coriander)

½ cup olive oil

¼ cup each: vegetable oil, distilled white vinegar

¼ teaspoon each: salt, freshly ground pepper

1. Cut chayote lengthwise into quarters. Cook in lightly salted water until tender, about 12 minutes. Drain; rinse under cold water to stop the cooking.

2. Cut each chayote quarter crosswise into slices. Put into large bowl. Add corn, red pepper, green pepper, onions and cilantro; toss to mix.

3. Mix oils, vinegar, salt and pepper in jar with tight-fitting lid. Shake well. Pour over chayote mixture; toss to mix. Refrigerate, covered, at least 6 hours or overnight.

■ *Reserve some of the sesame seeds to sprinkle over this salad before serving. Be stingy when measuring the sesame oil. It has a powerful flavor and a little goes a long way.*

SESAME BROCCOLI AND CAULIFLOWER SALAD

4 servings
Preparation time: 20 minutes
Cooking time: 10 minutes

1 **pound broccoli, cut into 2-inch pieces**
1 **pound cauliflower, separated in flowerets**
¼ **cup each: chopped green onions, soy sauce**
1 **tablespoon each: toasted sesame seeds, Oriental sesame oil**
1½ **teaspoons honey**
¼ **teaspoon chili oil or pinch cayenne pepper**
Salt to taste
Lettuce leaves
Tomato wedges

1. Cook broccoli and cauliflower separately in boiling water until crisp-tender, about 10 minutes. Rinse under cold water to stop the cooking; drain well. Refrigerate.

2. Mix green onions, soy sauce, sesame seeds, sesame oil, honey, chili oil and salt. Taste and adjust seasonings. Toss with broccoli and cauliflower. Serve on lettuce leaves. Garnish with tomato wedges.

Chicago cook Kay Keehn takes great pains to make her coleslaw tender and creamy. She removes all the tough white veins from the cabbage and uses only the tenderest pale green portions. Nothing is wasted, however, because she uses the white veins when she makes stuffed cabbage or soup. The addition of vinegar to the coleslaw helps wilt the cabbage slightly.

CREAMY COLESLAW

10 servings
Preparation time: 30 minutes
Chilling time: 1 hour

2 **medium heads cabbage, about 1½ pounds each**
1 **small onion, minced**
1 **small carrot, finely diced**
1 **tablespoon water**
2 **teaspoons white distilled vinegar**
1 **teaspoon salt or to taste**
  Freshly ground pepper to taste
1 **cup mayonnaise, about**

1. Cut cabbage into quarters. Remove core. Cut away all of the thickest white veins; use only tender green parts for coleslaw. Cut cabbage into very fine shreds on German cabbage cutter or by hand with a sharp knife.

2. Mix cabbage and remaining ingredients except mayonnaise in large bowl. Add 1 cup mayonnaise; toss to mix well. Add additional mayonnaise to make a creamy mixture but not saturated. Refrigerate, covered, about 1 hour.

This spicy cucumber salad comes from Mary Kaiser, grandmother of JeanMarie Brownson, The Tribune Test Kitchen director, who inherited her cooking skills from a family of talented cooks.

CUCUMBER SALAD WITH PAPRIKA
(Umorkasalat)

8 to 10 servings
Preparation time: 20 minutes
Standing time: 1 hour
Chilling time: 2 hours

3   **large cucumbers**
2   **cloves garlic, crushed in garlic press**
2   **tablespoons salt**
2   **tablespoons white distilled vinegar**
1   **teaspoon imported sweet paprika**
⅛   **teaspoon each: ground allspice, freshly ground black pepper or to taste**
1½ **cups sour cream**

1. Peel cucumbers. Slice very thinly. Put into large bowl; add garlic and salt; toss to coat. Let stand 1 to 2 hours to draw the water from the cucumbers.

2. Squeeze out as much liquid as you can from the cucumbers. Put into clean bowl. Stir in vinegar, paprika, allspice and pepper. Toss to mix. Add sour cream; stir until salad is smooth and creamy and cucumbers are well coated. Refrigerate, covered, until cold. Taste and adjust seasonings.

Indian cuisine takes advantage of the cooling tastes of yogurt and cucumbers. They are served under various forms as condiments to meals. This recipe unites the two. Serve it as a refresher with spicy foods.

CUCUMBER AND MINT SALAD

4 servings
Preparation time: 20 minutes

1   **medium cucumber**
    Salt to taste
¾   **cup plain yogurt**
¼   **cup sour cream**
1   **teaspoon minced fresh mint**
⅛   **teaspoon cayenne pepper**
    Freshly ground black pepper
    Fresh mint leaves

1. Peel strips of cucumber skin lengthwise at ½-inch intervals. Cut cucumber lengthwise in half; scoop out seeds. Slice crosswise into ⅛-inch-thick crescents. Sprinkle with salt; drain on paper towel 15 minutes.

2. Meanwhile, mix yogurt, sour cream, minced mint, cayenne and black pepper in medium bowl. Stir in cucumber. Garnish with mint leaves.

When buying asparagus look for straight, bright green stalks of uniform size with tight tips and moist bases. When properly cooked, the color will remain bright green and the stalks firm. Allow about half a pound (8 to 10 stalks) per person.

DILLED ASPARAGUS VINAIGRETTE

6 servings
Preparation time: 15 minutes
Cooking time: 4 minutes
Marinating time: 1 hour

3 pounds fresh asparagus

DRESSING
1 cup olive or vegetable oil
6 tablespoons fresh lemon juice
¾ teaspoon salt, or to taste
¼ teaspoon each: dry mustard, freshly ground white pepper

¼ cup minced shallots
5 tablespoons minced fresh dill or 2 teaspoons dried dill weed
3 tablespoons each: minced fresh parsley, freshly grated lemon rind

1. Snap off tough ends of asparagus. Lightly peel stalks. Cook asparagus spears in simmering water in large skillet until crisp-tender, 4 to 6 minutes. Drain thoroughly.

2. Meanwhile, mix oil, lemon juice, salt, mustard and pepper in jar with tight-fitting lid; shake well to blend.

3. Put drained asparagus in shallow serving dish. While still warm, sprinkle shallots, dill, parsley and lemon rind over asparagus. Drizzle with dressing. Toss gently; season to taste with additional salt and pepper, if needed.

4. Cover; let stand 1 hour. Serve asparagus at room temperature or chilled, as desired.

Sautéed eggplant, peppers, garlic and tomatoes meld together into a Mediterranean salad that is delicious served at room temperature or chilled.

EGGPLANT AND PEPPER SALAD

6 servings
Preparation time: 10 minutes
Standing time: 30 minutes
Cooking time: 8 minutes

1 **pound eggplant or zucchini, cubed**
Salt to taste
3 **tablespoons olive oil**
2 **cloves garlic, minced**
1 **each, seeded, sliced: red bell pepper, green pepper**
2 **tomatoes, peeled, seeded, chopped**
1 **teaspoon paprika**
½ **teaspoon each: ground coriander seed, ground cumin**
Fresh lemon juice, to taste
Black olives, lemon wedges for garnish

1. Sprinkle eggplant cubes with salt. Drain on paper towel 30 minutes. Pat dry.

2. Heat oil in large skillet; add garlic. Cook and stir until soft but not browned, about 2 minutes. Stir in eggplant; cook and stir until golden on all sides. Stir in peppers, tomatoes, paprika, coriander and cumin. Cook and stir until vegetables are tender, about 5 minutes. Cool.

3. Stir in lemon juice. Taste and adjust seasonings. Serve at room temperature. Garnish with black olives and lemon wedges.

Key to the success of this vegetable plate is vigilance. Don't overcook the vegetables because preserving the texture of each type contributes to the interesting texture. Gear cooking time according to the thickness or thinness of each piece. For an added garnish, sprinkle with fresh, chopped cilantro.

GRILLED VEGETABLES WITH SPICY BEAN SALAD

8 servings
Preparation time: 30 minutes
Cooking time: 15 minutes

BEAN SALAD

- 2 cans (15 ounces each) great northern beans
- 1 pint cherry tomatoes, hulled, halved
- 1 jar (12 ounces) mild salsa
- ¼ cup minced fresh cilantro (coriander)
- 1 small jalapeño pepper, seeded, minced, optional

    Salt, freshly ground black pepper to taste

GRILLED VEGETABLES

- 2 medium each: red, yellow and green bell peppers
- 2 medium eggplants
- 4 each: yellow squash, zucchini

    Extra-virgin olive oil

    Lettuce leaves

1. For bean salad, drain and rinse beans. Put into large bowl. Stir in cherry tomatoes, salsa, cilantro and jalapeño. Add salt and pepper. Mix well and refrigerate at least 1 hour. Let stand at room temperature for 30 minutes before serving.

2. Prepare charcoal grill or preheat broiler. Put peppers onto grill and cook, turning until skin is golden brown and flesh is crisp-tender, 10 to 15 minutes.

3. Meanwhile, cut eggplant into 1-inch-thick slices. Cut yellow squash and zucchini lengthwise in half. Put eggplant slices, squash and zucchini onto grill. Cook, turning once and brushing with olive oil until golden and crisp-tender, about 10 minutes.

4. Remove seeds and cores from peppers and cut into quarters. Put lettuce leaves onto center of large serving platter. Fill leaves with the bean salad. Arrange grilled vegetables around the bean salad. Drizzle vegetables with olive oil. Sprinkle with salt and pepper. Serve at room temperature.

■ *This is an interesting salad because it mixes some unusual ingredients, such as hearts of palm, fresh bean sprouts and artichoke hearts, in the same bowl. If you don't have time to make dressing, use a commercially prepared ranch or creamy Italian one spiked with some fresh lemon juice.*

HERBED HEARTS OF PALM SALAD

6 to 8 servings
Preparation time: 15 minutes
Chilling time: 1 hour

1 **pound fresh bean sprouts, rinsed**

1 **can (8 ounces) water chestnuts, drained, thinly sliced**

1 **can (14 ounces) hearts of palm, drained, cut into ½-inch-thick slices**

1 **can (8 ounces) artichoke hearts, drained, halved**

1 **cup mayonnaise**

3 **tablespoons vinegar**

2 **tablespoons Dijon mustard**

1½ **teaspoon dried marjoram**

1 **teaspoon chili powder**

½ **teaspoon each: salt, cayenne pepper**

1 **clove garlic, minced**

⅛ **teaspoon freshly ground pepper**

2 **small heads Boston lettuce, rinsed**

1. Mix bean sprouts, water chestnuts, hearts of palm and artichoke hearts in large bowl. Mix remaining ingredients, except lettuce, in small bowl. Stir into vegetable mixture. Toss to coat. Refrigerate covered at least 1 hour. Serve on lettuce leaves.

Cabbage's cousin, kohlrabi, could double for a pale green turnip in the looks department. What sets it apart, however, is a unique nut-like flavor. This recipe is a variation on carrot slaw but with a Middle Eastern taste from ground cumin.

KOHLRABI SLAW

4 servings
Preparation time: 25 minutes
Cooking time: 2 minutes
Chilling time: 2 hours

3 **large kohlrabi, peeled**
2 **large carrots, peeled**
1 **egg, slightly beaten**
2 **tablespoons white**
   wine vinegar
⅓ **cup vegetable oil**
½ **cup plain yogurt**
½ **teaspoon ground cumin**
⅛ **teaspoon cayenne**
   pepper
   Salt, freshly ground
   pepper to taste
½ **cup diced green onions**

1. Cut kohlrabi and carrots into julienne strips about 2 inches by ¼ inch. Drop into boiling water; cook until crisp-tender, about 2 minutes. Drain; rinse under cold water until cool. Pat dry.

2. Beat egg and vinegar in medium bowl until smooth. Gradually whisk in oil in slow, steady stream until thick and smooth. Whisk in yogurt, cumin, cayenne, salt and pepper. Taste and adjust seasonings. Add kohlrabi, carrots and onions. Toss to coat. Refrigerate, covered, 2 hours.

Zucchini, by nature, holds quite a bit of water. That is why many recipes calling for the vegetable require the cook to pat slices dry with paper toweling. In this recipe the towel absorbs extra moisture which would otherwise dilute the strength of the dressing.

KOREAN ZUCCHINI SALAD

10 to 12 servings
Preparation time: 25 minutes
Cooking time: 10 minutes

5 **pounds zucchini**
   (about 8 medium)
4 **carrots, peeled, diced**
8 **green onions, diced**
¼ **cup soy sauce**
2 **tablespoons each:**
   Oriental sesame oil,
   rice vinegar
1 **tablespoon sugar**

1. Drop whole zucchini into large pot of boiling water. Boil until crisp-tender and bright green, about 5 minutes for small zucchini and 10 minutes for large ones. Drain; cool.

2. Cut zucchini crosswise in half. Cut each half into thin lengthwise slices. Pat slices dry with paper towel. Mix remaining ingredients in large bowl. Add zucchini slices. Toss to mix well.

3. Let stand, covered, at room temperature for 1 to 2 hours. Or refrigerate covered, up to several hours. Stir occasionally.

■ *This is the quintessential summer salad: crisp green beans, fresh tarragon and fresh chives, all served in a garden-ripe tomato shell.*

TARRAGON GREEN BEAN SALAD IN TOMATO CUPS

4 servings
Preparation time: 30 minutes
Marinating time: 1 to 2 hours

1½ **pounds fresh green beans**

3 **tablespoons white wine tarragon vinegar**

2 **teaspoons Dijon mustard**

2 **tablespoons each: vegetable oil, olive oil**

1 **tablespoon minced fresh chives**

½ **teaspoon minced fresh tarragon or ¼ teaspoon dried**

¼ **teaspoon each: salt, freshly ground pepper**

1 **small red bell pepper, cored, diced**

4 **small tomatoes**

1. Trim ends from beans. Cut into 1-inch pieces. Cook in a large amount of boiling water until bright green and crisp-tender, about 8 minutes. Drain; rinse under cold water to stop cooking.

2. Mix vinegar and mustard in bottom of large bowl. Stir in oils, chives, tarragon, salt and pepper. Add beans and red bell pepper. Marinate about 1 hour at room temperature.

3. To serve, cut off tops of tomatoes. Hollow out centers, leaving shells. (Reserve centers for soups or stock.) Serve bean mixture in tomato shells.

■ *Bless the microwave for getting the cook out of the kitchen fast. In this recipe the microwave is relied on for softening the mushrooms, onions and sun-dried tomatoes. Roasted peppers, an apt substitute for the sun-dried tomatoes, will impart a slightly smoky, nutty flavor.*

MUSHROOM AND SUN-DRIED TOMATO SALAD

4 servings
Preparation time: 15 minutes
Microwave cooking time: 8 minutes
Chilling time: 2 hours

1 **pound fresh mushrooms, wiped clean, quartered**
1 **small onion, chopped**
1 **tablespoon olive oil (or oil from bottle of sun-dried tomatoes)**
1 **small jalapeño pepper, seeded, minced**
2 **small cloves garlic, minced**
½ **cup minced, bottled sun-dried tomatoes (roasted red peppers may be substituted)**
2 **green onions, white and first 2 inches of green, chopped**
2 **tablespoons chopped fresh parsley**

1. Put mushrooms, onion, oil, jalapeño and garlic in 2-quart microwave-safe casserole. Do not cover. Microwave on high (100 percent power), stirring twice, until mushrooms are crisp-tender, about 6 minutes.

2. Stir in sun-dried tomatoes. Microwave on high 2 minutes. Cover and refrigerate at least 2 hours. Stir in green onions. Sprinkle with parsley.

When Tribune *writer Patricia Tennison wrote about the newfound interest in cabbage in 1987, the test kitchen created several recipes that raised the vegetable from humble origins (corned beef's time-honored partner) to the realm of trendy and versatile. In this recipe, cabbage finds a niche with pasta and apples.*

RED CABBAGE AND NOODLE SLAW

6 to 8 servings
Preparation time: 25 minutes
Standing time: 20 minutes

1 **small head red cabbage, shredded, about 3½ cups**
8 **ounces shell-shaped noodles, cooked, drained**
2 **ribs celery, diced**
5 **green onions, sliced**
1 **large tart apple, peeled, cored, diced**

DRESSING
1 **cup each: plain yogurt, mayonnaise**
2 **tablespoons fresh lemon juice**
½ **teaspoon each: salt, freshly ground pepper**

1. Mix cabbage, noodles, celery, onions and apple in large bowl.

2. For dressing, mix all ingredients until smooth. Spoon over cabbage mixture. Mix well. Let stand 20 minutes before serving.

NOTE: Two cans (7 ounces each) water-packed tuna, well drained and flaked, can be added if you wish.

Okra is a love/hate affair. Some diners love the delicate flavor similar to a mildly acidic eggplant. Others abhor the slimy texture. Our thanks to Chicagoan Roger Brown, for this recipe which highlights one of okra's selling points, crispness. When shopping for okra, look for shiny, small, crisp green pods.

SPICY OKRA AND TOMATO SALAD

4 to 6 servings
Preparation time: 25 minutes
Cooking time: 5 minutes

1 **pound fresh okra, sliced**

Lettuce leaves

2 **tomatoes, sliced**

Chili powder

2 **hard-cooked eggs, chopped**

3 **green onions, minced**

2 **tablespoons chopped fresh parsley**

DRESSING

1 **cup olive oil**

½ **cup red wine vinegar**

2 **teaspoons Dijon mustard**

1 **teaspoon each: freshly ground black pepper, paprika, sugar**

½ **teaspoon salt**

¼ **teaspoon cayenne pepper**

3 **dashes Worcestershire sauce**

1. Steam sliced okra over boiling water until bright green and crisp-tender, 3 to 5 minutes. Drain well.

2. Make a bed of lettuce leaves on large serving plate. Top with tomato slices, then the okra. Sprinkle with chili powder. Top with hard-cooked eggs, green onions and parsley.

3. For dressing, mix all ingredients in jar with tight-fitting lid. Shake well. Drizzle dressing over salad. Serve.

Cobb salad brings out the artist in the cook, says food write Marcy Goldman-Posluns. If care is given in how the strips of chicken, the rows of cheese and avocado are arranged, it is truly a visual feast befitting one of your best glass serving bowls. An advantage of poaching, rather than baking chicken, is preserving its moisture. Skin and bones are easier to remove if the chicken is still warm.

ORIGINAL COBB SALAD

6 to 8 servings
Preparation time: 30 minutes

VINAIGRETTE

⅓ cup white wine vinegar

¼ cup olive oil

1 small clove garlic, crushed

1 teaspoon each: fresh lemon juice, Dijon mustard

½ teaspoon salt

¼ teaspoon each: basil, freshly ground pepper

SALAD

½ head iceberg lettuce

1 small head curly endive

1 small bunch watercress

2 medium tomatoes, peeled, seeded, diced

Salt, freshly ground pepper to taste

3 hard-cooked eggs, coarsely chopped

6 slices bacon, cooked, drained, crumbled

1 whole chicken breast, poached, skinned, boned, diced (see note)

2 green onions, chopped

1 teaspoon minced yellow onion

3 ounces blue cheese, crumbled

1 large avocado, peeled, cut into ½-inch dice, tossed with juice of ½ fresh lemon

1 small Belgian endive, separated into spears

1. For vinaigrette, mix all ingredients in jar with tight-fitting lid. Shake well to blend.

2. To assemble salad, prepare iceberg lettuce and curly endive by shredding with a knife and then cutting crosswise. Put in bottom of large glass serving dish. Add watercress and toss.

3. Arrange tomatoes, seasoned with salt and pepper, in two rows at either side of the salad bowl. Working toward the center, make two similar rows of chopped eggs, then two of crumbled bacon.

4. Make two rows of diced chicken over greens, inside the rows of bacon. Mix green onions and yellow onion and sprinkle over chicken. Make two rows of the blue cheese and finally a center row of avocado slices. Salad may be chilled up to 2 hours before serving.

5. To serve, drizzle vinaigrette over the salad and gently toss to combine. Serve on glass plates and garnish with an endive leaf.

NOTE: To poach chicken, heat a pot of salted water to a boil. Drop in chicken and reduce heat to a simmer. Cover, and let chicken poach until juices no longer run clear, 15 to 20 minutes. Chicken should be tender but thoroughly cooked. Remove and drain. Refrigerate.

Italy springs to mind with this salad—a standard issue on many Italian menus. To capture the genuine flavor, buy a top-quality grade of mozzarella and stick with fresh basil, not dried. Toasting the pine nuts enhances their flavor.

TOMATO, MOZZARELLA AND BASIL SALAD

4 servings
Preparation time: 15 minutes
Marinating time: 3 hours

4 **large tomatoes, cored, thinly sliced**
  Salt, freshly ground pepper to taste
¼ **cup extra-virgin olive oil**
2 **tablespoons white wine vinegar**
½ **pound soft mozzarella cheese, thinly sliced**
1 **cup fresh basil leaves, chopped**
¼ **cup pine nuts**

1. Put tomato slices on serving platter. Sprinkle with salt and pepper. Drizzle with some of the oil and vinegar.

2. Top with cheese slices. Sprinkle basil and pine nuts over all. Sprinkle again with salt, pepper, oil and vinegar. Serve at room temperature.

The heady flavor of garlic reigns in this potato salad from Chicago's Cafe Ba-Ba-Reeba! Four cloves are used in the dressing. Be sure to eat it with very close friends or alone. The richness of mayonnaise can be cut, if desired, by adding a few dollops of plain yogurt.

GARLIC POTATO SALAD

4 servings
Preparation time: 20 minutes
Cooking time: 20 minutes
Standing time: 1 hour

15 **small red potatoes**
 1 **cup mayonnaise**
¼ **cup minced fresh parsley**
 4 **cloves garlic, minced**
½ **teaspoon salt**
  Freshly ground white pepper

1. Boil potatoes in water to cover until tender but not mushy, 10 to 20 minutes. Drain; cool. Peel potatoes. Cut in half.

2. Mix remaining ingredients in large bowl. Add potatoes; toss gently. Refrigerate 1 hour before serving.

Potato salad with a red wine/mustard vinaigrette is simplicity itself. For the best flavor, use a top-quality olive oil and cook the potatoes only until just tender. That way, they will keep their texture after being mixed with the acidic dressing. This recipe comes from Carol Segal, co-owner of Chicago-based Crate & Barrel stores.

FRENCH POTATO SALAD

6 to 8 servings
Preparation time: 30 minutes
Cooking time: 20 minutes
Chilling time: 2 to 3 hours

3 pounds red potatoes
⅓ cup dry white wine
1 small red bell pepper, seeded, diced

VINAIGRETTE
3 tablespoons red wine vinegar
2 tablespoons Dijon mustard
¾ teaspoon salt
½ teaspoon freshly ground pepper
½ cup olive oil

3 medium shallots, minced
Chopped fresh parsley for garnish

1. Boil potatoes in salted water until just tender, 15 to 20 minutes. Drain and cool until slightly warm.

2. Peel and cube potatoes. Toss the warm potatoes with white wine. Add red bell pepper.

3. Whisk together vinegar, mustard, salt and pepper in medium bowl until blended. Gradually whisk in olive oil to make a thick vinaigrette.

4. Pour dressing over salad. Add the shallots and toss well. Chill 2 to 3 hours. Garnish with parsley before serving.

■ *Garlic, when baked, loses some of its harshness and takes on a slight sweetness. When combined with goat cheese and served with potato salad on the side, it creates a rich-tasting pairing. Our thanks to Jennifer Newbury, co-owner of Chez Jenny and Sole Mio restaurants, for such a heady union.*

POTATO SALAD WITH BAKED GARLIC AND GOAT CHEESE

4 appetizer servings
Preparation time: 45 minutes
Cooking time: 2 hours

WHOLE BAKED GARLIC

- **4 whole heads garlic**
- **8 tablespoons olive oil**
- **4 tablespoons butter**
  - **Pinch each: minced fresh thyme, salt, freshly ground pepper**

POTATO SALAD

- **¾ pound new red potatoes**
- **1 tablespoon balsamic vinegar**
- **1 small leek, sliced paper thin, about ½ cup**
- **⅛ teaspoon each: salt, freshly ground pepper**
  - **Toasted, sliced French bread**
- **6 ounces mild goat cheese, sliced**

1. Heat oven to 275 degrees. For whole baked garlic, using a small knife, cut through outside skin on garlic, going around the diameter. Try not to puncture cloves. Peel outside skin away so that top half of garlic is exposed. Do not peel individual cloves.

2. Put garlic into small baking dish; put 2 tablespoons olive oil on each head. Put 1 tablespoon of butter on top of each garlic. Sprinkle with thyme, salt and pepper. Cover tightly with foil and bake for 20 minutes.

3. Remove foil and baste garlic well with oil and butter in the bottom of the pan. Continue baking, uncovered, basting every 10 minutes, until soft, about 1½ hours.

4. For potato salad, cook potatoes in boiling water until tender but still firm, about 15 minutes. Drain. Allow to cool until just slightly warm.

5. Cut potatoes into ½-inch cubes and toss with 3 to 4 tablespoons oil from the garlic pan and balsamic vinegar. Stir in thinly sliced leek. Season with salt and pepper.

6. Serve potato salad with toasted bread, mild goat cheese and whole baked garlic. To eat, spread bread with cheese, squeeze garlic cloves out of skins and eat on bread. Potato salad is served on the side.

For a hearty salad, nothing is as satisfying or easy to prepare in advance as this combination of cooked sausage and red potatoes. Italian sausage substitutes well for Polish. Be sure to leave the skins on the potatoes for color contrast.

POTATO SALAD WITH POLISH SAUSAGE

8 servings
Preparation time: 30 minutes
Cooking time: 20 minutes

3 **pounds red potatoes**
½ **pound fully cooked Polish sausage, sliced into ¼-inch slices**
4 **ribs celery, diced**
3 **green onions, sliced**
1 **tablespoon minced flat-leaf parsley**

DRESSING

6 **tablespoons white wine tarragon vinegar**
½ **teaspoon each: Dijon mustard, salt, freshly ground pepper**
¾ **cup olive oil**

Lettuce leaves, optional

1. Cook potatoes in boiling water until just tender, 15 to 20 minutes. Drain. Cool slightly. Cut into chunks or ¼-inch slices.

2. Put potatoes in large bowl. Add sausage, celery, green onions and parsley. Toss gently to mix.

3. For dressing, put vinegar, mustard, salt and pepper in small bowl. Whisk to blend. Gradually whisk in oil. Pour dressing over potato mixture; toss gently to mix. Serve while still warm over lettuce leaves if desired.

Darrell Dodson, owner of Seafruit restaurant, Chicago, Illinois, changes his potato salad recipe according to whim and what's freshest in the market. The following recipe is a warm summer day version. Pimientos, peppers, parsley and dill give the salad a colorful eye-appeal.

POTATO SALAD WITH RED PEPPERS AND DILL

8 to 10 servings
Preparation time: 30 minutes
Cooking time: 20 minutes
Chilling time: Several hours

3 **pounds red potatoes**
2 **medium red bell peppers, diced**
¼ **cup diced pimientos**
1 **tablespoon each, minced fresh parsley, dill**
1 **teaspoon each: minced garlic, dried leaf oregano**
1¾ **cups mayonnaise**
1 **tablespoon prepared mustard**
½ **teaspoon salt**
1 **or 2 hard-cooked eggs, sliced**

1. Cook potatoes in boiling water until just tender, 15 to 20 minutes. Drain; cool slightly. Peel potatoes and cut into chunks. Put potatoes in large bowl; add red peppers, pimientos, parsley, dill, oregano and garlic. Toss to mix.

2. Mix mayonnaise with mustard and salt until well blended. Spoon over potato salad while potatoes are still warm. Toss gently to mix. Arrange sliced eggs attractively on top. Refrigerate.

■ *Fresh walnuts and homemade walnut oil add a heady flavor to this otherwise classic potato salad from the California Walnut Board. Cooked peas, beans or carrots make colorful additions to this versatile salad. To keep nut oil fresh, store in the refrigerator. But before using, bring to room temperature.*

RED JACKET PICNIC SALAD

4 to 6 servings
Preparation time: 30 minutes

¼ **cup homemade walnut oil (see recipe, page 649)**

1½ **tablespoons white wine vinegar**

1 **teaspoon Dijon mustard**

½ **teaspoon sugar**
Salt, freshly ground pepper to taste

2 **pounds small red potatoes, cooked, drained**

½ **cup coarsely chopped walnuts**

4 **green onions, sliced diagonally**

¼ **cup chopped fresh dill or 1 teaspoon dried dill weed**
Lettuce leaves

1. Mix walnut oil, vinegar, mustard, sugar, salt and pepper in large bowl. Cut hot potatoes in half; add to bowl, tossing to coat with dressing. Cool, tossing occasionally.

2. Add nuts, onions and dill. Toss again. Serve at room temperature on lettuce-lined plate.

NOTE: If small red potatoes are unavailable, substitute large red potatoes, cut into cubes. Steamed or fresh raw vegetables may be added, such as green beans.

The secret to Chicagoan Marilyn Heiberger's German potato salad is to make it 48 hours in advance and then reheat it just before serving. This allows all of the flavors to blend together.

WARM GERMAN POTATO SALAD

10 servings
Preparation time: 30 minutes
Cooking time: 40 minutes
Chilling time: 48 hours

4 **pounds large red potatoes**
½ **pound bacon, diced**
½ **large onion, minced**
2 **ribs celery, minced**
½ **cup distilled white or cider vinegar**
½ **cup each: water, sugar**
2 **eggs, beaten well**
1½ **teaspoons minced fresh parsley**
½ **teaspoon salt**
¼ **teaspoon freshly ground pepper**
4 **hard-cooked eggs, chopped**

1. Cook potatoes in boiling water to cover until fork-tender but not mushy, about 20 minutes. Drain; cool under cold water. Peel; cut into thick slices.

2. Cook bacon in large dutch oven until brown. Do not discard fat. Add onion and celery; cook and stir over low heat until crisp-tender, about 15 minutes.

3. Mix vinegar, water, sugar, beaten eggs, parsley, salt and pepper in small bowl. Add potatoes and hard-cooked eggs to bacon mixture. Stir in vinegar mixture. Cook and stir gently until mixture thickens. Remove from heat; cool slightly. Refrigerate, covered, up to 48 hours.

4. To reheat, put into 300-degree oven, stirring occasionally, until hot. Garnish with additional hard-cooked egg slices if you wish.

■ *The flavor of pork loin, fresh picnic or smoked, is extended in this salad that knows no season. Hardly dainty, it satisfies with lots of bulk from cabbage. For a flavor twist, some grated apple or caraway seed can be added to the cabbage sauté. To round out a menu, try bread sticks or crusty rolls, perfect for lapping up the dressing.*

PORK SALAD ON RED CABBAGE WITH SHALLOTS

4 servings
Preparation time: 25 minutes
Cooking time: 15 minutes

½ **pound leftover cooked pork loin, fresh or smoked**

DRESSING

2 **tablespoons white wine tarragon vinegar**

1 **tablespoon country-style Dijon mustard**

1 **egg yolk**

¼ **teaspoon each: ground cumin, crumbled tarragon leaves**

½ **cup olive oil**
Salt, freshly ground pepper to taste

CABBAGE

4 **thick slices hickory smoked bacon, diced**

2 **large shallots, minced**

4 **cups shredded red cabbage, about ¾ pound**

1. Cut pork into thin strips.

2. For dressing, put vinegar, mustard, egg yolk, cumin and tarragon into blender or food processor. Process until smooth. With machine running, add oil in slow, steady stream until smooth and emulsified. Add salt and pepper.

3. For cabbage, cook bacon and shallots in large skillet until bacon is almost crisp. Add shredded cabbage. Sauté until crisp-tender, about 5 minutes.

4. To serve, use a slotted spoon to pile cabbage onto plate. Top with pork strips. Pass dressing.

This version is reportedly the one created by the Solari Restaurant in San Francisco, says food writer Marcy Goldman-Posluns. Cold lobster or shrimp can be used instead of the crab. For an accompaniment, stick with something crunchy, such as crackers or breadsticks.

CRAB SALAD LOUIS

4 servings
Preparation time: 25 minutes

DRESSING
- 1 cup mayonnaise
- ½ cup half-and-half
- ¼ cup each: chili sauce, chopped green onions, chopped green pepper
- 2 tablespoons chopped green olives
- Juice of ½ lemon
- Salt, freshly ground pepper to taste

SALAD
- Lettuce or mixed greens
- 2 cups cold, cooked crabmeat chunks
- 3 hard-cooked eggs, sliced
- ¾ cup black olives

1. For dressing, mix all ingredients in small bowl.

2. Line a shallow serving dish with lettuce. Toss crabmeat with salad dressing. Spoon crabmeat over lettuce. Garnish with sliced eggs and olives. Sprinkle with salt and fresh black pepper.

■ *Transform this salad into a meal by adding shredded cooked chicken or thinly sliced strips of cooked lamb or beef. Almonds add crunch to the salad. Toasting them enhances their flavor.*

COUSCOUS SALAD

8 to 10 servings
Preparation time: 30 minutes
Chilling time: 2 to 3 hours

1½ cups precooked
    medium-grain
    couscous
2 cups warm beef broth
    or reserved meat
    juices from Moroccan
    meat pie (see recipe,
    page 310)
1 cup raisins
1 tablespoon butter
½ cup sliced almonds
3 ribs celery, chopped
1 Granny Smith apple,
    cored, diced
2 green onions, minced
1 tablespoon minced
    fresh cilantro
    (coriander)
1 teaspoon minced fresh
    mint
    Grated rind of 1 lemon
    Juice of 1 lemon
    Salt, freshly ground
    pepper to taste

1. Put couscous in large bowl, add broth; stir to mix.

2. Put raisins in small cup, add warm water to cover. Let stand until softened, about 10 minutes. Drain.

3. Melt butter over medium heat in small skillet and cook almonds, stirring until golden. Remove from heat.

4. Add raisins, almonds and remaining ingredients to couscous mixture. Toss to mix. Cover with plastic wrap. Refrigerate 2 to 3 hours. Toss once or twice with fork to fluff during chilling. Serve cold or at room temperature.

Kathy Kirby, a creative Chicago cook, serves this salad in individual brioche. She hollows out the centers of the rolls and fills each with salad for an impressive luncheon entree.

CURRIED TURKEY SALAD

8 servings
Preparation time: 40 minutes
Chilling time: 2 to 3 hours

2 pounds cooked turkey breast, cut into ½-inch cubes, about 6 cups

2 cups each: diced Granny Smith apples, diced celery

1½ cups coarsely chopped dry roasted peanuts

1 cup golden raisins

1½ cups mayonnaise

⅓ cup mango chutney

¼ cup each: fresh lemon juice, cider vinegar

2 tablespoons curry powder (see note)

1 teaspoon turmeric

½ teaspoon each: cayenne pepper, salt, freshly ground pepper

1 head leaf lettuce, washed

½ cup minced fresh cilantro (coriander)

1. Put turkey, apples, celery, peanuts and raisins into large mixing bowl. Toss to mix.

2. Mix remaining ingredients except lettuce and cilantro in small mixing bowl. Mix until well blended and smooth. Pour over turkey mixture; toss to coat.

3. Arrange several lettuce leaves on individual serving plates. Mound curried turkey salad on top. Sprinkle with cilantro.

NOTE: For homemade curry powder, put ¼ teaspoon ground cardamom, 3 whole cloves, 2 teaspoons coriander seeds, 1½ teaspoons ground turmeric, ½ teaspoon each: cumin seeds, mustard seeds, black peppercorns and fenugreek seeds, ½ teaspoon ground ginger, ½ stick cinnamon, broken up, and ⅛ teaspoon cayenne pepper into spice grinder or blender. Process until a fine powder. Store in a tightly covered jar.

This recipe is merely a springboard for ideas. If you're out of beef, use cooked chicken and switch the broth accordingly. Stretch bulgur's nutty flavor and the recipe yield by including leftover cooked vegetables. For a Middle Eastern accent, add chopped, dried fruit or toasted nuts.

MAIN-DISH BULGUR SALAD

6 servings
Preparation time: 40 minutes
Cooking time: 20 minutes
Chilling time: 2 hours or overnight

1 **eggplant, peeled, cubed**
Salt
1 **cup uncooked bulgur (cracked wheat)**
2 **cups beef or vegetable broth**
3 **tablespoons olive oil**
1 **pound piece leftover cold, rare roast beef**
1 **large red onion, chopped**
1 **large tomato, seeded, chopped**
1 **cup frozen peas, thawed**
¼ **pound mushrooms sliced**
1 **package (7 ounces) feta cheese, drained, cubed, about 1¾ cup**
1 **cup each: sliced calamata olives, minced fresh parsley**
Oregano dressing (see recipe, page 485)
Lettuce leaves

1. Sprinkle eggplant with salt. Drain on paper towel 20 minutes; pat dry. Meanwhile, put bulgur and broth into large saucepan. Simmer, covered, until tender, about 15 minutes. Transfer to large bowl; cool completely.

2. Sauté eggplant in oil in large skillet until slightly brown, about 5 minutes. Drain on paper towels. Stir into bulgur. Cut beef into thin strips about 2 by ¼ inches. Stir into bulgur. Stir in onion, tomato, peas, mushrooms, cheese, olives and parsley.

3. Pour half of the oregano dressing over salad. Toss to coat. Refrigerate covered at least 2 hours. Serve salad in lettuce cups; pass remaining dressing.

This tabbouleh (wheat salad), from the late food writer, Roy Andries de Groot, can be stretched into a dinner salad by adding shredded cooked chicken or turkey. Tabbouleh can also be enjoyed as a stuffing for pita bread sandwiches or a not-so-filling appetizer. Instead of bread, serve it on spears of crisp romaine lettuce.

MIDDLE EASTERN TABBOULEH

8 servings
Preparation time: 40 minutes
Chilling time: 2 to 8 hours

1 **cup uncooked bulgur (cracked wheat)**

1¼ **cups loosely packed chopped flat-leaf parsley**

1 **cup loosely packed chopped fresh mint leaves**

1 **medium yellow onion, cut into eighths, about 1 cup**

1 **large bunch green onions, including tops, diced**

6 **to 8 canned Italian-style plum tomatoes, seeded, squeezed dry, chopped, or 4 ripe tomatoes, chopped**

Juice of up to 4 fresh lemons

¼ **to ½ cup top-quality extra-virgin olive oil**

1 **teaspoon coarse (kosher) salt**

½ **teaspoon freshly ground pepper**

1. Put bulgur into bowl, then place it under a stream of cold water. Dig your fingers down among the grains to separate them and break up all lumps. Drain off this first washing water, then cover the wheat with enough fresh water so the grains are submerged by at least 2 inches. Let soak until al dente. Some types of wheat might be ready in 10 minutes, others might require an hour or several hours.

2. Drain off remaining water and, taking the grain by handfuls, squeeze out as much excess water as possible. It also helps to squeeze and twist the grain inside a clean towel. Finally, dry out the bowl and add the now-dry bulgur.

3. Lightly rinse parsley and mint leaves; pat dry with paper towels. Put into food processor or blender. Process with on/off turns until minced. Stir into bulgur. Mince onions; stir into bulgur.

4. Add tomatoes. Stir in ¼ cup each of lemon juice and oil; mix thoroughly. Add salt and pepper as needed. Add remaining lemon juice, oil, salt and pepper to taste.

5. Refrigerate, covered, for 2 or up to 8 hours.

6. Just before serving, taste and make any final adjustments of lemon, oil, salt and pepper.

Frequently The Tribune *Food Guide* features recipes submitted by readers. One from Chicagoan Margie Irr in 1985 is almost a meal in a bowl. It is beautiful and full of texture and taste.

ORIENTAL NOODLE SALAD

4 servings
Preparation time: 15 minutes

½ **head cabbage, chopped**
4 **green onions, chopped**
1 **package (3 ounces) vegetable-flavored instant ramen noodles**
½ **cup slivered almonds, toasted**
2 **tablespoons sesame seeds, toasted**

DRESSING

⅓ **cup vegetable or peanut oil**
3 **tablespoons distilled white vinegar**
2 **tablespoons sugar**
  Salt, freshly ground pepper to taste

1. Put cabbage and onions into large bowl. Reserve the seasoning packet from the package of noodles. Crumble the noodles (uncooked, straight from the package) over the cabbage. Add almonds and sesame seeds. Toss to mix.

2. Mix reserved seasoning packet from noodles with oil, vinegar, sugar, salt and pepper in jar with tight-fitting lid. Shake well.

3. Just before serving, pour dressing over salad. Toss well to mix. Serve immediately.

Need a refreshing entree for a sweltering day? Try this seafood salad, a cousin to salad Niçoise. Unlike France's classic salad, this one features boneless salmon fillets, instead of tuna, and a sassy mustard dressing with chervil and tarragon, rather than the standard herb vinaigrette.

POACHED SALMON SALAD WITH MUSTARD DRESSING

2 servings
Preparation time: 30 minutes
Cooking time: 10 minutes

MUSTARD DRESSING

- ¼ **cup sherry wine or white wine vinegar**
- 2 **teaspoons each: country-style Dijon mustard, dried chervil**
- ¼ **teaspoon dried tarragon**
- ⅛ **teaspoon freshly ground pepper**
  Pinch salt
- ⅓ **to ½ cup extra-virgin olive oil**

SALAD

- 6 **small new potatoes**
- ¼ **pound very thin green beans, ends trimmed**
- 1 **cup each: water, dry white wine**
- 1 **pound boneless salmon fillets**
- 4 **cups torn, assorted lettuces**
- 1 **small cucumber, peeled, halved, seeded, sliced**

1. For dressing, mix vinegar, mustard, chervil, tarragon, pepper and salt in jar with tight-fitting lid. Add ⅓ cup of the oil; shake until well mixed. Taste and adjust seasonings adding more oil as desired.

2. Cook potatoes in boiling water to cover until fork-tender, about 10 minutes. Drain. Cook green beans in boiling water, uncovered, until crisp-tender, about 3 minutes. Drain; rinse under cold water to stop the cooking.

3. Meanwhile, heat water and wine to simmer in medium skillet. Add fish fillets. Cover and simmer gently until fish barely flakes, 5 to 8 minutes. Immediately remove from water with slotted spatula. Remove skin. Cool.

4. Arrange lettuces on serving plates. Slice potatoes and toss with some of the dressing in small bowl. Arrange potato slices over the lettuce in a ring about 2 inches in from edge of plate. Mix cucumber slices with some of the dressing in small bowl. Arrange cucumbers in center of lettuce. Break salmon into large hunks; toss with some of the dressing. Arrange salmon over the cucumbers. Toss green beans with some of the dressing. Arrange beans around salmon. Serve immediately; pass any remaining dressing.

Salads & Salad Dressings

Take a hint from Chicago's caterers: To cut down on last-minute preparation, salad greens can be rinsed and torn 24 hours in advance. Refrigerate the greens wrapped in paper towel in a plastic bag. It keeps them crisp.

QUICK CHEF'S SALAD

4 servings
Preparation time: 15 minutes

DRESSING
¼ cup each: mayonnaise, sweet pickle relish
2 tablespoons catsup
1 tablespoon lemon juice

SALAD
6 cups torn, assorted, salad greens, such as iceberg, romaine, curly endive, leaf lettuce or escarole
½ pound cooked turkey breast, cut into ½-inch cubes
2 cups fresh bean sprouts, rinsed, optional
1 tomato, cored, thinly sliced
1 cup cubed Swiss cheese

1. For salad dressing, mix all ingredients in small bowl.

2. For salad, put greens into large bowl. Top with turkey, sprouts, tomato slices and cheese. Add dressing; toss to mix. Serve immediately.

The variety and availability of fresh seafood allow the cook freedom to change the ingredients according to whim or budget. A hint of cumin in this vinaigrette enlivens the slightly briny taste of shrimp and mussels that reign in this colorful main-dish salad. A basket of crackers, a crisp, dry white wine and fresh fruit round out the menu.

SHRIMP AND MUSSEL SALAD WITH CUMIN VINAIGRETTE

2 servings
Preparation time: 30 minutes
Cooking time: 5 minutes

CUMIN VINAIGRETTE

- ¼ **cup cider vinegar**
- 1 **large egg**
- ¾ **teaspoon imported sweet paprika**
- ½ **teaspoon dried leaf thyme**
- ¼ **teaspoon each: cayenne pepper, ground cumin**
- ½ **cup peanut oil**
  Salt, freshly ground pepper to taste

SALAD

- ¾ **pound large raw shrimp**
- 1½ **dozen fresh mussels (or substitute shelled, smoked mussels)**
- 4 **cups torn assorted lettuces**
- 1 **small red bell pepper, seeded, diced**
- 1 **cup blanched fresh peas or defrosted frozen peas**
- ½ **small cucumber, peeled, seeded, sliced**

1. For cumin vinaigrette, put vinegar, egg, paprika, thyme, cayenne and cumin into food processor or blender. Process until mixed. With machine running, add oil in slow steady stream until smooth. Season to taste with salt and pepper.

2. For salad, drop shrimp into simmering water; simmer until pink and barely opaque, 2 to 3 minutes. Drain; peel and devein.

3. Put mussels into large pot with 1 inch of boiling water. Cover and steam until shells barely open, 2 to 3 minutes. Drain. Remove mussels from shells, reserving 4 in the shell for garnish. (Omit this step if using smoked mussels.)

4. Mix lettuce, red pepper, peas and cucumber in large bowl. Divide between serving plates. Arrange shrimp and mussels over lettuce mixture. Garnish with mussels in their shells.

5. At tableside, pour vinaigrette over salads. Toss before eating.

Two types of rice make this salad interesting in color and texture. The rices, dressing and shrimp may be prepared in advance and stored in the refrigerator until the salad is ready to assemble.

SHRIMP AND VEGETABLE RICE SALAD

6 to 8 servings
Preparation time: 40 minutes
Cooking time: 7 to 10 minutes
Chilling time: Several hours or overnight

1 cup raw long-grain brown rice
1 box (4 ounces) wild rice

DRESSING

½ cup vegetable oil
¼ cup white wine vinegar
2 teaspoons Dijon mustard
1 teaspoon sugar
½ teaspoon each: salt, freshly ground pepper

SALAD

1 each: red bell pepper, green bell pepper
1 pound frozen, shelled medium-size shrimp, cooked, cooled
2 ribs celery, diced
½ small red onion, diced
½ cup pitted black olives, sliced
2 tablespoons finely chopped fresh parsley
4 ripe avocados
Lemon juice
2 to 3 ripe tomatoes, sliced

1. Cook rices separately according to package directions. Mix in large bowl.

2. Put dressing ingredients into jar with tight-fitting lid. Shake well to blend. Pour over the warm rice. Toss to mix.

3. Remove ends from peppers; cut in half; remove seeds. Dice. Add peppers, shrimp, celery, onion, olives and parsley to the rice. Toss gently to mix. Cover with plastic wrap. Refrigerate several hours or overnight.

4. Peel and slice avocados. Rub with a little fresh lemon juice so that the avocado slices do not brown. Spoon a serving of salad on each plate and encircle with avocado slices. Arrange sliced tomatoes as garnish.

Details make a big difference in making a genuine salad Niçoise. Take time to rub the bottom and side of the salad bowl with a clove of garlic. And do toss the potatoes, beans and tomatoes with a bit of dressing. With attention and care, the result will be a perfectly balanced salad, a testimonial to the French art of salad making.

SALAD NIÇOISE

4 servings
Preparation time: 45 minutes
Cooking time: 10 minutes

6 **small new potatoes**

1 **cup tiny French green beans (haricot vert) or regular**

¼ **cup basil wine vinegar or white wine vinegar**

¼ **teaspoon Dijon mustard**

6 **tablespoons olive oil**

1 **tablespoon minced fresh parsley**

2 **teaspoons minced fresh basil**

   Salt, freshly ground black pepper to taste

1 **cup cherry tomatoes, halved**

1 **clove garlic, halved**

6 **cups torn Boston or assorted lettuces**

1 **can (7 ounces) albacore tuna, drained, flaked**

3 **hard-cooked eggs, peeled, quartered**

6 **to 8 anchovy fillets**

½ **cup Niçoise olives**

1. Cook potatoes in boiling water until fork-tender, 5 to 10 minutes. Drain well; rinse under cold water to stop the cooking. Refrigerate.

2. Drop beans in boiling water; cook until crisp-tender, about 3 minutes. Drain well; rinse under cold water to stop the cooking. Refrigerate.

3. Put vinegar and mustard in small bowl. Whisk until smooth. Gradually whisk in oil until smooth. Whisk in parsley, basil, salt and pepper.

4. Mix beans with a little of the dressing and toss well. Slice potatoes and mix with a little of the dressing and toss well. Mix tomatoes with a little of the dressing and toss well.

5. Rub bottom and sides of large salad bowl with cut sides of garlic. Put lettuce leaves in salad bowl. Drizzle remaining dressing over the lettuce and toss to coat.

6. Mound beans over lettuce at one side of the salad bowl. Arrange potatoes at another side, tomatoes at another and tuna in the center. Put egg quarters around edge of bowl. Lay anchovy fillets over all. Sprinkle with olives. Serve immediately.

■ *When* The Tribune *Food Guide asked readers to send in their favorite chicken salad recipes in November 1987, we learned the bird had at least 250 personalities. Jane Napolitano, of Naperville, won first place with her Oriental-inspired salad. It uses rice sticks (available at Oriental food markets), bok choy, sesame seeds and sesame oil.*

ORIENTAL CHICKEN SALAD

4 to 6 servings
Preparation time: 30 minutes
Cooking time: 20 minutes

3 large whole chicken
   breasts, boned, split
1 bundle (3 to 4 ounces)
   Chinese rice stick
   noodles
   Vegetable oil for
   deep-frying

DRESSING

⅓ cup vegetable oil
4 to 5 tablespoons rice
   vinegar
1 tablespoon each:
   Oriental sesame oil,
   soy sauce, sugar
2 teaspoons lemon juice
1 teaspoon each: ground
   ginger, dry mustard
1 small clove garlic,
   crushed
   Salt, freshly ground
   pepper to taste

1 small head iceberg
   lettuce, shredded
½ bunch romaine lettuce,
   thinly sliced
3 ribs celery or bok
   choy, diced
4 green onions (include
   tops), thinly sliced
¼ cup chopped fresh
   parsley or fresh
   cilantro (coriander)
½ cup sliced almonds,
   toasted

2 to 3 tablespoons
   sesame seeds,
   toasted

1. Cook chicken breasts by simmering in salted water until tender and juices no longer run pink, 15 to 20 minutes. Cool, remove and discard skin, and shred chicken.

2. Break rice stick noodles into small bundles. Deep-fry in wok or saucepan in very hot oil, a few at a time, for just a few seconds until they puff up. Remove with slotted spoon and drain on paper towel. (Can be prepared ahead of time and stored in an airtight container or zippered plastic storage bag for up to 3 days.)

3. Mix ⅓ cup vegetable oil, vinegar, sesame oil, soy sauce, sugar, lemon juice, ginger, mustard, garlic, salt and pepper in a jar. Cover tightly and refrigerate.

4. Mix salad greens, celery, onions and parsley in large bowl. Just before serving add chicken, rice sticks, almonds and sesame seeds. Add dressing; toss well. Serve immediately while crisp and crunchy.

James Bannos cooks for a living. Ask him about his hobbies, and he answers "cooking, eating and traveling." A trip to New Orleans inspired the owner of the Garland Restaurant, Chicago, Illinois, to develop this recipe.

CAJUN CHICKEN SALAD WITH HONEY JALAPEÑO DRESSING

4 servings
Preparation time: 45 minutes
Cooking time: 10 minutes

1 cup all-purpose flour
1½ teaspoons Cajun seasoning for poultry, such as Chef Paul Prudhomme's Poultry Magic
¾ teaspoon paprika
¼ teaspoon each: freshly ground black pepper, cayenne pepper, salt, sugar
⅛ teaspoon each: celery salt, garlic salt, onion salt, white pepper
   Pinch each, ground: cinnamon, nutmeg
4 boneless chicken breast halves, 4 to 5 ounces each
2 large eggs, beaten
   Vegetable oil for deep-frying

DRESSING
1 cup mayonnaise
¾ cup whipping cream or half-and-half
2 tablespoons honey
2 green onions, finely chopped
1 jalapeño pepper, seeded, minced
½ teaspoon each: hot red pepper sauce, Worcestershire sauce
⅛ teaspoon each: black pepper, cayenne pepper, white pepper

Assorted lettuces, such as iceberg, romaine and green leaf
4 tomatoes, cut in wedges
8 cherry peppers
   Black olives
½ pound fresh mushrooms, sliced
   Alfalfa sprouts

1. Combine flour and spices in a bowl. Dredge chicken breasts in spiced flour mixture. Dip in beaten eggs; dredge again in spiced flour mixture so chicken is well coated.

2. Heat oil in deep-fryer or saucepan until 350 degrees. Deep-fry chicken, turning, until light brown, about 5 minutes. Drain on paper towels. Cool.

3. For dressing, whisk together mayonnaise, whipping cream, honey, onions, jalapeño, hot pepper sauce, Worcestershire sauce and peppers in a bowl. Thin with additional whipping cream if desired. Refrigerate until serving.

4. Chop all lettuce and mix well. Place the lettuce in individual or serving bowl. Add tomato wedges at the 12 o'clock and 6 o'clock positions. Place the cherry peppers at the 3 o'clock and 9 o'clock positions.

5. Garnish with black olives, mushrooms and alfalfa sprouts to your liking. Dice the chicken into large pieces and place on the center of the salad. Just prior to serving, pour honey dressing on salad.

Eadie Levy, of the Chicago restaurant family, is quite a cook. When she gave us this salad recipe in May 1987, it became an instant hit with readers. And we heard about it. The Tribune *was deluged with phone calls regarding the ingredients. Yes, it does call for two boxes of flavored gelatin.*

BLUEBERRY GELATIN

6 to 8 servings
Preparation time: 15 minutes
Chilling time: 2 hours

1 can (16 ounces)
   crushed pineapple in
   syrup
1 can (16 ounces)
   blueberries in water
2 cups water
2 boxes (6 ounces each)
   red raspberry–
   flavored gelatin
1½ cups sour cream
½ cup pecan pieces

1. Strain juice from pineapple and blueberries into large saucepan. Set fruits aside. Add water to juice. Heat to boil. Remove from heat. Dissolve gelatin in juice mixture. Mix thoroughly. Cool.

2. Gradually mix pineapple and blueberries into sour cream in large bowl. (This must be done gradually or the sour cream will curdle.)

3. Add sour cream mixture to gelatin. Mix well. Pour into 13 by 9-inch pan. Sprinkle pecans over top. Refrigerate until firm, about 2 hours.

This yogurt-based dressing marries well with any combination of fruit. The dressing can be made ahead of time and stored in a covered container in the refrigerator for about a week.

CARROT APPLE SALAD

4 servings
Preparation time: 20 minutes
Chilling time: 2 hours

1 cup each: grated
   carrots, drained
   crushed pineapple
1 large apple, cored,
   diced
½ cup walnuts, chopped
1 cup plain yogurt
3 tablespoons honey
1 tablespoon lemon juice
1 teaspoon grated
   orange rind
   Pinch ground nutmeg

1. Toss carrots, pineapple, apple and walnuts in serving bowl. Mix yogurt, honey, lemon juice, orange rind and nutmeg; pour over fruit mixture. Toss. Chill 2 hours.

This fruit salad can double as dessert when served in balloon wine or parfait glasses. Any fruit-flavored yogurt will do. If less richness or sweetness is desired, cut the whipped salad dressing or whipping cream with plain yogurt.

FRESH FRUIT SALAD WITH CREAMY YOGURT DRESSING

6 to 8 servings
Preparation time: 25 minutes

1 **pineapple, peeled, cored, sliced**

1 **cantaloupe, peeled, seeded, sliced**

2 **pears, cored, sliced**

1 **or 2 ripe bananas**

1 **medium bunch seedless grapes**

DRESSING

½ **cup each: whipping cream, whipped salad dressing (such as Miracle Whip)**

1 **carton (8 ounces) fruit-flavored yogurt**

1. Prepare fruit. Arrange on serving platter.

2. For dressing, whip cream until soft peaks form. Fold in whipped salad dressing and yogurt. Serve dressing over fruit.

■ *Cucumbers and/or zucchini play minor roles in this salad which highlights luscious fresh fruit. It may be served as a refreshing side dish for poultry, a luncheon entree or between an entree of roast leg of lamb and dessert.*

LAYERED GARDEN SALAD WITH FRUIT

8 servings
Preparation time: 30 minutes
Standing time: 30 minutes
Chilling time: 4 hours

CREAMY MINT DRESSING

- 2 **large egg yolks**
- 2 **tablespoons white wine vinegar**
- 1½ **teaspoons sugar**
- 1 **clove garlic**
- ½ **teaspoon salt**
- ¾ **cup oil**
- ¼ **cup plain yogurt**
- 2 **teaspoons minced fresh mint**

SALAD

- 2 **medium cucumbers or zucchini or 1 of each**
- 1 **honeydew melon, halved, seeded, cut into balls**
- 3 **peaches, peeled, pitted, sliced**
- 2 **cups seedless green grapes, about ½ pound**
- ¾ **cup coarsely chopped walnuts**
  Fresh mint leaves for garnish

1. For dressing, put egg yolks, vinegar, sugar, garlic and salt into blender or food processor. Process until mixed. With machine running, add oil in slow steady stream until thickened and smooth. Pour into small bowl. Stir in yogurt and chopped mint.

2. Peel cucumber; cut lengthwise in half; remove seeds. Cut crosswise into slices. Sprinkle with salt. Let drain on paper towel 30 minutes. Rinse off salt; pat dry.

3. Put cucumber slices over bottom of large clear serving bowl. Drizzle 2 tablespoons of the dressing over cucumber slices. Put melon balls in layer over cucumber. Top with a layer of the peaches. Top with the grapes. Pour remaining dressing over all. Sprinkle with walnuts. Garnish with mint leaves. Refrigerate, covered, at least 4 hours before serving.

■ *What's chicken or turkey dinner without a fruit salad? This is the Thanksgiving dinner classic, an uncomplicated tag-along with sweet and crunchy overtones, from Marcy Goldman-Posluns. Sweetness can be enhanced by adding raisins or a few pinches of sugar to the mayonnaise. If tartness is desired, a few splashes of fresh lemon juice tossed with the apples will do the trick.*

SIMPLE WALDORF SALAD

4 servings
Preparation time: 10 minutes

2 **apples (preferably 1 tart, 1 sweet apple)**

3 **ribs celery, diced**

¼ **cup mayonnaise (preferably homemade)**

Lettuce leaves, optional

1. Peel and core apples. Chop into ½-inch dice. Combine apples with celery. Toss with mayonnaise. Serve on a bed of lettuce, if desired.

Here is a complex version of Waldorf salad also from Marcy Goldman-Posluns. Adventuresome diners will go for the mayonnaise-based dressing laced with mustard and curry powder and the multitude of textures, thanks to nuts, currants and grapes.

WALDORF SALAD WITH CURRIED MAYONNAISE

6 to 8 servings
Preparation time: 25 minutes

MAYONNAISE DRESSING

- 1 egg, room temperature
- 1 egg yolk, room temperature
- 1 tablespoon fresh lemon juice
- ¾ teaspoon salt
- ¼ teaspoon Dijon mustard
- ⅛ teaspoon curry powder
- ¾ cup safflower oil
- ¼ cup salad oil
- ¼ cup whipping cream, whipped

SALAD

- 2 medium red Delicious apples, unpeeled, cored, diced
- 1 tablespoon each: fresh lemon juice, orange juice
- 1½ cups coarsely chopped walnuts
- 4 medium ribs celery, cut into ½-inch pieces
- 2 tablespoons currants
- 2 small heads Bibb or Boston lettuce
- 1 tablespoon julienned orange rind
- Green grapes for garnish

1. For mayonnaise, put egg, egg yolk, lemon juice, salt, mustard and curry powder in food processor or blender. Process until mixed. With machine running, add oils in slow, steady stream; process until oil is incorporated and mayonnaise is smooth. Fold whipped cream into mayonnaise and cover and refrigerate. (Can be stored up to 3 days.)

2. For salad, toss apples with lemon juice and orange juice. Add walnuts, celery and currants. Toss with the mayonnaise until mixed.

3. Form lettuce into cups arranged on individual serving plates. Fill with salad mixture. Garnish with orange rind and green grapes.

A honey-lime dressing enlivens this fruit salad made with apples, pineapple and papaya. The dressing is also delicious with fresh strawberries when they are in season.

TROPICAL FRUIT SALAD WITH HONEY-LIME DRESSING

8 servings
Preparation time: 25 minutes
Cooking time: 5 minutes
Chilling time: 1 hour

DRESSING

⅓ **cup honey**
¼ **cup fresh lime juice**
1 **large egg, beaten**
 Pinch salt
1 **tablespoon rum,**
 optional
1 **cup sour cream**

SALAD

 Bibb or Boston lettuce leaves
1 **each: red Delicious apple, golden Delicious apple**
1 **fresh pineapple, peeled, cut into spears**
1 **small honeydew melon, peeled, seeded, cut into chunks**
1 **papaya, peeled, seeded, sliced**
1 **banana, peeled, cut into chunks**

 Chopped nuts

1. Mix honey, lime juice, egg and salt in small saucepan. Cook and stir over low heat until thickened. Do not boil. Remove from heat; stir in rum. Cool. Fold in sour cream. Refrigerate until cold, about 1 hour.

2. Arrange lettuce leaves over large serving platter. Core and slice apples. Arrange fruits over lettuce leaves. Spoon dressing over fruits. Sprinkle with nuts.

The ingredients in this salad know no season. They are available all year around. Prepare fruit ahead of time and store in a covered container in the refrigerator. A splash of rum or orange-flavored liqueur helps spark the flavor.

CURRIED CABBAGE AND FRUIT SALAD

6 to 8 servings
Preparation time: 15 minutes

CURRY DRESSING

½ **cup each:**
 yogurt, sour cream

2 **tablespoons white wine vinegar**

1 **tablespoon each: lemon juice, sugar**

¼ **teaspoon each: curry powder, ground cumin**

 Dash salt

SALAD

3 **cups shredded cabbage**

2 **apples, cored, diced**

2 **ribs celery, thinly sliced**

1 **cup green grapes, seeds removed**

½ **cup pecan halves, chopped**

2 **large avocados, peeled, diced**

2 **bananas, peeled, sliced**

 Lettuce leaves, optional

1. Mix dressing ingredients in small bowl. Refrigerate until cold.

2. Mix cabbage, apples, celery, grapes and pecans in large bowl. Add dressing; toss to combine. Add avocados and bananas. Toss gently until mixed. Serve on lettuce leaves, if you wish.

This creamy salad dressing is delicious served over crisp romaine leaves or shredded cabbage. Freshly ground pepper is a must here, but if a less spicy dressing is desired, use less. When buying peppercorns, make sure they are stored in tightly covered containers and are evenly shaped and colored.

CREAMY BLACK PEPPERCORN DRESSING

About 3 cups
Preparation time: 10 minutes

1   **carton (8 ounces) plain yogurt**
1   **cup each: buttermilk, mayonnaise**
¼   **cup minced fresh parsley**
2   **tablespoons minced fresh chives or green onion tops**
1   **to 1½ tablespoons coarsely ground fresh black pepper**
1   **tablespoon dried basil**
1   **teaspoon dried tarragon**
¼   **teaspoon dried leaf thyme**
   Several dashes salt-free herb seasoning, such as Mrs. Dash
   Dash of paprika
   Salt to taste

1. Mix yogurt, buttermilk and mayonnaise in large jar. Add remaining ingredients. Shake well. Refrigerate 30 minutes before using. Taste and adjust seasonings. Salad dressing will keep about 2 weeks in the refrigerator.

Jeffrey Tomchek, chef at The Set, in Chicago, transforms a bunch of cilantro (coriander) into a wonderful dressing. The size of a bunch can vary, so be flexible, Tomchek says, adding more or less half-and-half and sour cream as needed. And for a little kick, add a dash of hot pepper sauce and a few drops of balsamic vinegar.

CREAMY CILANTRO DRESSING

About 2 cups
Preparation time: 10 minutes

1 **bunch fresh cilantro (coriander), rinsed, picked over**
¾ **cup each: half-and-half, sour cream**
¼ **cup white vinegar**
   Salt, white pepper to taste

1. Puree cilantro and half-and-half in blender or food processor. Put puree in mixing bowl. Add sour cream and vinegar; whisk until blended. Add salt and pepper to taste. Chill until serving time.

A pot of chives not only looks terrific on the windowsill of the kitchen, they're useful. Snip the tops and sprinkle on boiled potatoes, in bread batter or blend with butter for an herb spread. They provide a delicate onion flavor in this dressing.

CHIVE VINAIGRETTE

About ¾ cup
Preparation time: 10 minutes

¼ **cup white wine vinegar**
2 **teaspoons Dijon mustard**
1 **teaspoon caraway seeds**
½ **cup olive oil**
2 **tablespoons chopped fresh garlic-chives or regular chives**
¼ **teaspoon each: salt, freshly ground pepper**

1. Mix vinegar, mustard and caraway seeds in small bowl. Gradually whisk in oil in slow steady stream until mixed. Stir in chives, salt and pepper.

This vinaigrette dressing gets a delicious sting from sharp Creole mustard. Serve it over sliced avocados.

CREOLE MUSTARD VINAIGRETTE

About 1¼ cups
Preparation time: 10 minutes

¾ cup salad oil
¼ cup red wine vinegar
2 to 3 tablespoons finely chopped green onion tops
2 tablespoons Creole mustard
1½ teaspoons fresh ground pepper
2 cloves garlic, minced
¼ teaspoon salt

1. Mix all ingredients in jar with tight-fitting lid. Shake vigorously before using.

Homemade dressing doesn't have to be complicated or exotic. This basic dressing can be used to marinate shrimp for cocktail appetizers or to splash over cooked pasta for salad. Vary the flavor by changing the herb.

OREGANO DRESSING

About 1⅔ cups
Preparation time: 10 minutes

1 cup olive oil
⅓ cup each: fresh lemon juice, red wine vinegar
1 tablespoon oregano
2 cloves garlic, minced
½ teaspoon salt
¼ teaspoon freshly ground pepper

1. Mix all ingredients in jar with tight-fitting lid. Shake vigorously before using. Taste and adjust seasoning.

■ *Here is a dressing that is as basic as a black dress. It is excellent on cabbage salads, over cooked seafood or drizzled on warm spinach leaves.*

SHALLOT VINAIGRETTE

About ¾ cup
Preparation time: 5 minutes

¼ **cup sherry wine**
  vinegar
1 **tablespoon each:**
  country-style Dijon
  mustard, minced
  fresh parsley, minced
  shallots
½ **teaspoon dried basil**
  Salt, freshly ground
  pepper to taste
¼ **cup olive oil**
2 **tablespoons vegetable**
  oil

1. Mix all ingredients, except oils, in jar with tight-fitting lid. Shake vigorously. Add oils and shake again. Let stand at least 15 minutes before using.

■ *Fresh greens and warm salad dressing? It sounds strange, but the combination is wonderful. Prove it by trying this dressing, which combines the saltiness of bacon with the sweet-sour appeal of sugar and red wine vinegar. Use a variety of hearty, bitter greens such as endive, escarole, dandelion, flowering purple kale or radicchio.*

WARM BACON AND SHALLOT DRESSING WITH BASIL SHREDS

About ⅔ cup
Preparation time: 10 minutes
Cooking time: 10 minutes

6 **slices bacon, diced**
2¼ **teaspoons sugar**
3 **tablespoons minced**
  shallots
⅓ **cup red wine vinegar**
1 **teaspoon Dijon**
  mustard
⅛ **teaspoon salt**
  Freshly ground black
  pepper to taste
3 **tablespoons finely**
  shredded, fresh basil
  leaves or 1
  tablespoon dried

1. Cook bacon in large skillet until crisp. Remove bacon with slotted spoon. Add sugar to bacon fat in pan. Cook and stir until lightly browned.

2. Stir in shallots; cook and stir until shallots are crisp-tender, about 2 minutes. Stir in vinegar, mustard, salt and pepper. Heat until sugar is dissolved. Remove from heat; add basil.

3. Serve immediately over torn, assorted lettuces. Add crisp bacon. Toss to mix. Serve immediately.

Mayonnaise is as basic a staple as you can get. It marries with everything from BLT sandwiches and party dips to grilled cheese and cold shrimp. Once this basic recipe is mastered, variations will abound.

BASIC MAYONNAISE

About 1⅓ cups
Preparation time: 15 minutes

2 **large egg yolks, at room temperature**
1 **teaspoon fresh lemon juice**
¼ **teaspoon salt**
   Dash cayenne or hot pepper sauce
1¼ **cups vegetable oil**

1. Whisk egg yolks, lemon juice, salt and cayenne in medium bowl until light and lemon colored.

2. Put oil into glass measure with pouring spout. In slow, steady stream, pour oil into yolk mixture while whisking vigorously. (Start slowly by adding only about 1½ teaspoons at a time.) Whisk vigorously after each addition. When about one-quarter of the oil has been added, you can add oil a little faster. When all of the oil has been added, whisk until light.

3. Taste and adjust seasonings, adding more salt, lemon juice or cayenne as desired.

Blender or food processor mayonnaise: Put all ingredients except oil in blender or food processor. Process until well mixed. With machine running, add oil in very slow, steady stream. Process until light and fluffy.

Use this mayonnaise for cold fish, roast chicken or beef, or as a dip for vegetables. The handsome shade of pale green contrasts well with poached salmon. Experiment with different fresh herbs.

HERB MAYONNAISE

About 1 cup
Preparation time: 15 minutes

1 **cup basic mayonnaise (see recipe, above)**
2 **teaspoons each: minced fresh chives, minced parsley, minced watercress**
1 **to 2 teaspoons minced fresh basil**

1. Mix all ingredients in small bowl. Use for cold poached fish, cold roast chicken or beef, or as a dip for vegetables.

Salads & Salad Dressings

BREADS

Nothing is more inviting than the aroma of freshly baked bread wafting though the house.

And with such time-saving devices as food processors, electric mixers with dough hooks and microwave ovens to cut down on preparation time, a new generation is creating wonderful aromas as it embraces the art of baking breads, muffins or light-as-a-feather biscuits.

In this selection of recipes, you'll find some of the best breads, muffins and doughnuts tested in *The Tribune*'s kitchen. For those with a "healthy" conscience, we've updated classics by incorporating such contemporary ingredients as natural cereals, rolled oats, raisins and whole-grain flour into doughs and batters.

We've included traditional recipes for Easter, St. Patrick's Day, Christmas and Rosh Hashanah. Somehow, these holidays just wouldn't be the same without Easter twists, Irish soda bread, Christmas stollen or challah.

Quick breads that follow include muffins, biscuits, popovers and batter breads. The beauty of these recipes is that they are cooked or baked as soon as they are mixed. So in no time at all, you'll be slathering pats of sweet butter on buttermilk-cranberry muffins, hot buttered corn-bread or pineapple-macadamia scones.

Yeast breads, which require several risings and kneadings before baking, are wonderful despite the extra effort. To prove the point, take serious note of the raisin bread deluxe, the incredibly rich sticky caramel pecan rolls or the country Parmesan herb bread.

So, get out the jams and preserves, a crock of butter and a hot cup of freshly brewed tea. The baking is about to begin.

HOW TO MAKE A PERFECT MUFFIN

Sift the dry ingredients together in a bowl. Make a well in the center of the dry ingredients and add the liquid. Combine just until the dry ingredients are moistened. Overmixing will result in tough-textured breads. Fill muffin tins two-thirds full. To test for doneness, muffins should be springy to the touch and should have slightly pulled away from the sides of the tins.

How Yeast Works

Working with yeast is still the most difficult hurdle for novice bread bakers to master. Yeast is a very small plant, a fungus that activates by feeding on sugar and warmth. As it feeds, it ferments the sugar-producing carbon dioxide. Small bubbles of the carbon dioxide are trapped in the dough, helping the dough to stretch and rise. Punching the dough breaks the large bubbles into smaller ones, resulting in a finer texture.

Regular dry yeast must be dissolved in water for best results. The water temperature should range between 105 to 115 degrees Fahrenheit. If the water is too hot, it will kill the yeast's rising action; if it is too cold, it retards the yeast's expansion capabilities.

The microwave oven comes to the rescue here. If using dry yeast, water can be heated in the microwave oven with a probe until it reaches 115 degrees Fahrenheit, the maximum temperature needed in most traditional bread recipes.

Fast Yeast

Fast yeast, a newer, more active strain of yeast, feeds on the sugar faster and helps the dough to rise about 50 percent faster. It works best when mixed with the dry ingredients; dissolving fast yeast in a liquid makes it lose its fast rising ability.

Flours for Yeast Breads

Flour provides the frame of the bread. Its protein (gluten) is developed in kneading and stretches as the yeast rises and stabilizes during baking. There are several types of flour and grains used to make breads.

All-purpose flour: A mixture of two kinds of milled wheat, hard wheat which has a high protein content and soft wheat which has a low protein content. This flour may absorb slightly less liquid than unbleached.

Unbleached all-purpose flour: Unbleached and is usually more expensive than all-purpose.

Bread flour: Has a higher amount of protein than all-purpose. A mixture of high-gluten flour and malted barley flour to which potassium bromate has been added.

Whole-wheat flour: Comes from whole-wheat kernels that have been milled into a lightly textured flour. Because it is lower in gluten, whole-wheat flour results in heavier breads. So if you wish to substitute whole-wheat flour for all-purpose flour, we suggest you use a combination of the two flours instead.

One Final Note

It's perfectly acceptable to use margarine instead of butter in these bread recipes. Keep in mind, however, that most margarines contain salt, and these recipes call for unsalted butter. So either use unsalted margarine or omit the added salt listed as an ingredient.

BREADS

YEAST BREADS

Basic white bread
Challah bread
Homemade rye buns
Black pumpernickel bread
Whole-wheat millet bread
Country Parmesan herb bread
Raisin bread deluxe
Cinnamon-topped raisin bread
Giant cinnamon rolls
Sticky caramel pecan rolls
Easter twists
Greek Easter bread
Polish sauerkraut rye bread
Hungarian walnut cake
Hot cross buns
Classic German stollen

QUICK BREADS

Hot buttered cornbread
Skillet cornbread
Cranberry-banana nut bread
Harvest loaf
Irish soda bread

MUFFINS, BISCUITS, ETC.

Buttermilk cranberry muffins
Cherry pecan muffins
Cheddar-onion corn muffins
Oat bran muffins
Herbed biscuits
Whole-wheat biscuits
Rich scones
Pineapple-macadamia scones
Never-fail popovers
Apple cider doughnuts

This basic white bread recipe offers you the option of using several different mixing and kneading techniques. The bread either can be prepared in the food processor, the electric mixer fitted with dough hook or by hand. The first method listed in each of the preparation steps is the fastest. You pick which one you want to use.

BASIC WHITE BREAD

2 loaves
Preparation time: 30 minutes
Rising time: 2 to 3 hours
Baking time: 40 minutes

6½ **cups all-purpose flour**
2 **tablespoons sugar**
1 **tablespoon salt**
1 **package quick-rise or regular active dry yeast**
1¼ **cups water**
1 **cup milk**
1 **tablespoon butter**
1 **large egg mixed with 1 tablespoon milk**

1. *Combine.* Mix 5½ cups of the flour, sugar, salt and yeast in one of the following:
    A. Food processor with metal blade or dough blade.
    B. Large bowl of electric mixer with dough hook.
    C. Large bowl for making bread by hand.

2. *Heat liquids.* Use one of the following techniques.
    A. Put water, milk and butter into 1-quart microwave-safe glass measure. Microwave on high (100 percent power) until liquids register 130 degrees for quick-rise yeast or 110 degrees for regular yeast on a microwave probe or instant-read thermometer.
    B. Put water, milk and butter into medium saucepan. Heat until mixture registers 130 degrees for quick-rise yeast or 110 degrees for regular yeast on instant-read thermometer.

3. *Mix.* Use one of the following methods:
    A. *Food processor.* With machine running, pour heated liquid ingredients through feed tube into flour mixture. Stop machine when mixture forms a ball and pulls away from sides, 1 to 2 minutes. If dough is sticky, add flour one tablespoon at a time through feed tube and process with on/off turns to mix.
    B. *Electric mixer with dough hook.* Add heated liquids to flour mixture. Beat on low speed until blended, then on high until mixture pulls away from sides of bowl, about 10 minutes. If dough is sticky, add flour by tablespoons.

C. *Hand mixing.* Use large spoon to beat heated liquids into flour mixture until dough is elastic, about 10 minutes. Scrape dough from bowl and put on lightly floured surface to knead.

4. *Knead.* If you mixed dough with a food processor or electric mixer with dough hook, you don't have to knead the dough. If you mixed by hand, you must knead the dough. Grease hands lightly to make it easier to handle dough. Gather up dough and fold over toward you. Then, use heel of hand to press dough away from you. Rotate dough a quarter-turn and knead again. Repeat until dough is smooth and elastic, 5 to 10 minutes, adding flour to work surface as needed. When dough is properly kneaded, it has a satiny surface and will no longer stick to work surface.

5. *Rising.* Put dough into large, greased bowl. Turn dough over so entire surface is lightly greased. Cover bowl with clean cloth. Put bowl in draft-free spot with temperature of 75 to 85 degrees. Let rise, 1 to 2 hours, until doubled in bulk and an imprint from a fingertip remains in dough. At this point, use fist to punch down dough; turn dough over. If you have time, allow dough to rise again until doubled in bulk; it will have a finer grain.

6. *Shaping.* Punch down dough; divide in half. Put each half on lightly floured surface. Use rolling pin or palms to press it down evenly. Roll up jelly-roll fashion; tuck in short ends. Put, seam side down, into 2 greased 9 by 5-inch loaf pans. Each end of loaf should touch pan sides to help support dough as it rises. Brush top with egg mixture. Cover and let dough rise again until almost doubled in bulk, about 1 hour.

7. *Baking.* Heat oven to 450 degrees. Gently brush egg mixture over bread again. Bake 10 minutes. Reduce oven temperature to 350 degrees; bake until loaf has shrunk in from sides of pan and bottom sounds hollow when tapped, about 30 more minutes. Remove loaves from pans immediately; cool completely on wire racks.

A Rosh Hashanah and Sabbath favorite, challah is a braided bread with a hint of sweetness to it. This recipe is contributed by Food Guide reader Agnes Ellegant. Leftovers are perfect as breakfast toast.

CHALLAH BREAD

2 large braided loaves
Preparation time: 15 minutes
Rising time: 2 to 3 hours
Baking time: 30 to 35 minutes

2 packages active dry yeast
1¾ cups warm water (105 to 115 degrees)
½ cup vegetable oil
¼ cup sugar
2 large eggs, beaten
2 teaspoons vanilla extract
1 teaspoon salt
6 to 7 cups sifted all-purpose flour, about
1 egg yolk, beaten

1. Grease two 9 by 5-inch loaf pans. Line bottom and sides with wax paper.

2. Dissolve yeast in ¼ cup of the water in small bowl; let stand until bubbly.

3. Mix remaining 1½ cups water, oil and sugar in large bowl. Stir in 2 eggs, vanilla, salt and dissolved yeast. Gradually stir in flour to form stiff dough. Knead on lightly floured surface, adding more flour as needed, until smooth and elastic, about 10 minutes.

4. Put into large greased bowl. Cover loosely with damp towel. Let rise in warm place until doubled in bulk, 1 to 1½ hours.

5. Punch down dough; divide in half. Divide one half into 3 pieces; roll each piece into long rope. Braid the 3 ropes together; tuck ends under. Put into prepared pan. Brush with egg yolk. Repeat with other half. Let rise, covered, until doubled in bulk, 1 to 1½ hours.

6. Heat oven to 350 degrees. Bake until golden and bottom sounds hollow when tapped, 30 to 35 minutes. Remove loaves from pans immediately; cool completely on wire racks.

Rye flour, with its slightly bitter taste, is what makes these buns a special treat. Check health food stores or specialty food shops for availability. These buns can be made small to use as dinner rolls or made large to use for hamburger or sandwich buns.

HOMEMADE RYE BUNS

16 buns
Preparation time: 25 minutes
Rising time: 1½ hours
Baking time: 15 minutes

¾ **cup milk**

⅓ **cup unsalted butter or margarine**

¼ **cup sugar**

1 **teaspoon salt**

2 **packages active dry yeast**

¾ **cup warm water (105 to 115 degrees)**

1 **cup rye flour**

3 **to 3½ cups all-purpose flour**

Melted butter, poppy seeds for garnish

1. Heat milk to simmer in small saucepan; add butter, sugar and salt. Stir until sugar dissolves and butter melts. Transfer to large bowl; cool to lukewarm. Dissolve yeast in water in small bowl; let stand until bubbly. Stir into milk mixture.

2. Stir in rye flour. Stir in 1 cup of the all-purpose flour; stir until smooth. Gradually stir in remaining flour to form a stiff dough. Knead on lightly floured surface until smooth and elastic, about 10 minutes.

3. Put into greased bowl; turn to grease top. Cover with towel. Let rise in warm place until doubled in bulk, about 1 hour.

4. Punch down dough. Roll on lightly floured surface to ¾-inch thickness. Cut into 16 rounds with 3½-inch cookie cutter. Put onto greased baking sheets. Brush each with melted butter; sprinkle with poppy seeds. Let rise, covered, until doubled in bulk, about 30 minutes.

5. Heat oven to 425 degrees. Bake until golden brown and bottoms sound hollow when tapped, 10 to 14 minutes. Cool completely on wire racks.

Nicole's Bake Shop in Chicago gave us this recipe for dense, rich pumpernickel bread. For the best texture, owner Nicole Bergere suggests using a medium grind rye flour rather than a fine grind. She also uses quick-rise yeast to cut down on the rising time.

BLACK PUMPERNICKEL BREAD

2 loaves
Preparation time: 40 minutes
Rising time: 2 hours
Baking time: 45 minutes

4   cups unbleached
     all-purpose flour
3½ cups medium-grind rye
     flour (see note)
2   cups uncooked oat
     bran cereal
2   tablespoons caraway
     seeds
1   tablespoon salt
1   tablespoon instant
     minced onion flakes
2   teaspoons Postum,
     optional (see note)
2   packages quick-rise
     active dry yeast
1   ounce bitter or semi-
     sweet chocolate
⅓ cup dark molasses
¼ cup each: cider
     vinegar, olive oil
2½ cups very warm water
     (120 to 130 degrees)
½ teaspoon cornstarch
     dissolved in ¼ cup
     cold water

1. Mix 1 cup of the all-purpose flour, 1 cup rye flour, oat bran, caraway seeds, salt, onion flakes, Postum and yeast in large bowl. Mix molasses, vinegar, oil and chocolate in medium saucepan; cook and stir over low heat until chocolate melts. Remove from heat. Add water; stir well.

2. Add chocolate mixture to dry ingredients. Beat 2 minutes in heavy-duty mixer or by hand with spoon 3 minutes. Slowly beat in 1½ cups of the rye flour. When machine starts to labor, put dough onto floured work surface.

3. Knead while adding remaining 1 cup rye flour. Then knead in remaining all-purpose flour, a little at a time. Work the dough after each addition until it is no longer sticky. Do not allow dough to get too stiff or it will make loaf too dense. Cover with towel; let rest 15 minutes.

4. Knead dough on lightly floured surface until smooth and elastic, about 6 minutes. Put into large greased bowl. Cover tightly with plastic wrap; let rise in warm place until doubled in bulk, about 1 hour.

5. Punch down dough; divide in half. Shape each into oblong or round shape; put onto greased baking sheets. Cover with 2 towels; let rise until doubled in bulk, about 45 minutes.

6. Heat oven to 375 degrees. Bake until bottom sounds hollow when tapped, about 45 minutes. Remove loaves from sheets; immediately cool on wire racks. Cook cornstarch mixture in small saucepan until it becomes clear. Paint loaves with mixture as soon as they are out of oven. Cool completely on wire racks.

This much-asked-for recipe by readers originated from Jerome's restaurant on Clark Street in Chicago. Millet, a tiny yet very nutritious grain, can be found at health food stores. Bulgur is a wheat that has been cracked, parched, steamed and then dried. It, too, can be found at health food stores.

WHOLE-WHEAT MILLET BREAD

2 large loaves or 4 small loaves
Preparation time: 45 minutes
Rising time: 3½ hours
Baking time: 45 minutes

¾ cup honey
3 cakes (0.6 ounces each) compressed yeast (see note)
3 cups warm water (90 to 100 degrees)
4½ cups whole-wheat flour
¼ cup vegetable oil
1 tablespoon salt
1 cup millet
⅓ cup bulgur wheat, optional
2 to 3 cups all-purpose flour
1 egg beaten with 1 teaspoon milk

1. Dissolve honey and yeast in warm water in large bowl; let stand until bubbly. Stir in 3½ cups of the whole-wheat flour, oil and salt until smooth. Let rise, covered, in warm place until doubled in bulk, about 1 hour.

2. Stir in remaining 1 cup whole-wheat flour, millet and bulgur. Stir in all-purpose flour, ½ cup at a time, until stiff dough forms and pulls away from sides of bowl. Knead on lightly floured surface until dough is very stiff, smooth and elastic.

3. Put dough into greased bowl; turn dough to grease top. Let rise, covered, in warm place until doubled, about 1 hour.

4. Punch down dough; turn dough over; cover and let rise in warm place, until doubled in bulk.

5. Punch down dough; cut in half or quarters. Shape each piece into round loaf. Put loaves onto greased baking sheets; cover and let rise 20 minutes. Brush loaves with beaten egg.

6. Heat oven to 350 degrees. Bake until nicely browned and bottom sounds hollow when tapped, 30 to 45 minutes. Cool completely on wire racks.

NOTE: You may substitute 3 packages active dry yeast for the compressed yeast; heat water to 105 to 115 degrees.

■ *Imported Parmesan cheese adds a robust flavor to this homemade country bread, says food processor columnist and cookbook author Jane Salzfass Freiman. She adds that domestic cheese is a suitable and less expensive substitute, however.*

Bread flour, which is available in most supermarkets and health food stores, is a mixture of high-gluten flour and malted barley flour to which potassium bromate (a chemical which makes the gluten more elastic) has been added.

With the help of a food processor, it takes just 2 minutes to mix and knead the dough.

COUNTRY PARMESAN HERB BREAD

3 loaves
Preparation time: 45 minutes
Rising time: 3½ hours
Baking time: 20 to 25 minutes

1⅓ **cups warm water
     (105 to 115 degrees)**
 1 **tablespoon sugar**
 1 **package active dry
     yeast**
 6 **ounces imported
     Parmesan cheese,
     rind removed, cut
     into 1-inch chunks**
3½ **cups bread flour**
 2 **tablespoons pure mild
     olive oil or vegetable
     oil**
 ¾ **teaspoon salt**
1½ **teaspoons dried leaf
     oregano**
 ⅜ **teaspoon freshly
     ground pepper
     Vegetable shortening**
 1 **egg white**

1. Mix ⅔ cup of the water, sugar and yeast in small bowl; let stand until bubbly.

2. Insert metal blade in dry food processor container. Process Parmesan cheese until powdery; measure ½ cup and set remainder aside. Put flour, ½ cup cheese, oil and salt in container. Process, adding remaining ⅔ cup warm water in thin stream within 15 seconds. Stir yeast mixture well. Process, adding yeast mixture in thin stream within 15 seconds. Process until dough forms a soft, moist ball, about 45 seconds.

3. Rinse large bowl with warm water; do not dry. Add dough. Cover with plastic wrap. Let rise in warm place until tripled in bulk, 1½ to 2 hours.

4. Remove dough from bowl without kneading; divide into 3 even pieces. Remove ⅓ cup of dough from each piece.

5. To shape each loaf, keep a ruler on hand. Sprinkle 1 tablespoon Parmesan cheese on work surface. On the cheese-sprinkled surface, roll out large piece of dough to 12 by 8-inch rectangle, turning to coat both sides evenly with cheese. Sprinkle 1½ tablespoons Parmesan cheese, ½ teaspoon oregano and ⅛ teaspoon pepper evenly over top of dough. Fold into thirds lengthwise to make a long, thin dough rectangle. Pinch two long edges together tightly to form a cigar-shaped loaf.

6. For dough strips, sprinkle work surface with 1 tablespoon Parmesan cheese. On cheese-sprinkled surface, roll out a ⅓-cup piece of dough to 12 by 4-inch rectangle. Cut in half lengthwise to form two long flat strips.

7. With cheese side of dough strip facing the cigar-shaped loaf, wrap and stretch strip around loaf clockwise; pinch both ends firmly. Attach the second strip where the first ended and wrap it counterclockwise around the loaf to form a criss-cross diamond pattern. Pinch dough strips at both ends to fasten securely. Repeat with other loaves.

8. Coat a curved metal French bread pan or baking sheet generously with vegetable shortening. Put each loaf seam side down in pan. Gently press 1 tablespoon Parmesan cheese on top of each loaf. Cover with lightweight towel. Let rise in warm place until doubled in bulk, about 1 hour.

9. Adjust oven rack to lowest position. Heat oven to 425 degrees. Wet a soft pastry brush and dip it into egg white. Brush tops with egg white. Bake until golden brown and bottom sounds hollow when tapped, 20 to 25 minutes. Loosen from bread pan; cool completely on wire racks.

Raisin bread deluxe originally appeared in The Tribune *food pages in 1951. That recipe called for cake yeast, but it works just as well with active dry yeast. If you only have hard raisins on hand, soak them in hot water for about 10 minutes to soften them up.*

RAISIN BREAD DELUXE

2 loaves
Preparation time: 30 minutes
Rising time: About 2 hours
Baking time: 45 minutes

DOUGH

- ½ **cup (1 stick) unsalted butter or margarine**
- 2 **cups milk**
- 1 **cup sugar**
- 1 **teaspoon salt**
- ½ **teaspoon ground cardamom**
- ¼ **teaspoon mace**
- 3 **packages active dry yeast**
- 3 **large eggs, lightly beaten**
- 9 **cups all-purpose or bread flour, about**
- 3 **to 4 cups raisins**

TOPPING

- ½ **cup (1 stick) unsalted butter, melted**
- 1 **tablespoon ground cinnamon**

1. For dough, melt butter in large saucepan. Add milk, sugar, salt, cardamom and mace. Heat to lukewarm (105 degrees to 115 degrees). Transfer to large bowl; add yeast and let stand until bubbly.

2. Stir in eggs; gradually add flour, 1 cup at a time, to form a soft dough. Knead on lightly floured surface until dough is smooth and elastic, 8 to 10 minutes.

3. Put into large greased bowl. Let rise, covered, in warm place until doubled in bulk, about 1 hour.

4. Turn dough onto lightly floured work surface. Knead in raisins. Divide dough in half. Shape each into loaf. Put into two well-greased 9 by 5-inch loaf pans. Cover and let rise in warm place until doubled in bulk, about 1 hour.

5. Heat oven to 400 degrees. Bake at 400 degrees for 10 minutes. Reduce oven temperature to 350 degrees; bake until loaves are well browned, about 45 more minutes.

6. Remove loaves from pans immediately; put onto wire racks. For topping, mix melted butter and cinnamon together. Brush over top and sides of bread. Cool completely.

If you only have about an hour to make a yeast bread from start to finish, this recipe is for you. The microwave oven is what makes it possible. Remember to use microwave-safe or glass loaf pans. It is crucial that the dough be raised at low power, for even a notch higher may kill the yeast and prevent the dough from rising. The lack of a crisp crust is not a problem because the bread is best served sliced and toasted.

CINNAMON-TOPPED RAISIN BREAD

2 loaves
Preparation time: 40 minutes
Microwave cooking time: 11 minutes

DOUGH

- **5 cups all-purpose flour**
- **1 cup raisins**
- **3 tablespoons granulated sugar**
- **2 packages active dry yeast**
- **1½ teaspoons ground cinnamon**
- **½ teaspoon salt**
- **1½ cups half-and-half**
- **½ cup water**
- **2 large eggs, beaten**

TOPPING

- **¼ cup packed dark brown sugar**
- **2 teaspoons ground cinnamon**

- **2 tablespoons butter, melted**

1. For dough, mix flour, raisins, granulated sugar, yeast, 1½ teaspoons cinnamon and salt in large bowl. Put half-and-half and water into microwave-safe medium bowl. Microwave on high (100 percent power) until 120 degrees, about 2 minutes. Stir in eggs. Stir into flour mixture to make a stiff batter.

2. Generously butter two 8 by 4-inch or two 9 by 5-inch microwave-safe loaf pans. For topping, mix brown sugar and 2 teaspoons cinnamon. Coat bottom and sides of each pan with some of the sugar mixture.

3. Divide batter between pans; smooth tops. Cover with towel. Microwave on low (30 percent power) 1 minute. Let rest 10 minutes: repeat microwaving and resting 2 more times. Dough should double in bulk.

4. Brush tops of loaves with butter. Sprinkle with remaining sugar mixture. Microwave each loaf separately on medium (50 percent power) until top springs back when touched, 6 to 9 minutes. (Surface of loaf will be flat and just slightly moist.) Remove loaves from pans immediately; cool completely on wire racks.

5. To serve, slice and toast; spread with butter.

■ *The rich, seductive aroma of warm cinnamon seldom fails to send people to the kitchen in search of something good. These rolls will certainly draw a crowd. They were created in* The Tribune *test kitchen to duplicate those sold at the popular cinnamon roll shops around town.*

For perfect rolls, use a piece of thread to cut the rolled dough into 2-inch pieces. Using a knife will result in squashed rolls.

GIANT CINNAMON ROLLS

6 rolls
Preparation time: 45 minutes
Rising time: 2½ hours
Baking time: 30 minutes

DOUGH

4 cups all-purpose flour, about

1 package active dry yeast

1¼ cups milk

¼ cup each: granulated sugar, unsalted butter

1 teaspoon salt

1 large egg

CINNAMON FILLING

¼ cup granulated sugar

2 tablespoons packed dark brown sugar

1 tablespoon ground cinnamon

5 tablespoons butter, melted

GLAZE

1 cup confectioners' sugar, sifted

½ teaspoon vanilla extract

Half-and-half or milk

1. For dough, mix 1½ cups of the flour and yeast in large mixer bowl. Heat milk, ¼ cup sugar, ¼ cup butter and salt in small saucepan, stirring constantly, just until warm (115 to 120 degrees). Add to yeast mixture; add egg. Beat at low speed for 30 seconds; scrape sides of bowl. Beat at high speed 3 minutes. Using a wooden spoon, stir in enough remaining flour to form a soft dough.

2. Turn out onto lightly floured surface and knead until smooth and elastic, about 8 minutes. Shape into ball.

3. Put into lightly greased bowl; turn once to grease top. Let rise, covered, in warm place until double, 1½ to 2 hours. Punch down; turn out onto floured surface. Cover; let rest 10 minutes.

4. For cinnamon filling, mix sugars and cinnamon. Brush 9-inch round cake pan, at least 2 inches deep, with 1 tablespoon of the melted butter.

5. Roll dough on lightly floured surface into thin rectangle measuring 20 by 12 inches. Brush dough generously with melted butter. Sprinkle with cinnamon mixture. Roll up jelly-roll fashion starting at one 12-inch end. You should end up with a fat log that is 12 inches in length.

6. Cut rolls at 2-inch intervals, using the following method: Place a piece of thread under rolled dough and pull up and around sides. Crisscross thread at top, then pull quickly. (Using thread to cut dough eliminates applying pressure with a knife, which would squash rolls.)

7. Put rolls, cut side up (so the cinnamon spiral shows) into prepared pan. Drizzle any remaining melted butter over all. Let rise, covered, in warm place 20 minutes.

8. Heat oven to 375 degrees. Bake until puffed and golden brown, 25 to 30 minutes. Cool in pan 10 minutes.

9. Meanwhile, for glaze, mix confectioners' sugar, vanilla extract and enough half-and-half to make a medium-thick glaze. Invert pan over serving platter. Drizzle rolls with glaze. Serve warm.

■ *If it's totally self-indulgent, incredibly rich, unbelievably delicious breakfast rolls you want, then these caramel rolls from test kitchen director JeanMarie Brownson are for you.*

For Sunday brunch, start the dough the night before so the rolls can be baked fresh the next morning. Or, skip the refrigerator rising time and make the rolls the same day. Simply punch the dough down after the first rising and let it rise a second time in a warm place until doubled in volume, about 1 hour. Then proceed as directed.

STICKY CARAMEL PECAN ROLLS

1 dozen rolls
Preparation time: 1 hour
Rising time: 1½ hours plus overnight
Baking time: 40 minutes

½ cup milk
¼ cup granulated sugar
¾ teaspoon salt
1 cup (2 sticks) unsalted butter
½ cup warm water (105 to 115 degrees)
1 package active dry yeast
1 whole large egg
1 large egg yolk
4 cups sifted all-purpose flour, about
3 tablespoons water
1 cup packed dark brown sugar
1½ cups pecan halves

FILLING

¼ cup melted butter
½ cup each: packed dark brown sugar, chopped pecans
1 teaspoon ground cinnamon

1. Put milk, granulated sugar, salt and 6 tablespoons of the butter into small saucepan. Heat until hot and sugar dissolves. Remove from heat; cool to warm.

2. Put water and yeast into large bowl. Let stand until bubbly. Stir in butter mixture, egg, egg yolk and 2 cups of the flour until smooth. Stir in remaining flour as needed to form a soft dough. Knead on lightly floured surface until smooth and elastic, about 10 minutes.

3. Put into large well-buttered bowl; turn once to butter top. Let rise, covered, in warm place until doubled in bulk, about 1 hour.

4. Punch down dough. Refrigerate dough, well covered, overnight. Let dough sit in warm place about 30 minutes before shaping.

5. Mix 1½ tablespoons water, 5 tablespoons of the remaining butter, melted and ½ cup dark brown sugar in bottom of 9-inch round cake pan or well-seasoned cast-iron skillet. Sprinkle ¾ cup pecan halves over mixture. Repeat with a second cake pan.

6. Roll dough on lightly floured surface into 18 by 12-inch rectangle. Brush with ¼ cup melted butter. Sprinkle with ½ cup dark brown sugar, ½ cup chopped pecans and 1 teaspoon cinnamon.

7. Roll up dough jelly-roll fashion to end with 18-inch roll. Cut into 12 rolls using the following method: Place a piece of thread under the rolled dough and pull up and around sides. Crisscross thread at top, then pull quickly. (Using thread to cut dough eliminates applying pressure with a knife, which would flatten the rolls.)

8. Put 6 rolls, cut sides facing up and down, in each prepared pan. Let rise covered in warm place until double, about 30 minutes.

9. Heat oven to 350 degrees. Bake until golden and puffed, 35 to 40 minutes. Let cool in pan 5 minutes. Then invert onto serving platter. Cool to warm and serve.

Katina Vaselopulos gave us this recipe for a Greek Easter bread, called tsourekia, *with a dough so soft it is best to knead it in a mixing bowl. The resulting fragrant loaves are heavy with the scent of mahlepi seeds. The seeds, which have a cardamom-like perfume, generally are available at Greek and Middle Eastern food markets.*

EASTER TWISTS

3 large braids
Preparation time: 1 hour
Rising time: 8 to 8½ hours
Baking time: 20 minutes

¼ **cup warm water (105 to 115 degrees)**

1 **envelope active dry yeast**

1 **tablespoon flour**

1 **teaspoon sugar**

1 **cup (2 sticks) unsalted butter or margarine**

1 **cup milk**

2 **cups sugar**

¼ **teaspoon salt**

2 **teaspoons mahlepi seeds, finely ground (see note)**

7 **large eggs, at room temperature**

10 **to 12 cups all-purpose flour, about**

   Softened butter

   Sesame seeds or almond slices

1. Mix water, yeast, 1 tablespoon flour and 1 teaspoon sugar in small bowl. Let stand until bubbly, about 10 minutes.

2. Melt butter in large saucepan. Add milk, 2 cups sugar and salt; stir until sugar is almost dissolved. Let stand until lukewarm (105 to 115 degrees). Stir in ground mahlepi seeds. Stir in 6 of the eggs and 1 egg white (reserve egg yolk for glaze) until mixed. Stir in yeast mixture.

3. Put 10 cups of the flour in large bowl. Make well in center of flour. Pour butter mixture into well. Using large spoon, gradually stir flour into butter mixture. Knead, on lightly floured surface, adding more flour, to form a soft, sticky dough.

4. Put mixture into large well-buttered bowl. Smear softened butter over top of dough. Cover with plastic wrap and then a clean towel. Let rise in warm place until doubled in bulk, at least 5 hours. (Dough also can rise in the refrigerator overnight; remove from refrigerator and let stand at room temperature 1 hour before shaping.)

5. Divide dough into 3 equal portions. Divide each portion into three pieces; roll each piece into long rope. (If dough is too sticky to handle, butter hands and work surface.) Braid 3 ropes together. Repeat to shape other 2 dough portions.

6. Put onto greased baking sheets; cover with plastic wrap and a light towel. Let rise in warm place until doubled in bulk, 3 to 3½ hours.

7. Heat oven to 375 degrees. Beat 1 teaspoon water with reserved egg yolk. Brush braids lightly with mixture. Sprinkle with sesame seeds.

8. Bake until golden and bottom sounds hollow when tapped, 20 to 25 minutes. Remove from sheets to wire racks. Cool completely.

NOTE: If mahlepi seeds, also called mahleb, are unavailable, grind together 2 inches cinnamon stick, 3 whole cloves and 1 bay leaf. Use 2 teaspoons of this mixture in place of the ground mahlepi.

This slightly sweet Greek Easter bread, lambropsomo, *from Food Guide reader Georgia Botsis, is usually served as a counterpoint to the salty flavor of the feta cheese traditionally offered at Greek Easter tables. The secret to the success of this bread is three kneadings and three risings.*

GREEK EASTER BREAD

4 loaves
Preparation time: 1 hour
Rising time: 5 hours
Baking time: 35 minutes

2   **envelopes active dry yeast**
½   **cup warm water (105 to 115 degrees)**
½   **teaspoon sugar**
1   **cup each: milk, water**
½   **cup (1 stick) unsalted butter or margarine**
¼   **cup vegetable shortening**
4   **teaspoons salt**
¾   **cup sugar**
4   **large eggs**
8   **to 10 cups all-purpose flour, about**
    Vegetable oil
    Hard-cooked eggs tinted red, or shelled walnut halves
1   **egg beaten with 1 teaspoon water**
    Sesame seeds

1. Mix yeast, ½ cup warm water and ½ teaspoon sugar in small bowl. Let stand until bubbly, about 5 minutes.

2. Meanwhile, heat milk with 1 cup water, butter, shortening, salt and ¾ cup sugar in medium saucepan just until butter melts. Cool to lukewarm (105 to 115 degrees).

3. Put eggs in large mixer bowl. Beat until blended. Gradually add lukewarm milk mixture. Stir in yeast mixture. Beat in enough flour to make a smooth batter, 3 to 4 cups. Then, using a mixing spoon, continue adding flour, 1 cup at a time, to form a soft but firm dough. Knead dough in bowl or on counter until smooth and elastic, about 10 minutes.

4. Put into large well-oiled bowl. Turn once to oil top. Let rise, covered, in warm place until almost doubled in bulk, about 1½ hours.

5. Punch down dough. Repeat risings and punches 2 more times.

6. Divide dough into 4 equal portions. Grease four 8-inch round cake or pie pans. Remove an egg-size piece of dough from each portion for decorations. Shape large portion of dough into a smooth round ball. Put into prepared pans.

7. Cut a cross, about ¼-inch deep, in center of bread. Gently press hard-cooked egg or several walnut pieces into center of bread. Roll reserved piece of dough into 2 ropes and crisscross over bread and egg. Repeat shaping with remaining three portions of dough. Cover with clean towels; let rise until doubled in bulk.

8. Heat oven to 375 degrees. Brush surface of bread very lightly with egg-water mixture; sprinkle with sesame seeds. Bake until evenly browned and bottom sounds hollow when tapped, 30 to 40 minutes. Remove from pans immediately; cool completely on wire racks.

This recipe was adapted from Tuzik's bakery, in Chicago, which uses large mixing equipment to make its bread, but you can duplicate the effort at home with a food processor.

POLISH SAUERKRAUT RYE BREAD

2 loaves
Preparation time: 20 minutes
Rising time: 2 to 3 hours
Baking time: 30 to 40 minutes

5½ cups all-purpose flour
1 cup rye flour
2 tablespoons butter
1 tablespoon each: salt, sugar
1 package dry active yeast
¾ cup well-drained sauerkraut
2 cups warm water (105 to 115 degrees)
2 teaspoons cornmeal
1 egg yolk
1 tablespoon milk
2 teaspoons caraway seeds

1. Put 4½ cups of the all-purpose flour into food processor fitted with metal blade. Add rye flour, butter, salt, sugar and yeast; process until mixed. Add sauerkraut; process until mixed. With machine running, slowly pour warm water through feed tube. Add remaining flour 1 tablespoon at a time until dough no longer sticks to sides of bowl and begins to gather into a ball.

2. Put into large oiled bowl. Turn once to oil top. Let rise, covered, in warm place until doubled in bulk, about 1 hour.

3. Punch down dough. Let rise, covered a second time until doubled in bulk, about 1 hour.

4. Punch down dough; divide in half. Roll each piece to 1-inch-thick rectangle. Roll up jelly-roll fashion; tuck in short ends. Grease large baking sheets; sprinkle with cornmeal. Put loaves onto baking sheets. Let rise, covered, until almost doubled in bulk, about 1 hour.

5. Heat oven to 400 degrees. Mix egg yolk and milk; lightly brush over loaves. Sprinkle with caraway seeds. Using a sharp knife, make 4 to 5 slashes on top of each loaf. Bake 20 minutes. Reduce oven temperature to 350 degrees; continue baking until bottom is golden and sounds hollow when tapped, 10 to 15 more minutes. Remove from baking sheet; cool completely on wire rack.

■ *Bob Kasser, of Franklin Park, Illinois, calls this recipe a cake, but it really is more like a sweet-bread recipe. It is especially delicious served warm.*

HUNGARIAN WALNUT CAKE

4 loaves
Preparation time: 30 minutes
Rising time: 2 hours
Baking time: 20 to 25 minutes

2 **cups milk**
1 **cup (2 sticks) unsalted butter, softened**
1¾ **cups sugar**
2 **packages active dry yeast**
¼ **cup warm water (105 to 115 degrees)**
1 **whole large egg**
2 **large egg yolks**
6 **cups all-purpose flour, about**
1½ **pounds fresh walnut pieces**

1. Heat milk in medium saucepan to simmer. Add ½ cup of the butter and ¼ cup of the sugar. Let cool.

2. Dissolve yeast in warm water with pinch sugar in large bowl. Let stand until bubbly.

3. Stir cooled milk mixture into yeast mixture. Stir in egg and egg yolks. Stir in flour, 1 cup at a time, to form a soft dough. Knead on lightly floured surface until smooth and elastic, about 10 minutes.

4. Put into greased bowl; turn once to grease top. Let rise, covered, in warm place until doubled in bulk, 1 to 1½ hours.

5. Meanwhile, for walnut filling, chop walnuts in food processor with on/off turns until very fine. Mix walnuts with remaining 1½ cups sugar.

6. Punch down dough; divide into 4 pieces. Let rest, covered, 15 minutes. Roll each piece on lightly floured surface to 13 by 10-inch rectangle. Spread with 2 tablespoons of the remaining butter. Sprinkle one-quarter of the nut mixture over dough, leaving 1-inch border on all sides. Roll up jelly-roll fashion, starting with short side. Pinch seams and ends closed. Put seam side down onto greased baking sheet. Repeat to roll and fill remaining dough pieces.

7. Let rise, covered, in warm place until almost doubled in bulk, about 30 minutes.

8. Heat oven to 350 degrees. Bake until golden brown, 20 to 25 minutes. Remove loaves from baking sheet immediately; cool completely on wire racks.

Here's an easy recipe for hot cross buns, which in pagan times were thought to have curative powers. They are best served warm; therefore, when making ahead, cut down a bit on the baking time to keep them from overbrowning when reheating in the oven.

HOT CROSS BUNS

About 20 buns
Preparation time: 45 minutes
Rising time: About 3 hours
Baking time: 15 to 20 minutes

¼ **cup warm water (105 to 115 degrees)**
1 **package active dry yeast**
Pinch sugar
¾ **cup plain yogurt, at room temperature**
⅓ **cup sugar**
¼ **cup butter or margarine, softened**
2 **large eggs**
1 **teaspoon salt**
½ **cup whole-wheat flour**
1 **teaspoon ground cinnamon**
½ **teaspoon ground nutmeg**
¼ **teaspoon ground cardamom**
3 **cups all-purpose flour, about**
½ **cup currants**
⅓ **cup chopped crystallized ginger**
¼ **cup chopped pitted prunes**
1 **egg yolk**
2 **tablespoons whipping cream**

GLAZE
1½ **cups confectioners' sugar**
2 **to 3 tablespoons fresh lemon juice**

1. Mix water, yeast and pinch of sugar in large bowl. Let stand until bubbly. Mix yogurt, ⅓ cup sugar, butter, eggs and salt in small bowl. Stir into yeast mixture.

2. Stir in whole-wheat flour, cinnamon, nutmeg and cardamom. Gradually stir in enough of the all-purpose flour to form a soft, slightly sticky dough. Knead on lightly floured surface until smooth and elastic, about 10 minutes.

3. Put dough into large buttered bowl. Turn once to butter top. Let rise, covered, in warm place until doubled in bulk, about 1½ hours.

4. Punch down dough. Knead in currants, ginger and prunes until evenly dispersed throughout. Return to bowl. Let rise a second time until doubled in bulk, about 1 hour.

5. Punch down dough and turn out onto floured surface. Pat dough to ½-inch thickness. Cut dough with a lightly floured round cutter about 2½ inches in diameter. Put onto greased baking sheets about 1 inch apart. Reroll scraps and cut to use up all the dough. Let rise until doubled in bulk, about 30 minutes.

6. Heat oven to 375 degrees. Just before baking, use floured scissors to snip a cross on top of each. Beat egg yolk and cream; brush lightly over tops.

7. Bake until golden, 15 to 20 minutes. Cool on wire racks until warm.

8. When cooled, mix confectioners' sugar and lemon juice to a thick drizzling consistency. Using a spoon, drizzle a cross over each bun. Serve warm.

Lutz Olkiewicz presided over the Drake Hotel's pastries for 25 years, 6 days a week. Now he's at The Sara Lee Company developing fresh cakes for bakeries and delicatessen counters in supermarkets.

His stollen is legendary in Chicago. Its deep flavor comes from the rum-soaked fruit, the use of the very finest ingredients and aging in the freezer.

This is not an easy recipe to make. Be sure to follow it exactly. Even though you may be tempted to forego brushing the baked stollen with all that butter, don't. The final butter not only adds flavor and acts as a preservative, but it is essential to the finished texture.

You can eat the stollen immediately, but after storage in the refrigerator or freezer it gets even better. It will keep up to a year if wrapped twice, then stored in a heavy plastic freezer bag with a twister seal to secure.

CLASSIC GERMAN STOLLEN

Three 3-pound loaves
Soaking time: 24 hours
Preparation time: 1½ hours
Rising time: About 6 hours
Baking time: 30 minutes
Standing time: Overnight

FRUIT MIXTURE

- ¾ pound golden raisins, about 2¼ cups
- ½ cup each, chopped: candied citron, candied orange rind
- ½ cup good quality dark rum

SPONGE

- 4 envelopes active dry yeast
- 1½ cups milk, scalded, cooled to 105 to 115 degrees
- 1¾ cups bread flour

BASE DOUGH

- 2¾ cups (5½ sticks) unsalted butter, softened
- ½ cup granulated sugar
- 1 teaspoon each: salt, vanilla extract
- ½ teaspoon almond extract

- Grated rind of 2 lemons
- 6¾ cups bread flour, about
- 2½ cups sliced blanched almonds

SEALER/TOPPING

- 2 cups (4 sticks) unsalted butter, melted, strained through cheesecloth
- 1 jar (12 ounces) apricot preserves
- ½ cup granulated sugar
- Few drops vanilla extract
- Confectioners' sugar

1. Put raisins, citron, orange rind and rum into large nonaluminum bowl. Cover; let stand, stirring occasionally, up to 24 hours.

2. For the sponge, put yeast in large bowl. Add cooled milk; stir until smooth. Stir in 1¾ cups flour until smooth again. (Mixture should be about the consistency of thin mashed potatoes.)

3. Sprinkle top with a little flour. Let rise in warm place until 1½ times its original size, 10 to 15 minutes. Keep checking it: Once the flour develops tracks and cracks in its surface, this will indicate that the sponge has risen. If it rises too much, it will collapse when you touch the top. If this happens, don't use it, as it will have become too sour and strong.

4. Meanwhile, for base dough, cream butter in large mixer bowl until light. Beat in sugar, salt, vanilla, almond extract and lemon rind, until creamy. Gradually beat in 6 cups of the flour.

5. Using your hands, a wooden spoon or the paddle or dough hook of a heavy-duty electric mixer, add the risen sponge to the base dough, mixing well.

6. Turn dough out onto floured work surface. Knead in remaining ¾ cup flour to form a soft dough. Knead and squeeze dough for a few seconds. Put into large greased bowl; sprinkle top lightly with flour. Let rise, covered, in warm place until doubled in bulk, 2 to 3 hours. (Because this is a heavy dough with lots of butter, it takes a long time to rise.)

7. Knead in fruit mixture and almonds on lightly floured surface until well mixed. Put into large bowl; cover and let rise a second time until doubled in bulk, 2 to 3 hours.

8. Punch down dough; divide into 3 pieces. Lightly press 1 piece on floured surface into thick rectangle. Repeat with remaining dough. Let rest, covered, about 10 minutes.

9. With your knuckles, make a lengthwise indentation down center of 1 rectangle. Press a round stick of wood about the thickness of a broom handle and about 20 inches long, into indentation. Remove wood and roll dough so it resembles a partly unrolled piece of paper with a flat center and rolls on either side. One of the rolls, however, should be twice as full as the other. Then fold the stollen in half so the two rolls are put on top of each other. Repeat with remaining dough.

continued on next page

10. Transfer each stollen to lightly greased baking sheet. Let rise, covered, until 1½ times its bulk (not more), 30 to 45 minutes.

11. Heat oven to 375 degrees. Bake until golden and wooden pick comes out dry, about 30 minutes. Let sit on baking sheet on wire rack at room temperature about 15 minutes. Pick off and discard any burned raisins or nuts.

12. Carefully, transfer stollen to second tray topped with parchment. Liberally brush all surfaces of stollen 3 times with hot butter. Continue to coat stollen with butter until all of butter is used. Cover stollen tightly. Let rest overnight in cool place.

13. Heat apricot preserves in small saucepan to boil; push though fine sieve into small bowl. Lightly brush over all surfaces of stollen. Cool.

14. Meanwhile, put granulated sugar into small bowl; sprinkle a few drops of vanilla extract over sugar. With fingers, work vanilla into sugar to form a streusel-like consistency. When stollen are cool, cover with sugar mixture. Then dust thickly with confectioners' sugar.

15. Store stollen in plastic bags in refrigerator if using within 1 week. If not, wrap each individually in plastic wrap; then wrap again in foil. Put into plastic bags and secure with twister seals. Freeze at least 1 week. Stollen will store beautifully up to a year in the freezer and improves with age.

For many families, Sunday dinner just wouldn't be Sunday dinner if cornbread were not on the table. Chicago caterer Tondalaya Thomas gave us her recipe for this Southern specialty which begs to be served alongside succotash, smothered chicken and rice and caramel cake.

Mix the batter just until moistened or the texture of the bread will be coarse. The addition of buttermilk gives the bread a distinct flavor.

HOT BUTTERED CORNBREAD

6 to 8 servings
Preparation time: 10 minutes
Baking time: 20 to 25 minutes

1 cup yellow or white cornmeal
1 cup cake flour, sifted
1 teaspoon baking powder
½ teaspoon baking soda
¼ teaspoon sugar
2 tablespoons vegetable oil
½ cup buttermilk
⅓ cup whole milk
2 large eggs, slightly beaten
¼ cup (½ stick) butter or margarine, softened

1. Heat oven to 400 degrees. Mix all dry ingredients in large bowl.

2. Put vegetable oil into 9-inch pie pan or 8-inch square cake pan. Put into oven while mixing other ingredients. Add buttermilk, whole milk and eggs to dry mixture. Mix gently until dry ingredients are moistened. Do not overmix.

3. Remove pan from oven; pour half of the oil into cornbread mixture. Stir just enough for oil to be absorbed. Pour mixture into pan. Bake until golden, 20 to 25 minutes. Immediately spread butter over entire top of cornbread. Cool on wire rack. Serve warm.

The following cornbread is ideal for using in poultry stuffings or as a simple bread to accompany a meal. It can also be jazzed up with other ingredients such as crumbled, cooked bacon, parsley, herbs or shredded cheese.

SKILLET CORNBREAD

6 servings
Preparation time: 10 minutes
Baking time: 20 to 25 minutes

1¼ cups yellow cornmeal
¾ cup all-purpose flour
4 teaspoons baking powder
1 teaspoon sugar
½ teaspoon salt
1 cup milk
4 tablespoons corn oil
1 large egg

1. Sift cornmeal, flour, baking powder, sugar and salt together in large bowl. Mix milk, 2 tablespoons of the corn oil and egg together in small bowl.

2. Heat oven to 450 degrees. Spoon remaining 2 tablespoons corn oil into 9-inch cast-iron skillet. Heat skillet in oven 10 minutes.

3. While skillet heats, add milk mixture to sifted dry ingredients; mix lightly just until dry ingredients are moistened. Do not overmix.

4. Pour batter into hot skillet (batter will sizzle). Return skillet to oven; reduce oven temperature to 425 degrees. Bake until bread is golden, crusty at edges and pulls away slightly from sides of skillet, 20 to 25 minutes. Cool completely on wire rack.

Mrs. Anton Zalesky of Western Springs, Illinois, submitted this quick bread recipe, which successfully combines the tartness of cranberries with the mellow flavor of bananas. The bread slices and tastes best if made one day ahead.

CRANBERRY-BANANA NUT BREAD

One 9-inch loaf
Preparation time: 30 minutes
Baking time: 1 hour, 15 minutes
Standing time: Overnight

2 **cups all-purpose flour**
1 **tablespoon baking powder**
½ **teaspoon each: salt, ground cinnamon**
¼ **cup (½ stick) butter or margarine, softened**
1 **cup sugar**
1 **large egg**
1 **cup cranberries, fresh or frozen, coarsely chopped**
1 **teaspoon grated orange rind**
½ **cup milk**
1 **cup each: mashed ripe banana, chopped pecans**

1. Heat oven to 350 degrees. Grease 9 by 5-inch loaf pan. Sift flour, baking powder, salt and cinnamon into medium bowl.

2. Cream butter and sugar in large mixer bowl until light and fluffy. Beat in egg. Add cranberries and orange rind; mix well. Stir in milk, then banana. Stir in dry ingredients and pecans just until blended.

3. Pour into prepared pan. Bake until wooden pick inserted comes out clean, about 1 hour and 15 minutes. Cool on wire rack 5 minutes. Invert on wire rack and cool completely. Wrap in foil or wax paper. Let stand overnight before slicing.

■ *This is a wonderful recipe from* Once Upon a Thyme, *a collection of recipes by the Young Women's Auxiliary of the Women's Club of Evanston, Illinois. The moist loaf makes good use of fall's anticipated harvest of pumpkins. For the best results, allow the bread to ripen for at least 6 hours before slicing.*

HARVEST LOAF

One 9-inch loaf
Preparation time: 20 minutes
Baking time: 1 hour, 5 minutes
Standing time: 6 hours

1¾ cups sifted all-purpose flour
1 teaspoon each: baking soda, ground cinnamon
½ teaspoon each: salt, ground nutmeg
¼ teaspoon each, ground: ginger, cloves
½ cup (1 stick) butter or margarine, softened
1 cup granulated sugar
2 large eggs
¾ cup mashed or solid-pack canned pumpkin
1 package (6 ounces) semisweet chocolate chips
¾ cup chopped walnuts or pecans

SPICE GLAZE

½ cup confectioners' sugar, sifted
⅛ teaspoon each, ground: nutmeg, cinnamon
1 to 2 teaspoons milk

1. Heat oven to 350 degrees. Mix flour with baking soda and spices in medium bowl. Cream butter in large mixer bowl until light and fluffy. Beat in sugar; beat in eggs.

2. Alternately beat dry ingredients and pumpkin into batter, beginning and ending with dry ingredients. Stir in chocolate chips and ½ cup of the nuts. Pour into well-greased 9 by 5-inch loaf pan. Sprinkle with remaining nuts.

3. Bake until golden and wooden pick inserted in center is withdrawn clean, 65 to 70 minutes. Cool in pan on wire rack 5 minutes. Turn out onto rack to cool completely.

4. For glaze, mix confectioners' sugar, nutmeg and cinnamon in small bowl. Stir in enough milk to form a thin glaze. Drizzle over cooled bread; let stand, covered loosely with foil, at least 6 hours before slicing.

This Irish recipe is an adaptation of one used at Winston's, a delightful butchery/ grocery/bakery in Chicago, that stocks a variety of British foodstuffs. Dark raisins can be substituted for golden raisins.

IRISH SODA BREAD

2 round loaves
Preparation time: 20 minutes
Baking time: 1 hour

4　cups sifted all-purpose flour
⅔　cup sugar
1　tablespoon baking powder
1　teaspoon each: baking soda, salt
1½　cups golden raisins or currants
1¾　cups buttermilk
2　large eggs, well-beaten
2　tablespoons butter, melted

1. Heat oven to 350 degrees. Sift dry ingredients into large bowl. Stir in raisins. Add remaining ingredients and mix briefly to moisten dry ingredients. Do not overmix; dough will be sticky.

2. Divide dough in half. Shape each on lightly floured surface into round loaves. Put onto greased baking sheets. Cut a cross on the top of each; sprinkle with flour. Bake until wooden pick inserted in center comes out clean, about 1 hour. Cool completely on wire rack.

If fruit is part of your muffin repertoire, make sure the tartness of the fruit contrasts with the slightly sweet batter, as in this cranberry muffin recipe. Fill the muffin tins about two-thirds full, bake and serve warm for optimum flavor.

BUTTERMILK CRANBERRY MUFFINS

1 dozen
Preparation time: 15 minutes
Baking time: 25 minutes

2　cups all-purpose flour
1　cup fresh cranberries
⅓　cup sugar
1　tablespoon baking powder
2　teaspoons finely grated orange rind
¼　teaspoon salt
1　cup buttermilk
¼　cup (½ stick) unsalted butter or margarine, melted
1　large egg, slightly beaten

1. Heat oven to 375 degrees. Lightly grease muffin tins. Mix ¼ cup of the flour and cranberries in small bowl. Mix remaining 1¾ cups flour, sugar, baking powder, orange rind and salt in large bowl.

2. Stir in buttermilk, melted butter and egg until dry ingredients are moistened. Stir in cranberry mixture. Do not overmix.

3. Spoon into prepared tins, filling two-thirds full. Bake until puffed and golden, 20 to 25 minutes. Cool on wire rack.

Dried cherries with a slightly tart bite sets these muffins apart from all others. This recipe is from Justin Rashid, the owner of American Spoon Foods in Petoskey, Michigan, who produces the cherries in addition to other fine foodstuffs.

The muffin batter should be stirred very briefly. Overmixing will result in coarse muffins with air tunnels.

CHERRY PECAN MUFFINS

1 dozen
Preparation time: 15 minutes
Baking time: 20 minutes

2 cups all-purpose flour
¼ cup sugar
2 teaspoons baking powder
½ teaspoon salt
½ cup (1 stick) unsalted butter, melted, cooled
¾ cup milk
2 large eggs, lightly beaten
1 teaspoon vanilla extract
1 cup (4 ounces) pecans, coarsely chopped
1 cup (4 ounces) dried red tart cherries
Grated rind of 1 lemon

1. Heat oven to 400 degrees. Lightly grease muffin tins. Mix flour, sugar, baking powder and salt in large bowl. Mix butter, milk, eggs and vanilla in another bowl.

2. Pour egg mixture into dry mixture. Add pecans, cherries and lemon rind. Stir until dry ingredients are moistened. Do not overmix.

3. Spoon into prepared muffin tins, filling two-thirds full. Bake until golden and wooden pick inserted into center of muffin comes out clean, about 20 minutes. Cool on wire rack.

Sharp Cheddar cheese and onion add interest and flavor to these basic corn muffins from chef Charlie Orr, owner of the Maple Tree Inn in Chicago. The muffins taste best when served warm with a little softened butter.

CHEDDAR-ONION CORN MUFFINS

About 1½ dozen
Preparation time: 15 minutes
Baking time: 40 minutes

1½ cups all-purpose flour
1 cup yellow cornmeal
1½ tablespoons baking powder
1 tablespoon sugar
½ teaspoon salt
1 cup shredded sharp Cheddar cheese
½ cup minced onion
1½ cups milk
¼ cup melted butter
2 eggs, lightly beaten

1. Heat oven to 350 degrees. Lightly grease muffin tins. Mix flour, cornmeal, baking powder, sugar and salt in large bowl. Add cheese and onion; mix well. Add milk, melted butter and eggs; stir just until dry ingredients are moistened. Do not overmix.

2. Spoon into prepared muffin tins, filling two-thirds full. Bake until puffed and golden, 30 to 40 minutes. Cool on wire rack.

These dense, good-for-you muffins, adapted from a recipe by the Quaker Oats Corporation, use a minimum of fat and lots of oat bran. Stir just until the dry ingredients are moistened and bake immediately because the leavening power of the baking powder and soda begins to diminish as soon as they get moist. If the batter must be held, put it in the refrigerator. Bring to room temperature before baking.

OAT BRAN MUFFINS

1 dozen
Preparation time: 15 minutes
Baking time: 20 minutes

1 **cup each: uncooked oat bran cereal, all-purpose flour**

⅓ **cup packed light brown sugar**

1½ **teaspoons baking powder**

1 **teaspoon baking soda**

½ **teaspoon each: salt, ground cinnamon**

¾ **cup skim milk**

⅓ **cup vegetable oil**

1 **large egg, slightly beaten**

1 **teaspoon grated orange rind**

TOPPING

¼ **cup each: packed light brown sugar, chopped almonds**

2 **tablespoons vegetable oil margarine, melted**

5 **teaspoons all-purpose flour**

¼ **teaspoon ground cinnamon**

1. Heat oven to 400 degrees. Lightly grease muffin tins. Mix cereal, 1 cup flour, ⅓ cup brown sugar, baking powder, baking soda, salt and cinnamon in large bowl. Add milk, oil, egg and orange rind; stir just until dry ingredients are moistened. Do not overmix.

2. Spoon into prepared muffin tins, filling two-thirds full. Mix topping ingredients in small bowl. Sprinkle over batter. Bake until puffed and golden, about 20 minutes. Cool on wire rack.

■ *Herbed biscuits were a featured recipe in a story about the Cook's Garden, a real vegetable and herb garden created by* The Tribune *in conjunction with Cantigny Gardens and Museums in Winfield, Illinois.*

HERBED BISCUITS

About 1 dozen
Preparation time: 20 minutes
Baking time: 20 to 30 minutes

BISCUITS
- 2 **cups all-purpose flour**
- 1 **tablespoon baking powder**
- 2 **teaspoons each: sugar, minced fresh oregano (or ¾ teaspoon dried)**
- 1 **teaspoon each: salt, minced fresh basil (or ¼ teaspoon dried)**
- ¼ **teaspoon garlic powder**
- 6 **tablespoons cold butter or margarine, cut into pieces**
- ⅔ **cup milk**
- 2 **teaspoons Dijon mustard**
- 3 **green onions, finely chopped**
- 2 **tablespoons finely chopped fresh parsley**

GLAZE
- 1 **large egg**
- ½ **teaspoon salt**

1. Heat oven to 375 degrees. Mix flour, baking powder, sugar, oregano, salt, basil and garlic powder in large bowl. Cut in butter with pastry blender until mixture resembles coarse crumbs. Mix milk and mustard in small bowl until well blended. Add onions and parsley; mix. Stir milk mixture into flour mixture just until soft dough forms. Do not overmix.

2. Turn out onto well-floured surface. Pat out to ½-inch thickness. Cut into 2½-inch rounds, using a floured biscuit cutter. Put 1 inch apart onto lightly greased baking sheet.

3. For glaze, mix egg and salt. Brush over biscuits. Bake until golden, 20 to 30 minutes. Cool on wire rack. Serve warm.

The addition of whole-wheat flour to these baking powder biscuits adds a nutty taste and slightly dense texture.

WHOLE-WHEAT BISCUITS

About 1 dozen
Preparation time: 10 minutes
Baking time: 15 minutes

1 cup each: whole-wheat flour, all-purpose flour
1 tablespoon baking powder
½ teaspoon salt
⅓ cup vegetable shortening, cold
¾ cup buttermilk

1. Heat oven to 450 degrees. Mix flours, baking powder and salt in large bowl. Cut in shortening until mixture resembles coarse crumbs. Stir in buttermilk just until soft dough forms. Do not overmix.

2. Turn out onto well-floured surface. Pat out to ½-inch thickness. Cut into 2½-inch rounds using a floured biscuit cutter. Put 1-inch apart onto ungreased baking sheet. Bake until golden, 12 to 15 minutes. Cool on wire rack. Serve warm.

When the Carlton Tower in London was selected in 1984 as the best British tea place, we had to have their recipe for scones. The secret for these rich biscuits is to use unsalted butter, not margarine. Do not overmix the ingredients or you'll be serving something similar to hockey pucks.

RICH SCONES

About 1 dozen
Preparation time: 20 minutes
Baking time: 15 minutes

2 cups all-purpose flour
⅓ cup sugar
1½ teaspoons baking powder
¼ cup (½ stick) cold unsalted butter, cut into pieces
⅓ cup currants
2 large eggs
½ cup milk
Unsalted butter, whipped cream or jam for serving

1. Heat oven to 450 degrees. Sift flour, sugar and baking powder into large bowl. Cut in butter until mixture resembles coarse crumbs. Stir in currants. Mix 1 egg and milk in small bowl. Stir into flour mixture with large fork just until soft dough forms.

2. Turn out onto lightly floured surface. Pat dough into ½-inch-thick circle. Cut into 2½-inch rounds using a floured biscuit cutter. Put onto greased baking sheet.

3. Beat remaining egg; brush over biscuits. Bake until puffed and tops are golden, about 15 minutes. Cool on wire rack. Serve warm with unsalted butter, whipped cream or jam.

NOTE: Do not overmix the dough, just combine ingredients until free of lumps. Brush tops twice with eggs for a beautiful shine.

These sweet scones are studded with candied pineapple and macadamia nuts. Instead of cutting into rounds, cut these into pie-shaped wedges before baking.

PINEAPPLE-MACADAMIA SCONES

8 scones
Preparation time: 20 minutes
Baking time: 15 to 18 minutes

1 jar (3½ ounces) macadamia nuts, coarsely chopped
2 cups sifted all-purpose flour
2 teaspoons sugar
1 teaspoon each: cream of tartar, baking soda
½ teaspoon salt
½ cup (1 stick) cold unsalted butter, cut into pieces
¾ cup buttermilk
¼ cup dark rum
½ cup coarsely chopped candied pineapple
2 tablespoons each: milk, sugar

1. Heat oven to 400 degrees. Add nuts to boiling water in small saucepan for 10 seconds. Drain; pat dry on paper towels.

2. Sift flour, 2 teaspoons sugar, cream of tartar, baking soda and salt in large bowl. Cut in butter until mixture resembles coarse crumbs. Stir in buttermilk and rum just until soft dough forms. Stir in nuts and candied pineapple. Do not overmix.

3. Turn out onto lightly floured surface; divide into half. Pat each into ¾-inch-thick circle. Cut into quarters. Put onto greased baking sheet.

4. Brush tops with milk; sprinkle with sugar. Bake until golden, 15 to 18 minutes. Cool on wire rack. Serve warm.

Food Guide reader Alyce LaVine from Hillside, Illinois, submitted her fail-proof recipe for popovers. Because popovers are made with a batter containing no yeast or baking powder, the batter should be beaten vigorously for 3 to 4 minutes to activate the gluten in the flour.

NEVER-FAIL POPOVERS

10 popovers
Preparation time: 10 minutes
Baking time: 1 hour, 10 to 15 minutes

6 large eggs
2 cups milk
6 tablespoons butter or margarine, melted
2 cups sifted all-purpose flour
1 teaspoon salt

1. Heat oven to 375 degrees. Beat eggs in large bowl; stir in milk and butter and mix well. Add flour and salt; stir vigorously 3 to 4 minutes.

2. Divide batter evenly between 10, well-buttered, 6-ounce custard cups placed on baking sheet.

3. Bake 60 minutes. Slit each open popover on one side to let out steam. Return to oven; bake until well browned, 15 more minutes. Serve immediately.

Light, slightly sweet and with a delicate taste of apple, these glazed, walnut-laden doughnuts won't hang around in the kitchen for long. Pay close attention to the temperature of the oil while frying. Oil that is too hot will result in undercooked doughnuts and oil that is too cool will produce greasy ones.

APPLE CIDER DOUGHNUTS

About 10 doughnuts
Preparation time: 15 minutes
Chilling time: 15 minutes
Frying time: 15 minutes

2　cups sifted all-purpose flour
3½ teaspoons baking powder
¾　teaspoon salt
½　teaspoon ground nutmeg
¼　cup each: vegetable shortening, sugar
1　large egg
1¼ cups buttermilk
½　cup chopped walnuts
　　Oil or vegetable shortening for deep-frying

APPLE CIDER GLAZE
1　pound confectioners' sugar, sifted
6　tablespoons unsweetened apple cider or juice

1. Sift flour, baking powder, salt and nutmeg in large bowl. Cream ¼ cup shortening, sugar and egg in large mixer bowl until smooth. Alternately beat in flour mixture and buttermilk. Dough should be moderately stiff. Stir in walnuts. Refrigerate dough about 15 minutes.

2. Heat oil in deep-fryer or large, deep saucepan to 375 degrees. Put dough into doughnut maker; press a few doughnuts at a time into hot oil. Deep-fry, turning frequently, until golden brown, 3 to 5 minutes. Remove with slotted spoon. Drain on wire rack set over paper towels.

3. Mix confectioners' sugar with enough of the apple cider to make a thin smooth glaze. Dip one doughnut at a time into glaze; allow excess to drip off. Put onto rack set over baking sheet; let stand until glaze is set.

DESSERTS

OK, we all know by now that we need to cut back on fat, on the cholesterol. Many of us go jogging in the morning, work out at lunchtime, have an exercycle in the bedroom and count laps in the pool.

But we still love our desserts. "We go out jogging and then get home and reach for a piece of chocolate cake," said a food consultant one afternoon as she demonstrated working with chocolate in *The Tribune* test kitchen.

After all, what is more American than apple pie? Or flourless chocolate cake? Or macadamia nut tart? Or bread pudding?

We love our desserts, so when we eat them, let's eat the best. Dessert may not be for every night, but when we do indulge, we should do so with the finest. Dessert should be the grand finale to a meal.

The desserts in this chapter come from many sources and have a vast variety. Several are from well-known Chicago chefs, who have shared their favorite sweet endings with *The Tribune* over the years. Others are from Chicagoans who have sent us their favorite recipes. Most have been created in *The Tribune* test kitchen and then heartily enjoyed by all the members of the food staff.

There are comfort desserts here, pound cakes, puddings and custards reminiscent of childhood. There are also light desserts, such as the tangerine sherbet and cinnamon ice cream. And there are the sinfully decadent desserts like that macadamia nut tart—the kind of dessert where you cut yourself just a thin piece because you know it's so rich and then help yourself to a second slice.

We have enjoyed them all. So will you.

DESSERTS

CAKES

Carrot nut cake

Chocolate angel food cake

Chocolate fudge peanut butter cake

Deluxe chocolate zucchini cake

Chocolate hazelnut cake

Flourless chocolate cake with
orange liqueur

Fudgy flourless chocolate cake

Mary Meade's white fruitcake

Dacquoise meringue cake

Peanut butter cookie cake

Pineapple macadamia upside-down
cake

Buttermilk lemon cake

Semolina pound cake

Peach cake roll

White chocolate coconut cake

CHEESECAKES

Amaretto cheesecake

Chocolate cheesecake

Layered strawberry cheesecake

PIES & TARTS

Basic pie crust

Fast food processor pie crust

Apple slices

All-American apple pie

Blue-ribbon apple pie

Buttered toffee apple pie

Classic cherry pie

Ginger peach pie

Key lime pie

Lemon meringue pie

Pumpkin pecan pie

Strawberry rhubarb lattice pie

Fresh fruit tarts

Fresh nectarine tart

Hot French apple tart

Macadamia nut tart

COBBLERS, PUDDINGS & SHORTCAKE

Easy pear crisp

Mixed berry cobbler

Peach buckle

Bourbon pecan pumpkin pudding

Bread pudding soufflé

Raisin bread pudding with
whiskey sauce

Crème caramel

Crème brulée with berries

Golden rice pudding

Tiramisu

Chocolate strawberry shortcake

OTHER DELIGHTS

Baklava

Chocolate mousse

Chocolate satin

Cold cranberry soufflé

Passion fruit soup

Poached cinnamon pears

Profiteroles with chocolate
cream sauce

ICE CREAMS, SHERBET & SORBET

Bittersweet chocolate ice cream

Cinnamon ice cream

Coffee ice cream

Prune and Armagnac ice cream

Strawberry ice cream

Superb vanilla custard ice cream

Cassis and blackberry sorbet

Frozen mango whip

Pear lemon ice

Tangerine sherbet

DESSERT SAUCES

Crème Anglaise

Luscious chocolate sauce

Fresh strawberry sauce

Rhubarb orange sauce

Carrots improve your eyesight, of course, so here's a recipe for your vision and your sweet-tooth. This version of carrot cake, from food consultant Suzanne Checchia of Evanston, Illinois, with almonds and a cream cheese frosting, is a definite winner.

CARROT NUT CAKE

One 9-inch cake, 10 servings
Preparation time: 35 minutes
Baking time: 40 to 45 minutes

1 cup whole blanched almonds
½ cup plus 3 tablespoons fine, dry bread crumbs
6 large eggs, separated, at room temperature
1½ teaspoons grated orange rind
¾ teaspoon ground cinnamon
¼ teaspoon salt
⅔ cup plus ¼ cup sugar
1 cup finely shredded carrots, lightly packed
Cream cheese frosting (recipe follows)

1. Heat oven to 350 degrees. Process almonds in food processor with on/off turns, until very finely ground and powdery. Grease 9-inch springform pan well; coat evenly with 3 tablespoons of the bread crumbs.

2. Beat egg yolks in small mixer bowl until thick, lemon colored and doubled in volume. Beat in orange rind, cinnamon and salt. Gradually beat in ⅔ cup sugar until thick and fluffy. Transfer to large bowl. Fold in almonds and remaining ½ cup bread crumbs; fold in carrots.

3. Beat egg whites in large mixer bowl until foamy; gradually beat in remaining ¼ cup sugar until stiff peaks form. Stir one-quarter of the egg whites into yolk mixture; fold in remaining egg whites. Spread batter evenly in prepared pan.

4. Bake until wooden pick inserted into center comes out clean, 40 to 45 minutes. Cool completely in pan on wire rack. Cake will settle slightly. Remove side of pan; frost top of cake with cream cheese frosting.

CREAM CHEESE FROSTING

About 1½ cups

1 package (3 ounces) cream cheese, softened
¼ cup (½ stick) unsalted butter, softened
1 teaspoon vanilla extract
¼ teaspoon grated orange rind
2½ to 3 cups sifted confectioners' sugar

1. Beat cream cheese and butter in smaller mixer bowl until light and fluffy. Beat in vanilla extract and orange rind. Gradually beat in sugar until spreading consistency.

Chocolate angel food cake manages to taste incredibly rich while keeping that light, airy, egg-white texture that we associate with angel food. The only trick is to avoid overbeating the whites, or overmixing when the other ingredients are folded into the beaten whites.

CHOCOLATE ANGEL FOOD CAKE

One 10-inch tube cake, 10 servings
Preparation time: 25 minutes
Baking time: 35 minutes

1¼ cups sifted cake flour
1¾ cups granulated sugar
½ cup unsweetened Dutch-processed cocoa
12 large egg whites, room temperature
1½ teaspoons cream of tartar
½ teaspoon salt
1 teaspoon vanilla extract
2 ounces bittersweet chocolate, grated
Confectioners' sugar

TO SERVE, OPTIONAL
Pureed strawberries
Crème Anglaise (see recipe, page 600)
Whipped cream, sliced strawberries, mint sprigs, for garnish

1. Heat oven to 375 degrees. Sift together cake flour, ¾ cup of the granulated sugar and cocoa 3 times; set aside.

2. Beat egg whites, cream of tartar and salt in large mixer bowl until soft peaks form. Beat in remaining 1 cup of sugar, ¼ cup at a time, until stiff peaks form when beater is raised.

3. Carefully fold in vanilla extract. Sift one-quarter of the cocoa-flour mixture over beaten egg whites. Fold carefully (about 15 strokes). Repeat until all of the dry mixture is incorporated.

4. Fold in grated chocolate. Pour into ungreased 10-inch tube pan. Smooth out top. Make 20 or 30 cuts through the batter with a knife to remove any large air pockets.

5. Bake until cake springs back when touched lightly, about 35 minutes. Take out of oven and invert pan to cool for 2 hours. Remove from pan. Put onto platter. Sprinkle with confectioners' sugar.

SERVING SUGGESTION: Pour pureed strawberries over half of a large serving plate. Spoon crème Anglaise carefully over the other half of the plate. Put a wedge of the cake in center of plate. Garnish with whipped cream, sliced strawberries and mint sprigs.

■ *Chocolate and peanut butter are two perennial favorites, and this cake recipe from* The Tribune *test kitchen happily combines the two.*

CHOCOLATE FUDGE PEANUT BUTTER CAKE

One 13 by 9-inch cake, 10 servings
Preparation time: 25 minutes
Baking time: 40 to 50 minutes

CHOCOLATE BATTER

- **1 cup (2 sticks) unsalted butter or margarine, softened**
- **2 cups granulated sugar**
- **2 teaspoons vanilla extract**
- **4 large eggs**
- **1½ cups all-purpose flour**
- **¾ cup unsweetened Dutch-processed cocoa**
- **1 teaspoon baking powder**
- **½ cup peanut butter chips**

PEANUT BUTTER BATTER

- **¾ cup smooth peanut butter**
- **⅓ cup butter or margarine, softened**
- **⅓ cup granulated sugar**
- **2 tablespoons all-purpose flour**
- **2 large eggs**
- **¾ teaspoon vanilla extract**
- **Chocolate frosting (recipe follows)**

1. Heat oven to 350 degrees. Grease 13 by 9-inch baking pan.

2. For chocolate batter, cream 1 cup butter and 2 cups sugar in large mixer bowl until light and fluffy. Beat in 2 teaspoons vanilla extract; beat in 4 eggs, one at a time. Beat in 1½ cups flour, cocoa and baking powder until mixed. Stir in peanut butter chips.

3. For peanut butter batter, cream peanut butter and ⅓ cup butter in small mixer bowl. Beat in ⅓ cup sugar, 2 tablespoons flour, 2 eggs and ¾ teaspoon vanilla. Beat until smooth.

4. Spread half of the chocolate batter over bottom of prepared pan. Spread peanut butter mixture over chocolate mixture. Spread remaining chocolate mixture over all. Use a spatula to swirl layers together creating a marbled effect.

5. Bake until tops springs back when touched lightly, 40 to 50 minutes. Cool completely on wire rack. Frost top of cake with chocolate frosting. Let stand until frosting sets. Cut into bars.

CHOCOLATE FROSTING | About 1½ cups

3 ounces unsweetened
   chocolate
3 tablespoons butter or
   margarine
2⅔ cups confectioners'
   sugar, sifted
¾ teaspoon vanilla
   extract
¼ teaspoon salt
4 to 5 tablespoons water

1. Melt chocolate and butter in small saucepan. Remove from heat; stir in confectioners' sugar, vanilla and salt. Stir in enough water to form a spreading consistency.

How big did you say that zucchini was in your garden? Everyone who grows zucchini needs lots of zucchini recipes, and here's one that combines that fast-growing vegetable with rich chocolate for a tasty, not hard-to-make cake. If you don't have a garden, this cake is even worth a stop at the vegetable stand.

DELUXE CHOCOLATE ZUCCHINI CAKE

One 12-inch Bundt cake, 12 servings
Preparation time: 25 minutes
Baking time: 1 hour

2 cups all-purpose flour
1 cup whole-wheat flour
1¼ teaspoons each: baking
   powder, baking soda
1 teaspoon salt
⅛ teaspoon ground
   cinnamon
4 large eggs
2 cups sugar
1¼ cups vegetable oil
3 ounces unsweetened
   chocolate, melted,
   cooled
1½ teaspoons vanilla
   extract
½ teaspoon almond
   extract
1 cup chopped pecans or
   walnuts
½ cup raisins or chopped
   dates

3 cups coarsely shredded
   zucchini, patted dry
   Confectioners' sugar

1. Heat oven to 350 degrees. Butter 12-cup Bundt pan and dust lightly with flour. Sift dry ingredients together and set aside.

2. Beat eggs and sugar in large mixer bowl until thick and fluffy. Beat in oil; beat in chocolate and extracts. Fold in dry ingredients, nuts and raisins. Fold in zucchini. Spread batter evenly in prepared pan.

3. Bake until wooden pick inserted in center comes out clean, about 1 hour. Let cool in pan 10 minutes, then invert onto wire rack; cool completely. Sprinkle with confectioners' sugar.

■ *Cooking teacher Jean True's chocolate hazelnut cake is moist, dense and full of hazelnuts. It is delicious frosted with a chocolate frosting made with bittersweet chocolate. The unfrosted cake also freezes well.*

CHOCOLATE HAZELNUT CAKE

One 13 by 9-inch cake, 10 servings
Preparation time: 30 minutes
Baking time: 1 hour

8 **ounces shelled hazelnuts (filberts)**
1 **cup (2 sticks) unsalted butter, softened**
1 **cup sugar**
1½ **teaspoons vanilla extract**
7 **large eggs, separated**
½ **pound bittersweet chocolate, finely grated (see note)**
¾ **cup all-purpose flour**
   Pinch salt
   Chocolate frosting (see recipe, page 537) or your favorite chocolate or vanilla buttercream icing

1. Heat oven to 400 degrees. Put hazelnuts into baking pan. Bake until nuts are golden and outer skins are loose, about 15 minutes. Immediately put nuts into clean towel. Then rub together in towel to remove skins. Let nuts cool. Process nuts in food processor with on/off turns until finely ground and powdery. (Or chop on a cutting board until finely minced.)

2. Reduce oven temperature to 300 degrees. Butter and flour 13 by 9-inch baking pan.

3. Cream butter and sugar in large mixer bowl until light and fluffy. Beat in vanilla extract. Beat in egg yolks, one at a time.

4. Mix ground nuts, grated chocolate and flour. Add chocolate mixture, a few tablespoons at a time, to butter mixture until smooth.

5. Put egg whites and pinch of salt in large mixer bowl. Beat until stiff peaks form. Gently stir one-quarter of the whites into batter to lighten it. Then fold in remaining whites. Spread batter evenly in prepared pan.

6. Bake until wooden pick inserted in center is withdrawn clean, about 1 hour. Cool completely on wire rack. Frost top of cake with chocolate frosting. Let stand until frosting sets. Cut into squares.

NOTE: To grate chocolate in food processor fitted with metal blade, put chunked chocolate and 1 teaspoon sugar in machine, process with on/off turns until grated.

■ *Rich and dense, here is a chocolate lover's dream. Former chef/owner Jean Banchet, of Le Français in Wheeling, Illinois, serves this cake with a few spoonfuls of custard sauce, but it's rich enough to forgo the sauce. Don't be dismayed by the crust that forms and then cracks on top of the cake. Simply sprinkle the top with confectioners' sugar before serving.*

FLOURLESS CHOCOLATE CAKE WITH ORANGE LIQUEUR

One 12-inch cake, 12 to 14 servings
Preparation time: 30 minutes
Baking time: 1½ hours
Chilling time: Several hours or overnight

14 **ounces bittersweet baking chocolate, finely chopped**
¾ **cup plus 2 tablespoons (1¾ sticks) unsalted butter**
1¼ **cups granulated sugar**
10 **large eggs, separated**
2 **tablespoons orange-flavored liqueur**
1 **tablespoon vanilla extract**
Confectioners' sugar

1. Put chocolate and butter into top of double boiler. Cook and stir over simmering water until melted. Stir in ¾ cup of the sugar. Continue stirring until sugar is almost dissolved.

2. Beat egg yolks in large mixer bowl until light. Beat in a little of the warm chocolate until well combined. Continue adding chocolate until fully combined. Return chocolate mixture to top of double boiler; cook, stirring until slightly thickened. Do not boil. Remove from heat.

3. Heat oven to 250 degrees. Butter and flour 12-inch springform pan. Line sides of pan with a strip of buttered wax paper.

4. Beat egg whites in large mixer bowl until foamy. Beat in remaining ½ cup sugar, 1 tablespoon at a time, until mixture holds stiff peaks.

5. Stir liqueur and vanilla into chocolate mixture, mixing well. With a rubber spatula, scrape chocolate mixture over egg whites. Fold together gently but thoroughly.

6. Spoon batter into prepared pan. Bake until set and top is crusty, about 1½ hours. Cool on wire rack to room temperature. Refrigerate until cold.

7. Loosen edge of cake from sides of pan. Remove sides of pan. Put cake onto platter. Sprinkle heavily with confectioners' sugar. Top will be brittle.

This recipe, originated by chef John Terczak in 1982 at Chicago's Gordon Restaurant, was printed twice in The Tribune: *the second time because a reader desperately wrote that she had lost her original copy. With its fudgy texture and deep chocolate flavor it's certainly worth saving.*

FUDGY FLOURLESS CHOCOLATE CAKE

One 8-inch cake, 8 servings
Preparation time: 30 minutes
Baking time: 60 to 70 minutes
Chilling time: Several hours or overnight

7 **tablespoons unsalted butter**

9 **ounces semisweet chocolate, finely chopped**

7 **large eggs, separated Pinch salt**

⅓ **cup sugar Whipped cream for garnish**

1. Generously coat 8-inch round by 3-inch deep cake pan or springform pan using 1 tablespoon of the butter. Dust pan with flour; refrigerate until needed.

2. Put chocolate and remaining 6 tablespoons butter into top of double boiler set over simmering water. Cook and stir until well mixed and melted.

3. Mix egg yolks in small bowl; add a little of the warm chocolate; stir well. Scrape mixture into remaining chocolate and stir well; then set aside in warm place, uncovered.

4. Heat oven to 250 degrees. Beat egg whites and salt in large mixer bowl until soft peaks form. Beat in sugar, 1 teaspoon at a time, until stiff and glossy, but not dry.

5. Scrape chocolate mixture over egg whites; fold together carefully but thoroughly. Spoon batter into pan.

6. Bake until center is set but still wiggles, 50 to 60 minutes. Cool on wire racks 10 minutes. As it begins to cool, cake will pull away from side of pan. Remove sides of springform or, if using ordinary cake pan, invert cake onto serving plate to cool. Cool completely. Refrigerate until cold.

7. Cut cake in wedges. Serve each wedge topped with a large dollop of whipped cream.

Like Betty Crocker, Mary Meade sprang full-blown from an editor's head in an era when it was customary to attribute recipes to a fictional persona. She may not really exist, but the rich, easy-to-make white fruitcake that still bears her name is a longtime favorite. It stores well for months and the flavor improves with age.

MARY MEADE'S WHITE FRUITCAKE

4 cakes, 12 servings each
Preparation time: 40 minutes
Standing time: Overnight
Baking time: 3 hours
Aging time: 1 week or longer

1 **pound each: candied pineapple, candied cherries, golden raisins**

½ **pound each, candied: lemon rind, orange rind, citron**

1½ **cups orange-flavored liqueur or white wine**

3 **cups (6 sticks) unsalted butter or margarine, softened**

2 **cups sugar**

12 **large eggs**

6 **cups sifted all-purpose flour**

1½ **teaspoons baking powder**

1 **teaspoon salt**

1½ **pounds pecan or walnut halves, coarsely chopped**

Light corn syrup

Whole candied cherries, pecan or walnut halves for garnish

1. Cut pineapple in pieces of varying size. Slice cherries in half. Put pineapple, cherries, raisins, rinds and citron into large bowl. Add liqueur; let stand, covered, overnight.

2. Heat oven to 250 degrees. Cream butter and sugar in large mixer bowl until light and fluffy. Beat in eggs, one at a time, until mixture is fluffy. Add dry ingredients and mix well. Stir into fruit mixture; add nuts. Blend until well mixed.

3. Grease four 10 by 3-inch or 9 by 5-inch pans. Line pans with heavy brown paper. Grease paper. Spoon batter lightly into pans.

4. Put shallow pan of water into oven on lowest rack. Bake cakes on center rack until golden and pulled away from sides of pans, about 3 hours. Cool cakes in pans on wire racks 20 minutes. Unmold; remove paper. Cool completely on wire racks.

5. Brush with additional liqueur if desired. Store wrapped in foil in covered container 1 week or more. Before you give away or serve, brush with light corn syrup, decorate with fruit and nuts and brush again with corn syrup. Let them dry somewhat before wrapping in plastic.

At the end of one summer, Tribune *food writers decided to rejoice in the fact that bathing-suit, calorie-counting days were almost over, so we printed some of the most decadently rich dessert recipes available. This one was developed by Jeanne McInerney-Lubeck of Fresh Start Bakery and Catering in Flossmoor, Illinois. It immediately became an absolute favorite.*

DACQUOISE MERINGUE CAKE

One 9-inch layer cake, 14 servings
Preparation time: 1½ hours
Baking time: 45 minutes
Chilling time: 1 hour

MERINGUE LAYERS
- 8 **large egg whites, about 1 cup**
- ⅛ **teaspoon salt**
- 1 **cup sugar**
- ½ **cup finely ground pecans**

BUTTERCREAM
- 1 **cup water**
- 3 **cups sugar**
- 5 **whole eggs**
- 5 **egg yolks**
- 4½ **cups (9 sticks) unsalted butter, softened**

GARNISH
- 1 **package (8 ounces) pecans, coarsely chopped**
- 4 **ounces bittersweet or semisweet chocolate, melted**

1. Heat oven to 300 degrees. Cut parchment paper or brown paper to fit baking sheets. Trace three 9-inch circles on the paper.

2. For meringue layers, beat egg whites and salt in large mixer bowl until soft peaks form. Gradually beat in sugar until stiff peaks form. Fold in ground nuts.

3. Fit large pastry bag with ½-inch round tip. Fill bag with some of the meringue mixture. Starting in center of circle on prepared paper, pipe out meringue in concentric circles to completely fill in the traced circle.

4. Bake until golden and crisp, about 30 minutes. Reduce oven temperature to 225 degrees; continue baking until dry and crisp, 15 to 20 minutes. Turn off oven; let cool in oven at least 1 hour to dry out meringue.

5. For buttercream, heat water and sugar to boil in small, heavy saucepan. Cover and boil 2 minutes. Uncover, insert candy thermometer and boil until candy thermometer registers 250 to 260 degrees.

6. Meanwhile, beat 5 whole eggs and 5 egg yolks in large mixer bowl until light. With mixer running, slowly pour boiling sugar-water into eggs. Beat continuously until mixture is very light and cool to the touch, about 10 minutes. Gradually beat in softened butter until fluffy and spreading consistency. (If buttercream begins to separate, set mixer bowl over pan of simmering water; beat until smooth again.)

7. To assemble, slip a long metal spatula under meringue layers to loosen from paper. Put one layer onto platter. Spread generously with buttercream. Top with second meringue layer. Spread generously with buttercream. Top with remaining meringue layer. Frost top and sides of cake with remaining buttercream.

8. Press chopped pecans onto top and sides of cake. Drizzle melted chocolate in center of cake. Refrigerate until buttercream is firm, at least 1 hour. Slice with serrated knife.

NOTE: As with most meringue recipes, the cake layers are best made on a cool, dry day. If making in advance, be sure they are thoroughly dry and crisp, then store in a covered tin or in a closed, dark oven.

Ever wonder what else to do with Girl Scout cookies besides eat them right out of the box? Well, 16 Chicago-area restaurants, hotels, schools and other food businesses competed to see who could come up with the most innovative recipes using the cookies. This was one of the favorites, created by Tribune *test kitchen director JeanMarie Brownson, and it uses Girl Scout peanut butter sandwich cookies.*

PEANUT BUTTER COOKIE CAKE

One 9-inch layer cake, 14 servings
Preparation time: 1¼ hours
Baking time: 35 minutes
Chilling time: 1 hour

CAKE
- **1 cup all-purpose flour**
- **¾ cup granulated sugar**
- **3½ teaspoons baking powder**
- **¼ teaspoon salt**
- **1¾ cups finely crushed peanut butter sandwich cookies**
- **¾ cup (1½ sticks) margarine, softened**
- **1 cup plus 2 tablespoons milk**
- **1½ teaspoons vanilla extract**
- **2 large eggs**

FILLING
- **1½ cups milk**
- **4 large egg yolks, beaten**
- **½ cup granulated sugar**
- **6 tablespoons all-purpose flour**
- **1 tablespoon butter**
- **1½ teaspoons vanilla extract**

FROSTING
- **1 cup (2 sticks) unsalted butter, softened**
- **½ cup smooth peanut butter**
- **2 to 2½ cups confectioners' sugar, sifted**

GARNISH
- **9 peanut butter sandwich cookies**

1. Heat oven to 375 degrees. Lightly grease two 9-inch round cake layer pans. Line bottoms of pans with circle of wax paper. Lightly grease paper.

2. For cake, sift flour, sugar, baking powder and salt into large mixer bowl. Stir in crushed cookies. Add margarine, milk and vanilla extract. Beat on low speed until dry ingredients are moistened. Beat on medium speed 2 minutes. Beat in eggs, one at a time, until mixed.

3. Pour batter into prepared pans. Bake until tops spring back when lightly touched, about 25 minutes. Cool 10 minutes on wire racks. Remove from pans; remove paper. Cool completely on wire racks.

4. For custard filling, heat milk in large saucepan to simmer. Put egg yolks, sugar and flour in medium bowl. Stir in 1 cup of the hot milk; stir until smooth. Pour egg mixture back into pan with remaining milk. Cook and stir over medium heat until mixture is smooth and thick and some bubbles break on the surface. Immediately strain through fine sieve into large bowl. Stir in butter and vanilla. Refrigerate, covered, until very cold.

5. For frosting, cream butter and peanut butter in large mixer bowl until very light and fluffy. Beat in confectioners' sugar until mixture is spreading consistency.

6. To assemble, slice cake layers horizontally in half. Be careful; layers are very fragile. Put one layer onto platter. Spread with one-third of the custard mixture. Top with second cake layer. Spread with another one-third of custard. Top with third cake layer; spread with remaining custard. Top with remaining cake layer.

7. Frost top and sides of the cake. Make swirls in frosting with the tip of a spatula. Crush remaining cookies and sprinkle over top of cake for garnish. Refrigerate until chilled, about 1 hour.

NOTE: You may substitute one 3-ounce box of instant or regular vanilla pudding mix prepared according to the package directions for the filling.

This is a classic upside-down cake updated with fresh pineapple, bourbon and macadamia nuts. The recipe was given to us by Philadelphia cooking teacher and author Julie Dannebaum.

PINEAPPLE MACADAMIA UPSIDE-DOWN CAKE

One 8-inch cake, 6 to 8 servings
Preparation time: 15 minutes
Cooking time: 40 minutes

½ **cup (1 stick) unsalted butter**
⅔ **cup pure maple syrup**
3 **cups ¼-inch cubes fresh pineapple**
2 **tablespoons bourbon**
½ **cup chopped macadamia nuts, toasted**
⅔ **cup sugar**
1 **large egg**
1 **teaspoon vanilla extract**
1¼ **cups all-purpose flour**
2 **teaspoons baking powder**
   Pinch salt
⅔ **cup milk**

1. Heat oven to 350 degrees. Melt ¼ cup of the butter in 8-inch square or round baking pan. Add maple syrup and pineapple cubes. Cook over low heat to remove the raw taste of the fruit, about 5 minutes. Sprinkle with bourbon and macadamia nuts.

2. Cream remaining ¼ cup butter and sugar in small bowl. Beat in egg and vanilla extract. Beat until light and fluffy, about 5 minutes. Combine dry ingredients; add alternately with milk to egg mixture until smooth. Pour batter over pineapple mixture.

3. Bake until cake springs back when touched lightly in center, 40 to 45 minutes. Cool 10 minutes; invert onto platter. Cool completely.

This recipe by Nancy Solomon is adapted from the 1983 book, Parker Cooks, *a collection from the alumni and friends of Francis W. Parker School in Chicago.*

BUTTERMILK LEMON CAKE

One 10-inch tube cake, 16 servings
Preparation time: 45 minutes
Baking time: 1½ hours

Fine bread crumbs
Rind of 2 large
  lemons, very finely
  grated
3 tablespoons lemon
  juice
3 cups all-purpose flour,
  sifted
½ teaspoon each: baking
  soda, salt
1 cup (2 sticks) unsalted
  butter, softened
3 cups sugar
5 large eggs
1 cup buttermilk

GLAZE
¼ cup plus 1 tablespoon
  lemon juice
1 tablespoon water
½ cup sugar

1. Heat oven to 350 degrees. Line bottom of 10-inch tube pan with wax paper cut to fit. Butter pan and paper; dust completely with fine bread crumbs.

2. Mix lemon rind and juice in small bowl. Sift together flour, baking soda and salt; set aside.

3. Cream butter in large mixer bowl until light. Gradually beat in sugar until light and fluffy. Beat in eggs, one at a time, beating well after each addition. Beat another 3 minutes.

4. Alternately beat in dry ingredients and buttermilk, beginning and ending with the dry ingredients. Stir in lemon rind and juice.

5. Pour into prepared pan. Bake in center of oven until wooden pick is withdrawn clean and cake has pulled away from sides of pan, about 1½ hours.

6. Mix glaze ingredients in small bowl; let stand while cake bakes.

7. When cake is done, remove from oven and cool in pan 5 minutes only. Invert onto platter; remove wax paper. Apply glaze with pastry brush until absorbed. Let stand until completely cool.

■ *The anise in this pound cake, from Suzanne Checchia, gives it a slight licorice flavor. Pound cakes can be topped with just about anything of your choice, from fruit to whipped cream or both.*

SEMOLINA POUND CAKE

One 8 by 4-inch cake, 12 to 16 servings
Preparation time: 35 minutes
Baking time: 65 to 70 minutes

1¼ **cups sifted cake flour**
¼ **cup plus 2 tablespoons semolina (see note)**
⅔ **cup unsalted butter, softened**
2⅓ **cups sifted confectioners' sugar**
3 **large eggs, room temperature**
¾ **teaspoon vanilla extract**
½ **teaspoon anise seeds, crushed, optional**
Confectioners' sugar

1. Heat oven to 325 degrees. Grease 8 by 4-inch loaf pan; dust with flour and tap out excess.

2. Sift flour and semolina together onto plate. Cream butter in large mixer bowl until light and fluffy. Gradually beat in 2⅓ cups sugar; continue beating until very light and fluffy.

3. Beat in eggs, one at a time, beating well on high speed after each addition. Beat in vanilla extract and crushed anise seeds. Add one-quarter of the flour mixture at a time, mixing on low speed after each addition just until smooth and blended. Spread batter evenly in prepared loaf pan.

4. Bake until wooden pick inserted into center comes out clean, 65 to 70 minutes. Cool cake in pan on wire rack 5 minutes. Loosen edges; remove from pan. Cool completely on rack.

5. Wrap cake in aluminum foil; let stand overnight at room temperature. Sprinkle with confectioners' sugar before serving. Cut into thin slices.

NOTE: Semolina, fine, hard wheat particles that do not pass into flour in milling, is used in pasta, pudding, soup-thickenings, etc. It can be found in Italian groceries and some gourmet food stores. Yellow cornmeal may be substituted if necessary.

Fresh peaches, cream cheese and confectioners' sugar team up for the filling of this cake roll from Food Guide reader Ann Zorek of Chicago.

PEACH CAKE ROLL

10 to 12 servings
Preparation time: 40 minutes
Baking time: 12 to 15 minutes

CAKE

- 1 cup sifted cake flour
- 1 teaspoon baking powder
- ¼ teaspoon salt
- 3 large eggs
- 1 cup granulated sugar
- ⅓ cup water
- 1 teaspoon vanilla extract

PEACH FILLING

- 1 package (8 ounces) cream cheese, softened
- ½ cup confectioners' sugar, sifted
- ⅛ teaspoon almond extract
- 1 cup finely diced fresh peaches
- Confectioners' sugar for garnish

1. Heat oven to 375 degrees. Line 15 by 10-inch jelly-roll pan with greased wax paper. For cake, sift together cake flour, baking powder and salt in small bowl; set aside.

2. Beat eggs in large mixer bowl until thick and lemon colored, about 5 minutes. Gradually beat in granulated sugar. Add water and vanilla extract; beat on low speed. Gradually add dry ingredients; beat just until batter is smooth.

3. Spread batter evenly into prepared pan. Bake until wooden pick inserted in center comes out clean, 12 to 15 minutes.

4. Remove cake from oven and loosen cake from edges of pan. Immediately invert cake onto a clean towel that has been sprinkled heavily with confectioners' sugar. Carefully remove wax paper. Trim off stiff edges of cake if necessary. While cake is still hot, use the towel to roll cake, beginning with the narrow end. Let cake cool completely on wire rack wrapped in towel.

5. For peach filling, beat cream cheese in small mixer bowl until light and fluffy. Beat in confectioners' sugar and almond extract; mix well. Add peaches; mix gently.

6. Carefully unroll cake and spread with peach filling. Carefully roll cake up again. Sprinkle outside with confectioners' sugar. Wrap loosely with towel and store in refrigerator until serving.

White chocolate has taken a definite spot in the American heart and palate. This cake, with coconut in the frosting, looks like a yummy, giant snowflake.

WHITE CHOCOLATE COCONUT CAKE

One 9-inch layer cake, 12 to 14 servings
Preparation time: 1 hour
Baking time: 35 minutes
Chilling time: 2 hours

CAKE

- ⅓ **pound white chocolate**
- ½ **cup water**
- 1 **cup (2 sticks) unsalted butter or margarine, softened**
- 2 **cups granulated sugar**
- 4 **large eggs, separated**
- 2½ **cups sifted cake flour**
- 1½ **teaspoons baking powder**
- ½ **teaspoon salt**
- 1 **cup buttermilk**
- 1 **teaspoon vanilla extract**
- 1 **cup chopped almonds or pecans**
- 1 **can (3½ ounces) flaked coconut**

FROSTING

- 2 **cups whipping cream**
- 2 **tablespoons confectioners' sugar**
- 2 **teaspoons vanilla extract**
- 1 **cup flaked coconut**

1. Heat oven to 350 degrees. Grease three 9-inch round cake pans. Line bottoms with wax paper. Grease paper.

2. Put white chocolate and water into top of double boiler; cook and stir over simmering water until melted. (Water should not touch bottom of top boiler.) Whisk until smooth; cool. Cream butter and 1½ cups sugar in large mixer bowl until light and fluffy. Beat in egg yolks, one at a time, beating well after each addition.

3. Sift flour with baking powder and salt. Add flour mixture to butter mixture in thirds, alternately with buttermilk, vanilla extract and white chocolate mixture, beating until smooth after each addition.

4. Beat egg whites in small mixer bowl until soft peaks form. Gradually beat in remaining ½ cup sugar; beat until stiff but not dry. Fold into batter; gently fold in nuts and coconut.

5. Spoon batter evenly into prepared pans. Bake until wooden pick inserted in center is withdrawn clean, 30 to 35 minutes. Cool on wire racks 10 minutes. Remove from pans; cool completely on wire racks. Remove wax paper.

6. For frosting, beat cream until frothy. Beat in sugar and vanilla extract. Beat until soft peaks form. Fold in coconut. Put one cake layer onto platter; frost. Repeat layers. Frost top and sides of cake. Refrigerate up to 2 hours before serving.

Chicago is known for its cheesecake. This is one of those classic, delicious cakes with a touch of amaretto for a little extra zing from columnist Beverly Dillon.

AMARETTO CHEESECAKE

One 8-inch cheesecake, 8 to 10 servings
Preparation time: 30 minutes
Baking time: 1 hour, 10 minutes
Standing time: 1 to 2 hours
Chilling time: Overnight

CRUST

1¼ cups finely crushed vanilla wafer crumbs

½ cup finely ground blanched almonds

6 tablespoons melted butter

FILLING

3 packages (8 ounces each) cream cheese, softened

1 cup sugar

½ teaspoon almond extract

¼ teaspoon salt

1 cup sour cream

3 large eggs

¼ cup amaretto liqueur

1. Heat oven to 350 degrees. Lightly butter an 8- or 9-inch springform pan.

2. For crust, put vanilla wafer crumbs, ground almonds and butter in bowl; mix until moistened. Press into prepared pan.

3. For filling, beat cream cheese in large mixer bowl until smooth. Add sugar, almond extract and salt. Continue to beat until light and fluffy, about 3 minutes. Beat in sour cream. Beat in eggs, one at a time, beating well after each addition. Slowly beat in amaretto. Continue to beat at medium speed until well blended, 3 to 4 minutes.

4. Pour filling into prepared pan. Bake until top is golden and filling is set, about 1 hour, 10 minutes. Turn off oven. Prop oven door open a few inches. Let cake cool in oven 1 to 2 hours.

5. Cool completely on wire rack. Refrigerate, covered, overnight.

You pay a lot to buy a slice of chocolate cheesecake in the deli department; this recipe gives you 14 servings of creamy chocolate cheesecake. A bit of rum is used instead of vanilla extract and enhances the flavor.

CHOCOLATE CHEESECAKE

One 10-inch cheesecake, 14 to 16 servings
Preparation time: 35 minutes
Baking time: 50 to 55 minutes
Standing time: 1 to 2 hours

1 **cup crushed chocolate wafers**

¼ **cup each: melted butter, chopped walnuts**

¼ **teaspoon ground cinnamon**

3 **packages (8 ounces each) cream cheese, softened**

1 **cup sugar**

3 **large eggs**

2 **cups sour cream**

2 **teaspoons dark rum**

1 **large package (12 ounces) semisweet chocolate chips, melted**

1 **square (1 ounce) unsweetened chocolate, melted**

1. Heat oven to 350 degrees. Mix wafer crumbs, butter, walnuts and cinnamon in small bowl. Press mixture over bottom of buttered 10-inch springform pan. Bake 10 minutes. Cool on wire rack. Line sides of springform pan with buttered wax paper.

2. Reduce oven temperature to 325 degrees. Beat cream cheese and sugar in large mixer bowl until light and fluffy. Beat in eggs, one at time, beating well after each addition. Beat in sour cream and rum. Fold in chocolates until smooth.

3. Pour batter into prepared pan. Bake until center is almost set, 40 to 45 minutes. Turn off oven. Prop oven door open a few inches. Let cake cool in oven 1 to 2 hours.

4. Cool completely on wire rack. Refrigerate, covered, overnight.

■ *Chicago chef/restaurateur Dennis Terczak's cheesecake is like a combination cheesecake and cheesepie. The sour cream topping is added to the top of the baked cheesecake, and then the entire cake is baked for a few more minutes. Strawberries and apricot glaze give an elegant finish, plus added richness.*

LAYERED STRAWBERRY CHEESECAKE

One 8-inch cheesecake, 8 to 10 servings
Preparation time: 35 minutes
Baking time: 1 hour
Chilling time: Overnight

6 **tablespoons butter, melted**

1½ **cups graham cracker crumbs**

2 **packages (8 ounces each) cream cheese, softened**

1¾ **cups sour cream**

1¼ **cups sugar**

4 **large eggs**

2 **tablespoons vanilla extract**

1 **pint fresh strawberries, hulled, halved**

¾ **cup apricot preserves**

1. Heat oven to 325 degrees. Use 1 tablespoon butter to grease bottom and sides of 8-inch springform pan. Mix remaining butter with crumbs; carefully press crumbs over bottom and up sides of the pan.

2. Beat cream cheese, half of the sour cream, half of the sugar, eggs and half of the vanilla extract in large mixer bowl until smooth. Carefully pour into pan; put pan onto baking sheet.

3. Bake until risen slightly and center is set, about 1 hour. Cool on wire rack to room temperature; do not unmold.

4. Increase oven temperature to 425 degrees. Mix remaining sour cream and sugar and vanilla extract in small bowl. Spread over cheesecake. Bake until slightly set, 10 to 15 minutes. Cool on wire rack to room temperature. Remove sides from pan.

5. Arrange strawberries on top of cheesecake. Heat preserves in small saucepan; push through fine sieve. Brush warm preserves over strawberries.

NOTE: This cheesecake tastes best eaten the day it is made, and at room temperature. It may be refrigerated, but never frozen.

It's the crust—or rather, the fear of the crust—that keeps many cooks from attempting pie. All it takes is one mastered recipe, and the rest is as easy as, yes, apple pie. This recipe is taped to the cabinet in The Tribune *test kitchen.*

BASIC PIE CRUST

For 1 double-crust 9-inch pie
Preparation time: 10 minutes
Chilling time: 30 minutes

2 cups all-purpose flour

1 teaspoon salt

⅔ cup vegetable shortening or lard, cold

2 tablespoons unsalted butter, cold

5 to 6 tablespoons ice water

1. Mix flour and salt in large bowl. With pastry blender or two table knives, cut in shortening and butter until mixture resembles coarse crumbs. With fork, stir in just enough water so that mixture gathers easily into ball. With hands, shape into ball. Cover in plastic wrap. Refrigerate at least 30 minutes.

2. Roll and fit into pan as directed below.

METHOD FOR A TWO-CRUST PIE

1. Divide chilled dough into 2 portions, one slightly larger than the other. Chill smaller portion until ready to roll out.

2. For bottom crust, place larger portion on lightly floured board or pastry cloth. Roll with quick strokes of rolling pin, working away from the center to make a round circle 1 inch larger than top of pie pan and about ⅛-inch thick.

3. Fold dough in half and lift into pie pan. Unfold and fit lightly into pan. Trim edge with scissors or sharp knife, allowing about 1 extra inch to hang over edge.

4. Gently heap filling high in the center.

5. For top crust, roll out reserved dough as for bottom crust. After folding in half, cut several slits near center or pierce with a fork after unfolded.

6. Brush edge of bottom crust with water. Fit top crust over filling. Fold edge of top crust over bottom crust. Press together lightly with fingers or fork. Bake according to specific pie recipe directions.

Desserts

METHOD FOR A ONE-CRUST PIE

1. Arrange bottom crust as directed in steps 2 and 3 for two-crust pie. Or, for fluted rim, roll dough ¼-inch thick and 3 inches larger than pie pan. Fit into pan, leaving a 1½-inch dough overhang. Double back dough overhanging edges so it stands upright. Shape with fingers into fluted edges.

2. Chill thoroughly, at least 15 minutes. Put in filling. Bake according to specific pie recipe directions.

METHOD FOR UNFILLED PIE

1. To bake a one-crust pie without filling (or "blind," as the English call it), first pierce the bottom of the crust with a fork. Chill thoroughly, at least 15 minutes. Line loosely with foil and fill with dried peas, beans or pie crust weights to keep crust from rising and bubbling. Bake in a preheated 450-degree oven 8 minutes.

2. Remove beans and foil. Put crust back in oven to finish baking until lightly browned, about 2 minutes. Cool completely before filling.

GENERAL TIPS

1. Chill the ingredients and utensils.

2. Use all-purpose or pastry flour.

3. Measure carefully. The correct proportions can make the difference between flaky and crumbly.

4. Butter has the finest flavor, but an all-butter crust can be hard and brittle.

5. Lard makes a fine, flaky crust but is best combined with butter for flavor. Such a pie usually tastes better when eaten warm.

6. Enough water is needed to make the dough hold together and easy to roll out. Too much will make the pastry tough.

7. Mix dough quickly. Overworking will make it tough.

8. In warm weather, refrigerate the flour-fat mixture for an hour before adding liquid.

9. Roll on a wooden board, if possible. A pastry cloth and rolling pin cover will keep dough from sticking.

10. To prevent sticking and shrinking later, chill dough and avoid pressing down on dough with rolling pin. Lift the dough occasionally with a broad spatula and sprinkle the board or pastry cloth again with flour.

11. If patching is needed, cut a piece to fit. Moisten with water. Press into place.

12. If possible, hook fluted edge over edge of pie plate to prevent shrinking.

13. To glaze the upper crust, brush with ice water, cream or a beaten egg before baking.

Jane Salzfass Freiman developed this easy pie crust for the food processor. Her precise directions ensure a tender, flaky crust. The prebaked crust is suitable for pumpkin pie and most fruit or custard pies.

FAST FOOD PROCESSOR PIE CRUST

For 1 single crust
Preparation time: 25 minutes
Chilling time: 1 hour
Baking time: 15 minutes

1¼ cups all-purpose flour
½ cup cake flour
2 tablespoons sugar
½ teaspoon salt
⅔ cup vegetable shortening
¼ to ⅓ cup cold milk

1. Insert metal knife blade in food processor. Put flours, sugar, salt and shortening into container. Process with half-second pulses until shortening disappears. Add milk to container and process to mix dough thoroughly with half second pulses, or until dough begins to clump. Gather dough into ball and wrap in plastic. Refrigerate 1 hour.

2. Heat oven to 350 degrees. Generously flour work surface and dough, using 3 to 4 tablespoons flour. Roll out dough to 13-inch circle. Loosen from work surface and carefully roll up on rolling pin. Unroll over a 9-inch pie plate, working carefully as dough is brittle. If dough crumbles, add a tablespoon or two of milk, reroll, and replace in pie plate.

3. Trim dough to ¼ inch beyond plate rim. Turn edges under, doubling dough along rim. Dough will crack; push together and flute rim of crust. Flatten bottom and sides gently against pie plate. Pierce bottom and rim of crust at even intervals. Refrigerate 10 minutes to firm. Bake 15 minutes. Cool. Crust is partly baked and ready to fill.

This frequently requested recipe for apple slices originally ran in 1951 when the food editor was the fictitious Mary Meade. You can tell it is an older recipe because it calls for lard instead of vegetable shortening; you can use either.

APPLE SLICES

12 servings
Preparation time: 30 minutes
Baking time: 50 minutes

FILLING

- 3 **pounds tart cooking apples**
- 1 **cup water**
- 1¼ **cups granulated sugar**
- 1 **teaspoon ground cinnamon**
- ¼ **teaspoon salt**
- 2 **tablespoons cornstarch**
- ¼ **cup cold water**

CRUST

- 2 **cups all-purpose flour**
- ½ **teaspoon each: baking powder, salt**
- ¾ **cup lard (see note)**
- 1 **teaspoon lemon juice**
- 2 **egg yolks, beaten**
- ½ **cup water**

ICING

- 1 **cup confectioners' sugar**
- 2 **to 3 tablespoons lemon juice or water**

1. For filling, peel and core apples. Cut into eighths. Heat water, sugar, cinnamon and salt to boil in large saucepan. Add apples and cook gently for 10 minutes. Blend cornstarch and ¼ cup cold water until smooth and add to hot mixture. Cook 5 minutes longer, stirring gently. Cool.

2. For crust, sift together flour, baking powder and salt into large bowl. Cut in lard until mixture resembles coarse crumbs. Mix lemon juice, egg yolks and water together. Sprinkle over flour mixture, 1 tablespoon at a time, mixing with fork, until flour is moistened and soft dough forms. Divide into 2 parts, one slightly larger than the other.

3. Heat oven to 450 degrees. Roll out the larger piece to fit bottom and sides of 13 by 9-inch pan. Fill with apple mixture. Roll other half of dough to fit top; crimp top and bottom edges together. Cut out a design on top for steam vents.

4. Bake at 450 degrees 20 minutes. Reduce oven temperature to 350 degrees; bake until crust is golden, about 30 more minutes.

5. Cool slightly on wire rack. Ice with a thin frosting made from the confectioners' sugar and lemon juice.

NOTE: The original recipe calls for lard. Solid vegetable shortening, butter or margarine can be used, if desired.

The late Bert Greene was a well-known American cook and food author, and this apple pie recipe is an example of his culinary abilities. He uses many ingredients—orange rind in the crust, ginger in the crumb topping, and several spices mixed with the apples. The result is bursting with flavor.

ALL-AMERICAN APPLE PIE

One 9-inch pie, 6 to 8 servings
Preparation time: 45 minutes
Standing time: 1 hour
Baking time: 1 hour
Chilling time: 1 hour

PIE CRUST
2½ cups all-purpose flour
 ½ teaspoon salt
 ½ cup each: cold,
    unsalted butter,
    vegetable shortening
 ¼ teaspoon grated
    orange rind
 2 to 3 tablespoons each:
    very cold orange
    juice, ice water

CRUMB TOPPING
 ⅓ cup each: all-purpose
    flour, packed dark
    brown sugar
 ¼ teaspoon ground
    cinnamon
    Dash each: salt,
    ground ginger
 2 tablespoons cold,
    unsalted butter

FILLING
 7 to 8 medium Granny
    Smith apples
 1 to 1½ tablespoons
    all-purpose flour
 ¾ cup granulated sugar
 ½ teaspoon each: ground
    cinnamon, orange
    rind, vanilla extract
 ⅛ teaspoon ground
    nutmeg
    Dash salt
 ½ cup honey

1½ tablespoons unsalted
    butter
 1 egg, beaten

1. For pie crust, sift flour and salt into large bowl. Cut in butter and shortening until mixture resembles coarse crumbs. Add orange rind. Sprinkle in juice and water, 1 tablespoon at a time, mixing with fork until flour is moistened and soft dough forms. Shape into ball. Refrigerate, covered, 1 hour.

2. For crumb topping, mix flour, brown sugar, cinnamon, salt and ginger. Work in butter with fingers until mixture is crumbly.

3. For filling, peel, core and cut apples into ½-inch slices. Put slices in large bowl; toss with 1 to 1½ tablespoons flour. Add sugar, cinnamon, orange rind, vanilla extract, nutmeg and salt. Stir in honey; let stand 1 hour.

4. Heat oven to 450 degrees. Roll half of dough into a circle; fit in metal, 9-inch pie pan. Trim edge. Drain liquid from apples; reserve. Set ¼ cup of the crumb topping aside. Layer apples with remaining crumbs in dough-lined pan. Use crumbs like mortar to build fruit up. Dot apples with 1½ tablespoons butter. Sprinkle with 5 tablespoons reserved apple liquid.

5. Roll out remaining dough; cut with knife or fluted pastry wheel into ½-inch-wide strips. Weave strips into lattice over fruit. Seal strips at edge of pan, moistening with apple liquid. Flute edge. Sprinkle reserved crumbs in holes of lattice. Brush only crust edge and strips with beaten egg.

6. Bake on foil-lined baking sheet at 450 degrees, 5 minutes. Reduce oven temperature to 350 degrees; bake until apples are tender, 50 to 55 more minutes (or only 40 minutes if you like crunchier apples). Cool on wire rack to room temperature.

NOTE: Serve with vanilla ice cream or whipped cream flavored with vanilla sugar and orange-flavored liqueur.

John McBride took second place in The Tribune*'s Great Apple Pie contest. He told us he has made hundreds of these pies and has won many local contests; the secret, he said, is the simplicity of the recipe and the combination of apples that he uses.*

BLUE-RIBBON APPLE PIE

One 9-inch pie, 6 to 8 servings
Preparation time: 40 minutes
Baking time: 1 hour

PIE CRUST
- 2 **cups all-purpose flour**
- 1 **teaspoon salt**
- ⅔ **cup lard or vegetable shortening, cold**
- 6 **to 7 tablespoons cold water**

FILLING
- 1 **cup sugar**
- ¼ **teaspoon ground cinnamon**
- ⅛ **teaspoon ground allspice**
- 8 **to 9 medium-size tart apples (a mix of Granny Smith and McIntosh is best), peeled, thinly sliced**
- 1 **tablespoon milk**
- 2 **tablespoons sugar**

1. Heat oven to 375 degrees. For pie crust, put flour and salt into large bowl. Cut in lard until mixture resembles coarse crumbs. Sprinkle in water, 1 tablespoon at a time, mixing well with fork until flour is moistened and soft dough forms. Divide into 2 parts, one slightly larger than the other. Refrigerate covered, 30 minutes.

2. Roll out the larger piece on lightly floured surface to fit 9-inch pie pan. Fit into pan. Roll out other half for top crust.

3. Mix 1 cup sugar, cinnamon and allspice in a large bowl, add apple slices; mix well. Turn coated apples into dough-lined pan. Cover with top crust; flute edges. Brush crust lightly with milk; sprinkle with 2 tablespoons sugar. Cut out a design on top crust for steam vents.

4. Bake at 375 degrees 20 minutes. Reduce oven temperature to 350 degrees; bake until crust is golden, about 40 more minutes. Cool on wire rack.

Chicago schoolteacher Elaine Michura took top honors in the first Great Apple Pie contest held by The Tribune *food section. She said she cooks for relaxation, and you may feel like curling up for a nap after filling up with this wonderful pie. The toffee topping adds a candy bar richness that's irresistible.*

BUTTERED TOFFEE APPLE PIE

One 9-inch pie, 6 to 8 servings
Preparation time: 40 minutes
Baking time: 40 to 45 minutes

PIE CRUST

- 2 **cups all-purpose flour**
- ½ **teaspoon salt**
- 1 **cup (2 sticks) cold unsalted butter**
- 4 **to 8 tablespoons cold water**

FILLING

- ⅓ **cup light corn syrup**
- 3 **tablespoons granulated sugar**
- 1 **tablespoon each: melted butter, cornstarch**
- 1½ **teaspoons ground cinnamon**
- ½ **teaspoon salt**
- 6 **tart apples, such as Granny Smith, peeled, cored, sliced**

TOFFEE TOPPING

- ½ **cup plus 2 tablespoons packed dark brown sugar**
- ¼ **cup chopped walnuts**
- 3 **tablespoons each: light corn syrup, melted butter**
- 2 **tablespoons all-purpose flour**

1. For pie crust, put flour and salt into large bowl. Cut in butter until mixture resembles coarse crumbs. Sprinkle in water, 1 tablespoon at a time, mixing well with fork until flour is moistened and soft dough forms. Divide in half and shape into 2 balls. Refrigerate, covered, until needed.

2. Mix corn syrup, sugar, butter, cornstarch, cinnamon and salt in large bowl. Add apples; mix well.

3. Heat oven to 425 degrees. Roll out 1 ball on well-floured surface to fit 9-inch pie pan. Fit into pan. Fill with apple mixture. Roll out remaining dough for top crust. Put over filling. Seal and flute edges. Make 4 large slashes on top for steam vents.

4. Bake at 425 degrees 10 minutes. Reduce oven temperature to 350 degrees; bake until crust is golden, about 30 more minutes.

5. Meanwhile, for topping, mix ingredients in small bowl. Pour topping over pie. Return to oven for 5 minutes. Cool on wire rack. Serve warm.

Here's the two-crust cherry pie that George Washington might have been familiar with. If you like the taste of almonds, a few drops of almond extract can be used instead of the kirsch (cherry brandy).

CLASSIC CHERRY PIE

One 9-inch pie, 6 to 8 servings
Preparation time: 40 minutes
Baking time: 50 minutes

PIE CRUST

- 2 **cups all-purpose flour**
- 1 **teaspoon salt**
- ⅔ **cup lard or vegetable shortening, cold**
- 2 **tablespoons cold butter**
- 4 **to 5 tablespoons ice water**

FILLING

- 5 **to 6 cups fresh or individually quick-frozen sour cherries**
- 1⅓ **cups sugar**
- ¼ **cup kirsch (cherry brandy)**
- 2 **tablespoons plus 2 teaspoons quick-cooking tapioca**
- 1 **teaspoon finely grated lemon rind**
- 2 **tablespoons butter**

1. For pie crust, put flour and salt into large bowl. Cut in lard and butter until mixture resembles coarse crumbs. Sprinkle in water, 1 tablespoon at a time, mixing well with fork until flour is moistened and soft dough forms. Shape into 2 balls.

2. Roll out 1 ball on well-floured surface to fit 9-inch pie pan. Fit into pan. Roll out remaining dough for top crust.

3. Heat oven to 450 degrees. For filling, rinse, drain and pit fresh cherries or thaw if using frozen cherries. Mix with sugar, kirsch, tapioca and lemon rind in large bowl. Let mixture stand for 15 minutes.

4. Pour fruit into dough-lined pan. Dot top with butter. Put top crust over filling. Seal and flute edges. Make 4 large slashes on top for steam vents.

5. Bake at 450 degrees 10 minutes. Reduce oven temperature to 350 degrees; bake until crust is golden brown, about 40 more minutes. Cool on wire rack.

This deep-dish, double-crust peach pie would be a true American classic except for the addition of a couple of simple ingredients: ginger and gingersnaps. The ginger adds to the flavor (not to mention the aroma) while the gingersnap crumbs absorb liquid that could otherwise make the lower crust soggy. Call it a neoclassic peach pie.

GINGER PEACH PIE

One 9-inch pie, 6 to 8 servings
Preparation time: 30 minutes
Chilling time: 30 minutes
Baking time: 1 hour

PIE CRUST

- 2 cups all-purpose flour
- 1 teaspoon salt
- ⅔ cup vegetable shortening or lard, cold
- 2 tablespoons cold unsalted butter
- 4 to 5 tablespoons ice water

FILLING

- 7 cups sliced, peeled fresh peaches, about 12 medium peaches
- ⅓ cup each: granulated sugar, packed light brown sugar
- 3 tablespoons cornstarch
- 1 tablespoon fresh lemon juice
- 1 teaspoon minced lemon rind
- ½ teaspoon ground ginger
- ¼ teaspoon ground cinnamon
- ¼ cup finely crushed gingersnaps
- 2 tablespoons whipping cream
- 1 tablespoon granulated sugar

1. For pie crust, put flour and salt into large bowl. Cut in shortening and butter until mixture resembles coarse crumbs. Sprinkle in water, 1 tablespoon at a time, mixing well with fork until flour is moistened and soft dough forms. Shape into 2 balls. Refrigerate covered at least 30 minutes.

2. Heat oven to 425 degrees. For filling, mix peaches, ⅓ cup granulated sugar, brown sugar, cornstarch, lemon juice, lemon rind, ginger and cinnamon in large bowl.

3. Roll out 1 ball on well-floured surface to fit a deep, 9-inch pie pan. Fit into pan. Sprinkle bottom with gingersnap crumbs. Add peach mixture. Roll out remaining dough for top crust. Put over filling. Seal and flute edges. Make 4 large slashes on top for steam vents.

4. Brush crust all over with whipping cream. Sprinkle with 1 tablespoon sugar. Put pie onto baking sheet. Bake at 425 degrees 20 minutes. Reduce oven temperature to 350 degrees; bake until crust is golden brown, 30 to 40 minutes. Cool on wire rack.

BOB FILA

CHICKEN CURRY WITH BAMBOO SHOOTS, GARLIC PRAWNS

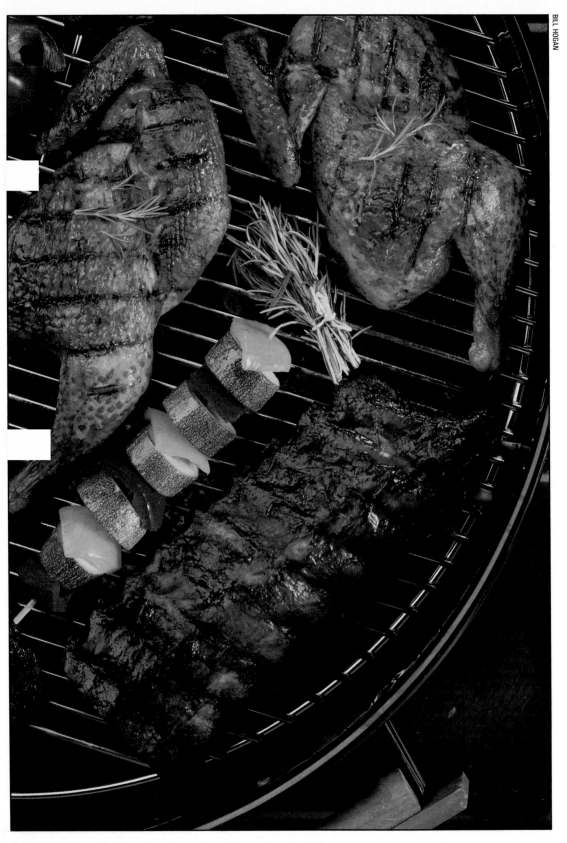

BILL HOGAN

Chicago-style Barbecued Ribs, Greek-style Grilled Chicken

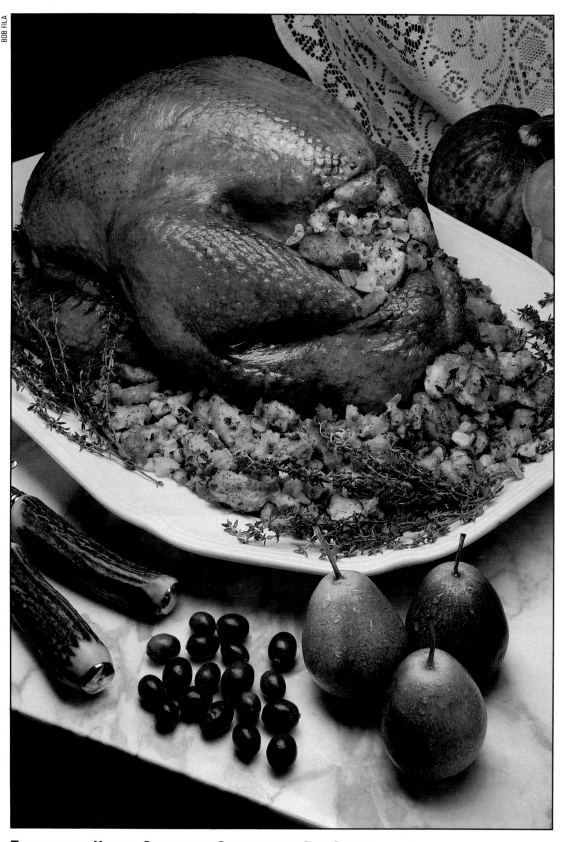

TURKEY WITH HERBED CORNBREAD STUFFING AND PAN GRAVY

BAKED WHOLE GARLIC

COLORFUL BROCCOLI STIR-FRY

PRESERVES

GRILLED VEGETABLES WITH ROSEMARY VINAIGRETTE

CAESAR SALAD

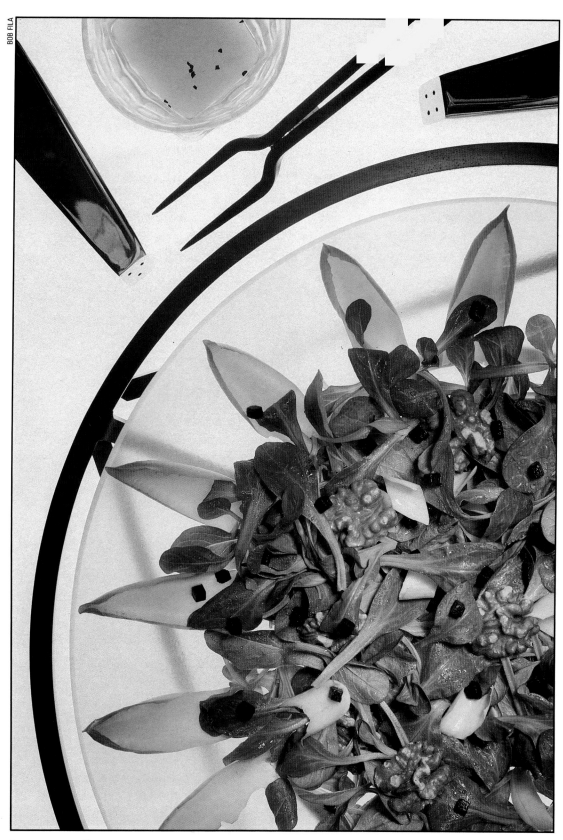

BOB FILA

BEET AND MÂCHE SALAD WITH WALNUTS

BASIC WHITE BREAD, CHALLAH BREAD

FRESH FRUIT TARTS

CHOCOLATE SATIN, PASSION FRUIT SOUP

KEY LIME PIE

PEANUT BUTTER COOKIES

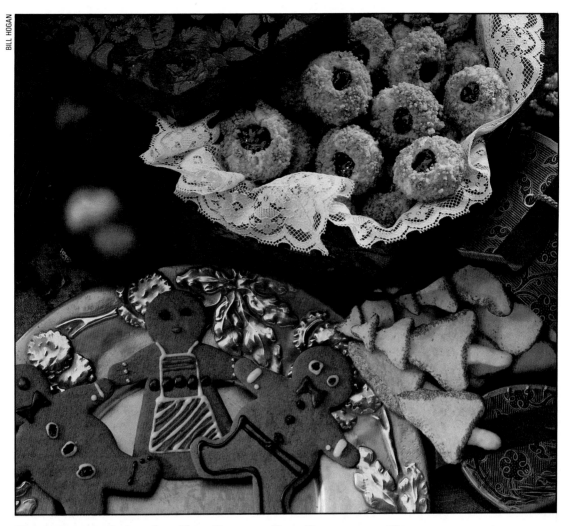

THUMBPRINTS, CHRISTMAS TREE COOKIES, BEST GINGERBREAD COOKIES

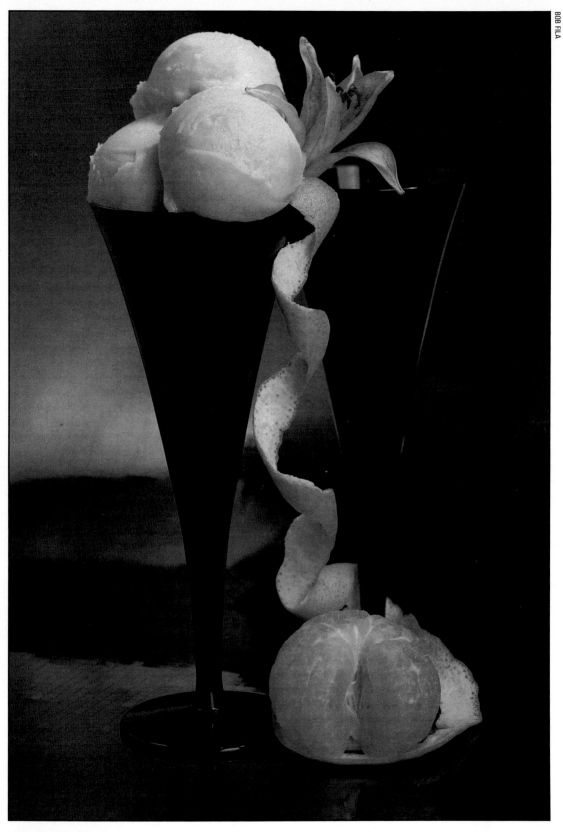

TANGERINE SHERBET

Key lime pie has the unusual characteristics of being both sweet and tart, light yet rich. This version, from The Tribune *test kitchen, is a combination of several recipes. Since we couldn't decide between a standard pie crust and a graham cracker crust we have included both. The choice is yours.*

KEY LIME PIE

One 9-inch pie, 6 to 8 servings
Preparation time: 45 minutes
Baking time: 20 minutes
Chilling time: 4 hours

Basic pie crust (see recipe, page 553)
1 can (14 ounces) sweetened condensed milk
⅔ cup fresh lime juice
4 large egg yolks, lightly beaten
1 tablespoon grated lime rind
2 large egg whites
1½ teaspoons sugar
1 cup whipping cream, for garnish
1 lime slice for garnish

1. Make basic pie crust using method for unfilled pie.

2. Heat oven to 375 degrees. Mix sweetened condensed milk, lime juice, egg yolks and lime rind in large bowl. Beat egg whites and sugar in small mixer bowl until soft peaks form. Fold whites into lime mixture. Pour into prepared crust.

3. Bake until filling sets, about 10 minutes. Cool completely on wire rack. Refrigerate at least 4 hours.

4. Beat whipping cream in small bowl until soft peaks form. Spoon into pastry bag fitted with ½-inch star tip. Pipe around edge of pie. Pipe a dollop of whipped cream in center of pie. Top with lime slice. Serve immediately.

VARIATION: For graham cracker crust, mix 1½ cups graham cracker crumbs, 2 tablespoons light brown sugar and ⅛ teaspoon ground cinnamon in medium bowl. Stir in ⅓ cup unsalted butter, melted, until crumbs are moistened. Press crumbs over bottom and up sides of 9-inch pie pan. Bake at 375 degrees until crisp, 8 to 10 minutes. Cool completely on wire rack. Fill and bake as directed.

■ *Jolene Worthington is a Chicago cook and vice president of production at Eli's Chicago's Finest Cheesecake, who has made many contributions to* The Tribune's *food section. To increase the lemony flavor of her lemon meringue pie, she advises to add more lemon rind rather than increasing the lemon juice; the rind contains the lemon oil, and the oil contains the flavor, color and aroma.*

LEMON MERINGUE PIE

One 10-inch pie, 8 servings
Preparation time: 30 minutes
Chilling time: 3½ hours
Cooking time: 50 minutes

PIE CRUST

1½ **cups all-purpose flour**
 ½ **cup (1 stick) cold unsalted butter or vegetable shortening**
 3 **to 4 tablespoons ice water**
 1 **teaspoon sugar**
 ¼ **teaspoon salt**

FILLING

 9 **large egg yolks**
 ½ **cup plus 3 tablespoons sugar**
 1 **cup fresh lemon juice**
2½ **teaspoons grated lemon rind**
 ½ **cup egg whites, about 4 to 5**
 Pinch salt
 ½ **cup plus 1 tablespoon sugar**

1. For pie crust, put flour into large bowl. Cut in butter until mixture resembles coarse crumbs. Mix 3 tablespoons water, sugar and salt in small bowl; stir until sugar and salt dissolve. Gradually drizzle water over flour mixture while mixing with fork until flour is moistened and soft dough forms. Shape into ball; flatten into disk. Refrigerate, covered, at least 3 hours or overnight.

2. Roll dough on lightly floured surface to fit 10-inch pie pan or tart pan with removable bottom. Fit into pan; trim and flute edges. Refrigerate 30 minutes. Pierce bottom and sides with fork.

3. Heat oven to 450 degrees. Line pie shell with foil and dried beans or pie weights. Bake on lowest oven rack, 12 minutes; remove foil and beans. Reduce oven temperature to 400 degrees. Continue to bake until brown, about 10 minutes. Cool on wire rack.

4. Reduce oven temperature to 350 degrees. For filling, whisk egg yolks and ½ cup plus 3 tablespoons sugar in top of double boiler until light; stir in lemon juice. Put over simmering water; cook, stirring constantly, until mixture thickens and heavily coats a spoon, about 10 minutes. Stir in 1½ teaspoons of the lemon rind. Remove from heat. Remove and reserve ⅓ cup of the lemon filling for decoration/topping.

5. Beat egg whites and salt in large mixer bowl until soft peaks form. Gradually beat in ½ cup plus 1 tablespoon sugar until stiff peaks form. Beat in remaining 1 teaspoon lemon rind. Gently fold half of the whites into warm lemon filling (do not overfold). Pour into prepared crust, slightly mounding in the center.

6. Bake at 350 degrees 10 minutes. Remove pie from oven. Filling will be firm to fingertips, but slightly soft in center.

7. Increase oven temperature to 400 degrees. Fill large pastry bag fitted with ½-inch star tube with remaining egg whites. Pipe lattice design over baked filling. Bake until meringue browns, about 5 minutes. While hot, spoon reserved lemon filling into lattice diamonds. Cool completely on wire rack.

The filling is pumpkin, the topping is pecans and the garnish is whipped cream. It's a classic fall and winter dessert from Jane Salzfass Freiman.

PUMPKIN PECAN PIE

One 9-inch pie, 6 to 8 servings
Preparation time: 45 minutes
Chilling time: 1 hour
Baking time: 1 hour

Fast pie crust, prebaked (see recipe, page 556)

TOPPING
- ¾ **cup pecan halves**
- 3 **tablespoons butter, slightly softened**
- 2 **tablespoons dark brown sugar**

FILLING
- 2 **cups solid-pack canned pumpkin**
- ⅔ **cup packed dark brown sugar**
- ⅓ **cup granulated sugar**
- 2 **teaspoons ground cinnamon**
- 1 **teaspoon ground ginger**
- ½ **teaspoon ground nutmeg**
- ¼ **teaspoon each: ground cloves, mace**
- 1 **cup whipping cream**
- 3 **large eggs**
- ¼ **cup milk**
- ¼ **cup bourbon or rum**
  Whipped cream for garnish

1. Prepare pie crust.

2. Heat oven to 350 degrees. For topping, chop pecans in food processor fitted with metal blade with four 1-second pulses; set aside. Cut butter in 3 pieces and add to container with brown sugar. Process to mix 10 seconds; scrape down container sides. Add chopped pecans and mix with two 1-second pulses; refrigerate until ready to use.

3. For filling, put pumpkin, brown sugar, granulated sugar, cinnamon, ginger, nutmeg, cloves and mace into food processor. Process to mix 5 seconds; scrape down container sides. Add cream, eggs, milk and bourbon. Process to mix 10 seconds; scrape down container sides; process 5 seconds. Pour filling into partly baked crust.

4. Bake 35 minutes. Remove pie from oven and spoon topping around rim. Return pie to oven; bake until knife inserted in center is withdrawn clean, about 25 minutes. Cool completely on wire rack.

5. Serve cold or at room temperature. Garnish with whipped cream.

The combination of strawberries and rhubarb has become a classic. Here the two harbingers of spring are paired in a pie with a decorative lattice top.

STRAWBERRY RHUBARB LATTICE PIE

One 9-inch pie, 6 to 8 servings
Preparation time: 45 minutes
Chilling time: 1 hour
Cooking time: 1 hour

PIE CRUST

- 2 **cups all-purpose flour**
- ¾ **teaspoon salt**
- ⅔ **cup vegetable shortening or lard, cold**
- 2 **tablespoons cold unsalted butter**
- 4 **to 5 tablespoons ice water**

FILLING

- 2 **cups diced fresh rhubarb, ¼-inch pieces**
- ¾ **cup sugar**
- ¼ **teaspoon salt**
- 1 **tablespoon cornstarch**
- ½ **teaspoon grated lemon rind**
- 1½ **pints strawberries, halved**
- 3 **tablespoons finely crushed vanilla wafers**
- 2 **tablespoons whipping cream**

   Whipped cream for serving

1. For pie crust, put flour and salt into large bowl. Cut in shortening and butter until mixture resembles coarse crumbs. Sprinkle in water, 1 tablespoon at a time, mixing well with fork until flour is moistened and soft dough forms. Shape into 2 balls, making 1 slightly larger than the other. Refrigerate, covered, at least 30 minutes.

2. Roll out larger half on lightly floured surface to ⅛-inch thickness. Fit into 9-inch pie pan. Refrigerate while making filling.

3. For filling, put rhubarb, sugar and salt in medium bowl; let stand 30 minutes. Strain accumulated rhubarb liquid into medium saucepan. Add cornstarch and lemon rind. Cook and stir over medium heat until smooth and thickened, about 5 minutes. Remove from heat. Stir in rhubarb and strawberries.

4. Heat oven to 450 degrees. Sprinkle vanilla wafer crumbs over dough-lined pan. Top with rhubarb mixture. Roll out remaining dough on lightly floured surface to ¼-inch thickness. Cut into ½-inch-wide strips. Arrange strips over pie in lattice fashion.

5. Brush strips lightly with cream. Put pie on baking sheet. Bake 15 minutes at 450 degrees. Reduce oven temperature to 350 degrees; bake until crust is crisp and brown and fruit is tender, about 35 more minutes. Cool on wire rack. Serve warm with whipped cream.

Pastry, fresh fruits and custard team up to make these small tarts an elegant ending to a meal.

FRESH FRUIT TARTS

16 to 18 small tarts
Preparation time: 1 hour
Chilling time: 1 hour
Baking time: 15 minutes

TART DOUGH

2¾ cups all-purpose flour
½ cup sugar
   Rind of 1 lemon, finely grated
½ teaspoon salt
1 cup (2 sticks) cold unsalted butter, cut into pieces
6 tablespoons half-and-half
2 egg yolks

CUSTARD FILLING

2 cups milk
½ cup sugar
5 tablespoons cornstarch
4 large egg yolks
   Pinch salt
1 tablespoon brandy

TO ASSEMBLE

5 to 6 cups prepared fruit (such as seedless grapes, sliced peeled papaya, sliced pear, sliced fig, sliced plum, etc.)
   Melted apple jelly

1. For dough, put flour, sugar, lemon rind and salt into food processor. Process until mixed. Add butter. Process with on/off turns until mixture resembles coarse crumbs. Mix half-and-half and egg yolks; add through feed tube with machine running. Process just until mixture starts to form a ball. Remove to sheet of wax paper and press dough together into a flat disk. Refrigerate until firm, about 30 minutes.

2. Heat oven to 350 degrees. Roll dough on lightly floured surface to ⅛-inch thickness. Cut to fit into 16 to 18 small individual tart pans. Press dough into pans. Line with foil and fill with dried beans or pie weights. Put tart pans onto baking sheets. Bake 5 minutes. Remove foil and beans. Continue baking until golden, about 10 more minutes. Cool completely on wire racks.

3. For custard filling, mix ½ cup of the milk, sugar, cornstarch and egg yolks in medium bowl until smooth. Heat remaining 1½ cups milk and salt in large saucepan. Gradually pour cornstarch mixture into hot milk. Whisk constantly, over medium heat until smooth and thickened. Do not boil. Strain through fine sieve into bowl. Stir in brandy. Cover with plastic wrap touching the surface and refrigerate until chilled, at least 30 minutes.

4. To assemble, remove tart shells from pans. Fill with chilled custard. Cut and prepare fruit. Arrange fruit over custard. Brush with melted jelly. Serve within 2 hours of assembly.

Fresh summer fruit gets an added richness from sour cream in the following tart.

FRESH NECTARINE TART

One 10-inch tart, 8 servings
Preparation time: 30 minutes
Chilling time: 30 minutes
Cooking time: 40 minutes

TART DOUGH

1 **cup all-purpose flour**
½ **teaspoon salt**
⅓ **cup vegetable shortening or lard, cold**
1½ **teaspoons cold butter**
2 **to 3 tablespoons ice water**

FILLING

1 **cup sour cream**
⅔ **cup granulated sugar**
2 **tablespoons all-purpose flour**
1 **large egg, beaten**
2 **tablespoons dark rum**
½ **teaspoon vanilla extract**
¼ **teaspoon each, ground: cinnamon, nutmeg**

TOPPING

½ **cup each: all-purpose flour, chopped pecans**
¼ **cup each: packed light brown sugar, softened butter**
2 **cups sliced, peeled nectarines or peaches, about 4 medium (see note)**

1. For dough, put flour and salt into large bowl. Cut in shortening and butter until mixture resembles coarse crumbs. Stir in water, 1 tablespoon at a time, tossing with a fork until flour is moistened and soft dough forms. Refrigerate, covered, at least 30 minutes.

2. Heat oven to 425 degrees. Roll out dough on lightly floured surface to ⅛-inch thickness. Fit into 10-inch tart, quiche or pie pan; flute edge. Line bottom with foil; fill with dried beans or pie weights. Bake at 400 degrees 8 minutes. Remove foil and beans; bake until golden, 8 to 10 minutes. Cool completely on wire rack.

3. For filling, mix sour cream, granulated sugar, 2 tablespoons flour, egg, rum, vanilla extract, cinnamon and nutmeg in large bowl. For topping, mix ½ cup flour, pecans, sugar and butter with fingers until crumbly.

4. Reduce oven temperature to 375 degrees. Sprinkle two-thirds of the topping over dough-lined pan. Pour filling on top. Arrange nectarine slices over filling. Sprinkle with remaining topping.

5. Bake until puffed and golden, 35 to 40 minutes. Cool completely on wire rack. Serve at room temperature.

NOTE: To peel nectarines or peaches, add to large saucepan of boiling water for 1 minute. Drain; rinse under cold water. Lift off peel with sharp knife.

Jean Banchet, former chef/owner of the famed Chicago-area Le Français restaurant, loves apple tarts served on puff pastry with sauce Anglaise.

HOT FRENCH APPLE TART

4 servings
Preparation time: 15 minutes
Baking time: 25 minutes

8 ounces puff pastry (see note)

2 Northern Spy apples

4 teaspoons each: superfine granulated sugar, unsalted butter

½ cup apricot preserves

1 cup crème Anglaise, slightly chilled (see recipe, page 600)

1. Heat oven to 350 degrees. Roll out dough on lightly floured surface to ⅛-inch thickness. Cut dough into 4 circles, each about 5 inches in diameter.

2. Peel and core apples; cut into very thin slices. Arrange apples in overlapping fashion in circles, beginning at outside edge of tart and working inward, until no pastry shows. Sprinkle each with 1 teaspoon sugar; dot top of each with 1 teaspoon butter.

3. Bake until both pastry and apples are golden brown, about 25 minutes.

4. Meanwhile, put apricot preserves in blender; process until smooth. Transfer to small saucepan. Heat to boil; push through fine sieve into small bowl. Brush hot preserves over tarts; the glaze will harden slightly as it cools. Serve warm with crème Anglaise on the side.

NOTE: Jean Banchet uses all-butter puff pastry, available in the freezer section of gourmet food stores. Thaw according to package directions.

Fresh Start Bakery and Catering is a Flossmoor, Illinois gourmet food shop that's well known for its exceptionally rich and delicious desserts. Here is one of them.

MACADAMIA NUT TART

One 10-inch tart, 8 servings
Preparation time: 1 hour
Chilling time: 20 to 30 minutes
Baking time: 25 minutes

TART DOUGH
- ½ cup (1 stick) unsalted butter, softened
- ½ cup granulated sugar
- 2 egg yolks
- 1 teaspoon vanilla extract
- 1½ cups all-purpose flour

FILLING
- 1 cup packed light brown sugar
- ⅓ cup unsalted butter
- 3 tablespoons whipping cream
- 2 tablespoons, plus 1 teaspoon each: pure maple syrup, light corn syrup
- ¾ pound unsalted macadamia nut halves
- Whipped cream for garnish

1. For tart dough, beat together ½ cup butter and granulated sugar in small mixer bowl until light and fluffy. Beat in egg yolks, one at a time. Beat in vanilla extract. Stir in flour with wooden spoon. Mix just until dough forms.

2. Roll out dough into ½-inch-thick circle between 2 sheets of wax paper. Refrigerate on baking sheet 20 to 30 minutes.

3. Heat oven to 350 degrees. Remove one sheet of wax paper. Put dough, paper side up, into greased 10-inch tart pan with removable bottom. Remove second sheet of wax paper. (Dough is very fragile and may break; if it does, simply press dough over bottom and up sides of pan.)

4. Trim excess dough off top with sharp knife. Line bottom with aluminum foil; fill with dried beans or pie weights. Bake until light gold, about 15 minutes. Remove foil and beans. Bake until golden 5 to 10 more minutes. Cool on wire rack.

5. For filling, put brown sugar, butter, whipping cream, maple syrup and corn syrup into medium saucepan. Heat to boil; boil until sugar is dissolved, about 1 minute.

6. Fill crust with nuts. Pour hot filling over nuts. Bake just until filling bubbles, 3 to 5 minutes. Cool completely on wire rack. Remove sides of pan. Serve with dollop of whipped cream.

This is one of those classic recipes using an oats, brown sugar and butter mixture, as in the old apple brown crisp recipes. However, this one uses pears instead. Topped with whipped cream or ice cream, it has a tart-sweet flavor that's hard to resist.

EASY PEAR CRISP

8 servings
Preparation time: 20 minutes
Baking time: 40 to 50 minutes

½ **cup packed light brown sugar**

¼ **cup all-purpose flour**

2 **tablespoons quick-cooking rolled oats**

½ **teaspoon ground cinnamon**

¼ **teaspoon ground ginger**

¼ **cup unsalted butter or margarine, cold, cut into small pieces**

¼ **cup finely chopped pecans**

6 **large, ripe pears**
Juice of 1 lemon
Whipped cream or vanilla ice cream, optional

1. Heat oven to 375 degrees. Put sugar, flour, oats, cinnamon and ginger in large bowl. Stir to mix. Cut in butter until mixture resembles coarse crumbs. Add nuts; toss to mix.

2. Peel pears; cut in half and remove cores. Slice into ¼-inch-thick slices. Arrange half of the pears in single layer in well-buttered 13 by 9-inch baking dish. Sprinkle with half of the lemon juice. Crumble half of the oat mixture over top. Repeat layering.

3. Bake until top is lightly browned and pears are tender, 40 to 50 minutes. Cool on wire rack. Serve warm with whipped cream.

This recipe was included in a column by Jane Salzfass Freiman, who quite correctly commented that few desserts offer such delicious simplicity as old-fashioned cobblers filled with berries and topped with a thick, tender pastry crust. This cobbler can be made in the morning and then set aside until serving time. You can serve it with whipped cream, ice cream, custard sauce or all by its wonderful self.

MIXED BERRY COBBLER

6 to 8 servings
Preparation time: 30 minutes
Baking time: 30 minutes

DOUGH

Rind of 1 medium lemon

3 tablespoons sugar

1½ cups cake flour

2 teaspoons baking powder

Pinch salt

¼ cup each, cold: unsalted butter, vegetable shortening

⅓ cup milk

FILLING

2 pints mixed berries, including 1 pint blueberries and ½ pint each strawberries and raspberries

2 tablespoons cornstarch

3 tablespoons water

1 tablespoon fresh lemon juice

½ cup sugar

Whipped cream or vanilla ice cream, optional

1. For dough, strip off lemon rind with vegetable peeler, allowing strips to fall into food processor container fitted with metal blade. Add 3 tablespoons sugar; process until rind is minced, usually 1 minute. Add cake flour, baking powder and salt. Process 5 seconds to mix.

2. Cut butter into pieces; add butter and vegetable shortening to processor container. Process with 1-second pulses until butter and shortening disappear. Add milk and process with ½-second pulses until dough begins to clump. Wrap and refrigerate dough 20 minutes.

3. Heat oven to 350 degrees. Generously butter 8-inch square heat-resistant baking dish. Rinse and stem berries as necessary; put in large bowl. Dissolve cornstarch in water and lemon juice in small bowl; add ½ cup sugar and toss completely with berries. Transfer mixture to prepared dish.

4. Roll out dough on generously floured work surface. Transfer to baking dish and adjust to completely cover filling. Bake until crust is golden, 30 to 35 minutes. Cool on wire rack until warm. Serve warm with whipped cream.

Plain yogurt is used in this recipe, giving a nice tang to the fruit that sits under a traditional, sweet topping.

PEACH BUCKLE

8 servings
Preparation time: 30 minutes
Baking time: 1¼ hours

½ cup (1 stick) unsalted butter or margarine, softened
½ cup sugar
1 egg, lightly beaten
2 cups all-purpose flour
2½ teaspoons baking powder
¼ teaspoon salt
¾ cup plain yogurt
6 to 7 large peaches, peeled, pitted, sliced

TOPPING

½ cup each: sugar, all-purpose flour
¾ teaspoon ground cinnamon
½ cup (1 stick) unsalted butter
Vanilla ice cream, optional

1. Heat oven to 375 degrees. Cream butter and sugar in large mixer bowl until light; beat in egg. Sift together flour, baking powder and salt. Stir into butter mixture alternately with yogurt, beginning and ending with dry ingredients.

2. Spread batter across bottom of well-greased 12 by 7-inch baking pan. Arrange peach slices over batter.

3. For topping, mix sugar, flour and cinnamon in small bowl. Cut in butter until mixture is crumbly. Sprinkle evenly over peaches.

4. Bake until buckle is puffed and nicely browned, about 1¼ hours. Cool on wire rack. Serve warm with ice cream.

■ *This sounds like the ultimate Thanksgiving dessert, a combination of pecans and pumpkin with a dash of bourbon thrown in for good measure, from Paul A. Camp. And in truth, this exceptionally moist pudding is a quick and tasty alternative to the usual pie and eliminates making a crust. No need to limit it to Thanksgiving, however. It is good anytime, warm or cold.*

BOURBON PECAN PUMPKIN PUDDING

10 servings
Preparation time: 20 minutes
Baking time: 35 minutes

1¼ cups sugar

¼ cup (½ stick) unsalted butter or margarine, softened

6 large eggs

¼ teaspoon each: salt, ground cinnamon, ground cloves, ground nutmeg

2 cups pureed cooked fresh or solid-pack canned pumpkin

⅓ cup bourbon

½ teaspoon finely grated lemon rind

½ cup finely chopped pecans

1 cup whipping cream

Pecan halves for garnish

Whipped cream flavored with 1 teaspoon bourbon for serving

1. Heat oven to 350 degrees. Generously butter 2-quart soufflé or baking dish. Sprinkle dish with sugar; tap out excess sugar.

2. Beat 1¼ cups sugar and butter in large mixer bowl. Beat in eggs, one at a time, until smooth and light. Beat in salt, cinnamon, cloves and nutmeg. Add pumpkin, bourbon and lemon rind. Beat until smooth. Stir in chopped pecans.

3. Beat 1 cup whipping cream to soft peaks. Gently fold into pumpkin mixture. Do not overmix.

4. Scrape into prepared dish. Bake until fork inserted into middle is withdrawn clean, about 35 minutes. Cool on wire rack.

5. Garnish with pecan halves. Serve warm with flavored whipped cream. The pudding is also good cold or at room temperature.

Bread pudding is definitely comfort food that we all remember from childhood. This one from Commander Palace's Restaurant, in New Orleans, is a little time-consuming to prepare and calls for whiskey or brandy (which we probably didn't have as children), but makes a wonderful, soothing soufflé.

BREAD PUDDING SOUFFLÉ

8 servings
Preparation time: 1 hour, 20 minutes
Baking time: 45 minutes

BREAD PUDDING

- 10 slices day-old French bread, broken in pieces
- 1 quart milk, scalded
- 1 cup whipping cream
- 4 large eggs
- 1 cup granulated sugar
- 1 tablespoon vanilla extract
- 1 teaspoon ground cinnamon
- ½ teaspoon ground nutmeg
- ¼ cup (½ stick) butter, melted
- ½ cup raisins

SAUCE

- 1½ cups milk
- ½ cup granulated sugar
- 1 tablespoon cornstarch
- ¼ cup water
- 3 egg yolks
- 1 teaspoon vanilla extract
- 3 tablespoons whiskey or brandy

SOUFFLÉ MIXTURE

- 6 large eggs, separated
- ½ cup each: granulated sugar, confectioners' sugar

1. Heat oven to 350 degrees. For bread pudding, mix bread, milk and cream in large bowl. Beat eggs in large bowl; add sugar and mix well. Stir in bread mixture, vanilla extract, cinnamon and nutmeg. Stir in butter and raisins. Pour into buttered 3-quart baking dish. Set dish into large pan of warm water about 1 inch deep.

2. Bake until knife inserted comes out clean, about 1 hour. Cool on wire rack. Put 2½ cups of the bread pudding in a large mixing bowl; set aside for soufflé. (Remaining bread pudding can be eaten warm with maple syrup.)

3. For sauce, put milk and sugar in top of double boiler over simmering water. Mix cornstarch and water until smooth. Stir into milk mixture. Cook and stir over simmering water until thickened. Beat 3 egg yolks in small bowl. Stir some of the hot milk mixture into egg yolks. Pour egg yolk mixture back into remaining milk mixture. Cook and stir until thickened. Do not boil. Remove from heat; stir in vanilla extract and whiskey. Cool.

4. For soufflé mixture, butter and lightly sugar a 2-quart soufflé dish. Heat oven to 375 degrees. Mix 6 egg yolks and granulated sugar in top of double boiler over very low heat. Whisk yolks and sugar until frothy and shiny. Whisk into reserved bread pudding until smooth.

5. Beat 6 egg whites until frothy. Gradually beat in confectioners' sugar until stiff but not dry. Gently fold into bread pudding mixture.

6. Turn the soufflé mixture into prepared dish. Wipe edges clean. Bake until soufflé is puffed and golden, 30 to 45 minutes. Serve immediately topped with sauce.

Most of us remember bread pudding from our childhood. This one is just as delicious as the one in our memory but with two differences; using the microwave oven has made it an exceptionally simple dish to make and it is topped with a rich whiskey sauce.

RAISIN BREAD PUDDING WITH WHISKEY SAUCE

6 servings
Preparation time: 20 minutes
Microwave cooking time: 15 minutes

7 slices raisin bread, cubed, about 4 cups

¼ cup packed light brown sugar

¼ teaspoon salt

2 cups milk

¼ cup (½ stick) unsalted butter or margarine, cut into pieces

2 large eggs, beaten

WHISKEY SAUCE

⅓ cup granulated sugar

2 tablespoons bourbon whiskey

¼ cup (½ stick) unsalted butter or margarine, cut into pieces

1 large egg

1. Spread bread cubes in 10 by 6-inch microwave-safe baking dish. Sprinkle with brown sugar and salt. Put milk and butter into 1-quart microwave-safe glass measure. Microwave on high (100 percent power) until hot, about 4 minutes.

2. Whisk eggs into milk mixture; pour over bread cubes. Microwave on high, rotating dish once, until knife inserted in center comes out clean, about 9 minutes. Cool on wire rack.

3. For sauce, mix sugar and bourbon in 2-cup microwave-safe glass measure; stir in butter. Microwave on high until mixture is bubbly, about 2 minutes. Beat egg in small bowl. Stir some of the sugar mixture into egg; pour egg back into remaining mixture; whisk until smooth. Microwave on high just until warm, 30 seconds. Whisk vigorously. Serve warm sauce over bread pudding.

This recipe comes from the well-known restaurant, Jamin, in Paris. The crème caramel couldn't be richer, but then it couldn't be better, either.

CRÈME CARAMEL

4 servings
Preparation time: 20 minutes
Baking time: 5 minutes
Chilling time: 1½ hours

1 **vanilla bean**
3 **large egg yolks**
⅓ **cup granulated sugar**
1¼ **cups whipping cream**
¼ **cup milk**
   Brown sugar

1. Heat oven to 325 degrees. Split vanilla bean lengthwise in half with sharp knife. Scrape out the small granules from each half; reserve granules. (Save pod for other use.)

2. Put egg yolks into medium bowl. Whisk in granulated sugar and vanilla granules until smooth. Gradually whisk in whipping cream and milk. Fill 4 small, shallow, oven-to-table custard cups with mixture. Set cups in large pan. Fill pan with hot water to come halfway up sides of cups.

3. Bake until mixture is almost set but center still wiggles slightly, about 50 minutes. Remove cups from water; cool on wire rack.

4. Refrigerate for no more than 1 hour. Sprinkle each with brown sugar.

5. Broil, 10 inches from heat source, until sugar is melted and golden, about 30 to 60 seconds. Refrigerate at least 30 minutes before serving.

Simplicity is the key to this version of the classic crème brulée by executive chef Roland Liccioni, formerly of Carlos' restaurant in Highland Park. The sweet-tart flavor of the berries he uses in the custard cups adds a delightful dimension to the rich custard.

CRÈME BRULÉE WITH BERRIES

10 servings
Preparation time: 10 minutes
Baking time: 45 minutes

2½ **cups whipping cream**
½ **cup milk**
½ **vanilla bean**
⅔ **cup granulated sugar**
6 **large egg yolks**
2 **cups berries, such as raspberries, blackberries, blueberries, sliced strawberries, etc.**
Confectioners' sugar

1. Heat oven to 325 degrees. Put cream, milk and vanilla bean into medium saucepan. Heat to boil. Remove from heat and remove vanilla bean; cool slightly.

2. Mix sugar and egg yolks in large bowl. Stir in cream mixture.

3. Divide berries among 10 individual 6-ounce custard cups. Pour cream mixture over berries. Set cups in large pan. Fill pan with hot water to come halfway up sides of cups.

4. Bake until knife inserted in center is withdrawn clean, 30 to 45 minutes. Remove from water; cool on wire rack. Refrigerate until cold.

5. To serve, sprinkle each with confectioners' sugar over tops. Broil, 10 inches from heat source, until sugar is melted and golden, 30 to 60 seconds. Serve immediately.

Chef Lutz Olkiewicz created this rice pudding while he was pastry chef at Chicago's Drake Hotel. The only ingredient missing here is a whole almond—a must for Scandinavians eating this dessert on New Year's Day. According to their folk tales, the person who gets the almond will be blessed with good luck for the coming year.

GOLDEN RICE PUDDING

8 to 10 servings
Preparation time: 30 minutes
Cooking time: 45 minutes

EGG CUSTARD

- 2 **cups milk**
- ⅔ **cup each: sugar, half-and-half**
- 3 **large eggs**
  Pinch salt
- ½ **teaspoon vanilla extract**
- 4 **drops yellow food coloring, optional**

PUDDING MIXTURE

- 2 **cups milk**
- 1 **cup raw rice (do not use instant rice)**
- 3 **cups half-and-half**
- ½ **cup sugar**
- ½ **teaspoon vanilla extract**
  Pinch salt
- 1 **cup golden raisins**

1. Mix all the custard ingredients together in large bowl. Strain through fine sieve.

2. For pudding mixture, put milk and rice into top of double boiler. Cook and stir over boiling water until rice is soft. Remove from heat; stir in half-and-half, sugar, vanilla extract and salt; mix well. Stir egg custard mixture and pudding mixture together well.

3. Heat oven to 375 degrees. Sprinkle raisins over bottom of well-buttered 13 by 9-inch baking dish. Pour egg mixture over raisins. Set baking dish into larger pan. Fill large pan with boiling water to come halfway up sides of dish.

4. Bake until set and top is golden, about 45 minutes. Cool on wire rack. Serve lukewarm or at room temperature. Do not refrigerate. Custard should be made the day it is to be served.

NOTE: To reheat, set custard in a larger pan of boiling water and cover. Heat in a low oven for a few minutes or until just slightly warmed.

This classic Italian dessert drew such raves when it was served one night at Chicago's Metropolis Cafe that we immediately asked for the recipe. The two cups of espresso coffee used in the recipe explains the name—"pick-me-up."

TIRAMISU

10 to 12 servings
Preparation time: 25 minutes
Chilling time: At least 2 hours

6 **large eggs, separated**

½ **cup sugar**

1 **pound marscapone, softened (see note)**

1 **cup whipping cream**

1 **package (10¾ ounces) pound cake, thinly sliced**

2 **cups espresso or very strong coffee**

1 **to 2 tablespoons dark rum, optional**

8 **ounces bittersweet chocolate, finely chopped**

1. Beat egg yolks with sugar in large mixer bowl set over pan of simmering water just until sugar dissolves. Remove from heat; beat until light and lemon colored. Beat in marscapone.

2. Beat whipping cream in small bowl until soft peaks form. Fold into marscapone mixture. Beat egg whites in small clean bowl until stiff but not dry; fold into marscapone mixture.

3. Cover bottom of 13 by 9-inch dish with cake slices. Mix espresso and rum. Brush over cake slices until very moist. Spoon half of marscapone mixture over cake. Sprinkle with half of the chocolate. Top with remaining cake slices. Sprinkle with remaining espresso mixture. Top with remaining marscapone mixture, then chocolate.

4. Refrigerate at least 2 hours before serving. Spoon into individual serving bowls.

NOTE: Marscapone is a soft, mild Italian cheese. It can be found at Italian markets and gourmet food shops. Although the flavor will be different, two packages (8 ounces) cream cheese, softened, may be substituted.

Strawberry shortcake topped with whipped cream is the ultimate for many. This recipe, which uses chocolate-dipped strawberries, comes from Michael Stuart's, a Chicago restaurant.

CHOCOLATE STRAWBERRY SHORTCAKE

12 servings
Preparation time: 45 minutes
Baking time: 10 to 15 minutes

STRAWBERRY SAUCE

2 cans (16 ounces each) frozen strawberries in syrup, thawed

3 tablespoons orange-flavored liqueur, optional

SHORTCAKES

2 cups all-purpose flour

½ cup granulated sugar

5 tablespoons unsweetened Dutch-process cocoa

1 tablespoon baking powder

½ teaspoon baking soda

½ cup (1 stick) cold unsalted butter or margarine, cut into 8 pieces

½ cup each: milk, buttermilk

CHOCOLATE-DIPPED STRAWBERRIES

4 pints fresh strawberries

1 package (6 ounces) semisweet chocolate chips

TO ASSEMBLE

2 cups whipping cream

¼ cup confectioners' sugar

1. For strawberry sauce, put thawed strawberries into food processor or blender. Add liqueur. Process until almost smooth. Transfer to nonaluminum container; cover and refrigerate. (This can be made one day in advance.)

2. Heat oven to 400 degrees. For shortcakes, put flour, sugar, cocoa, baking powder and baking soda into food processor. Process 1 minute. Add butter pieces; process until mixture resembles coarse crumbs. Add milk and buttermilk; process just until mixture is moistened.

3. Spoon batter into 18 lightly greased muffin tins, filling two-thirds full. Bake until firm, 10 to 15 minutes. Cool in pan 10 minutes. Remove from pans; cool completely on wire rack. (This can be made one day in advance or carefully wrapped and frozen.)

4. For chocolate-dipped strawberries, choose 12 of the most perfect berries with stems attached. Wipe the 12 carefully with damp cloth; pat dry. Melt chocolate chips in top of double boiler. When chocolate is melted, pick up 1 strawberry, hold it carefully by stem; immerse it two-thirds deep into melted chocolate. Shake off excess chocolate. Put onto wax paper–lined tray. Repeat with remaining 11 strawberries. Do not refrigerate. (Dip only on day to be used.) Reserve remaining melted chocolate.

5. Cut undipped strawberries into quarters if large, halves if small. Refrigerate until needed.

6. To assemble, beat cream in large mixer bowl until foamy. Beat in confectioners' sugar until soft peaks form. Cut each shortcake horizontally in half.

7. Spoon about 3 tablespoons of the strawberry sauce into bottom of 12 dessert bowls. Put 2 shortcake halves side by side into each bowl. Top with some of the quartered strawberries. Top with large mound of whipped cream. Put a third short-cake half over whipped cream. Spoon about 1 tablespoon strawberry sauce over top of shortcake. Top with heaping tablespoon of whipped cream.

8. Put 1 chocolate-dipped strawberry on top. Drizzle with some of the remaining melted chocolate lightly over all. Repeat with other shortcakes. Serve immediately.

This classic Greek dessert, which literally drips sweet richness, doesn't have to wait for a Greek meal. Sometimes it even calls you from the refrigerator in the middle of the night.

BAKLAVA

12 to 14 servings
Preparation time: 1 hour
Baking time: 1½ to 2 hours

1 **box (16 ounces) frozen filo dough**
1 **pound walnut pieces**
¼ **cup sugar**
1 **teaspoon ground cinnamon**
2 **cups (4 sticks) unsalted butter**

SYRUP
3 **cups sugar**
1½ **cups water**
2 **cinnamon sticks**
¼ **teaspoon whole cloves**
½ **lemon**

1. Thaw filo dough according to package directions. Process nuts in grinder or food processor until finely ground. Mix ground nuts, ¼ cup sugar and ground cinnamon in large bowl. Melt butter in small saucepan.

2. Heat oven to 300 degrees. Butter 14 by 10-inch baking pan. Lay filo dough out on clean towel. Cover with slightly damp towel. Remove 1 sheet of filo at a time to work surface covered with another towel. Brush with butter. Put into prepared pan. Repeat until there are 5 buttered filo sheets in pan.

3. Sprinkle with 1 cup of the nut mixture. Put 1 buttered sheet of filo over nuts. Sprinkle with 1 cup of the nut mixture. Repeat layering with buttered filo and nut mixture until nut mixture is used up. Then layer remaining filo sheets, buttered, over all. Tuck any overhanging filo into pan. Brush top with remaining butter.

4. Cut through layers with sharp knife into diamonds before baking. Bake until golden brown and crisp, 1½ to 2 hours. Cool on wire rack.

5. For syrup, put sugar, water, cinnamon sticks and cloves into heavy saucepan. Squeeze juice from lemon half into mixture, then put lemon shell into mixture, too. Heat to boil until sugar is dissolved. Reduce heat; simmer, uncovered, 6 minutes. Strain. Pour hot syrup slowly over cooled baklava. Cool completely on wire rack.

Here is an uncomplicated, light-tasting, but nevertheless rich chocolate mousse that is easy to make, elegant to eat and a sure pleaser.

CHOCOLATE MOUSSE

8 servings
Preparation time: 20 minutes
Chilling time: Several hours

¾ cup (1½ sticks) unsalted butter

¾ cup unsweetened Dutch-processed cocoa (or 4 ounces unsweetened chocolate)

3 large eggs, separated

¾ cup sugar

1¼ cups whipping cream

3 tablespoons orange-flavored liqueur

2 teaspoons vanilla extract

Whipped cream and chocolate curls for garnish

1. Melt butter in medium saucepan. Remove from heat; stir in cocoa until smooth. Cool.

2. Beat egg yolks in large mixer bowl until thick and lemon colored; gradually beat in ¼ cup of the sugar. Beat until light and fluffy. Beat in cocoa mixture on low speed. Stir in ¼ cup of the cream and liqueur.

3. Beat egg whites in small mixer bowl until stiff but not dry. Fold into chocolate mixture. Beat remaining 1 cup cream, ½ cup sugar and vanilla extract in small mixer bowl until soft peaks form. Fold into chocolate mixture. Spoon into individual dessert dishes or 1½-quart mold.

4. Refrigerate several hours or overnight. Garnish with whipped cream and chocolate curls.

■ *Charlie Trotter's is a Chicago restaurant located in a classic old brownstone where food is handled and served with innovation, seriousness and love. The desserts always look too elegant to eat, but diners manage—with great gusto. This rich and colorful concoction of chocolate, butter, cream and raspberries (to name just a few of the ingredients) isn't something you'll whip up in a few minutes, but wait until you see and taste the results! This was developed by pastry chef, Mary Cech.*

CHOCOLATE SATIN

6 servings
Preparation time: 1 hour
Freezing time: 3 hours or overnight
Cooking time: 5 minutes

CHOCOLATE FILLING

- **2 tablespoons hazelnut-flavored liqueur**
- **1 tablespoon each: crème de cocoa liqueur, rum**
- **2 large eggs, separated**
- **2 tablespoons confectioners' sugar**
- **8 ounces semisweet chocolate**
- **2 tablespoons butter**
- **1 cup whipping cream**
- **¼ cup granulated sugar**

RASPBERRY CREAM

- **1 cup fresh or frozen raspberries**
- **½ cup whipping cream**
- **1 tablespoon confectioners' sugar**

GLAZE

- **1 cup plus 2 tablespoons granulated sugar**
- **½ cup (1 stick) butter**
- **1 cup each: whipping cream, unsweetened Dutch-processed cocoa, sifted**
- **1 ounce semisweet chocolate, chopped**
- **Pesticide-free rose petals for garnish**

1. For chocolate filling, mix liqueurs and rum in large bowl. Beat egg yolks and confectioners' sugar in small mixer bowl until light and lemon colored, about 5 minutes. Fold into liqueur mixture.

2. Melt chocolate and butter together in small saucepan over low heat. Let cool; add to yolk mixture.

3. Beat cream in small mixer bowl until soft peaks form. Add one-quarter of whipped cream to chocolate mixture; mix well. Gently fold in remaining cream.

4. Beat egg whites with granulated sugar until stiff but not dry. Fold into chocolate mixture just until blended. Pour mixture into 6 well-buttered 6-ounce custard cups. Freeze 3 hours or overnight.

5. For raspberry cream, put raspberries, cream and confectioners' sugar into food processor or blender. Process until smooth. Strain through fine sieve to remove seeds. Refrigerate until cold.

6. For glaze, put sugar, butter and cream in small saucepan. Cook over low heat until butter melts. Remove from heat. Add cocoa powder and chocolate; stir until melted. Strain through fine sieve into medium bowl. Cool to room temperature.

7. Shortly before serving, dip each custard cup into warm water 5 seconds. Run a knife around edges and invert onto wire racks. Return to freezer for a few minutes to firm.

8. Quickly pour glaze over top of each and let glaze drip down sides. Put into refrigerator to set glaze.

9. To serve, pour some raspberry cream onto center of each serving plate. Remove chocolate satins from wire rack and place on plate. Decorate plate with rose petals and a sprinkling of confectioners' sugar, if desired.

Cranberries don't have to be relegated to an accompaniment to turkey or chicken. This soufflé is a sweet and different way to use the fresh berries.

COLD CRANBERRY SOUFFLÉ

6 to 8 servings
Preparation time: 25 minutes
Chilling time: 4 hours or overnight

½ **pound fresh cranberries, finely chopped (about 2 cups)**

1½ **cups sugar**

½ **cup cranberry-flavored liqueur**

½ **teaspoon finely grated lemon rind**

2 **envelopes plain gelatin**

2 **cups whipping cream, whipped**

Cranberry-flavored liqueur

1. Sprinkle chopped cranberries with sugar in medium bowl; let stand 20 minutes. Drain; reserve ¼ cup juice. Mix ½ cup liqueur and lemon rind with cranberries.

2. Sprinkle gelatin over ¼ cup reserved juice in glass measure to soften; put measure in pan of boiling water and stir until dissolved; cool.

3. Stir gelatin into cranberry mixture; fold in whipped cream. Pour into 1½-quart soufflé dish or mold. Refrigerate until set, 4 hours or overnight. Serve with a drizzle of cranberry liqueur.

Pastry chef Gale Gand, of Bice restaurant in Chicago, devised this refreshing, fruit-filled dessert, which she serves in a soup bowl and calls a passion fruit soup. But don't let the word "soup" throw you off. It's definitely dessert.

PASSION FRUIT SOUP

4 servings
Preparation time: 15 minutes
Cooking time: 3 minutes
Chilling time: 3 hours

½ **teaspoon unflavored gelatin**
½ **cup passion fruit puree (see note)**
⅓ **cup sugar**
½ **cup whipping cream**

CITRUS JUICE

½ **cup fresh orange juice**
1 **tablespoon each: lemon juice, passion fruit puree**

GARNISH

½ **pint citrus sorbet, such as orange or lemon**
Assorted fresh fruits such as peeled, sliced kiwi, papaya, blueberries, raspberries, strawberries

1. Sprinkle gelatin over ½ cup passion fruit puree in small saucepan; let stand until soft. Add sugar and heat until gelatin dissolves, 2 to 3 minutes. Transfer to large bowl. Cool to room temperature.

2. Beat cream in electric mixer until soft peaks form. Fold one-quarter of the cream into cooled gelatin. Gently fold gelatin mixture into remaining cream. Pour into 4 individual soup bowls. Cover and refrigerate until firm, about 3 hours.

3. For citrus juice, mix orange juice, lemon juice and 1 tablespoon passion fruit puree.

4. To serve, pour some of the juice mixture over each soup. Garnish with a scoop of sorbet and assorted prepared fruits.

NOTE: Passion fruit puree can be made by scooping out the pulp from fresh passion fruit and pushing it through fine sieve. You may substitute passion fruit drink, coulis or juice available at specialty food stores.

Winter pears taste great when poached in a cinnamon-flavored liquid. Serve them with some of the syrupy cooking liquid while still warm, because the syrup thickens as it cools.

POACHED CINNAMON PEARS

4 servings
Preparation time: 15 minutes
Cooking time: 30 minutes

4 winter pears, such as Bosc
1 cup each: sugar, water
½ cup fresh orange juice
1 cinnamon stick

1. Use paring knife to cut spiral design in skin of each pear. Cut small slice from bottom of each so they stand upright; remove core from its base, if you wish, for easy eating.

2. Heat sugar and water to boil in medium saucepan just large enough to hold pears. Stir juice and cinnamon stick into saucepan. Set pears upright in liquid. Cook gently over medium heat until tender, 20 to 30 minutes. Spoon syrup over pears frequently as they cook.

3. Transfer pears to warm serving dish; pour syrup over them. Serve while still warm.

The following recipe is inspired by the excellent profiteroles served at Julien, a bistro in Paris. The shells require a long baking time to make them very crisp. To save time, make the chocolate sauce while they bake. The best quality vanilla ice cream will yield the richest results.

PROFITEROLES WITH CHOCOLATE CREAM SAUCE

4 to 6 servings
Preparation time: 10 minutes
Cooking time: 50 minutes

1 **cup water**
½ **cup (1 stick) unsalted butter**
1 **cup all-purpose flour**
4 **large eggs**
1 **egg yolk**
1 **tablespoon whipping cream or milk**
   Chocolate cream sauce (recipe follows)
   Vanilla ice cream

1. Heat oven to 375 degrees. Heat water and butter in medium saucepan to boil. Reduce heat; stir in flour all at once until well mixed. Cook, stirring vigorously, over low heat, until mixture forms a ball and pulls away from sides of pan, 4 to 5 minutes. Dough should not stick to your fingers. Remove from heat; transfer to bowl. Let cool 5 minutes.

2. Beat in 4 eggs, one at a time, until thoroughly incorporated. Beat until smooth.

3. Put dough into pastry bag fitted with ½-inch round tip. Pipe dough onto ungreased baking sheet into 1½-inch round mounds about 1 inch high. Repeat to make 12 mounds.

4. Brush tops with beaten egg yolk mixed with whipping cream. Bake until puffed and golden, 45 to 50 minutes. Cool completely on wire rack.

5. Meanwhile, make chocolate sauce; keep warm. To serve, cut tops off baked shells. Scoop out any moist dough. Fill with ice cream. Replace tops; put onto serving plates. Ladle warm sauce over all. Serve immediately.

CHOCOLATE CREAM SAUCE

About 2 cups

½ **cup whipping cream**
2 **tablespoons sugar**
2 **egg yolks**
8 **ounces bittersweet or semisweet chocolate, finely grated**
3 **tablespoons cognac or brandy**
1 **tablespoon butter**

1. Mix cream, sugar and egg yolks in small heavy saucepan. Cook, stirring constantly with wooden spoon, over medium-low heat until mixture thickens and coats back of spoon. Do not boil. Remove from heat. Stir in chocolate until melted. Stir in cognac and butter. Cool slightly; serve warm.

Although it's rich and chocolatey, this recipe is not overly sweet. If you like your chocolate sweet, increase the sugar to ¾ cup. Be sure to use high-quality chocolate for the best flavor.

BITTERSWEET CHOCOLATE ICE CREAM

About 1 quart, 4 servings
Preparation time: 20 minutes
Chilling time: Several hours
Freezing time: Varies with machine

4 ounces each: semisweet chocolate, unsweetened chocolate

½ cup each: sugar, water

⅛ teaspoon salt

2 cups each: whipping cream, half-and-half

1 teaspoon vanilla extract

1. Chop chocolate in food processor or on cutting board until very fine. Put sugar, water and salt into medium saucepan. Cook and stir over low heat until sugar dissolves. Stir in chocolate. Cook and stir until chocolate melts. Whisk in cream and half-and-half. Cook over medium heat, stirring constantly until mixture is slightly thickened, about 15 minutes. Do not boil. Strain through fine sieve into large bowl. Refrigerate, covered, until very cold.

2. Stir in vanilla extract. Freeze in ice-cream freezer according to manufacturer's directions. Then put in freezer at least 15 minutes before serving.

NOTE: Transfer the ice cream from the machine container to another container once it has frozen. Otherwise it will freeze harder at the edges of the container and may be uneven in texture.

The cinnamon flavor in this ice cream goes well with pumpkin, apple, pecan and sweet potato pies, making it a natural for Thanksgiving dinner—as well as any other time of year.

CINNAMON ICE CREAM

About 5 cups, 5 servings
Preparation time: 15 minutes
Chilling time: Several hours
Freezing time: Varies with machine

3 **cups whipping cream**
1 **cup milk**
1 **scant cup packed dark
    brown sugar**
4 **large egg yolks**
2 **cinnamon sticks**
1 **cup chopped walnut**

1. Put cream, milk and sugar in large saucepan. Cook and stir until sugar dissolves and mixture is hot. Put egg yolks in small bowl; whisk to combine. While whisking, slowly pour in about 1 cup of the hot cream mixture. Mix well. Stir egg yolk mixture back into saucepan. Add cinnamon sticks.

2. Cook over medium-low heat, stirring constantly, just until mixture thickens slightly and coats back of spoon or to 180 degrees on instant-read thermometer. Do not boil. Strain mixture through fine sieve into large bowl. Add cinnamon sticks to the bowl. Refrigerate, covered, until very cold.

3. Strain mixture through fine sieve into ice-cream machine container. Freeze in ice-cream freezer according to manufacturer's directions. Remove ice cream from machine; stir in walnuts. Then put in freezer at least 15 minutes before serving. Serve in small scoops.

NOTE: This ice cream, as well as most homemade ice creams, tastes best when used within 2 or 3 days.

Leslee Reis, whose Cafe Provençal, in Evanston, Illinois, is a hallmark of exquisitely good food, gave us this recipe for ice cream. It's not difficult to make, and it tastes of creamy coffee, just right after a big dinner. Or a small dinner.

COFFEE ICE CREAM

About 1½ quarts, 6 servings
Preparation time: 35 minutes
Chilling time: Several hours
Freezing time: Varies with machine

6 **large egg yolks, lightly beaten**
1 **cup sugar**
2 **cups half-and-half**
1½ **cups whipping cream**
  Grated rind of 1 lemon
1 **tablespoon vanilla extract**
3 **tablespoons instant espresso or coffee dissolved in 3 tablespoons hot prepared coffee**

1. Beat yolks with sugar in top of double boiler set over simmering water until thick and lemon colored (they should form a ribbon when beaters are lifted). Whisk in small portion of the half-and-half. Then whisk in remaining half-and-half and cream over heat. Whisk in lemon rind. Continue cooking, whisking constantly, until mixture thickens slightly and coats back of spoon or is 180 degrees on instant-read thermometer. Do not boil.

2. Strain through fine sieve into large bowl. Stir in vanilla extract and coffee. Refrigerate, covered, until very cold.

3. Freeze in ice-cream freezer according to manufacturer's directions. Then put in freezer at least 15 minutes before serving.

While on a tour of this country, French Chef Andre Daguin demonstrated making this classic French ice cream for a group of culinary students at Evanston's Kendall College.

PRUNE AND ARMAGNAC ICE CREAM

About 1 quart, 4 servings
Preparation time: 30 minutes
Marinating time: 2 weeks or more
Chilling time: Several hours
Freezing time: Varies with machine

1 **pound dried, pitted prunes**
  Armagnac or cognac or brandy
1 **quart milk**
8 **large egg yolks**
1 **to 1¼ cups sugar to taste**

1. Two weeks or more in advance, put prunes into large clean jar or crock. Add Armagnac to cover. Cover jar or crock; store in cool place.

2. Measure out 1 cup moderately packed prunes and fill up remainder of cup with Armagnac; set aside.

3. Scald milk in medium saucepan; set aside. Whisk egg yolks over low heat in large, nonaluminum saucepan until warm. Continue whisking, adding sugar gradually. When all sugar is added and sugar has begun to dissolve, remove saucepan from heat. Whisk in hot milk. Return saucepan to low heat. Cook and stir well until thickened enough to coat a spoon heavily. Do not boil. Cool 2 hours; beat very vigorously with whisk or electric beaters.

4. Strain mixture through fine sieve into ice-cream machine container. Freeze according to manufacturer's directions. When ice cream is just beginning to set, drop in prunes one by one (while machine is in operation) and drizzle in Armagnac. Continue freezing until ice cream is firm. Then put in freezer at least 15 minutes before serving.

5. To serve, scoop out ice cream, top with a prune, and drizzle some Armagnac over, if desired.

NOTE: Chef Andre Daguin suggests finding the least expensive Armagnac for this recipe; it will have the strongest flavor.

The secret to this rich, intensely flavorful ice cream lies in cooking the strawberries after they're pureed. If you're concerned about the admittedly high butterfat content, the richness can be cut by reducing the number of egg yolks to 6 and using all half-and-half instead of whipping cream.

STRAWBERRY ICE CREAM

About 2 quarts, 8 servings
Preparation time: 25 minutes
Cooking time: 20 minutes
Chilling time: Several hours
Freezing time: Varies with machine

3 **cups half-and-half**
2 **cups whipping cream**
1 **cup sugar**
8 **large egg yolks, beaten**
1½ **teaspoons vanilla extract**
Pinch salt
4 **pints fresh ripe strawberries, hulled**

1. Put half-and-half and cream into large heavy saucepan. Heat to simmer; stir in sugar; cook and stir until sugar dissolves. Whisk egg yolks in medium bowl. Stir in about 1 cup of hot cream. Stir egg yolk mixture back into remaining cream mixture in saucepan. Cook and stir over low heat, until mixture lightly coats back of spoon, about 180 degrees on instant-read thermometer. Do not boil.

2. Immediately strain into large bowl. Stir in vanilla extract and salt. Refrigerate, covered, until very cold.

3. Meanwhile, puree strawberries in food processor or blender. Strain into large heavy saucepan. Cook and stir over medium heat, until puree reduces to 2 cups. Strain into bowl. Refrigerate until very cold.

4. Stir chilled strawberry puree into chilled custard.

5. Freeze in ice-cream machine according to manufacturer's directions. Then put into freezer at least 15 minutes before serving.

Of all the hundreds of different ice-cream flavors available today, simple vanilla remains one of the favorites.

SUPERB VANILLA CUSTARD ICE CREAM

1 quart, 4 servings
Preparation time: 5 minutes
Cooking time: 10 minutes
Chilling time: Several hours
Freezing time: Varies with machine

3　cups whipping cream
1　cup half-and-half
¾　cup sugar
4　large egg yolks
1　vanilla bean, about 4
　　inches long

1. Heat cream, half-and-half and sugar in medium saucepan over medium heat. Stir occasionally until sugar is dissolved and mixture is hot.

2. Whisk egg yolks in medium bowl. Stir in about 1 cup of the hot cream. Stir egg yolk mixture back into remaining cream in saucepan. Cut vanilla bean lengthwise in half. Scrape out seeds; add seeds and pod to mixture.

3. Cook and stir over medium heat until mixture thickens and lightly coats back of spoon, about 180 degrees on an instant-read thermometer. Do not boil. Strain mixture through fine sieve into large bowl. Refrigerate, covered, until very cold.

4. Freeze in ice-cream freezer according to manufacturer's directions. Then put into freezer at least 15 minutes before serving.

■   *This dessert is made with a ruby-colored liqueur called crème de cassis, a luscious, black-currant liquid with a sweet-tangy flavor. The most popular use for cassis in this country is for kir (white wine and a few drops of cassis), but in this recipe, it becomes the key to a most refreshing finish to a rich dinner.*

CASSIS AND BLACKBERRY SORBET

About 3 cups, 4 servings
Preparation time: 15 minutes
Freezing time: Varies with machine

½ **pint fresh or frozen blackberries**
1 **cup crème de cassis liqueur or cassis syrup**
Juice of ½ small lemon
1 **cup water**
Brandy for serving, optional

1. Put blackberries into food processor or blender. Process until berries are a coarse puree. Push through fine sieve into nonaluminum bowl. Stir in crème de cassis, lemon juice and water. Chill thoroughly.

2. Transfer mixture into container of ice-cream machine; freeze according to manufacturer's directions. Then put in freezer at least 15 minutes before serving. (See note.)

3. Serve in small scoops in a stemmed glass. Drizzle a little brandy over sorbet before serving.

NOTE: If an ice-cream machine is unavailable, mixture may be still-frozen in shallow nonaluminum bowl or pan. Put in freezer and allow to freeze until mixture is solid 2 inches in from sides. Beat vigorously with fork. Repeat freezing and beating 2 more times. Freeze solid.

The clean, exotic taste of fresh mangoes makes the fruit a natural for a crisp, refreshing frozen dessert. It's a perfect finishing touch to a big meal.

FROZEN MANGO WHIP

6 servings
Preparation time: 20 minutes
Freezing time: Overnight

4 or 5 mangoes
½ cup sugar
½ cup whipping cream
¼ cup brandy
  Crystallized ginger or
    shredded coconut,
    optional

1. Peel, seed and cut mangoes into small chunks. Mix with sugar; freeze in large metal bowl until firm.

2. Remove mixture from freezer and break up. Put in food processor or blender and process until light and smooth, about 1 minute.

3. With machine running, add cream and brandy. Process until mixture is smooth and creamy. Put mixture in large metal bowl; cover and freeze overnight.

4. To serve, soften slightly at room temperature. Put into food processor or blender; process until smooth. Serve immediately. Garnish with ginger.

This easily made ice gets dressed up when served in hollowed-out lemon shells.

PEAR LEMON ICE

8 servings
Preparation time: 10 minutes
Cooking time: 4 minutes
Freezing time: 6 hours

1½ cups each: sugar,
    water
 4 very ripe pears,
    peeled, cored
 1 tablespoon grated
    lemon rind
 9 lemons, halved, juiced,
    shells reserved
    Fresh mint leaves,
    pomegranate seeds
    for garnish

1. Heat sugar and water to boil in large saucepan. Cook and stir until sugar dissolves; cook, covered, 4 minutes. Cool; set aside.

2. Put pears, lemon rind and 1 cup lemon juice into food processor or blender. Add 1 cup of the syrup and process until smooth. Taste and adjust for sweetness. Add more syrup if desired. Pour into large metal bowl; freeze until almost firm, about 2 hours.

3. Clean lemon shells. Cut thin slice off each bottom so it stands upright.

4. Put frozen lemon mixture into food processor or blender. Process until smooth. Spoon into lemon shells. Freeze until firm.

5. Serve garnished with mint leaves.

This refreshing sherbet can either be made in an ice-cream machine or frozen in a large bowl, beaten several times while freezing. It's a nice summery dessert from pastry chef and author Lindsey Remolif Shere of Chez Panisse in Berkeley, California. Try it on a hot day or after a rich meal.

TANGERINE SHERBET

6 to 8 servings
Preparation time: 25 minutes
Freezing time: Varies

4 to 5 pounds tangerines (10–12 medium), such as Minneola, Fairchild, Kinnow or Honey

1 cup minus 1 tablespoon sugar

Cognac, brandy or orange liqueur to taste

Mint leaves for garnish

1. Using a zester or a flat grater with $\frac{1}{16}$-inch holes, make long shreds from rind of 1 tangerine. Reserve the shreds.

2. Cut tangerines in half. Squeeze juice from tangerines into large nonaluminum bowl. Save shells if desired to use as serving cups.

3. Put 1 cup of the juice and sugar into nonaluminum saucepan. Heat just until sugar dissolves. Stir warmed mixture into remaining juice. Add reserved shreds. Stir in cognac 1 teaspoon at a time to desired taste.

4. Refrigerate until cold. Then freeze in ice-cream machine according to manufacturer's directions. Then put in freezer at least 15 minutes before serving. (See note.)

5. Let soften slightly before serving if necessary. Garnish with mint leaves.

NOTE: If an ice-cream machine is unavailable, mixture may be still-frozen in shallow nonaluminum bowl or pan. Put into freezer and allow to freeze until mixture is solid 2 inches in from sides. Beat vigorously with fork. Repeat beating and freezing 2 more times.

Desserts

CRÈME ANGLAISE

About 1¼ cups
Preparation time: 5 minutes
Cooking time: 10 minutes

1 **cup milk**
5½ **tablespoons sugar**
½ **vanilla bean**
2 **large egg yolks**

1. Heat milk, 3 tablespoons sugar and vanilla bean to simmer in large saucepan. Beat egg yolks and 2½ tablespoons sugar in mixer bowl until mixture forms ribbons. Beat in some of the hot milk mixture. Return mixture to saucepan.

2. Cook and stir over low heat until mixture coats back of spoon and registers 180 degrees on instant-read thermometer. Do not boil. Strain through fine sieve into bowl. Cool completely. Refrigerate, covered, up to 1 week.

LUSCIOUS CHOCOLATE SAUCE

About 3 cups
Preparation time: 5 minutes
Cooking time: 10 minutes

5 **ounces unsweetened chocolate, finely chopped**
⅓ **cup unsalted butter**
3 **cups confectioners' sugar**
1 **can (13 ounces) evaporated milk**
1 **teaspoon vanilla extract or favorite liqueur to taste**

1. Put chocolate and butter into medium-size, heavy saucepan. Cook and stir over low heat just until chocolate melts. Remove pan from heat and alternately stir in sugar and milk.

2. Cook over low heat, stirring constantly, until thickened, 5 to 8 minutes. Add vanilla extract. Refrigerate, covered, up to 3 weeks.

This fresh, natural strawberry topping is rich in fresh flavor. Use it for ice cream, puddings or pound cakes.

FRESH STRAWBERRY SAUCE

About 1½ cups
Preparation time: 5 minutes
Cooking time: 5 minutes

1 **pint strawberries, hulled, sliced**
⅓ **cup sugar**
1 **tablespoon fresh lemon juice**
½ **teaspoon vanilla extract or orange-flavored liqueur**

1. Crush strawberries lightly in medium nonaluminum saucepan. Stir in sugar and lemon juice. Cook and stir over medium heat until sugar dissolves. Boil hard for 1 minute. Remove from heat. Cool. Stir in vanilla extract. Refrigerate, covered, up to 2 weeks.

Fresh rhubarb is a natural for the microwave. All that's needed for this sauce is the fruit, a little water, sugar and the flavoring of your choice (allspice is used in this recipe); the rhubarb creates its own juices and the cooking time is minimal. The sauce can be served over cake, ice cream, pudding or pie.

RHUBARB ORANGE SAUCE

About 2 cups
Preparation time: 5 minutes
Microwave cooking time: 6 minutes

1 **orange**
½ **pound rhubarb, cut into ½-inch pieces**
⅓ **cup sugar**
1 **tablespoon each: cornstarch, water**
¼ **teaspoon ground allspice**
   Cake, ice cream or pudding for serving

1. Grate rind from orange. Cut off white membrane and section orange. Put rhubarb and sugar into 1-quart microwave-safe glass measure. Microwave on high (100 percent power) 3 minutes.

2. Mix cornstarch and water. Stir into rhubarb with orange sections, rind and allspice. Microwave on high, stirring once, until thickened, about 3 minutes. Let stand 5 minutes. Serve warm or cold over cake, ice cream or pudding.

COOKIES & CANDIES

Cookies are like old friends—easy to take, forgiving and satisfying. Landing a couple of freshly baked cookies, warm from the oven, is one of the perks associated with being a member of *The Tribune* Food Guide staff.

In an average year, we test over 1,000 recipes, and about half of them are sweet. When cookies are on the testing schedule, *The Tribune* kitchen has more surprise visitors than usual. Cookies are widely preferred over layer cake, pizza or a soufflé, because a cookie can be discretely escorted back to a desk without fanfare or fear of kidnapping by a ravenous coworker.

During a typical Christmas cookie contest, for example, more than 200 readers send us their favorite recipes. It is not unusual by the end of a day of holiday cookie testing to have 36 dozen goodies stacked on the kitchen counters. Editors and writers "stop by" in droves.

Now you, too, can have a taste of some of those cookies baked in our test kitchen, including a good array of the classics, from sugar cookies, chocolate chip and peanut butter to snappy peppercorn cookies and lemon delights. Enjoy.

WHEN IS A COOKIE DONE?

Most cookie recipes require little in terms of skill or exactitude. Unlike cakes, cookies are forgiving. They can be baked successfully within a temperature range of 325 to 375 degrees. Cookies with molasses, fruits or nuts bake well at 325 degrees. How to tell when they are done? Look for an even golden color, with a dry, glossy surface and firm edges. A bar cookie is done when it shrinks a bit from the edges and the top springs back when touched.

A DO-AHEAD NOTE

Saving a block of time isn't necessary to make cookies. The harried baker can prepare the dough and store it in the refrigerator up to a week or in the freezer up to a month.

COOKIE TYPES

Thanks to a variety of cookie types, boredom is rarely a problem. Basically, there are four types:

Dropped: Chocolate chip and old-fashioned oatmeal cookies are included in this category. The batter is dropped onto a sheet by spoonfuls. If the batter is thin, leave about 1 inch between dough balls to allow for spread; if the batter is thick, flatten with the tines of a fork or spread with a knife dipped in water or flatten with the bottom of a glass that has been floured. Cookies flattened before baking will have a more uniform shape than if allowed to spread naturally.

Rolled: Work with about a cup of chilled dough at a time and keep remaining dough in the refrigerator. Dust cutting board with confectioners' sugar or flour to prevent sticking. Unless a recipe specifies, this type of dough does not require a greased baking sheet.

Refrigerated: The typical cut-out sugar Christmas cookie falls into this area. These doughs need to be well chilled before slicing and baking. The dough can be made hours, or even days, ahead of time and refrigerated. Unless a recipe specifies, this type of cookie does not require a greased baking sheet. Doughs that store especially well have a ratio of ¼ cup of shortening to 1 cup flour. A dough with less fat will crumble and dry out.

Bars: This type of cookie is generally richer and chewier than most cookies. Due to their moisture, they don't keep fresh as long as cookies do. These cut more easily when warm. Control the thickness of the bar cookie by selecting the right pan size. For a thinner bar cookie, use a larger pan.

WHAT GOES INTO A COOKIE?

Flour: Pastry flour makes cookies that spread out during baking. It is preferred for thin, delicate cookies. All-purpose flour makes firm cookies which hold their shape during baking. It is not necessary to sift flour for most cookie recipes.

Fats: For a richer-tasting cookie, use butter. Vegetable shortening is used when the flavor of butter is not necessary or the flavors of seasonings and spices are designed to be more assertive. Cookies made with shortening tend to be lighter. Have fats at room temperature so they blend more easily.

Eggs: Eggs are easier to separate when chilled, but they yield greater volume when used at room temperature. To deepen the color of a cookie, add another egg yolk.

COOKIE SHEET TIPS

To bake cookies, use cookie sheets without sides because high sides will deflect the heat and cookies will not bake properly. When cookies have a high-fat content, greasing the sheet isn't necessary.

TIMING THE BAKING

If you like cookies chewy and slightly soft, shorten baking time. If a crisper texture is desired, lengthen it. If you have underestimated the baking time by a minute or two, let the cookies remain on the warm baking sheet. The residual heat will finish the baking process.

HOW TO STORE COOKIES

Store baked cookies in covered jars or tins in a cool, dry place. Cookies tend to pick up flavors, so pack different kinds of cookies separately. If cookies are delicate, place sheets of wax paper between layers. To keep soft cookies from drying out, add a slice of bread or section of an apple in the tin or storage jar and replace every few days. If cookies become soggy, freshen them up for a few minutes in a 300-degree oven.

COOKIES

Amish sugar cookies

Back-to-school cookies

Best gingerbread cookies

Easy butter cookies

Christmas tree cookies

Chocolate biscotti cookies

Danish brown spice cookies

Kolacky

Molasses cookies

Praline cookies

Peanut butter cookies

Peppercorn cookies

Oatmeal thins

Walnut refrigerator cookies

Sesame seed cookies

Coriander shortbread

Cornmeal shortbread

Sugar cookies

Thumbprints

BAR COOKIES

Almond nougat crispies

Brownies

Frango chocolate brownies

Coconut-chip layer bars

Lemon delights

Passover lemon bars

OTHERS

Lemon madeleines

Nut horns

CANDIES

Brittle breakup

Rio bravo pralines

Caramel truffles

Coconut joys

Peanut butter bonbons

Sparkling pretzels

Oven caramel corn

Reader Nancy Jackson, of Wilmette, Illinois, snagged $10 through The Tribune*'s favorite recipe column in October 1980, with these sugar cookies. Using two types of sugar contributes to their tenderness. Because the dough is sticky, chilling makes handling easier.*

AMISH SUGAR COOKIES

About 5 dozen
Preparation time: 20 minutes
Chilling time: 2 hours
Baking time: 8 to 10 minutes, 30 minutes total

1 **cup (2 sticks) unsalted butter, softened**
1 **cup granulated sugar**
2 **large eggs, beaten**
1 **cup confectioners' sugar**
2 **teaspoons vanilla extract**
¾ **teaspoon cream of tartar**
½ **teaspoon salt**
1 **cup vegetable oil**
4½ **cups all-purpose flour**

1. Cream butter and granulated sugar in large mixer bowl until light and fluffy. Beat in eggs. Beat in confectioners' sugar, vanilla extract, cream of tartar and salt. Alternately beat in oil and flour; beat until smooth and fluffy. Refrigerate dough, covered, 2 hours or until cold.

2. Heat oven to 350 degrees. Roll rounded tablespoons of dough into balls. Put 2 inches apart onto lightly greased baking sheets. Flatten each with bottom of a glass that has been lightly oiled and dipped in granulated sugar.

3. Bake until bottoms are golden, 8 to 10 minutes. Cool on wire racks.

When Food Guide reader Gloria Scolaro sent this cookie recipe to the test kitchen in 1986, the Hinsdale, Illinois, baker included the following tips: Vary the quantities of raisins, chocolate chips and coconut to suit taste. The batter, divided into two parts, can be used as a base for two different cookies. And, she said, you can toast the oats for a more interesting texture and flavor.

BACK-TO-SCHOOL COOKIES

About 4 dozen
Preparation time: 25 minutes
Baking time: 8 to 10 minutes, 20 minutes total

1 cup (2 sticks) unsalted butter or margarine, softened
1 cup each: granulated sugar, packed light brown sugar
2 large eggs
1 teaspoon vanilla extract
2 cups all-purpose flour
1 teaspoon baking soda
½ teaspoon baking powder
2 cups quick-cooking oats
2 cups crisp rice cereal or 1 cup corn flakes and 1 cup crisp rice cereal
1 cup raisins or chocolate chips or flaked coconut

1. Cream butter and sugars in large mixer bowl until light and fluffy. Gradually beat in eggs and vanilla extract. Sift flour, baking soda and baking powder together. Using a wooden spoon, gradually add flour mixture to creamed mixture. Stir in oats, cereal and raisins. Dough will be stiff.

2. Heat oven to 350 degrees. Roll dough into balls about the size of a walnut. Put 2 inches apart onto greased baking sheets.

3. Bake until golden, 8 to 10 minutes. Cool on wire racks.

These spicy gingerbread cookies won Gloria Heeter of Oak Brook, Illinois, the third-place spot in The Tribune*'s Christmas Cookie Contest in 1988.*

BEST GINGERBREAD COOKIES

About 3 dozen
Preparation time: 25 minutes
Chilling time: 8 hours or overnight
Baking time: 7 to 10 minutes, 30 minutes total

1 cup (2 sticks) corn oil margarine, softened
1 cup each: sugar, molasses
1 large egg
4 cups all-purpose flour
1 tablespoon ground cinnamon
2 teaspoons each: baking powder, ground cloves, ground ginger
1 teaspoon each: baking soda, ground nutmeg
Currants, raisins, silver balls and candy, for decoration
1 large egg yolk mixed with 1 teaspoon water
Icing for decorating (recipe follows)

1. Cream margarine, sugar and molasses in large mixer bowl until light and fluffy. Beat in egg. Sift together flour, cinnamon, baking powder, cloves, ginger, baking soda and nutmeg. Using a wooden spoon, stir into butter mixture; mix well.

2. Divide dough into 4 equal portions. Wrap each piece in plastic wrap; shape into flat disk about 1-inch thick. Refrigerate until firm, about 8 hours. (Dough can be refrigerated up to 3 days.)

3. Heat oven to 350 degrees. Working with 1 piece at a time, roll out on well-floured surface, dusting rolling pin as you work, to ⅛-inch thickness. Dough is soft and can be difficult to work with, so work quickly and use plenty of flour. Using cookie cutters dipped in flour, cut into desired shapes. Put cookies 1 inch apart onto ungreased baking sheets. Use currants or candy for eyes or buttons, if desired.

4. Bake until lightly puffed, 7 to 10 minutes. (First batch may be puffier because they will have less flour rolled in them.) While still warm, paint with egg yolk mixture. Cool on wire racks. Decorate as desired with icing.

For icing, mix 1 cup sifted confectioners' sugar with small amount of water until thick and spreading consistency. Add food coloring if desired; put into small plastic bag. Cut small hole in one corner and drizzle icing onto cookies.

Butter cookies are standard issue in any Easter basket created by Joan Saltzman, owner of Good Taste, a food shop in Chicago. This versatile cookie can be frosted, dipped or sandwiched with preserves.

EASY BUTTER COOKIES

About 3 dozen
Preparation time: 15 minutes
Chilling time: 2 hours
Baking time: 8 to 10 minutes, 20 minutes total

1 cup (2 sticks) unsalted butter, softened
½ cup confectioners' sugar
1 teaspoon vanilla extract
2 cups sifted all-purpose flour
Melted chocolate, chopped nuts, optional

1. Cream butter and sugar in large mixer bowl until light and fluffy. Beat in vanilla extract. Add flour and mix well. Gather into ball. Divide dough into 4 parts. Shape into logs on wax paper. Roll up in wax paper. Refrigerate until firm, 2 hours or more.

2. Heat oven to 375 degrees. Cut cookies into ¼-inch-thick slices. Put onto ungreased baking sheet. Bake until bottoms are golden, 10 to 12 minutes. Cool on wire racks.

3. Dip half of each cookie in melted chocolate and sprinkle with nuts.

Pat Egan of Dolton, Illinois, took second place in The Tribune*'s 1988 Christmas Cookie Contest. The rich dough can be easily shaped into trees that are edged with glittery green sugar.*

CHRISTMAS TREE COOKIES

About 6 dozen
Preparation time: 20 minutes
Chilling time: 4 hours
Baking time: 10 minutes, 30 minutes total

2½ **cups all-purpose flour**
1 **cup sugar**
1 **cup (2 sticks) butter or margarine, softened**
1 **large egg**
1½ **teaspoons baking powder**
½ **teaspoon almond extract**
¼ **teaspoon salt**
¼ **cup each: green sugar crystals, confetti or nonpareil candy decorations, optional**

1. Put flour, sugar, butter, egg, baking powder, almond extract and salt into large mixer bowl. Beat on low speed until mixed. Dough will be crumbly. Then knead dough with hands until mixture holds together.

2. Remove ⅓ cup of the dough; wrap and refrigerate. Using hands, roll remaining dough into a log about 1¾ inches in diameter. Put sugar crystals onto wax paper. Roll log in sugar crystals to coat well; use the wax paper as a guide to press in crystals. Shape log by pressing gently on wax paper to give 3 sharp corners with 2 sides longer than the third side (this will result in triangular-shaped slices). Wrap well; refrigerate until firm enough to slice, at least 4 hours.

3. Heat oven to 350 degrees. Slice logs crosswise into ¼-inch-thick slices. Put slices 1 inch apart onto ungreased baking sheets. For each cookie, shape about ½ teaspoon of reserved dough into a tree trunk. Attach to bottom underside of each cookie to form a tree. Sprinkle lightly with candy decorations, if desired.

4. Bake until bottoms are golden, about 10 minutes. Carefully remove to wire racks. Cool completely.

NOTE: The logs can be divided and shaped into 3 sizes and sliced to form a 3-tiered tree. (See photograph.)

■ *Italians celebrate St. Joseph's Day in March by donating homemade food to the poor or sharing it at home with friends. The table is a dazzling performance of every cook's repertoire. For one such menu,* Tribune *columnist Beverly Dillon created for dessert a chocolate version of* biscotti, *a crisp, not-too-sweet cookie that is perfect for dunking into coffee or milk.*

CHOCOLATE BISCOTTI COOKIES

About 3 dozen cookies
Preparation time: 30 minutes
Baking time: 55 minutes total

4 ounces unsweetened chocolate
1 cup (2 sticks) unsalted butter
3 large eggs, separated
1¼ cups sugar
½ teaspoon each: anise extract, almond extract
3¼ cups all-purpose flour
½ teaspoon baking powder
2 cups sliced almonds
1 egg white, lightly beaten

1. Melt chocolate and butter in top of double boiler over simmering water. Let cool. Beat egg yolks and ¾ cup of the sugar in large mixer bowl until thick and pale lemon colored. Slowly beat in melted chocolate mixture, anise extract and almond extract.

2. Heat oven to 350 degrees. Beat 3 egg whites and remaining ½ cup sugar in small mixer bowl until stiff but not dry. Fold into chocolate mixture. Sift together flour and baking powder. Gently fold flour mixture into chocolate mixture. Fold in almonds.

3. Divide dough into 4 portions. Using floured hands, form dough into cylinder-shaped logs (1½ inches wide and 10 inches long). Put onto lightly greased baking sheets; brush with lightly beaten egg white.

4. Bake until firm, about 45 minutes. Cut on diagonal into ½-inch-thick slices. Arrange on baking sheets, cut side down.

5. Return to oven; bake, turning once, until slightly dry, about 10 minutes. Cool on wire racks. (Cookies can be stored in airtight container.)

Reader Julie Cook of Chicago snagged first prize in the 1986 Tribune *Christmas cookie contest with this spicy Danish butter cookie. These cookies keep their flavor and texture when stored in a covered tin box at room temperature.*

DANISH BROWN SPICE COOKIES
(Sirups kager)

About 5 dozen
Preparation time: 45 minutes
Chilling time: 1 hour
Baking time: 8 to 10 minutes, 30 minutes total

1 **cup (2 sticks) butter or margarine, softened**
1 **cup each: sugar, dark corn syrup**
2 **teaspoons ground cinnamon**
1 **teaspoon ground cloves**
½ **teaspoon baking soda mixed with 1 teaspoon water**
3¾ **to 4 cups all-purpose flour, as needed**

1. Cream butter with sugar and corn syrup in large mixer bowl until light and fluffy. Beat in cinnamon, cloves and baking soda mixture. Add flour a little at a time, mixing well after each addition until stiff dough forms. Cover and refrigerate until firm, about 1 hour.

2. Heat oven to 400 degrees. Roll dough to ⅛-inch thickness on floured surface. Cut with cookie cutters into reindeer or other desired shapes. (Or roll dough into logs about 1 inch in diameter and slice crosswise into ⅛-inch-thick rounds.) Put onto ungreased baking sheets.

3. Bake until light brown, 8 to 10 minutes. Cool on wire racks.

Test Kitchen Director JeanMarie Brownson salutes her mother, Dolores Kaiser, who shared this recipe with readers in December 1984. Kolacky, a tender, rich-tasting cookie with Eastern European roots, is made with cream cheese. It can be filled with jam or poppy seed filling, pinched together like a three-cornered hat and, after baking, sprinkled with confectioners' sugar. They are irresistible when warm.

KOLACKY

About 3 dozen
Preparation time: 30 minutes
Chilling time: 1 to 2 hours
Baking time: 15 minutes, 30 minutes total

½ **cup (1 stick) butter, softened**

1 **package (3 ounces) cream cheese, softened**

1 **cup all-purpose flour**
Jam or preserves
Confectioners' sugar

1. Mix butter and cream cheese with a fork in medium bowl until smooth. Gradually work in flour until dough forms. Gather into ball; wrap in wax paper. Refrigerate until firm, 1 to 2 hours.

2. Heat oven to 375 degrees. Roll out dough on well-floured board or pastry cloth until very thin. Cut out circles with 2-inch round cutter. Dot center of each circle with about ¼ teaspoon jam. (If you use too much jam it will run out of cookies onto baking sheet.) Fold 2 edges of circle to center. Press edges together tightly. Put onto ungreased baking sheets.

3. Bake until golden, 10 to 15 minutes. Cool on wire racks. Sprinkle lightly with confectioners' sugar while warm.

When Tribune restaurant critic Paul A. Camp asked his mother for some of her holiday cookie recipes for an article in December 1984, Jean Camp replied with one of his boyhood favorites. A pinch of ginger will make these molasses cookies full-bodied.

MOLASSES COOKIES

About 2 dozen
Preparation time: 15 minutes
Chilling time: 1 hour
Baking time: 8 to 10 minutes total

¾ cup (1½ sticks) butter
   or margarine,
   softened
1 cup sugar
1 large egg
¼ cup light molasses
2 cups all-purpose flour
2 teaspoons baking soda
1 teaspoon ground
   cinnamon
½ teaspoon ground
   cloves
¼ teaspoon salt
   Sugar for rolling

1. Cream butter and sugar in large mixer bowl until light and fluffy. Beat in egg, molasses, flour, baking soda, ground cinnamon, cloves and salt, one at a time. Dough will be soft. Turn out of bowl and wrap in plastic or wax paper. Refrigerate 1 hour.

2. Heat oven to 375 degrees. Form dough into large walnut-size balls. Roll in granulated sugar. Put 2 inches apart on well-greased baking sheets.

3. Bake until brown, 8 to 10 minutes. Let sit a few minutes before removing cookies. Cool on wire racks.

Memories of sore hands and a stiff back enhance Jean McGree's enjoyment of this Christmas cookie recipe. When the Flossmoor, Illinois, reader was growing up in the South, the pecan trees in her grandmother's yard in South Carolina provided work—plucking, sorting and shelling—as well as pleasure. Every Christmas, when relatives ship a box of nuts to her home, she yanks out the recipe and "bores everyone" with the pecan story.

PRALINE COOKIES

About 2 dozen
Preparation time: 25 minutes
Baking time: 10 to 12 minutes total

½ cup (1 stick) butter,
   softened
1½ cups packed brown
   sugar
1 large egg
1½ cups all-purpose flour
1 teaspoon vanilla
   extract
1 cup chopped pecans

1. Heat oven to 350 degrees. Cream butter, sugar and egg in large mixer bowl until light and fluffy. Using a wooden spoon stir in flour, vanilla extract and pecans. Shape into balls about the size of walnuts. Put onto greased baking sheets; flatten to about ⅛ inch.

2. Bake until bottoms are brown, 10 to 12 minutes. Cool completely on wire racks.

■   *About one billion pounds of peanuts are used every year to make peanut butter. While much of it is used in tandem with bread and jelly, another healthy chunk of it goes into peanut butter cookies. After all, who can resist them? Certainly not young folks or, it seems, most adults.*

This rendition, from cookbook author and columnist Abby Mandel, has an extra dose of peanut butter, preferably chunky style; so there's no mistaking what kind of cookie it is.

PEANUT BUTTER COOKIES

About 3 dozen
Preparation time: 15 minutes
Baking time: 12 minutes, 24 minutes total

½ **cup (1 stick) unsalted butter, softened**

¾ **cup each: granulated sugar, packed light brown sugar**

2 **large egg whites**

1½ **teaspoons vanilla extract**

1¼ **cups chunky peanut butter**

1 **cup all-purpose flour**

½ **teaspoon baking soda**

¼ **teaspoon salt**

1. Heat oven to 375 degrees. Cream butter and both sugars in large mixer bowl until light and fluffy. Beat in egg whites and vanilla extract. Add peanut butter; beat until smooth. Add flour, baking soda and salt; mix just until flour disappears.

2. Roll dough into 1½-inch balls. Put 2½ inches apart onto ungreased baking sheets. Flatten with tines of fork.

3. Bake until set, about 12 minutes. Transfer to wire racks. Cookies can be stored in an airtight container for several days or frozen.

NOTE: To make dough in food processor, process butter, both sugars, egg whites and vanilla extract until completely smooth, about 1 minute, stopping once to scrape down sides of work bowl. Add peanut butter; process until combined, 10 seconds. Add flour, baking soda and salt; process just until combined. Bake as directed.

The late food authority James Beard popularized one of his beloved condiments, pepper, in a favorite dessert, fresh strawberries rolled in coarsely ground pepper. The taste of the fruit's sweetness is enhanced by the pepper's astringency. The sweet/pepper theme continues in these butter cookies where warm spices—ginger, ground cinnamon, cloves—complement pepper's bitterness.

PEPPERCORN COOKIES

About 3 dozen
Preparation time: 30 minutes
Baking time: 10 minutes, 20 minutes total

3 cups all-purpose flour

2 teaspoons baking powder

1 cup (2 sticks) unsalted butter, softened

1¾ cups sugar

1 generous teaspoon coarsely ground fresh black pepper

Pinch cayenne pepper

1 tablespoon ground ginger

2 teaspoons ground cinnamon

½ teaspoon ground cloves

1 large egg

1. Heat oven to 400 degrees. Sift flour and baking powder together in bowl.

2. Cream butter in large mixer bowl until light and fluffy. Beat in sugar until well mixed. Beat in black pepper, cayenne pepper, ginger, cinnamon and cloves. Beat in egg until incorporated.

3. Gradually beat in flour. Knead dough on lightly floured surface a few times. Divide dough into 3 pieces. Roll each piece to ⅛-inch thickness with a lightly floured rolling pin on well-floured work surface. Cut into cookie shapes with cookie cutters.

4. Put 1 inch apart on ungreased baking sheets. Bake until edges are golden, 10 to 12 minutes. Cool on wire rack.

■ *Perfect crispness results by combining two fats, butter and margarine. Butter provides rich flavor while margarine makes the cookie light and extra crisp.*

OATMEAL THINS

About 5 dozen
Preparation time: 10 minutes
Chilling time: 2 to 3 hours
Baking time: 10 minutes, 30 minutes total

1 cup (2 sticks) each, softened: butter, margarine
1 cup granulated sugar
2¼ cups all-purpose flour
3 cups rolled oats (not quick-cooking)
Confectioners' sugar

1. Cream butter, margarine and granulated sugar in large mixer bowl until light and fluffy. Stir in flour and oatmeal. Refrigerate, covered, until firm.

2. Heat oven to 350 degrees. Roll dough into balls and put onto ungreased baking sheets. Flatten balls with tines of a fork making a crosshatch pattern.

3. Bake until bottoms are golden, 10 to 15 minutes. Remove to wire racks; cool until warm. Sprinkle cookies with confectioners' sugar while still slightly warm.

■ *These cookies are great for two reasons. One, they taste great. Two, the dough holds in the refrigerator for weeks.*

WALNUT REFRIGERATOR COOKIES

About 5 dozen
Preparation time: 20 minutes
Chilling time: Overnight
Baking time: 10 to 12 minutes, 30 minutes total

¾ cup (1½ sticks) butter or margarine
2 large eggs, well beaten
2 cups firmly packed brown sugar
3 cups sifted all-purpose flour
2 teaspoons baking powder
1 teaspoon salt
1 cup chopped walnuts
1 teaspoon vanilla extract

1. Melt butter; let cool. Beat eggs in large mixer bowl until light. Beat in sugar until smooth. Beat in melted butter. Blend thoroughly.

2. Mix together flour, baking powder and salt. Beat into butter mixture. Add nuts and vanilla extract; blend thoroughly. Dough will be thick, but not firm.

3. Turn out dough; shape into 3 logs about 2 inches in diameter. Wrap in plastic or wax paper. Refrigerate at least overnight.

4. Heat oven to 375 degrees. Slice logs into ⅛-thick slices. Put onto well-greased baking sheets. Bake until golden, 10 to 12 minutes. Remove immediately to wire racks. Cool completely.

THE CHICAGO TRIBUNE COOKBOOK

Vegetable shortening is preferred in this recipe over butter because it provides crunch without a flavor. Toasting enhances the flavor of sesame seeds and a splash of cream sherry complements it. If you're out of sherry, try marsala wine or vanilla extract.

SESAME SEED COOKIES

About 6 dozen
Preparation time: 15 minutes
Chilling time: 2 hours
Baking time: 15 minutes, 45 minutes total

½ **cup vegetable shortening**
¾ **cup sugar**
1 **large egg**
½ **cup toasted sesame seeds**
2 **cups all-purpose flour**
1 **teaspoon baking powder**
¼ **teaspoon salt**
2 **tablespoons cream sherry**

1. Cream shortening and sugar in large mixer bowl until light and fluffy. Beat in egg until well blended. Stir in one-third of the sesame seeds. Mix flour, baking powder and salt. Add flour mixture alternately with sherry to egg mixture. Mix well.

2. Divide dough in half; shape into 2 logs about 1½ inches in diameter. Refrigerate, covered, 2 hours or more.

3. Heat oven to 350 degrees. Slice logs into ⅛-inch-thick rounds. Put onto greased baking sheets. Sprinkle with remaining sesame seeds; press lightly into dough. Bake until golden, 12 to 15 minutes. Cool on wire racks.

These buttery, crisp cookies are infused with the flavor and aroma of coriander seed. They are great served warm with hot tea.

CORIANDER SHORTBREAD

About 4 dozen
Preparation time: 15 minutes
Baking time: 20 to 25 minutes, total

2 teaspoons coriander seeds
1 cup (2 sticks) unsalted butter, softened
1 teaspoon vanilla extract
Pinch salt
½ cup confectioners' sugar, sifted
1¾ cups all-purpose flour

1. Put seeds into small skillet. Heat over medium heat until seeds are aromatic and very lightly toasted. Immediately remove from pan to paper towel. Cool.

2. When seeds are cool, grind to a very fine powder in spice grinder or coffee mill. There will be about 1 teaspoon powder.

3. Cream butter in large mixer bowl until light and fluffy. Beat in vanilla extract and salt. Beat in sugar and coriander powder until light and fluffy.

4. Heat oven to 350 degrees. Using a wooden spoon, stir in flour until mixed. Do not overmix. Turn dough out onto a floured surface. Press dough into ½-inch-thick rectangle. Using a floured knife, cut dough into 1-inch squares. Put squares onto ungreased baking sheet, about ½ inch apart.

5. Bake until golden and crisp, 20 to 25 minutes. Cool on wire racks.

Classic shortbread is transformed in the following recipe by using light brown sugar instead of white sugar and substituting yellow cornmeal for some of the flour.

CORNMEAL SHORTBREAD

About 2 dozen
Preparation time: 20 minutes
Baking time: 20 minutes total

1 cup (2 sticks) unsalted butter, softened
⅓ cup each: packed light brown sugar, confectioners' sugar
2 teaspoons vanilla extract
1½ cups all-purpose flour
½ cup yellow cornmeal
Pinch salt

1. Heat oven to 350 degrees. Cream butter and sugars in large mixer bowl until light and fluffy. Add vanilla extract and beat well. Mix flour, cornmeal and salt. Stir into butter mixture until well blended.

2. Roll out dough on lightly floured surface to ¼-inch thickness. Cut into 3-inch rounds. Put on ungreased baking sheets. Pierce each cookie 3 times with a fork.

3. Bake until edges are light brown, 15 to 20 minutes. Cool on wire racks.

These sugar cookies taste great just rolled in sugar and baked, but they can be dressed up with a nut half or candied fruit before baking.

SUGAR COOKIES

About 2 dozen
Preparation time: 15 minutes
Baking time: 10 minutes total

½ cup (1 stick) butter or margarine, softened
1 cup sugar
1 teaspoon each: salt, vanilla extract
1 large egg
2 cups all-purpose flour
1 teaspoon baking powder
¼ teaspoon baking soda
Nut halves or candied fruit, optional

1. Cream butter and sugar in large mixer bowl until light and fluffy. One at a time beat in salt, vanilla extract, egg, flour, baking powder and baking soda until dough forms into a clump. Remove dough from bowl, wrap in plastic, chill 1 hour.

2. Heat oven to 375 degrees. Remove dough from refrigerator and form into walnut-size dollops. Press each side of the dough into granulated sugar. Put on well-greased baking sheet. If desired, top each with a nut half or piece of candied fruit.

3. Bake until golden brown, 8 to 10 minutes. Cool on wire racks.

The winning recipe in The Tribune's 1988 Christmas Cookie Contest is a delightful buttery cookie that crumbles as it melts in your mouth. Fay Kuhn of Earlville, Illinois, received the honors.

THUMBPRINTS

About 2 dozen
Preparation time: 20 minutes
Chilling time: 1 hour
Baking time: 15 to 18 minutes total

½ cup (1 stick) unsalted butter, softened
¼ cup sugar
1 large egg, separated
½ teaspoon vanilla extract
1 cup all-purpose flour
¼ teaspoon salt
1¼ cups finely chopped nuts
¼ cup raspberry jam

1. Cream butter and sugar in large mixer bowl until light and fluffy. Beat in egg yolk and vanilla extract. Mix well. Mix flour and salt. Stir into butter mixture and mix well. Cover; refrigerate at least 1 hour.

2. Heat oven to 325 degrees. Shape dough into 1-inch balls. Beat egg white lightly in small bowl. Put nuts in another small bowl. Dip each ball into egg white, then roll in nuts. Put balls 1 inch apart onto ungreased baking sheet. Press thumb in the center of each to make an indentation.

3. Bake until bottoms are golden, 15 to 18 minutes. Cool on wire racks. Fill indentation with a small amount of raspberry jam.

Here's an updated recipe that elevates crispy, marshmallow treats from elementary school fare to the ranks of graduate school. It goes black tie with the addition of Swiss-made white almond candy and toasted almonds.

ALMOND NOUGAT CRISPIES

8 squares
Preparation time: 20 minutes
Cooking time: 5 minutes

3 bars (3 ounces each) white almond and honey nougat candy, such as Toblerone
5 cups crisp rice cereal
1½ cups sliced almonds, toasted
¾ cup (1½ sticks) unsalted butter
4 cups miniature marshmallows

1. Butter an 8-inch square baking pan and set aside. Chop the nougat bars finely. Toss cereal and nuts in bowl to mix.

2. Melt butter in large saucepan. Add marshmallows; cook, stirring constantly with wooden spoon, until melted. Add chopped nougat, stirring until melted. Remove from heat. Add cereal mixture; toss until well coated.

3. Using buttered spatula, press mixture evenly into prepared pan. Cut into squares when cool.

Ah, the classic brownie. Topped with a scoop of vanilla ice cream, it is definitely one of life's simple pleasures.

BROWNIES

12 squares
Preparation time: 15 minutes
Baking time: 25 minutes

2 ounces unsweetened chocolate

½ cup (1 stick) butter

⅔ cup all-purpose flour

½ teaspoon baking powder

⅛ teaspoon salt

2 large eggs

1 cup granulated sugar

1 teaspoon vanilla extract

½ cup chopped nuts, optional

Confectioners' sugar, optional

1. Put chocolate and butter in top of double boiler to melt. Meanwhile, mix flour, baking powder and salt in small bowl. Heat oven to 350 degrees.

2. Beat eggs in large mixer bowl until light. Gradually beat in granulated sugar; then add chocolate mixture and vanilla extract, mixing well. Stir in flour mixture. Then stir in nuts if using. Spread batter evenly in greased 8-inch square baking pan.

3. Bake until brownies just begin to pull away from sides of pan and top is set, about 25 minutes. Cool on wire rack. Cut into squares. Sprinkle with confectioners' sugar, if desired.

Among the recipes most often requested by our readers is this one for Marshall Field's Frango brownies, which canonizes the company's chocolate, mint-flavored candy. The texture should be fudgy, not cake-like, and the top, shiny. Watch the clock closely and do not overbake. For best results, use the genuine candy.

FRANGO CHOCOLATE BROWNIES

9 squares
Preparation time: 10 minutes
Baking time: 25 minutes

½ cup (1 stick) unsalted butter

2 ounces unsweetened chocolate, chopped fine

2 large eggs, at room temperature

1 cup sugar

1 teaspoon vanilla extract

½ cup all-purpose flour

⅛ teaspoon salt

½ cup coarsely chopped pecans

8 Frango Mint Chocolates (dark) or your favorite Frango flavor, chopped fine to measure about ½ cup

1. Heat oven to 350 degrees. Butter an 8-inch square baking pan.

2. Melt butter in medium saucepan over low heat. Remove from heat, add chopped unsweetened chocolate; stir until chocolate is melted. Let mixture cool until tepid.

3. Beat eggs in large mixer bowl until light and fluffy, about 2 minutes. Gradually beat in sugar, then beat for an additional minute. Beat in melted chocolate mixture and vanilla extract. Using a rubber spatula, fold in flour and salt. Fold in pecans and chopped Frango chocolates. Spread batter evenly in prepared pan.

4. Bake until wooden pick inserted halfway between center and edge comes out with a moist crumb, about 25 minutes. Do not overbake; brownies should be moist. Cool completely on wire rack. Using a sharp knife, cut the brownies into 9 squares. Store the brownies in an airtight container at room temperature.

NOTE: Brownies can be baked up to 2 days in advance.

Names for this recipe are as numerous as the calorie count is high. But the flavor is worth it. Coconut and chopped, dry-roasted nuts add crunch and chewiness. Chopped raisins, sunflower seeds or cereal can be combined with or substituted for the nuts.

COCONUT-CHIP LAYER BARS

2 dozen squares
Preparation time: 15 minutes
Baking time: 15 minutes

¾ cup (1½ sticks) butter or margarine, melted

2 cups graham cracker crumbs

1½ cups chopped, dry-roasted, unsalted cashews or pecans

1 package (12 ounces) semisweet chocolate chips

2 cups flaked coconut, toasted

1 can (14 ounces) sweetened condensed milk

1. Heat oven to 350 degrees. Put butter into 13 by 9-inch baking pan. Put into oven just until butter melts, 5 to 10 minutes.

2. Stir in graham cracker crumbs. Press evenly over bottom of pan. Sprinkle with nuts. Then sprinkle with chocolate chips, then coconut. Drizzle with sweetened condensed milk.

3. Bake until golden, about 15 minutes. Cool completely on wire rack. Cut into squares.

The late Chicago Mayor Harold Washington and his fiancée, Mary Ella Smith, competed with 16 other celebrity teams at a March of Dimes Gourmet Gala in May 1984. His Honor's KP detail for the evening? Stirring the batter for this lemon delight dessert.

LEMON DELIGHTS

2 dozen squares
Preparation time: 20 minutes
Baking time: 45 minutes

CRUST

- 1 **cup (2 sticks) unsalted butter, softened**
- ½ **cup sifted confectioners' sugar**
- 2 **cups sifted all-purpose flour**

FILLING

- 4 **large eggs**
- 1½ **cups granulated sugar**
- ¼ **cup sifted all-purpose flour**
- 1 **teaspoon baking powder**
- ¼ **cup fresh lemon juice**
- 2 **tablespoons grated lemon rind**

GLAZE

- 1½ **cups sifted confectioners' sugar**
- 3 **tablespoons hot water, about**

1. Heat oven to 350 degrees. For crust, cream butter and ½ cup confectioners' sugar in large mixer bowl until light and fluffy. Stir in 2 cups flour until evenly blended. Spread into ungreased 13 by 9-inch baking pan. Bake until light brown, about 15 minutes.

2. Meanwhile, for filling, beat eggs and granulated sugar in large mixer bowl until very light and fluffy. Stir in ¼ cup flour, baking powder, lemon juice and lemon rind.

3. Pour over hot crust. Return to oven and continue baking until filling is set, about 30 minutes. Cool 10 minutes on wire rack.

4. For glaze, mix confectioners' sugar and enough hot water to drizzling consistency. Drizzle over top of lemon bars. Finish cooling on wire rack. Cut into squares.

Cooking teacher Lois Carol Levine, of Chicago, contributed this variation of the classic lemon bar cookie, making it suitable for Passover.

PASSOVER LEMON BARS

16 squares
Preparation time: 10 minutes
Baking time: 45 minutes

1 cup matzo cake meal, sifted
½ cup (1 stick) margarine
¼ cup "confectioners' sugar" (see note)
4 large eggs
2 cups granulated sugar
1 teaspoon "baking powder" (see note)
¼ teaspoon salt
⅔ cup fresh lemon juice

1. Heat oven to 350 degrees. Beat together cake meal, margarine and "confectioners' sugar" until well blended. Press into bottom of 9-inch square pan. Bake until lightly browned, 15 to 20 minutes.

2. Combine eggs, granulated sugar, "baking powder," salt and lemon juice; beat until smooth. Pour over baked crust and return to oven until bubbly and lightly browned, about 30 minutes.

3. Cool; top with "confectioners' sugar" and cut into bars.

NOTE: To make a kosher confectioners' sugar, use ¼ cup granulated sugar. Remove ½ tablespoon from the sugar and replace with ½ tablespoon potato starch. To make a kosher baking powder, mix ½ teaspoon baking soda plus ½ teaspoon cream of tartar.

Madeleines are small, shell-shaped French sponge cakes baked in a special pan. They make an elegant addition to a sweet table or formal tea party. The pans are available at specialty cookware shops. Cake flour is used to make the texture as delicate as possible.

LEMON MADELEINES

About 3 dozen
Preparation time: 20 minutes
Baking time: 10 minutes, 30 minutes total

4 **large eggs**
¾ **cup sugar**
1 **teaspoon vanilla**
    extract
    Grated rind of 1 lemon
1½ **cups sifted cake flour**
½ **teaspoon baking**
    powder
    Dash salt
¾ **cup (1½ sticks)**
    unsalted butter,
    melted, cooled
    Confectioners' sugar

1. Heat oven to 400 degrees. Generously butter madeleine pan.

2. Beat eggs in large mixer bowl until very thick, lemon colored and tripled in volume. Eggs should fall in ribbons when beaters are lifted. Gradually beat in sugar. Stir in vanilla extract and lemon rind.

3. Sift flour with baking powder and salt. Alternately fold melted butter and flour mixture into egg batter. Fill each madeleine shell with about 1 tablespoon batter.

4. Bake until puffed and delicately browned, about 10 minutes. Remove from pans and cool on wire rack. Sprinkle with confectioners' sugar just before serving.

Robin Swartzman learned to make nut horns from her grandmother. Now, the mother of two sells them in her bakery, Robin's Incredible Edibles, in Northbrook, Illinois. The marriage of butter and cream cheese in the dough produces a tender texture, a perfect foil to the granular nut filling. Refrigerating the dough makes rolling, cutting and shaping easier.

NUT HORNS

15 to 16 pieces
Preparation time: 25 minutes
Chilling time: Overnight
Baking time: 20 to 25 minutes total

DOUGH

- ½ cup (1 stick) butter, softened
- 4 ounces cream cheese, softened
- 2 tablespoons granulated sugar
- 1 cup all-purpose flour

NUT MIXTURE

- 2 tablespoons each: finely chopped walnuts, golden raisins
- 1 tablespoon granulated sugar
- ½ teaspoon cinnamon

Confectioners' sugar

1. For dough, cream butter and cream cheese in large mixer bowl until light. Beat in 2 tablespoons sugar. Gradually beat in flour. Gather into ball and refrigerate overnight.

2. Roll dough out between sheets of lightly floured wax paper into a 10-inch circle; chill 30 minutes.

3. Heat oven to 350 degrees. For nut mixture, mix walnuts, raisins, 1 tablespoon granulated sugar and cinnamon in small bowl.

4. Remove one sheet of wax paper from dough. Sprinkle dough with nut mixture. Cut dough into 15 or 16 triangular wedges as if you were cutting a pizza. Starting at widest edge of the wedge, roll up and shape into a crescent shape. Put onto lightly greased baking sheet.

5. Bake until golden, 20 to 25 minutes. Cool on wire rack. Sprinkle with confectioners' sugar.

Although staff members have access to all recipes before they appear in the paper, this recipe—an easy version of English toffee—gets lost frequently. And when one of the writers or editors needs a candy fix or a homemade gift idea from the kitchen, the call goes out to "make an extra copy of the brittle for me." Store the candy in a covered glass jar or tin box at room temperature.

BRITTLE BREAKUP

About 1 pound
Preparation time: 10 minutes
Cooking time: 15 minutes

1 cup (2 sticks) butter
1 cup sugar
2 tablespoons water
1 tablespoon light corn syrup
1 cup semisweet chocolate chips
⅔ cup finely chopped nuts

1. Melt butter in medium saucepan over low heat. Add sugar; cook and stir until melted, 3 to 4 minutes. Add water and corn syrup. Continue cooking over low heat without stirring until small amount of syrup dropped into cold water becomes brittle (300 degrees on a candy thermometer), 15 to 20 minutes. Do not undercook. Remove from heat. Immediately pour onto greased baking sheet. Cool until hardened.

2. Melt chocolate over hot water. Spread over candy base. Sprinkle nuts over chocolate; press in. Cool. Break into pieces.

Making candy in the microwave is easy with Mary Jo Bergland's version of a Southern favorite.

RIO BRAVO PRALINES

About 3 dozen
Preparation time: 10 minutes
Microwave cooking time: 12 minutes

2 cups pecan halves
1 cup sugar
1 cup firmly packed brown sugar
¾ cup evaporated milk
2 tablespoons butter
⅛ teaspoon salt

1. Put all ingredients into 4-quart microwave-safe glass bowl. Microwave on high (100 percent power) stirring every 3 minutes for 12 minutes. Beat mixture vigorously by hand until tacky. Drop by teaspoons onto buttered wax paper–lined baking sheet. Cool on wire rack until firm.

Added to desserts or candy, caramel—refined sugar that has been cooked to a rich brown color—provides a handsome color and assertive flavor. In this sophisticated candy recipe, from Eric Singer, pastry chef and owner of Bertram's Bakery in Chicago, it functions to contrast the sweet taste of chocolate as well.

CARAMEL TRUFFLES

About 30
Preparation time: 45 minutes
Cooking time: 15 minutes
Chilling time: Several hours

½ cup each: sugar, water
2 tablespoons cold whipping cream
¾ cup (1½ sticks) unsalted butter, cut into small pieces
1 pound bittersweet chocolate, finely chopped
1 cup finely crushed chocolate wafers (about half of an 8-ounce box of chocolate wafer cookies)

1. Put sugar and water into medium-size heavy saucepan. Cook, stirring constantly with a wooden spoon, over medium heat until mixture is smooth and a bit darker in color than butterscotch. Immediately remove from heat. Stir in cream to cool mixture.

2. Gradually add butter in small pieces, stirring constantly with a wooden spoon. Refrigerate, stirring occasionally, until firm, about 1½ hours.

3. Roll into balls slightly larger than a hazelnut. Put onto wax paper–lined baking sheet. Refrigerate or freeze until hardened.

4. Melt chocolate in top of double boiler over hot (but not boiling) water. Cool until slightly thickened. Using a fork, dip each caramel ball into melted chocolate. Allow excess chocolate to drip off. Put onto wax paper–lined baking sheet. Refrigerate until chocolate hardens.

5. Redip centers in chocolate; then roll in crushed wafers to coat on all sides. Refrigerate until firm.

NOTE: Truffles may be stored in a covered container in refrigerator up to 1 week or in freezer up to 2 months.

No baking is required with these Christmas cookies/candies. Reader Shere Case, of Hickory Hills, Illinois, has been making these fuss-free treats for 18 years. For easy removal, drop cookies onto wax paper before chilling.

COCONUT JOYS

About 3 dozen
Preparation time: 30 minutes
Chilling time: 1 hour

½ cup (1 stick) butter
2 cups confectioners' sugar
3 cups flaked coconut
1 tablespoon milk
2 squares (2 ounces) semisweet chocolate, melted

1. Melt butter in large saucepan. Remove from heat. Add sugar, coconut and milk. Mix well. Shape rounded teaspoons of mixture into balls. Make a dent in center of each. Put onto baking sheet lined with wax paper.

2. Fill center with drops of melted chocolate. Refrigerate until chocolate is firm. Store in refrigerator or freezer.

In December 1984, Tribune *microwave columnist Mary Jo Bergland appeased hundreds of readers by answering requests for Christmas goodies. With kitchen staples such as peanut butter and crisp rice cereal, this recipe can be made without a pilgrimage to the grocery store.*

PEANUT BUTTER BONBONS

About 72 pieces
Preparation time: 30 minutes
Microwave cooking time: 3 minutes, total
Chilling time: 1 hour

½ cup (1 stick) butter or margarine, melted
2 cups each: confectioners' sugar, creamy or crunchy peanut butter, crushed crisp rice cereal
½ cup finely chopped, dry-roasted, unsalted peanuts or walnuts
1 pound milk chocolate or compound chocolate coating, cut into chunks

1. Mix butter, sugar, peanut butter, cereal and nuts in large bowl. Stir and knead until well blended. Refrigerate until firm, about 30 minutes. Roll into 1-inch balls; put onto baking sheet. Refrigerate until firm, about 30 minutes.

2. Put chocolate into 1-quart microwave-safe glass measure. Microwave on high (100 percent power), stirring once, until melted, 2 to 3 minutes. Cool until slightly thickened.

3. Using wooden skewer or fork, dip each ball into melted chocolate. Allow excess chocolate to drip off. Put onto wax paper–lined baking sheet. Refrigerate until firm. Store in the refrigerator.

Got some leftover pretzels from a poker party? Turn them into candy. Dip pretzel sticks or rods into melted almond bark. The microwave performs the melting chore without sticking or scorching.

SPARKLING PRETZELS

2 dozen
Preparation time: 15 minutes
Microwave cooking time: 3 minutes

1 **pound almond bark or green compound coating, finely chopped**
2 **tablespoons vegetable oil**
24 **pretzel rods**
    Decorative sugar

1. Put almond bark and oil into 1-quart microwave-safe glass measure. Microwave on high (100 percent power), stirring once, until melted and smooth, 2½ to 3 minutes.

2. Dip two-thirds of each pretzel stick or rod in coating. Let excess coating drip off. Roll in decorative sugar. Put onto wax paper–lined baking sheet until firm.

Neither adults nor children can resist buttery rich caramel corn. This version, from The Tribune *test kitchen, requires some patience while the glazed corn bakes but is well worth the wait.*

OVEN CARMEL CORN

12 servings
Preparation time: 15 minutes
Baking time: 1 hour

6 **quarts popped popcorn, about 2 cups raw**
1 **cup chopped nuts, optional**
2 **cups packed light brown sugar**
1 **cup (2 sticks) unsalted butter**
½ **cup light corn syrup**
1 **teaspoon each: salt, baking soda**

1. Heat oven to 200 degrees. Carefully remove all unpopped kernels from popcorn. Mix popcorn and nuts in very large greased baking pan.

2. Put sugar, butter, syrup and salt into medium saucepan. Heat to boil and sugar dissolves; boil, uncovered, for 5 minutes. Remove from heat and stir in baking soda.

3. Gradually, but quickly, pour mixture over popcorn, tossing with 2 large wooden spoons to coat popcorn evenly.

4. Bake popcorn stirring every 15 minutes, until crisp, about 1 hour. Cool on wire rack. Store popcorn in covered tin.

PRESERVES

Back when the grandparents were still children, in the days before Velcro and remote controls and radar ranges, before fresh fruits and vegetables were available in the supermarket 12 months a year, cooks spent a generous amount of time and energy "putting up" produce for the leaner months.

Ripe fruits and vegetables would be gathered at harvest time and hours would be spent cooking and processing the produce into heavy glass jars like so many preserved laboratory specimens.

Those pickles and beans and tomatoes, that applesauce and jam, would be accessible from the shelves in the fruit cellar when the cold set in. Preserving was almost a necessity and certainly economical.

Today's supermarkets, however, often contain as many as 250 varieties of fresh produce year-round, and the prices vary only slightly. So it is rather unimportant and unnecessary to can tomatoes or beans or fruits for the winter.

It also is much simpler just to freeze many of the products that once required canning. About the only reason to put up preserves is for the taste and for the fun and good feeling one gets from working with food the way grandmother did. Your own put-up jellies, jams, relishes, chutneys always taste better than anything purchased in the store. They make excellent gifts for holidays, tied up in gingham and ribbon, because they include the loving labor of personal preparation.

In the contemporary kitchen, devices such as the food processor and the microwave oven have joined the now-venerable pressure cooker as tools that save time and effort in making preserves. It is hardly any effort at all to get great-tasting jams and sauces. Most of the recipes in this section do not require complicated canning procedures.

But, if for no other reason than to experience a little bit of American history and to take pride in doing something extra, it is nice to try traditional canning once in a while. If you do, be sure to read an up-to-date guide to processing food such as that put out by the U.S. Department of Agriculture called the "Complete Guide to Home Canning" (Agricultural Information Bulletin No. 539, usually available from the local county extension office) or those published by companies who manufacture canning jars.

Canning and freezing are ways to keep food and, more important today, to preserve treasured family recipes and experiment with new ones.

PRESERVES

Jonathan applesauce

Spiced applesauce

Savory strawberry-rhubarb chutney

Fresh strawberry jam

Fresh pineapple jam

Nectarine-honeydew conserve

Cranberry conserve

Colorful garden relish

Zucchini bread and butter pickles

Cilantro chutney

Mint chutney

Raspberry vinegar

Walnut oil

Homemade mincemeat

Sliced beets with Vidalia onions

Raw-pack carrots with dill

Raw-pack lima beans with
   roasted red peppers

Okra with hot peppers

Stewed tomatoes

When baskets of shiny apples grace the fall farmstands it's easy to buy more than you can eat. Even if you don't stock up, this simple applesauce recipe is worth keeping on hand. The recipe may be doubled or quadrupled as desired.

JONATHAN APPLESAUCE

About 1½ cups
Preparation time: 15 minutes
Cooking time: 20 minutes

5 Jonathan apples, about 1 pound

½ cup water
Sugar, cinnamon to taste

1. Cut apples into quarters. (Peel and core apples if you do not have a food mill.)

2. Put apples into large nonaluminum saucepan. Add water. Cook, covered, stirring often, over medium heat until apples are very soft, 10 to 20 minutes. Push apples through food mill to remove seeds and skin. (Or mash the peeled apples.)

3. If applesauce is too thin, return to saucepan and cook over low heat until excess moisture has evaporated. Add sugar and cinnamon as desired.

4. Cool; refrigerate in covered containers up to 1 week. Or freeze up to 2 months.

This spicy applesauce is delicious served with simple roast pork, potato pancakes or plain waffles.

SPICED APPLESAUCE

About 2½ cups
Preparation time: 25 minutes
Cooking time: 30 minutes

1½ **pounds cooking apples, such as Winesap or Jonathan**
2 **tablespoons water**
½ **cup sugar**
2 **tablespoons unsalted butter**
1 **tablespoon fresh lemon juice**
½ **teaspoon each: grated lemon rind, ground cinnamon, ground ginger**
⅛ **teaspoon each, ground: cloves, allspice**

1. Rinse, core, peel and coarsely chop apples. Put into large nonaluminum saucepan with tight-fitting lid. Add water; cook, covered, stirring often, over low heat until apples are tender, about 20 minutes. Drain off any excess water.

2. Put apples into food processor or blender. Process until smooth, or put into saucepan and mash until smooth. Add sugar, butter, lemon juice, lemon rind, cinnamon, ginger, cloves and allspice.

3. Return apple mixture to saucepan. Heat to boil; reduce heat; cook over medium heat until slightly thickened, 5 to 10 minutes. Pour into bowl. Serve warm or cold.

4. Cool; refrigerate in covered containers up to 1 week. Or freeze up to 2 months.

Serve this chutney alongside roast duck, Cornish hens or pork tenderloin. It is also delicious when used to glaze a baked ham.

SAVORY STRAWBERRY-RHUBARB CHUTNEY

About 5 cups
Preparation time: 15 minutes
Cooking time: 30 minutes

1 **quart each: diced rhubarb, halved strawberries**
1¾ **cups sugar**
1½ **cups raisins**
½ **cup each: chopped onion, white vinegar**
1 **teaspoon each: salt, ground ginger, ground cinnamon, ground allspice**
½ **cup chopped walnuts**

1. Put all ingredients, except walnuts, in a large nonaluminum saucepan. Heat to boil; reduce heat to simmer. Simmer, stirring frequently, until thickened, about 30 minutes.

2. Cool. Stir in walnuts. Refrigerate in covered containers up to 3 weeks. Or freeze up to 3 months.

Patricia Tennison created the following strawberry and pineapple jams especially for the microwave oven. She offers this tip, "If you guess wrong and refrigerate the jam before it has cooked enough to firm up, just return the cold, soupy jam to the bowl and cook it some more."

FRESH STRAWBERRY JAM

About 1 cup
Preparation time: 20 minutes
Microwave cooking time: 22 to 27 minutes

½ **tart apple, such as Granny Smith**
1 **quart fresh whole strawberries**
1 **cup sugar**
1 **teaspoon lemon juice**

1. Remove and discard seeds from apple but leave skin on; chop apple finely. Put in 1-cup microwave-safe glass measure. Microwave on high (100 percent power) until softened, about 2 minutes.

2. Rinse strawberries, remove hulls and cut away any underripe, overripe or spoiled areas. Put in 3-quart microwave-safe bowl with high sides (not a flat casserole). Use potato masher to gently mash strawberries.

3. Stir in apple and sugar. Cover loosely with wax paper. Microwave on high 5 minutes. Stir well. Remove paper. Microwave on high until jam becomes quite thick (see note), 15 to 20 minutes, skimming off foam and stirring every 3 to 5 minutes. Stir in lemon juice.

4. Cool. Refrigerate in covered containers up to 3 weeks. Or freeze up to 3 months.

NOTE: To test if jam is cooked enough, put a drop on a very cold plate. If the drop clings to the plate without spreading, the jam is done. If the edges of the drop look quite watery and spread quickly, return jam to microwave and continue to cook. Stir and test the jam every 1 to 2 minutes.

Try this jam on French toast or as a topping for ice cream and sherbet.

FRESH PINEAPPLE JAM

About 1 cup
Preparation time: 20 minutes
Microwave cooking time: 22 to 27 minutes

½ **tart apple (Granny Smith is good)**
1 **quart fresh peeled pineapple cubes**
1 **cup sugar**
  Grated rind of 1 lemon
1 **tablespoon fresh lemon juice**

1. Remove and discard seeds from apple but leave skin on; chop apple finely. Put in 1-cup microwave-safe glass measure. Microwave on high (100 percent power) until softened, about 2 minutes.

2. Put pineapple in food processor. Use metal blade and process with on/off pulses until chunks are fine, about ¼ inch, but not smooth. Or chop pineapple chunks with knife until fine, saving the juices.

3. Mix pineapple, sugar and lemon rind in 3-quart microwave-safe bowl with high sides (not a flat casserole). Cover with wax paper. Microwave on high (100 percent power) 5 minutes. Stir well. Remove paper. Microwave on high until jam becomes quite thick (see note), 15 to 20 minutes, skimming off foam and stirring every 3 to 5 minutes. Stir in lemon juice.

4. Cool. Refrigerate in covered containers up to 3 weeks. Or freeze up to 3 months.

NOTE: To test if jam is cooked enough, put a drop on a very cold plate. If the drop clings to the plate without spreading, the jam is done. If the edges of the drop look quite watery and spread quickly, return jam to microwave and continue to cook. Stir and test the jam every 1 to 2 minutes.

Preserving the taste of summer is essential when you think of the taste of sweet, perfectly ripe nectarines. This recipe pairs the juicy fruit with the aromatic honeydew melon.

This recipe and others that follow are processed in a water bath canner to seal the jars properly for shelf storage. A water bath canner is simply a large kettle of boiling water. Filled jars are submerged into the water on a rack. Processing times should be followed closely and seals checked after the jars are cool.

The recipes may also be stored in the refrigerator in covered containers for several weeks.

NECTARINE-HONEYDEW CONSERVE

About 4½ cups
Preparation time: 20 minutes
Cooking time: 45 minutes
Processing time: 15 minutes

1½ **pounds semi-ripe nectarines, peeled, pitted, cut into ½-inch dice, about 3½ cups**

Rind of 2 medium oranges, finely grated

½ **cup fresh orange juice**

½ **large honeydew melon, cut into ½-inch cubes, about 5 cups**

3 **cups sugar**

½ **cup slivered almonds, optional**

1. Put nectarines, orange rind and juice in wide 2½-quart saucepan; heat to boil over high heat, stirring. Reduce heat so mixture boils slowly or until fruit is tender when pierced with a wooden pick, 10 to 15 minutes. Stir often to prevent sticking.

2. Remove from heat; add honeydew and sugar. Return to heat; heat to boil, stirring to dissolve sugar. Boil steadily until honeydew changes from bright to pale green, about 10 minutes.

3. Remove from heat; pour into colander over heatproof bowl. Let drain thoroughly, about 1 hour or more. Then return syrup to pan; boil rapidly until thick and reduced by half, about 10 minutes.

4. Return fruit to pan along with any syrup remaining in bowl. If you wish, spoon a little onto a plate and refrigerate long enough to check its consistency. Heat to boil. Cook longer, if necessary. Otherwise, pack hot into hot, sterilized jars, leaving ¼ inch headspace.

5. Seal according to jar manufacturer's directions. Process in boiling water bath 15 minutes. Cool completely. Check seal. Store in cool, dry place.

Stockpile this microwave conserve when the cranberry season is at its peak in the fall. A conserve need not be as thick as a jam.

CRANBERRY CONSERVE

About 3 cups
Preparation time: 10 minutes
Microwave cooking time: 25 minutes

1 bag (12 ounces) fresh
  cranberries
2 cups sugar or to taste
⅔ cup apple cider
½ pound golden raisins
2 tablespoons minced
  crystallized ginger
1 small orange or ½
  large, seeded, diced
1 cup chopped walnuts,
  pecans or almonds

1. Put all ingredients except nuts into 3-quart microwave-safe bowl. Rub edge of dish with butter about 1 inch of the way down inside of bowl.

2. Microwave, covered, on high, stirring every 2 minutes, for 10 minutes. Uncover; microwave, stirring every 2 minutes, until slightly thickened, about 10 more minutes.

3. Let stand for 10 minutes. Stir in nuts. Cool. Refrigerate in covered containers up to 3 weeks. Or freeze up to 3 months.

This recipe shows that great amounts of salt are not necessary to enhance the taste of nature's bounty.

COLORFUL GARDEN RELISH

About 3 quarts
Preparation time: 20 minutes
Cooking time: 20 minutes
Processing time: 10 minutes

1 quart diced celery
1½ cups chopped white
  onions
¼ cup water
3 green peppers, seeded,
  diced
3 medium yellow squash
  or zucchini or a
  combination, chopped
2 cups cider vinegar
2 tablespoons sugar, or
  to taste
2 teaspoons each: celery
  seeds, mustard seeds
1 teaspoon dry mustard

2 jars (4 ounces each)
  chopped pimiento,
  drained or 2 red bell
  peppers, seeded,
  diced

1. Cook celery and onions in water in large non-aluminum saucepan 10 minutes. Drain off water. Add remaining ingredients, except pimiento. Heat to boil; boil, uncovered, until vegetables are crisp-tender. Pack hot mixture into hot, sterilized canning jars leaving ¼ inch headspace.

2. Seal according to jar manufacturer's directions. Process in boiling water bath 10 minutes. Cool completely. Check seal. Store in cool, dry place.

What to do with the gardenful of zucchini? Make pickles of course.

ZUCCHINI BREAD AND BUTTER PICKLES

About 2½ quarts
Preparation time: 25 minutes
Standing time: 1½ hours
Cooking time: 10 minutes
Processing time: 10 minutes

14 to 16 small zucchini, sliced crosswise
 8 small onions, sliced
 ⅓ cup coarse (kosher) salt
 3 cups distilled white vinegar
 2 cups sugar
 2 tablespoons mustard seeds
 1 tablespoon dry mustard
 1 teaspoon each: celery seeds, turmeric, peppercorns
 2 medium green peppers, seeded, diced

1. Alternate layers of zucchini, onions and salt in large glass bowl. Cover with ice cubes; let stand 1½ hours. Drain off liquid and rinse. Pat dry with paper towels.

2. Mix vinegar, sugar, mustard seeds, mustard, celery seeds, turmeric and peppercorns in large nonaluminum saucepan. Heat to boil; add zucchini, peppers and onions. Return to boil. Remove from heat. Pack hot mixture and liquid into hot, sterilized canning jars leaving ¼ inch headspace.

3. Seal according to jar manufacturer's directions. Process in boiling water bath 10 minutes. Cool completely. Check seal. Store in cool, dry place.

Andre Schaack, of Chicago, serves this cilantro chutney with his vegetable couscous recipe on page 176. It is also good with grilled meats, boiled cauliflower and broccoli or as a dip for raw vegetables.

CILANTRO CHUTNEY

About 3 cups
Preparation time: 15 minutes

1 teaspoon cumin seeds
1 carton (16 ounces) plain low-fat yogurt
2 cups packed, chopped fresh cilantro (coriander)
2 tablespoons lemon juice
1 teaspoon salt
½ teaspoon cayenne pepper
¼ teaspoon freshly ground pepper

1. Cook cumin seeds in small heavy skillet, stirring constantly, until roasted and fragrant, about 4 minutes. Cool on paper plate. Grind to powder in mortar and pestle or spice grinder.

2. Mix cumin into yogurt with remaining ingredients in medium bowl. Refrigerate covered up to 1 week.

This mint chutney is excellent served with the Indian appetizer called samosa (see recipe, page 44). It also makes a delicious dip for raw vegetables.

MINT CHUTNEY

About ½ cup
Preparation time: 10 minutes

1 **bunch fresh cilantro (coriander) leaves**
16 **to 18 mint sprigs**
¼ **cup water**
3 **tablespoons lemon juice**
2 **tablespoons dry-roasted peanuts or 1 ripe banana**
6 **small green chiles, seeded, or to taste**
1 **teaspoon salt or to taste**
1 **teaspoon dry-roasted cumin seeds**

1. Put all ingredients into blender or food processor. Process until smooth. Refrigerate covered up to 3 weeks.

Chef Carolyn Buster contributed this recipe for raspberry vinegar. Her method could be used to make any flavor berry vinegar. In addition to use in sauces and salad dressings, some people enjoy a drop or two of fruit vinegar in sparkling water for a thirst-quenching beverage.

RASPBERRY VINEGAR

About 3 cups
Preparation time: 10 minutes
Aging time: 2 weeks

3 **cups distilled white vinegar**
1 **package (10 ounces) quick-thaw frozen raspberries**
1 **cinnamon stick, optional**

1. Put all ingredients into medium-size nonaluminum saucepan. Let stand, covered, 8 hours or overnight.

2. Heat over low heat to simmer. Remove from heat. Cool completely. Strain into storage jars. Store, covered, at least 2 weeks before using.

The California Walnut Board created this delicious walnut oil. Try it with pistachios or almonds for variety.

WALNUT OIL

About 1 cup
Preparation time: 5 minutes
Aging time: 3 days

⅔ **cup walnut pieces**
1⅓ **cups vegetable oil**

1. Put walnuts into small skillet. Cook and stir over medium heat until lightly toasted and aromatic.

2. Spread warm toasted walnut pieces on wax paper. Crush with rolling pin. Put walnuts and oil into clean, dry, glass quart jar. Stir. Cover. Let stand in cool room or refrigerator for 3 days. Strain through fine sieve.

PRESSURE CANNING

Pressure canning is not difficult: It requires a canner and a good set of directions which should be followed for every recipe you wish to can.

A pressure canner lid has a safety valve, a vent and a pressure gauge. The vent allows steam to escape under a controlled pressure. If it should become clogged inadvertently, a safety valve is designed to pop, releasing pressure and preventing the kettle from exploding.

Before starting be sure the vent is not clogged. Some suggest that a string be drawn through the vent and safety valve openings before the canner is used to make sure that they are free from obstruction.

Prescribed times and temperatures should be followed. All of the recipes that follow can be stored in the refrigerator up to 2 weeks if you do not wish to can them.

This recipe for mincemeat has been handed down for generations in Jeannette McCullough's family, of Rockford, Illinois, as were the now old-fashioned wire and glass-topped canning jars. Over the years, short ribs have replaced beef suet as the meat in the mincemeat.

HOMEMADE MINCEMEAT

About 5 quarts
Preparation time: 45 minutes
Processing time: 25 minutes

13 pounds of green
    tomatoes, about 40
    small, ground
2 pounds short ribs,
    boiled, boned, cut up,
    with 1 cup of
    reserved cooking
    juices
2 pounds brown sugar
2 pounds seedless
    raisins
1 cup cider vinegar
1 tablespoon ground
    cinnamon
2 teaspoons ground
    cloves
1 tablespoon salt, about
8 apples, peeled, ground

1. Put tomatoes in large kettle with enough water to cover. Heat to boil. Drain. Cover again with water. Cook until tender. Drain.

2. Put drained tomatoes and remaining ingredients in heavy nonaluminum saucepan. Mix well. Simmer, stirring often, 2 hours.

3. Put canning jars, lids and rings into boiling water. Pack hot, cooked mincemeat into hot jars, leaving 1 inch headspace. Seal according to jar manufacturer's instructions.

4. Process pints and quarts 25 minutes at 10 pounds pressure in pressure canner according to manufacturer's directions. Cool jars; check seals.

These recipes are adapted from the Ball Corporation, in Indiana, makers of canning jars and lids for many years.

SLICED BEETS WITH VIDALIA ONIONS

Preparation time: 20 minutes
Cooking time: 10 minutes
Processing time: 30 to 35 minutes

Beets
Vidalia onions, sliced
Salt

1. Wash beets. Leave 2 inches of stems and the tap roots. Boil until skins can be slipped. Remove skins, trim beets; slice.

2. Alternate layers of sliced beets and sliced Vidalia onions in hot jars, leaving 1 inch headspace. Add ½ teaspoon salt to each pint or 1 teaspoon salt to each quart. Cover with boiling water, leaving 1 inch headspace.

3. Remove air bubbles. Seal according to jar manufacturer's instructions. Process pints 30 minutes, quarts 35 minutes, at 10 pounds pressure in pressure canner according to manufacturer's directions. Cool jars; check seals.

RAW-PACK CARROTS WITH DILL

Preparation time: 20 minutes
Processing time: 25 to 30 minutes

Carrots
Fresh dill sprigs
Salt

1. Wash and scrape carrots. Slice, dice or leave whole if small. Pack tightly into hot jars, adding a few dill sprigs to each, leaving 1 inch headspace. Add ½ teaspoon salt to each pint, or 1 teaspoon salt to each quart. Cover with boiling water, leaving 1 inch headspace.

2. Remove air bubbles. Seal according to jar manufacturer's instructions. Process pints 25 minutes, quarts 30 minutes, at 10 pounds pressure in pressure canner according to manufacturer's directions. Cool jars; check seals.

RAW-PACK LIMA BEANS WITH ROASTED RED PEPPERS

Preparation time: 20 minutes
Processing time: 40 to 50 minutes

Fresh lima beans
Red bell peppers, roasted, peeled, diced
Salt

1. Wash, drain and shell tender young beans. Wash again. Pack beans and red peppers loosely into hot jars, leaving 1 inch headspace. Do not press or shake down. Add ½ teaspoon salt to each pint, or 1 teaspoon salt to each quart. Cover with boiling water, leaving 1 inch headspace.

2. Remove air bubbles. Seal according to jar manufacturer's instructions. Process pints 40 minutes, quarts 50 minutes, at 10 pounds pressure in pressure canner according to manufacturer's directions. Cool jars; check seals.

OKRA WITH HOT PEPPERS

Preparation time: 20 minutes
Processing time: 25 to 40 minutes

Young, tender okra
Small, dried hot red chili peppers
Salt

1. Use young, tender okra. If it is to be added to soup, it should be sliced; otherwise, can pods whole. Wash and drain okra. Remove stem and blossom ends without cutting into pod. Boil 2 minutes. Pack hot okra and peppers into hot jars, leaving 1 inch headspace. Add ½ teaspoon salt to each pint, or 1 teaspoon salt to each quart. If needed, add boiling water to cover, leaving 1 inch headspace.

2. Remove air bubbles. Seal according to jar manufacturer's instructions. Process pints 25 minutes, quarts 40 minutes, at 10 pounds pressure in pressure canner according to manufacturer's directions. Cool jars; check seals.

Stewed tomatoes are a standard canning recipe coming back into vogue for its fresh flavor, low calorie count and versatility. You can add chopped fresh jalapeño peppers for a spicy version if desired. Serve the tomatoes as a side dish with roast or grilled poultry or as a base of a salsa, soup or sauce.

STEWED TOMATOES

About 7 pints
Preparation time: 45 minutes
Cooking time: 10 minutes
Processing time: 15 to 20 minutes

4 **quarts peeled, cored, chopped tomatoes, about 2 dozen large**
1 **cup chopped celery**
½ **cup chopped onion**
¼ **cup chopped green pepper**
1 **tablespoon sugar**
2 **teaspoons salt**

1. Mix all ingredients in large nonaluminum saucepan; cover and cook 10 minutes, stirring occasionally to prevent sticking. Pour hot, into hot jars, leaving ½ inch headspace.

2. Remove air bubbles. Seal according to jar manufacturer's instructions. Process pints 15 minutes, quarts 20 minutes, at 10 pounds pressure in pressure canner according to manufacturer's directions. Cool jars; check seals.

APPENDIX

Glossary of Ingredients

achiote (annatto) small, irregularly shaped, rusty-red seeds from the annatto tree with a pungent, musty taste; used in Latin American and Caribbean cooking

allspice from the myrtle family, this round, brown berry gets its name from its flavor which is reminiscent of a combination of several spices—primarily cinnamon, nutmeg and clove

anchovy tiny, salted fish that comes either packed in oil or dry-packed in salt; especially popular in Mediterranean cuisines

anise licorice-tasting seed used widely in the Middle East and Europe

arrowroot starch used for thickening (Some cooks prefer arrowroot to cornstarch or flour because of its more delicate taste.)

baking powder leavening agent made of baking soda and cream of tartar

baking soda sodium bicarbonate; when mixed with an acid such as lemon juice or buttermilk, it acts as a leavening agent

basil common green, leafy herb which tastes slightly of licorice; available dried or fresh

bay leaf pungent flavored leaf from bay trees, native to the Mediterranean; available dried

beans, dried legume eaten as a vegetable; comes in many varieties; best vegetable source for protein

Belgian endive variety of chicory with a creamy-white to light green, compact bunch of leaves with a slightly bitter taste

beurre French word for butter (Beurre blanc is a foamy, white butter sauce.)

bouillon French word for broth made from meat, poultry or assorted vegetables cooked in water

bouquet garni flavoring packet usually comprised of bay leaves, parsley and thyme tied together in cheesecloth *broth*   flavored liquid made by cooking beef, chicken or seafood and carrots, onions, celery and seasonings in water

bulgur   whole-wheat kernels that are steamed, dried and crushed

buttermilk   portion of the cream that remains after the butter has been made; used as a liquid in breads and desserts

calamari   Italian word for squid

capers   small, unopened flower buds with a pickle-like flavor from a Mediterranean bush; usually packed in brine, vinegar or salt

carambola   tropical fruit, also called star fruit; has a waxy yellow exterior and resembles a star when sliced (Some varieties are sweet; others are as sour as lemons.)

caraway seed   small, oval seed with a slight licorice taste used frequently in European and Indian cooking

cardamom   expensive, tropical spice belonging to the ginger family; very aromatic with a slightly sweet taste; used in baked goods

caviar   eggs, or roe, from sturgeon, treated with salt (Eggs from other fish can be called caviar but must clearly state the fish of origin on the label.)

cayenne pepper   bright red powder made from ground, dried hot chilies

celery root   also known as celeriac and celery rave, this root, a relative of the celery family, is round in shape with a mottled brown exterior and a celery flavor

celery seed   a tiny seed from wild celery

chayote   light green, pear-shaped squash with a bland taste similar to zucchini; common to Latin American, Caribbean, Creole and Cajun cooking (also known as mirliton, christophene, vegetable pear)

chervil   feathery green herb with a slight licorice taste; available fresh or dried

chestnuts   sweet and starchy nut; must be cooked before eaten; available fresh or canned (Served roasted or used to flavor stuffings, desserts and ice cream.)

chilies   from the capsicum family; more than 100 varieties with flavors ranging from mild to hot; available fresh or dried (Typically, the smaller the chilies, the hotter they are. Most of the heat is concentrated in the seeds and membranes.)

chives   long, green, skinny member of the onion family with a delicate onion taste; available fresh, dried or frozen

chorizo   Mexican sausage links made with fresh pork and spicy seasonings

chutney   spicy condiment made from fruit, spices, sugar and vinegar; served as a relish; important component of Indian cuisine

cilantro   distinctive pungent, aromatic herb; used in Latin, Oriental, and Indian cuisines; also called fresh coriander or Chinese parsley; available fresh or dried

clarified butter butter that has been melted and had milky solids and whey removed (To clarify butter, heat to simmer in saucepan over low heat about 10 minutes. Disturb white foam on top from time to time to see when it is clarified. It is ready when you can see to the bottom clearly: It will no longer be cloudy. At this point, pour through several layers of cheesecloth or a piece of flannel to remove any lingering milk solids.)

cloves an aromatic spice; available in berries or powdered (Used sparingly in desserts, soups, stews, beverages, pork.)

coconut milk clear liquid from the coconut (Canned, unsweetened coconut milk used in Asian cooking is often a combination of the liquid plus milk or water.)

confectioners' sugar granulated sugar pulverized into a satiny powder with cornstarch added to prevent caking; also called powdered sugar

coriander seed tiny husk-like seed often combined with cumin and other spices to produce the distinctive flavor found in Middle Eastern and Southeast Asian cuisines; has the flavor of lemon and caraway; used in salads, marinades and breads

cornmeal ground sweet corn; yellow, white or blue hues; used in tortillas, polenta, cornbread, stuffings, crepes and mush

cornstarch corn flour used as a thickener, binder or coating for foods

couscous delicate grain made from semolina flour; used as a substitute for rice and other grains; national dish of Morocco and Algeria

cream of tartar acid salt; used in baking, baking powders and self-rising flour; also used as a stabilizer for whipped egg white

crème fraîche cream that has been allowed to ferment; thicker than whipping cream but has a flavor similar to sour cream; popular in France (To make, mix 2 cups whipping cream with 2 tablespoons buttermilk, cover and let stand at room temperature about 24 hours. Then refrigerate up to 1 week.)

cumin intensely flavored spice; related to the caraway family; used to flavor pork, cordials, breads, cheeses and Middle Eastern and Mexican dishes

currants tart red or black berries widely used in preserves and jellies (Black currants are the main ingredient of crème de cassis.)

curry powder hot or mild commercial blend of as many as 15 to 20 spices including cinnamon, cloves, fenugreek, ginger, red pepper and turmeric

dashi transparent fish and seaweed flavored stock; base of many Japanese dishes; faint flavor; available in granules

dill herb with delicate feathery leaves and a lemony flavor; used as a garnish and in sauces, fish dishes, pickles and vinegars; available fresh or dried (labeled dillweed)

escargot French word for snail; available fresh or canned

extract intense flavoring extracted from meat, vanilla beans, almonds, lemons, etc.

fennel   a licorice-flavored member of the parsley family; both bulb and leaves are used in fish dishes, salads; available fresh or dried (Scandinavians also use fennel seed to flavor pastries, sweet breads and cookies.)

fenugreek   bitter red-brown seeds with a taste similar to burnt sugar; used in curries, chutneys and Middle Eastern dishes such as halva

filé powder   ground leaves from the sassafras tree; flavor resembles thyme and savory; used as a flavor enhancer and thickener for gumbos and stews

five-spice powder   combination of five spices such as star anise, cinnamon, nutmeg, Szechwan peppercorns, cloves, fennel or licorice root; used as a seasoning in Oriental marinades

garlic   pungent bulb with a distinctive flavor; crushed cloves from the bulb used in savory dishes such as meats, fondues, omelets, Italian specialties and vegetables; available fresh, powdered, dried or preserved

gelatin   tasteless, odorless powder extracted by boiling animal bones, hoofs and tissues; used to gel foods such as aspics and desserts

ghee   nutty-flavored clarified butter used as fat in Indian cooking

ginger   root with a pleasant, biting-hot taste; usually grown in the Asian tropics; used in Oriental dishes, pickles, cakes, cookies and pies; available fresh, ground, crystallized or preserved

honey   thick, syrup-like liquid; a by-product of flower pollination by bees; used to sweeten desserts, beverages, stews, cereals, breads

horseradish   spicy hot, fleshy root; adds pizazz to dips, roast beef, fish and salad dressings; available fresh or preserved

hot pepper sauce   liquid condiment mixture of hot peppers and vinegar

jicama   starchy root vegetable with a flavor similar to a slightly sweet radish without the hot bite; crisp and white; used for salads and as a vegetable

juniper berries   bittersweet berry from the juniper bush; used as a flavoring for game, gin, pork, salmon and duck

kelp   brown sheets of edible seaweed; used in Oriental dishes such as sushi and for making dashi

lard   internal pig fat which has been melted, strained and cooled; white solid is used for deep-frying, pie crusts and cakes

mace   husk around the nutmeg seed (similar flavor but slightly milder); used in savory and sweet dishes; available powdered

mahlepi seeds   also called mahleb, available at Greek or Assyrian groceries; if unavailable grind together 2 inches of cinnamon stick, 3 whole cloves and 1 bay leaf

marinades   mixture of oil, vinegar, wine and seasonings; used to flavor and tenderize meat, poultry and fish before cooking

marjoram   herb in the mint family; related to thyme; often substituted for oregano, although marjoram tastes sweeter and milder; available fresh or dried

millet   nutty-flavored grain high in protein; used in breads and ground into flour

mirin   sweet rice wine used in Japanese dishes as a seasoning or cooking ingredient

molasses   dark, sweet syrup from the refining of sugar cane (Light or dark molasses is sold bottled.)

monosodium glutamate   also known as MSG; white, crystalline vegetable extract (an additive); used as a flavor enhancer; available powdered (Some researchers believe the seasoning causes some people allergic reactions.)

mustard seeds   spice with a recognized reputation for enhancing savory dishes; three main types: brown (pungent), white (mild) and black (extra-strong); gives a hot flavor to savory dishes such as sauces, pickles and deviled foods; available in seeds or powdered or prepared

nam pla   thin Thai fish sauce; salty with a pungent flavor

nutmeg   aromatic spice used in baking and in some savory dishes; available ground or as a nut.

oils   edible oil used as a cooking medium; derived from a number of sources such as fruits, vegetables, legumes and nuts

oregano   herb similar to marjoram; used in spaghetti sauces, soups, pizzas and tomato dishes; available fresh, dried or powdered

pancetta   unsmoked Italian bacon

paprika   red powder made from ground red chilies; sweet or hot depending on type of chilies used; used in savory dishes and as decoration for light-colored dishes

parsley   herb with a dozen varieties with the most common being the curly and the stronger-flavored Italian flat-leafed

passion fruit   sweet fruit of the passion flower tree; jelly-like flesh; used in desserts and mousses and made into juice

pasta   generic term for noodles; available fresh or dried

pectin   found in cell walls of many plants such as apples or citrus fruit; when combined with sugar it causes jams and jellies to set

pesto   Italian; uncooked sauce of basil, Parmesan cheese, garlic, pine nuts and olive oil

pimiento   cooked sweet red pepper; available bottled

poppy seeds   tiny black or white seeds used in stuffings, strudels, breads

prosciutto   Italian word for ham which has been rubbed with salt and seasonings and air-dried

quince   Latin American fruit that looks like a large pear but is very hard and sour; usually cooked with sugar

quinoa   originating in South America; called the "super grain" because it's high in protein (Tiny, ivory-colored grains are used like rice, wheat and corn.)

radicchio   Italian chicory; color ranges from rose-pink to red; used in salads

rosemary   pungent herb that subtly alters in various dishes; used in casseroles, bouquet garni, fish, rice, apples and dumplings; available fresh or dried

rosewater   fragrant water made by distilling fresh rose petals; used in Turkish cuisine

saffron   the stigmas from crocus flowers; said to be the most expensive food in the world; used as a flavoring and gives food a yellow hue (Red threads are slightly medicinal in taste.)

sage   lime-scented herb that is highly aromatic; commonly used in poultry dishes, stuffings, sausage, game and marinades; available fresh or dried

salsify   root vegetable with texture and taste similar to a parsnip; also called oyster plant

savory   herb traditionally used in bean dishes; also used with pork and stuffings; available fresh or dried (Summer savory is aromatic and delicious while winter savory has a bitter bite.)

semolina   particles of fine wheat made from the endosperm of durum wheat; used in Middle Eastern, Italian and Indian cuisines

sesame   small nutty-flavored seed; can be red, brown, black or light beige; used in breads, pastries, cookies, salads and meats; often toasted

shallot   member of the onion family; milder taste with a slight garlic flavor

sorbet   French word for sherbet; ice flavored with fruit or liqueur

sorrel   herb used by the French for making soup; strong aroma; also used with rice and fish dishes and as a substitute for spinach; available fresh or bottled

sour cream   cream soured and thickened by a lactic acid

soy sauce   salty brown sauce extracted from fermented soy beans; used widely in Oriental dishes; available in three grades: light, medium and thick (or dark)

sprouts   sprout of a legume seed such as mung; used in salads and sandwiches

star anise   eight-pointed seed that comes from the magnolia family; used to season Oriental dishes, including marinades, stews and braised dishes

tamari   thick, unrefined soy sauce; used as a dipping sauce and condiment

tamarind   fruit that resembles a long bean pod with a sweet, lime flavor; large pulpy seeds are used to flavor fruit drinks and sweets; available fresh, frozen or in concentrate

tarragon   licorice-flavored herb that is the essential ingredient of the famous French sauce, bearnaise; also used in lamb and poultry dishes; available fresh or dried *thyme*   aromatic herb most universally used in stuffings for pork or chicken; also used to flavor kebabs, cheese dishes and marinades; available fresh, powdered or dried

tofu   also called bean curd; made from soybeans which have been soaked, pureed and cooked; sold in square cakes or blocks packed in water; excellent source of protein

tomatillos   small, green Mexican ground tomatoes related to the Cape gooseberry; enveloped in a brown paper-like husk; used in Latin and Tex-Mex dishes; small green tomatoes may be substituted

tortillas   Latin American flat, circular bread made with wheat flour or cornmeal

truffles   pungent black fungi with an earthy flavor; very expensive because they are rare; grow underground and are dug up from the base of oak trees by trained pigs or dogs; available fresh or canned or in paste form

turmeric   deep-yellow spice related to ginger; important component of curries; also used in pickles and chutneys; available powdered

ugli fruit   hybrid of grapefruit, orange and tangerine; labeled "ugli" because of its bumpy exterior; popular in Caribbean islands; used in salads and sherbets

vanilla   sweet aromatic flavoring from long, black, wrinkled pods; available in pods or in extract form

vegetable shortening   cooking fat made from the oils of vegetables

vinegar   acetic acid; can be flavored with herbs, shallots, garlic or spices; used in salad dressings, pickles and marinades

wasabi   pungent Japanese green horseradish; usually served with sushi; available powdered or in tubes (A little goes a long way.)

water chestnuts   nut-like seed of an aquatic plant found in East Asia; slightly sweet taste with crisp texture; available canned, occasionally fresh

watercress   green plant that is a member of the mustard family; spicy flavor; used in salads and for garnishing

wheat germ   seeds of wheat; may be sprinkled on food or added to breads

wild rice   acquatic grass grown in bogs or swamps; nutty flavor; requires longer cooking time than white rice

Worcestershire sauce   commercial piquant sauce of vinegar, molasses, sugar, anchovies, tamarind, onions, garlic, shallots and spices; used as a marinade ingredient, or to enhance flavor of soups, stews and sauces

yeast   small plant that feeds on sugar and warmth and expands rapidly when mixed with flour; used in making breads, cakes, beer and wine; available in cakes or granules

zest   colored, sweet part of citrus rind

Glossary of Cooking Terms

al dente   an Italian phrase which literally means "to the tooth"; used primarily to indicate doneness for pasta—tender but still firm

au gratin   a dish, topped with cheese or bread crumbs, or both, and browned in the oven

au jus   food served in its own juices, usually roast beef

bake   to cook by dry heat in the oven

barbecue   to cook on a grill over hot coals; also refers to food cooked in a spicy sauce

baste   the process of moistening food while it cooks with its pan juices or some other flavored liquid

batter   a mixture, thin enough to pour, before cooking

beard   to remove the hairy fibers off an unshucked mussel

beat   to mix ingredients together with a vigorous motion using a spoon or electric mixer to incorporate air

blanch   to precook foods, or remove their outer skin, usually by immersing in large quantity of boiling water

boil   to heat liquid until large bubbles break on the surface (212 degrees Fahrenheit for water at sea level)

braise   to cook slowly, usually covered, in a small amount of liquid or fat

broil   to cook under high, direct heat

brown   to cook with high heat so foods take on a brown appearance; can be done on top of the stove or under the broiler

brulée   the French word for "burned"; usually for foods that have a caramelized appearance

butterfly   to split open through the middle without completely separating the two halves; used for meats and shrimp

can   to preserve food by sealing it in an airtight container

candy   to cook food in sugar or heavy sugar syrup

caramelize   to cook sugar until it melts and becomes brown in color; also, to cook food with caramelized sugar

chop   to cut into small pieces with a knife or food chopper

clarify   to make cloudy liquids clear by filtering (Clarified butter is melted butter with the frothy top and the milk solids on the bottom removed.)

coat   to evenly cover food with crumbs, flour or batter

combine   to mix two or more ingredients together

confit a French preserving method in which meats are salted and then cooked in fat and sealed in fat in an earthenware crock

core to remove the core from fruits and vegetables

cream to vigorously beat butter, or other fat, sometimes with sugar or other ingredients added, until light and fluffy

crimp to seal the edge of a pastry dough

crisp-tender to cook food to the stage where it is tender but still slightly crisp

crush to pulverize food into crumbs

cube to cut food into pieces that are the same size on all sides, usually ⅛ or ¼ inch

cut in to mix fat with dry ingredients by using a pastry blender or two knives until mixture resembles coarse crumbs

deep-fry to cook food by complete immersion in hot fat or oil

deglaze to scrape the browned bits up off a skillet or roasting pan by adding liquid and cooking and scraping (This liquid in then used for its flavor.)

degrease to remove the grease or fat from the surface of foods, such as soups, stocks and sauces

dice to cut into small even pieces, usually cubes between ⅛ and ¼ inch

dot to evenly distribute small bits of food over another food, such as butter, over the top of a pie before baking

drain to pour off and discard the liquid

drizzle to lightly distribute a liquid, such as melted butter or syrup, over another food

drop to drop from a spoon, such as cookie dough onto a baking sheet or fritter batter into hot oil

dust to cover food lightly with flour, sugar or fine bread crumbs

emulsify to mix two foods into an emulsion such as egg yolks with oil

filet a boneless piece of beef tenderloin, as in filet mignon

fillet a boneless piece of meat or fish

flake to break food apart with a fork into flakes or small pieces

flour to lightly coat with flour

fluff to lightly mix with a fork until fluffy

flute to decorate food with small impressions; pie crusts are fluted by pressing the edge into various shapes

fold to gently mix ingredients together by using a spatula and cutting down and up through the mixture, while turning the bowl, until incorporated

Appendix

frost   to cover top and sides of a cake with frosting

fry   to cook in shallow amount of hot fat

fumet   a concentrated stock; used to flavor soups and sauces

ganache   a thick, rich frosting made with butter and chocolate

garnish   to decorate a finished dish before serving

glaze   to brush a glossy mixture over surface of food to make it shine

grate   to cut food into small granules using a grater

grease and flour   to coat a pan with shortening and then lightly with flour to prevent foods from sticking

grill   to cook foods over hot coals

grind   to pulverize food into small particles using a grinder or mortar and pestle

hot water bath   a small pan placed inside a larger pan; the larger pan is then filled with hot or boiling water

husk   to remove the coarse outer husk

jelly-roll style   a flat piece of food rolled up around a filling to resemble a jelly roll

julienne   to cut into thin matchstick shapes

knead   to manipulate dough, using the hands or an electric mixer with a dough hook, in a rhythmic folding and pressing motion in order to develop the gluten in flour

marinate   to cover food in a flavored liquid, usually containing an acid such as vinegar, wine or lemon juice, to tenderize and add flavor

mash   to make soft food into a pulp

melt   to heat until liquified

mince   to chop very finely into irregular pieces

mortar and pestle   mortar is a bowl-shaped container made of a hard material; pestle is a blunt instrument of the same material used for crushing the contents of the mortar

pan-broil   to cook, uncovered, in a pan using as little fat as possible

pan-fry   to cook, uncovered, in a pan in a shallow amount of fat (The French word is sauté.)

partially set   to chill gelatin mixtures until set enough to resemble the consistency of raw egg whites

peel (pare)   to remove the skin or outer peels from fruits or vegetables

pickle   to preserve food in salt or vinegar solutions sometimes containing spices

pierce   to make small holes in food with the tip of a knife or tines of a fork *pipe*   to squeeze a soft (but not runny) food through a pastry bag

plump   to soak dried fruits in liquid until they swell

poach   to cook food submerged in simmering liquid so it retains its shape

pound   to flatten food with a mallet

preheat   to heat oven or broiler to required temperature before adding food

preserve   to save food for future use by pickling, canning, curing, smoking or freezing

proof   to test yeast for potency by dissolving it and watching for bubbles

puree   to mash to a smooth consistency

reconstitute   to rehydrate dried foods in liquid

reduce   to boil liquid gently until volume has been reduced and flavors concentrated

render   to make solid fat into liquid by heating slowly

rice   to push food through a ricer

roast   to cook, uncovered, by dry heat in an oven (Pot roasting refers to braising in liquid.)

roll out   to roll dough into a thin flat sheet using a rolling pin

roux   a mixture of melted fat and flour used as a thickener

sauté   French word for cooking on top of the stove using a small amount of fat and stirring occasionally

scald   to heat a liquid just below the boiling point (To scald a food means to drop it briefly in boiling water.)

score   to make shallow cuts into meat or fish to help retain its shape while cooking

sear   to cook at very high heat in order to seal in the juices

shell   to remove the shell

shred   to cut food into thin strips using a shredder

shuck   to remove the shells from mollusks or the husks from corn

sieve   to push food or strain liquid through a sieve

sift   to remove lumps and to lighten the ingredients by passing them through a sifter or fine sieve

simmer   to heat liquid just until tiny bubbles begin to form

skewer   to thread pieces of food onto metal or wooden skewers

skin   to remove the skin from poultry and meats

sliver   to cut food into fine thin pieces

soft peaks   to beat a mixture until light enough to hold soft peaks that curl over at the top when the beater is lifted

steam   to cook foods over rapidly boiling water and allow the steam to circulate

stew   to cook slowly in liquid

stiff peaks   to beat a mixture until light enough to hold stiff peaks that stand erect when the beater is lifted

stir-fry   to cook food quickly, in a small amount of fat, over fairly high heat, stirring or tossing as food cooks

stock   the broth strained from cooked meats, poultry, fish or vegetables

strain   to separate liquids from solids in a manner in which the solids and liquid are saved

tenderize   to make tender, by pounding, scoring or with chemical tenderizers

terrine   an earthenware container used for baking pâtés; also the dish so cooked

toss   to mix with a gentle tossing motion

truss   to bind poultry so it will keep its shape while cooking

turn   to turn food over as it cooks or marinates; also, to flute or cut scallops into a food with a small paring knife

whip   to lighten and increase the volume with a beater

whisk   to beat with a whisk (an instrument made of looped wires)

zest   the colored part of a citrus rind; also, the action of removing the colored part from the fruit

CHICAGO SHOPPING SOURCES

Here is a list of specialty food shops in the Chicago area, where some of the special ingredients called for in several of the recipes could be located. They are listed by their specialty, although most of these stores carry an assortment of products. Please keep in mind that this is but a sampling of the many fine food shops in the Chicago area.

A caveat: Although this list was accurate at the time of publication, specialty food shops come and go out of business. Unless otherwise noted, all the addresses are in Chicago. They all are in Illinois.

FISH

Burhop's, One Fish Plaza, 745 N. LaSalle Street, 60610, plus other locations

Chicago Fish House, 1250 W. Division Street, 60622

Supreme Lobster and Seafood, 220 E. North Avenue, P.O. 669, Villa Park, 60181

GOURMET SHOPS
(carrying a wide variety of items)

Beautiful Food, 718 Elm Street, Winnetka, 60093

Chalet Wine & Cheese Shop, 40 E. Delaware Street, 60610, plus other locations

Foodstuffs, 338 Park Avenue, Glencoe, 60022, plus other locations

Kenessey's Gourmets International, Hotel Belmont, 403 W. Belmont Avenue, 60657

LaBelle Gourmet, 16 W. Calendar Court, La Grange, 60525

Marshall Field & Co., gourmet foods and wines, 111 N. State Street, 60602, plus other locations

Mitchell Cobey Cuisine, 100 E. Walton Street, 60611

Neiman-Marcus Epicure Shop, 737 N. Michigan Avenue, 60611

Spice 'N Easy, 528 Crescent Blvd., Glen Ellyn, 60137

Zambrana's Food Emporium, 2346 N. Clark Street, 60614

GERMAN

Kuhn's Delicatessen, 3551 N. Lincoln Avenue, 60657

ITALIAN

Conte di Savoia, 1440 W. Taylor Street, 60607

Convito Italiano, Plaza del Lago, 1515 Sheridan Road, Wilmette, 60091, plus other locations

D'Andrea & Son, 7055 W. Cermak Road, Berwyn, 60402

Pasta Shoppe, 3755 N. Harlem Avenue, 60634

MEATS

Czimer's, 13136 W. 159th Street, Lockport, 60441

E&M Provisions, Inc., 3358 W. Dempster Street, Skokie, 60076

Elegance in Meats, 3135 Dundee Road, Northbrook, 60052

Gepperth's Meat Market, 1970 N. Halsted Street, 60614

Honey Baked Hams, 3018 W. Belmont Avenue, 60618

McChesney & Miller, 460 Crescent Boulevard, Glen Ellyn, 60137

Paulina Market, 3501 N. Lincoln Avenue, 60657

Purtill's Foods, Inc., 1129 N. State Street, 60610

Wild Game, Inc., 2315 W. Huron Street, 60612

MEXICAN

Armando's Finer Foods, 2627 S. Kedzie Avenue, 60623

Carniceria Atotonilco, 3917 W. 26th Street, 60623

El Milagro, 3050 W. 26th Street, 60623

La Guadalupana, 3215 W. 26th Street, 60623

La Justicia, 3644 W. 26th Street, 60623

ORIENTAL

Diho Market, 665 Pasquinelli Drive, Westmont, 60559

Oriental Food Market, 2801 W. Howard Street, 60645

Star Market, 3349 N. Clark Street, 60657

Thai Grocery, 5014 N. Broadway Street, 60640

Thai Market, 3920 N. Broadway Street, 60640

PRODUCE

Big Apple Finer Foods, 2345 N. Clark Street, 60614

Carrot Top, 1430 Paddock Drive, Northbrook, 60062

Foodworks, 1002 W. Diversey Avenue, plus other locations

Rogers Park Fruit Market, 7401 N. Clark Street, 60616

SWEDISH

Erickson's Delicatessen, 5250 N. Clark Street, 60640

Wikstrom Scandinavian Gourmet Foods, 5247 N. Clark Street, 60640

ACKNOWLEDGMENTS

The cookbook committee would like to thank *Chicago Tribune* photographers Tony Berardi, Bob Fila, Bill Hogan and Chris Walker whose works are featured here. We also appreciate the support of Jack Corn, director of photography, and the photo lab staff. We would also like to thank Beverly Dillon, Lenni Gilbert and Susie Goldstein for their food styling, recipe development and recipe testing.

Thank you to *The Chicago Tribune* editors who believed in this book, particularly James D. Squires, Colleen Dishon, Paul A. Camp and Owen Youngman.

Ruthellyn Roguski, Kevin Dabe and John Lux at *The Chicago Tribune* graciously handled all the business aspects of putting together such a volume. A sincere thanks to the reference room staff at *The Chicago Tribune*, especially John Jansson, Mary Huschen and Mary Wilson.

Amy Teschner, cookbook editor at Chicago Review Press, made the project exciting and fun.

A very special thanks to all those cooks, chefs, authors, restaurateurs and readers who have allowed us to use their recipes over the years. In particular we would like to thank those whose recipes are included in this volume: Nancy Abrams, American Grill, Elsa and Marco Amidei, Carol and Darwin Apel, Arun's restaurant, Melanie Atkinson, Avanzare restaurant, Ball Corporation, Jean Banchet, Annamarie Bannos, Jim Bannos, Barclay Hotel, Michael Beck, Victoria Becker, Sophie Berger, Nicole Bergere, Mary Jo Bergland, Rajana Bhargava, Ann Bloomstrand, Blue Mesa restaurant, Judy Borree, Georgia Botsis, Lamar Brantley, Roger Brown and Carolyn Buster.

Cafe Ba-Ba-Reeba!, California Walnut Board, Jean Camp, Carlucci's restaurant, Michael Carmel, Shere Case, Mary Cech, Robert Chavis, Suzanne Checchia, Chicago Baking Company, Bob Chinn's Crab House, City Tavern restaurant, Mitchell Cobey, Commander's Palace restaurant, Convito Italiano, Julie Cook, Steve Cotsirilos, Andre Daguin, Pat Dailey, Julie Dannebaum, Martha F. Davis, Ed Debevic's restaurant, Geri DeStefano, Dorothy DeVries-Wolf, Beverly Dillon, Aydin Dincer, Darrell Dodson, Pat Egan and Agnes Ellegant.

Judy and Joseph Fell, Jane Salzsfass Freiman, Fresh Starts Bakery and Catering, Michael Foley, Gale Gand, Gandhara restaurant, Gilroy Garlic

Festival, Marcy Goldman-Posluns, Elaine Gonzalez, Bert Greene, Myrna Greenspan, Roy Andries de Groot, Angie Gulino, Jim Guth, Hamburger Hamlet, Jim Haring, Gloria Heeter, Marilyn Heiberger, Helmand restaurant, Terri Hemmert, Judy Hevrdejs, Ken Hom, Honora family, Monique Hooker, House of Hunan, Diane Hugh, John Husar, Marjie Irr, Nancy Jackson, Jamin restaurant, Jerome's restaurant, Jerry's Kitchen, Jeanne Jones, Dolores E. Kaiser, Martin and Mary Kaiser, Bob Kasser, Kay Keehn, Kathy Kirby, Joyce Klein, Saard Kongsuwan, Marjie Korshak, Barbara Kuck, Fay Kuhn, Peter Kump, Alyce LaVine, Lois Carol Levine, Eadie Levy, Roland Liccioni and Linda Lynn.

Abby Mandel, Marion Mandeltort, Tony Mantuano, Rosalyn Markette, Marshall Field's, John McBride, Peter McGinley, Jean McGree, Jeanne McInerney-Lubeck, Metropolis Cafe, Elaine Michura, Le Mikado, Maurice Moore-Betty, Younghee Na, Jane Napolitano, Jennifer Newbury, Lutz Olkiewicz, Charlie Orr, Stuart Parsons, Le Perroquet, Harlan "Pete" Peterson, Silvio Pinto, Les Plumes restaurant, Pomodoro restaurant, Sadie Porto, Paul Prudhomme, The Pump Room, Quaker Oats Company, David Radwine, Justin Rashid, Chanpen Ratana, Jean E. Reeb, Madeleine Reinke, Leslee Reis and Terry Roy.

Romeo Salta, Joan Saltzman, Andre Schaak, William H. Schmitt III, Eli Schulman, Gloria Scolaro, Carole Segal, Shaw's Crab House, Lindsay Remolif Shere, Kevin Shikami, Shilla restaurant, Eric Singer, Jennifer Smith, Nancy Solomon, Michael Stuart's restaurant, Suntory restaurant, Robin Swartzman, Susan M. Swett, Louis Szathmary, Tallgrass restaurant, Tango restaurant, Dennis Terczak, John Terczak, Tony Terlato, Tondalaya Thomas, Lee Thompson, Jeffrey Tomchek, Lam Ton, Ann Topham, Jean True, Barbara Tuleja and Tuzik's Bakery.

Yvonne Uhlianuk, Irene Ulanov, Valentino's restaurant, Katina Vaselopulos, Winston's Bakery, Women's Club of Evanston, Jolene Worthington, Mrs. Anton Zalesky, Cathy Zordan and Ann Zorek.

INDEX

Egg(s)
    bacon and cheese bake, 77
    baked with mushrooms and potatoes,
        73
    Benedict, 85
    crab foo yung, 76
    crepes with red peppers and
        mushrooms, 78
    curried salad, 75
    Mexican omelet with avocado topping,
        81
    morel and asparagus omelet, 83
    omelet, basic, 80
    omelet with chicken, tomato and
        cheese, 82
    poached, make-ahead, 79
    potato and pepper frittata, 84
    scrambled with chorizo (huevos con
        chorizo), 84
Eggnog
    classic Southern, 65
    Mary Meade's, 66
Eggplant
    baked with yogurt sauce, 398
    caponata in red cabbage leaves, 45
    Parmesan, 399
    and pepper salad, 446
    soup, curried cream of, 130
    spread, 18
    terrine with sun-dried tomato
        mayonnaise, 28
Enchiladas
    chicken, 332
    chicken and cilantro, 275
    picadillo, 274
Endive. See Belgian endive
English-style roast beef with gravy and
    Yorkshire pudding, 266
Escarole and bean soup, 103

F

Fennel and celery root au gratin, 424
Feta and spinach stuffed tomatoes, 419
Fettucini

Alfredo, 150
    with wild mushrooms, 151
Filipino sausage and bok choy, 299
Fish, 207–36. See also Shellfish
    about buying and preparing, 207–209
    balls for Vietnamese combination soup,
        121
    bass, marinated grilled, with green
        tomato relish, 228
    catfish, cornmeal-fried, with barbecue
        sauce and sweet potato hush
        puppies, 230
    catfish, grilled fillet of, with Dijon
        mustard, 229
    cod, oven-baked with tomatoes, 211
    and crab spread, 19
    halibut, grilled with mustard cream
        sauce, 211
    orange roughy with tarragon, 225
    porgy, pan-fried, 212
    red snapper
        firepot, 213
        in orange sauce, 214
        sweet and sour, 215
        Thai whole fried, 216
    salmon
        broiled with sesame-sauced green
        beans, 217
        grilled with anchovy butter, 218
        mousse with beurre blanc, 220
        Oriental, 219
    sea bass provencal, 221
    shark, grilled with tomato-feta relish,
        222
    skate and onions, deep-fried, 223
    smelt, Cajun, batter-fried, 236
    smelt, spicy fried, 235
    smoked, lemon-dill dry cure for, 249
    stock (fumet), 135
    swordfish with spicy basil butter, 224
    tilefish, puffy broiled, 224
    tuna fillets Creole, 226

Mâche and beet salad with walnuts, 434
Madeleines, lemon, 630
Mango whip, frozen, 598
Margarita, 65
Martini, Cajun, 62
Mary Meade's
  eggnog, 66
  white fruitcake, 541
Mayonnaise. *See also* Salad dressing
  basic, 487
  chili, 46
  curried, 480
  herb, 487
  lemon basil, 194
  sun-dried tomato, 29
Meat
  ball(s)
    minestrone, 112
    and sausage, Italian, spaghetti
    sauce with, 143
    soup, Mexican, 114
    and spaghetti sauce, fiesta, 144
  -filled turnovers, 39
  less burritos, 192
  loaf Cajun, 273
  loaf, just great, 272
  pie, Moroccan, 310
Meaty baked lasagna, 148
Meringue cake, dacquoise, 542
Mexican
  chicken and avocado soup, 109
  chicken and cilantro enchiladas, 275
  chicken enchiladas, 332
  meatball soup, 114
  meatless burritos, 192
  melted cheese casserole (queso
    fundido), 23
  omelet with avocado topping, 81
  open-face bean and cheese
    sandwiches, (molletes), 198
  picadillo enchiladas, 274

pork braised in tortillas, 288
salsa, 20
scrambled eggs with chorizo (huevos
  con chorizo), 84
-style pot roast with vegetables, 277
tortilla soup, quick, 115
Microwave dishes
  butternut squash steamed with ginger,
    414
  cauliflower or broccoli steamed with
    red pepper sauce, 394
  chicken enchiladas, 332
  chicken in the, 337
  crab and fish spread, 19
  eggplant spread, 18
  flank steak, stuffed, 280
  goulash soup, 111
  mushroom ginger soup, 106
  mushroom and sun-dried tomato salad,
    451
  orange roughy with tarragon, 225
  peanut butter bonbons, 634
  pork roast, garlic and spinach, 292
  pralines, Rio Bravo, 632
  pretzels, sparkling, 635
  raisin bread, cinnamon-topped, 503
  raisin bread pudding with whiskey
    sauce, 577
  red snapper in orange sauce, 214
  salmon mousse with beurre blanc, 220
  turbot with basil, 227
Millet whole-wheat bread, 499
Mincemeat, homemade, 650
Minestrone, meatball, 112
Mint
  chutney, 648
  creamy dressing, 478
  julep, sparkling orange, 61
Mirliton. *See* Chayote squash
Molasses cookies, 617
Molletes (Mexican bean and cheese
  sandwiches, open-face), 198

Salad dressing
    bacon and shallot, warm, with basil
        shreds, 486
    black peppercorn, creamy, 483
    Camembert, 438
    cilantro, creamy, 484
    honey jalapeño, 475
    mayonnaise. *See* Mayonnaise
    mint, creamy, 478
    oregano, 485
    vinaigrette. *See* Vinaigrette
    vinegar, raspberry, 648
    walnut oil, 649
Salmon
    with basil vinaigrette, 49
    broiled with sesame-sauced green
        beans, 217
    coho Berteau, 233
    grilled with anchovy butter, 218
    mousse with beurre blanc, 220
    Oriental, 219
    poached, salad with mustard dressing,
        469
Salsa, 20. *See also* Sauce
    smoky, steak fajitas with, 279
    verde, 19
Salt, herb and spice, 357
Samosas with mint chutney, 44
Sandwich(es), 191–204
    avocadowiches, 191
    cheese and bacon dogs, 202
    chicken, with lemon basil mayonnaise,
        194
    chili dogs, 203
    corned beef loaf, layered, 196
    duck breast, smoked, with leeks, 200
    ham and cheese, grilled (croque
        monsieur), 195
    loaf, chorizo bread, 193
    meatless burritos, 192
    Mexican open-face bean and cheese,
        198

    muffalata, 197
    pan bagnat in pita, 198
    pizza, summer, 202
    Reuben hot dogs, 204
    shrimp poor boys, 199
    steak and cheese, 201
    tabbouleh for, 467
Sauce
    apricot dipping, 32
    barbecue, good-old-boy, 290
    barbecue, homemade, 231
    Bolognese, 145
    dessert
        chocolate cream, 590
        chocolate, luscious, 600
        crème Anglaise, 600
        rhubarb orange, 601
        strawberry, fresh, 601
    four cheese, 146
    ginger, 76
    hollandaise, basic, 383
    mushroom, 286
    mustard,
        cream, 43
        dipping, hot, 236
        hot, 77
    peanut, 35
    pesto, 129
    pesto, special, 147
    quick red, 192
    raspberry pink peppercorn, 369
    red pepper, 394
    remoulade dipping, quick, 237
    rouille, 117
    salsa, 20
    smoky salsa, 279
    spaghetti, 143, 144
    spicy, 38
    spinach pesto, 147
    sweet and sour (for fish), 215
    teriyaki, 240

Yorkshire pudding, 267

Z

Zucchini
  bread and butter pickles, 647
  chocolate cake, deluxe, 537
  or green beans in fresh tarragon
    marinade, 420
  salad, Korean, 449

Index to People and Places

Cooking and Hospitality Institute of
Chicago, 107
Cotsirilos, Steve, 337
The Cottage restaurant, 368, 416
Crate & Barrel, 456

D

Daguin, Andre, 594
Dailey, Pat, 302
Dannebaum, Julie, 545
David, Elizabeth, 392
Davis, Martha F., 119
de Groot, Roy Andries, 43, 102, 467
DeStefano, Geri, 144
DeVries-Wolf, Dorothy, 226
Dillon, Beverly, 76, 78, 87, 88, 102,
154 194, 196, 201, 218, 230, 241,
263, 265, 277, 285, 286, 295, 310,
348, 550, 614
Dincer, Aydin, 321
Dodson, Darrell, 459
Drake Hotel, 580
Drechsler, Erzwin, 161

E

Ed Debevic's restaurant, 153
Edwardo's restaurant, 189
Egan, Pat, 613
Eli's Chicago's Finest Cheesecake, 564
Eli's, The Place for Steak, 320
Ellegant, Agnes, 496
Eurasia restaurant, 386

F

Fell, Judy and Joseph, 346
Finney, Leon, 289
Foley, Michael, 89, 340
Foley's restaurant, 89
Le Francais, 539, 570
Freiman, Jane Salzfass, 329, 500, 556,
566, 573

Fresh Starts Bakery and Catering, 239,
542, 571

G

Gand, Gale, 588
Gandhara restaurant, 413
Garland restaurant, 475
Gino's East Pizzeria, 183
Giordano's restaurant, 184
Goldman-Posluns, Marcy, 454, 463, 479,
480
Gonzalez, Elaine, 288
Good Taste, 612
Gordon restaurant, 540
Greene, Bert, 558
Greenspan, Myrna, 330
Gulino, Angie, 211
Guth, Jim, 228

H

Haddix, Carol, 359
Hamburger Hamlet, 270, 271
Haring, Jim, 147, 305
Harlan "Pete" Peterson, 234, 433.
Heeter, Gloria, 611
Heiberger, Marilyn, 461
The Helmand restaurant, 170, 264, 398
Hemmert, Terri, 276
Henri de Jonghe's Monroe Street Hotel,
246
Hevrdejs, Judy, 20, 23, 84
Hom, Ken, 343
The Home-Run, 186
Honora family, 191
Hooker, Monique, 352
House of Hunan, 166
Hugh, Diane, 31
Husar, John, 235

I

Inn at Union Pier, 77
Irr, Margie, 468